T0214156

Lecture Notes in Computer Science 11857

More information about this series at http://www.springer.com/series/7412

Zhouchen Lin · Liang Wang ·
Jian Yang · Guangming Shi ·
Tieniu Tan · Nanning Zheng ·
Xilin Chen · Yanning Zhang (Eds.)

Pattern Recognition and Computer Vision

Second Chinese Conference, PRCV 2019
Xi'an, China, November 8–11, 2019
Proceedings, Part I

 Springer

Editors
Zhouchen Lin
School of EECS
Peking University
Beijing, China

Jian Yang
Nanjing University of Science
and Technology
Nanjing, China

Tieniu Tan
Institute of Automation
Chinese Academy of Sciences
Beijing, China

Xilin Chen
Chinese Academy of Sciences
Beijing, China

Liang Wang
Institute of Automation
Chinese Academy of Sciences
Beijing, China

Guangming Shi
Xidian University
Xi'an, China

Nanning Zheng
Institute of Artificial Intelligence
Xi'an Jiaotong University
Xi'an, China

Yanning Zhang
Northwestern Polytechnical University
Xi'an, China

ISSN 0302-9743   ISSN 1611-3349   (electronic)
Lecture Notes in Computer Science
ISBN 978-3-030-31653-2   ISBN 978-3-030-31654-9   (eBook)
https://doi.org/10.1007/978-3-030-31654-9

LNCS Sublibrary: SL6 – Image Processing, Computer Vision, Pattern Recognition, and Graphics

This Springer imprint is published by the registered company Springer Nature Switzerland AG
The registered company address is: Gewerbestrasse 11, 6330 Cham, Switzerland

Preface

Welcome to the proceedings of the Second Chinese Conference on Pattern Recognition and Computer Vision (PRCV 2019) held in Xi'an, China!

PRCV merged from CCPR (Chinese Conference on Pattern Recognition) and CCCV (Chinese Conference on Computer Vision), which are both the most influential Chinese conferences on pattern recognition and computer vision, respectively. Pattern recognition and computer vision are closely inter-related and the two communities are largely overlapping. The goal of merging CCPR and CCCV into PRCV is to further boost the impact of the Chinese community in these two core areas of artificial intelligence and further improve the quality of academic communication. Accordingly, PRCV is co-sponsored by four major academic societies of China: the Chinese Association for Artificial Intelligence (CAAI), the China Computer Federation (CCF), the Chinese Association of Automation (CAA), and the China Society of Image and Graphics (CSIG).

PRCV aims at providing an interactive communication platform for researchers from academia and from industry. It promotes not only academic exchange, but also communication between academia and industry. In order to keep track of the frontier of academic trends and share the latest research achievements, innovative ideas, and scientific methods in the fields of pattern recognition and computer vision, international and local leading experts and professors are invited to deliver keynote speeches, introducing the latest advances in theories and methods in the fields of pattern recognition and computer vision.

PRCV 2019 was hosted by Northwestern Polytechnical University and was co-hosted by Xi'an Jiaotong University, Xidian University, and Shaanxi Normal University. We received 412 full submissions. Each submission was reviewed by at least three reviewers selected from the Program Committee and other qualified researchers. Based on the reviewers' reports, 165 papers were finally accepted for presentation at the conference, including 18 oral and 147 posters. The acceptance rate is 40%. The proceedings of the PRCV 2019 are published by Springer.

We are grateful to the keynote speakers, Prof. Kyros Kutulakos from the University of Toronto in Canada, Prof. Licheng Jiao from Xidian University, Prof. Tinne Tuytelaars from the University of Leuven in Belgium, and Prof. Kyoung Mu Lee from Seoul National University in South Korea.

We give sincere thanks to the authors of all submitted papers, the Program Committee members and the reviewers, and the Organizing Committee. Without their contributions, this conference would not be a success. Special thanks also go to all of the sponsors and the organizers of the special forums; their support made the conference a success. We are also grateful to Springer for publishing the proceedings and especially to Ms. Celine (Lanlan) Chang of Springer Asia for her efforts in coordinating the publication.

We hope you find the proceedings enjoyable and fruitful.

November 2019

Tieniu Tan
Nanning Zheng
Xilin Chen
Yanning Zhang
Zhouchen Lin
Liang Wang
Jian Yang
Guangming Shi

Organization

Steering Committee Chair

Tieniu Tan — Institute of Automation, Chinese Academy of Sciences, China

Steering Committee

Xilin Chen — Institute of Computing Technology, Chinese Academy of Sciences, China

Chenglin Liu — Institute of Automation, Chinese Academy of Sciences, China

Long Quan — The Hong Kong University of Science and Technology, SAR China

Yong Rui — Lenovo, China

Hongbin Zha — Peking University, China

Nanning Zheng — Xi'an Jiaotong University, China

Jie Zhou — Tsinghua University, China

Steering Committee Secretariat

Liang Wang — Institute of Automation, Chinese Academy of Sciences, China

General Chairs

Tieniu Tan — Institute of Automation, Chinese Academy of Sciences, China

Nanning Zheng — Xi'an Jiaotong University, China

Xilin Chen — Institute of Computing Technology, Chinese Academy of Sciences, China

Yanning Zhang — Northwestern Polytechnical University, China

Program Chairs

Zhouchen Lin — Peking University, China

Liang Wang — Institute of Automation, Chinese Academy of Sciences, China

Jian Yang — Nanjing University of Science and Technology, China

Guangming Shi — Xidian University, China

Organizing Chairs

Jianru Xue   Xi'an Jiaotong University, China
Peng Wang   Northwestern Polytechnical University, China
Wei Wei   Northwestern Polytechnical University, China

Publicity Chairs

Shiguang Shan   Institute of Computing Technology, Chinese Academy
                          of Sciences, China
Qiguang Miao   Xidian University, China
Zhaoxiang Zhang   Institute of Automation, Chinese Academy of Sciences,
                          China

International Liaison Chairs

Jingyi Yu   ShanghaiTech University, China
Jiwen Lu   Tsinghua University, China
Zhanyu Ma   Beijing University of Posts and Telecommunications,
                          China

Publication Chairs

Xiang Bai   Huazhong University of Science and Technology,
                          China
Tao Yang   Northwestern Polytechnical University, China

Special Issue Chairs

Ming-Ming Cheng   Nankai University, China
Weishi Zheng   Sun Yat-sen University, China

Tutorial Chairs

Deyu Meng   Xi'an Jiaotong University, China
Yuxin Peng   Peking University, China
Feiping Nie   Northwestern Polytechnical University, China

Workshop Chairs

Huchuan Lu   Dalian University of Technology, China
Yunhong Wang   Beihang University, China
Qingshan Liu   Nanjing University of Information Science
                          and Technology, China

Sponsorship Chairs

Tao Wang	iQIYI, China
Jinfeng Yang	Civil Aviation University of China, China
Xinbo Zhao	Northwestern Polytechnical University, China

Demo Chairs

Huimin Ma	Tsinghua University, China
Runping Xi	Northwestern Polytechnical University, China

Competition Chairs

Nong Sang	Huazhong University of Science and Technology, China
Wangmeng Zuo	Harbin Institute of Technology, China
Hanlin Yin	Northwestern Polytechnical University, China

PhD Forum Chairs

Junwei Han	Northwestern Polytechnical University, China
Xin Geng	Southeast University, China
Si Liu	Beihang University, China

Web Chairs

Guofeng Zhang	Zhejiang University, China
Di Xu	Northwestern Polytechnical University, China

Financial Chairs

Jinqiu Sun	Northwestern Polytechnical University, China
Lifang Wu	Beijing University of Technology, China

Registration Chairs

Yu Zhu	Northwestern Polytechnical University, China
Shizhou Zhang	Northwestern Polytechnical University, China

Area Chairs

Xiang Bai	Huazhong University of Science and Technology, China
Songcan Chen	Nanjing University of Aeronautics and Astronautics, China
Jian Cheng	Chinese Academy of Sciences, China

Ming-Ming Cheng	Nankai University, China
Junyu Dong	Ocean University of China, China
Jianjiang Feng	Tsinghua University, China
Shenghua Gao	ShanghaiTech University, China
Xin Geng	Southeast University, China
Huiguang He	Institute of Automation, Chinese Academy of Sciences, China
Qinghua Hu	Tianjin University, China
Shuqiang Jiang	Institute of Computing Technology, China Academy of Science, China
Yu-Gang Jiang	Fudan University, China
Lianwen Jin	South China University of Technology, China
Xiaoyuan Jing	Wuhan University, China
Liping Jing	Beijing Jiaotong University, China
Xi Li	Zhejiang University, China
Zhouchen Lin	Peking University, China
Guangcan Liu	Nanjing University of Information Science and Technology, China
Qingshan Liu	Nanjing University of Information Science and Technology, China
Huchuan Lu	Dalian University of Technology, China
Jiwen Lu	Tsinghua University, China
Deyu Meng	Xi'an Jiaotong University, China
Qiguang Miao	Xidian University, China
Yadong Mu	Peking University, China
Yuxin Peng	Peking University, China
Yu Qiao	Shenzhen Institutes of Advanced Technology, Chinese Academy of Sciences, China
Nong Sang	Huazhong University of Science and Technology, China
Hongbin Shen	Shanghai Jiao Tong University, China
Linlin Shen	Shenzhen University, China
Mingli Song	Zhejiang University, China
Zhenan Sun	Chinese of Academy of Sciences, China
Kurban Ubul	Xinjiang University, China
Hanzi Wang	Xiamen University, China
Jingdong Wang	Microsoft, China
Lifang Wu	Beijing University of Technology, China
Yihong Wu	Institute of Automation, Chinese Academy of Sciences, China
Guisong Xia	Wuhan University, China
Yong Xia	Northwestern Polytechnical University, China
Shiming Xiang	Chinese Academy of Sciences, China
Xiaohua Xie	Sun Yat-sen University, China
Junchi Yan	Shanghai Jiao Tong University, China

Jinfeng Yang	Civil Aviation University of China, China
Xucheng Yin	University of Science and Technology Beijing, China
Xiaotong Yuan	Nanjing University of Information Science and Technology, China
Zhengjun Zha	University of Science and Technology of China, China
Changshui Zhang	Tsinghua University, China
Daoqiang Zhang	Nanjing University of Aeronautics and Astronautics, China
Zhaoxiang Zhang	Chinese Academy of Sciences, China
Weishi Zheng	Sun Yat-sen University, China
Wangmeng Zuo	Harbin Institute of Technology, China

Additional Reviewers

Peijun Bao	Jiaqing Fan	Rui Huang
Jiawang Bian	Qingnan Fan	Sheng Huang
Jinzheng Cai	Jianjiang Feng	Rongrong Ji
Ziyun Cai	Wei Feng	Kui Jia
Xiangyong Cao	Jingjing Fu	Ming Jiang
Yang Cao	Xueyang Fu	Shuqiang Jiang
Boyuan Chen	Chenqiang Gao	Tingting Jiang
Chusong Chen	Jin Gao	Yu-Gang Jiang
Dongdong Chen	Lin Gao	Liang Jie
Juncheng Chen	Shaobing Gao	Lianwen Jin
Songcan Chen	Shiming Ge	Xin Jin
Tianshui Chen	Xin Geng	Jianhuang Lai
Xilin Chen	Guoqiang Gong	Chenyi Lei
Yingcong Chen	Shuhang Gu	Chunguang Li
Jingchun Cheng	Xiaojie Guo	Kai Li
Ming-Ming Cheng	Yiwen Guo	Shijie Li
Li Chi	Yulan Guo	Stan Li
Yang Cong	Zhenhua Guo	Wenbo Li
Peng Cui	Chunrui Han	Xiangyang Li
Daoqing Dai	Hu Han	Xiaoxiao Li
Yuchao Dai	Tian Han	Xin Li
Cheng Deng	Yahong Han	Yikang Li
Weihong Deng	Huiguang He	Yongjie Li
Chao Dong	Fan Heng	Yufeng Li
Jiangxin Dong	Qibin Hou	Zechao Li
Weisheng Dong	Tingbo Hou	Zhanqing Li
Xiwei Dong	Changhui Hu	Zhizhong Li
Lijuan Duan	Lanqing Hu	Wei Liang
Lixin Duan	Qinghua Hu	Minghui Liao
Bin Fan	Xiaowei Hu	Zicheng Liao
Dengping Fan	Qingqiu Huang	Shuoxin Lin

Weiyao Lin
Zhouchen Lin
Bing Liu
Bo Liu
Chenchen Liu
Chenglin Liu
Dong Liu
Guangcan Liu
Jiawei Liu
Jiaying Liu
Liu Liu
Mengyuan Liu
Miaomiao Liu
Nian Liu
Qingshan Liu
Risheng Liu
Sheng Liu
Shuaicheng Liu
Si Liu
Siqi Liu
Weifeng Liu
Weiwei Liu
Wentao Liu
Xianglong Liu
Yebin Liu
Yiguang Liu
Yu Liu
Yuliang Liu
Yun Liu
Xihui Liu
Yaojie Liu
Mingsheng Long
Cewu Lu
Jiang Lu
Sihui Luo
Bingpeng Ma
Chao Ma
Huimin Ma
Lin Ma
Zhanyu Ma
Zheng Ma
Lin Mei
Deyu Meng
Qiguang Miao
Weiqing Min
Yue Ming

Yadong Mu
Feiping Nie
Yuzhen Niu
Gang Pan
Jinshan Pan
Yu Pang
Xi Peng
Yuxin Peng
Xiaojuan Qi
Yu Qiao
Jianfeng Ren
Jimmy Ren
Min Ren
Peng Ren
Wenqi Ren
Nong Sang
Mingwen Shao
Dongyu She
Shuhan Shen
Tianwei Shen
Lu Sheng
Boxin Shi
Jian Shi
Yukai Shi
Zhenwei Shi
Tianmin Shu
Dongjin Song
Xinhang Song
Jian Sun
Ke Sun
Qianru Sun
Shiliang Sun
Zhenan Sun
Ying Tai
Mingkui Tan
Xiaoyang Tan
Yao Tang
Youbao Tang
Yuxing Tang
Jun Wan
Changdong Wang
Chunyu Wang
Dong Wang
Guangrun Wang
Hanli Wang
Hanzi Wang

Hongxing Wang
Jian Wang
Le Wang
Liang Wang
Limin Wang
Lingjing Wang
Nannan Wang
Qi Wang
Tao Wang
Weiqun Wang
Wenguan Wang
Xiaosong Wang
Xinggang Wang
Xintao Wang
Yali Wang
Yilin Wang
Yongtao Wang
Yunhong Wang
Zilei Wang
Hongyuan Wang
Xiushen Wei
Junwu Weng
Kwanyee Wong
Yongkang Wong
Baoyuan Wu
Fei Wu
Jianlong Wu
Jianxin Wu
Lifang Wu
Shuzhe Wu
Xiaohe Wu
Xinxiao Wu
Yihong Wu
Guisong Xia
Fanyi Xiao
Xiaohua Xie
Xianglei Xing
Peixi Xiong
Yu Xiong
Xiangyu Xu
Yongchao Xu
Yuanlu Xu
Zheng Xu
Jianru Xue
Shipeng Yan
Sijie Yan

Hao Yang	Lin Zhang	Yue Zhao
Jufeng Yang	Runze Zhang	Haiyong Zheng
Meng Yang	Shanshan Zhang	Wenming Zheng
Shuang Yang	Shengping Zhang	Guoqiang Zhong
Wei Yang	Shiliang Zhang	Yiran Zhong
Yang Yang	Tianzhu Zhang	Chunluan Zhou
Jingwen Ye	Wei Zhang	Hao Zhou
Ming Yin	Xiangyu Zhang	Jiahuan Zhou
Dongfei Yu	Xiaoyu Zhang	Xinzhe Zhou
Gang Yu	Yongqiang Zhang	Yipin Zhou
Jiahui Yu	Yu Zhang	Siyu Zhu
Tan Yu	Zhaoxing Zhang	Chao Zhu
Yang Yu	Feng Zhao	Guangming Zhu
Zhenbo Yu	Jiaxing Zhao	Tyler (Lixuan) Zhu
Ganzhao Yuan	Kai Zhao	Xiaoke Zhu
Jiabei Zeng	Kaili Zhao	Yaohui Zhu
Dechuan Zhan	Qian Zhao	Liansheng Zhuang
Daoqiang Zhang	Qijun Zhao	Nan Zhuang
He Zhang	Qilu Zhao	Dongqing Zou
Juyong Zhang	Tiesong Zhao	Qi Zou
Lei Zhang	Ya Zhao	Wangmeng Zuo

Contents – Part I

Object Detection, Tracking and Recognition

Channel Feature Enhanced Detector for Small Ball Detection   3
Shambel Ferede, Xuemei Xie, Xing Jin, Jiang Du, and Guangming Shi

High-Order Graph Convolutional Network for Skeleton-Based Human
Action Recognition   14
Zhimin Bai, Hongping Yan, and Lingfeng Wang

Multi-scale Spatial-Temporal Attention for Action Recognition   26
Qing Zhang, Hongping Yan, and Lingfeng Wang

Reading Digital Numbers of Water Meter with Deep Learning
Based Object Detector   38
Shirong Liao, Pan Zhou, Lianglin Wang, and Songzhi Su

Exploiting Category-Level Semantic Relationships for Fine-Grained
Image Recognition   50
*Xianjie Mo, Jiajie Zhu, Xiaoxuan Zhao, Min Liu, Tingting Wei,
and Wei Luo*

On the Multi-scale Real-Time Object Detection Using ResNet   63
Zhengyao Bai and Dong Jiang

Learning Attention Regularization Correlation Filter for Visual Tracking   74
Zhuling Qiu, Yufei Zha, Peng Zhu, and Fei Zhang

Target Tracking via Two-Branch Spatio-Temporal Regularized
Correlation Filter Network   86
Peng Sun, Wenbo Guo, and Songhao Zhu

A Real-Time Rock-Paper-Scissor Hand Gesture Recognition System
Based on FlowNet and Event Camera   98
*Xuemei Xie, Shu Zhang, Jinjian Wu, Xun Xu, Guangming Shi,
and Jianyu Chen*

Cross-Category Cross-Semantic Regularization for Fine-Grained
Image Recognition   110
Yelin Chen, Xianjie Mo, Zijun Liang, Tingting Wei, and Wei Luo

The Multi-task Fully Convolutional Siamese Network with Correlation
Filter Layer for Real-Time Visual Tracking   123
Shiyu Xuan, Shengyang Li, Zifei Zhao, and Mingfei Han

Table Detection Using Boundary Refining via Corner Locating   135
  Ningning Sun, Yuanping Zhu, and Xiaoming Hu

Dictionary Learning and Confidence Map Estimation-Based Tracker
for Robot-Assisted Therapy System.   147
  *Xiaolong Zhou, Sixian Chan, Junwei Li, Shengyong Chen,
  and Honghai Liu*

Power Line Corridor LiDAR Point Cloud Segmentation Using
Convolutional Neural Network   160
  *Jisheng Yang, Zijun Huang, Maochun Huang, Xianxian Zeng, Dong Li,
  and Yun Zhang*

Face Liveness Detection Based on Client Identity Using
Siamese Network   172
  Huiling Hao, Mingtao Pei, and Meng Zhao

Learning Weighted Video Segments for Temporal Action Localization   181
  Che Sun, Hao Song, Xinxiao Wu, and Yunde Jia

REAPS: Towards Better Recognition of Fine-Grained Images
by Region Attending and Part Sequencing   193
  Peng Zhang, Xinyu Zhu, Zhanzhan Cheng, Shuigeng Zhou, and Yi Niu

Weakly-Supervised Action Recognition and Localization
via Knowledge Transfer.   205
  Haichao Shi, Xiaoyu Zhang, and Changsheng Li

Visual Tracking with Levy Flight Grasshopper Optimization Algorithm.   217
  Huanlong Zhang, Zeng Gao, Jie Zhang, and Guanglu Yang

Exploring Context Information for Accurate and Fast Object Detection   228
  Zhenjun Shi, Xiaoqi Li, and Bin Zhang

A Novel Method for Thermal Image Based
Electrical-Equipment Detection   239
  *Futian Wang, Songjian Hua, Xiao Wang, Zhengzheng Tu,
  Cheng Zhang, and Jin Tang*

State Detection of Electrical Equipment Based on Infrared Thermal
Imaging Technology   251
  Hejin Yuan, Xiuxin Chen, Yu Wang, and Ming Su

Attention Based Convolutional Recurrent Neural Network
for Environmental Sound Classification   261
  *Zhichao Zhang, Shugong Xu, Tianhao Qiao, Shunqing Zhang,
  and Shan Cao*

Salient Object Detection via Light-Weight Multi-path
Refinement Networks   272
    Kang Ma, Jun Feng, Tuo Zhang, Rui Wang, and Qirong Bu

Visual Object Tracking via an Improved Lightweight Siamese Network.   284
    Mingyang Liu, Qing Lei, Li Yu, Yun Gao, and Xuejie Zhang

A Simple and Robust Attentional Encoder-Decoder Model for License
Plate Recognition   295
    Linjiang Zhang, Peng Wang, Fan Dang, and Shaojie Zhang

Semi-supervised Deep Neural Networks for Object Detection in Video
Surveillance Systems.   308
    Jinshan Chen, Yujun Liu, Kaiming Ding, Shimin Li, Songxin Cai,
    Jinhe Su, Zongyue Wang, and Guorong Cai

Machine Learning

YNBIRDS: A System for Fine-Grained Bird Image Recognition.   325
    Yili Zhao and Hua Zhou

Quadratic Approximation Greedy Pursuit for Cardinality-Constrained
Sparse Learning   337
    Fanfan Ji, Hui Shuai, and Xiao-Tong Yuan

Iterative Discriminative Domain Adaptation   349
    Xiaofu Wu, Jiahui Fu, Suofei Zhang, and Quan Zhou

Common Structured Low-Rank Matrix Recovery
for Cross-View Classification   361
    Zihan Long, Jiamiao Xu, Fangzhao Wang, Chuanwu Yang,
    and Xinge You

Pruning Convolutional Neural Networks via Stochastic Gradient
Hard Thresholding   373
    Xin Yang, Haiwei Lu, Hui Shuai, and Xiao-Tong Yuan

Channel and Constraint Compensation for Generative
Adversarial Networks   386
    Wei Wang, Haifeng Hu, and Dihu Chen

Faster Real-Time Face Alignment Method on CPU.   398
    Pengfei Duan, Xin Ning, Yuan Shi, Shaolin Zhang, and Weijun Li

A Siamese Pedestrian Alignment Network for Person Re-identification   409
    Yi Zheng, Yong Zhou, Jiaqi Zhao, Meng Jian, Rui Yao, Bing Liu,
    and Xuning Liu

Training Low Bitwidth Model with Weight Normalization
for Convolutional Neural Networks   421
    Haoxin Fan, Jianjing An, and Dong Wang

Virtual Adversarial Training on Graph Convolutional Networks
in Node Classification   431
    Ke Sun, Zhouchen Lin, Hantao Guo, and Zhanxing Zhu

Brain Functional Connectivity Augmentation Method
for Mental Disease Classification with Generative Adversarial Network   444
    Qi Yao and Hu Lu

Attention-Based Label Consistency for Semi-supervised Deep Learning   456
    Jiaming Chen and Meng Yang

Semantic Reanalysis of Scene Words in Visual Question Answering   468
    Shiling Jiang, Ming Ma, Jianming Wang, Jiayu Liang, Kunliang Liu,
    Yukuan Sun, Wei Deng, Siyu Ren, and Guanghao Jin

A Dustbin Category Based Feedback Incremental Learning Strategy
for Hierarchical Image Classification   480
    Ying Chen, Wen Shen, Qianwen Li, and Zhihua Wei

Spatial-temporal Fusion Network with Residual Learning and Attention
Mechanism: A Benchmark for Video-Based Group Re-ID   492
    Qiling Xu, Hua Yang, and Lin Chen

Architectural Style Classification Based on DNN Model   505
    Peipei Zhao, Qiguang Miao, Ruyi Liu, and Jianfeng Song

DAEimp: Denoising Autoencoder-Based Imputation of Sleep
Heart Health Study for Identification of Cardiovascular Diseases   517
    Xiaoyun Dong, Jingjing Zhang, Gang Wang, and Yong Xia

Fabric Defect Detection Based on Lightweight Neural Network   528
    Zhoufeng Liu, Jian Cui, Chunlei Li, Miaomiao Wei, and Yan Yang

Person Re-identification with Neural Architecture Search   540
    Shizhou Zhang, Rui Cao, Xing Wei, Peng Wang, and Yanning Zhang

Deep Convolutional Center-Based Clustering   552
    Qinhong Yan, Meihan Tang, Weifu Chen, and Guocan Feng

Exponential Moving Averaged Q-Network for DDPG   562
    Xiangxiang Shen, Chuanhuan Yin, Yekun Chai, and Xinwen Hou

Multi-scale Convolutional Neural Network Based on 3D Context Fusion
for Lesion Detection   573
    Zebiao Wu, Jinshan Chen, Zongyue Wang, Jinhe Su, and Guorong Cai

Orientation Adaptive YOLOv3 for Object Detection in Remote
Sensing Images.   586
    Jiahui Lei, Chongjun Gao, Jing Hu, Changxin Gao, and Nong Sang

Neural Ordinary Differential Equations with Envolutionary Weights   598
    Lingshen He, Xingyu Xie, and Zhouchen Lin

Infrared Image Segmentation for Photovoltaic Panels Based on Res-UNet . . .   611
    Hao Zhang, Xianggong Hong, Shifen Zhou, and Qingcai Wang

Author Index   623

Contents – Part II

Image/Video Processing and Analysis

Multiscale Entropy Analysis of EEG Based on Non-uniform Time 3
  Hongxia Deng, Jinxiu Guo, Xiaofeng Yang, Jinxiu Hou, Haoqi Liu,
  and Haifang Li

Recurrent Deconvolutional Generative Adversarial Networks
with Application to Video Generation 18
  Hongyuan Yu, Yan Huang, Lihong Pi, and Liang Wang

Functional Brain Network Estimation Based on Weighted BOLD Signals
for MCI Identification 29
  Huihui Chen

ESNet: An Efficient Symmetric Network for Real-Time
Semantic Segmentation 41
  Yu Wang, Quan Zhou, Jian Xiong, Xiaofu Wu, and Xin Jin

Assignment Problem Based Deep Embedding 53
  Ruishen Zheng, Jin Xie, Jianjun Qian, and Jian Yang

Auto Data Augmentation for Testing Set 66
  Wanshun Gao and Xi Zhao

Dense Activation Network for Image Denoising 79
  Yan Shen, Liao Zhang, Shuqin Lou, and Zhongli Wang

The Optimal Graph Regularized Sparse Coding with Application
to Image Representation 91
  Zhenqiu Shu, Xiaojun Wu, Zhen Liu, Congzhe You, and Honghui Fan

Robust Embedding Regression for Face Recognition 102
  Jiaqi Bao, Jianglin Lu, Zhihui Lai, Ning Liu, and Yuwu Lu

Deep Feature-Preserving Based Face Hallucination:
Feature Discrimination Versus Pixels Approximation 114
  Xiaoyu Zheng, Heng Liu, Jungong Han, and Shudong Hou

Lung Parenchymal Segmentation Algorithm Based on Improved Marker
Watershed for Lung CT Images 126
  Ying Chen and Ding Wang

Fine Grain Lung Nodule Diagnosis Based on CT Using 3D Convolutional
Neural Network   138
    Qiuli Wang, Jiajia Zhang, Sheng Huang, Chen Liu, Xiaohong Zhang,
    and Dan Yang

Segmentation Guided Regression Network for Breast Cancer Cellularity   150
    Yixuan Wang, Li Yu, and Shengwei Wang

Automatic Inspection of Yarn Locations by Utilizing Histogram
Segmentation and Monotone Hypothesis   161
    Yu Han and Ling Luo

Membranous Nephropathy Identification Using Hyperspectral
Microscopic Images.   173
    Xueling Wei, Tianqi Tu, Nianrong Zhang, Yue Yang, Wenge Li,
    and Wei Li

A Level Set Method Combined with Gaussian Mixture Model
for Image Segmentation   185
    Xin Lu, Xuewu Zhang, Min Li, Zhuo Zhang, and Haiyan Xu

Nonstandard Periodic Gait Energy Image for Gait Recognition
and Data Augmentation   197
    Kejun Wang, Liangliang Liu, Yilong Lee, Xinnan Ding, and Junyu Lin

A Temporal Attentive Approach for Video-Based Pedestrian
Attribute Recognition   209
    Zhiyuan Chen, Annan Li, and Yunhong Wang

An Effective Network with ConvLSTM for Low-Light
Image Enhancement   221
    Yixi Xiang, Ying Fu, Lei Zhang, and Hua Huang

Self-Calibrating Scene Understanding Based on Motifnet   234
    Xiangyu Yin

BDGAN: Image Blind Denoising Using Generative Adversarial Networks . . .   241
    Shipeng Zhu, Guili Xu, Yuehua Cheng, Xiaodong Han,
    and Zhengsheng Wang

Single Image Reflection Removal Based on Deep Residual Learning.   253
    Zhixin Xu, Xiaobao Guo, and Guangming Lu

An Automated Method with Attention Network for Cervical
Cancer Scanning.   267
    Lijuan Duan, Fan Xu, Yuanhua Qiao, Di Zhao, Tongtong Xu,
    and Chunli Wu

Graph-Based Scale-Aware Network for Human Parsing   279
Beibei Yang, Changqian Yu, Jiahui Liu, Changxin Gao, and Nong Sang

Semi-supervised Lesion Detection with Reliable Label Propagation
and Missing Label Mining   291
Zhuo Wang, Zihao Li, Shu Zhang, Junge Zhang, and Kaiqi Huang

Image Aesthetic Assessment Based on Perception Consistency   303
Weining Wang, Rui Deng, Lemin Li, and Xiangmin Xu

Image De-noising by an Effective SURE-Based Weighted
Bilateral Filtering   316
Jian Ji, Sitong Li, Guofei Hou, Fen Ren, and Qiguang Miao

Automatic Detection of Pneumonia in Chest X-Ray Images Using
Cooperative Convolutional Neural Networks   328
Kun Wang, Xiaohong Zhang, Sheng Huang, and Feiyu Chen

Siamese Spatial Pyramid Matching Network with Location Prior
for Anatomical Landmark Tracking in 3-Dimension Ultrasound Sequence . . .   341
Jishuai He, Chunxu Shen, Yibin Huang, and Jian Wu

Local Context Embedding Neural Network for Scene
Semantic Segmentation   354
Junxia Li, Lingzheng Dai, Yu Ding, and Qingshan Liu

Retinex Based Flicker-Free Low-Light Video Enhancement   367
Juanjuan Tu, Zongliang Gan, and Feng Liu

Transfer Learning for Rigid 2D/3D Cardiovascular Images Registration   380
Shaoya Guan, Cai Meng, Kai Sun, and Tianmiao Wang

Temporal Invariant Factor Disentangled Model
for Representation Learning   391
Weichao Shen, Yuwei Wu, and Yunde Jia

A Multi-frame Video Interpolation Neural Network for Large Motion   403
Wenchao Hu and Zhiguang Wang

One-Shot Video Object Segmentation Initialized with Referring Expression . . .   416
*XiaoQing Bu, Jianming Wang, Jiayu Liang, Kunliang Liu, Yukuan Sun,
and Guanghao Jin*

Scalable Receptive Field GAN: An End-to-End Adversarial Learning
Framework for Crowd Counting   429
Yukang Gao and Hua Yang

Lightweight Video Object Segmentation Based on ConvGRU.   441
*Rui Yao, Yikun Zhang, Cunyuan Gao, Yong Zhou, Jiaqi Zhao,
and Lina Liang*

Crowd Counting via Conditional Generative Adversarial Networks   453
    Tao Xu, Yinong Duan, Jiahao Du, and Caihua Liu

Gemini Network for Temporal Action Localization   463
    Hongru Li, Ying Wang, and Yuan Zhou

SS-GANs: Text-to-Image via Stage by Stage Generative
Adversarial Networks   475
    Ming Tian, Yuting Xue, Chunna Tian, Lei Wang, Donghu Deng,
    and Wei Wei

Face Super-Resolution via Discriminative-Attributes   487
    Ning Dong, Xiaoguang Li, Jiafeng Li, and Li Zhuo

RefineNet4Dehaze: Single Image Dehazing Network Based on RefineNet . . .   498
    Kuan Ma, Hongwei Feng, Jie Luo, and Qirong Bo

Level Set Image Segmentation Based on Non-independent
and Identically Distributed   508
    Yaxin Wang, Yuanfeng Lian, Dianzhong Wang, and Jianbin Zhang

KSLIC: K-mediods Clustering Based Simple Linear Iterative Clustering   519
    Houwang Zhang and Yuan Zhu

Social Behavior Recognition in Mouse Video Using Agent Embedding
and LSTM Modelling   530
    Zhenchuan Zhang, Yingchun Yang, and Zhaohui Wu

Unsupervised Global Manifold Alignment for Cross-Scene Hyperspectral
Image Classification   542
    Wei Feng, Yuan Zhou, and Dou Jin

Poleward Moving Aurora Recognition with Deep Convolutional Networks. . .   551
    Yiping Tang, Chuang Niu, Minghao Dong, Shenghan Ren,
    and Jimin Liang

Robust Hyperspectral Image Pan-Sharpening via Channel-Constrained
Spatial Spectral Network   561
    Na Li and Licheng Liu

Ensemble Transductive Learning for Skin Lesion Segmentation   572
    Zhiying Cui, Longshi Wu, Ruixuan Wang, and Wei-Shi Zheng

MobileCount: An Efficient Encoder-Decoder Framework for Real-Time
Crowd Counting   582
    Chenyu Gao, Peng Wang, and Ye Gao

Multi-scale Densely 3D CNN for Hyperspectral Image Classification   596
    Yong Xiao, Qin Xu, Dongyue Wang, Jin Tang, and Bin Luo

No-Reference Image Quality Assessment via Multi-order Perception
Similarity.   607
  Ziheng Zhou, Wen Lu, Jiachen Yang, and Shishuai Han

Blind Quality Assessment for DIBR-Synthesized Images Based
on Chromatic and Disoccluded Information   620
  Mengna Ding, Yuming Fang, Yifan Zuo, and Zuowen Tan

Gait Recognition with Clothing and Carrying Variations Based on GEI
and CAPDS Features.   632
  Fengjia Yang, Xinghao Jiang, Tanfeng Sun, and Ke Xu

Stage-by-Stage Based Design Paradigm of Two-Pathway Model
for Gaze Following.   644
  Zhongping Cao, Guoli Wang, and Xuemei Guo

Multi-modal Feature Fusion Based on Variational Autoencoder for Visual
Question Answering   657
  Liqing Chen, Yifan Zhuo, Yingjie Wu, Yilei Wang, and Xianghan Zheng

Local and Global Feature Learning for Subtle Facial Expression
Recognition from Attention Perspective.   670
  Shaocong Wang, Yuan Yuan, and Yachuang Feng

Multi-label Chest X-Ray Image Classification via Label
Co-occurrence Learning.   682
  Bingzhi Chen, Yao Lu, and Guangming Lu

Asymmetric Pyramid Based Super Resolution from Very Low Resolution
Face Image   694
  Xuebo Wang, Yao Lu, Xiaozhen Chen, Weiqi Li, and Zijian Wang

A Hybrid Pan-Sharpening Approach Using Nonnegative Matrix
Factorization for WorldView Imageries   703
  Guiqing He, Jiaqi Ji, Qiqi Zhang, and Zhaoqiang Xia

Distinguishing Individual Red Pandas from Their Faces.   714
  Qi He, Qijun Zhao, Ning Liu, Peng Chen, Zhihe Zhang, and Rong Hou

Facial Expression Recognition: Disentangling Expression Based
on Self-attention Conditional Generative Adversarial Nets   725
  Haohao Li, Qiong Liu, Xiaoming Wei, Zhenhua Chai, and Wenbai Chen

Image Enhancement of Shadow Region Based on Polarization Imaging.   736
  Mohamed Reda, Linghao Shen, and Yongqiang Zhao

Multi-scale Convolutional Capsule Network for Hyperspectral
Image Classification   749
   Dongyue Wang, Qin Xu, Yong Xiao, Jin Tang, and Bin Luo

Dark Channel Prior Guided Conditional Generative Adversarial Network
for Single Image Dehazing.   761
   Yan Zhao Su, Zhi Gao Cui, Ai Hua Li, Tao Wang, and Ke Jiang

A Fast Region Growing Based Superpixel Segmentation for Hyperspectral
Image Classification   772
   Qianqian Xu, Peng Fu, Quansen Sun, and Tao Wang

Complexity Reduction for Depth Map Coding in 3D-HEVC.   783
   Shifang Yu, Guojun Dai, Hua Zhang, and Hongfei Huang

Super Resolution via Residual Restructured Dense Network.   794
   Yifeng Wang, Yaru Rong, Haihong Zheng, and Aoli Liu

Author Index   807

Contents – Part III

Data Analysis and Optimization

Modality Consistent Generative Adversarial Network
for Cross-Modal Retrieval 3
    Zhiyong Wu, Fei Wu, Xiaokai Luo, Xiwei Dong, Cailing Wang,
    and Xiao-Yuan Jing

Retrieval by Classification: Discriminative Binary Embedding
for Sketch-Based Image Retrieval 15
    Yufeng Shi, Xinge You, Wenjie Wang, Feng Zheng, Qinmu Peng,
    and Shuo Wang

Robust Subspace Segmentation via Sparse Relation Representation 27
    Lai Wei and Hao Liu

An Approach to the Applicability Evaluation of Moving Target
Tracking Algorithm. 38
    Runping Xi, Shaohui Xue, Qianqian Han, and Jiaxin Chen

A Cooperative Particle Swarm Optimization Algorithm Based
on Greedy Disturbance 52
    Xing Huo, Fei Zhang, Chao Luo, Jieqing Tan, and Kun Shao

Jointing Cross-Modality Retrieval to Reweight Attributes for Image
Caption Generation 62
    Yuxuan Ding, Wei Wang, Mengmeng Jiang, Heng Liu, Donghu Deng,
    Wei Wei, and Chunna Tian

Pseudo Label Guided Subspace Learning for Multi-view Data 75
    Shudong Hou, Heng Liu, and Xiujun Wang

MVB: A Large-Scale Dataset for Baggage Re-Identification and Merged
Siamese Networks. 84
    Zhulin Zhang, Dong Li, Jinhua Wu, Yunda Sun, and Li Zhang

Personalized Travel Recommendation via Multi-view
Representation Learning. 97
    Yujun Zhang, Bin Han, Xinbo Gao, and Haoran Li

FollowMeUp Sports: New Benchmark for 2D Human
Keypoint Recognition 110
    Ying Huang, Bin Sun, Haipeng Kan, Jiankai Zhuang,
    and Zengchang Qin

Partial Order Structure Based Image Retrieval   122
  Zhuoyi Li, Guanghua Gu, and Jiangtao Liu

Computer Vision Applications

Semantic Object and Plane SLAM for RGB-D Cameras   137
  Longyu Zheng and Wenbing Tao

Crime Scene Sketches Classification Based on CNN   149
  Kaixuan Wang, Houlu Zhang, and Yunqi Tang

Image-Based Air Quality Estimation   161
  Qin Li and Bin Xie

Rotational Alignment of IMU-camera Systems with 1-Point RANSAC   172
  Banglei Guan, Ang Su, Zhang Li, and Friedrich Fraundorfer

Bidirectional Adversarial Domain Adaptation with Semantic Consistency. . . .   184
  Yaping Zhang, Shuai Nie, Shan Liang, and Wenju Liu

A Novel Hard Mining Center-Triplet Loss for Person Re-identification   199
  Xinbi Lv, Cairong Zhao, and Wei Chen

Kinematic Feature-Based Evaluation Method for Elderly Balance Ability
by Using Factor Analysis.   211
  Rui Ming, Xing-Rong Fan, and Guoliang Xu

Efficient Automatic Meta Optimization Search for Few-Shot Learning.   223
  Xinyue Zheng, Peng Wang, Qigang Wang, Zhongchao Shi, and Feiyu Xu

Visual Odometry with Deep Bidirectional Recurrent Neural Networks   235
  Fei Xue, Xin Wang, Qiuyuan Wang, Junqiu Wang, and Hongbin Zha

Fuzzy Control Reversing System Based on Visual Information   247
  Shaofeng Liu, Yingchun Fan, Yuliang Tang, Xin Jing, Jintao Yao,
  and Hong Han

Adversarial Domain Alignment Feature Similarity Enhancement Learning
for Unsupervised Domain Adaptation   259
  Jun Zhou, Fei Wu, Ying Sun, Songsong Wu, Min Yang,
  and Xiao-Yuan Jing

ADSRNet: Attention-Based Densely Connected Network
for Image Super-Resolution   272
  Weiqi Li, Yao Lu, Xuebo Wang, Xiaozhen Chen, and Zijian Wang

Robust and Efficient Visual-Inertial Odometry with Multi-plane Priors   283
  Jinyu Li, Bangbang Yang, Kai Huang, Guofeng Zhang, and Hujun Bao

Contour-Guided Person Re-identification   296
Jiaxing Chen, Qize Yang, Jingke Meng, Wei-Shi Zheng,
and Jian-Huang Lai

Robust License Plate Detection Through Auxiliary Information and Context
Fusion Model   308
Ning Wang, Feng Liu, and Zongliang Gan

PointNet-Based Channel Attention VLAD Network   320
Rongrong Fan, Hui Shuai, and Qingshan Liu

Multi-scale Deep Residual Network for Satellite Image
Super-Resolution Reconstruction   332
Wen Xu, Chuang Zhang, and Ming Wu

CG Animation Creator: Auto-rendering of Motion Stick Figure Based
on Conditional Adversarial Learning   341
Jie Lin, Jian Cui, Guangming Shi, and Danhua Liu

Deep Eyes: Binocular Depth-from-Focus on Focal Stack Pairs   353
Xinqing Guo, Zhang Chen, Siyuan Li, Yang Yang, and Jingyi Yu

Small Defect Detection in Industrial X-Ray Using Convolutional
Neural Network   366
Long Cheng, Ping Gong, Guanghui Qiu, Jing Wang, and Ziyuan Liu

ODCN: Optimized Dilated Convolution Network
for 3D Shape Segmentation   378
Likuan Qian, Yuanfeng Lian, Qian Wei, Shuangyuan Wu,
and Jianbin Zhang

Style Consistency Constrained Fusion Feature Learning for Liver
Tumor Segmentation   390
Yunfeng Liu, Xibin Jia, Zhenghan Yang, and Dawei Yang

Hierarchical Correlation Stereo Matching Network   397
Xuliang Chen and Yue Zhou

An Accurate LSTM Based Video Heart Rate Estimation Method   409
Mingyun Bian, Bo Peng, Wei Wang, and Jing Dong

Self-supervised Homography Prediction CNN for Accurate Lane
Marking Fitting.   418
Yiman Chen, Wentao Du, Zhiyu Xiang, Nan Zou, Shuya Chen,
and Chengyu Qiao

Scenario Referring Expression Comprehension via Attributes of Vision
and Language.   430
  Shaonan Wei, Jianming Wang, Yukuan Sun, Guanghao Jin, Jiayu Liang,
  and Kunliang Liu

Incremental Poisson Surface Reconstruction for Large Scale
Three-Dimensional Modeling   442
  Qiang Yu, Wei Sui, Ying Wang, Shiming Xiang, and Chunhong Pan

Deep Voice-Visual Cross-Modal Retrieval with Deep Feature
Similarity Learning   454
  Yaxiong Chen, Xiaoqiang Lu, and Yachuang Feng

Exploiting Human Pose for Weakly-Supervised Temporal
Action Localization.   466
  Bing Zhu, Tianyu Li, and Xinxiao Wu

Combing Deep and Handcrafted Features for NTV-NRPCA Based Fabric
Defect Detection.   479
  Junpu Wang, Chunlei Li, Zhoufeng Liu, Yan Dong, and Yun Huang

A Cost-Sensitive Shared Hidden Layer Autoencoder for Cross-Project
Defect Prediction   491
  Juanjuan Li, Xiao-Yuan Jing, Fei Wu, Ying Sun, and Yongguang Yang

Person ReID: Optimization of Domain Adaption Though Clothing Style
Transfer Between Datasets   503
  Haijian Wang, Meng Yang, Hui Li, and Linbin Ye

Shellfish Detection Based on Fusion Attention Mechanism
in End-to-End Network   516
  Guangyao Li, Zhenbo Li, Chuyue Zhang, Yaodong Li, and Jun Yue

Multi-branch Structure for Hierarchical Classification in Plant
Disease Recognition   528
  Zihao Mao, Jiaming Chen, and Meng Yang

Author Index   539

Object Detection, Tracking and Recognition

Channel Feature Enhanced Detector
for Small Ball Detection

Shambel Ferede[1,2], Xuemei Xie[1(✉)], Xing Jin[1], Jiang Du[1],
and Guangming Shi[1]

[1] Xidian University, Xi'an 710071, China
xmxie@mail.xidian.edu.cn
[2] Assosa University, 18, Assosa, Ethiopia

Abstract. We propose the channel feature enhanced detector (CFED) for ball detection, a challenging small object detection task. The proposed method achieves a good performance on small ball detection since we design a channel feature enhanced module to increase the discriminability of the target features. Moreover, we set up the BALL dataset for training and evaluation. Experimental results show that our method achieves a mAP of 90.2% on BALL dataset with an inference time of 11.4 milliseconds per image. The proposed lightweight network makes it possible to apply real-time detection to mobile devices.

Keywords: Channel feature enhanced detector · Ball detection ·
Single shot multi-box detector · Real-time

1 Introduction

Recent achievements in artificial intelligence (AI) have shown great influence in humans life. Intelligent physical education, which borrows the power of AI to bring convenience to teaching, is gaining more popularity. The main role that AI plays in this application is visual semantic information pursuit [17]. At an early stage of AI, object detection [10] is a very fundamental task for visual perception unit pursuit.

Contemporarily, remarkable advances have been achieved in deep neural networks (DNN) for object detection. Some of the classical methods like Faster R-CNN [23], SSD [18], YOLO [21] have been proposed and they obtain the ability for detecting hundreds of categories of objects. This is because of the exploding rise of computational capability of GPUs, so that we can design deeper and larger DNN models, and some largescale datasets like PASCAL VOC [5] and MS COCO [3] have been set up for training and evaluation.

Although we have obtained remarkably high scores in public datasets, there are still a lot of challenges for object detection in reality tasks. For example, in intelligent physical education, detecting the ball would be helpful for the coach

---

This paper will compete the Best Student Paper Award.

© Springer Nature Switzerland AG 2019
Z. Lin et al. (Eds.): PRCV 2019, LNCS 11857, pp. 3–13, 2019.
https://doi.org/10.1007/978-3-030-31654-9_1

to grasp the accuracy of students who play the ball. However, when placing the camera in the sports room, the balls takes up just a few pixels, which is small objects for detection. This makes the current DNN-based detector difficult to catch the visual perception unit of the ball.

The key challenge in ball detection is that the feature of small balls tends to be very weak and ambiguous in this task, due to deformation, motion blur, and analogous image background whose color and shading is similar to the balls. Existing methods for small object detection [1] employ the combination of different layers in SSD, which introduce the contextual information to help the detection. While this fails in ball detection, since the distribution of contextual feature of the ball in these tasks varies in a wide range.

Considering these challenges, we use the classical object detector SSD to detect the ball. We propose channel feature enhancement module based on SSD for precision and speed trade-offs. To compute the channel enhancement effectively, we squeeze the spatial dimension of the input feature map into a feature vector. This increases the difference between target features and redundant features that enhanced a good performance on the ball detection.

In summary, our main contributions are as follows:

– We propose channel feature enhanced detector for small ball detection.
– We propose channel feature enhanced module to enhance the discriminability of target feature map.
– We set up the BALL dataset for detection.
– Proposed detector achieves a good performance with a mAP of 90.2%

The remaining of the paper is organized as follows - Sect. 2 presents the general related work, in Sect. 3 we discuss the enhanced feature detector, Sect. 4 dataset preparations and an experimental result is explained, and in Sect. 5 conclusions is drawn.

2   Related Work

2.1   Object Detection

Object detection is the identification of an object in an image along with its localization and classification [2]. Most of the object detection methods are based on the slidingwindow paradigm for many years using the handcrafted features, such as HOG [4]. In the recent years the accuracy and inference speed of detection greatly improved, because of the development of ConvNets that can integrate feature learning and classifier in to one framework. According to StairNet [26], R-CNN [8] achieves amazing performance by integrating object proposal mechanism and a powerful CNN classifier.

The R-CNN detector has been modified over the time in terms of speed and accuracy. Fast R-CNN [7] is fast and reliable framework than R-CNN for object detection with deep ConvNets. Lately, Faster-RCNN combined proposal generation module and the Fast R-CNN classifier into a single CNN together. Then

YOLO and SSD have been emerged for real-time detection. Both are fast single stage methods which divide an image in to a multiple grids and concurrently predict bounding boxes and class confidences. SSD combine predictions from multiple feature maps with different resolutions to naturally handle objects of various sizes. This makes SSD more robust to detect different shapes and sizes of objects than YOLO. Consequently, a number of studies show that using multiple layers within CNN can improve detection and segmentation.

2.2 Small Object Detection

Small object detection enriched by increasing the input image resolution [16, 18, 27] or by fusing high-resolution features with high dimensional features from the low-resolution image [20]. However, using higher resolution raises computational overhead and does not address the disproportion between small and large objects [16]. The performance of detecting small object instances is still not appropriate because of the deficit of semantic information on shallow features [16, 27]. For the top semantic features, the representations of fine details for small objects are highly dispersed. SSD uses the features from the shallower layers to detect small objects, while exploits the features from the deeper layers for bigger objects detection. To solve this DSSD [6] adds extra deconvolution layers in the end of SSD to increase the accuracy of small objects. Feature-fused SSD [1] uses a multi-level feature fusion method to introduce contextual information in SSD and improves the accuracy of small object detection.

2.3 Real-Time Object Detection

In recent years, there have been many studies aimed at improving the speed and accuracy of target detection. YOLOv3 [22] uses the onestage method to directly predict object position and category, which greatly increases the speed of detection. However, the detection accuracy is not satisfactory. SSD [18] performs well in both accuracy and speed, by using multiscale predicted layers.

But YOLOv3 and SSD don't detect small targets very well. In order to improve this, [13, 28, 29] use top-down feature fusion models to enhance the feature of small objects, thereby improving the accuracy of small object detection.

In this paper, we use channel feature enhanced module (CFEM) by exploiting the inter-channel relationship of features to end-to-end manner to detect a ball in a real time video.

3 Channel Feature Enhanced Detector

This section introduces our channel feature enhanced detector based on SSD model, which makes a trade-off between detection accuracy and speed. We first introduce SSD and our improvements on it. Then we elaborate the channel feature enhanced module.

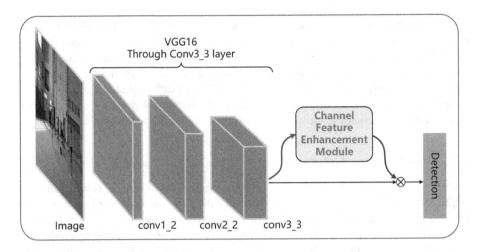

Fig. 1. Architecture of channel feature enhanced detector. It includes improved SSD and channel feature enhanced module.

3.1   Single Shot Multibox Detector

The emergence of the single shot multibox detector (SSD) provides an effective and efficient detection method. First of all, SSD takes the idea of one-stage, which greatly improves the speed of the network. Secondly, SSD learns from the anchor idea of Faster R-CNN in RCNN series. And based on this, SSD proposes the idea of multi-layer feature extraction to adapt to multi-scale object detection. It predicts objects from conv4_3 layer to conv11_2 layer with different size default boxes. SSD achieves a good performance on PASCAL VOC and MS COCO dataset which contains objects of various sizes and shapes.

3.2   Proposed Architecture

The proposed architecture, as shown in Fig. 1, is based on SSD and has been modified on SSD to make it suitable for small ball detection. All the balls are too small in our dataset, resulting in a poor detection results of SSD. We calculated the size of the effective receptive fields of several convolution layer of SSD and counted the size distribution of the balls in our dataset. In order to match the sizes of the receptive field and the ball, we add a new predicted layer on conv3_3 instead of using the original prediction layer of SSD, as shown in Fig. 1. We removed the other layers after conv3_3 layer in the SSD. So our network has very few parameters that is particularly critical for real-time detection. And we only use one size default box to avoid too much computation burden and lead convergence easily. The default boxes with a scale of 16×16 and an aspect ratio of 1:1 are evenly set on the conv3_3 prediction layer. We use this modified SSD as our baseline and add a channel feature enhanced module to improve the feature of prediction layer.

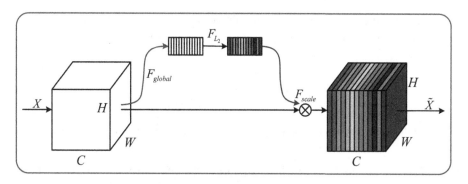

Fig. 2. Architecture of channel feature enhanced module. It uses prediction feature map as input and outputs the enhanced feature map.

3.3   Channel Feature Enhanced Module

Convolution neural network (CNN) learns features in a layer-by-layer manner to generate sufficiently rich features. Therefore, researchers usually design a deeper [11] and wider [25] network structure to generate more features, thereby improving the accuracy of the algorithm. However, when these large networks are used for small dataset, there will be many redundant features which reduce the discriminability of useful features. We apply Squeeze-and-Excitation block [12] as our channel feature enhanced module (CFEM) by exploiting the inter-channel relationship of features for the task on our BALL dataset, as shown in Fig. 2. This module quantifies the importance of each convolution kernel of the feature layer. To compute the channel enhancement effectively, we squeeze the spatial dimension of the input feature map into a feature vector. The feature vector representing the importance weights is used to adjust the feature map of each channel. This approach increases the difference between target features and redundant features, making the target feature more discriminative. The enhanced target features will lead a good performance on the target detection. Next, we introduce the details of CFEM.

Global Average Pooling. The input of the CFEM is the feature map of the predicted layer. We use a global average pooling layer to get the strongest response value of each channel feature map, as shown in Eq. (1).

$$z_i = F_{global}(X) = \frac{1}{H \times W} \sum_{m=1}^{H} \sum_{n=1}^{W} x_i(m,n), i = 1, 2, ..., C \qquad (1)$$

Where $F_{global}(X)$ stands for the global average pooling. H and W are the height and width of the input feature map X. $x_i(m,n)$ represents the value of each point on the i-th feature map. This equation represents summing all the pixel values in the feature map of the i-th channel and then taking the mean to get the response z_i of the i-th channel. It will output a vector $Z = [z_1, z_2, ..., z_C]$ with dimension C (usually C = 256).

Normalize Layer. To prevent the amplitude of the vector from being too large, we normalize it using the L_2 function [19], as Eq. (2) shows.

$$s_i = F_{L_2}(Z) = \frac{z_i}{\|z\|_2} = \frac{z_i}{\sqrt{\sum_{i=1}^{C} z_i^2}} \tag{2}$$

We will get a new vector S representing the response weight of each channel.

Scale Layer. We apply a scale layer to obtain the final output, which consists of the weight vector and original features. We use the vector S to scale the overall amplitude of each channel feature map. The original prediction feature maps are multiplied by the weight vector S to get new enhanced feature maps, as shown in Eqs. (3) and (4). This means that each point on the feature map x_i is multiplied by s_i.

$$\tilde{x}_i = F_{scale}(s_i, x_i) = s_i \cdot x_i \tag{3}$$

$$\tilde{X} = [\tilde{x}_1, \tilde{x}_2, ..., \tilde{x}_C] \tag{4}$$

Where $\tilde{x}_i$ means one of the new feature and $\tilde{X}$ means all output features. F_{scale} means that the original feature map x_i of each channel is multiplied by the corresponding scalar s_i.

The response of the target feature is greater than the redundant feature. Therefore, the weight of the target feature to be multiplied is large. By the scaling of the Eq. (3), the discriminability between the target feature and the redundant feature is more obvious.

4   Experiments

In this section, we firstly analyze the effectiveness of our framework on our BALL dataset, then evaluate the channel feature enhanced module, finally introduce the inference time. And the experimental details are also given.

4.1   Dataset Preparation

In this paper, all methods and experiments are designed for the BALL dataset, as shown in Fig. 3. The collected BALL dataset is acquired at Shaanxi Provincial Sports Training Center. We shot some videos while the athletes were training with balls. For all videos, the resolution is 1920×1080 and we captured one target image per 10 frames. The whole dataset contains 1,754 images with 1,315 images for training and 439 images for testing. Training and testing samples are annotated one category – ball. Images from the train and test sets come from different videos. There are 7,082 ball instances in whole dataset, with an average of 4 balls per image. In the BALL dataset, the balls are distributed in various positions and have different shapes.

Fig. 3. Some examples of our BALL dataset in different scenes. The ball will be deformed, occluded or blurred while moving.

Figure 3 shows the ball in different scenes. The ball will be blurred due to the quick throw. When squeezed or dropped to the ground, the ball will deform. And the ball will be blocked, when the athlete takes the ball. Moreover, the features of the ball will not be obvious when there is a shadow.

4.2   Detection Results on BALL Dataset

Our network is implemented based on SSD built on the Caffe framework [15], and the VGG16 [24] architecture, all of which are available online. The VGG16 network is reduced of fully connected layers when used as the framework of SSD. We improves SSD using conv3_3 to predict small balls and add channel feature enhanced module to enhance the discriminability of target feature map. All layers in our network initialized with 'Xavier' weight [9]. We add a batch normalization layer [14] and a scale layer after each convolution layer. The training process starts with the learning rate at 10^{-3} for the first 10K iterations, and decreases to 10^{-4} and 10^{-5} at 15K and 20K. We resize the input image to 300×300. We do all experiments with the batch size 16 and test the model with batch size 1 using a single NVIDIA GTX-1080Ti GPU (12 GB memory), CUDA 8.0, cuDNNv6.0 with Intel Core i7-7700k@4.2GHz.

Table 1 shows comparison results of CFED with other detectors. It can be seen that CFED achieves a mAP of 90.2% on BALL dataset. CFED is much more accurate than other detectors. It takes an average of 11.4 ms to inference a image because of the low-computational-cost algorithm. In summary, our proposed detector achieves a good performance on small ball detection.

Table 1. The ball detection results and inference time of CFED and other detectors on the BALL dataset.

Method	mAP (%)	Inference time (ms)
Faster R-CNN	68.3	121.5
SSD	71.8	21.3
YOLOv3	74.4	14.9
CFED	90.2	11.4

We show some qualitative results on BALL test dataset in Fig. 4. A score threshold of 0.3 is used to display these images. As shown in Fig. 4, CFED achieves a good performance on small ball detection, even if the ball is deformed, occluded or blurred due to rapid motion. For the sake of aesthetics, we use circles to represent the boxes of test results. (x, y, w, h) of the rectangular default box is still used as the learning parameter during training.

4.3   Ablation Study

To demonstrate the effectiveness of different components in CFED, we design several variants and validate them on BALL dataset. We set same training iteration, batch size and input size to achieve a fair comparison. The model is trained and tested on our BALL dataset.

Table 2. The ball detection results and inference time of ablative experiments for the CFEM model and BN layer on the BALL dataset.

Method	CFED			Baseline
CFEM	√		√	
BN	√	√		
mAP (%)	90.2	88.9	88.1	85.0

Table 3. The ball detection results and inference time of ablative experiments for the CFEM with two different global pooling layer.

	mAP (%)	Inference time (ms)
Global average pooling	90.2	11.4
Global maximum pooling	89.6	12.3

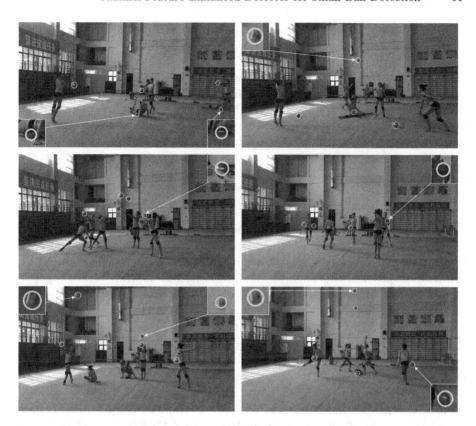

Fig. 4. Some examples of our CFED ball detection results. We zoomed in on some small balls that were difficult to detect, such as deformed, occluded or blurred balls.

Channel Feature Enhanced Module. To validate the effectiveness of channel feature enhancement module, we compare the test results with and without CFEM. Table 2. of col 3 and col 4 shows the results of the two models. The accuracy increases from 85.0% to 88.1% by adding CFEM. The results validate the effectiveness of CFEM. Without CFEM, the presence of redundant features can interfere with detection results. CFEM can improve the detection accuracy by increasing the discriminability of the target features.

Batch Normalization. To evaluate the effectiveness of the batch normalization (BN), we compare the test results with and without the BN layers. Table 2 of col 2 and col 4 shows the results of the two models. The accuracy increases from 85.0% to 88.9% by adding the batch normalization layer. It evaluates that the batch normalization is a valid training method for random initialization. It can accelerate network convergence speed and make a good optimization result.

Global Pooling Layer. We use the global average pooling method to get the weight of each channel in our network. We also do the experiment with the global maximum pooling approach. The test results of the two models are shown in Table 3. It is clear that global average pooling in CFEM shows a better performance than global maximum pooling. It is because the maximum value can only represent one point value and does not reflect the entire feature map. And the complexity of calculating the maximum value leads to a longer inference time. So we use global average pooling in our network.

5   Conclusions

This paper proposes a lightweight framework for real-time small ball detection. We use the channel feature enhanced module to increase the discriminability of the target feature. The proposed network achieves remarkable performance on BALL dataset. This work is of great significance since it plays an important role in intelligent physical education. In the future, we will implement the proposed framework on mobile devices to detect the small balls online.

Ackonwledgement. This work is supported by Natural Science Foundation (NSF) of China (61836008).

References

1. Cao, G., Xie, X., Yang, W., Liao, Q., Shi, G., Wu, J.: Feature-fused SSD: fast detection for small objects. In: Ninth International Conference on Graphic and Image Processing (ICGIP 2017), vol. 10615, p. 106151E. International Society for Optics and Photonics (2018)
2. Chahal, K.S., Dey, K.: A survey of modern object detection literature using deep learning. arXiv preprint arXiv:1808.07256 (2018)
3. Chen, X., et al.: Microsoft coco captions: data collection and evaluation server. arXiv preprint arXiv:1504.00325 (2015)
4. Dalal, N., Triggs, B.: Histograms of oriented gradients for human detection (2005)
5. Everingham, M., Van Gool, L., Williams, C.K., Winn, J., Zisserman, A.: The pascal visual object classes (VOC) challenge. Int. J. Comput. Vision **88**(2), 303–338 (2010)
6. Fu, C.Y., Liu, W., Ranga, A., Tyagi, A., Berg, A.C.: DSSD: deconvolutional single shot detector. arXiv preprint arXiv:1701.06659 (2017)
7. Girshick, R.: Fast R-CNN. In: Proceedings of the IEEE International Conference on Computer Vision, pp. 1440–1448 (2015)
8. Girshick, R., Donahue, J., Darrell, T., Malik, J.: Rich feature hierarchies for accurate object detection and semantic segmentation. In: Proceedings of the IEEE Conference on Computer Vision and Pattern Recognition, pp. 580–587 (2014)
9. Glorot, X., Bengio, Y.: Understanding the difficulty of training deep feedforward neural networks. In: Proceedings of the Thirteenth International Conference on Artificial Intelligence and Statistics, pp. 249–256 (2010)
10. Han, J., Zhang, D., Cheng, G., Liu, N., Xu, D.: Advanced deep-learning techniques for salient and category-specific object detection: a survey. IEEE Signal Process. Mag. **35**(1), 84–100 (2018)

11. He, K., Zhang, X., Ren, S., Sun, J.: Deep residual learning for image recognition. In: Proceedings of the IEEE Conference on Computer Vision and Pattern Recognition, pp. 770–778 (2016)
12. Hu, J., Shen, L., Sun, G.: Squeeze-and-excitation networks. In: Proceedings of the IEEE Conference on Computer Vision and Pattern Recognition, pp. 7132–7141 (2018)
13. Hu, P., Ramanan, D.: Finding tiny faces. In: Computer Vision and Pattern Recognition, pp. 1522–1530 (2017)
14. Ioffe, S., Szegedy, C.: Batch normalization: accelerating deep network training by reducing internal covariate shift. arXiv preprint arXiv:1502.03167 (2015)
15. Jia, Y., et al.: Caffe: convolutional architecture for fast feature embedding. In: Proceedings of the 22nd ACM International Conference on Multimedia, pp. 675–678. ACM (2014)
16. Kisantal, M., Wojna, Z., Murawski, J., Naruniec, J., Cho, K.: Augmentation for small object detection. arXiv preprint arXiv:1902.07296 (2019)
17. Liu, D., Bober, M., Kittler, J.: Visual semantic information pursuit: a survey (2019)
18. Liu, W., et al.: SSD: single shot multibox detector. In: Leibe, B., Matas, J., Sebe, N., Welling, M. (eds.) ECCV 2016. LNCS, vol. 9905, pp. 21–37. Springer, Cham (2016). https://doi.org/10.1007/978-3-319-46448-0_2
19. Liu, W., Rabinovich, A., Berg, A.C.: ParseNet: looking wider to see better. arXiv preprint arXiv:1506.04579 (2015)
20. Menikdiwela, M., Nguyen, C., Li, H., Shaw, M.: CNN-based small object detection and visualization with feature activation mapping. In: 2017 International Conference on Image and Vision Computing New Zealand (IVCNZ), pp. 1–5. IEEE (2017)
21. Redmon, J., Divvala, S., Girshick, R., Farhadi, A.: You only look once: unified, real-time object detection. In: Proceedings of the IEEE Conference on Computer Vision and Pattern Recognition, pp. 779–788 (2016)
22. Redmon, J., Farhadi, A.: YOLOv3: an incremental improvement. arXiv preprint arXiv:1804.02767 (2018)
23. Ren, S., He, K., Girshick, R., Sun, J.: Faster R-CNN: towards real-time object detection with region proposal networks. In: Advances in Neural Information Processing Systems, pp. 91–99 (2015)
24. Simonyan, K., Zisserman, A.: Very deep convolutional networks for large-scale image recognition. arXiv preprint arXiv:1409.1556 (2014)
25. Szegedy, C., Ioffe, S., Vanhoucke, V., Alemi, A.A.: Inception-v4, inception-ResNet and the impact of residual connections on learning. In: Thirty-First AAAI Conference on Artificial Intelligence (2017)
26. Woo, S., Hwang, S., Kweon, I.S.: StairNet: top-down semantic aggregation for accurate one shot detection. In: 2018 IEEE Winter Conference on Applications of Computer Vision (WACV), pp. 1093–1102. IEEE (2018)
27. Xu, M., et al.: MDSSD: multi-scale deconvolutional single shot detector for small objects. arXiv preprint arXiv:1805.07009 (2018)
28. Zhang, S., Wen, L., Bian, X., Lei, Z., Li, S.Z.: Single-shot refinement neural network for object detection. In: Proceedings of the IEEE Conference on Computer Vision and Pattern Recognition, pp. 4203–4212 (2018)
29. Zhang, S., Zhu, X., Lei, Z., Shi, H., Wang, X., Li, S.Z.: S^{3}fd: single shot scale-invariant face detector. In: Proceedings of the IEEE International Conference on Computer Vision, pp. 192–201 (2017)

High-Order Graph Convolutional Network for Skeleton-Based Human Action Recognition

Zhimin Bai[1], Hongping Yan[1], and Lingfeng Wang[2](✉)

[1] Institute of Information Engineering, China University of Geosciences,
Beijing, China
{zmbai,yanhp}@cugb.edu.cn
[2] Institute of Automation, Chinese Academy of Sciences, Beijing, China
lfwang@nlpr.ia.ac.cn

Abstract. Skeleton-based action recognition plays an important role in the field of human action recognition. Recently, with the introduction of Graph Convolution Network (GCN), GCN has achieved superior performance in the field of skeleton-based human action recognition. In this work, we propose a high-order GCN model. In this model, we introduce the expression of high-order skeletons and establish a new high-order adjacency matrix. Through this matrix, the relationship between skeleton nodes and non-neighbor nodes has being established. In addition, based on the degree of node association of different hierarchical neighborhoods, the value of the matrix expresses the importance of different hierarchies. As a result, the proposed model extracts the co-occurrence feature of the skeleton which is superior to the local features and improves the recognition rate. We evaluate our model on two human skeleton action datasets, Kinetics-skeleton and NTU RGB+D, and then further explore the influence of skeleton nodes based on different hierarchies on the recognition results.

Keywords: Human action recognition · High-order skeleton information · Graph convolution network

1 Introduction

Human action recognition is an important and challenging research field of computer vision, and has received extensive attention in recent years. At present, the RGB image sequence is the main research field of human action recognition [1–8]. However, it is greatly affected by the environment, such as light and background. In addition, human action recognition based on RGB image sequences is difficult to distinguish subtle motion differences between similar actions. Currently, with

This work is supported by the National Natural Science Foundation of China (Grant Number 61773377 and 61573352).

the continuous development of software and hardware equipment, advanced algorithms for extracting skeleton sequences [9] and human action datasets based on skeleton [10] have been proposed. Based on this, skeleton-based human action recognition algorithm is proposed [12–14]. These Convolutional Neural Network (CNN) based models tend to be complex and difficult to obtain skeleton spatial features. For example, the TCN model [14] proposed by Kim et al. only considers the temporal information of the skeleton and ignores the spatial relationship between the skeleton nodes. In order to solve these problems, Yan et al. [18] proposed a new model, which breaks through the traditional CNN method and uses GCN to extract temporal and spatial information of the skeleton.

CNN has been able to efficiently process Euclidean data. It refers to grids, sequences, etc. For instance, images can be viewed as 2D grids data. There are many non-Euclidean data in reality, however, such as the human skeleton. Kipf et al. [23] formally proposed GCN to deal with non-Euclidean data, and also achieved good results in the field of human action recognition [18]. Compared with the traditional CNN method, the GCN is simpler and more precise.

At present, the GCN-based model extracts feature information through connections between nodes. This makes the feature representation of human skeleton simpler and more comprehensive than CNN. However, there is a correlation between multiple joints of the human skeleton when the person is moving. For example, in Fig. 1, when the person is drinking water, the wrist, elbow, shoulder, neck and head will have relative movement, even the interaction of the left and right arms is required to fully realize the behavior of drinking water. Therefore, when using GCN to implement skeleton-based human action recognition, only the skeleton nodes and their adjacent nodes are considered, that is limited.

(a)

(b)

Fig. 1. People need to interact with multiple joints when drinking water, such as wrists, elbows, shoulders, neck and head.

In this paper, we propose a graph convolutional network model based on higher-order skeletons. Based on the current best network model ST-GCN [18], we consider the spatial-temporal information of the skeleton during motion and the kinematics theorem of the body. Furthermore, the expressions of higher-order skeleton nodes and higher-order adjacency matrices are introduced. In addition, we establish connections between non-neighboring nodes and express the importance of joint points of different hierarchies by parameters, which is determined by the degree of correlation between the nodes. The main details and superiors of this work are listed as follows:

(1) Based on the ST-GCN network, we propose a high-order graph convolution network model based on skeleton. Through this model, the relationship between the high-order skeletons is expressed, and the co-occurrence characteristics of the skeleton are extracted. We verified the effectiveness of the method through experiments.
(2) We propose a new high-order neighborhood representation that achieves the importance of different neighborhood nodes by defining parameters and learnable weights. It reduces the noise and experimentally verifies that the method can improve the result.

2   Related Work

The current mainstream models and methods for human action recognition are based on RGB video, such as C3D [4,5], Two-stream [1–3] and Long Short Term Memory (LSTM) [6,7], etc. However, with the introduction of the human skeleton extraction method [9] and the establishment of related datasets [10], the skeleton-based human action recognition has gradually developed. Early traditional methods mainly used the sliding window [15] or relative position between joints [16] to obtain characteristic information of skeleton. With the popularization of deep learning in the field of computer vision, deep networks based on skeleton-based human action recognition is proposed. It is mainly divided into two methods: One is to convert the node coordinate information of the skeleton [11] or the distance between the joint points and the angle between the skeletons into a picture [12], and then extract features through the CNN. Li et al. [17] proposed a new end-to-end hierarchical feature learning network, which realizes the aggregation from the point level to the global co-occurrence feature. On the other hand, Song et al. [19] introduced the spatial-temporal attention mechanism based on the RNN neural network of LSTM and achieved good results. Liu et al. [20] optimized the spatial-temporal attention model and improved the performance of the network. Wang et al. [21] used two-stream RNN to realize the extraction of spatial-temporal features. Zhang et al. [22] proposed a new idea, which is a new viewpoint adaptive scheme. The coordinates of the skeleton are rotated to the appropriate angle of view, and the action recognition is performed through the RNN. Its has been greatly improved compared to the previous method.

With the emergence of many datasets in the form of graphs or networks, neural networks based on graph structure are an emerging topic in current deep learning research. In the past few years, many researchers have paid attention to the problem of generalizing neural networks to handle arbitrary graph structures. For example: Bruna et al. [24] first proposed the application of irregular grids on CNN, and proposed two methods: spatial domain and spectrum domain. For the spectral domain, Henaff et al. [25] proposed using a smooth kernel to implement a local filter. For the spatial domain, Niepert et al. [26] proposed to use the CNN to efficiently process the graph structure data by labeling the graph nodes and then convolving the nodes according to the sequence. Thomas et al. [23] proposed an extensible semi-supervised learning convolutional neural network method to process graph-based data and formally propose GCN. Meantime, with the introduction of GCN, it provides new research directions for data application based on graph structure [27,28], such as skeleton-based human action recognition. Although CNN and LSTM perform well in skeleton-based human action recognition, they have problems such as complex models and difficulty in training. Therefore, Yan et al. [18] proposed using GCN to realize skeleton-based human action recognition (ST-GCN), which shows better performance than the most advanced model.

3   Method

Actions of the human body is a range of local motion centered on certain joint points. Therefore, an important step of human action recognition based on high-order skeleton is to divide the skeleton based on kinematics. In addition, since the establishment of the network framework is based on the graph convolution, it is necessary to transform the skeleton into the expression form of the graph structure, and then realize the representation, division and graph convolution method of the high-order skeleton.

3.1   Skeleton Graph Construction

(a) Spatial diagram   (b) Spatial-Temporal diagram

Fig. 2. Skeleton spatial-temporal structure diagram. (a): The spatial relationship of the skeleton is represented by the connection between joint points. (b): The temporal relationship of the skeleton is represented by connecting the same joint points between consecutive frames.

The human skeleton is a typical graph structure. When describing the behavior of the human body, we need to obtain the spatial and temporal information of the skeleton. Therefore, the joint point set of the skeleton can be expressed as $V = \{v_{tn}|t = 1, 2, \ldots, T, n = 1, 2, \ldots, N\}$, where T represents the number of video frames and N represents the number of joint nodes. First, one connects the joint points in the same frame, then each edge represents the spatial relationship of the joint points, as shown in Fig. 2(a). We use a subset to represent the spatial relationship of the edges, denoted as $E_s = \{v_{ti}v_{tj}|(i, j) \in S\}$, where S represents the natural connection of the human joint. Temporal relationship is established by connecting the same joint point between consecutive frames. The set of temporal relational edges can be expressed as $E_t = \{v_{ti}v_{(t+1)i}|t = 1, 2, \ldots, T - 1, i = 1, 2, \ldots, N\}$. The set E of skeleton edges can be expressed as: $E = E_s \bigcup E_t$. Skeleton spatial-temporal relationship diagram is shown in Fig. 2(b).

The spatial relationship of the skeleton can be converted into an adjacency matrix. In t frame, if there is a connection between two nodes: $v_{ti}v_{tj} \in E_s$. It can be expressed as $A_{ij} = 1$ in the adjacency matrix A. In addition, taking into account the impact of the joint itself, we set $A_{ii} = 1$. If there is no association between nodes, i.e. $v_{ti}v_{tj} \notin E_s$ and $i \neq j$, then $A_{ij} = 0$. The temporal relationship of the skeleton, we recall, is constructed by connecting the same nodes of consecutive frames. Therefore, based on the spatial relationship, it can be easily extended to the spatial-temporal relationship. Suppose we operate on the skeleton in the time range θ, the spatial-temporal relationship $ST(v_{ti})$ can be expressed as:

$$ST(v_{ti}) = \{v_{qi}|d(v_{ti}, v_{tj}) < n, |t - q| \leq \lfloor \theta/2 \rfloor\} \tag{1}$$

3.2   Division Strategy

Skeleton High-Order Adjacency Matrix. According to the graph structure of the skeleton, we can establish the 1-order adjacency matrix of the skeleton. However, based on the kinematics of the human body, the human body needs multiple coordination of the body to complete the exercise. In this regard, we can obtain the co-occurrence characteristics of the skeleton joint by establishing a high-order adjacency matrix. To distinguish the joint points of different hierarchies, we use the shortest path length of the two joints, $d(v_i, v_j)$, to express the relationship between the joint points. Then the nodes in the n-order that affect each other need to satisfy: $d(v_i, v_j) \leq n$, where if $i = j$, set $d(v_i, v_j) = 1$. It is known that the adjacency matrix A represents the spatial relationship information between the node and the neighbor nodes. The n-order adjacency matrix A_n can be expressed by a 1-order adjacency that extends the expression of the spatial relationship to non-neighbor nodes:

$$A_n = A^n \tag{2}$$

Where A is the 1-order adjacency matrix, n means n^{th} order. The n-order adjacency matrix established by Eq. (2) implements the adjacency matrix parameter to represent the shortest distance between the joint points of the skeleton. The equation is as follows:

$$A_n^{ij} = \begin{cases} 0 & d(v_i, v_j) > n \\ d(v_i, v_j) & d(v_i, v_j) \leq n \end{cases} \tag{3}$$

High-Order Skeleton Division. Human action is based on the local motion of some joint nodes within a range, so it is necessary to divide the skeleton. Referring to the division method in [18], the division of the skeleton needs to consider the kinematics of the human skeleton. For simplicity, we only consider skeleton partitioning within a single frame. The division of the skeleton is mainly divided into two parts, as shown in Fig. 3. Firstly, the multi-order neighborhood of skeleton node is divided. We set $N_n(v)$ is the nth-order neighborhood of node v. Therefore, assuming that the 3-order node neighborhood of the skeleton is divided, the n-order neighbor nodes of node v can be expressed as:

$$N(v) = N_1(v) + N_2(v) + N_3(v) \tag{4}$$

where $N_1(v)$ includes node v itself.

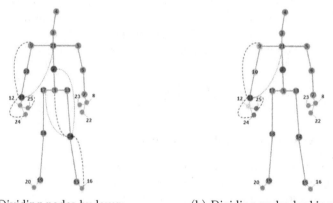

(a) Dividing nodes by layer   (b) Dividing nodes by kinematics

Fig. 3. Division strategy. Taking the division of the 3-order skeleton as an example, the skeleton is divided according to the division strategy. (a): The red dashed line indicates the connection of the 2nd-order neighborhood joint point, and the green dashed line indicates the connection of the 3rd-order neighborhood joint point. (b): The red node represents the center point. We further divide the nodes of different hierarchies, and different colors represent different divided regions.

We divided the skeleton according to the kinematics theory of the human body. Then, considering that all movements of the human body belong to centripetal or eccentric motion, we select the central node c of the skeleton as the center of the motion range. The nth-order neighborhoods of the skeleton are respectively divided, and a label map r is set for each partition. We divide the skeleton according to the following method: (i). According to the law of motion, the first division should be the node itself. The corresponding mapping is $r = 0$. (ii). For a neighboring node in a hierarchy, if the distance from the node to the center point is closer or equal to the distance from the feature node to the center point, then the neighboring node belongs to the second partition. The corresponding mapping is $r = 1$. (iii). The remaining nodes, that is, the distance from the node to the central point is farther than the distance from the feature node to the central point, belonging to the third partition. The corresponding mapping is $r = 2$.

According to the partitioning strategy and label mapping, correspondingly, the adjacency matrix A_n can be divided. Assume that A_{N_i} is used to represent the adjacency matrix of the i-th neighbor node. Then, A_{N_i} is further divided according to the partitioning strategy, and finally the high-order adjacency matrix can be expressed as:

$$A_n = \sum_{i=1}^{n} \sum_{r=0}^{2} A_{N_i}^r \tag{5}$$

where $A_{N_i}^r$ represents the matrix after A_{N_i} is partitioned.

In addition, considering the different degrees of association between different hierarchies, we define a parameter Φ represent the importance of different hierarchies, the setting of which is related to the hierarchy of the node. In summary, the expression of the higher-order adjacency matrix is as follows:

$$A_n = \Phi(N_i) \sum_{i=1}^{n} \sum_{r=1}^{2} A_{N_i}^r \tag{6}$$

3.3   Spatial-Temporal Graph Convolution

We learn the spatial feature information of the skeleton on a single frame. The convolution operation acts on the node. If the n-order neighbor of v_{ti} is sampled, the sampling function is: $p(v_{ti}, v_{tj}) = \{v_{tj} | d(v_{ti}, v_{tj} \leq n)\}$.

Compared with the sampling function, the definition of the weight function has a relatively large change. The node spatial structure of the graph structure is not fixed, and the number of neighbor is different. The weight of the graph structure can be expressed in another form, that is, the adjacency matrix of the graph. The adjacency matrix is another expression of the spatial relationship of the graph structure. The parameter of the adjacency matrix is the weight of the graph convolution. Therefore, the weight function W can be written as: $W(v_{ti}, v_{tj}) = A_n(v_{ti}, v_{tj})$. Spatial graph convolution can be expressed as:

$$Fs_{out} = \sum_{v_{tj} \in p(v_{ti}, v_{tj})} f_{in}(p(v_{ti}, v_{tj})) \cdot A_n(v_{ti}, v_{tj}) \tag{7}$$

The convolution operation in the temporal direction is relatively simple. After determining the node information in the spatial direction, the convolution in the time direction needs to implement the convolution of the same node in a certain period of time. We set the input of the convolution network to $X(v_{qi}, t)$. It represents v_{qi} node within the t frame range. Therefore, the convolution operation in the time direction is as follows:

$$Ft_{out}(v_{qi}) = \sum_{|t-q|=0}^{\theta/2} X(v_{qi}, t) \cdot w(t, 1) \tag{8}$$

In addition, we consider that even the nodes in the same neighborhood have different effects on motion. Therefore, when extracting the features in the spatial direction, we set a parameter matrix M that can be learned. Set all the parameters in M to 1, multiply with A_n by element, and learn the parameters of each node through deep learning network. Therefore, higher-order graph convolution operation can be expressed by:

$$f_{out} = \sum_n \Lambda_n^{-1/2} M \otimes A_n \Lambda_n^{-1/2} f_{in} \cdot W_t \tag{9}$$

where $\Lambda_n^{ij} = \sum_k A_n^{ik} + \alpha$, we set $\alpha = 0.001$ to avoid empty rows in A_n. W_t is a weight function in the time direction. f_{in} is the characteristic function of the input skeleton. $\otimes$ represents multiplication of the M matrix and the A_n matrix by elemental correspondence.

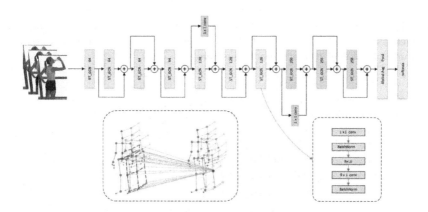

Fig. 4. High-order graph convolutional network model.

Before performing feature learning, the data needs to be pre-processed to fit the graph convolution network. The human skeleton data of a video is converted into a 3-dimensional tensor (C, T, V). C represents the number of channels, which corresponds to the 3-dimensional coordinates of the skeleton. T represents the number of video frames, and V represents the number of nodes. The extraction of spatial-temporal information is realized by convolution operations on spatial dimensions and temporal dimensions. The network frame of the spatial-temporal graph convolution is shown in Fig. 4.

4   Experiment

We verified that our approach can achieve better accuracy. We separately evaluated the human motion datasets based on 2D and 3D skeletons, and discussed the experimental results based on different high-order skeleton data. In order to make the experimental result data more objective, we set the same experimental environment for the experiments under each dataset.

4.1   2D Skeleton Data

The 2D skeleton data we used is Kinetics-skeleton, which is extracted from the Kinetics human action video dataset [29] via openpose [9]. Then use openpose to identify the 18 joint points of the skeleton, and extract the skeleton of the human behavior in each frame. The storage form of the skeleton node is (X, Y, C), and (X, Y) represents the 2D coordinates of the skeleton node, C represents the confidence score of the skeleton node. According to the recommendations of the dataset authors, we use $Top - 1$ and $Top - 5$ to evaluate their performance. The probability of correct classification. The performance of this dataset on the graph convolution network of the nth-order skeleton is shown in the following table. In this experiment, we set $batchsize = 100$, $epoch = 60$ and experiment with $n = 1, 2, 3, 4$ respectively.

Table 1. Action recognition performance for high-order skeleton based models on the Kinetics database. 2-order ST-GCN* means that parameters Φ that represent the importance of different orders are not considered

Method	Top-1	Top-5
Deep LSTM [10]	16.6	35.3
TCN [14]	20.5	40.4
ST-GCN [18]	31.6	53.7
1-order GCN	31.5	54.2
2-order GCN*	32.7	55.4
2-order GCN	33.3	56.2
3-order GCN	**33.8**	**56.4**
4-order GCN	33.7	56.0

Under this dataset, when only 1-order neighbor nodes are considered, our method is similar to st-gcn and the result is basically the same. If we only increase the order of the skeleton and regardless of the importance of different classes (the 2-order GCN* in Table 1), the results show that the accuracy rate will increase 1%. When we add a parameter that expresses the importance of the hierarchy, the accuracy increased by a further 0.5%.

4.2 3D Skeleton Data

The 3D skeleton dataset used in this study is NTU RGB+D [10], which is the largest dataset of behavior recognition research based on 3D skeleton data. The preservation form is the 3D coordinates (X, Y, Z) of the skeleton node, and the skeleton sequence includes 25 joint points whose center point is the joint point located at the center point of the human skeleton. This dataset divides all skeletons into two themes: X-sub and X-view. X-sub implements training and testing of different skeletons, that is, training with some actors and testing with other actors; X-view realizes skeleton training and testing from different perspectives, that is, training with two perspectives and testing with another perspective. We use $Top-1$ to evaluate its performance. The performance of the dataset in the high-order spatial-temporal graph convolution network is shown in the following table. In this experiment, we set $batchsize = 30$, $epoch = 100$ and experiment with $n = 1, 2, 3, 4$ respectively. In addition, we changed the center point of the 3D skeleton to the center of the human body (It is 1-order GCN in Table 2). The experimental results were improved compared with ST-GCN.

Table 2. Skeleton based action recognition performance on NTU-RGB+D datasets. 2-order ST-GCN* means that parameters Φ that represent the importance of different orders are not considered

Method	X-sub	X-view
Deep LSTM [10]	60.5	67.0
TCN [14]	74.2	82.9
C-CNN+MTLN [11]	79.0	84.2
ST-GCN [18]	79.5	86.4
1-order GCN	80.5	88.0
2-order GCN*	80.8	88.7
2-order GCN	**81.1**	**89.3**
3-order GCN	80.6	89.2

4.3 Discussion

The two datasets in experiments have very different natures. The 2D skeleton dataset is extracted by openpose and the 3D skeleton dataset is obtained by depth sensor. The number of skeleton nodes and the saved form are different, which makes the performance on the high-order spatial-temporal convolution network also very different. The experimental results based on 2D data show that before the 3-order, the accuracy rate is on the rise, and the accuracy is stable after the 3rd order. However, based on 3D data, it is bounded by 2-order. We suspect that this is due to the large noise generated by the 3D skeleton data annotation. Therefore, when the order is gradually increased, the error will accumulate and accumulate more and more, which may affect the accuracy of the high-order skeleton data. However, based on the above results, we can still conclude that for any human skeleton data, when performing human behavioral motion, the feature information of a certain node should consider all neighbor information in the 2nd or 3rd order neighborhood.

5   Conclusion

In this work, we propose a high-order spatial-temporal graph convolutional network model, which is mainly to redefine the structure of the high-order skeleton and to divide the skeleton based on it. The divided skeleton is inputted into the Spatial-Temporal graph convolution network to realize the action recognition of the human body. The model shows good performance on different datasets, but it is difficult to express the skeleton nodes that are far away, which makes the expression of higher order features limited. In addition, certain behaviors of the human body are accomplished by the cooperation of various parts of the body. At this time, there are different degrees of correlation between different parts. We can learn this correlation through the network to get higher accuracy, which is reserved for future work.

References

1. Simonyan, K., Zisserman, A.: Two-stream convolutional networks for action recognition in videos (2014)
2. Feichtenhofer, C., Pinz, A., Zisserman, A.: Convolutional two-stream network fusion for video action recognition. In: 2016 IEEE Conference on Computer Vision and Pattern Recognition (CVPR) (2016)
3. Wang, L., Qiao, Y., Tang, X.: Action recognition with trajectory-pooled deep-convolutional descriptors (2015)
4. Tran, D., Bourdev, L., Fergus, R., et al.: Learning spatiotemporal features with 3D convolutional networks (2015)
5. Carreira, J., Zisserman, A.: Quo vadis, action recognition? A new model and the kinetics dataset (2017)
6. Donahue, J., Hendricks, L.A., Rohrbach, M., et al.: Long-term recurrent convolutional networks for visual recognition and description. IEEE Trans. Pattern Anal. Mach. Intell. **39**(4), 677–691 (2014)
7. Sharma, S., Kiros, R., Salakhutdinov, R.: Action recognition using visual attention. Comput. Sci. (2015)
8. Wang, Y., Zhou, W., Zhang, Q., et al.: Weighted multi-region convolutional neural network for action recognition with low-latency online prediction (2018)
9. Cao, Z., Simon, T., Wei, S.E., Sheikh, Y.: Realtime multi-person 2D pose estimation using part affinity fields (2016)
10. Shahroudy, A., Liu, J., Ng, T.T., Wang, G.: NTU RGB+D: a large scale dataset for 3D human activity analysis. In: 2016 IEEE Conference on Computer Vision and Pattern Recognition (CVPR), pp. 1010–1019 (2016)
11. Ke, Q., Bennamoun, M., An, S., et al.: A new representation of skeleton sequences for 3D action recognition (2017)

12. Ding, N.Z., Wang, N.P., Ogunbona, P.O., Li, N.W.: Investigation of different skeleton features for CNN-based 3D action recognition. In: 2017 IEEE International Conference on Multimedia Expo Workshops (ICMEW) (2017)
13. Liu, J., Shahroudy, A., Xu, D., Wang, G.: Spatio-temporal LSTM with trust gates for 3D human action recognition (2016)
14. Kim, T.S., Reiter, A.: Interpretable 3D human action analysis with temporal convolutional networks (2017)
15. Wang, J., Liu, Z., Wu, Y., Yuan, J.: Learning actionlet ensemble for 3D human action recognition. In: IEEE Conference on Computer Vision Pattern Recognition (2012)
16. Du, Y., Wang, W., Wang, L.: Hierarchical recurrent neural network for skeleton based action recognition. In: CVPR, pp. 1110–1118 (2015)
17. Li, C., Zhong, Q., Xie, D., Pu, S.: Co-occurrence feature learning from skeleton data for action recognition and detection with hierarchical aggregation (2018)
18. Yan, S., Xiong, Y., Lin, D.: Spatial temporal graph convolutional networks for skeleton-based action recognition (2018)
19. Song, S., Lan, C., Xing, J., et al.: An end-to-end spatio-temporal attention model for human action recognition from skeleton data (2016)
20. Liu, J., Wang, G., Duan, L.Y., Abdiyeva, K., Kot, A.C.: Skeleton-based human action recognition with global context-aware attention LSTM networks. IEEE Trans. Image Process. **PP**(99), 1 (2017)
21. Wang, H., Wang, L.: Modeling temporal dynamics and spatial configurations of actions using two-stream recurrent neural networks (2017)
22. Zhang, P., Lan, C., Xing, J., et al.: View adaptive neural networks for high performance skeleton-based human action recognition. IEEE Trans. Pattern Anal. Mach. Intell. **PP**(99) (2018)
23. Kipf, T.N., Welling, M.: Semi-supervised classification with graph convolutional networks (2016)
24. Bruna, J., Zaremba, W., Szlam, A., LeCun, Y.: Spectral networks and locally connected networks on graphs (2014) arXiv:1312.6203
25. Henaff, M., Bruna, J., Lecun, Y.: Deep convolutional networks on graph-structured data. Comput. Sci. (2015)
26. Niepert, M., Ahmed, M., Kutzkov, K.: Learning convolutional neural networks for graphs. In: International Conference on Machine Learning, 2014C2023 (2016)
27. Yu, B., Yin, H., Zhu, Z.: Spatio-temporal graph convolutional networks: a deep learning framework for traffic forecasting (2017)
28. Mahdi, K., Jianhui, W.: Spatio-temporal graph deep neural network for short-term wind speed forecasting. IEEE Trans. Sustain. Energy, 1 (2018)
29. Kay, W., Carreira, J., Simonyan, K., et al.: The kinetics human action video dataset (2017)

Multi-scale Spatial-Temporal Attention for Action Recognition

Qing Zhang[1], Hongping Yan[1], and Lingfeng Wang[2(✉)]

[1] Institute of Information Engineering, China University of Geosciences,
Beijing, China
{qingzhang,yanhp}@cugb.edu.cn
[2] Institute of Automation, Chinese Academy of Sciences, Beijing, China
lfwang@nlpr.ia.ac.cn

Abstract. In this paper, we propose a new attention model by integrating multi-scale features to recognize human action. We introduce multi-scale features through different sizes of convolution kernel on both spatial and temporal fields. The spatial attention model considers the relationship between detail and integral of the human action, therefore our model can focus on the significant part of the action on the spatial field. The temporal attention model considers the speed of action, in order that our model can concentrate on the pivotal clips of the action on the temporal field. We verify the validity of multi-scale features in the benchmark action recognition datasets, including UCF-101 (88.8%), HMDB-51 (60.0%) and Penn (96.3%). As a result that the accuracy of our model outperforms the previous methods.

Keywords: Action recogniztion · Multi-scale · Spatial-temporal attention

1 Introduction

Action Recognition (AR) aims to recognize the action of interested target from video sequences. It's one of the most important and challenging missions in the computer vision flied. Successful action recognition techniques could facilitate a large group of applications such as motion detection, understanding, *etc.* The key of action recognition algorithm is to gain a strong feature which influenced by complicated internal factors (*e.g.*, complex and sundry behavior, fickle perspective, action speed and action range) and external factors (*e.g.*, complex background occlusion and light).

Currently, various methods [1–26] based on Deep Learning Networks demonstrate excellent results on several action recognition benchmarks. One of the key elements to these successful methods is the good feature learned by Convolution Neural Network (CNN). The feature is adaptable to the environment and

---

The first author of this paper is an undergraduate.

© Springer Nature Switzerland AG 2019
Z. Lin et al. (Eds.): PRCV 2019, LNCS 11857, pp. 26–37, 2019.
https://doi.org/10.1007/978-3-030-31654-9_3

requires low shooting conditions. However, there are also many factors that exciting methods can't solve, such as complex human action, background occlusion and unfixed temporal length.

In this regard, attention based methods for action recognition have gradually attracted a lot of attentions of researchers. The key of attention model is to focus on the focal point and ignore the others, *i.e.*, background and irrelevant video frame. For example, Sharma *et al.* [1] exploit LSTMs to gain the attention score. LSTM assists to distinguish the focal point and background, while it is limited by the input of continuous vector sequence which omit the relationship in spatial neighbor areas. Yu *et al.* [2] solve the defect through score map obtained by convolution layer and *softmax* layer which can identify the significant part of the video and considers the spatial neighbor areas. However, the score map of [2] ignores the relationship of different scales in spatial and temporal fields.

Recently, researches on biological nerves have shown that action observation of human will be affected by background, distance, speed, angle and other factors of the action. Namely, the significant area of action, the key-frames, *etc.* which obtained by different factors of action are not same (see Fig. 1). It means that multi-scale features are useful to action recognition. As we mention above, most attention models loss the information of scales. In order that, our aim is to design a multi-scale spatial-temporal attention model.

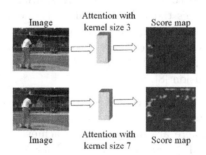

Fig. 1. Feature maps with different scales.

1.1 Contribution

In this paper, we propose a new multi-scale spatial-temporal attention based model for human action recognition. By combining multi-scale 3D convolution and softmax layers, the spatial attention module with multi-scale implementation can focus on the true action area on the spatial field. The multi-scale temporal attention module obtains the key video clips through bidirectional LSTM which think over the previous, the present and the future information. In order to introduce multi-scale information to the temporal module, we also take different speed video in consider. Specifically, the details and superiors of this work are summarized as follows:

- We propose a new multi-scale spatial attention module for action recognition. Its innovation is the increase of detail and integral information of human action which can promote the identification of significant part.
- We present a temporal attention model with multi-scale features for action recognition. It considers the speed of human action which can conduce to recognize the key clips of video.
- We introduce multi-scale features on spatial-temporal attention model. It outperforms the single-scale method on 3 datasets (see Table 4). It is also compact and efficient to compute.

2   Related Work

Our purpose is to complete the multi-scale attention based action recognition. In order that, we mainly concern how to eliminate irrelevant information and preserve significant areas. Our model draws inspiration from many areas, including Deep Convolution Neural Network (DCNN), Typical Attention based Action Recognition and Multi-Scale Features.

DCNN. For the last few years, mostly outstanding algorithms about computer vision mission are based on DCNN. There are two main directions: 3D Convolutional Network (C3D) [3] and Two-Stream Convolutional Networks [4]. Specifically, the former uses 3d convolution to obtain spatial and temporal features in video. The latter divides the video into single frame and optical flow information which used to catch spatial and temporal information separately. After that, there are many excellent algorithms based on C3D and two-stream convolution networks. Such as: I3D [5], P3D [6], Very Deep Two-Stream ConvNets [7], Two-Stream Network Fusion [8], etc.

Typical Attention Based Action Recognition. In computer vision field, the attention model is mainly used on image classification, behavior recognition and target detection. There are many ways to achieve attention mechanisms. For instance, Hierarchical Attentive Recurrent Tracking [9] adds Gaussian kernel to process the original image to get the preliminary location of the object (See Eq. 1). Then the Appearance Attention further extracts the appearance information of the image and eliminates the background information.

$$g_t = A_t^y X_t (A_t^x)^T \tag{1}$$

where g_t is the preliminary location of object. $x_t \in \mathbb{R}^{H \times W}$ is the original image. A_X and A_Y are two Gaussian kernel matrices based on the image.

Residual Attention Network for Image Classification [10] proposes a residual attention learning method. The attention score α can be expressed as:

$$\alpha = \phi(W \times X_t) \tag{2}$$

where X_t is the tensor of middle feature that handled by the residual convolution block. $W \in \mathbb{R}^{1 \times 1}$ is the learnable 2D convolution parameters. ϕ is the *sigmod* activation.

Squeeze-and-Excitation Networks [11] puts forward to learn the attention feature on channels, its attention score α is:

$$\alpha = \phi(W_2\sigma(W_1z)) \tag{3}$$

where z is the distribution of C feature maps, in other words z is global information. It can be obtained by global pooling. $W_1 \in \mathbb{R}^{\frac{c}{r} \times C}$ indicates fully connection which can reduce the parameters. $W_2 \in \mathbb{R}^{C \times \frac{c}{r}}$ is also fully connection, which tends to calculate dependencies between different channels. σ is $ReLU$ activation.

Recurrent Models of Visual Attention [12] selects a range of regions or locations through the attention network, then only selects the area with high resolution. The temporal weight β obtained via:

$$\beta = Wx + b \tag{4}$$

here W is weight matrix, x is the input vector and b is model biases.

Joint Spatial-Temporal Attention (JSTA) [2] uses bidirectional LSTM to gain temporal weight β. The formula is as follows:

$$\beta = \sigma(Wh_t + b) \tag{5}$$

Multi-scale Feature. It is known that multi-scale features are useful to computer vision missions. It has been confirmed in image segmentation [13,14]. Typical multi-scale feature based networks are skip-net and share-net [13]. Skip-net combines features from different network layers, because different layers have different features. For example, the Fully Convolutional Networks [15] uses features from lower layers to gain more accurate prediction and uses coarser-scale features from higher layers to initialize. Share-net takes multi-scale images as input of the networks those share the same weight. For instance, Efficient piecewise training of deep structured models for semantic segmentation [16] applies 3 different scale images as input of the network.

3   Method

The network we proposed is shown in Fig. 2, it based on JSTA [2] and ResNet3D [17]. The input of network is a variable length video clips $V \in \{V_1, V_2, \ldots, V_n\}, V_i \in \mathbb{R}^{a \times b \times c}, i = 1, \ldots, n$, where a, b, c are the corresponding video width, video height and channel numbers. V passes through several residual convolutional blocks (there are 3 residual blocks in our work) to obtain the intermediate features which can be input into multi-scale spatial attention model. The 3d convolution output M can be defined as:

$$M = \mathbf{K} * V = \sum_c \sum_{p=1}^P \sum_{q=1}^Q \sum_{r=1}^R \mathbf{K}^{pqr} * V^{(x+p)(y+q)(z+r)} \tag{6}$$

where $*$ is 3D convolution. $\mathbf{K}$ is the convolution kernel. P, Q, R are the kernel width, kernel height and kernel depth, respectively. x, y, z are space and time index.

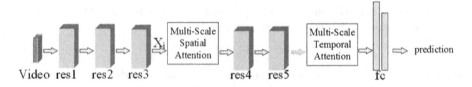

Fig. 2. Multi-scale spatial-temporal attention network. In this figure, *res i* presents residual convolutional block.

3.1 Muliti-scale Spatial Attention Model

Analysis. When people know the world, they instinctively pay attention to the remarkable area. Owing to different angles, distance and other factors of observation, the significant area judged by the human is different. Therefore it is meaningful to add multi-scale features on attention model to imitate human. The multi-scale spatial attention model (see Fig. 3) takes the intermediate features as input, and forms the base model with 3D convolution and *softmax* activation. The advantages of multi-scale spatial attention model can be summarized as: *a*. Independent multi-scale feature extraction branches can visualize the diversity of different scales. *b*. The spatial-temporal convolution branches of each scale have better robust to the environment.

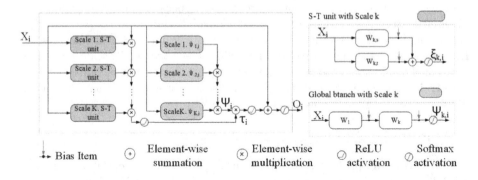

Fig. 3. Multi-scale spatial attention module

First of all, randomly extract several segments clips in each video, that each clip has 8 frames. Then obtain intermediate feature $X \in \{x_1, x_2, \ldots, x_t\}, x \in \mathbb{R}^{w \times h \times d}, i = 1, 2, \ldots, t$ through the residual convolution blocks, where w is the video clips width, h is the video clips height, d is the video clips channels and t is the number of video clips. The residual convolution block is based on Resnet3D [17], namely in our experiments $w = h = 28$ and $d = 128$, thus $X_i \in \mathbb{R}^{28 \times 28 \times 128}$.

We choose K scales to explore our multi-scale vision. For each scale, X_i is divided into two branches of space-time to obtain the weight score map. On spatial branch, we choose 2D convolution to obtain attention. Since the action also changes on time, we use 1D convolution to get the corresponding time guidance. The spatial-temporal branches ($S - T$ unit with Scale k) can be formulated as:

$$\begin{cases} S_{k,i} = X_i * W_{k,s} + B_{k,s} \\ T_{k,i} = X_i * W_{k,t} + B_{k,t}. \end{cases} \quad (7)$$

here $W_{k,s} \in \mathbb{R}^{y \times y \times 1}$ and $W_{k,t} \in \mathbb{R}^{1 \times 1 \times y}$ are learnable 3D convolution parameters. $B_{k,s}$ and $B_{k,t}$ are biases. $S_{k,i}$ and $T_{k,i}$ are output of spatial and temporal convolution at k scale separately. Then these outputs are merged into a $S - Tunit$ and activated by $softmax$ (δ)

$$\xi_{k,i} = \delta(S_{k,i} + T_{k,i}) \quad (8)$$

Then fusion the multi-scale $S - Tunit$ as:

$$\tau_i = \sigma(X_i \otimes \xi_{1,i} \otimes \xi_{2,i} \otimes, \dots, \otimes \xi_{K,i}) \quad (9)$$

where $\otimes$ denotes element-wise multiplication.

To ensure accurate results, we also increase multi-scale information on global attention branch, the formula is:

$$\psi_{k,i} = \delta((X_i * W_1 + B_1) * W_k + B_k) \quad (10)$$

$$\psi_i = \psi_{1,i} \otimes \psi_{2,i} \otimes, \dots, \otimes \psi_{K,i} \quad (11)$$

where $\psi_{k,i}$ is the attention weight score of the global branch with the k scale. ψ_i is the fusion of $\psi_{k,i}$. $W_1 \in \mathbb{R}^{1 \times 1 \times 1}$ and $W_k \in \mathbb{R}^{y \times y \times y}$.

The output of multi-scale spatial attention model is

$$o_i = \delta(\sigma(\tau_i \otimes \psi_i) + X_i) \quad (12)$$

After spatial attention model, o_i still need to pass two residual blocks. Details of the network can be found in next section. Importantly, the kernel number of last convolution layer is set to be 512, after global average pooling, the final output is $o'_i \in \mathbb{R}^{1 \times 1 \times 512}$.

3.2   Muliti-scale Temporal Attention Model

Analysis. Human focus on the key frames and ignore the extraneous noisy frames, which means our attention can't be distributed evenly. Actually, due to the speed of the action is different, the key frames we noticed would be different as well. Therefore, introduce multi-scale features in temporal attention is necessary. We decide to add multi-scale temporal guidance on the $S - Tunit$ (see Fig. 4a). The spatial resulting feature vector o'_i is used as input to the temporal attention model (see Fig. 4b). The temporal model obtains importance score by bidirectional LSTM. Compared to normal LSTM, bidirectional LSTM subjoins a future hidden state and it has higher accuracy and better stability.

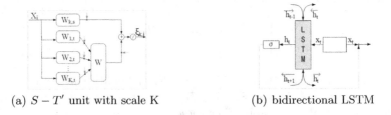

(a) $S - T'$ unit with scale K   (b) bidirectional LSTM

Fig. 4. Multi-scale temporal attention module

The new time guidance $T'_{k,i}$ formula is defined as

$$T'_{k,i} = [(X_i * W_{1,t} + b_{1,t})\bullet, \ldots, \bullet(X_i * W_{K,t} + b_{K,t})] * W_1 + b_1 \qquad (13)$$

where $\bullet$ is concat merge.

The integrated hidden state of bidirectional LSTM is

$$h_t = \overrightarrow{h_t} \circ \overleftarrow{h_t} \qquad (14)$$

where $\overrightarrow{h_t}$ named forward hidden state, $\overleftarrow{h_t}$ named backward hidden state, $\circ$ represents average, sum or concat merge.

The temporal importance score can be got via:

$$\beta_t = \sigma(W_T h_t + b) \qquad (15)$$

The normalized importance is obtained via *softmax* activation

$$\overline{\beta_t} = \delta(W_t^T \beta_t) \qquad (16)$$

4   Experimental Evaluations

In this section, we contrast to our proposed algorithm with other state-of-art algorithms (*e.g.*, C3D [3], ResNet3D [17], FSTCN [22], Optical Flow [26], etc.) on three benchmark datasets (UCF-101, HMDB-51 and Penn).

4.1   Datasets and Implementation Details

UCF-101 [27] consists of $13,320$ videos that can be divided into 101 categories. It is a challenging action recognition dataset with large videos in different background, viewpoint and light.

HMDB-51 [28] contains $6,849$ videos of 51 action classes. The source of videos is YouTube and films which have better diversity and randomness. HMDB-51 is more challenging than UCF-101.

Penn [29] is a smaller dataset with $2,326$ videos which can be segmented into 15 categories. It provides human joints annotation in addition to RGB frames.

Specific Experimental Parameter Settings. Our network is built using *Caffe* and *Keras*. We revise the source code of *Caffe* to read random video clips. For the spatial network, the optimizer is Stochasical Gradient Descent (SGD) with learning rate $lr = 0.001$ and the maximum iteration is $40,000$. For temporal network, *RMSprop* or *Adagrad* is employed as optimizer, its learning rate is $lr = 0.001$ and the number of iteration is 10. All experiments are based on a single Titan X GPU.

4.2   Analysis of Multi-scale Spatial Attention Model

First of all, we analysis the effectiveness of multi-scale spatial attention model. In Table 1, we compare the multi-scale spatial attention model with baseline method JSTA [2] in three datasets. We can draw conclusion that our proposed model is superior than the spatial attention model of JSTA. The reason is addition action information provided by multi-scale features.

Table 1. Testing accuracy of spatial attention model. The results are re-implemented with the same training and testing strategies.

Method	Penn	HMDB-51	UCF-101
JSTA (spatial)	93.4	56.8	86.2
Our spatial model	94.2	57.2	86.4

Besides, we provide the visualization of feature maps (as illustrated in Fig. 5) to understand the multi-scale spatial attention model better. From Fig. 5 we can conclude that the multi-scale feature maps have more information than the single-scale feature maps.

Finally, we test the effect of numbers of scales on the results in table 2. First line JSTA is the baseline and single scale method. The second set of method, *e.g.*, kernel size $= (3,5),(3,7),(5,7)$, increases an input scale. The accuracy of the second set of methods improves weakly. After adding another scale, accuracy improves 1% superlatively. Table 2 illustrates two points: (a) The influence of number of scales is not equal. (b) The best performance is obtained with three input scales. However, we consider that it is no more meaning to increase the number of scale. The advantages brought by multi-scale are no longer enough to offset the consumption of compute.

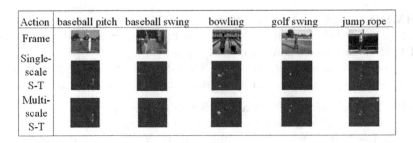

Fig. 5. Contrast of spatial attention visualization on Penn dataset.

Table 2. Testing accuracy of multi-scale S-T on Penn, HMDB-51 and UCF-101

	Penn	HMDB-51	UCF-101
Baseline: JSTA (spatial)	93.4	56.8	86.2
Kernel size = (3, 5)	93.5	56.7	86.5
Kernel size = (3, 7)	93.4	56.7	86.3
Kernel size = (5, 7)	93.1	56.6	86.1
Kernel size = (3, 5, 7)	94.2	57.2	86.4

4.3 Analysis of Multi-scale Temporal Attention

We analysis the practicability of the multi-scale temporal attention model. Table 3 presents that multi-scale temporal features outperform the single-scale one on three datasets.

Table 3. Testing accuracy of temporal attention model on Penn, HMDB-51 and UCF-101.

	Penn	HMDB-51	UCF-101
JSTA	94.7	59.8	88.6
MSTA (ours)	96.3	60.0	88.8

4.4 Comparison with State-of-Art Methods

In this section, we validate the effectiveness of the multi-scale spatial-temporal attention model. Compared to other advanced algorithms on three datasets, where JSTA [2] is employed as the baseline.

Table 4 shows the results of datasets. Due to the human joints annotations provided by Penn, we choose the pose based methods and their trajectory-based improvement methods [29–31]. Surprisingly, our proposed model without the annotations performs better than these algorithm.

For HMDB and UCF datasets with large data, methods based on DCNN are usually more effective. Our proposed model has surpassed the classical C3D [3] and ResNet3D [17] algorithms in terms of accuracy. Final compared to JSTA, our attention model which increase multi-scale features has better results on three datasets.

Table 4. Testing accuracy of multi-scale STA on Penn, HMDB-51 and UCF-101.

Method	Penn	HMDB-51	UCF-101
iDT [30]	73.4	51.9	76.2
IDT+FV [30]	89.7	57.2	85.9
ACPS [31]	79.0	–	–
Actemes [29]	79.4	–	–
MST-AOG [29]	74.0	–	–
ACPS+iDT+FV [31]	92.9	–	–
ConvNet [20]	–	–	63.3
LSTM [21]	–	44.0	75.8
C3D [3]	86.0	–	81.5
ResNet3D [17]	86.8	46.9	82.6
FSTCN [22]	87.8	58.6	87.9
Attention Poolingv [23]	–	52.2	–
TSB C3D [24]	92.6	52.2	82.7
JSTA [2]	94.7	59.8	88.6
MSTA (ours)	**96.3**	**60.0**	**88.8**

5 Conclusion

In this paper, we propose a multi-scale spatial-temporal attention model to recognize human action in video. Visually, the spatial multi-scale attention appears as the difference in the size of the observed objects, so the spatial attention model processes the video frames with different kernel sizes to obtain salient regions in the video. The temporal multi-scale attention is expressed as the speed of the action. We change the $S-T$ unit on spatial model to gain the multi-scale temporal features. Then explore the importance score of video clips with bidirectional LSTM. Results show that our multi-scale spatial-temporal attention (MSTA) model is more effective than single-scale attention methods, e.g., JSTA, especially on the small dataset.

In the future, we will explore different ways to acquire multi-scale features, such as different sample rates.

Acknowledgments. This work is supported by the National Natural Science Foundation of China (Grant Number 61773377 and 61573352).

References

1. Sharma, S., Kiros, R., Salakhutdinov, R.: Action recognition using visual attention. Comput. Sci. (2015)
2. Yu, T.Z., Guo, C.X., Wang, L.F., Gu, H.X., Xiang, S.M., Pan, C.H.: Joint spatial-temporal attention for action recognition. Pattern Recogn. Lett. **112**, 226–233 (2018)
3. Dempsey, P.W., Allison, M.E.D., Akkaraju, S., et al.: C3d of complement as a molecular adjuvant: bridging innate and acquired immunity. Science **271**(5247), 348–350 (1996)
4. Simonyan, K., Zisserman, A.: Two-stream convolutional networks for action recognition in videos (2014)
5. Balaguer, J.F., Gobbetti, E.: i3D: a high-speed 3D Web browser. In: Proceedings ACM Symposium on VRML, pp. 69–76 (1995)
6. Qiu, Z., Yao, T., Mei, T.: Learning spatio-temporal representation with pseudo-3D residual networks (2017)
7. Wang, L., Xiong, Y., Wang, Z., et al.: Towards good practices for very deep two-stream ConvNets. Comput. Sci. (2015)
8. Feichtenhofer, C., Pinz, A., Zisserman, A.: Convolutional two-stream network fusion for video action recognition. In: Computer Vision Pattern Recognition (2016)
9. Kosiorek, A.R., Bewley, A., Posner, I.: Hierarchical attentive recurrent tracking (2017)
10. Wang, F., Jiang, M., Qian, C., et al.: Residual attention network for image classification (2017)
11. Hu, J., Shen, L., Albanie, S., et al.: Squeeze-and-excitation networks (2017)
12. Mnih, V., Heess, N., Graves, A., et al.: Recurrent models of visual attention. In: Advances in Neural Information Processing Systems (2014)
13. Chen, L.C., Yi, Y., Jiang, W., et al.: Attention to scale: scale-aware semantic image segmentation. In: IEEE Conference on Computer Vision Pattern Recognition (2016)
14. Florack, L., Romeny, B.T.H., Viergever, M., et al.: The Gaussian scale-space paradigm and the multiscale local jet. Int. J. Comput. Vision **18**(1), 61–75 (1996)
15. Long, J., Shelhamer, E., Darrell, T.: Fully convolutional networks for semantic segmentation. IEEE Trans. Pattern Anal. Mach. Intell. **39**(4), 640–651 (2014)
16. Lin, G.S., Shen, C.H., Hengel, A., Reid, I.: Efficient piecewise training of deep structured models for semantic segmentation. In: CVPR, pp. 3194–3203 (2016)
17. He, K., Zhang, X., Ren, S., et al.: Deep residual learning for image recognition (2015)
18. Clement, F., Couprie, C., Najman, L., et al.: Learning hierarchical features for scene labeling. IEEE Trans. Pattern Anal. Mach. Intell. (2013)
19. Wang, L., et al.: Temporal segment networks: towards good practices for deep action recognition. In: Leibe, B., Matas, J., Sebe, N., Welling, M. (eds.) ECCV 2016. LNCS, vol. 9912, pp. 20–36. Springer, Cham (2016). https://doi.org/10.1007/978-3-319-46484-8_2
20. Karpathy, A., Toderici, G., Shetty, S., Leung, T., Sukthankar, R., Feifei, L.: Large-scale video classification with convolutional neural networks. In: CVPR, pp. 1725–1732 (2014)
21. Donahue, J., et al.: Long-term recurrent convolutional networks for visual recognition and description. In: CVPR, pp. 2625–2634 (2015)

22. Sun, L., Jia, K., Shi, B.: Human action recognition using factorized spatio-temporal convolutional networks. In: ICCV, pp. 57–65 (2015)
23. Rohit, G., Deva, R.: Attentional pooling for action recognition. In: NIPS, pp. 33–44 (2017)
24. Cao, C., Zhang, Y., Zhang, C., Lu, H.: Body joint guided 3D deep convolutional descriptors for action recognition, CoRR. abs/1704.07160 (2017)
25. Yu, T., Gu, H., Wang, L., Xiang, S., Pan, C.: Cascaded temporal spatial features for video action recognition. In: ICIP, pp. 1552–1556 (2017)
26. Feichtenhofer, C., Pinz, A., Zisserman, A.: Convolutional two-stream network fusion for video action recognition. In: CVPR, pp. 1933–1941 (2016)
27. Soomro, K., Zamir, A.R., Shah, M.: UCF101: a dataset of 101 human actions classes from videos in the wild, CoRR. abs/1212.0402 (2012)
28. Kuehne, H., Jhuang, H., Garrote, E., Poggio, T., Serre, T.: HMDB: a large video database for human motion recognition. In: ICCV, pp. 2556–2563 (2011)
29. Zhang, W., Zhu, M., Derpanis, K.: From actemes to action: a strongly-supervised representation for detailed action understanding. In: ICCV, pp. 2248–2255 (2013)
30. Wang, H., Schmid, C.: Action recognition with improved trajectories. In: ICCV, pp. 3551–3558 (2013)
31. Iqbal, U., Garbade, M., Gall, J.: Pose for action-action for pose. In: FG, pp. 438–445 (2017)

Reading Digital Numbers of Water Meter with Deep Learning Based Object Detector

Shirong Liao[1], Pan Zhou[1], Lianglin Wang[2], and Songzhi Su[1(✉)]

[1] School of Informatics, Xiamen University,
Xiamen 361005, People's Republic of China
ssz@xmu.edu.cn
[2] Ropeok Technology Group Co., Ltd., Xiamen, China

Abstract. Automatically reading water meter is a classical OCR problem, typical method includes four major components: region of interests (ROIs) detection, skew correction of bounding boxes, single digital character segmentation, and digital classification. Disadvantage of the traditional method is that the pipeline is too complex and coupled to the accuracy of the final recognition result. Deep learning based object detection has achieved promising results on many computer vision tasks. As one of the representatives of the deep learning object detection framework, YOLOv3 perform detection task quickly and accurately. Inspired by this, we formulate the water meter reading problem as a detection problem, which is a true end-to-end solution. In order to attack the half-character problem of water meter, we proposed a heuristic rule to guarantee that there is only one bounding box in the vertical direction within a grid. Experimental results on our own built XMU-W-M dataset showed that the 0-error recognition rate reaches 96.67% and the 1-error recognition rate is up to 99.81%, which outperforms the traditional water meter recognition system in both time and precision. Both the code and dataset are available: https://github.com/sloan96/water-meter-recognition.

Keywords: Water meter recognition · Traditional method · Deep learning · YOLOv3 · Rule

1 Introduction

Reading the water meter automatically makes our daily life more convenient. The general meter-reading process is as follows: the camera is fixed above the water meter waiting for power-on command, the picture is taken and its binary code is sent to the terminal immediately once the command is received. Terminal collects the binary code and sends data to the platform software while issuing a power-off command to the camera. The platform software decodes the received binary data into an image format, recognizes the water meter number and analyzes the result.

Supported by organization x.

Optical Character Recognition (OCR) refers to converting text on an image into computer-editable text content. There are already large numbers of studies in this area, such as license plate recognition. Digital character recognition is a traditional research topic of pattern recognition and it's still studied by many researchers and widely used in many domains. However, due to the specific application scenarios, the situation is different and problems are of great diversity. In this paper, we focus on the image digital recognition part of the above process and regard the recognition problem as a detection problem.

As we can see from Fig. 1, the collected images mainly lead to four challenges for recognition. (1) Camera installation and uneven illumination of the light source lead to image distortion. (2) Irrelevant characters existed in the dial will affect the recognition. (3) The rotation of the water meter makes the numbers not in a horizontal line. (4) Uncertainty caused by digital rotation changes.

Fig. 1. The examples of water meter images. All the three sub-images have difficulty (1) and (2), the second and third sub-image significantly have difficulty (3) and (4).

In this work, we turn to a deep learning framework – YOLOv3. You only look once (YOLO) [1] is a state-of-the-art, real-time object detection system. We no longer need to perform tedious preprocessing such as digital segmentation and skew correction thanks to the one stage pipeline of YOLOv3 [3]. However, one mainly trouble is the half-word problem, namely, more than one detected bounding boxes in a digital grid caused by the above mentioned difficulty (4). In order to handle this situation, we add a heuristic rule to the network.

The main contributions of this paper are: (1) recognizing multiple digits without digital segmentation, (2) modeling ROIs localization as detection problem, so that the slope is not required to be estimated by basic image processing techniques, (3) proposing a heuristic method to tackle the half-word problem. We also introduce a new dataset of both realistic and virtual water meter dial images generated by using GAN [12], and experimentally evaluate our adjusted model.

2   Related Work

The traditional water meter recognition system generally includes five modules: (1) water meter digital area detection, (2) digital rectangle area location, (3) rectangular box skew correction, (4) digital segmentation, and (5) digital recognition.

As Fig. 2 shows, inputting an image containing a water meter, after jpeg compression, thresholding, tilt angle detection and correction, throw the image at this time into the trained Support Vector Machine (SVM) classifier [10], where the HOG [9] feature is usually used. Getting the water meter digital area, scaling it to the specified size, generally using the method based on the maximum interval width of adjacent characters for digital segmentation, sometimes we discard this step but regard single-character recognition as end-to-end multi-label classification and throw it into the trained Convolutional Neural Networks, finally we could obtain the recognition result.

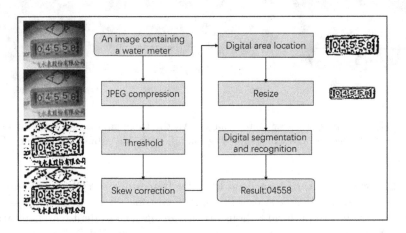

Fig. 2. The pipeline of traditional water meter recognition, mainly including region of interests (ROIs) detection, skew correction of bounding boxes, single digital character segmentation, and digital recognition

Over the years, a large number of digital recognition methods have been put forward. The traditional approach is to design and extract features, and input them to the classifier, then a digital classifier model could be established. However, feature design is very time-consuming and single designed features tends to result in low generalization ability, therefore [11] proposed to replace hand crafted features with features learned by unsupervised algorithms like K-means [13]. Another method is character template matching, generally including digital template definition, digital area segmentation and digital matching. However, it is too simple to be applied to a slightly complicated situation. Lately, the emergence of powerful deep learning techniques has led to plenty of digital recognition methods based on neural network. For example, the famous LeNet-5 [4] proposed by Yann LeCun, which has 7 layers. The input 2D image is first passed through the convolution layer to the pooling layer, then through the fully connected layer, and finally using the softmax classification as the output layer. Based on [4,5] presents a feed-forward network architecture for recognizing an unconstrained handwritten multi-digit string. Lately, Qiang Guo proposed a method to combine the Hidden Markov Model (HMM) and deep learning methods to locate and identify the numbers in the natural scene [6]. But a problem is that training networks needs a large number of data and better hardware condition.

In our paper, we are committed to water meter digital recognition. For the purpose of achieving a high accuracy within a really short time, we take inspiration from YOLOv3 framework to regard the localization of ROIs as a detection problem and simplify the pipeline. In addition, we specially design several rules to iron out problems arising from the detection process. Surprisingly, under our attempts, the final model could hit a high accuracy level.

3   Self-built Water Meter Dataset

3.1   Data Generation

The original idea was to use pix2pixHD [7] open source framework to simulate the generation of water meter data.

pix2pixHD is a variant of GAN whose input consists of a digital map x and a true label y corresponding to x. Training generator G and generating $G(x)$ to make it realistically true to the true label y. D is a discriminator, the input x and the generated image $G(x)$ are determined to be false as much as possible, in contrast, the input x and the real label image y are determined to be true as much as possible. VGG is used for calculating the perceptual reconstruction loss [8] between the real label image and the generated image.

Using pygame and font library to generate a label image corresponding to the real water meter number, i.e. '08281' image with white background. The image generated by pygame rendering should be the same size as the real water meter image. The corresponding white background label image is rendered according to the label of the real water meter, and the generator $G(x)$ is trained by the pix2pixHD framework. The training and transfer process is shown in Fig. 3(a). We only need to generate the digital image X' we want, that is, we can render the corresponding water meter digital image $G(x')$.

As shown in Fig. 3(b), we find that there is still a gap between the data generated by this method and the real data. The improvement of the effect requires a large number of real samples, which is of little significance for our training, but can be considered for image noise rendering. Considering that the training requires a large number of real samples, we simulate the actual scene to capture the water meter image, as shown in Fig. 3(c). These data are more in line with the real scene, followed by data labeling issues.

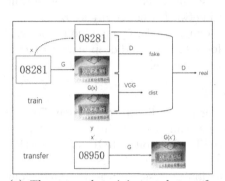

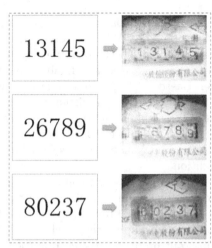

(a) The general training and transfer process of data generation

(b) Actual generation effect

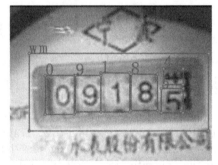

(c) Real samples obtaining

(d) Water meter data annotation

Fig. 3. Data generation and annotation

3.2 Data Annotation

We use the open source tool labelImg[1] for data annotation. As shown in Fig. 3(d), we mark each number in the water meter image and also add a 'wm' category, which is convenient for post-processing to distinguish the numbers inside and outside the box. For the area where the digital rotation changes, the numbers appearing above and below should both be marked, and the marked box should be as close as possible to the number, which can ensure that the predicted bounding box can also fit the number as much as possible, which helps us to apply rules to reduce errors. When we encounter a blurred digital area that is unrecognizable to the human eye, no marking is required, because this type of area contains too much noise. Once labeled, it is easy to make the model learn the wrong information and increase the background false detection rate.

---

[1] Tzutalin. LabelImg. Git code (2015). https://github.com/tzutalin/labelImg

4 Proposed Method

In this section, we first briefly introduce the principles and framework of YOLOv3, then introduce how to regard digital recognition as a detection problem, and finally detail how the additional rules are to reduce the error rate step by step.

4.1 YOLOv3

YOLO divides the input image into $S \times S$ grids, and each grid unit is responsible for detecting targets falling into it. Each grid unit predicts a confidence score corresponding to the B bounding boxes and the bounding box, the confidence reflecting whether the bounding box contains the likelihood of the target. As Eq. (1) shows, the confidence is defined as Pr (Object) $*\mathrm{IOU}_{pred}^{truth}$. If no object exists in that cell, the confidence scores should be zero. Otherwise the confidence score should equal the intersection over union (IOU) between the predicted box and the ground truth.

$$Confidence\,score = P_r(Object) \times IOU_{pred}^{truth} \qquad (1)$$

If the grid cell does not contain a target, the confidence should be 0, otherwise the confidence is equal to the prediction box and the Ground Truth's IOU. Each bounding box contains 5 predicted values: x, y, w, h, confidence. The (x, y) coordinates represent the center point of the bounding box, and w and h represent the width and height of the bounding box. Each grid unit also predicts C (the number of categories) conditional category probabilities $P_r(Class|Object)$, and the prior condition is that the grid unit contains the target. Regardless of how many bounding boxes are predicted, each grid unit only predicts a set of category probabilities. If there are 20 categories, then each grid unit will only predict a set of 20 categories of probabilities, so a map corresponds to a predicted value of $S \times S \times (B * 5 + C)$.

YOLOv3 uses the cluster center as the anchor box. But it uses logistic regression instead of the previous softmax, which effectively improves the case where a bounding box predicts only one category and the near-small target detection rate is not high. YOLOv3 predicts the bounding box at three different scales, where the author uses a similar feature pyramid network. At the same time, a hybrid method for Darknet-19 and novel residual network is proposed to realize feature extraction, which is named Darknet-53 because it has 53 convolution layers. The specific structure is shown in Fig. 4.

4.2 Regard as a Detection Problem

An example of recognition is shown in Fig. 5. We have no needs to do any splitting on the numbers on the image but input the full image to the trained YOLOv3 model, then locations of ROIs will be directly detected and presented with bounding boxes sorted from small to large according to the x coordinate of

Type	Filters	Size	Output
Convolutional	32	3 × 3	256 × 256
Convolutional	64	3 × 3 / 2	128 × 128
1× Convolutional	32	1 × 1	
Convolutional	64	3 × 3	
Residual			128 × 128
Convolutional	128	3 × 3 / 2	64 × 64
2× Convolutional	64	1 × 1	
Convolutional	128	3 × 3	
Residual			64 × 64
Convolutional	256	3 × 3 / 2	32 × 32
8× Convolutional	128	1 × 1	
Convolutional	256	3 × 3	
Residual			32 × 32
Convolutional	512	3 × 3 / 2	16 × 16
8× Convolutional	256	1 × 1	
Convolutional	512	3 × 3	
Residual			16 × 16
Convolutional	1024	3 × 3 / 2	8 × 8
4× Convolutional	512	1 × 1	
Convolutional	1024	3 × 3	
Residual			8 × 8
Avgpool		Global	
Connected		1000	
Softmax			

Fig. 4. Darknet-53

Fig. 5. Water meter recognition flowchart in this paper, YOLOv3 for RoIs regression and classification, then additional algorithm to solve half-word problem

the upper left corner. At the same time, classification results are also generated. When the rules are formulated, the converted string is finally outputted. See Algorithm 1 for details.

4.3 Additional Rules

As we all know, there are five digits in the water meter. Predictably, three scenarios are predicted, as shown in Fig. 6:

a. The number of predicted bounding boxes is greater than five except 'wm' category
b. The number of predicted bounding boxes is equal to five except 'wm' category
c. The number of predicted bounding boxes is less to five except 'wm' category

In the second case, the digital length is 5, however, there may be a situation in which the prediction is wrong or even there are two bounding boxes in the nearly vertical position while some positions have no bounding box. This kind of

Algorithm 1. Detection into recognition

Require: Water meter image IMAGE
Ensure: Water meter number NUMBER

1: r = YOLOv3.detect(IMAGE) //r contains the predicted N categories C[N] and their corresponding bounding box position information P[N] and score S[N],where $P^{(i)} = [x_{min}^{(i)}, y_{min}^{(i)}, w^{(i)}, h^{(i)}]\ i \in [1, N]$;

2: Construct a new empty list of boxes;

3: **for** $i \leftarrow 1$ to N **do**

4:     **if** $C^{(i)} \neq$ "wm" and $IoU(P^{(i)}, P^{wm}) > threshold$ **then**

5:         $boxes^{(i)} = [C^{(i)}, x_{min}^{(i)}, y_{min}^{(i)}, w^{(i)}, h^{(i)}, S^{(i)}]$

6:     **end if**

7: **end for**

8: $sorted\_boxes = sorted(boxes, key = lambda\ x : x[2])$ //sorted from small to large according to the x coordinate of the upper left corner;

9: $checked\_boxes = check(sorted\_boxes)$ //the check function will be introduced in section 4.3;

10: $detect\_number = [checked\_boxes^{(i)}[1]]\ i \in [1, length(checked\_boxes)]$;

11: $NUMBER = ListToString(detect\_number)$ //convert list to string;

12: **return** $NUMBER$;

---

situation is likely to occur in the case of blurred images with rotating numbers. At this time, strengthening the training corresponding to the error sample can effectively reduce the prediction error, and the second case is likely to become the first case. The third case means there are misses, If it is a blurred image that is unrecognizable to the human eye, this situation can be ignored. If not, a simple way is to lower the threshold and perform the YOLOv3 detection again, which can add some new predicted bounding boxes, but the time cost increases. One feasible way is to increase the number of unpredicted digital samples to join the training. We focus on applying the rules to solve the first case, which is also the case with the most exceptions.

The digital rotation changes have 36 cases like xxx09-xxx10, xx099-xx100, x0999-x1000, 09999-10000. We strictly label the digital appearing in the digital

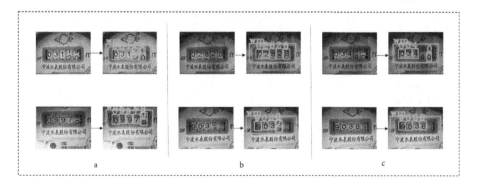

Fig. 6. Three main situations with different number of predicted bounding boxes

area of the water meter when marking, so almost all of the following 36 cases can predict more than five bounding boxes except 'wm' category, and in most cases, the predicted bounding boxes fit the digital well. Since the last step of YOLOv3 has added non-maximum suppression, we do not need to consider the case where the two predicted bounding boxes have a large overlap. We first find out if two or more predicted bounding boxes appear in the same vertical area, which is the so-called half-word problem, then suppress this situation, and finally ensure that there is only one predicted bounding box for each vertical area. We propose a suppression strategy (Algorithm 2): finding the closest two boxes of X_{min} in each loop, then proposing an evaluation function value_func(), comparing the scores of the two boxes found, and suppressing the predicted box with a lower score, simultaneously recording whether the above or below box is reserved. The subsequent loop only needs to compare the y_{min} of the two boxes, keeping the same as the previous record. Exit the loop until the number of predicted bounding boxes is less than or equal to five. For the evaluation function value_func(), we propose three scheme comparisons, which are comparing the height of the predicted bounding box, the score, and the combination of height normalization and score. See Eqs. 3, 4 and 5 for details. box_i is the i_{th} box, $height_{box_i}$ is the height of i_{th} box, and $score_{box_i}$ is the score of i_{th} box.

Algorithm 2. check() function

Require: sorted boxes SBOXES
Ensure: checked boxes CBOXES
 1: $flag \leftarrow -1$;
 2: **while** $(length(SBOXES) - 5) \neq 0$ **do**
 3:     Find the box_{idx} and box_{idx+1} of the current x_{min} minimum difference in SBOXES;
 4:     **if** $flag = -1$ **then**
 5:         **if** $value\_func(box_{idx}, box_{idx+1}) > value\_func(box_{idx+1}, box_{idx})$ **then**
 6:             Remove box_{idx+1} from SBOXES;
 7:         **else**
 8:             Remove box_{idx} from SBOXES;
 9:         **end if**
10:         Record flag is 1 or 0, corresponding to whether the reserved box is above or below;
11:     **else**
12:         Compare the y_{min} of box_{idx+1} and box_{idx}, and keep the box consistent with the flag;
13:     **end if**
14: **end while**
15: $CBOXES_i \leftarrow SBOXES_i$ $i \in [1,5]$;
16: **return** $CBOXES$;

$$value\_func(box_i, box_j)_1 = height_{box_i} \qquad (2)$$

$$value\_func(box_i, box_j)_2 = score_{box_i} \qquad (3)$$

$$value\_func(box_i, box_j)_3 = \lambda * \frac{height_{box_i}}{height_{box_i} + height_{box_j}} + (1 - \lambda) * score_{box_i} \quad (4)$$

5   Experiments

In this section, we compare the performance of the traditional version with the version of YOLOv3 combined with the rules on the test set. In order to compare the three evaluation functions, we also prepared 3,000 more fuzzy water meter images for evaluation.

5.1   Experimental Settings

The traditional version uses OpenCV's[2] own contour algorithm to extract digital regions as positive samples, and other regions as negative samples, training SVM classifiers. The recognition part uses a simple convolutional network of three convolutional layers and two fully connected layers, using maximum pooling and dropout. We prepared 10, 510 water meter images that have been labeled, divided into training and test sets in a ratio of 8:2 after data cleaning, and use the official YOLOv3-voc network structure to train, modify the number of categories to 11, and add random transformations. All of our experiments are on Intel Core i7 8700K, 16G Memory, 1T HDD, Ubuntu 16.04, a GeForce GTX 1080Ti graphics card with 11G memory.

5.2   Comparison Results

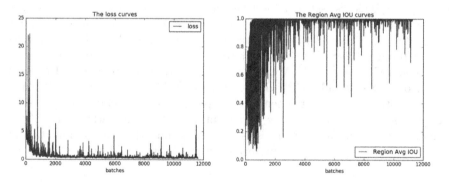

Fig. 7. Training loss and average IoU

Figures 7 and 8 show that training 10,000 batches basically leads to converge, and the 11 categories of training have achieved super-high AP, and the mAP of 11 categories is up to 0.9893.

---

[2] https://opencv.org/.

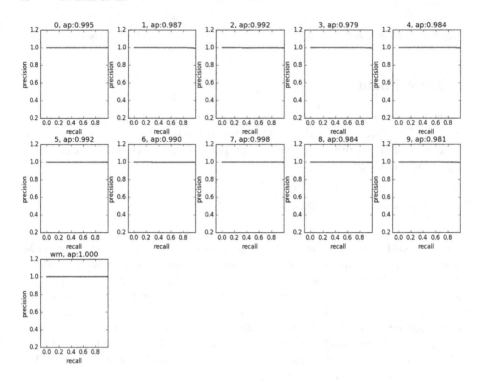

Fig. 8. PR curve for each category

On 2102 test sets, it can be found that the proposed method improves the 0-error accuracy by about 11.2% and the 1-error accuracy by about 4%. With 3000 blurred images as test sets, the performance gap is even greater. The proposed method improves the 0-error accuracy by about 26.8% and the 1-error accuracy by about 12.1%. The speed of the traditional method is about 100 ms/image, and our proposed method takes about 30 ms/image and 450 ms/images respectively under GPU and CPU. We also trained a tiny structure, with a 1-error of 99.57% on test2012 and a CPU time of 150 ms. Taking actual product demand into account, customers often tend to accept an error of 1 cubic meter, so the accuracy of 1-error may be more important. Based on the performance of the evaluation function on the two test sets, we can find that the combination of height normalization and score performs better (Tables 1 and 2).

Table 1. Accuracy on two types of test sets.

Method	Test 2102		Test 3000	
	0-error	1-error	0-error	1-error
Traditional method	0.8692	0.9600	0.7500	0.8877
Proposed method	**0.9667**	**0.9981**	**0.9570**	**0.9953**

Table 2. Accuracy in three evaluation functions.

Value function	Test 2102		Test 3000	
	0-error	1-error	0-error	1-error
Function(1)	0.9662	0.9981	0.9667	0.9940
Function(2)	0.9577	0.9972	0.9433	0.9950
Function(3), $\lambda = 0.65$	**0.9667**	**0.9981**	0.9570	**0.9953**

6 Conclusion

In this paper, we have established a water meter image dataset for training our model, as well as a novel water meter digital recognition method to tackle the recognition problem as a detection task. In contrast to traditional approaches, our work gets rid of time-consuming feature design thanks to the deep learning technology, instead it is a simple pipeline that directly receives images as input data and detect the location of ROIs, as well as classification. Detailed experiments evidence the benefit of our YOLOv3-based framework, it is a really accurate and real-time system, which has met the commercial standard. In particular, due to the wide application of water meter in both industries and our daily life, our water meter recognition work is of great practicability.

References

1. Redmon, J., Ali, F.: You only look once: unified, real-time object detection. IEEE (2015)
2. Redmon, J., Ali, F.: YOLO9000: better, faster, stronger. IEEE (2017)
3. Redmon, J., Ali, F.: YOLOv3: an incremental improvement. IEEE (2018)
4. LeCun, Y., Bottou, L., Bengio, Y., Haffner, P.: Gradient-based learning applied to document recognition. IEEE (1998)
5. Matan, O., Burges, C.J.C., LeCun, Y., Denker, J.S.: Multi-digit recognition using a space displacement neural network. In: NIPS (1991)
6. Guo, Q., Lei, J., Tu, D., Li, G.: Reading numbers in natural scene images with convolutional neural networks. In: Proceedings of the IEEE Conference on Computer Vision and Pattern Recognition (2014)
7. Wang, T.C., Liu, M.Y., Zhu, J.Y.: High-resolution image synthesis and semantic manipulation with conditional gans. In: Proceedings of the IEEE Conference on Computer Vision and Pattern Recognition (2018)
8. Johnson, J., Alahi, A., Fei-Fei, L.: Perceptual losses for real-time style transfer and super-resolution. In: European Conference on Computer Vision (2016)
9. Dalal, N., Triggs, B.: Histograms of oriented gradients for human detection. IEEE (2005)
10. Vapnik, V.N.: An overview of statistical learning theory. IEEE (1999)
11. Netzer, Y., et al.: Reading digits in natural images with unsupervised feature learning. In: NIPS (2011)
12. Goodfellow, I.J., Pouget-Abadie, J., Mirza, M.: Generative adversarial nets. In: NIPS (2014)
13. Jain, A.K.: Data clustering: 50 years beyond K-means. In: ECML/PKDD (2008)

Exploiting Category-Level Semantic Relationships for Fine-Grained Image Recognition

Xianjie Mo[1], Jiajie Zhu[1], Xiaoxuan Zhao[1], Min Liu[2], Tingting Wei[1], and Wei Luo[1(✉)]

[1] College of Mathematics and Informatics, South China Agricultural University, Guangzhou 510642, GD, People's Republic of China
cedricmo.cs@gmail.com, {Zhujiajie,zhaobear}@stu.scau.edu.cn, weitingting@scau.edu.cn, cswluo@gmail.com
[2] School of Computer, National University of Defense Technology, Changsha 410003, HN, People's Republic of China
gfsliumin@gmail.com

Abstract. We present a label-based, semantic distance induced regularization learning method for Fine-grained image recognition (FGIR). In contrast to previous label-based methods that involve a nontrivial optimization in multi-task metric learning, our approach can be integrated into an end-to-end network without introducing any extra parameters, thus easy to be optimized. To this end, a category-level hierarchical distance matrix (HDM) that encodes semantic distance between subcategories through a tree-like label hierarchy is constructed. HDM is then incorporated into a DCNN to aggregate misclassified prediction probabilities for model learning, thus providing additional discriminative information for fine-grained feature learning. Experiments on three fine-grained benchmark datasets (Stanford Cars, FGVC-Aircraft, CUB-Birds) validate the effectiveness of our approach and demonstrate its improvements over previous methods.

Keywords: Fine-grained image recognition · Deep convolutional neural networks · Label structure

1 Introduction

Fine-grained image recognition (FGIR) aims at distinguishing images of subordinate categories that belong to the same base class, e.g., bird [22] species, car models [10], aircraft model variants [16], etc. Different from the base-class recognition, the differences between subordinate categories are subtle and usually exist in local regions, which make recognition models difficult to learn effective discriminative feature to distinguish them, e.g., for a car dataset with four-level

---

The first author is a student.

© Springer Nature Switzerland AG 2019
Z. Lin et al. (Eds.): PRCV 2019, LNCS 11857, pp. 50–62, 2019.
https://doi.org/10.1007/978-3-030-31654-9_5

hierarchical annotations—year, model, make and type, the visual differences in appearance between cars of the same type but from different makers and models are difficult to be ascertained. Intuitively, it is important to delve deeply into the rich semantic relationship inherited in fine-grained categories to learn better representations for FGIR.

Exploiting semantic relationships between categories for FGIR is usually proceeded from three aspects—parts [6,7,29,30], objects [24,34], and labels [23,25, 33]. Leveraging parts and bounding box annotations to propose geometry constraints for part detector learning [29,30] possesses the advantage of reducing the number of false positive parts compared to that of unsupervised part learning methods [20,26]. However, the application of this method is limited due to its requirements of annotations. Utilizing the relationship between objects is implicitly implemented in the configuration of weakly-supervised learning, which minimizes averaging prediction loss across training samples with only image-level labels available [24,34]. This methodology relaxes the requirements of data annotation but with a trade-off between data annotation and prediction accuracy. Constructing the hierarchy of fine-grained labels for FGIR was also studied in the community. A number of methods propose to learn different-granularity features from different label granularities [23], and several other approaches make efforts to utilize similarities among categories through multi-task metric learning [33]. Although the idea of learning fine-grained features by leveraging label relationships is straightforward, it is usually difficult to well define the relationships between labels and involves a nontrivial optimization procedure to learn the model, like the metric learning presented in [33].

In this paper, we propose a simple but effective regularization method that exploits the semantic relationship between categories by constructing a hierarchy distance matrix from fine-grained labels for FGIR. Our method leverages the hierarchical structure inherited in fine-grained labels to build a category-level hierarchical distance matrix (HDM), in which each entity represents the semantic distance between two fine-grained categories. To this end, a tree-like hierarchy based on semantics or domain knowledge is built with the coarsest and finest granularity labels located on the root and leaf nodes, respectively. For example, a car with year, model, maker, and type, like '2012 BMW M3 coupe', forms a four-level hierarchical structure—year, model, maker and type respectively represent the leaf, the penultimate layer, the second top, and the root nodes. Then a path from the root node to a leaf node naturally defines a kind of inclusion relationship in which a son node contains more fine-grained information than its parent node. Therefore, the semantic distance between any two fine-grained categories is defined as the smallest number of edges travelled through from one leaf node to another via the tree. In order to incorporate HDM into deep convolutional neural networks (DCNNs) for fine-grained feature learning, a regularization term based on the inner product between DCNNs' output class-probability and columns of HDM indexed by the true label is established. This regularizer can effectively aggregate large amounts of supervising information from misclassified categories in the training stage, especially from those with extreme similarities in appearance but with large semantic distances. Experiments on three public available fine-grained datasets—Stanford Cars, CUB-Birds, and FGVC-aircraft, validate the effectiveness of our approach and demonstrate a clear improvement over existing methods. In summary, we make the following three concrete contributions:

- We propose a method to exploit the semantic relationship between categories by constructing a category-level hierarchical distance matrix (HDM) for fine-grained labels.
- We study a regularization method to aggregate misclassified information by using HDM to guide the fine-grained feature learning for FGIR.
- We construct a four-level tree-like label hierarchy—year, model, makers, and type—for images from Stanford Cars and make it publicly available for community research.

The remainder of this paper is organized as follows: Sect. 2 reviews related work. Section 3 details the construction of the hierarchical distance matrix (HDM) and our model learning with HDM. Experimental results and analysis are presented in Sect. 4 and we conclude our work in Sect. 5.

2   Related Work

2.1   Label Induced FGIR

Exploiting label relationships for performance improvement has been widely adopted in many applications [17,36]. The motivation behind this idea is that there is a latent semantic relationship between categories. For FGIR, the relationship between categories is apparent since all subcategories are derived from the same base category, namely, they generally share the same structure and attributes [10,16,22]. Therefore, [1] investigates attribute-based label embeddings for FGIR. [4,25] propose to augment training samples from external sources either to build super-type and factor-type super categories or combine with attributes for FGIR respectively. Developing similarities between categories from fine-grained labels was studied in [18,33,35], where [33] employs metric learning with triplet loss to facilitate feature learning, [35] groups fine-grained labels into several independent coarse label groups and learns features cooperatively, and [18] tries to maximize the entropy between visually very similar subcategories to prevent the classifier from being too confident in its outputs for feature learning. These methods normally involve a nontrivial optimization procedure to learn their models effectively. Besides, the hierarchy inherited in fine-grained labels was also studied, in which [2] incorporates predictions for high-level categories as prior knowledge to guide the feature learning of the low-level fine-grained categories while [23] combines features from different label granularities for prediction. Our work in this paper also focuses on exploiting label relationships and extends to man-made objects, which are limited in [2,23]. In addition, our work establishes a semantic distance between fine-grained categories while not a regularization relationship between different-granularity labels like that in [2,35].

Further, our model only involves a single network for model learning. This is different from previous work [2,23,33], which need to train an ensemble of networks.

2.2 Part Localization Based FGIR

Another line of research focuses on semantic parts localization [8,19,24,29]. The idea behind this viewpoint is that the discriminative structures are subtle and existed in local areas. Thus it is practical to first localize these areas and then extract feature from these local areas for FGIR. Early work in this line of research utilizes parts or bounding box annotations to guide part detectors learning [31,32] and then employ the learned detectors for part detection and feature extraction [29,30]. However, the requirements of part annotations limit its applications. With the increasing understanding of the functionality of neurons in DCNNs [3,15,28], developing detectors from DCNNs dominates the research. [20] finds constellations of neural activation patterns computed in DCNNs. [34] also studies this idea to select neural channels for detectors learning. Combining bottom-up and top-down information for part detectors discovering was also studied in [24]. Although improvements have been achieved by these methods, they involves a multi-stage optimization. Recent work unifies the detector learning and parts feature extraction in a single model, in which [13] explore the idea of visual attention for model learning by employing reinforcement learning while [14,27] learn fine-grained models by localizing semantic parts through exploiting the high-level feature maps. A weakness of these methods is that they either need to train an ensemble of networks or occasionally involve a separate initialization. Although our work in this paper does not involve localizing semantic parts, our model on the other hand can be trained end-to-end without introducing any extra parameters, and is thus easy to be extended to large-scale datasets. Moreover, our work is orthogonal to the part-based methods and can be easily integrated into these models.

3 Approach

We detail our approach in this section. Our approach includes two key components: (1) Constructing a category-level hierarchical distance matrix (HDM) based on a tree-like label hierarchy from fine to coarse (Sect. 3.1); and (2) Guiding fine-grained feature learning by aggregating misclassified output probabilities through HDM (Sect. 3.2). An overview of our approach is depicted in Fig. 1.

3.1 The Construction of HDM

Existing methods for FGIR by exploiting label relationships either utilize label granularities to augment the amount of training samples [23,25] or build similarity relationships between categories [33,35]. These methods usually need to train an ensemble of networks with each corresponding to one granularity or involve

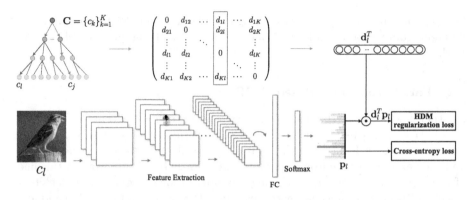

Fig. 1. An overview of our approach. The top row is an exemplification of the construction of HDM. The bottom row is a DCNN that extracts features and outputs prediction probabilities. The probabilities are regularized through a weighted sum, with weights from the column of HDM indexed by the ground-truth label, e.g., c_l and $\mathbf{d}_l^T$. The whole model is then trained end-to-end with gradients from the HDM regularization loss and the cross-entropy prediction loss.

a nontrivial optimization procedure. In this section, we propose a method to exploit label relationships for FGIR by constructing HDM from fine-grained labels, which can then be integrated into a network for end-to-end training.

Given a set of fine-grained categories with labels from set $\mathbf{C} = \{c_k\}_{k=1}^K$, we can construct a label hierarchy from $\mathbf{C}$ since the fine-grained label usually contain a full description of its derivative information, i.e., '2012 BMW M3 Coupe'. Supposing a M-layer relationship can be explored from $\mathbf{C}$, we can then construct a $M + 1$-level hierarchy with the leaf and root nodes representing the finest and coarsest labels, respectively. Consequently, a path from the root node to a leaf node naturally defines a kind of inclusion relationship in which the son node contains more fine-grained information than its parent node. The distance between two fine-grained categories can then be defined as the smallest number of edges needed to be traveled through from one leaf node to another. Figure 2 illustrates the idea of our HDM.

Formally, for two different fine-grained categories c_i and c_j, represented by two leaf nodes i and j respectively, with a common parent node in layer L_m ($0 < m \leq M$), the category-level semantic distance between them can be simply defined as:

$$d_{ij}(m) = 2me \quad i,j \in L_0, \tag{1}$$

where e is a constant denoting the length of the edge. We set $e = 1$ in this work. Thus the distance between two categories is completely determined by m. Therefore, for a set of K fine-grained labels, we encode the semantic distances between every two fine-grained categories into a matrix $\mathbf{D}^{K \times K}$, in which the entries on the main diagonal are all zeros (that is, the matrix is a hollow matrix). Compared to previous designs of label relationships between fine-grained categories [33,35], our design is simple yet effective and easy to be optimized (see Sect. 4).

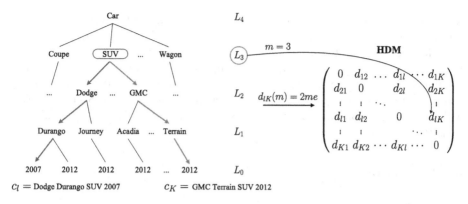

Fig. 2. An illustration of the construction of HDM on Stanford Cars. A 5-layer hierarchical tree is exemplified on the left by exploring derivative information inherited in the fine-grained labels. We build the 5-layer hierarchy according to the inclusion relationship of year-model-maker-type. Based on this hierarchy, the semantic distance between any pair of categories (e.g., c_l and c_K on the left) can be determined by the smallest number of edges needed to be traveled through between their corresponding nodes. The right is the constructed HDM.

3.2 Regularization Learning with HDM

HDM explicitly encapsulates the prior knowledge of category similarities into its design. Thus we can incorporate HDM into DCNNs for feature learning. Intuitively, this can be implemented in a regularization term that guides the fine-grained feature learning by providing more discriminative information through aggregating misclassified probabilities.

Given $\mathbf{D}^{K \times K} = [\mathbf{d}_1, \mathbf{d}_2, \cdots, \mathbf{d}_K]^T$, where each column $\mathbf{d}_t$ is a K-dimensional vector. Let p_{lj} be the output class-probability for c_j given an image with ground-truth label c_l, which could be predicted by the softmax layer. Then the regularization loss introduced by HDM can be defined as (see Fig. 1):

$$L_r = \frac{1}{N} \sum_{l=1}^{N} \sum_{k=1}^{K} b_l^{(k)} \mathbf{d}_k^T \mathbf{p}_l \tag{2}$$

where N is the total number of training samples, $b_l^{(k)} \in \{0, 1\}$ is a binary variable. $b_l^{(k)} = 1$ indicates that sample l belongs to c_k, otherwise $b_l^{(k)} = 0$. $\mathbf{d}_k$ denotes the kth column from $\mathbf{D}^{K \times K}$. $\mathbf{p}_l$ represents the prediction probability from our model for sample l. Together with the HDM regularization loss, $\mathbf{p}_l$ is also employed in a cross-entropy loss for model training:

$$L_c = -\frac{1}{N} \sum_{l=1}^{N} \sum_{j=1}^{K} t_{lj} \log p_{lj} \tag{3}$$

Therefore, our model can be learned by minimizing:

$$L = L_c + \lambda L_r \tag{4}$$

where λ is a balance weight. Compared to canonical cross-entropy learning where misclassified prediction probabilities are unused, the HDM regularization term can effectively aggregate misclassified prediction probabilities to guide the model training. Therefore, it provides additional supervising discriminative information for fine-grained feature learning, especially for those categories with extreme similarities in appearance but with large semantic distance (see Sect. 4.6). We will develop our approach on DCNNs in this paper, e.g., ResNet [5] and SE-ResNet [9].

4   Experiments

4.1   Datasets

The empirical evaluation of our method is performed on Stanford Cars [10], FGVC-Aircraft [16], and CUB-200-2011 [22]. Statistics numbers of training and testing samples of all 3 datasets are shown in Table 1. FGVC-Aircraft organizes its labels in a Model-Family-Manufacturer hierarchy. We use the hierarchical labels for CUB-200-2011 from [2], which is organized based on a Species-Genera-Family-Order taxonomy. We construct a hierarchy based on a Year-Model-Maker-Type taxonomy for Stanford Cars since its fine-grained labels have already include such information. Finally, we obtain 16 years, 178 models, 49 makers, and 9 types on Stanford Cars. We will make the hierarchical labels publicly available.

Stanford Cars. Stanford Cars dataset contains 16,185 images of 196 classes of cars. The data is split into 8,144 training images and 8,041 testing images, where each class has been split roughly in a 50-50 split.

FGVC-Aircraft. FGVC-Aircraft is a dataset containing 10,000 images of aircraft, spanning 100 aircraft models, and organized in a three-level hierarchy. It includes 6667 and 3333 samples for training and testing respectively.

CUB-200-2011. CUB-200-2011 includes 11,788 bird images from 200 subspecies with 5,994 images for training and 5,794 images for testing.

4.2   Implementation

We experiment our model with ResNet-50 [5] and SE-ResNet-50 [9] on 4 NVIDIA GTX 1070 GPUs in PyTorch. We train our model 30 epochs with the batch size of 32 and momentum 0.9 by SGD [12]. The initial learning rate is 0.01 and decayed by 0.1 every 15 epochs. The images are first resized to 600×600 and then randomly cropped a region of size 448×448 as the input with a horizontal flipping probability of 0.5. A Center crop of 448×448 without horizontal flipping is used in testing. The balance weights, λ, are determined on the validation sets and set to 0.1, 0.2 and 0.1 for Stanford Cars, FGVC-Aircraft, and CUB-200-2011, respectively.

Table 1. Statistics of benchmark datasets

Datasets	#class	#Train	#Test
CUB-200-2011	200	5,994	5,794
Stanford Cars	196	8,144	8,041
FGVC Aircraft	100	6,667	3,333

Table 2. Performance evaluation on Stanford Cars. 1-stage means end-to-end learning.

Method	1-stage	Accuracy
TLAN [24]	×	–
Part-CNN w/o bbox [30]	×	–
MG-CNN w/o bbox [23]	×	–
PDFR [34]	×	–
HAR-CNN [25]	×	80.8%
ELS [33]	√	88.4%
ResNet-50 [5]	√	91.1%
SE-ResNet-50 [9]	√	91.2%
ResNet-50 + HDM (ours)	√	91.6%
SE-ResNet-50 + HDM (ours)	√	**92.2%**

Results of ResNet and SE-ResNet are from our reimplementation. The results of three label-induced methods—HAR-CNN [25], ELS [33], and MG-CNN [23], are from the authors reports. HAR-CNN acquires a large number of hyper-class-labeled images for mode training. ELS embeds label structures into a multi-task learning framework with a generalized triplet loss. MG-CNN learns an ensemble of networks for different label granularities. We develop our HDM regularization and report its performance based on ResNet-50 and SE-ResNet-50.

4.3   Results on Stanford Cars

The experimental results are presented in Table 2. HAR-CNN [25] and ELS [33] are correspondingly based on AlexNet [11] and GoogleNet [21]. From comparison, it shows clearly advantages of advanced network architectures, as we achieve 91.1% and 91.2% for ResNet-50 [5] and SE-ResNet-50 [9], respectively. The effectiveness of HDM is significant since it improves by 0.5% and 1.0% for ResNet-50 and SE-ResNet-50 respectively. Considering the simplicity of our HDM, the improvements effectively demonstrate the usefulness of misclassified probabilities in training for providing more supervised information to fine-grained feature learning.

Table 3. Performance evaluation on FGVC-Aircraft. The 1st group are methods with bbox annotations. The 2nd group are weakly-supervised methods. 1-stage means end-to-end learning.

Method	1-stage	Accuracy
Part-CNN w/bbox [30]	×	–
MG-CNN w/bbox [23]	×	86.6%
SPDA [29]	×	–
TLAN [24]	×	–
Part-CNN w/o bbox [30]	×	–
MG-CNN w/o bbox [23]	×	82.5%
PDFR [34]	×	–
HAR-CNN [25]	×	–
ELS [33]	√	–
ResNet-50 [5]	√	89.5%
SE-ResNet-50 [9]	√	90.8%
ResNet-50 + HDM (ours)	√	89.8%
SE-ResNet-50 + HDM (ours)	√	**91.2%**

4.4 Results on FGVC-Aircraft

Table 3 shows the performance of methods on this dataset. We achieve the best performance of 91.2%. Compared to MG-CNN [23], our approach only needs to train one network to make full use of information from different label granularities, while MG-CNN trains an ensemble of networks with each corresponding to one label granularity. This can save huge of training time for our model over that of MG-CNN. In addition, We can find the bounding box (bbox) annotations have a big influence on MG-CNN since it drops by 4.1% in performance when without bbox. Moreover, compared to the two supporting frameworks—ResNet-50 and SE-ResNet-50, training with HDM steadily improves their performance, which indicates the robustness of our approach.

4.5 Results on CUB-Birds

Table 4 demonstrates the prediction accuracy on CUB birds. Our approach achieves almost the best result on this dataset. Compared to the best result of methods with bbox (85.7%), our result is comparable (84.4%), considering only image-level labels are employed in our approach. Our approach surpasses almost all methods that employs multi-stage training while without annotations, like TLAN [24], Part-CNN [30], and MG-CNN [23]. The comparable performance with PDFR [34] advocates the effectiveness of our approach. In comparison with PDFR, our approach is much more simple and easy to extend to large-scale datasets since it does not introduce any extra parameters into its supporting

Table 4. Performance evaluation on CUB-200-2011. The 1st group are methods with bbox annotations. The 2nd group are weakly-supervised methods. 1-stage means end-to-end learning.

Method	1-stage	Accuracy
Part-CNN w/bbox [30]	×	76.4%
MG-CNN w/bbox [23]	×	83.0%
SPDA [29]	×	**85.7%**
TLAN [24]	×	69.7%
Part-CNN w/o bbox [30]	×	73.9%
MG-CNN w/o bbox [23]	×	81.7%
PDFR [34]	×	**84.5%**
HAR-CNN [25]	×	–
ELS [33]	√	–
ResNet-50 [5]	√	81.6%
SE-ResNet-50 [9]	√	83.6%
ResNet-50 + HDM (ours)	√	82.0%
SE-ResNet-50 + HDM (ours)	√	**84.4%**

(a)   (b)   (c)

Fig. 3. The left image in every group is misclassified into the category of the right image in the corresponding group by SE-ResNet since they have a very similar visual appearance. However, by exploiting the semantic relationships between categories, our SE-ResNet+HDM can correctly predict their true categories. The images in (a) Stanford Cars, (b) FGVC-Aircraft, and (c) CUB-Birds, from left to right, are respectively from categories 'Bentley Continental GT Coupe 2007', 'Aston Martin Virage Coupe 2012', 'A340-300', 'A340-200', 'Hooded Oriole', and 'Baltimore Oriole'.

networks and can be trained end-to-end. PDFR, however, involves a multi-stage training and needs to select filters in a DCNN to train part detectors for localizing parts before training a classification network.

4.6   Improvements Inspection

It is essential to inspect in which aspect HDM contributes to FGIR. To this end, we select the SE-ResNet-50 as our observation model since it surpasses ResNet-50 and achieves the best performance on all datasets. Figure 3 illustrates our findings. We find that, by exploiting semantic distance between fine-grained categories, HDM can effectively distinguish objects that come from different categories but with an extremely similar visual appearance. The objects with this kind of properties are difficult to be correctly classified as demonstrated by SE-ResNet-50. Thus, we conclude that HDM contributes to correctly classify images that are almost indistinguishable in visual appearance.

5   Conclusion

In this paper, we proposed a method to exploit semantic relationships between subcategories by constructing a hierarchical distance matrix from fine-grained labels. In order to take advantage of this relationship to improve the performance of FGIR, we studied an HDM-induced regularization approach that aggregates misclassified prediction probabilities to guide the model learning. With more supervised discriminative information from the HDM regularizer, our approach improves the performance of FGIR significantly. Experiments on benchmark datasets validate the effectiveness of our approach and demonstrate its improvements over existing methods.

Acknowledgement. This work was supported in part by the National Natural Science Foundation of China under Grant 61702197, in part by the Natural Science Foundation of Guangdong Province under Grant 2017A030310261, in part by the program of China Scholarship Council.

References

1. Akata, Z., Reed, S., Walter, D., Lee, H., Schiele, B.: Evaluation of output embeddings for fine-grained image classification. In: CVPR (2015)
2. Chen, T., Wu, W., Gao, Y., Dong, L., Luo, X., Lin, L.: Fine-grained representation learning and recognition by exploiting hierarchical semantic embedding. In: ACM MM (2018)
3. Fong, R., Vedaldi, A.: Net2vec: quantifying and explaining how concepts are encoded by filters in deep neural networks. In: CVPR (2018)
4. Gebru, T., Hoffman, J., Li, F.F.: Fine-grained recognition in the wild: a multi-task domain adaptation approach. In: ICCV (2017)
5. He, K., Zhang, X., Ren, S., Sun, J.: Deep residual learning for image recognition. In: CVPR (2016)
6. He, X., Peng, Y.: Fine-grained image classification via combining vision and language. In: CVPR (2017)
7. He, X., Peng, Y.: Weakly supervised learning of part selection model with spatial constraints for fine-grained image classification. In: AAAI (2017)
8. He, X., Peng, Y., Zhao, J.: Which and how many regions to gaze: focus discriminative regions for fine-grained visual categorization. Int. J. Comput. Vis., 1–21 (2019)
9. Hu, J., Shen, L., Sun, G.: Squeeze-and-excitation networks. In: CVPR (2017)
10. Krause, J., Stark, M., Deng, J., Li, F.F.: 3D object representations for fine-grained categorization. In: 4th IEEE Workshop on 3D Representation and Recognition at ICCV (2013)

11. Krizhevsky, A., Sutskever, I., Hinton, G.E.: ImageNet classification with deep convolutional neural networks. In: NIPS (2012)
12. LeCun, Y., Bottou, L., Bengio, Y., Haffner, P.: Gradient based learning applied to document recognition. Proc. IEEE **86**(11), 2278–2324 (1998)
13. Li, Z., Yang, Y., Liu, X., Wen, S., Xu, W.: Dynamic computational time for visual attention. In: ICCV (2017)
14. Liu, X., Xia, T., Wang, J., Lin, Y.: Fully convolutional attention localization networks: efficient attention localization for fine-grained recognition. In: arXiv preprint arXiv:1603.06765 (2016)
15. Mahendran, A., Vedaldi, A.: Understanding deep image representations by inverting them. In: CVPR (2015)
16. Maji, S., Rahtu, E., Kannala, J., Blaschko, M., Vedaldi, A.: Fine-grained visual classification of aircraft. In: arXiv preprint arXiv:1306.5151 (2013)
17. Mostajabi, M., Maire, M., Shakhnarovich, G.: Regularizing deep networks by modeling and predicting label structure. In: CVPR (2018)
18. Dubey, A., Gupta, O., Raskar, R., Naik, N.: Maximum entropy fine-grained classification. In: NIPS (2018)
19. Peng, Y., He, X., Zhao, J.: Object-part attention model for fine-grained image classification. IEEE Trans. Image Process. **27**(3), 1487–1500 (2017)
20. Simon, M., Rodner, E.: Neural activation constellations: unsupervised part model discovery with convolutional networks. In: ICCV (2015)
21. Szegedy, C., et al.: Going deeper with convolutions. In: CVPR (2015)
22. Wah, C., Branson, S., Welinder, P., Perona, P., Belongie, S.: The Caltech-UCSD birds-200-2011 dataset. Technical report, California Institute of Technology (2011)
23. Wang, D., Shen, Z., Shao, J., Zhang, W., Xue, X., Zhang, Z.: Multiple granularity descriptors for fine-grained categorization. In: ICCV (2015)
24. Xiao, T., Xu, Y., Yang, K., Zhang, J., Peng, Y., Zhang, Z.: The application of two-level attention models in deep convolutional neural network for fine-grained image classification. In: CVPR (2015)
25. Xie, S., Yang, T., Wang, X., Lin, Y.: Hyper-class augmented and regularized deep learning for fine-grained image classification. In: CVPR (2015)
26. Yang, S., Bo, L., Wang, J., Shapiro, L.G.: Unsupervised template learning for fine-grained object recognition. In: NIPS (2012)
27. Yang, Z., Luo, T., Wang, D., Hu, Z., Gao, J., Wang, L.: Learning to navigate for fine-grained classification. In: Ferrari, V., Hebert, M., Sminchisescu, C., Weiss, Y. (eds.) Computer Vision – ECCV 2018. LNCS, vol. 11218, pp. 438–454. Springer, Cham (2018). https://doi.org/10.1007/978-3-030-01264-9_26
28. Zeiler, M.D., Fergus, R.: Visualizing and understanding convolutional networks. In: Fleet, D., Pajdla, T., Schiele, B., Tuytelaars, T. (eds.) ECCV 2014. LNCS, vol. 8689, pp. 818–833. Springer, Cham (2014). https://doi.org/10.1007/978-3-319-10590-1_53
29. Zhang, H., et al.: SPDA-CNN: unifying semantic part detection and abstraction for fine-grained recognition. In: CVPR (2016)
30. Zhang, N., Donahue, J., Girshick, R., Darrell, T.: Part-based R-CNNs for fine-grained category detection. In: Fleet, D., Pajdla, T., Schiele, B., Tuytelaars, T. (eds.) ECCV 2014. LNCS, vol. 8689, pp. 834–849. Springer, Cham (2014). https://doi.org/10.1007/978-3-319-10590-1_54
31. Zhang, N., Farrell, R., Darrell, T.: Pose pooling kernels for sub-category recognition. In: CVPR (2012)
32. Zhang, N., Farrell, R., Iandola, F., Darrell, T.: Deformable part descriptors for fine-grained recognition and attribute prediction. In: ICCV (2013)

33. Zhang, X., Zhou, F., Lin, Y., Zhang, S.: Embedding label structures for fine-grained feature representation. In: CVPR (2016)
34. Zhang, X., Xiong, H., Zhou, W., Lin, W., Tian, Q.: Picking deep filter responses for fine-grained image recognition. In: CVPR (2016)
35. Zhou, F., Lin, Y.: Fine-grained image classification by exploring bipartite-graph labels. In: CVPR (2016)
36. Zlateski, A., Jaroensri, R., Sharma, P., Durand, F.: On the importance of label quality for semantic segmentation. In: CVPR (2018)

On the Multi-scale Real-Time Object Detection Using ResNet

Zhengyao Bai[✉] and Dong Jiang

School of Information Science and Engineering, Yunnan University,
Kunming 650500, China
baizhy@ynu.edu.cn, 1012833912@qq.com

Abstract. Real-time target detection and location has important values in video surveillance. Aimed at the low accuracy of existing real-time object detection algorithms, this paper proposes a multi-scale real-time target detection algorithm based on residual convolution neural network. Firstly, the residual convolutional neural network is introduced into the YOLOv3-Tiny algorithm. The jump connection of the low-level and high-level networks forms the residual module in the YOLOv3-Tiny algorithm to effectively prevent network degradation while increasing the depth of the neural network. Secondly, a new prediction layer is added to the neural network to improve the results of small target detection. Finally, the trained model is tested on the Pascal VOC public dataset. The experimental results show that the proposed algorithm achieves 64.6% accuracy on the validation dataset, and the speed of 60FPS in the video detection. The detection accuracy is improved to a higher level at a small cost of a little lower speed still meeting the real-time detection requirements, and small targets in the image can be effectively detected. The algorithm is effective and robust.

Keywords: Real-time object detection · Residual convolutional neural network · YOLOv3-Tiny

1   Introduction

The task of object detection is to find the objects in the image or video, determine their position, size and category. Therefore, fast and accurate object detection has always been one of the research hotspots in the field of computer vision. In early stage, Viola [1] train the neural network to achieve face target detection based on the AdaBoost algorithm, although the method can process images quickly and it has high accuracy, but category is single and can't be widely used. With the development of deep learning, the convolutional neural network has achieved breakthrough results in image classification and object detection. Object detection algorithms based on deep learning can be divided into two categories, one is based on candidate regions, the other one is based on regression.

The typical algorithm based on regression is the YOLO [2] (You Only Look Once) series of algorithms. The YOLOv1 algorithm directly uses a convolution network to complete the classification and localization of targets. Due to the reduced amount of repetitive calculation, the YOLOv1 algorithm is fast. However, the detection accuracy

Z. Lin et al. (Eds.): PRCV 2019, LNCS 11857, pp. 63–73, 2019.
https://doi.org/10.1007/978-3-030-31654-9_6

is slightly lower. In the YOLOv2 [3] algorithm, Redmon used the anchor box strategy in Faster RCNN, but unlike the empirically driven anchor box in Faster RCNN [4], YOLOv2 uses the clustering method to analyze the anchor box, and the final object detection result is better. In order to further improve the detection effect of the network on small targets, Redmon borrowed the idea of Feature Pyramid Networks [5] (FPN) to perform object detection on multiple scales, and proposed the YOLOv3 [6] algorithm, which makes the detection effect of small target better.

The faster detection speed in the YOLO series is the YOLOv3-Tiny algorithm, but its detection accuracy is lower. In view of this problem, this paper combine the residual convolution network with YOLOV3-Tiny network to improve the processing of image features in convolutional networks and improve the detection accuracy of the algorithm. On the basis of the fusion of the convolutional neural network, a layer of prediction is added to improve the detection effect on small targets. The experimental results show that the combination network improves the detection accuracy and improves the detection effect on small targets, while the detection speed can still meet the requirements of real-time detection.

2 YOLOv3-Tiny Network Modifications

2.1 Detection Procedure in YOLO

The YOLO series algorithm does not need to generate candidate boxes for the classification and detection, it can directly output the target categories and positions simultaneously after the neural network training. First, the YOLO series algorithm extracts the input image through the convolutional neural network, and obtains a fixed-size feature map through a series of convolution processing and down sampling operations. For example, for image size is 416 × 416, through the YOLO-Tiny network processing, a feature map with a size of 13 × 13 can be obtained. According to the obtained feature map, the YOLO-Tiny network divides the input image into several grids. When the center coordinates of the target are within a certain grid, the grid is responsible for predicting it. When predicting, each grid predicts a fixed number of bounding boxes. The detection step of YOLO-Tiny algorithm is shown in Table 1.

Table 1. YOLO-Tiny algorithm

1: Input an image and resize to 416x416
2: Divides the image into an S×S grid
3: Whether the target center is in some grid
if target's center in some grid:
this grid is responsible for predict the target, it predicts B bound boxes, confidence for those boxes, and C class probabilities.
end if
4: repeat step 3.
end.

2.2   Multi-scale Prediction

In the YOLO algorithms, the number of bounding boxes predicted by each grid in the YOLOv1 network is two. In YOLOv2 network it is increased to five, and YOLOv2 predict 845 bounding boxes on a feature map of size 13 × 13. While in the YOLOv3 network the number of boxes is three, but it is predicted on three different size feature maps. Therefore, the actual number of bounding boxes is 10,647, which is more than ten times of YOLOv2. The number of bounding boxes increases, which makes the algorithms detect object more precise. Since the small-scale feature map extracted by the low-level network in the convolutional neural network contains more position information of the image, such as detecting on the feature map of size 52 × 52, more position information about the small target can be obtained, and the feature map extracted by the high-level network contains more detailed information of the image, which is beneficial to the recognition of the target category. Therefore, the feature map extracted by different layers can be detected separately to achieve multi-scale prediction of specific targets. In order to make the bounding box better predict the target, the author uses the k-means clustering method to cluster the labeled real positioning boxes in the coco dataset [7], and obtains nine different sizes of anchor boxes, as shown in Table 2.

Table 2. Anchor box for different size feature maps

Feature map	Anchor box
13 × 13	(116 × 90), (156 × 198), (373 × 326)
26 × 26	(30 × 61), (62 × 45), (59 × 119)
52 × 52	(10 × 13), (16 × 30), (33 × 23)

As can be seen from Table 2, because the feature map of size 13 × 13 has the largest receptive field and contains the most abundant feature information, it is suitable for detecting the large target existing in the image. Therefore, the three largest anchor boxes are used for detection this layer. The 26 × 26 feature map uses a medium-sized anchor box to detect medium-sized targets in the image. The 52 × 52 feature map receptive field contains more position information of the target, so it is suitable for detecting smaller targets in the image. Therefore, the prediction is performed using the smallest three anchor boxes.

2.3   Modifying YOLO-Tiny Using ResNet

YOLOv3-Tiny is a simplified version of YOLOv3 with fast detection speed but low accuracy. The YOLOv3-Tiny network only uses two scale feature maps to predict the object. The YOLOv3-Tiny network consists of only the convolutional layer and the pooling layer. The network layer is shallow and the calculation is low, but the feature extraction and processing of the input image is not sufficient. In general, the deeper the network level is, the more feature information is extracted from the image, but simply increasing the network level will lead to gradient dispersion or gradient explosion.

The solution to this problem is to introduce Batch Normalization [8] into the neural network. However, it is still easy to cause new problems, resulting in the saturation or decline of the accuracy of the network during the training process and the degradation of the neural network. In order to make the neural network fully extract the image feature information and avoid the above problems, this paper introduces the idea of residual convolutional neural network [9] (ResNet) to YOLO-Tiny network. The ResNet was proposed by He Kaiming et al in 2015. It has added direct channels to the lower and upper layers, which allows shallow input information to be directly connected to the deep network, as shown in Fig. 1. If the input information is x, the output F(x) is obtained after convolution processing, and the output node is connected with the input information. This not only can protect the integrity of the input information, but also can adjust and optimize the weight of the network. According to the input and output residuals of the network in the training process, which simplifies the learning objectives and computational complexity of the network. ResNet is widely used in image detection, recognition and segmentation because it can effectively extract image features, restrain network degradation and reduce error rate.

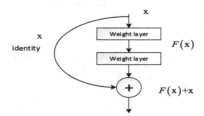

Fig. 1. Residual block

Inspired by residual convolution neural network, aimed at the problems of shallow YOLOv3-Tiny network and insufficient feature extraction, this paper introduces residual module structure to extract image features in YOLOv3-Tiny network. In addition, this paper adds another prediction layer to the network to improve the detection effect of small targets. Those networks shown in Fig. 2.

The Res-Tiny network use the same size feature map to perform object detection like YOLv3-Tiny. The experimental result shows that the detection accuracy of the Res-Tiny network is higher than YOLOv3-Tiny network 6%. In the convolutional neural network, because the feature map with larger size contains less feature details, but the location information is more abundant, this paper adds a predication layer based on the Res-Tiny network. Object detection is carried out to improve the detection effect on small targets. It is verified that the detection accuracy of the Res-Tiny-3 network for small targets is increased by more than 11% compared with the YOLOv3-Tiny network.

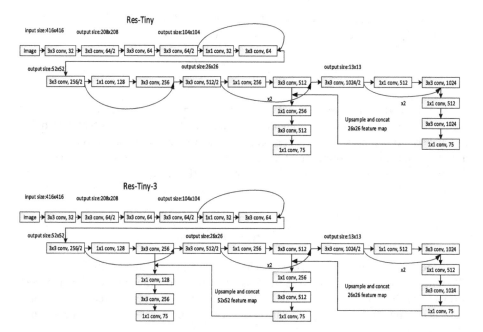

Fig. 2. Res-Tiny network and Res-Tiny-3 network

3 Evaluation Indexes

3.1 Confusion Matrix

At present, the evaluating indexes commonly used in object detection include confusion matrix, recall, precision, F1-score, Average Precision (AP), mean Average Precision (mAP) and so on. Among them, the definition of the confusion matrix is shown in Table 3.

Table 3. Confusion matrix

Truth	Prediction results	
	Positive example	Negative example
Positive example	True positives (TP)	False positives (FP)
Negative example	False negatives (FN)	True negatives (TN)

In Table 3, TP represents the number of samples that are actually positive samples and are correctly identified as positive. TN represents the number of samples that are actually negative samples and is correctly identified as negative samples. FP represents the negative sample is recognized as the number of positive samples. FN represents the number of positive samples identified as negative samples. Through the confusion matrix, two indicators, recall rate R and precision rate P can be calculated to evaluate the effect of target detection. They are defined as follows:

$$R = \frac{TP}{TP + FN}, P = \frac{TP}{TP + FP} \tag{1}$$

The recall rate and precision rate are contradictory measures. If the recall rate is high and accuracy rate remains high, the performance of the classifier is better. In order to balance the contradiction between recall rate and precision rate, a certain value is used to evaluate the performance of the classifier, and the F1-score is derived. Usually, the bigger the value of F1-score, the better the performance of the classifier. F1 is defined as follows:

$$F_1 = 2 \cdot \frac{precision \cdot recall}{precision + recall} \tag{2}$$

In addition, in object detection, each image often contains multiple targets of different categories. Therefore, the mAP is often used to evaluate the detection performance of the network. The AP is the area under the PR (precision-recall) curve and mAP is the sum of the Average Precision of each type of target divided by the number of categories.

3.2 Intersection Over Union (IoU)

The intersection over union represents the overlap degree between the detected and real object positioning box in the image. The optimal intersection over union ratio is 1, which is a complete overlap. The calculation method is shown in Fig. 3.

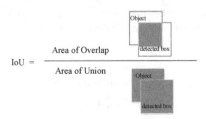

Fig. 3. Computation of intersection over union

4 Experimental Results and Analysis

First, we compare Res-Tiny and Res-Tiny-3 with other real-time detection systems on PASCAL VOC 2007. To understand the differences between Res-Tiny, Res-Tiny-3 and YOLOv3-Tiny, we explore the confusion matrix on VOC 2007 made by Res-Tiny, Res-Tiny-3 and YOLOv3-Tiny. We also present AP of each class on VOC 2007 test dataset. Finally, we show PR curve to analyze the difference between Res-Tiny-3 and YOLOv3-Tiny on small target detection.

4.1   Comparisons with Other Detection Algorithms

Many object detection algorithm focus on making detection speed fast. However, only Sadeghi [10] design algorithm that could runs in 30 frames per second (FPS). While the other efforts don't meet the real-time requirement we also compare their relative mAP and speed. YOLOv3-Tiny is the fastest object detection method on PASCAL with mAP 54.07%, it is more than twice as accurate as prior work on real-time detection. Res-Tiny pushes mAP to 60.92% while detection speed still can reach 63FPS. After add a prediction layer on Res-Tiny, the mAP increase about 4%, but it speed slower than Res-Tiny 3FPS.

Fastest DPM [11] effectively speeds up DPM without sacrificing much mAP but it still can't meet the real-time detection. It also is limited by DPM's relatively low accuracy on detection compared to neural network approaches. R-CNN minus R [12] use static bounding box proposals to locate target. Its mAP higher but slower.

Fast R-CNN [13] make the class classification faster but it still relies on selective search which can take around 2 s per image to generate bounding box proposals. Thus it has high mAP but it can't meet real-time detection. The Faster R-CNN [4] replaces selective search with region proposal networks. It most speed model achieves 18 FPS while less accurate. The Faster R-CNN VGG16 is 9 mAP higher but is also 9 times slower than Res-Tiny-3. The Zeiler Fergus Faster R-CNN [4] is 3 times slower than Res-Tiny-3 and less accurate.

Table 4. Detection accuracy and detection speed of each algorithm

Detection algorithm	Training data	mAP (%)	FPS (Frames Per Second)
100 Hz DPM [10]	2007	16.0	100
30 Hz DPM [10]	2007	26.1	30
Fastest DPM [11]	2007	30.4	15
R-CNN Minus R [12]	2007	53.5	6
Fast RCNN [13]	2007 + 2012	70.0	0.5
Faster RCNN VGG16 [4]	2007 + 2012	73.2	7
Faster RCNN ZF [4]	2007 + 2012	62.1	18
YOLO [2]	2007 + 2012	63.4	45
YOLOv2 [3]	2007 + 2012	76.8	36
YOLOv3-Tiny	2007 + 2012	**54.0**	**67**
Res-Tiny	2007 + 2012	**60.9**	**63**
Res-Tiny-3	2007 + 2012	**64.6**	**60**

From the data in Table 4, it can be seen that the previous YOLO and RCNN algorithms can't keep the detection accuracy and speed at a relatively ideal level at the same time. The rise of any one of mAP and FPS will lead to the decline of another, so it is difficult to apply in situations where the detection speed and accuracy are required to be higher. We compared with the YOLO series and RCNN series detection algorithms, the Res-Tiny-3 achieves a better balance between detection accuracy and detection speed.

4.2   Analysis of Confusion Matrix and IoU

To further illustrate the effectiveness of the proposed method, Table 5 shows the true positives (TP), false positives (FP), false negatives (FN), precision, recall, F1-score, and IoU.

Table 5. Confusion matrix parameters and IoU

Algorithm	TP	FP	FN	Precision	Recall	F1-score	IoU
YOLOv3-Tiny	5124	3229	6908	0.61	0.43	0.50	0.45
Res-Tiny	6508	3403	5524	0.66	0.54	0.59	0.50
Res-Tiny-3	7277	5466	4755	0.57	0.60	0.59	0.43

It can be seen from the data in Table 5 that the method can improve the recognition of true positives and reduce the number of detections of false negatives. After improving the basic network, the precision is increased by 5%, the recall is increased by 11%, and F1-score is also higher and more robust than the YOLOv3-Tiny network. Because the number of targets detected by the test set is huge, this paper calculates the average IoU to analyze the positioning accuracy of the algorithms. It can be seen from Table 5 that the average IoU of the Tiny algorithms is 45%. After use the residual network structure, the average IoU is increased by 5%, and the target location is more accurate. By adding the prediction layer based on the residual network, the number of detected true positives increased, but the number of false positives also increased, resulting in a 4% reduction in precision, but 17% increase in recall.

4.3   Analysis of Small Target Detection

In this paper, a layer of prediction layer is added to Res-Tiny-3 to improve the detection effect of small targets. In order to better analyze it, this paper calculates YOLOv3-Tiny network and Res-Tiny-3 AP value for each type of target is shown in Table 6.

Table 6. AP value of each type of object

Category	Algorithm	
	YOLOv3-Tiny	Res-Tiny-3
Aeroplane	61.83%	70.90%
Bicycle	66.64%	75.17%
Bird	**40.27%**	**55.79%**
Boat	39.77%	52.92%
Bottle	**25.29%**	**41.66%**
Bus	66.80%	72.48%
Car	71.26%	79.99%
Cat	59.61%	70.84%
Chair	32.46%	46.40%
Cow	55.80%	66.49%
Table	48.07%	59.64%
Dog	53.71%	67.02%
Horse	67.41%	76.97%

(continued)

Table 6. (*continued*)

Category	Algorithm	
	YOLOv3-Tiny	Res-Tiny-3
Motorbike	68.76%	73.13%
Person	63.98%	75.74%
Potted-plant	**26.38%**	**37.81%**
Sheep	56.05%	65.17%
Sofa	48.43%	62.69%
Train	70.02%	77.23%
TV monitor	**58.77%**	**64.10%**

The AP data in Table 6 show that the Res-Tiny-3 network has greatly improved the accuracy of 20 categories in the Pascal VOC dataset, especially for the four types of bird, bottle, potted-plant and tv monitor. The accuracy of four small target is improved by more than 11%. It is verified that the feature map extracted by the low-level network has more position information and use this feature map make the detection of small targets more accurate. Therefore, target detection on the feature map with small receptive field can improve the detection effect on small targets. The PR curve of four categories is shown in Fig. 4.

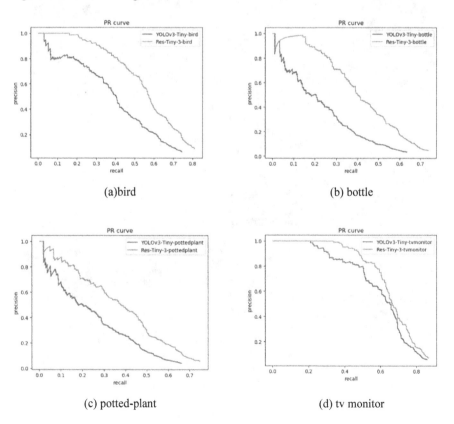

(a)bird

(b) bottle

(c) potted-plant

(d) tv monitor

Fig. 4. PR curves of bird, bottle, potted-plant and tv monitor

As can be seen from Fig. 4, as the recall increases, the accuracy of detection of objects by the YOLOv3-Tiny and Res-Tiny-3 networks decreases. Among them, the YOLOv3-Tiny network curve declines faster, and in order to improve the recall rate, more precision is lost, while the Res-Tiny-3 network's PR curve declines much slower than the YOLO-Tiny network, and the recall is improved. At the same time, it can still maintain a high precision, so the Res-Tiny-3 network is better than the YOLOv3-Tiny network for detecting small objects. The detection effect of the two algorithms is shown in Fig. 5.

(a) YOLOv3-Tiny algorithm detection result

(b) Res-Tiny-3 algorithm detection result

Fig. 5. Detection results

5 Conclusion

Based on the real-time target detection algorithm YOLOv3-Tiny, this paper introduces the idea of residual convolutional neural network for extraction of image features, which can effectively prevent network degradation and gradient dispersion while deepening the network level, and enhance the network's ability to understand and analyze image feature information. In this paper, the improved neural network is trained and tested on Pascal VOC dataset. Compared with YOLOv3-Tiny network, the improved neural network has higher detection accuracy, and better detection effect on small targets. The improved algorithm is more effective and robust. The algorithm improves the detection accuracy in real-time detection, but the detection speed still has a slight decrease during the experiment. The future work includes the network structure optimization, speeding the detection.

References

1. Viola, P., Jones, M.: Rapid object detection using a boosted cascade of simple features. In: Proceedings of the 2001 IEEE Computer Society Conference on Computer Vision and Pattern Recognition, pp. 511–518. IEEE, Kauai (2001)
2. Redmon, J., Divvala, S., Girshick, R.: You only look once: Unified, real-time object detection. In: Proceedings of the IEEE Conference on Computer Vision and Pattern Recognition, pp. 779–788 (2016)
3. Redmon, J., Farhadi, A.: YOLO9000: better, faster, stronger. In: 2017 IEEE Conference on Computer Vision and Pattern Recognition (CVPR), pp. 7263–7271. IEEE, Honolulu (2017)
4. Ren, S., He, K., Girshick, R.: Faster R-CNN: towards real-time object detection with region proposal networks. IEEE Trans. Pattern Anal. Mach. Intell. **39**(6), 1137–1149 (2015)
5. Lin, T., Dollár, P., Girshick, R.: Feature pyramid networks for object detection. In: Proceedings of the IEEE Conference on Computer Vision and Pattern Recognition, pp. 2117–2125 (2017)
6. Redmon, J., Farhadi, A.: Yolov3: an incremental improvement. arXiv preprint arXiv:1804. 02767 (2018)
7. Veit, A., Matera, T., Neumann, L.: Coco-text: dataset and benchmark for text detection and recognition in natural images. arXiv preprint arXiv:1601.07140 (2016)
8. Ioffe, S., Szegedy, C.: Batch normalization: accelerating deep network training by reducing internal covariate shift. In: Proceedings of the 32nd International Conference on International Conference on Machine Learning, pp. 448–456. JMLR.org, Lille (2001)
9. He, K., Zhang, X., Ren, S.: Deep residual learning for image recognition. In: 2016 IEEE Conference on Computer Vision and Pattern Recognition (CVPR), pp. 770–778. IEEE, Las Vegas (2016)
10. Sadeghi, M.A., Forsyth, D.: 30 Hz object detection with DPM V5. In: Fleet, D., Pajdla, T., Schiele, B., Tuytelaars, T. (eds.) ECCV 2014. LNCS, vol. 8689, pp. 65–79. Springer, Cham (2014). https://doi.org/10.1007/978-3-319-10590-1_5
11. Yan, J., Lei, Z., Wen, L.: The fastest deformable part model for object detection. In: Proceedings of the IEEE Conference on Computer Vision and Pattern Recognition, pp. 2497–2504. IEEE, Columbus (2014)
12. Lenc, K., Vedaldi, A.: R-CNN minus R. arXiv preprint arXiv:1506.06981 (2015)
13. Girshick, R.: Fast R-CNN. In: Proceedings of the IEEE International Conference on Computer Vision, pp. 1440–1448. IEEE (2015)

Learning Attention Regularization Correlation Filter for Visual Tracking

Zhuling Qiu, Yufei Zha[✉], Peng Zhu, and Fei Zhang

Aeronautics Engineering College, Air Force Engineering University, Xian, China
zhayufei@126.com

Abstract. Spatial regularization can effectively solve the unwanted boundary effect of discriminative correlation filters (DCF). However, the predefined mask is independent of the feature, which limits the performance improvement. In this paper, we take the mask as a variable that plays the same role as the filter, and an attention regularization correlation filter (ARCF) is proposed for visual tracking. Especially, the mask is no longer a binary but a real value between 0 and 1, used as the weight of the corresponding feature. Additionally, the temporal coherence is also considered when the filter and the mask are simultaneously optimizing via ADMM algorithm, so the filter can fit the variation of the target in the temporal domain. Extensive experiments on the OTB100 database prove that our algorithm is much better than the traditional SRDCF algorithm both in the performance and speed.

Keywords: Object tracking · Regularization · Correlation filters · Attention

1 Introduction

Visual tracking is an important task in many computer vision topics. One of the main challenges of this task is to address the target's appearance changes over time. Recent years, discriminative correlation filters (DCF) [8] have shown state-of-the-art performance in the fashion tracking data set [17] and competitions [11]. The advantages of DCF [8] benefit from the periodic assumption of training samples. However, such an assumption leads to unwanted boundary effects since the examples including many unrealistic, wrapped-around circularly shifted versions of the target due to the circularity. Thus, the discriminative power of the learned filter shown in Fig. 1(a) is limited, so that the tracking performance is difficult to further improve.

The above problem was addressed in the recent works [6,9,12]. Danneljan *et al.* [6] introduced predefined Inverse Gaussian distribution matrix as a spatial regularization to penalize filter values outside the target boundaries, which

Supported by the National Natural Science Foundation of China (No. 61773397) and the Fundamental Research Funds for the Central Universities (No. 3102019ZY1003).

Z. Lin et al. (Eds.): PRCV 2019, LNCS 11857, pp. 74–85, 2019.
https://doi.org/10.1007/978-3-030-31654-9_7

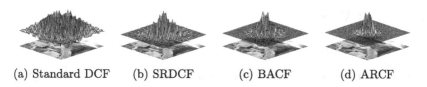

(a) Standard DCF   (b) SRDCF   (c) BACF   (d) ARCF

Fig. 1. Spatial Regularizations. Figure 1(a) shows filter of the standard discriminative correlation filters (DCF) [8], the filter regularized by the inverse Gaussian distribution matrix [6] and zero-padding mask [9] are shown in 1(b) and 1(c), respectively. The filter constrained by the proposed attention regularization is shown in 1(d).

is shown in Fig. 1(b). Different from the solution that was implemented by the Gauss-Seidel method with high computational complexity, STRCF tracker [12] trains the filter on the single sample via the alternating direction method of multipliers (ADMM) algorithm [3]. Galoogahi *et al.* [9] proposed zero-padding the filter shown in Fig. 1(c) to eliminate the background during training, then the optimization is also performed by the ADMM [3]. The ideas behind these methods are to design a predefined mask to overcome the boundary effects, however, there are some drawbacks: (1) The predefined regular shape of the mask can fit the appearance of the target (2) The value of the mask is binary that indicates whether this pixel is a target or not (3) The temporal coherence of the mask is not considered anymore.

To overcome these problems, an attention regularization correlation filter (ARCF) is proposed for visual tracking in this study. A spatial attention mask is learned with the filter and utilized to indicate the corresponding importance of each position in the filter. Unlike the existing methods that treat the mask as a hyper-parameter, we take the mask as a variable that plays the same role as the filter, then they are simultaneously optimized via ADMM algorithm. Here, the mask is no longer a binary but a real value between 0 and 1, used as the weight of the corresponding feature. Therefore, the position corresponding to the large weight forms the spatial attention of the image. Additionally, the temporal coherence is also considered when the filter and the mask are optimizing, so the filter can fit the variation of the target in the temporal domain. Figure 1(d) shows the learned filter by our spatial attention map. It can be seen that the discriminative ability of the features is enhanced by our method compared with the other methods. The contributions of this paper are summarized as follows:

- We propose a visual attention mechanism to regularize the correlation filter both in the spatial and temporal domain.
- The value of the spatial attention mask is released to [0, 1] replaced binary values {0, 1} to indicate the weights of the corresponding features.
- We propose to constrain the temporal coherence of the learned mask to adapt to the variation of the target in the temporal domain.

2   Related Work

2.1   Spatial Regularization

Unwanted boundary effects in correlation filter based tracking lead to inaccurate representation and insufficient discrimination of targets, especially in the cluttering background. Some works [6,12] wanted to solve this limitation by investigating the scale relationship between the training samples and filters. That is to say, the filter coefficients are penalized in terms of spatial locations [6] or temporal rank [12] to achieve more robust appearance modeling suitable for large variations. But the introduced noise of background became inevitable [10].

Different from those methods that perform regularization and filtering in a separated process with auxiliary features, our method is only required the features for visual tracking and simultaneously optimized the filter and spatial map. This is the motivation of this study.

2.2   Visual Attention

The visual attention derived from the cognitive neuroscience has been applied to some computer vision tasks, such as image classification [15] and image caption. It is so popular because the attention mechanism gives the model the discriminative ability between objects. The spatial weights, such as the cosine window map [2] and the Gaussian window map [8], are used as an attentional mechanism to be integrated into the correlation filter for visual tracking tasks.

However, these approaches emphasized attentive features and resort to additional attention modules to generate feature weights. In contrast to that, our method is self-attention, which exploited the attention map as a regularization term coupled with the standard correlation filter. And the attention map and the filter can be optimized simultaneously by the ADMM [3] algorithm for robust trackers.

3   Method

3.1   Learning Attention Regularization

Recently, the correlation filter received much attention with its ability to use circular matrix for dense sampling. But, the unwanted boundary effects derived from the periodic assumption of training samples limits the performance improvement further. To address this problem, an inverse Gaussian distribution matrix [6] is as a spatial regularization to penalize filter values outside the target boundaries. The spatial regularization correlation filter is rewritten with T training samples as:

$$\mathcal{L}(\Phi) = \sum_{k=1}^{T} \epsilon_k \left\| \sum_{l=1}^{D} \Phi^l * x_k^l - y_k \right\|^2 + \sum_{l=1}^{D} \|w \odot \Phi\|^2, \tag{1}$$

where $\Phi \in \mathbb{R}^D$ denotes the filter, the symbol $*$ represents correlation operation, y is the regression values of the feature $x \in \mathbb{R}^D$ and ϵ_k is the regularization term of the kth sample x_k. The size of feature x, filter Φ and regression y is $M \times N$. w is the spatial regularization matrix, which is the weight of the location in the filter Φ.

In this study, we introduce a attention mechanism, which makes the filter pay more attention to the target and the desired response lower at the background. Additionally, the temporal coherence is also considered constraining the regularization term w learning. We learn the spatial attention map correlation filter with the loss function:

$$\mathcal{L}(\Phi, w) = \underbrace{\frac{1}{2}\left\|\sum_{l=1}^{D}\Phi^l * x^l - y\right\|^2}_{Regression\ Term} + \underbrace{\frac{1}{2}\sum_{l=1}^{D}||w \odot \Phi^l||^2}_{Spatial\ Term} + \underbrace{\frac{\mu}{2}||w - w_0||^2}_{Temporal\ Term}, \quad (2)$$

where μ is temporal regularization coefficients, respectively. Unlike the existing works, the w is a variable to learn, not a hyper-parameter. Here, w_0 is an initial prior distribution which is predefined as an invert Gaussian distribution similar to the work [6].

The aim of minimizing the loss of Eq. (2) is to learn the filter Φ and the attention map w simultaneously. The first term is the regression term to learn the filter Φ with the feature x and the expected response y, which is same as the standard correlation filter. The spatial and temporal regularization terms are shown in the second term and third term to learn the attention regularization. According to the importance of the spatial position to learn the attention map w, the feature of the target are attached with the smaller spatial weights, and the background feature gives a bigger spatial constraint weight, which makes the learned filter more discriminative than that learned by the fixed spatial regularization. This can enhance the distinction between goals and background. Additionally, in order to deal with the variation of the target, the attention regularization is also constrained in the temporal domain which is represented in the third term of the Eq. (2). Temporal regularization terms make the filter change not too severe in the case of target occlusion, which can guarantee the performance of tracking.

According to the above theory, the flow chart of the algorithm is as shown in Fig. 2. By using the first frame I_0 information, the target frame is initialized and the spatial constraint weight w_0 in the first frame is assigned to the inverse Gaussian distribution, and the training is performed to obtain the filter Φ. The target position is predicted in the next frame by using the trained filter. At the same time, using the information of target position in the current frame can update the filter, and the weight map w is updated in the time domain and the frequency domain according to the position feature weight map in the current frame and the initial frame w_0, which can achieve more robust tracking.

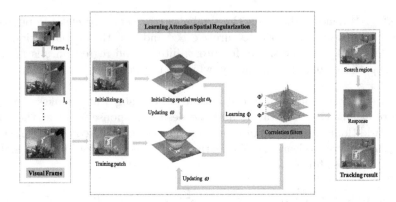

Fig. 2. Pipeline of learning attention regularization for correlation filter tracking. g_1 is the object bounding box in the first frame and w_0 is the spatial weight in the first frame. w is updated according to the spatial attention map in each subsequent frame during the learning process.

3.2   Model Optimization

In this subsection, we will introduce how to optimize the loss function Eq. (2), which is convex, and the optimal solution can be solved by iterative the alternating direction method of multipliers (ADMM) algorithm [3]. Therefore, through introducing the constraint condition $\Phi = \Theta$, Lagrangian equation of the Eq. (2) can be rewritten as:

$$
\mathcal{L}(\Phi, w, \Theta, \beta) = \frac{1}{2}||\sum_{l=1}^{D} \Phi^l * x^l - y||^2 + \frac{1}{2}\sum_{l=1}^{D}||w \odot \Theta^l||^2
$$
$$
+ \frac{\mu}{2}||w - w_0||^2 + \beta^T \sum_{l=1}^{D}(\Phi^l - \Theta^l) + \frac{\alpha}{2}\sum_{l=1}^{D}||\Phi^l - \Theta^l||^2, \tag{3}
$$

where β is the Lagrange multiplier and α is the penalty parameter.

When $\delta = \frac{\beta}{\alpha}$, the augmented Lagrangian equation can be written as:

$$
\mathcal{L}(\Phi, w, \Theta, \delta) = \frac{1}{2}\left\|\sum_{l=1}^{D} \Phi^l * x^l - y\right\|^2 + \frac{1}{2}\sum_{l=1}^{D}\left\|w \odot \Theta^l\right\|^2
$$
$$
+ \frac{\mu}{2}||w - w_0||^2 + \frac{\alpha}{2}\sum_{l=1}^{D}\left\|\Phi^l - \Theta^l + \delta^l\right\|^2. \tag{4}
$$

The ADMM algorithm is used to solve the following subproblems:

$$
\begin{cases}
\Phi^{(i+1)} = \underset{\Phi}{\arg\min} \left\|\sum_{l=1}^{D} \Phi^l * x^l - y\right\|^2 + \alpha \left\|\Phi - \Theta + \delta\right\|^2, \\
\Theta^{(i+1)} = \underset{\Theta}{\arg\min} \sum_{l=1}^{D} ||w \odot \Theta^l||^2 + \alpha \left\|\Phi - \Theta + \delta\right\|^2, \\
\delta^{(i+1)} = \delta^{(i)} + \Phi^{(i+1)} - \Theta^{(i+1)}.
\end{cases} \tag{5}
$$

Subproblem Φ. According to the iterative equation of ADMM algorithm, the solution of subproblem Φ can be converted to Fourier domain for solving,

$$\mathcal{L}(\hat{\Phi}) = \left\| \sum_{l=1}^{D} \hat{\Phi}^l \odot \hat{x}^l - \hat{y} \right\|^2 + \alpha \left\| \hat{\Phi} - \hat{\Theta} + \hat{\delta} \right\|^2, \tag{6}$$

where $\hat{\Phi}$ is the discrete Fourier transform of the filter Φ. By taking the derivative of $\hat{\Phi}$ be zero, the equation can be obtained as follows:

$$2(\hat{\Phi} \odot \hat{x} - \hat{y}) \odot \hat{x}^T + 2\alpha(\hat{\Phi} - \hat{\Theta} + \delta) = 0. \tag{7}$$

So, we have a closed-form solution of $\hat{\Phi}$:

$$\hat{\Phi} = \frac{\alpha \hat{\Theta} - \alpha \hat{\delta} + \hat{y} \odot \hat{x}^T}{\hat{x} \odot \hat{x}^T + \alpha I}. \tag{8}$$

Subproblem Θ. For the solution of subproblem Θ, we can take the derivative of Θ be zero in the time domain directly,

$$2w^T \odot w\Theta + 2\alpha(\Phi - \Theta + \delta) = 0. \tag{9}$$

And we can also get a closed-form solution for Θ:

$$\Theta = \frac{\alpha \Phi + \alpha \delta}{w^T \odot w + \alpha}. \tag{10}$$

Subproblem w. For updating the spatial weight w temporally, we can utilize Eq. (4) to take the derivative of w directly,

$$\frac{\partial \mathcal{L}(\Phi, \Theta, \delta)}{\partial w} = w \odot \sum_{l=1}^{D} (\Theta^l)^2 + \mu(w - w_0). \tag{11}$$

By solving $\frac{\partial \mathcal{L}(\Phi, \Theta, \delta)}{\partial w} = 0$ we get the closed-form solution

$$w = \frac{\mu w_0}{Q + \mu}, \tag{12}$$

where Q is $\sum_{l=1}^{D} (\Theta^l)^2$. By Eq. (12), we can update w which includes information about the target in the current frame.

Updating Penalty Parameter α. The stepsize parameter α is updated as:

$$\alpha^{(i+1)} = \min(\alpha^{max}, \rho \alpha^{(i)}), \tag{13}$$

where α^{max} is the maximum value of α and the scale factor ρ.

3.3 Object Tracking

Algorithm 1. Learning Attension Regulizaiton Correlation Filter for Visual Tracking

---

Input:
1: Frames: $I_t, t = 0, 1, 2, \cdots$; initial object bounding box: $g_1 = (x_1, y_1, w_1, h_1)$;
Output:
2: Prediction : $r_{t-1} = (x_{t-1}, y_{t-1}, w_{t-1}, h_{t-1})$;
3: **Initialization:**
4: initialize the correlation filters, initialize the spatial weight map: w_0 is an invert Gaussian distribution;
5: Learn Φ by minimizing Eq. (2), update w_1 by the solution Eq. (12) via the first frame with given bounding box, t = 2 ;
6: **while t $\geq$ 2 do**
7: Crop an image patch R_t from I_t at the last bounding g_t and extract its feature map x_t;
8: Detect the object location by calculating the response via x_t and Φ and the estimate the scale of the target, thus get g_t;
9: Update Φ_t by Eq. (2) using iterative ADMM algorithm via x_t and w_{t-1};
10: Learn w_t by the closed-form solusion Eq. (12) ;
11: $t = t + 1$;
12: **return** r_t

In this subsection, we describe the proposed tracking framework based on learning attention regularization. The overview of the proposed tracker is shown in Algorithm 1.

We use the information of the first frame to initialize the target frame and filter. The spatial regularization weight w0 in the first frame is assigned to the inverse Gaussian distribution. During the tracking process, the filters obtained by training in the previous frame are used to detect the position of the target in the search area of the next frame. After determining the target position, the training region centered on the target position of the current frame is extracted to update filter model. According to the spatial attention map, the spatial constraint weight w is adjusted.

4   Experiments

In this section, we present comprehensive experimental evaluations of the proposed algorithm using OTB100 [17] data set. First, we describe the implementation details and the evaluation protocols. Next, we demonstrate the effectiveness of each component in the proposed tracker in the form of experiment. Finally, the algorithm proposed in this paper is compared with other representative algorithms to obtain comprehensive experimental results.

4.1   Implementation Details

Tracker Parameters. Our filter is based on a regularized filter, but the proposed algorithm has a certain change in the parameter setting because the filter weight parameter is no longer a super parameter, but a real number from 0 to 1. Through many experiments, we set the hyperparameter in Eq. (2) to $\mu = 18$. Initial constraint parameters $\alpha^{(0)}$, maximum constraint parameters α^{max}, and scale factor ρ are set to 10,100 and 1.2.

Evaluation Protocols. In this paper, the algorithm is evaluated by the success rate and precision rate curve. The AUC is area under the curve for success rate. The DP is the value in the precision rate curve when the threshold is 20. Based on the benchmark library settings, we compare the proposed tracker with the state-of-the-art trackers using one-pass evaluation (OPE) (each tracker evaluates in the initial frame with the ground-truth box until the end of each sequence).

4.2   Overall Performance

The table below shows the algorithm presented in this paper performs significantly better than most of the competing trackers that use different tracking methods.

Table 1. The algorithm of this paper is compared with the regularization-based algorithm on the OTB100 [17] data set. The AUC, DP and the operation speed are used as evaluation criteria.

Tracker	AUC (%)	DP (%)	Speed (FPS)
OURS	**65.7**	**87.0**	27
SRDCF [6]	59.8	78.9	5
STRCF [12]	61.4	86.3	**36**
CSR-DCF [13]	59.8	73.3	15
BACF [9]	63.0	81.6	35

Comparison with the Trackers Based on Spatial Regularization. We evaluated the proposals for the four recently released trackers: STRCF [12], CSR-DCF [13], BACF [9], SRDCF [6]. The Table 1 and Fig. 3 shows that the tracker proposed in this paper achieves excellent results under two test criteria. As the benchmark algorithm SRDCF [6] uses Gauss-Seidel iterative method in the algorithm operation, its tracking speed is slower. Meawhile, because the temporal regularization isn't introduced to SRDCF [6], its performance is poor when facing videos such as occlusion. Therefore, the proposed algorithm has a larger improvement compared with the benchmark algorithm SRDCF [6]. And we can see the success plot has increased by about 8%, and the precision plot has increased by about 7%.

Table 2. The algorithm of this paper is compared with the algorithm based on neural network attention mechanism on the OTB100 [17] data set. The AUC, DP and the operation speed are used as evaluation criteria.

Tracker	AUC (%)	DP (%)	Speed (FPS)
OURS	65.7	87.0	27
DAT [14]	**66.3**	**90.2**	1
AFCN [4]	57.5	80.2	15
RASNet [16]	64.2	–	**83**

Comparison with the Trackers Based on Neural Network Attention Mechanisms. We evaluate the trackers proposed in this paper compared with state-of-the-art neural network attention-based trackers, including DAT [14], RASNet [16], and ACFN [4]. The algorithm improves the tracking effect by using a more flexible filter weight coefficient, which can improve filter response to the target and reduce background interference to the target. As are shown in Table 2 and Fig. 3, the algorithm perfors better than RASNet [16] and ACFN [4]. When compared with DAT [14], although the proposed algorithm is different from DAT [14] by about 3% in performance, it has an obvious performance in terms of tracking speed as this paper uses ADMM [3] (Alternating Direction Method of Multipliers) iterative algorithm. The improvement of the algorithm proposed in this paper is 27 times faster than DAT [14].

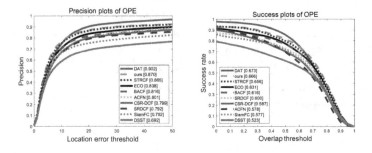

Fig. 3. The success plot and precision plot on the OTB100 [17] data set are quantitatively evaluated by the OPE method. The legend is the AUC and DP scores for each algorithm.

Compare with the Most Advanced and Classic Algorithms. SiamFC [1] and ECO [5] are currently advanced trackers, which uses different ways. SiamFC [1] classify the target using the method of joining the Alexnet network to improve the extraction accuracy of the target feature. However, due to the classification nature of the network, the problem of similar background interference cannot be solved, which makes tracking effect worse. The proposed algorithm solves the problem of similar interference by introducing temporal regularization, so it is far ahead of SiamFC [1] in performance. ECO [5] is due to the sparse update strategy, which makes the calculation process complicated and the operation speed slow down. The algorithm can be slightly weaker than the ECO [5], but the tracking speed is more than 4 times that of ECO [5]. DSST [7] is a relatively classic algorithm proposed in 2014. It adopts the method of feature fusion, which enables the algorithm to have a better adaptive process for scale variation of the target. As shown in Fig. 3, the proposed algorithm performs far better than DSST [7].

4.3   Ablation Study

The core idea of this paper mainly includes the real valued (learning attention) between the filter weight coefficient from fixed super-parameters to variable 0 to 1, and a regularization method in the time domain. In order to prove that each component improves the performance of the algorithm, a assessment of each part of the algorithm will be performed.

Regularization in the time domain can effectively solve the problem of occlusion of the target. We will remove the algorithm of time domain regularization with ARCFp. The change of the filter weight parameter can make the response value of the target larger and reduce the background interference. We will remove the learning attention algorithm by ARCFq. As is shown in Table 3, the results are compared.

Table 3. In this evaluation, the OTB100 [17] data set is used as the test sequence. Meanwhile, DP and AUC are used as the evaluation criteria, where DP is the value with a threshold of 20 and AUC is the area under the curve of success plot curve.

	ARCFp	ARCDq	ARCF
AUC (%)	61.5	47.7	65.7
DP (%)	82.6	69.3	87.0

4.4   Qualitative Analysis

We analyze the tracker performance using 11 annotation attributes in the OTB100 [17] data set: illumination variation, out-of-plane rotation, scale variation, occlusion, deformation, motion blur, etc. Figure 4 shows the results of a one-pass evaluation of these challenging attributes for visual object tracking. From the results, the tracker proposed in this paper in the illumination variation, out-of-plane rotation, scale change, occlusion, deformation, motion blur, fast motion, in-plane rotation, background clutter and low resolution can performe well and score at the top. Due to the fixed weight coefficient of the filter, other algorithms using similar methods have problems in poor ability of discriminating target and background and uneven mask distribution, resulting in poor

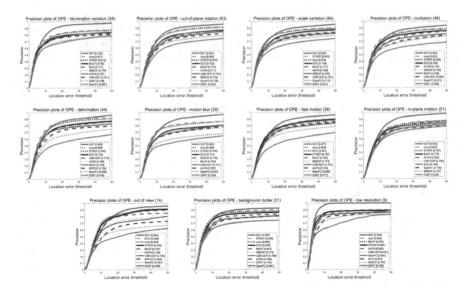

Fig. 4. The precision plot curve under each difficulty attribute, where the value after the curve is the value when the threshold is 20. (This evaluation method is the current mainstream qualitative analysis method)

overall tracking performance. However, the filter weight coefficient of the proposed algorithm is no longer a fixed weight or an inverse Gaussian distribution, but can vary from 0 to 1 depending on the target and background, so that the filter constraint weights at the background are gradually increasing as the target response increases. This can improve the tracking effect.

5   Conclusion

In this paper, we proposed an attention regularization correlation filter (ARCF) for visual tracking. The mask is treated as a variable that plays the same role as the filter, then they are simultaneously optimized via ADMM algorithm. Here, the greater the weight is, the more important the corresponding feature is. Additionally, the temporal coherence is also considered when the filter and the mask are optimizing, so the filter can fit the variation of the target in the temporal domain. Extensive experiments show that our method is much better than the traditional SRDCF tracker both in the performance and speed.

In the future, we want to investigate how to generally apply the proposed method with the CNN features that are powerful ability to describe the object in the semantic domain. This is helpful to distinguish the background, even distractors.

References

1. Bertinetto, L., Valmadre, J., Henriques, J.F., Vedaldi, A., Torr, P.H.S.: Fully-convolutional siamese networks for object tracking. In: Hua, G., Jégou, H. (eds.) ECCV 2016. LNCS, vol. 9914, pp. 850–865. Springer, Cham (2016). https://doi.org/10.1007/978-3-319-48881-3_56
2. Bolme, D.S., Beveridge, J.R., Draper, B.A., Lui, Y.M.: Visual object tracking using adaptive correlation filters. In: IEEE Conference on Computer Vision and Pattern Recognition, CVPR, pp. 2544–2550 (2010)
3. Boyd, S., Boyd, S., Vandenberghe, L., Press, C.U.: Convex Optimization. Cambridge University Press, Cambridge (2004)
4. Choi, J., Chang, H.J., Yun, S., Fischer, T., Demiris, Y., Choi, J.Y.: Attentional correlation filter network for adaptive visual tracking. In: CVPR, pp. 4828–4837. IEEE Computer Society (2017)
5. Danelljan, M., Bhat, G., Khan, F.S., Felsberg, M.: ECO: efficient convolution operators for tracking. In: Conference on Computer Vision and Pattern Recognition, CVPR, pp. 6931–6939 (2017)
6. Danelljan, M., Hager, G., Khan, F.S., Felsberg, M.: Learning spatially regularized correlation filters for visual tracking. In: International Conference on Computer Vision, (ICCV) (2015)
7. Danelljan, M., Häger, G., Khan, F.S., Felsberg, M.: Discriminative scale space tracking. IEEE Trans. Pattern Anal. Mach. Intell. 39(8), 1561–1575 (2017)
8. Henriques, J.F., Caseiro, R., Martins, P., Batista, J.: High-speed tracking with kernelized correlation filters. IEEE Trans. Pattern Anal. Mach. Intell. 37(3), 583–596 (2015)
9. Kiani Galoogahi, H., Fagg, A., Lucey, S.: Learning background-aware correlation filters for visual tracking. In: The IEEE International Conference on Computer Vision (ICCV), October 2017
10. Kiani Galoogahi, H., Sim, T., Lucey, S.: Correlation filters with limited boundaries. In: The IEEE Conference on Computer Vision and Pattern Recognition (CVPR), June 2015
11. Kristan, M., et al.: A novel performance evaluation methodology for single-target trackers. IEEE Trans. Pattern Anal. Mach. Intell. 38(11), 2137–2155 (2016)
12. Li, F., Tian, C., Zuo, W., Zhang, L., Yang, M.H.: Learning spatial-temporal regularized correlation filters for visual tracking. In: The IEEE Conference on Computer Vision and Pattern Recognition (CVPR), June 2018
13. Lukezic, A., Vojír, T., Zajc, L.C., Matas, J., Kristan, M.: Discriminative correlation filter tracker with channel and spatial reliability. Int. J. Comput. Vision 126(7), 671–688 (2018)
14. Pu, S., Song, Y., Ma, C., Zhang, H., Yang, M.H.: Deep attentive tracking via reciprocative learning. In: Neural Information Processing Systems (2018)
15. Wang, F., et al.: Residual attention network for image classification. In: The IEEE Conference on Computer Vision and Pattern Recognition (CVPR), July 2017
16. Wang, Q., Teng, Z., Xing, J., Gao, J., Hu, W., Maybank, S.J.: Learning attentions: residual attentional siamese network for high performance online visual tracking. In: CVPR, pp. 4854–4863. IEEE Computer Society (2018)
17. Wu, Y., Lim, J., Yang, M.: Object tracking benchmark. IEEE Trans. Pattern Anal. Mach. Intell. 37(9), 1834–1848 (2015)

Target Tracking via Two-Branch Spatio-Temporal Regularized Correlation Filter Network

Peng Sun[1], Wenbo Guo[2], and Songhao Zhu[1(✉)]

[1] School of Automatic, Nanjing University of Posts and Telecommunications,
Nanjing 210023, China
{1218053612, zhush}@njupt.edu.cn
[2] College of Overseas Education, Nanjing University of Posts
and Telecommunications, Nanjing 210023, China
H16000302@njupt.edu.cn

Abstract. In this paper, a spatio-temporal regularized correlation filter for object tracking method based on two-branch Siamese fully convolutional network learning. Firstly, a correlation filter layer is added into the Siamese fully convolutional network to achieve end-to-end learning representation; secondly, the semantic feature is combined with the appearance feature to further enhance the discriminative ability of Siamese fully convolutional network; finally, the spatio-temporal regularized correlation filter is utilized to reduce the training time and improve the tracking performance. Extensive experiments conducted on VOT2017 and OTB2015 dataset demonstrate the superior performance of the proposed approach over the examined state-of-the-art approaches.

Keywords: Two-branch siamese fully convolutional network · End-to-end learning · Spatio-temporal regularized correlation filter

1 Introduction

Recently, deep learning has achieved dominant results in object tracking. For example, some trackers integrate deep features into traditional tracking methods to make full use of convolution neural network feature expression capabilities, and some trackers employ convolution neural network as a classifier to implement the end to end training. Most of these methods employ online training to improve the tracking performance. For the large number of convolution neural network features and the complexity of deep neural network, the computation cost of online training is enormous. Therefore, most of the trackers based on convolution neural network runs much slower than traditional real-time tracking methods.

To simultaneously avoid online learning and achieve high tracking speed, two kinds of real-time tracker based on convolution neural network are proposed. One is the generic object tracking using regression network (GOTURN) based tracker as proposed in [1], which treats the object tracking problem as a box regression problem. The other is Siamese fully convolution network (SiamFCN) based tracker as proposed in [2, 3],

© Springer Nature Switzerland AG 2019
Z. Lin et al. (Eds.): PRCV 2019, LNCS 11857, pp. 86–97, 2019.
https://doi.org/10.1007/978-3-030-31654-9_8

which considers the object tracking problem as a problem of similarity learning through appearance. Siamese fully convolution network achieves much better performance than regression network, which demonstrates that the fully convolutional network architecture can make full use of offline learning data and to have highly discriminatory. However, when the tracking object has obvious appearance changes, the tracking performance of the Siamese network tracker will become very poor.

An end-to-end spatio-temporal regularization filter based tracking framework is proposed here to enhance the tracking performance and reduce the computational cost, as shown in Fig. 1. With the Siamese fully convolution network as mentioned in [4, 5], a two-branch Siamese fully convolution network is first constructed by adding semantic branch and appearance branch. Then, spatio-temporal regularization filters are integrated into the Siamese fully convolution network for discriminative correlation filter learning and model updating, which is beneficial to improve tracking accuracy and boundary effect. Here, conventional correlation filter is replaced by spatio-temporal correlation filter, which can be considered as a differentiable convolution neural network layer in the semantic branch network. Therefore, the difference between ground truth label and obtained label can be accurately transmitted back to the convolution neural network through the spatio-temporal correlation filter.

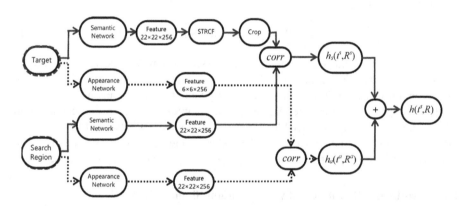

Fig. 1. Framework of the proposed approach.

Semantic branch network utilizes learned features to deal with the issue of object tracking, where the learned features contain abundant semantic information in the high-level. Appearance branch network utilizes learned features to deal with the issue of object tracking, where the learned features contain abundant appearance information in the low-level. To improve the tracking performance, the heat maps from these two branch networks are combined to maximize the strengths of both branch networks.

The main contributions of this paper contains the following two points. One is that Siamese fully convolution network is combined with the end-to-end learning framework to construct a two-branch Siamese fully convolution network based on semantic branches and appearance branches. The other is spatio-temporal regularization filters are added into the constructed two-branch Siamese fully convolution network to improve the target tracking accuracy and the boundary detection performance.

The rest of this paper is organized as follows. End to end learning network based on two-branch Siamese fully convolution network is detailed in Sect. 2. Spatial-temporal regularization correlation filter is detailed in Sect. 3. Experimental results and analyses are presented in Sect. 4. Section 5 concludes this work.

2   End to End Learning Based on Two-Branch SiamFCN

2.1   Correlation Filter Network

Recently, the correlation filter is integrated into the deep neural network to deal with the issue of object tracking, which greatly improves the computation speed. The correlation filter is utilized to train a linear template to distinguish the scale translation between successive frames, and the tracker can re-train every frame with the fast Fourier transform. For correlation filter network, the correlation filter with closed solution is considered as a differentiable layer, which makes the deep learning closely combined with the correlation filter. The closed solution of correlation filter network is formulated as follows:

$$h_{\psi,v,b}(t, R) = v \times \omega(f_\psi(t)) * f_\psi(R) + b \tag{1}$$

where t and R represent the tracking target and search region respectively, and scale variable v and bias b are introduced to obtain suitable fraction range for logistic regression. Furthermore, Ψ indicates the learning rate of convolutional neural network, and $f_\Psi(t)$ and $f_\Psi(R)$ represent the feature map of the tracking target z and search region X respectively. Correlation filter block $w = \omega(f_\Psi(t))$ is added between tracking target and cross-correlation to obtain a standard correlation filter template by solving the ridge regression problem in Fourier domain with respect to the feature maps $f_\Psi(t)$ and $f_\Psi(R)$.

2.2   Two-Branch Siamese Fully Convolution Siamese Network

The input of the network is taken from the first frame and the current frame of the video sequence is severed as the input for target tracking. Here, the symbols t^a, t^s and R represent the target, target with surrounding context and search region respectively. The size of t^a, t^s and R are denoted as $W_a \times H_a \times 3$, $W_s \times H_s \times 3$ and $W_s \times H_s \times 3$ respectively, where $W_s < W_a$ and $H_s < H_a$. Search region R can be regarded as a collection of candidate image region r in the search region with the same dimension as the target t. The output of each branch is a similarity feature map representing the target t and the candidate image region r within the search region R.

For the appearance branch of the constructed two-branch Siamese fully convolution network, the corresponding input is denoted as (t^a, R^a) and the corresponding extracted features are represented by $f_a(\cdot)$. The feature map of the appearance branch network is described as follows:

$$h_a(t^a, R^a) = corr(f_a(t^a), f_a(R^a)) \tag{2}$$

where *corr* represents the correlation operations. All parameters of the appearance branch network are trained through similarity learning, and is optimized by minimizing the logistic loss function described as follows:

$$\arg\min_{\theta_a} \frac{1}{N} \sum_{i=1}^{N} \{L(h_a(t_i^a, R_i^a; \theta_a), Y_i\} \tag{3}$$

where θ_a represents the parameters in the appearance branch network, and N represents the number of training samples. Furthermore, $Y_i \in \{+1, -1\}$ represents the corresponding ground truth response map of the search region, where $Y_i = +1$ represents positive examples and $Y_i = -1$ represents negative examples.

For the semantic branch of the constructed two-branch Siamese fully convolution network, the corresponding input is denoted as (t^s, R^s). Here, the pre-trained convolutional neural network is selected as the semantic branch network, and correlation filter block $w = \omega(f_s(t^s))$ is added between target images and cross-correlation operations to obtain the standard correlation filter block template. The feature map of the semantic branch network is formulated as follows:

$$h_s(t^s, R^s) = corr(v \times \omega(f_s(t^s)), f_s(R^s)) + b \tag{4}$$

A larger context region is needed to train correlation filters. Furthermore, the feature map is pre-multiplied by cosine window and the final template is cropped to reduce the influence of circular boundary.

Here, the minimization logic loss function is utilized to optimize the semantic branch, described as follows:

$$\arg\min_{\theta_s} \frac{1}{N} \sum_{i=1}^{N} \{L(h_s(t_i^s, R_i^s; \theta_s), Y_i\} \tag{5}$$

During the test process, the overall feature map is weighted average of feature maps from semantic branch network and appearance branch network, as formulated using the following equation:

$$h(t^s, R) = \lambda h_a(t^a, R^a) + (1 - \lambda) h_s(t^s, R^s) \tag{6}$$

where λ represents the weight parameter to balance the feature maps from different branch networks. The location of the maximum in $h(t^s, R)$ represents the center position of the tracking target, and multi-scale input is utilized to deal with the issue of scale change.

3 Spatial-Temporal Regularized Siamfcn

3.1 Spatial Regularized Correlation Filter

Spatial penalty is added into the discriminative correlation filter coefficients to deal with the boundary effect issue, formulated as follows:

$$\arg\min_w \sum_{k=1}^{T} \alpha_k \left\| \sum_{d=1}^{D} x_k^d * w^d - y_k \right\|^2 + \sum_{d=1}^{D} \left\| c \cdot w^d \right\|^2 \tag{7}$$

where W^d is the dth filter template, and a_k is the weight of the kth image. Furthermore, x_k^d is the dth feature map of the kth image, and y_k is the preset Gaussian shaped label of the kth image. Finally, $*$ and are the convolution operator and Hadamard product respectively, and c represents the regularization matrix of size $m \times n$.

3.2 Spatial-Temporal Regularized SiamFCN

Spatial-temporal regularized filter is added into the semantic Siamese fully convolutional network as the correlation filter layer, which constructs an end-to-end learning framework. By incorporating both temporal and spatial regularization, the boundary effect can be effectively handled without losing efficiency. For a new target, the algorithm first predicts its label and then updates its classifier according to the new target-label pair. The optimization formula is described as:

$$\arg\min_w \frac{1}{2} \left\| \sum_{d=1}^{D} x_k^d * w^d - y \right\|^2 + \frac{1}{2} \sum_{d=1}^{D} \left\| c \cdot w^d \right\|^2 + \frac{\mu}{2} \left\| w - w_{k-1} \right\|^2 \tag{8}$$

where w_{k-1} denotes the correlation filter in the $(k-1)$ image frame, and μ denotes the regularization parameter. Furthermore, w is the filter template, and y is the preset Gaussian shaped label. Finally, $\sum_{d=1}^{D} \left\| c \cdot w^d \right\|^2$ and $\left\| w - w_{k-1} \right\|^2$ denote the temporal regularization and spatial regularization respectively.

The model can be minimized to obtain the globally optimal solution via ADMM algorithm. Suppose s is the Lagrange multiplier, the auxiliary variable $\eta = w$, the step size parameter γ and $q = s/\gamma$, then the Augmented Lagrangian form of expression (8) is described as follows:

$$L(c, \eta, q) = \frac{1}{2} \left\| \sum_{d=1}^{D} x_k^d * w^d - y \right\|^2 + \frac{1}{2} \sum_{d=1}^{D} \left\| c \cdot \eta^d \right\|^2 + \frac{\gamma}{2} \sum_{d=1}^{D} \left\| w^d - \eta^d + q^d \right\|^2 + \frac{\mu}{2} \left\| w - w_{k-1} \right\|^2 \tag{9}$$

where μ is regularization parameter.

Then, parameters w, η, and γ can be obtained using the following equation set:

$$\begin{cases} w^{(i+1)} = \arg\min_{w} \left\| \sum_{d=1}^{D} x_k^d * w^d - y \right\|^2 + \gamma \|w - \eta + q\|^2 + \mu \|w - w_{k-1}\|^2 \\ \eta^{(i+1)} = \arg\min_{\eta} \sum_{d=1}^{D} \|c \cdot \eta^d\|^2 + \gamma \|w - \eta + q\| \\ q^{(i+1)} = q^{(i)} + w^{(i+1)} - \eta^{(i+1)} \end{cases} \tag{10}$$

Under the theorem of Parseval, w can be written in the Fourier domain as:

$$\arg\min_{\hat{w}} \left\| \sum_{d=1}^{D} \hat{x}_k^d * \hat{w}^d - \hat{y} \right\|^2 + \gamma \|\hat{w} - \hat{\eta} + \hat{q}\|^2 + \mu \|\hat{w} - \hat{w}_{k-1}\|^2 \tag{11}$$

where $\hat{w}$ denotes the discrete Fourier transform of the filter w. The jth element of the label $\hat{y}$ only depends on the jth element of the filter $\hat{w}$ and sample $\hat{x}_k$ across all D channels. Denote by $V_j(w) \in R^D$, the vector consisting of the jth elements of f along all D channels. The expression (11) can be further re-written as follows:

$$\arg\min_{V_j(\hat{w})} \left\{ \begin{array}{l} \left\| V_j(\hat{x}_k)^{\mathrm{T}} V_j(\hat{w}) - \hat{y}_j \right\|^2 + \\ \mu \left\| V_j(\hat{w}) - V_j(\hat{w}_{k-1}) \right\|^2 + \gamma \left\| V_j(\hat{w}) - V_j(\hat{\eta}) + V_j(\hat{q}) \right\|^2 \end{array} \right\} \tag{12}$$

Taking the derivative of expression (12) be zero, the corresponding closed-form solution for $V_j(\hat{w})$ can be described as below:

$$V_j(\hat{w}) = \left(V_j(\hat{x}_k) V_j(\hat{x}_k) \right)^{\mathrm{T}} + ((\mu + \gamma)I)^{-1} z \tag{13}$$

where the form of vector z is described as:

$$z = V_j(\hat{x}_k)\hat{y}_j + \gamma V_j(\hat{\eta}) - \gamma V_j(\hat{q}) + \mu V_j(\hat{w}_{k-1}) \tag{14}$$

Since $V_j(\hat{x}_k)V_j(\hat{x}_k)^T$ is rank-1 matrix, expression (14) can be solved with the Sherman Morrsion formula:

$$V_j(\hat{w}) = \frac{1}{\mu + \gamma} \left(I - \frac{V_j(\hat{x}_k)V_j(\hat{x}_k)^{\mathrm{T}}}{\mu + \gamma + V_j(\hat{x}_k)^{\mathrm{T}} V_j(\hat{x}_k)} \right) z \tag{15}$$

where w can be further obtained by the inverse discrete Fourier transform of $\hat{w}$.

It can be seen from the second formulation of formulation set (10), each element within η can be computed independently and the corresponding closed-form solution of η can be computed:

$$\eta = \left(W^T W + \gamma I\right)^{-1} \left(\gamma W + \gamma q\right) \tag{16}$$

where C represents the $DMN \times DMN$ diagonal matrix concatenated with D diagonal matrices $\text{Diag}(c)$.

The step size parameter γ is updated using the following equation:

$$\gamma^{(i+1)} = \min\left(\gamma^{\max}, \rho\gamma^{(i)}\right) \tag{17}$$

where $\gamma^{\max}$ denotes the maximum value of γ and the scale factor ρ.

4 Experiment and Analysis

To validate the effectiveness of the proposed approach, extensive evaluations are performed on VOT2017 video sequence [6] and OTB2015 video sequence [7]. Experimental settings are detailed in Sect. 4.1, algorithm performance comparison is described in Sect. 4.2, and experimental results are presented in Sect. 4.3.

4.1 Experimental Settings

In the current experiments, the size of each target image t is $127 \times 127 \times 3$, and the size of t^c and R are both $255 \times 255 \times 3$. For appearance branch network, the size of output features t and R are $6 \times 6 \times 256$ and $22 \times 22 \times 256$ respectively. For semantic branch network, the size of output features t^c and R are both $22 \times 22 \times 256$. Two sets of feature convolution networks both output 128 channels, and the size of feature map is 17×17.

Color images in ILSRC-2015 video dataset are used as the offline training set, which contains about 1 million 300 thousand frames and 2 million ground truth bounding boxes. Appearance branch network and semantic branch network are trained 30 times, where the learning rates of the first 25 times are 0.01 and the learning rates of the last 5 times are 0.001. We perform a grid search from 0.1 to 0.9, and experimental results demonstrate that the best performance is achieved when $\lambda = 0.3$. Regularization parameter μ is set to 16, and the proposed method is trained only with the current frame and ignores all historical information when $\mu = 0$. The initial step size parameter $\gamma^{(0)}$, the maximum value $\gamma^{\max}$ and scale factor ρ are set to 10, 100 and 1.2 respectively.

The proposed method is implemented with Matlab R2018a, and all the experiments are run on a PC equipped with Intel i7 8700 k CPU, 16 GB RAM and a single NVIDIA GTX 1080ti GPU.

4.2 Algorithm Comparison

In the current implementation, the proposed two-branch spatio-temporal regularized correlation filter network based target tracking approach is compared with other approaches based on the results obtained in their papers:

- Twofold Siamese network based tracking (SA-Siam for short) is proposed in [3], where the channel-wise weights are computed with respect to the channel activation around the target location and the inherited architecture from the Siamese fully convolutional network allows the tracker to run real-time.
- Correlation filter network based tracking (CFNet for short) is proposed in [4], which trains a linear template to discriminate between images and their translations and enables learning deep features that are tightly coupled to the correlation filter.
- Spatially regularized discriminative correlation filter tracker based tracking (SRDCF for short) is proposed in [8], where a spatial regularization function is introduced to penalize filter coefficients residing outside the target region to alleviate to the affection of increased size of the training and detection samples on the effective filter size.
- Spatio-Temporal Regularized correlation filter tracker based tracking (STRCF for short) is proposed in [9], where a spatio-temporal regularized correlation filter is introduced to track the target successfully under occlusion, and it can be well adapted to large changes in appearance.
- Color hough tracker based tracking (CHT for short) is proposed in [10], where colour histogram utilized as a global rotation-invariant model to separate object from the background and gradient orientation utilized as a Generalised Hough Transform to provide a localisation of the target are merged to estimate the object position, and model updating is done by computing independently two pixel-level confidence maps and by merging them.
- Discriminative scale space tracker based tracking (DSST for short) is proposed in [11], where a one-dimensional discriminative scale filter is learned to estimate the target size, and the intensity features is combined with the histogram of oriented gradient features to learn the translation filter.
- Staple tracker based tracking (Staple for short) is proposed in [12], which combines two image patch representations that are sensitive to complementary factors to train a model that is inherently robust to both colour changes and appearance deformations.
- The proposed context correlation information and discriminative correlation filer object tracking approach (Ours for short), which deal with the issue of object tracking by constructing spatio-temporal regularized discriminative correlation filer within a two-branch Siamese fully convolutional network.

Table 1. Performance comparison on the VOT2017 dataset.

Method	EAO	Accuracy	Robustness	Running speed (FPS)
SRDCF	0.119	0.483	46.833	2.5
STRCF	0.296	0.500	14.667	25
SA-Siam	0.236	0.500	20.833	50
CFNet	0.188	0.497	29.167	31
CHT	0.122	0.412	45.667	112
DSST	0.079	0.390	67.833	37
Staple	0.169	0.516	31.833	47
Ours	0.306	0.537	14.944	20

4.3   Experiment Results

Table 1 presents the comparative results based on the evaluation criterion of expected average overlap (EAO), accuracy, robustness and running speed. It can be seen from Table 1 that the proposed approach provides the best performance for different criteria. These results demonstrate the following two of the proposed approach: (1) the discriminative ability of Siamese fully convolutional network can be further enhanced by combining semantic features and appearance features, and (2) Although the training time is increased due to the addition of spatio-temporal regularized correlation filter layer, the training time is increased, the tracking performance can be further improved.

Figure 2 shows the accuracy-robustness plots of different approaches under various attributes including mean, weighted mean and pooled. Figure 3 show the comparative results based on the expected overlap curves and average expected overlap scores of different approaches respectively.

The same conclusions can be drawn from Fig. 3 that the proposed approach achieve better detection and tracking performance compared with other state-of-the-art approaches, which once demonstrate the importance of semantic feature and spatio-temporal regularization within a asymmetric Siamese neural network for the implementation of visual object tracking.

The proposed method is compared with six other methods on OTB2015 dataset. The OPE diagram is shown in Fig. 4. It can be seen from Fig. 4 that in the precision plots of OPE and success plots of OPE, the proposed approach obtain 0.853 and 0.645, respectively. the proposed approach achieve better detection and tracking performance compared with other state-of-the-art approaches, second only to ECO.

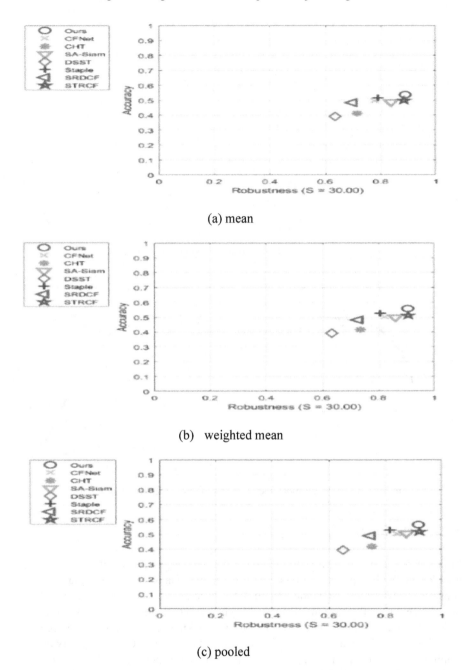

(a) mean

(b) weighted mean

(c) pooled

Fig. 2. Accuracy-robustness plot of different approaches under various attributes.

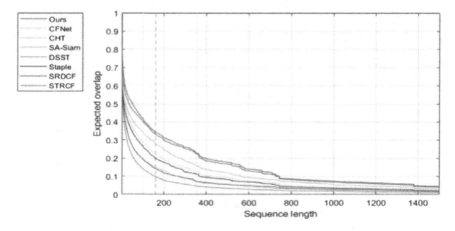

Fig. 3. Expected overlap on the VOT2017 dataset.

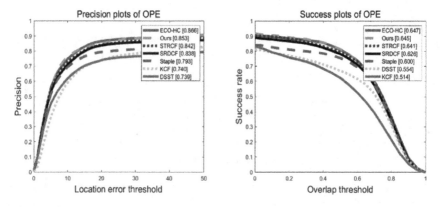

Fig. 4. The precision plots and success plots on OTB2015 benchmarks

5 Conclusions

In this paper, a two-branch spatio-temporal regularized correlation filter based target tracking method is proposed. Firstly, a two-branch Siamese network framework is constructed, where the semantic branch network is deep features and the appearance branch network is the baseline SiameseFC network. Then, the correlation filter layer is added into the semantic branch to improve the tracking speed and the tracking accuracy. Finally, the semantic branch network and the appearance branch network are combined to further optimize the tracking performance. Experimental results conducted on VOT2017 and OTB2015 dataset demonstrate that the proposed approach has lower robustness and better performance than other state-of-the-art approaches.

Acknowledgement. This work is supported by Natural Science Fund of Nanjing University of Posts and Telecommunications under No. NY217066 and NY219107.

References

1. Held, D., Thrun, S., Savarese, S.: Learning to track at 100 FPS with deep regression networks. In: European Conference on Computer Vision, pp. 749–765 (2016)
2. Tao, R., Gavves, E., Smeulders, A.: Siamese instance search for tracking. In: IEEE International Conference on Computer Vision and Pattern Recognition, pp. 1420–1429 (2016)
3. He, A., Luo, C., Tian, X., Zeng, W.: A twofold siamese network for real-time object tracking. In: IEEE International Conference on Computer Vision and Pattern Recognition, pp. 1–10 (2018)
4. Valmadre, J., Bertinetto, L., Henriques, J., Vedaldi, A., Torr, P.: End-to-end representation learning for correlation filter based tracking. In: IEEE International Conference on Computer Vision and Pattern Recognition, pp. 5000–5008 (2017)
5. Zhu, Z., Wu, W., Zou, W., Yan, J.: End-to-end flow correlation tracking with spatial-temporal attention. In: IEEE International Conference on Computer Vision and Pattern Recognition, pp. 548–557 (2017)
6. Kristan, M., Leonardis, A., Matas, J., et al.: The visual object tracking VOT2017 challenge results. In: European Conference on Computer Vision, pp. 1949–1972 (2017)
7. Wu, Y., Lim, J., Yang, M.H.: Object tracking benchmark. IEEE Trans. Pattern Anal. Mach. Intell. 37(9), 1834–1848 (2015)
8. Danelljan, M., Hger, G., Khan, F., Felsberg, M.: Learning spatially regularized correlation filters for visual tracking. In: IEEE International Conference on Computer Vision, pp. 4310–4318 (2015)
9. Li, F., Tian, C., Zuo, W., Zhang, L., Yang, M.: Learning spatial-temporal regularized correlation filters for visual tracking. In: IEEE International Conference on Computer Vision and Pattern Recognition, pp. 1–10 (2018)
10. Gundogdu, E., Alatan, A.: Good features to correlate for visual tracking. CoRR, abs/1704.06326, pp. 1–11
11. Danelljan, M., Hager, G., Khan, F., Felsberg, M.: Accurate scale estimation for robust visual tracking. In: British Machine Vision Conference, pp. 1–11 (2014)
12. Bertinetto, L., Valmadre, J., Golodetz, S., Miksik, O., Torr, P.: Staple: complementary learners for real-time tracking. In: IEEE International Conference on Computer Vision and Pattern Recognition, pp. 1401–1409 (2016)

A Real-Time Rock-Paper-Scissor Hand Gesture Recognition System Based on FlowNet and Event Camera

Xuemei Xie[✉], Shu Zhang, Jinjian Wu, Xun Xu, Guangming Shi, and Jianyu Chen

School of Artificial Intelligence, Xidian University, Xi'an 710071, Shaanxi, China
xmxie@mail.xidian.edu.cn

Abstract. Gesture recognition is one of the most popular tasks in computer vision, where convolutional neural networks (CNNs) based method has obtained the state-of-the-art performance. However, it is generally acknowledged that CNNs need a large amount of data to achieve such performance. Event Camera is a kind of biologically inspired event-based camera, which can keep the information of moving objects and remove the redundant background data. In this paper, we set up a rock-paper-scissor hand gesture recognition system based on FlowNet and Event Camera. Event camera is used to acquire event data. Then we propose an algorithm for the proposed gesture recognition. Specifically, FlowNet2.0 is employed to extract the motion representation of the pre-processed visual data, and a CNN classification network is applied to recognize the symbols extracted according to the motion representation. As a comparison, we also apply the rock-paper-scissor gesture recognition algorithm on traditional camera. The experimental results show that the proposed system based on Event Camera gets better performance, and to some extent, weaken the dependence on the training data. The whole system achieves 94.0% out-of-sample accuracy and allows computation at up to 30 fps.

Keywords: Gesture recognition · Event camera · FlowNet2.0 · Convolutional neural network

1 Introduction

Gesture recognition provides a means of natural and intuitive interaction between human and machine, and has high theoretical significance and practical value. With the development of gesture recognition technology, it shows its application potential in the field of natural Human-Computer Interaction (HCI) technology. However, the existing gesture data is mostly taken by a normal RGB camera with frame rate of 30 frames per second (fps). This frame-based data has a motion blur problem in the case of relatively fast gesture motion, which

© Springer Nature Switzerland AG 2019
Z. Lin et al. (Eds.): PRCV 2019, LNCS 11857, pp. 98–109, 2019.
https://doi.org/10.1007/978-3-030-31654-9_9

affects the gesture recognition performance. An naive solution to the problem of motion blur is increasing the frame rate of the normal camera, but the continuous image frames obtained by the high frame rate camera contain much static redundant information. The non-demand-driven shooting method records the complex background environment in the scene. Meanwhile, implicitly increasing the amount of training data for convolutional neural networks (CNNs) which have been demonstrated successfully on human gesture recognition.

Event Camera [4,6,12,18] is a new type of biomimetic sensor, with the advantages of removing redundant information, fast sensing capability, high dynamic range sensitivity and low power consumption. Compared to a normal frame-based camera, event camera acquires visual information in the completely different way, the frameless sampling allows continuous and asynchronous data in spatiotemporal domain. This demand-driven shooting method only record the illumination change caused by the gesture. The event stream generated in this way eliminates the redundant background, so low transmission bandwidth is needed. The microsecond time resolution of event camera ensures the continuity of gesture motion, without the limitation of exposure time and frame rate. In addition, event camera works well in the bright or dark environment due to its high dynamic range.

Since the advent of event camera, there have been multiple application scenarios in computer vision and robotics field. This paper mainly studies the dynamic gesture recognition method based on event camera. In this work, we set up a real-time rock-paper-scissor hand gesture recognition system. The rock-paper-scissor gesture is a good preliminary application, its interesting operation and presence of competing make it popular all over the world. Firstly, dynamic gesture data are gotten by using the event camera DAVIS240C to capture the preset gesture type. Secondly, the data conversion of three-dimensional event stream is needed. Thirdly, the converted data is segmented to extract meaningful gestures using FlowNet2.0 which estimate optical flow based on CNN structure. Finally, another CNN network is used to extract meaningful gesture features for final gesture recognition. The experimental results show that the performance of event camera is more accurate than normal RGB camera, further indicating that the event camera weaken the dependence on training data to a certain extent, and compared with normal RGB camera, can get the comparable results with less data.

2 Related Work on Event Camera Based Gesture Recognition

Owing to the complexity and diversity of hand gesture, most studies define specific gesture based on their own research purposes. In order to accurately recognize event streams, researchers use different methods for their specific gestures. The gesture recognition based on event camera can roughly be divided into three categories: specific hand shape recognition, gesture motion trajectory recognition and gesture motion change recognition.

The following works are specific hand shape recognition where the hand shape is fixed and shook slightly in front of the event camera. Rivera-Acosta et al. [19] convert the American sign language gesture events into images and digital image processing is applied to reduce noise, detect contour, extract and adjust characteristic pixel of contour. The Artificial Neural Network is used to classification and achieve 79.58% accuracy on 720 samples of 24 gestures. Lungu et al. [14] propose a method to recognizes the rock-paper-scissor gesture. Events are collected by slightly shaking fixed hand shape and accumulated into fixed event-number frames. These frames are fed into a CNN, which yielding 99.3% accuracy on 10% test data.

The following works are gesture motion trajectory recognition where hand shape is unchanged but hand position changes over time. Amir et al. [3] present the first gesture recognition system combined TrueNorth neurosynaptic processor with event camera and propose the first and the only one gesture event dataset(DvsGesture). A sequence of snapshots of event stream are collected and these concatenated snapshots are feed into CNN. Lee et al. [11] describes a gesture interface based on a stereo pair of event camera. The motion trajectory is detected by using leaky integrate-and-fire(LIF) neurons. Sixteen feature vectors are extracted from each spotted trajectory and classified by hidden Markov model gesture models. Achieved ranged from 91.9% to 99.5% accuracy depending on subject.

The following works are gesture motion change recognition where both hand shape and hand position change over time. Park et al. [17] propose a demosaicing method based on event-based images that offers substantial performance improvement of far-distance gesture recognition based on CNN. Ahn et al. [2] classify rock-paper-scissor gestures. Events within 20 ms are converted to a frame. Events number in one frame less than the given threshold can be regarded as delivery point (key frame is used in this paper). The statistical features like distribution of width within the hand or the number of connected components for each segment are extracted and achieving 89% accuracy on 60 rock-paper-scissor gestures.

3   Event Camera

The event camera used in this paper is the Dynamic and Active Pixel Vision Sensor(DAVIS) [4] which is produced by INIVATION company. More specifically, DAVIS240C of DAVIS series product is used, and the device is shown in Fig. 1(a). DAVIS combines Dynamic Vision Sensor (DVS) and CMOS Active Pixel Sensor (APS) technology to output both asynchronous event data and simultaneous image frames. DAVIS has independent and asynchronous pixels that in response to illumination change. The pixel schematic of DAVIS is shown in Fig. 1(b).

We only use the event data here, so we focus on introducing the intensity response principle of DVS, as shown in Fig. 2. Each pixel output a event whenever the logarithmic illumination change (V_p) greater than the user-defined threshold and output a stream of events over time. Polarity attribute is contained in each Event. Increasing in illumination is referred as ON event and decreasing in illumination is referred as OFF event.

The commonly used notation for an event is as follows:

$$e = [x, y, t, p]^T \tag{1}$$

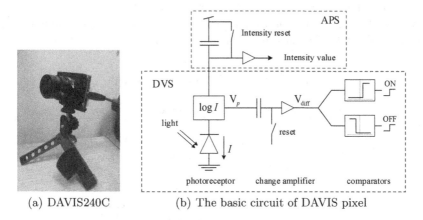

(a) DAVIS240C   (b) The basic circuit of DAVIS pixel

Fig. 1. Event camera and its pixel schematic

In which the event e indicates that the pixel located at $[x, y]^T$ on the pixel array of event camera output a event due to an illumination change at time t. The polarity attribute is encoded as $p \in [-1, 1]$, in which $p = 1$ is referred as ON event and $p = -1$ is referred as OFF event. It is worth mentioning that, events are conveyed at a temporal resolution of 1 μs and the event data rate is depend on the illumination change rate in the scene.

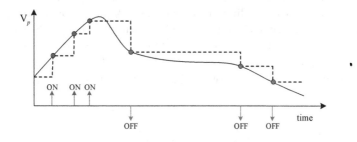

Fig. 2. Intensity response principle of DVS

4   Framework and System Components

Dynamic gestures usually have three phases of motion: preparation, stroke, and retraction [9]. The main information of gesture is mainly contained in the temporal sequence of the stroke phase. For the rock-paper-scissor gesture in this paper, there are also three phases, as shown in Table 1. The gestures in the preparation phase are consistent and cannot be distinguished. Key gesture is contained in stroke phase. The retraction phase is the transition phase to the next preparation phase. Therefore, it is necessary to divide the continuous dynamic gesture sequence, extract the key gesture, and then recognize the key gesture.

Table 1. Description of Gesture action

Three motion phases	Description of three phases
	Preparation: keep the fist form of hand, move the arm down.
	Stroke: delivery gesture(rock, paper or scissor) is needed to decide before reaching the lowest point. After reaching the lowest point, hand stays awhile.
	Retraction: the arm is pulled back up and the hand is slowly returned to the fist form of preparation.

How to deal with asynchronous event stream is the key basis for dynamic gesture recognition. Event stream is essentially a low-level visual spike signal. A single Event carries very limited information. A joint representation of multiple events can represent more descriptive information about the visual scene. Therefor, the three-dimensional event stream is mapped to a two-dimensional plane and low-level spike signal is converted to structural features. Our gesture recognition system has three major components, as shown in Fig. 3.

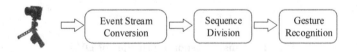

Fig. 3. Architecture of the proposed framework

4.1 Event Stream Conversion

There are two conversion methods. One is time-type conversion, which is related to time interval T. The other one is quantity-type conversion, which is related to the number of events N_e. The two conversion methods are shown in Fig. 4. It can be seen from Fig. 4(b) that the quantity-type conversion method cannot meet the real-time requirement because it does not consider the event occurrence time. Therefore, the time-type conversion method is chosen in this paper.

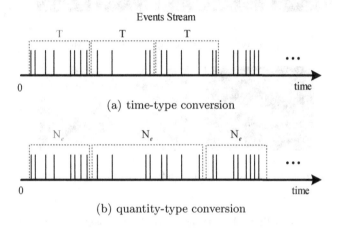

Fig. 4. Two conversion methods

A time interval value T is determined according to the gesture data to construct a sequence of images. The accumulated image frames of three different T values are shown in Fig. 5. The artifacts can be clearly seen in images of 30 ms. The artifact phenomenon is weakened, but it still exists in images of 20 ms. The artifact problem can be solved in images of 10 ms. It is more appropriate to choose the T value of 10 ms.

The accumulated Events image and the image of ordinary RGB camera are shown in Fig. 6. Further highlight the characteristic of event camera, with no redundant data. The dynamic gesture data of 11 subjects is collected using libcaer [1] software for about 60 s, and directly converted to AVI videos with a frame rate of 100.

4.2 Sequence Division

Optical Flow Estimation. The motion information caused by gesture movement is an important factor in image content changes. To reflect the motion information of the gesture, the motion of each pixel in the image can be described by optical flow. The purpose of optical flow is to approximate the spatial motion field that cannot be directly obtained from the image sequence.

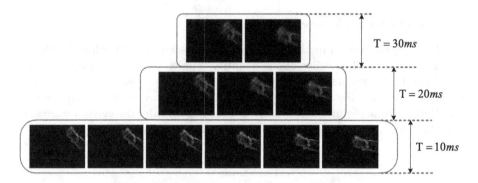

Fig. 5. Accumulated images for three T value

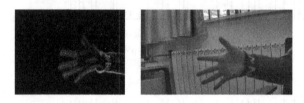

Fig. 6. Accumulated image (left) and RGB image (right)

Traditional optical flow algorithms [5,13,15,16] based on the main assumption that the invariance of light intensity under small movements are not applicable in real life. In general, traditional optical flow is difficult to achieve in both real-time and accuracy. Recently, state of the art deep learning optic flow FlowNet2.0 [7] focus on high-level motion and can be used for practical applications that require accurate and fast optical flow computation which can be applied in real-time scenarios.

It is necessary to verify whether the converted events image can be directly applied to the FlowNet2.0. The converted Events images are fed into FlowNet2.0, and the output results are shown in Fig. 7. It can be seen from the figure that the optical flow images have a clear boundary contour. Thus, the converted events images can be directly applied to FlowNet2.0.

Decision Module. It can be seen from Fig. 7 that the optical flow in y direction can be used to extract key gestures. The vertical optical flow information obviously and intuitively reflects the three stages of rock-paper-scissor. During the preparation phase, the moving speed is faster, the speed of stroke phase is gradually reduced until the hand is static, and then the speed gradually increases during the retraction phase.

In decision module, we use the changes of motion phases in velocity magnitude to get the frames contained desired hand posture. The magnitude of optical flow represents motion speed value of each pixel between adjacent frames. Considering

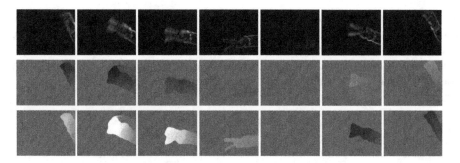

Fig. 7. The horizontal optical flow (second row) and the vertical optical flow (third row) for sample adjacent frames of "scissor" gesture (first row). The brighter or darker color in optical flow images means the greater velocity value.

the hand motion, two thresholds are set, T_v and T_n. When the number of magnitude in the interval $[-T_v, T_v]$ reaches T_n, the key frames are found.

Classification Network. After getting the key frames of the gesture, we take these key frames to train the CNN classification network. In the network designing, we employ a network proposed in [14] for rock-paper-scissor classification. This network is the enhanced version of LeNet, which consists of 5 convolutional layers and 1 fully connected layer. Each convolutional layer followed by RELU activation function and 2×2 max pooling. The structure of CNN network is shown in Fig. 8.

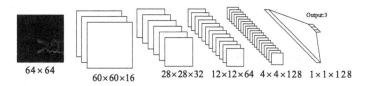

Fig. 8. Classification network structure.

Same classification task with [14], three symbols in rock-paper-scissor game are classified by the classification network. However, events are collected by slightly shaking fixed hand shape and accumulated into fixed event-number frames in [14].

5 Experiments

5.1 Results of Sequence Division

For the experimental setup of the decision module, if the number of key frames satisfying the decision condition is greater than 15, only 15 key frames are acquired, and vice versa, all key frames satisfying the decision condition are acquired. The first key frame is used as a judgment to determine whether the true key gesture image is lost. First, the T_n is fixed, and it is set to 1000. The key gesture image extraction result of different T_v is compared on 11 collected rock-paper-scissor converted events video. The results are shown in Table 2.

Table 2. Key gesture images of different T_v

T_v	T_n	Experimental data number											Missing number
		1	2	3	4	5	6	7	8	9	10	11	
3	1000	59	63	67	61	76	55	97	63	42	60	72	8
4	1000	59	59	67	61	72	55	93	61	42	60	75	19
5	1000	53	60	67	59	68	55	89	63	42	60	77	30
6	1000	56	62	67	60	66	55	93	63	42	58	74	19

* The red number in the table represent the missing key gesture image extraction results.

The red number in the table represent the missing key gesture image extraction results. It can be seen from the table that when the T_v is 3, the missing key gesture images are the least. Then, in the case of a fixed T_v, the key gesture image extraction results of different T_n are compared on 11 collected rock-paper-scissor converted events video. The results are shown in Table 3. As can be seen from the table, when the T_v is 3 and the T_n is 2000, the missing images are lost the least. Hence, T_v and T_n are set to 3 and 2000 respectively.

Table 3. Key gesture images of different T_n

T_v	T_n	Experimental data number											Missing number
		1	2	3	4	5	6	7	8	9	10	11	
3	1000	59	63	67	61	76	55	97	63	42	60	72	8
3	2000	59	63	67	61	76	55	97	63	42	60	75	5
3	3000	59	63	67	61	74	55	89	63	42	60	74	8
3	5000	59	62	66	55	73	55	88	42	36	60	21	106

* The red number in the table represent the missing key gesture image extraction results.

5.2 Results of Classification

Meanwhile, in order to stress the advantages of event-based pattern, we also use the traditional HIKVISION DS-2CD5A26FWD-IZ camera to collect the rock-paper-scissor gesture videos in different background. Then these video streams are fed into proposed key frames extraction module. The key frames extracted from that module are collected and finally we get 5205 images and 2539 images for DVS data and HIK data respectively. The difference in the number of two data sets is due to the equivalent frame rate of DVS video data different from the HIK videos. Then these images are divided into training dataset and out-of-sample validation dataset for the classification network. After that, we build up the unique DVS rock-paper-scissor static symbol dataset with accumulated events and the HIK rock-paper-scissor static symbol dataset.

It must be mentioned that, the storage capacity of DVS and HIK static symbol dataset are 32.6 MB and 381.8 MB respectively. DVS effectively remove the redundant background data, which enables efficient and low-power object recognition.

To verify the effectiveness of the 6-layer network used in this paper, we train a 6-layer model, and a AlexNet [10] model respectively on the dataset we collected. Besides, to evaluate the performance of the CNN network, images in 9 videos are selected as the training data, and the remaining images in 2 videos are reserved as out-of-sample validation. Considering the DVS dataset is gray-scale image, the strategies of training network on DVS data are learned from LeNet. Pixel values of DVS dataset is normalized to 0–1 range. For 6-layer network, the batch size is set to 8, and the base learning rates of DVS data and HIK data are 0.01 and 0.001 respectively. For AlexNet, the batch size is set to 16, and the base learning rates setting is the same as 6-layer network. The learning rate policy varies by data and network, e.g. 6-layer network for DVS data decrease the learning rate at iterations of 3000, 15000, 30000, 40000, and AlexNet for DVS data decrease the learning rate at iterations of 3000, 6000, 10000, 15000, 20000. All experiments are implemented with Caffe [8]. Our computer is equipped with Intel Core i7-6700 CPU with frequency of 3.4GHz, NVidia GeForce GTX Titan XP GPU, 128 GB RAM, and the framework runs on the Ubuntu 16.04 operating system.

We compare the performances of two limited training data on 6-layer and AlexNet network. The performances are reported in Table 4. In order to avoid the influence caused by random once selection of out-of-sample validation data, we randomly select 5 groups of 9 training data and 2 out-of-sample validation among the 11 videos. The final result is the average result of the 5 groups.

Table 4. Performance comparison with two limited training data on 6-layer and AlexNet network

Model	Data	Input	Out-of-sample acc.	Params.num	Net.forward (ms)
6-layer	DVS	64×64	0.940	114K	0.67
6-layer	HIK	64×64	0.662	115K	0.73
AlexNet	DVS	227×227	0.944	57M	8.96
AlexNet	HIK	227×227	0.668	57M	9.77

As shown in Table 4, the out-of-sample performance of DVS data on 6-layer network is better than HIK data, which benefit from eliminating redundant data and only keep the useful information. The performance of HIK data on 6-layer is unsatisfactory, largely because of limited amount of training data for complex backgrounds. Without enough training data, CNN cannot extract good features that are important for discrimination. It also makes the network not robust to image background interference, as poor performance is illustrated on data that the network has not seen before.

Besides, the DVS and HIK data show almost the same performance on AlexNet. Compared to AlexNet, the performance of 6-layer network is comparable. Moreover, 6-layer network has less parameters, and faster processing speed. The parameters in 6-layer network and AlexNet also shows that there is a lot of representation redundancy in AlexNet for DVS data. These experiments prove the effectiveness of the 6-layer on limited DVS training data used in this paper.

6   Conclusion

This paper proposes a system to classify dynamic gestures using event camera. Specifically, we focus on classifying three symbols in the rock-paper-scissor game, which is an preliminary application and the method can be extended to other real world applications. Combing DVS and CNNs to solve gesture recognition problem under complicated background, which also weaken the requirements for training data, to some extent. Different from other end-to-end gesture recognition without specific hand posture recognition. We utilize the FlowNet 2.0 to extract motion representation of the accumulated event frames, and motion representation is used to get the key frames. Then a 6-layer classification network is applied to recognize the symbols in key frames, which has very little time consumption.

However, the gesture recognition method in this paper still has some shortcomings. Since the two hard thresholds in decision module would inevitably result in data loss. This inflexible threshold setting method will make the extraction varies from person to person. And Converting the events into images dilute the asynchronous characteristic of events. In the future, a more efficient extraction of key gesture and a more rational use the asynchronous characteristics of events data will propose.

Acknowledgments. This work was supported by Young Fund for High Resolution Earth Observation Conference, Young Star Science and Technology Project (No. 2018KJXX-030) in Shanxi province.

References

1. https://github.com/inilabs/libcaer
2. Ahn, E.Y., Lee, J.H., Mullen, T., Yen, J.: Dynamic vision sensor camera based bare hand gesture recognition. In: 2011 IEEE Symposium On Computational Intelligence For Multimedia, Signal And Vision Processing, pp. 52–59. IEEE (2011)

3. Amir, A., et al.: A low power, fully event-based gesture recognition system. In: Proceedings of the IEEE Conference on Computer Vision and Pattern Recognition, pp. 7243–7252 (2017)
4. Brandli, C., Berner, R., Yang, M., Liu, S.C., Delbruck, T.: A 240 × 180 130 db 3 μs latency global shutter spatiotemporal vision sensor. IEEE J. Solid-State Circuits **49**(10), 2333–2341 (2014)
5. Horn, B.K., Schunck, B.G.: Determining optical flow. Artif. Intell. **17**(1–3), 185–203 (1981)
6. Huang, J., Guo, M., Chen, S.: A dynamic vision sensor with direct logarithmic output and full-frame picture-on-demand. In: 2017 IEEE International Symposium on Circuits and Systems (ISCAS), pp. 1–4. IEEE (2017)
7. Ilg, E., Mayer, N., Saikia, T., Keuper, M., Dosovitskiy, A., Brox, T.: Flownet 2.0: evolution of optical flow estimation with deep networks. In: Proceedings of the IEEE Conference on Computer Vision and Pattern Recognition, pp. 2462–2470 (2017)
8. Jia, Y., et al.: Caffe: convolutional architecture for fast feature embedding. In: Proceedings of the 22nd ACM International Conference on Multimedia, pp. 675–678. ACM (2014)
9. Kendon, A.: Current issues in the study of gesture. In: The Biological Foundations of Gestures: Motor and Semiotic Aspects, vol. 1, pp. 23–47 (1986)
10. Krizhevsky, A., Sutskever, I., Hinton, G.E.: Imagenet classification with deep convolutional neural networks. In: Advances in Neural Information Processing Systems, pp. 1097–1105 (2012)
11. Lee, J., et al.: Live demonstration: gesture-based remote control using stereo pair of dynamic vision sensors. In: 2012 IEEE International Symposium on Circuits and Systems, pp. 741–745. IEEE (2012)
12. Lichtsteiner, P., Posch, C., Delbruck, T.: A 128 × 128 120 db 15 μs latency asynchronous temporal contrast vision sensor. IEEE J. Solid-State Circuits **43**(2), 566–576 (2008)
13. Lucas, B.D., Kanade, T., et al.: An iterative image registration technique with an application to stereo vision (1981)
14. Lungu, I.A., Corradi, F., Delbrück, T.: Live demonstration: convolutional neural network driven by dynamic vision sensor playing roshambo. In: 2017 IEEE International Symposium on Circuits and Systems (ISCAS), pp. 1–1. IEEE (2017)
15. Nagel, H.H.: Displacement vectors derived from second-order intensity variations in image sequences. Comput. Vision Graph. Image Proc. **21**(1), 85–117 (1983)
16. Nagel, H.H.: On the estimation of optical flow: relations between different approaches and some new results. Artif. Intell. **33**(3), 299–324 (1987)
17. Park, P.K., et al.: Performance improvement of deep learning based gesture recognition using spatiotemporal demosaicing technique. In: 2016 IEEE International Conference on Image Processing (ICIP), pp. 1624–1628. IEEE (2016)
18. Posch, C., Matolin, D., Wohlgenannt, R.: A QVGA 143 dB dynamic range frame-free PWM image sensor with lossless pixel-level video compression and time-domain CDS. IEEE J. Solid-State Circuits **46**(1), 259–275 (2011)
19. Rivera-Acosta, M., Ortega-Cisneros, S., Rivera, J., Sandoval-Ibarra, F.: American sign language alphabet recognition using a neuromorphic sensor and an artificial neural network. Sensors **17**(10), 2176 (2017)

Cross-Category Cross-Semantic Regularization for Fine-Grained Image Recognition

Yelin Chen, Xianjie Mo, Zijun Liang, Tingting Wei, and Wei Luo[✉]

South China Agricultural University,
Guangzhou 510000, GD, People's Republic of China
{cvychen,liangzijun}@stu.scau.edu.cn, cedricmo.cs@gmail.com,
weitingting@scau.edu.cn, cswluo@gmail.com

Abstract. Fine-grained image recognition (FGIR) is challenging due to the local and subtle differences between subordinate categories. Existing methods adopt a two-step strategy by first detecting local parts from images, and then extracting features from them for classification. Although steady progress has been achieved, these methods localize object parts separately while neglecting the relationships between them. In this paper, we propose cross-category cross-semantic (C^3S), a regularization module that exploits the relationships between object parts from different images to regularize the fine-grained feature learning for FGIR. C^3S encourages the features of the same object part from different images to have strong correlations while decorrelating the features from different object parts as much as possible. C^3S can be incorporated into networks without introducing any extra parameters. Experiments on five benchmark datasets (CUB-200-2011, Stanford Dogs, Stanford Cars, FGVC-Aircraft and NABirds) validate the effectiveness of C^3S and demonstrate its comparable performance to existing methods.

Keywords: Fine-grained image recognition · Deep convolutional neural networks

1 Introduction

Fine-grained image recognition (FGIR) refers to distinguishing objects into subordinate categories, e.g., species of birds [29], models of cars [15], breeds of dogs [13], etc. Compared to base-class recognition, images from subordinate categories often exhibit more subtle and regional visual differences, which make recognition models difficult to learn discriminative and robust feature representations. The recognition performance of FGIR has undergone significant improvements in recent years, thanks to the progress in the design and training of deep neural networks. Generally, there are two broad types of attention mechanisms that

---

Y. Chen and X. Mo—Equal contributions. The first author is a student.

© Springer Nature Switzerland AG 2019
Z. Lin et al. (Eds.): PRCV 2019, LNCS 11857, pp. 110–122, 2019.
https://doi.org/10.1007/978-3-030-31654-9_10

are widely employed for weakly-supervised FGIR, namely, part detection that explicitly searches discriminative regions in raw images, and soft attention that constructs multiple output branches on one or more top-level layers to build higher-level attention-induced abstractions. Our study in this paper falls into the second category.

To better learn discriminative and robust feature representations, previous work [1] typically adopts a two-step strategy by first detecting local parts from images, and then extracting features from them for fine-grained classification. However, the application of this strategy is limited by a trade-off between recognition and localization ability. Based on these observations, the end-to-end learning framework has emerged that provides accurate fine-grained recognition predictions as well as highly informative regions during inference. These methods eliminate the need for alternative and multistage strategies, but lack a mechanism to exploit the relationships between object parts from different images, which usually results in degraded accuracy. [27] explores relationships between object parts by adapting a soft attention model. The model first extracts attention aware features through an one-squeeze multi-excitation structure (OSME), a module that takes input as a feature map and outputs multi-branch feature maps, and then employs a metric learning framework to mine semantic features. While achieving decent results, the complicated sample selection procedure and non-trivial optimization involved in the objective of metric learning limit its application.

In this paper, we propose C^3S, a simple but effective method that exploits relationships between object parts from different images to regularize the fine-grained feature learning for FGIR. Similar to [27], our method first extracts attention aware features through multiple excitation modules, but it further employs C^3S to guide the attention features to be extracted from distinct discriminative regions. In theory, for the attention features from different images but extracted from the same attention regions, they should be more correlated than those from different attention regions. To this end, C^3S encourages the features of the same object part from different images to have strong correlations while decorrelating the features from different object parts as much as possible. With constraints introduced by C^3S, the learned excitation modules are likely to localize distinct informative regions distributed over the whole object. Therefore, our proposed model can provides accurate fine-grained classification predictions as well as distinct discriminative regions during inference. Different from the metric learning framework, C^3S can be easily integrated into deep convolutional neural networks (DCNNs) without any sample selection procedure, resulting in increased computational efficiency. Experiments on five benchmark datasets (CUB-200-2011, Stanford Dogs, Stanford Cars, FGVC-Aircraft and NABirds) validate the effectiveness of C^3S and demonstrate its comparable performance to existing methods. Moreover, C^3S can be trained with standard back-propagation, allowing for end-to-end training of our method. Our main contributions can be summarized as follows:

– We propose a soft-attention based framework for FGIR, which learns to refine attention features end-by-end by unsupervised exploiting the relationships between the attended features.

- We design a novel regularizer, C^3S, to exploit the relationship between different attention features. C^3S encourages semantics of every attention by forcing the features of the same object part from different images to have strong correlations between each other while decorrelating the features from different object parts as much as possible.
- We conduct extensive experiments on five fine-grained benchmark datasets and present a detailed comparison analysis. The state-of-the-art performance validates the effectiveness of our method.

The remainder of this paper is organized as follows: Related work is reviewed in Sect. 2. In Sect. 3 we elaborate the OSME for attention feature extraction and C^3S. Experimental results are presented and analyzed in Sect. 4 and we conclude our work in Sect. 5.

2   Related Work

2.1   Fine-Grained Image Recognition

In computer vision, the recognition performance of coarse-grained learning has improved greatly thanks to the marked progress of deep learning architectures. However, Fine-grained image recognition (FGIR) is still a challenging task due to the subtle visual differences between subordinate classes in the object. In the task of classifying birds and dogs, it is difficult to distinguish categories owe to the distinct object postures and scenarios such as the flying bird across the forest and the standing dog in the crowd. A straightforward way of locating vital discriminative regions is to exploit manual object part annotations for better recognition. Yet it is laborious and expensive to obtain datasets with detailed annotations such as bounding box, which seriously limits the effectiveness of these methods in practice.

For the sake of implementing general networks, increasing weakly-supervised mechanisms have emerged to improve the fine-grained features learning. Jaderberg et al. [12] raise the Spatial Transformer, which allows spatial manipulation of data within the network in the weakly-supervised way. Lin et al. [18] utilize a bilinear network to capture discriminative features among subordinate categories. Other advanced methods, such as the way of leveraging the label hierarchy on fine-grained classes [38] and the strategy of integrating the average with bilinear pooling to learn a pooling way during the training [26]. These methods also perform the great prediction accuracy.

In comparison to previous methods, our method also devotes to extracting features in the weakly-supervised way but boosts the performance by encouraging the relationships between identical object parts and decorrelating the distinct parts, instead of operating spacial transform of the data or utilizing the bilinear extractor.

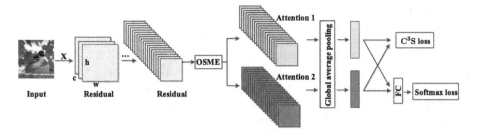

Fig. 1. Overview of our network architecture. Here we visualize the case of extracting two attention branches through OSME module in a residual network. The ultimate prediction according to softmax loss is regularized by C^3S loss which exploits the relationships between attention branches. Our model is trained end-to-end with gradients from C^3S loss and softmax loss.

2.2 Attention-Based Learning

Attention-based learning is a promising direction to address various issues of FGIR. There are two broad types of attention mechanisms that are effective for weakly-supervised FGIR. One is part detection, which explicitly searches discriminative regions in raw images. Faster R-CNN is a part detection method that contributes to perform without annotations by employing Region Proposal Network (RPN). Approaches like YOLO [25] and SSD [19] improve the detection speed in a single-shot architecture. Another attention mechanism is soft attention, which can lead the distribution of available processing resources to the most informative locations of images [10,11,16,21,24]. Wang et al. [31] propose the trunk-and-mask attention mechanism, which focuses on stacking Attention Modules for generating attention aware features that change adaptively as layers going deeper. The Squeeze-and-Excitation (SE) block [8] raised by Hu et al. exploits the channel-wise information to regulate channel weights. Above methods present the good performance in FGIR. What's more, our method is also part of soft attention, which utilizes the relationships between attention branches.

3   Method

In this section, we present our proposed method which can efficiently and accurately localize informative regions by exploiting the relationships between object parts from different images. As shown in Fig. 1, the framework of our method is composed of two parts: (1) Extracting attention features from multiple attention regions through the one-squeeze multi-excitation (OSME) module (Sect. 3.1); and (2) Guiding the attention features to represent distinct discriminative regions through C^3S (Sect. 3.2). Notably, our method can be easily integrated into existing backbone architecture; we use ResNet-50 with SE blocks as an instantiation.

3.1   Preliminaries

We briefly introduce the one-squeeze multi-excitation (OSME) [27] module for completeness before diving deep into the C^3S regularizer. OSME is a differential module that extracts attention features from multiple attention regions. Let $\mathbf{U} = [\mathbf{u}_1, \cdots, \mathbf{u}_C] \in \mathbb{R}^{W \times H \times C}$ be the output feature maps of the last residual block τ. In order to generate multiple attention-specific feature maps, the OSME module extends the original SE block by performing one-squeeze and multiple-excitation operations.

Formally, in the first one-squeeze step, OSME adopts global average pooling to shrink $\mathbf{U}$ and generates a channel-wise statistics $\mathbf{z} = [z_1, \cdots, z_C] \in \mathbb{R}^C$. In the second multi-excitation step, a gating mechanism is independently employed on $\mathbf{z}$ for each attention module $p = 1, \cdots, P$:

$$\mathbf{m}^p = \sigma\left(\mathbf{W}_2^p \delta\left(\mathbf{W}_1^p \mathbf{z}\right)\right) = [m_1^p, \cdots, m_C^p] \in \mathbb{R}^C, \tag{1}$$

where δ and σ denote Sigmoid and ReLU [23] functions respectively. To obtain the output attention-specific features map $\tilde{\mathbf{U}}^p$ of each attention module p, we use corresponding $\mathbf{m}^p$ to re-weight the channels of the original feature maps $\mathbf{U}$:

$$\tilde{\mathbf{U}}^p = [m_1^p \mathbf{u}_1, \cdots, m_C^p \mathbf{u}_C] \in \mathbb{R}^{W \times H \times C}. \tag{2}$$

The OSME block can extract multiple attention-specific features, but still lacks a mechanism to guarantee that these features come from distinct discriminative regions. [27] addresses this by formulating a metric learning framework to pull same-attention same-class features closer and push different-attention or different-class features away. However, optimizing the non-trivial objective of metric learning is still challenging in practice.

3.2   Cross-Category Cross-Semantic Regularizer

Different from the metric learning framework introduced in [27], we propose to regularize the attention-specific features learning by exploiting the relationships between object parts from different images and different excitation modules. In theory, for the attention features from different images but extracted from the same attention regions, they should be more correlated than those from different attention regions. To this end, we design the cross-category cross-semantic regularizer (C^3S) that encourages the features from the same excitation module to have strong correlations between each other while decorrelating the features from different excitation modules as much as possible.

To obtain the feature vector $\mathbf{f}^p \in \mathbb{R}^C$, we first adopt global average pooling (GAP) on corresponding attention-specific features map $\tilde{\mathbf{U}}^p$, and then we scale them down to unit vectors through ℓ_2 normalization ($\mathbf{f}^p \leftarrow \mathbf{f}^p / \|\mathbf{f}^p\|$). Thus we encode the relationships between all pairs of excitation module p and p' into a symmetric matrix S:

$$S_{|p,p'|} = \frac{1}{N^2} \sum \mathbf{F}^{p\mathrm{T}} \mathbf{F}^{p'}, \tag{3}$$

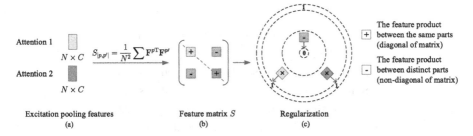

Fig. 2. An illustration of the cross-category cross-semantic regularizer. Assume the amount of excitation P in Eq. 4 is 2. (a) Each attention branch is composed of N image features extracted through OSME and GAP. (b) The interactive features between each branch are contained into a feature matrix. (c) Constraint leads feature products in symmetric matrix to the corresponding orientation to decrease the loss.

where $S_{|p,p'|}$ indicates an element of the matrix, N is the batch size, T is the transpose operator and $\mathbf{F}^p = [\mathbf{f}_1^p, \cdots, \mathbf{f}_N^p] \in \mathbb{R}^{C \times N}$ is a matrix storing the feature vectors from excitation module p for total samples in the batch.

The C^3S regularization loss is then constructed from two key components: (1) maximizing the diagonal of S to maximize the relationship between same -excitation features and (2) minimizing the non-diagonal of S to minimize the relationship between different-excitation features:

$$\mathcal{L}_{C^3S}(S) = \frac{1}{2}\left(\sum S - \mathrm{tr}\,(S)\right) + \left(P - \mathrm{tr}\,(S)\right) = \frac{1}{2}\left(\sum S - 3\mathrm{tr}\,(S) + 2P\right) \quad (4)$$

where $\mathrm{tr}(S)$ indicates the sum of the elements on the main diagonal of S. And in our method, we set the amount of excitation module P as 2. Different from the metric learning framework, C^3S regularization loss can be naturally inserted into the OSME block and is easily optimized without any sample selection procedure.

Therefore, we minimize the total loss:

$$L = L_s + \lambda L_{C^3S}, \quad (5)$$

where L_s is the softmax loss and λ is a balance weight. Our framework can be trained end-to-end using stochastic gradient descent (SGD).

4   Experiments

4.1   Datasets

Our experiments are carried out on five benchmark datasets, CUB-200-2011, Stanford Dogs, Stanford Cars, FGVC-Aircraft and NABirds, which are challenging to the network due to their complex textures and very subtle divergences among classes. All of these datasets are accompanied with additional bounding box despite of our weakly-supervised learning method needing no annotations but class labels. The statistics of these five datasets are shown in Table 1.

Table 1. Statistics of benchmark datasets.

Datasets	#total	#class	#train	#test
CUB-200-2011	11,788	200	5,994	5,794
Standford dogs	20,580	120	12,000	8,580
Standford cars	16,185	196	8,144	8,041
FGVG-Aircraft	10,000	100	6,667	3,333
NABirds	48,562	555	23,929	24,633

CUB-200-2011. CUB-200-2011 [29], extended on CUB-200 [32], has 11788 images in 200 categories and is diffusely used by most advanced models. Since the amount of images in each training class is only up to 30, it is a challenge to train a model in CUB-200-2011.

Stanford Dogs. This dataset covers 120 class labels and 20,580 images. Although dogs are easier to be distinguished compared to birds, it is also hard to recognize accurately in such a dataset owe to the complex background in images which disturbs operators to extract features.

Stanford Cars. Stanford Cars consists of 196 class labels and 16185 images. Various angles of cars are shoot in the images which enhance the difficulties in training. The production year and the model of cars are able to be identified through the labels.

FGVC-Aircraft. There are 10,000 images and 100 classes contained in the aircraft set. The ratio of the train set and the test set is approximately 1 : 2. FGVC-Aircraft was once used as part of the fine-grained recognition challenge FGComp 2013.

NABirds. NABirds, a dataset about North American birds, is the largest one in the datasets we exploit, which occupies 48562 images and 555 categories. There are abundant bird postures in the images (e.g. bending down to capture meats and pecking on the tree), which notably increase the classification difficulty. Each class label is noted by number.

4.2   Implementation

In our experiments, images are first resized to 448 × 448 and then disrupted randomly in training. Meanwhile, we apply the random cropping on the birds dataset such as cubbirds and nabirds in training while exerting the center cropping in testing. All experiments are conducted in 45 epochs with a batch of 32 images as input. The base learning rate is set to 0.01 in all datasets excluding stdogs which is set to 0.001 and decayed by 0.1 for every 15 epochs. Moreover, the momentum of the optimization function is set to 0.9 while the gamma is 0.1. The value of the balance weight λ in Eq. 5 is depended on the dataset we opt and the amount of excitations in OSME module is set to 2 in the whole experiments.

Table 2. Results on CUB-200-2011. "Anno." means extra annotations (bounding box or part) utilized in training. "Acc." stands for the top-1 accuracy in probabilities.

Method	Anno.	Acc.
DeepLAC [17]	√	80.3%
Part-RCNN [34]	√	81.6%
MG-CNN [30]	×	81.7%
ResNet-50 [6]	×	81.7%
PA-CNN [14]	√	82.8%
RAN [31]	×	82.8%
MG-CNN [30]	√	83.0%
B-CNN [18]	×	84.1%
ST-CNN [12]	×	84.1%
FCAN [20]	×	84.3%
MAMC-OSME-ResNet-50 [27]	×	**86.3%**
Ours (SE-ResNet-50)	×	82.8%
Ours (OSME-ResNet-50)	×	83.5%
Ours (OSME-ResNet-50+C^3S)	×	86.0%

To certify our C^3S constraint is effective and powerful, we undertake experiments on five datasets. Our baseline, OSME-ResNet-50, is on the basis of ResNet and the performance of the net can be promoted through our C^3S constraint prominently. To better illustrate the superiority of our novel method, we reimplement SE-ResNet as a contrast. At the same time, We compare our outcomes with other distinctive network cited from authors' papers, the according results are elucidated in tables. All the experiments testify that our method has the capacity to enhance the performance of the baseline.

4.3   Comparison with State-of-the-Arts

Quantitative experimental results are shown in Table 2, 3, 4, 5 and 6.

Results on CUB-200-2011. The experimental results are shown in Table 2. It's observed that with our C^3S, OSME-ResNet-50 excels most of state-of-the-art models. While the OSME-ResNet-50 exceeds the SE-resnet-50 by 0.7%, our method improve the performance of OSME-ResNet-50 by 2.5% significantly. What's more, for supervised methods with extra bounding box, such as MG-CNN [30], PA-CNN [14] and Part-RCNN [34], our method outperforms them by 3.0%, 3.2% and 4.4%, respectively. And compared to methods trained without extra annotations, our model surpasses FACN [20] and ST-CNN [12] by 1.7% and 1.5%. At the same time, our result is closed to the accuracy of MAMC-OSME-ResNet50 [27] which is running in the identical baseline as us and transcends ours by 0.3%. However our method is easier and more general to achieve compared

Table 3. Results on Stanford Dogs. "Anno." means extra annotations (bounding box or part) utilized in training. "Acc." stands for the top-1 accuracy in probabilities.

Method	Anno.	Acc.
PDFR [35]	×	72.0%
ResNet-50 [6]	×	81.1%
DVAN [36]	×	81.5%
RAN [31]	×	83.1%
FCAN [20]	×	84.2%
MAMA-ResNet-50 [27]	×	84.8%
MAMA-ResNet-101 [27]	×	85.2%
Ours (SE-ResNet-50)	×	83.7%
Ours (OSME-ResNet-50)	×	85.9%
Ours (OSME-ResNet-50+C^3S)	×	**87.3%**

Table 4. Results on Stanford Cars. "Anno." means extra annotations (bounding box or part) utilized in training. "Acc." stands for the top-1 accuracy in probabilities.

Method	Anno.	Acc.
DVAN [36]	×	87.1%
RAN [31]	×	91.0%
B-CNN [18]	×	91.3%
FCAN [20]	√	91.3%
MACNN [37]	×	92.8%
MAMC-ResNet-50 [27]	×	92.8%
MAMC-ResNet-101 [27]	×	93.0%
Ours (SE-ResNet-50)	×	91.7%
Ours (OSME-ResNet-50)	×	91.9%
Ours (OSME-ResNet-50+C^3S)	×	**93.7%**

to the MAMC for the reason that our model needn't compose three types of triplets to learn. Although CUB-200-2011 contains relatively fewer samples in the training set, our method still presents the good performance.

Results on Stanford Dogs. Table 3 exhibits the results on Stanford Dogs. We introduce the accuracy of methods operating without additional annotations as a contrast. The condition where our method compared to FCAN [20] which is on the basis of semantic segmentation and costs much computing resource, the outcomes claim explicitly that our method is effective (87.3% vs 84.4%). Especially in this dataset, our method surpasses the method of MAMC [27] greatly by 2.5% on the ResNet-50 as well as 2.1% on the ResNet-101. As for the original OSME-ResNet-50, our method can improve it by 1.4%.

Table 5. Results on Stanford FGVG-Aircraft. "Anno." means extra annotations (bounding box or part) utilized in training. "Acc." stands for the top-1 accuracy in probabilities.

Method	Anno.	Acc.
B-CNN [18]	×	84.1%
RA-CNN [5]	×	88.2%
HIHCA [2]	×	88.3%
Boost-CNN [22]	×	88.5%
MACNN [37]	×	89.9%
NTS-Net (K=2) [33]	×	90.8%
NTS-Net (K=4) [33]	×	91.4%
Ours (SE-ResNet-50)	×	89.8%
Ours (OSME-ResNet-50)	×	90.2%
Ours (OSME-ResNet-50+C^3S)	×	**91.9%**

Table 6. Results on NABirds. "Anno." means extra annotations (bounding box or part) utilized in training. "Acc." stands for the top-1 accuracy in probabilities.

Method	Anno.	Acc.
Branson et al. [1]	√	35.7%
PC-ResNet-50 [4]	×	68.2%
GoogLeNet [28]	×	70.7%
Lp + GoogLeNet [3]	×	72.0%
Van et al. [7]	√	75.0%
DenseNet-161 [9]	×	79.4%
Ours (SE-ResNet-50)	×	82.2%
Ours (OSME-ResNet-50)	×	82.8%
Ours (OSME-ResNet-50+C^3S)	×	**83.0%**

Results on Stanford Cars. Our experiments in cars are presented in Table 4 and the prediction accuracy of our method in Stanford Cars is the highest one among the experiments of five datasets we exerted due to the relatively obvious features in cars. In this dataset, our method also surpasses the MAMC-ResNet-101 [27] by 0.7%. On the contrast with B-CNN [18], a model commanding an extra net to capture features, our model is not only more outstanding but also much simpler and more exercisable(93.7% vs 91.3%).

Results on FGVG-Aircraft. Table 5 shows the outcomes about FGVG-Aircraft. Although NTS-Net [33], a method designed in a novel learning way that produces multiple proposal regions and ranks the regions to capture the features, carries out the great performance in FGIR. However, our method also has a capability to excels the NTS-Net by 0.5%.

Results on NABirds. The consequences conducted on NABirds are presented in Table 6. It is hard for networks to learn NABirds thanks to the diversity of attitude. Even DenseNet-161 [9] only achieves 79.4%, which executes in a radical dense linking mechanism that all layers are interconnected. Yet in such a complicated dataset, our C^3S maintains the excellent property to achieve 3.6% higher than DenseNet-161.

5   Conclusion

In this paper, we proposed a method, termed cross-category cross-semantic (C^3S), which exploits the relationships between object parts from different images to regularize the fine-grained features learning for FGIR. C^3S encourages the features from the same excitation module to have strong correlations between each other while decorrelating the features from different excitation modules as much as possible. Our method can be trained end-to-end in one stage without any bounding box or part annotations. Experiments on five benchmark datasets demonstrated the effectiveness and the state-of-the-art performance of our method.

Acknowledgements. This work was supported in part by the National Natural Science Foundation of China under Grant 61702197, in part by the Natural Science Foundation of Guangdong Province under Grant 2017A030310261, in part by the program of China Scholarship Council.

References

1. Branson, S., Horn, G.V., Belongie, S., Perona, P.: Bird species categorization using pose normalized deep convolutional nets. arXiv preprint arXiv:1406.2952 (2014)
2. Cai, S., Zuo, W., Zhang, L.: Higher-order integration of hierarchical convolutional activations for fine-grained visual categorization. In: ICCV (2017)
3. Dubey, A., Gupta, O., Guo, P., Raskar, R., Farrell, R., Naik, N.: Training with confusion for fine-grained visual classification. CoRR (2017)
4. Dubey, A., Gupta, O., Guo, P., Raskar, R., Farrell, R., Naik, N.: Pairwise confusion for fine-grained visual classification. In: ECCV (2018)
5. Fu, J., Zheng, H., Mei, T.: Look closer to see better: recurrent attention convolutional neural network for fine-grained image recognition. In: CVPR (2017)
6. He, K., Zhang, X., Ren, S., Sun, J.: Deep residual learning for image recognition. In: Computer Vision and Pattern Recognition, pp. 770–778 (2016)
7. Horn, G.V., et al.: Building a bird recognition app and large scale dataset with citizen scientists: the fine print in fine-grained dataset collection. In: CVPR (2015)
8. Hu, J., Shen, L., Sun, G.: Squeeze-and-excitation networks. In: CVPR (2018)
9. Huang, G., Liu, Z., Maaten, L.V.D., Weinberger, K.Q.: Densely connected convolutional networks. In: CVPR (2017)
10. Itti, L., Koch, C.: Computational modelling of visual attention. Nat. Rev. Neurosci. **2**(3), 194 (2001)
11. Itti, L., Koch, C., Niebur, E.: A model of saliency-based visual attention for rapid scene analysis. IEEE Trans. Pattern Anal. Mach. Intell. **20**(11), 1254–1259 (1998)

12. Jaderberg, M., Simonyan, K., Zisserman, A., et al.: Spatial transformer networks. In: NIPS (2015)
13. Khosla, A., Jayadevaprakash, N., Yao, B., Fei-Fei, L.: Novel dataset for fine-grained image categorization. In: CVPR (2011)
14. Krause, J., Jin, H., Yang, J., Feifei, L.: Fine-grained recognition without part annotations. In: CVPR (2015)
15. Krause, J., Stark, M., Deng, J., Li, F.F.: 3D object representations for fine-grained categorization. In: 4th IEEE Workshop on 3D Representation and Recognition at ICCV (2013)
16. Larochelle, H., Hinton, G.E.: Learning to combine foveal glimpses with a third-order Boltzmann machine. In: NIPS (2010)
17. Lin, D., Shen, X., Lu, C., Jia, J.: Deep LAC: deep localization, alignment and classification for fine-grained recognition. In: CVPR (2015)
18. Lin, T., Roychowdhury, A., Maji, S.: Bilinear CNN models for fine-grained visual recognition. In: International Conference on Computer Vision, pp. 1449–1457 (2015)
19. Liu, W., et al.: SSD: single shot multibox detector. In: ECCV (2016)
20. Liu, X., Xia, T., Wang, J., Yang, Y., Zhou, F., Lin, Y.: Fully convolutional attention networks for fine-grained recognition. arXiv preprint arXiv:1603.06765 (2016)
21. Mnih, V., Heess, N., Graves, A., et al.: Recurrent models of visual attention. In: NIPS (2014)
22. Moghimi, M., Belongie, S.J., Saberian, M.J., Yang, J., Vasconcelos, N., Li, L.: Boosted convolutional neural networks. In: BMVC (2016)
23. Nair, V., Hinton, G.E.: Rectified linear units improve restricted Boltzmann machines. In: ICML (2010)
24. Olshausen, B.A., Anderson, C.H., Essen, D.C.V.: A neurobiological model of visual attention and invariant pattern recognition based on dynamic routing of information. J. Neurosci. 13(11), 4700–4719 (1993)
25. Redmon, J., Divvala, S., Girshick, R., Farhadi, A.: You only look once: unified, real-time object detection. In: CVPR (2016)
26. Simon, M., Gao, Y., Darrell, T., Denzler, J., Rodner, E.: Generalized orderless pooling performs implicit salient matching. In: ICCV (2017)
27. Sun, M., Yuan, Y., Zhou, F., Ding, E.: Multi-attention multi-class constraint for fine-grained image recognition. In: ECCV (2018)
28. Szegedy, C., et al.: Going deeper with convolutions. In: CVPR (2015)
29. Wah, C., Branson, S., Welinder, P., Perona, P., Belongie, S.: The caltech-UCSD birds-200-2011 dataset. Tech. rep. California Institute of Technology (2011)
30. Wang, D., Shen, Z., Shao, J., Zhang, W., Xue, X., Zhang, Z.: Multiple granularity descriptors for fine-grained categorization. In: ICCV (2015)
31. Wang, F., et al.: Residual attention network for image classification. In: CVPR (2017)
32. Welinder, P., et al.: Caltech-UCSD Birds 200. Tech. rep. CNS-TR-2010-001. California Institute of Technology (2010)
33. Yang, Z., Luo, T., Wang, D., Hu, Z., Gao, J., Wang, L.: Learning to navigate for fine-grained classification. In: ECCV (2018)
34. Zhang, N., Donahue, J., Girshick, R.B., Darrell, T.: Part-based R-CNNs for fine-grained category detection. In: European Conference on Computer Vision (2014)
35. Zhang, X., Xiong, H., Zhou, W., Lin, W., Tian, Q.: Picking deep filter responses for fine-grained image recognition. In: CVPR (2016)

36. Zhao, B., Wu, X., Feng, J., Peng, Q., Yan, S.: Diversified visual attention networks for fine-grained object classification. IEEE Trans. Multimedia **19**(6), 1245–1256 (2017)
37. Zheng, H., Fu, J., Mei, T., Luo, J.: Learning multi-attention convolutional neural network for fine-grained image recognition. In: ICCV (2017)
38. Zhou, F., Lin, Y.: Fine-grained image classification by exploring bipartite-graph labels. In: CVPR (2016)

The Multi-task Fully Convolutional Siamese Network with Correlation Filter Layer for Real-Time Visual Tracking

Shiyu Xuan[1,2,3,4], Shengyang Li[1,2,3(✉)], Zifei Zhao[1,2,3,4], and Mingfei Han[1,2,3,4]

[1] Key Laboratory of Space Utilization, Beijing 100094, China
[2] Technology and Engineering Center for Space Utilization, Beijing 100094, China
{zhaozifei18,hanmingfei16,shyli,xuanshiyu17}@csu.ac.cn
[3] Chinese Academy of Sciences (CAS), Beijing 100094, China
[4] University of Chinese Academy of Sciences, Beijing 100094, China

Abstract. In recent years, the trackers based on the siamese network have achieved good performance on various benchmarks. However, most siamese trackers have difficulty in discriminating the similar objects and cannot benefit from the shallow features in the neural network. In this paper, we used three methods to solve the above problems. We use the VGGNet as the backbone of our networks instead of the most used AlexNet. We jointly train the correlation filter and the embedding similarity learning. The multi-task learning makes our tracker benefit from both the shallow and deep features in the neural network. We use the correlation filter as an attention module to make the tracker pay more attention to the object being tracked. Extensive experiments on benchmarks show that our approach yields 11.4% relative gain in OTB2015 and 33% relative gain in VOT2017 compared with the SiamFC. The proposed tracker can be real-time while achieving leading performance in OTB2013, OTB2015 and VOT2017.

Keywords: Visual tracking · Siamese network · Correlation filter

1 Introduction

Visual tracking is one of the most fundamental problems in computer vision. The goal of visual tracking is to locate the object being tracked in the video sequence. It has a large range of applications in many fields such as human-machine interaction, robotics, augmented reality, automatic driving and so forth. Although many researches have been done in recent years [2,4,5,8,12,17,25,26], there are still many challenging scenarios such as out-of-view, deformation, background cluttering, occlusions and other variations which require visual tracking algorithms to solve.

S. Xuan is a student.

© Springer Nature Switzerland AG 2019
Z. Lin et al. (Eds.): PRCV 2019, LNCS 11857, pp. 123–134, 2019.
https://doi.org/10.1007/978-3-030-31654-9_11

Recently, deep learning has made amazing achievements in many fields of computer vision. The visual tracking also benefits from the deep learning [2,6,9,10,15,17,22–24,27]. Amongst various deep learning tracking algorithms, the siamese network has drawn much attention because of its balance between accuracy and speed. The siamese trackers [2,9,15,21–24,27] formulate the object tracking as a matching problem and can be trained offline from a large set of videos. Most siamese trackers do not need to be updated online; therefore the trackers can be in real time. Although the accuracy of the algorithm has been greatly improved in recent years, there are still many inherent defects that constrain the further improvement of the algorithm performance:

- The goal of offline training is to make the network learning a general feature, therefore the network can only discriminate foreground from the nonsemantic background and the network cannot distinguish between similar objects as shown in Fig. 1. In order to improve the ability of the network to discriminate the foreground from the background, the network uses the deep features. Deep features contain more semantic features, which reduce the ability of the network to distinguish similar objects. When the number of similar objects in the search area is large, the performance of the algorithm will drop significantly.
- Most siamese trackers use the AlexNet [14] as their backbone which is not deep and robust enough. The discriminating power of the backbone network will directly affect the performance of the tracker.

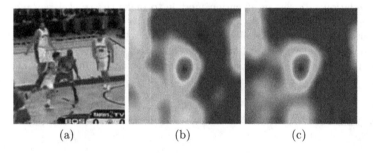

(a)   (b)   (c)

Fig. 1. Visualization of the response heatmaps of trackers. (a) the search image (b) produced by SiamFC (c) produced by MT-SiamFC_CF. Our approach can suppress the response of similar objects.

The correlation filter is another important algorithm in the visual tracking [3–5,11,12,16]. The correlation filter can be efficiently trained in the Fourier domain and quickly update online in the tracking procedure. It has strong discriminating power and is well suited to use the shallow features of neural networks [22,23]. The research of [22,23] further improves the algorithm performance by training the filter end-to-end. Inspired by the [22,23], we jointly train the correlation filter and the siamese network. These two tasks can be mutually improved through multi-task learning. Different from the original fully convolutional siamese network [2], our approach not only uses the semantic discriminating power of deep features but also preserves the ability of shallow features to distinguish between similar objects. Moreover, our approach uses the more powerful VGGNet [20] as our backbone.

In this paper our contributions can be divided into three-folds:

- A network that uses both shallow and deep features for tracking is proposed by multi-task learning. These two tasks make the network more robust for visual tracking.
- A novel method that regards the correlation filter layer as an attention module is proposed. The use of correlation filter layer makes the network distinguish similar objects better as shown in Fig. 1.
- We adapt the more advanced VGGNet into the framework of the original fully convolutional siamese network which makes the network has a better discrimination capability.

Based on the above contributions, the multi-task fully convolutional siamese network with correlation filter (MT-SiamFC_CF) tracker is presented. We did experiments on three benchmarks, OTB2013 [25], VOT2017 [13], OTB2015 [26]. The results of experiments demonstrated the effectiveness and real-time tracking ability of our algorithm.

2   Related Work

2.1   Siamese Trackers

The siamese trackers have drawn much attention in recent years [2,9,10,15,22–24,27]. These trackers cannot only track the object with high accuracy but also be real time. The goal of SiamFC [2] is to learn a metric of similarity in the embedding space. In the tracking procedure, the object position is determined by using cross convolution to find a position with the highest similarity to the exemplar image. The network does not need to online update, which makes the tracker can be real time. After SiamFC many researches have been done to make further improvement. The DSiam [9] made the network can update online by adding a fast transformation learning model. The SiamRPN [15] introduced the region proposal subnetwork (RPN) [18] in the siamese architecture and formulate it as a local one-shot detection framework. RPN can estimate the size of object more accuracy than the original scale pyramid method used in many siamese based trackers. The RASNet [24] improved the ability of the network to distinguish between similar objects by adding three different attention mechanisms.

2.2   The Correlation Filter

The correlation filter is another important type of tracking algorithm developed in recent years [3–8,11,12,16,22,23]. The correlation filter can be trained efficiently in Fourier Domain and has almost the same performance as the deep learning method with high speed. The correlation filter method was introduced in the visual tracking for the first time in [3]. The CSK [11] and KCF [12] further extended the correlation filter and made it benefits from the multi-channel features and kernel trick. The Deep-SRDCF [6] and CF2 [16] attempted to replace the hand-craft features but with the deep features and proved the shallow features in the neural network are more suitable for the correlation filter tracker. The CFNet [22], DCFNet [23] made the correlation filter can be trained end-to-end as a layer in the neural network. Inspired by these two studies, our work made a combination of correlation filter and the fully convolutional siamese network to retain the respective advantages of shallow and deep features of neural network.

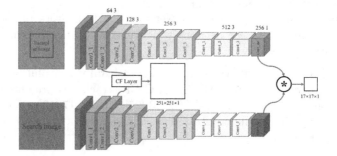

Fig. 2. The architecture of our network. The correlation filter layer only uses the features from the first two convolutional layers of our network. The embedding similarity learning uses the output of the last layer of the network. The numbers above the convolutional layers represent the number of channels and the size of kernel respectively. Moreover, we use the 1×1 convolution to reduce the number of channels to 256 in the last layer for lowering the computation cost.

3   Our Approach

We propose an architecture that combines the correlation filter layer and the fully convolutional siamese network. Moreover, we adapt the VGGNet into original siamese architecture. To adapt to the siamese architecture, the paddings of the VGGNet need to be removed. The correlation filter layer uses the shallow features of the network which have more detailed information of the object and are more robust to distinguish between the objects in the same class. The fully convolutional siamese network uses the deep features of the neural network. The deep features have more semantic information and are more robust to the rotation, variation and illumination change of the object. The correlation filter layer and the fully convolutional siamese network are jointly trained which force the network to remain the detail information of the shallow features. In the tracking procedure, we use the correlation layer as an attention module to enhance the ability of the fully convolutional siamese network. The architecture of our network is depicted in the Fig. 2.

3.1   The Correlation Filter Layer

In the standard discriminate correlation filters (DCF), the filter is trained using the ridge regression. Here we assume the feature of an image patch is $\varphi(x) \in R^{M \times N \times D}$ and the label is $y \in R^{M \times N}$ which is a Gaussian function. The value of y at the center is 1 and decays to 0 as the distance from center increasing. We can calculate the filter coefficients ω using (1),

$$\min_{\omega} \| \sum_{i=1}^{D} \omega^i \star \varphi^i(x) - y \|^2 + \lambda \sum_{i=1}^{D} \| \omega^i \|^2, \tag{1}$$

where ω^i is the filter coefficients of the channel i, $\star$ is the circular correlation and λ is the regularization coefficient of ridge regression to avoid over-fitting. Using the property of the Fourier transform, ω can be fast calculated through (2),

$$\hat{\omega}_i = \frac{\hat{x}_i^* \circ \hat{y}}{\sum_{i=1}^{D} \hat{x}_i^* \circ \hat{x}_i + \lambda}, \tag{2}$$

where $\hat{x}, \hat{y}, \hat{\omega}$ are the Discrete Fourier Transform (DCF) of x, y, ω respectively, $\hat{x}^*$ is the complex conjugation of $\hat{x}$, $\circ$ is the Hadamard product of matrix.

In the tracking procedure, first we get the feature $\varphi(z)$ from the search patch in the new frame, then we can get the response map g using (3)

$$g = \mathcal{F}^{-1} \left(\sum_{i=1}^{D} \hat{\mathbf{w}}_i^* \circ \hat{\varphi}_i(\mathbf{z}) \right). \tag{3}$$

The position of object can be calculated by finding the maximum value of the response map g.

In DCFNet [23] the correlation filter layer can be trained to make the features more suitable for the DCF. The loss function can be formulated as $L(\theta) = \| g - \widetilde{g} \|^2 + \gamma \| \theta \|^2$, where g can be calculated using (3), $\widetilde{g}$ is the ideal Gaussian label and $\gamma \| \theta \|^2$ is the L2-regularization of the network to prevent the over-fitting. The backpropagation can be calculated element by element:

$$\frac{\partial L}{\partial \hat{g}_{uv}^*} = \left(\mathcal{F} \left(\frac{\partial L}{\partial g} \right) \right)_{uv}, \tag{4}$$

$$\frac{\partial L}{\partial \hat{\varphi}_{uv}^i(\mathbf{x})} = \frac{\partial L}{\partial \hat{g}_{uv}^*} \frac{(\hat{\varphi}_{uv}^l(\mathbf{z}))^* \hat{\mathbf{y}}_{uv}^* - \hat{g}_{uv}^* (\hat{\varphi}_{uv}^l(\mathbf{x}))^*}{\sum_{k=1}^{D} \hat{\varphi}_{uv}^k(\mathbf{x}) (\hat{\varphi}_{uv}^k(\mathbf{x}))^* + \lambda}, \tag{5}$$

$$\frac{\partial L}{\partial (\hat{\varphi}_{uv}^i(\mathbf{x}))^*} = \frac{\partial L}{\partial \hat{g}_{uv}^*} \frac{-\hat{g}_{uv}^* \hat{\varphi}_{uv}^l(\mathbf{x})}{\sum_{k=1}^{D} \hat{\varphi}_{uv}^k(\mathbf{x}) (\hat{\varphi}_{uv}^k(\mathbf{x}))^* + \lambda}, \tag{6}$$

$$\frac{\partial L}{\partial \varphi^i(\mathbf{x})} = \mathcal{F}^{-1} \left(\frac{\partial L}{\partial (\hat{\varphi}^i(\mathbf{x}))^*} + \left(\frac{\partial L}{\partial \hat{\varphi}^i(\mathbf{x})} \right)^* \right). \tag{7}$$

The error can be propagated backwards to the feature maps; therefore the correlation filter can be used as a layer of the neural network. In our architecture only the layers from first two convolutional layers of VGGNet will be trained by the correlation layer since the shallow features are more suitable for the correlation filter. Our experiments show that simply using DCFNet formulation with a deeper network will reduce the performance of the tracker. In order to make the tracker benefit from the deep features of the network, the fully convolutional siamese network needs to be combined into the original DCFNet framework.

3.2   Fully Convolutional Siamese Network

The SiamFC addresses the visual tracking task as an embedding similarity learning process. The forward propagation of the images in the network can be regarded as transforming the images into an embedding space. Assuming the image is z and the image which is transformed into the embedding space is $\varphi(z)$, the similarity of two images z, x can be expressed as (8),

$$s = \frac{1}{mn} \sum_{i=0}^{m-1} \sum_{j=0}^{n-1} \varphi_{ij}(z) \circ \varphi_{ij}(x). \tag{8}$$

The advantage of the SiamFC architecture is that, we can easily calculate the similarity at all translation of a candidate image using the cross convolution operation. The candidate image x is much larger than the exemplar image z. The similarity at all translation of the candidate image can be calculated using (9),

$$f(z, x) = \varphi(z) * \varphi(x) + b1. \tag{9}$$

where $*$ is the general convolution operation, $b1$ is the bias which takes value $b \in R$ in every location. The $f(z, x)$ is a score map that represents the similarity of each translation. In the tracking procedure, the position of maximum score in the score map is the center of the object and therefore we can easily locate the object.

As a visual tracking task, the similarity of background and foreground should be low, while the similarity of the same object in the different frames of one video sequence should be high. Therefore, the network can be trained using the logistic loss $\ell(y, v) = \log(1 + \exp(-yv))$, where $y \in \{+1, -1\}$ is the groundtruth label and v is the similarity score of a single exemplar-candidate pair. The output of the network is a score map $f(z, x)$ and therefore we define the loss of the whole network as the mean of the individual losses,

$$L(y, f) = \frac{1}{|\mathcal{D}|} \sum_{u \in \mathcal{D}} \ell(y[u], f[u]), \tag{10}$$

where $y[u]$ represents the groundtruth label for each position $u \in \mathcal{D}$ in the score map and $f[u]$ represents the similarity score for each position in the score map.

The training samples are the exemplar-candidate pairs from a dataset of annotated videos. The exemplar-candidate pairs are extracted from two frames of a video with the object at the center of the image. Assuming the size of the object is (w, h), the exemplar image is croped from the original image with the size $(w + 2p) \times (h + 2p)$, $p = \frac{(w+h)}{4}$ is an added margin for context. Then the exemplar image is resized to 127×127 pixels. The size of search image is twice (255×255 pixels) than the exemplar image.

The object is at the center of the image; therefore the closer to the center, the greater the similarity to the object becomes. The elements in the score map are considered to be the positive example if they are within radius R of the center.

$$y[u] = \begin{cases} +1 & \text{if } \|u - c\| \leq R \\ -1 & \text{otherwise} \end{cases}. \tag{11}$$

3.3 Multi-task Learning and Correlation Filter Attention Tracking

To make the network benefit from both the shallow and deep features of the neural network, we jointly train two tasks: the correlation filter and the embedding similarity learning. The correlation filter is trained using the shallow features of the neural network, while the embedding similarity learning uses the deep feautres of the neural network. The multi-task loss function of our whole network is (12):

$$\ell_{all} = \lambda \ell_{cf} + \ell_{similarity\_learning}, \tag{12}$$

where ℓ_{cf} is the loss of correlation filter layer, $\ell_{similarity\_learning}$ is the loss of embedding similarity learning (10) and $\lambda > 0$ is a constant to balance between the two tasks. Moreover, the size of correlation filter must be the same as the size of search image and the size of search image is twice the size of the exemplar image in the embedding similarity learning. Therefore, in the multi-task learning there are some differences from the embedding similarity learning process. At first, the exemplar image is croped from the original image with size $2(w + 2p) \times 2(h+2p)$. Then the exemplar image is resized to 255×255 pixels and therefore we can get a exemplar image the same size as search image. Thirdly, the exemplar image and search image are used to train the correlation filter. At last, we make a center cropped in the exemplar image with size 127×127 pixels to get the image patch which is used for the embedding similarity learning.

For the ease of expression, the output of correlation filter layer is defined as O_{cf} and the score map is defined as O_s. In order to make a more accurate localization, we upsampling the score map 16X using bicubic interpolation in the tracking procedure. We make a combination of O_{cf} and $O_s^{upsampling}$ to help the final score map locate the object more accurately. The final response of the network is formulated as $O_{final} = \theta O_{cf} + O_s^{upsampling}$, where θ is a constant to control the weight of O_{cf} in the final response. If we only use the score map $O_s^{upsampling}$, the algorithm will drift to the similar objects easily. The network will pay more attention to the object being tracked through this way and the above drawback can be overcome.

In the tracking procedure, the $\varphi(z)$ in (9) is only calculated in the first frame and not updated during tracking. The correlation filter $\hat{\omega}_i$ in (2) is updated online like the standard DCF [11]: $\hat{\omega}_i^t = \eta \hat{\omega}_i + (1 - \eta)\hat{\omega}_i^{t-1}$, where η is the constant learning rate.

4 Experiments

In this section, first we introduce the implementation details of our tracker, then we analyse the contribution to the performance of each component of our tracker through the results of the ablation experiments. The results on OTB2013, OTB2015, VOT2017 demonstrate the effectiveness and robustness of our approach.

4.1 Implementation Details

The Training Dataset. To avoid the over-fitting, the training and testing should not be performed on the same data. We use the data from object detection from video of ImageNet Large Scale Visual Recognition Challenge (ILSVRC2015) [19] as our training dataset. This dataset is widely used by many trackers [2,9,10,15,22–24,27]. In each video of an object, we collect each pair of frames within the nearest 100 frames.

Training. The first ten convolutional layers of our network are initialized using pre-trained VGG-16 model on ImageNet. We apply stochastic gradient descent (SGD) with momentum of 0.9 to train the network and the weight of L2-regularization is set to 0.0005. The learning rate is annealed geometrically at each epoch from 10^{-3} to 10^{-6}. The training is performed for 50 epochs with a mini-batch size of 8. The λ in the (12) is set to 5. The radius R in the (11) is set to 2.

Tracking. To make the tracker adapt to the scale variations of object, we use the scale pyramid in the similar way to the original SiamFC [2]. The θ in the correlation filter attention tracking is set to 0.11 and does not change during tracking, the learning rate η of correlation filter is set to 0.1.

The proposed tracker is implemented on Python with the PyTorch and all the experiments are executed on the server with Intel(R) Xeon(R) Silver 4114 CPU @ 2.2 GHz and a NVIDIA GeForce RTX 2080Ti GPU.

4.2 Ablation Experiments

Our tracker uses three important components to improve the performance of SiamFC including the VGGNet as the backbone (Backbone), the joint training of correlation filter and embedding similarity learning (MT) and the correlation filter attention tracking (AT). We evaluate their contributions by checking the performance of the tracker when the examined component is missing. The trackers are evaluated on the benchmark of OTB2015 [26]. The results are shown in Table 1. The AUC is improved 3.1% by using the VGGNet as the backbone. The VGGNet is deeper than the AlexNet which provides more robust and discriminative features for the tracker. It gains most in the three components which proves features are the most important for the tracking algorithms. The multi-task learning improves 1.9% AUC. The joint training of the correlation filter and the embedding similarity learning makes the network benefit from both the shallow and deep features of neural network. The details of shallow features and the semantic information of deep features are both used. Moreover, the multi-task learning prevents the network to be over-fitted. The correlation filter attention tracking improves 1.5% AUC. The correlation filter is used as an attention module. This method further improves the discriminating ability of the network for similar objects and reduces the possibility of object drift.

Table 1. The results of ablation experiments

	AUC	OP	DP	FPS
SiamFC	58.2	70.2	77.1	**63**
SiamFC + Backbone	61.3	75.6	81.4	42
SiamFC + Backbone + MT	63.2	77.9	83.8	42
MT-SiamFC_CF	**64.7**	**80.9**	**86.4**	30

4.3   Comparison Results

OTB2013 and OTB2015 Dataset. The OTB2013 [25] and OTB2015 [26] are two commonly used online tracking benchmarks. OTB2013 has 51 realworld sequences. The OTB2015 adds 49 more challenging video sequences on the basis of OTB2013. It has a higher requirement on the robustness of trackers. Both OTB2013 and OTB2015 use bounding box overlap ratio and center location error as their metrics. The precision and success plots can be acquired by setting success threshold for each metric.

We use 9 state-of-the-art trackers to compare with our tracker. The CREST [21] is a deep tracker. The SiamFC [2] and CFNet [22] are the trackers based on the siamese network. The ECO [4] and SRDCF_deep [6] both use the deep features under the framework of the correlation filter. The SRDCF [7], ECO-hc [4], DSST [5], Staple [1] are the four outstanding trackers using the hand-craft features. As shown in Fig. 3, the MTSiamFC_CF achieves second best performance in success plots. In OTB2013, the MT-SiamFC_CF is slightly lower than the CREST [21] in precision plots, but a lot higher than the CREST in OTB2015. Since the OTB2015 is more difficult, it can be proved that our tracker is more robust than the CREST. Only the ECO [4] has a better performance than our trackers, but the speed of ECO is only 2–3 FPS while our tracker can be in real time. Our tracker has achieved relative improvement of 11.2%, 11.4% on the AUC over SiamFC in the OTB2013 and OTB2015 respectively. The results can prove that our approach is effective and maintains the real-time speed of the original SiamFC.

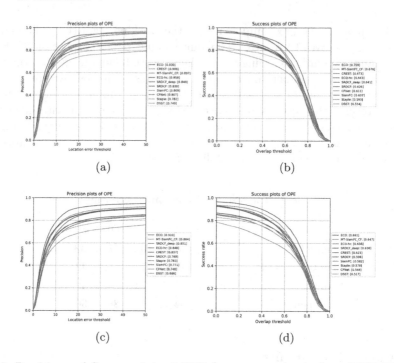

Fig. 3. Precision and Success plots of OPE (one pass evaluation) on OTB2013 and OTB2015 respectively. The numbers in the legend indicate the representative precisions at 20 pixels for precision plots and the AUC score for success plots, respectively.

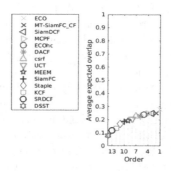

Fig. 4. Expected average overlap (EAO) ranking on VOT2017. We only show a part of trackers in this figure for clarity.

VOT2017 Dataset. Visual object tracking challenge is the most famous competition in visual tracking. The sequences are also used as the benchmark for evaluating the object tracking algorithms. VOT2017 has 60 sequences. The expected average overlap (EAO) considering both the bounding box overlap and the robustness of the trackers is the major evaluation metric on VOT2017. As shown in Fig. 4, only the ECO [4] has a higher EAO than our tracker but cannot be in real time. Compared with our baseline tracker SiamFC, our tracker can surpass its EAO by 33%. The results prove that our tracker is an outstanding real-time tracker. The using of VGGNet, multi-task learning and correlation filter attention tracking can overcome the drawbacks of original SiamFC.

5 Conclusion

In this work, we have improved SiamFC in three ways: (a) using the pretrained VGGNet as our backbone (b) jointly training the correlation filter and the embedding similarity learning (c) the correlation filter attention tracking. These three methods make the network benefit from both the shallow and deep features of the neural network and strengthen the ability of SiamFC to distinguish between similar objects. In evaluation experiments, our method can achieve leading performance in OTB2013, OTB2015 and VOT2017 while operating in real time.

References

1. Bertinetto, L., Valmadre, J., Golodetz, S., Miksik, O., Torr, P.: Staple: complementary learners for real-time tracking. In: Computer Vision & Pattern Recognition (2016)
2. Bertinetto, L., Valmadre, J., Henriques, J.F., Vedaldi, A., Torr, P.H.S.: Fully-convolutional siamese networks for object tracking. In: European Conference on Computer Vision (2016)
3. Bolme, D.S., Beveridge, J.R., Draper, B.A., Lui, Y.M.: Visual object tracking using adaptive correlation filters. In: Computer Vision & Pattern Recognition (2010)
4. Danelljan, M., Bhat, G., Shahbaz Khan, F., Felsberg, M.: ECO: efficient convolution operators for tracking. In: Proceedings of the IEEE Conference on Computer Vision and Pattern Recognition, pp. 6638–6646 (2017)
5. Danelljan, M., Häger, G., Khan, F.S., Felsberg, M.: Discriminative scale space tracking. IEEE Trans. Pattern Anal. Mach. Intell. **39**(8), 1561–1575 (2017)
6. Danelljan, M., Hager, G., Shahbaz Khan, F., Felsberg, M.: Convolutional features for correlation filter based visual tracking. In: Proceedings of the IEEE International Conference on Computer Vision Workshops, pp. 58–66 (2015)
7. Danelljan, M., Hager, G., Shahbaz Khan, F., Felsberg, M.: Learning spatially regularized correlation filters for visual tracking. In: Proceedings of the IEEE International Conference on Computer Vision, pp. 4310–4318 (2015)
8. Danelljan, M., Robinson, A., Shahbaz Khan, F., Felsberg, M.: Beyond correlation filters: learning continuous convolution operators for visual tracking. In: Leibe, B., Matas, J., Sebe, N., Welling, M. (eds.) ECCV 2016. LNCS, vol. 9909, pp. 472–488. Springer, Cham (2016). https://doi.org/10.1007/978-3-319-46454-1_29
9. Guo, Q., Feng, W., Zhou, C., Huang, R., Wan, L., Wang, S.: Learning dynamic siamese network for visual object tracking. In: Proceedings of the IEEE International Conference on Computer Vision, pp. 1763–1771 (2017)
10. He, A., Luo, C., Tian, X., Zeng, W.: A twofold siamese network for real-time object tracking. In: Proceedings of the IEEE Conference on Computer Vision and Pattern Recognition, pp. 4834–4843 (2018)

11. Henriques, J.F., Caseiro, R., Martins, P., Batista, J.: Exploiting the circulant structure of tracking-by-detection with kernels. In: Fitzgibbon, A., Lazebnik, S., Perona, P., Sato, Y., Schmid, C. (eds.) ECCV 2012. LNCS, vol. 7575, pp. 702–715. Springer, Heidelberg (2012). https://doi.org/10.1007/978-3-642-33765-9_50

12. Henriques, J.F., Caseiro, R., Martins, P., Batista, J.: High-speed tracking with kernelized correlation filters. IEEE Trans. Pattern Anal. Mach. Intell. **37**(3), 583–596 (2015)

13. Kristan, M., et al.: A novel performance evaluation methodology for single-target trackers. IEEE Trans. Pattern Anal. Mach. Intell. **38**(11), 2137–2155 (2016)

14. Krizhevsky, A., Sutskever, I., Hinton, G.E.: Imagenet classification with deep convolutional neural networks. In: Advances in Neural Information Processing Systems, pp. 1097–1105 (2012)

15. Li, B., Yan, J., Wu, W., Zhu, Z., Hu, X.: High performance visual tracking with siamese region proposal network. In: Proceedings of the IEEE Conference on Computer Vision and Pattern Recognition, pp. 8971–8980 (2018)

16. Ma, C., Huang, J.B., Yang, X., Yang, M.H.: Hierarchical convolutional features for visual tracking. In: Proceedings of the IEEE International Conference on Computer Vision, pp. 3074–3082 (2015)

17. Nam, H., Han, B.: Learning multi-domain convolutional neural networks for visual tracking. In: Proceedings of the IEEE Conference on Computer Vision and Pattern Recognition, pp. 4293–4302 (2016)

18. Ren, S., He, K., Girshick, R., Sun, J.: Faster R-CNN: towards real-time object detection with region proposal networks. In: Advances in Neural Information Processing Systems, pp. 91–99 (2015)

19. Russakovsky, O., et al.: Imagenet large scale visual recognition challenge. Int. J. Comput. Vision **115**(3), 211–252 (2015)

20. Simonyan, K., Zisserman, A.: Very deep convolutional networks for large-scale image recognition. arXiv preprint arXiv:1409.1556 (2014)

21. Song, Y., Ma, C., Gong, L., Zhang, J., Lau, R.W., Yang, M.H.: CREST: convolutional residual learning for visual tracking. In: Proceedings of the IEEE International Conference on Computer Vision, pp. 2555–2564 (2017)

22. Valmadre, J., Bertinetto, L., Henriques, J., Vedaldi, A., Torr, P.H.: End-to-end representation learning for correlation filter based tracking. In: Proceedings of the IEEE Conference on Computer Vision and Pattern Recognition, pp. 2805–2813 (2017)

23. Wang, Q., Gao, J., Xing, J., Zhang, M., Hu, W.: DCFNet: discriminant correlation filters network for visual tracking. arXiv preprint arXiv:1704.04057 (2017)

24. Wang, Q., Teng, Z., Xing, J., Gao, J., Hu, W., Maybank, S.: Learning attentions: residual attentional siamese network for high performance online visual tracking. In: Proceedings of the IEEE Conference on Computer Vision and Pattern Recognition, pp. 4854–4863 (2018)

25. Wu, Y., Lim, J., Yang, M.H.: Online object tracking: a benchmark. In: Proceedings of the IEEE Conference on Computer Vision and Pattern Recognition, pp. 2411–2418 (2013)

26. Wu, Y., Lim, J., Yang, M.H.: Object tracking benchmark. IEEE Trans. Pattern Anal. Mach. Intell. **37**(9), 1834–1848 (2015)

27. Zhu, Z., Wu, W., Zou, W., Yan, J.: End-to-end flow correlation tracking with spatial-temporal attention. In: Proceedings of the IEEE Conference on Computer Vision and Pattern Recognition, pp. 548–557 (2018)

Table Detection Using Boundary Refining via Corner Locating

Ningning Sun, Yuanping Zhu[✉], and Xiaoming Hu

Tianjin Normal University, No. 393 Binshuixi Road, Xiqing District, Tianjin, China
zhuyuanping@tjnu.edu.cn

Abstract. Table detection based on bounding-box method has achieved remarkable results. However, there still exists inaccurate table boundary locating. In this paper, a table detection method is proposed. Firstly, coarse table detection is implemented through Faster R-CNN. Secondly, corner locating is implemented through RPN and refined through Fast R-CNN. Corner grouping and filtering are implemented through post-processing algorithms. Therefore, unreliable corners are filtered. Thirdly, table boundaries are refined via reliable corners. Experimental results show that the proposed method obviously improves the precision of table boundary locating. We test on ICDAR2017 POD dataset, our method achieves an F-measure of 95.3%. Compared to Faster R-CNN method, the proposed method significantly increases by 3.2% in F-measure. Moreover, our method increases by 3.3% at pixel-level localization.

Keywords: Table detection · Corner locating · Table boundary refining

1 Introduction

Table detection has always been one of the most active research areas in layout analysis. Table detection is a challenge due to external and internal factors. External factors come from the environment, such as noise, blur, illumination, tilt and occlusion. There are some measures taken in weakening the interference, such as denoising, deblurring [1], illumination preprocessing [2], tilt refining [3], etc. Internal factors come from the attributes and changes of tables, such as, complex layout structure, table diversity, the interference of background. The factors mentioned above increase the difficulty of table detection.

So far, the methods used by people for table detection mainly include traditional methods and deep learning based methods. Traditional methods mainly include shape-based methods [4–6] and texture-based methods [7,8]. Shape-based methods are divided into top-down method [4], bottom-up method [5] and hybrid method [6]. Texture-based methods are divided into model-based method, feature-based method [7] and multiscale-based method [8]. Due to the limitation of traditional methods, it is gradually being replaced by deep learning based methods [9–11]. Deep learning based methods mainly include semantic

© Springer Nature Switzerland AG 2019
Z. Lin et al. (Eds.): PRCV 2019, LNCS 11857, pp. 135–146, 2019.
https://doi.org/10.1007/978-3-030-31654-9_12

Top-left corner 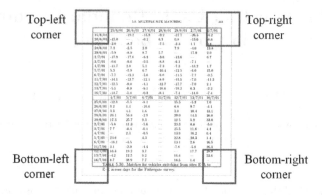 Top-right corner

Bottom-left corner Bottom-right corner

Fig. 1. The red bounding-boxes are corners and the green bounding-box is a table. (Color figure online)

segmentation method [9] and bounding-box based method [10,11]. Semantic segmentation method can classify each pixel. Therefore, it is suitable for natural scene detection instead of table detection. For example, Mask R-CNN [9] is a typical semantic segmentation method. Bounding-box based method can predict object box and is suitable for table detection. However, current technologies are still immature and need constant improvement.

In this paper, we propose a novel method called table detection using boundary refining via corner locating. The corners we mentioned refer to table corners (shown in Fig. 1). Compared to the previous methods, our method solves the problem of inaccurate table boundary locating. We have tested our method on a public dataset ICDAR2017 POD dataset [12]. According to the experimental results, the proposed method shows the best performance compared to several baselines, such as Faster R-CNN [10] and SSD [11].

The paper is organized as follows: we introduce related work and progress of table detection in Sect. 2. The methodology of table detection is then presented in the next section. In Sect. 4, experimental details, dataset and experimental results are described in details. Finally, we summarize in Sect. 5.

2 Related Work

Traditional Table Detection Methods. Table detection plays an important role, so people have done a lot of work in the field. Kieninger [13,14] takes the lead in doing basic work on table detection. However, his method is only applicable to specific tables. Subsequently, a new table detection method is proposed in [15] by detecting horizontal and vertical lines and determining the area surrounded by lines. In order to reduce the mistakes of candidate area, [16] adds intersect points detection. Inspired by [15,16], we think of refining table through table boundaries. Traditional table detection methods have made great progress. Meanwhile, there exists many problems, such as error detection and missed detection.

Deep Learning Based Methods. Table detection based on deep learning method is the trend nowadays. R-CNN (Region CNN) [17] takes the first step on deep learning based methods, but brings redundant computation problems. Girshick draws on the idea of SPP-net (Spatial Pyramid Pooling) [18] and proposes Fast R-CNN [19]. Fast R-CNN improves R-CNN by designing a special pooling layer. Subsequently, Faster R-CNN [10] emerges and introduces RPN (region proposal network). Faster R-CNN exponentially reduces computation complexity while also prevailing in speed and accuracy. Faster R-CNN based table detection is implemented in [20] and achieves good results.

Corners Based Detection Methods. Corners based detection methods is novel in object detection. In the DeNet [21] model, the RPN of Faster R-CNN is replaced by a corner detection layer and an analytical sampling layer. PLN (Point Linking Network) is proposed in [22], which regresses the bounding box and corresponding corner/center point. Lyu et al. [23] implement multi-oriented scene text detection with the help of corner localization and region segmentation. CornerNet model is represented in [24] for the purpose of detecting nature scene. The application of corners inspires us to use corners in table boundary refining.

3 Methodology

3.1 System Framework

In the network, we combine corner locating and table boundary refining methods. The network can predict four sets in representing the different location of table corners, one for the top-left corners, one for the top-right corners, one for the bottom-left corners and the other for the bottom-right corners. Through filtering unreliable corner groups, we could use reliable corners to refine table boundaries. The proposed method is also applicable to other datasets.

The framework is shown in Fig. 2. Table detection and corner locating are implemented through Faster R-CNN [10]. Then we apply post-processing algorithms to filter unreliable corner groups. Finally, table boundaries are adjusted and refined via reliable corners.

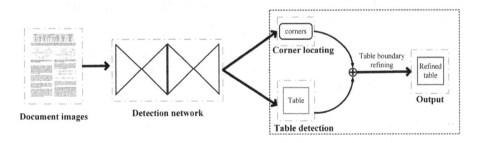

Fig. 2. System framework.

3.2   Table Detection

Table detection is implemented through Faster R-CNN. The process is divided into two steps, coarse table detection and table boundary refining. Firstly, document images are sent to Faster R-CNN. The backbone network is VGG16, followed by RPN and Fast R-CNN (shown in Fig. 3). VGG16 extracts feature maps from the input document images. Then feature maps are sent to RPN. RPN is used to generate region proposals. This layer uses softmax to determine that the anchors belong to the foreground or background, and then regresses the anchors to obtain accurate proposals. Through above steps, coarse table detection is implemented.

Secondly, the feature maps and the RoIs (Region of Interest) generated by the RPN are fed together to the RoI pooling layer. The layer generates fixed-size feature maps. Fast R-CNN acts as a detector to perform finer classification and location refining of the feature maps. Finally, feature maps are sent to the subsequent fully connected layer for object category determination.

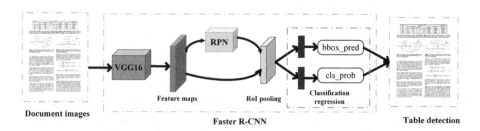

Fig. 3. Table detection network. The backbone network VGG16 is followed by two networks, RPN for coarse detection, Fast R-CNN for refining.

3.3   Corner Locating

Corner locating is implemented by corner detection, corner grouping and corner filtering. The process is shown in Fig. 4.

Corner Detection. Corner detection is implemented through RPN and slightly adjusted through Fast R-CNN [19]. Through refining, we obtain the accurate spatial location of corners. We name the corners belonging to the same table *corner1*, *corner2*, *corner3* and *corner4* respectively (in a clockwise direction). For convenience, they are abbreviated as $C1$, $C2$, $C3$ and $C4$. We refer to the corner group algorithm of CornerNet [24] and then apply post-processing algorithms to filter unreliable corner groups.

Corner Grouping. We hypothesize that corners belonging to the same table are respectively $C1(x_1, y_1)$, $C2(x_2, y_2)$, $C3(x_3, y_3)$ and $C4(x_4, y_4)$. Corner group determines a bounding-box. For convenience, we call the bounding-box R, described as:

$$R = \{C_i'(x_i', y_i') | i\epsilon\{1, 2\}\} \tag{1}$$

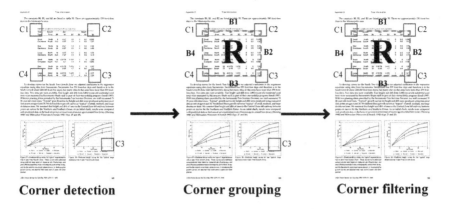

Corner detection   **Corner grouping**   **Corner filtering**

Fig. 4. An example of corner detection, grouping and filtering. The red bounding-boxes are corners and the green bounding-box is R. (Color figure online)

$$\begin{cases} x_1' = (x_1 + x_4)/2 \\ y_1' = (y_1 + y_2)/2 \\ x_2' = (x_2 + x_3)/2 \\ y_2' = (y_3 + y_4)/2 \end{cases} \tag{2}$$

Each corner group has a location constraint relationship. $C1$ and $C2$ are on the same horizontal table boundary, $C1$ and $C4$ are on the same vertical table boundary, etc. Adjacent corners that belong to the same table are named as corner pair. The prerequisites of corner pair are:

$$|(x_i - x_j)| \leq z \qquad \{i = 1, j = 4\} \quad or \quad \{i = 2, j = 3\} \tag{3}$$

$$|(y_i - y_j)| \leq z \qquad \{i = 1, j = 2\} \quad or \quad \{i = 3, j = 4\} \tag{4}$$

in which, z is related to image size. $z = \sqrt{\theta wh}$ ($0.0002 \leq \theta \leq 0.0005$), image is of size $w \times h$. Corner pair whose deviation more than z is rejected.

Corner Filtering. We hypothesize that boundaries link $C1$ and $C2$, $C2$ and $C3$, $C3$ and $C4$, $C1$ and $C4$ named $B1$, $B2$, $B3$ and $B4$ respectively. For each $B1$, there maybe multiple $B3$s that can match. This means that for each $C1$, there maybe multiple $C4$ that can match. Similarly, $C2$ and $C3$ will do the same. IOU (Intersection over Union) is used to exclude interference corners. For convenience, the table detected by RPN is called T. If IOU(R, T) is lower than the threshold we set (the default is 0.4), then those corner groups are filtered.

3.4   Table Boundary Refining

Observing table documents, we found that the upper and lower boundaries of table detection are basically accurate apart from the left and right boundaries. Therefore, we only take measures to refine left and right boundaries of tables.

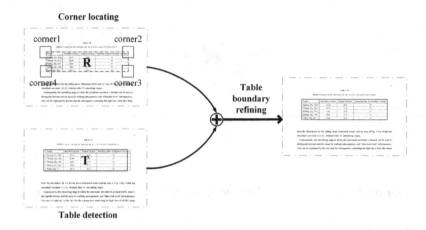

Fig. 5. An example of table boundary refining on ICDAR2017 POD dataset.

The more reliable $B2$ and $B4$, the more accurate table boundary locating. T is expressed as:

$$T = \{C_i''(x_i'', y_i'') | i \epsilon \{1, 2\}\} \qquad (5)$$

C_i'' is the vertex coordinate of detected table. The process of table boundary refining is shown in Fig. 5. The steps of table boundary refining are explained as follows:

– Reliable boundary checking. We hypothesize $angle1$ represents left deviation angle of $C1$ and $C4$, $angle2$ represents right deviation angle of $C2$ and $C3$, as shown in Fig. 6. Though there exists deviation error on left boundary of R (Fig. 6(a)), which plays a positive role in table boundary refining (Fig. 6(b)). This indicates that table boundaries can be refined via corner locating. The formulas of $angle1$ and $angle2$ are:

$$angle1 = \left| 90 - \left| \arctan\frac{(y_4 - y_1)}{(x_1 - x_4)} * \frac{180}{\pi} \right| \right| \qquad (6)$$

$$angle2 = \left| 90 - \left| \arctan\frac{(y_3 - y_2)}{(x_2 - x_3)} * \frac{180}{\pi} \right| \right| \qquad (7)$$

– Table refining via reliable boundaries. We hypothesize that (x_1', y_1', x_2', y_2'), $(x_1'', y_1'', x_2'', y_2'')$, $(x_1^*, y_1^*, x_2^*, y_2^*)$ represents the coordinates of R, T and $refined$ $table$ respectively. The calculation formulas are:

$$\begin{cases} x_1^* = \alpha x_1'' + (1 - \alpha)x_1' \\ y_1^* = y_1'' \\ x_2^* = \alpha x_2'' + (1 - \alpha)x_2' \\ y_2^* = y_2'' \end{cases} \qquad (8)$$

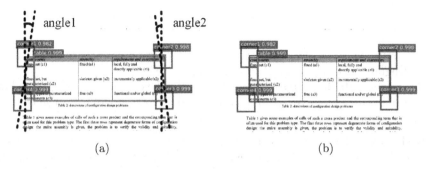

Fig. 6. Definition of deviation angles. (a) The red bounding-boxes are corners and the green bounding-box is a table. (b) The big red bounding-box is a refined table. (Color figure online)

The confidence factor α reflects the reliability of left and right boundaries of R. Deviation angle distribution histogram is shown in Fig. 7. Deviation angle is called t. We find that t more than 10 degrees only takes up a few. According to empirical rules, we set the threshold to 10 degrees. The function is derived from the sigmoid function, mapping variables between 0 and 1, defined as:

$$\alpha(t) = \frac{1}{1 + e^{\frac{10-t}{2}}} \tag{9}$$

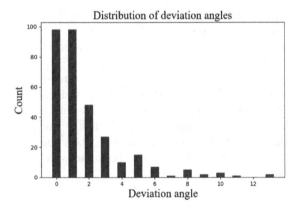

Fig. 7. Distribution of deviation angles.

3.5   Loss Function

Our method follows the spirit of Faster R-CNN [10]. It consists of two parts, classification loss and regression loss. Our method adopts the same multi-task loss on each sampled RoI as:

$$L = L_{cls} + L_{box}. \tag{10}$$

(1) L_{cls} represents the classification loss of classification layer. It plays a role in distinguishing foreground and background.

(2) L_{box} represents the regression loss of regression layer, which is used to predict the coordinates x, y, w and h of the proposal corresponding to the central anchor point.

Each sampled RoI is labeled with a ground-truth class p_i^* and predicted class p_i. We use a vector t_i^* representing ground-truth box coordinates and t_i representing the 4 parameterized coordinates of the predicted bounding box. The classification loss L_{cls} is expressed as:

$$L_{cls}(p_i, p_i^*) = -\log[p_i p_i^* + (1 - p_i^*)(1 - t_i^*)] \tag{11}$$

Where L_{cls} is implied the loss of foreground and background. The regression loss L_{reg} is expressed as:

$$L_{reg}(t_i, t_i^*) = Q(t_i - t_i^*) \tag{12}$$

Where Q is the robust loss function (smooth L1) defined in [19].

4   Experiment

4.1   Experimental Details

The experiment is trained in tensorflow 1.3.0 environment. Training the end-to-end version of network with GTX1080Ti, 11G of GPU memory is sufficient. During training, we set the input resolution to $600 \times h$ ($h \leq 1000$) and output resolution to 1200×1200 in the network. To reduce overfitting, we use random horizontally-flipped images for data augmentation.

We use a mini-batch size of 10 and 0.9 momentum to train the network, starting from a learning rate of 0.0001 and slowly reducing. The corner size is set to a fixed value (according to image size). Model continues to train for 80 k iterations. We put the bounding-boxes of all five branches together and apply non-maximum suppression to refine the object bounding-box. For detected tables, we use reliable corners to refine table boundaries, which promotes table detection precision.

4.2   Dataset

We choose the open dataset of ICDAR 2017 Page Object Detection Competition dataset [12]. Peking University rigorously labels such dataset. ICDAR2017 POD competition officially provides 792 (including tables) scanned document images, which contains 549 images for training and 243 images for testing. The dataset not only has complex page layout but also includes partial pixel loss. Therefore, those factors lead to higher difficulty in table detection. In order to verify the effectiveness of our method, we comprehensively evaluate our method on such dataset.

4.3   Experimental Result

Table 1 comprehensively compares between the proposed method and all results for latest. Please refer to the evaluation metrics of the ICDAR2017 POD competition. IOU (Intersection-over-Union) is set to 0.6, and the evaluation metrics including precision, recall and F-measure. We notice that SSD and CNN are not suitable for table detection. Faster R-CNN has achieved good result in table detection, but it doesn't achieve ideal result. Table 1 shows that the proposed method achieves the best result on ICDAR2017 POD dataset with F-measure of 95.3%.

Table 1. ICDAR2017 POD dataset test results.

Method head	Precision	Recall	F-measure
SSD [11]	0.071	0.959	0.132
CNN [17]	0.230	0.221	0.225
Faster R-CNN(VGG_CNN_M_1024) [10]	0.670	0.940	0.782
Faster R-CNN + edge_based information [12]	0.842	0.890	0.865
Faster R-CNN(VGG16)	0.924	0.918	0.921
Our method	**0.952**	**0.954**	**0.953**

As a further comparison, Faster R-CNN (VGG16) method and our method are trained for comparative experiments. We implement both methods and evaluate them. IOU indicates comparison at pixel-level localization. Table 2 indicates that the proposed method significantly increases by 3.2% in F-measure and 3.3% at pixel accurate. The evaluation metrics precision, recall and F-measure are the same as Table 1.

Table 2. Table boundary precision evaluation.

Method head	Precision	Recall	F-measure	IOU
Faster R-CNN(VGG16)	0.924	0.918	0.921	0.811
Our method	**0.952**	**0.954**	**0.953**	**0.844**

Comparative examples of Faster R-CNN (VGG16) method and our method are shown in Fig. 8(a) and (c) indicate that table detection based on Faster R-CNN method is inaccurate. (b) and (d) indicate that table detection based on the proposed method is accurate.

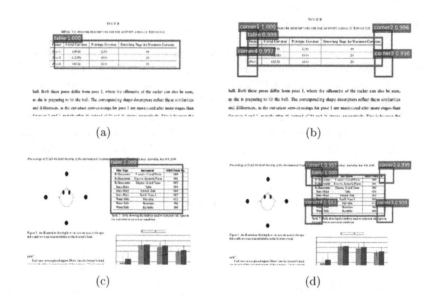

Fig. 8. Examples of table detection results on ICDAR2017 POD dataset. (a), (c): examples based on Faster R-CNN(VGG16) method; (b), (d): examples based on our method.

5   Conclusion

In this paper, we present a coarse-to-fine method for table detection. Our method takes advantage of corners in table boundary refining. Firstly, Faster R-CNN architecture is used to get coarse table detection and corner locating. Secondly, we apply post-processing algorithms to filter unreliable corners. Reliable corners are used to adjust and refine table boundaries. We conducts experiments on ICDAR2017 POD dataset, our method performs the best in all results for latest. Compared to Faster R-CNN method, the proposed method significantly increases by 3.2% in F-measure and 3.3% at pixel-level localization.

The proposed method has achieved the best result, but some problems still exist. Firstly, it is necessary to improve the accuracy of corner locating. Secondly, post-processing algorithms are too restrictive. We will continue to improve our method and make more achievements in the following work.

Acknowledgment. This work was supported by the Natural Science Foundation of Tianjin (Grant No. 18JCYBJC85000).

References

1. Sankhe, P.D., Patil, M., Margaret, M.: Deblurring of grayscale images using inverse and Wiener filter. In: International Conference & Workshop on Emerging Trends in Technology, pp. 145–148. ACM (2011)

2. Antal, G., Martinez, R., Csonka, F., Sbert, M., Szirmay-Kalos, L.: Combining global and local global-illumination algorithms. In: 19th Spring Conference on Computer Graphics, pp. 185–192. ACM (2003)

3. Rahman, M., Gustafson, S., Irani, P., Subramanian, S.: Tilt techniques: investigating the dexterity of wrist-based input. In: 27th International Conference on Human Factors in Computing Systems, Boston, MA, USA, pp. 1943–1952. ACM (2009)

4. Chang, F., Chu, S.Y., Chen, C.Y.: Chinese document layout analysis using an adaptive regrouping strategy. Pattern Recogn. **38**(2), 261–271 (2005)

5. Xi, J., Hu, J., Wu, L.: Page segmentation of Chinese newspapers. Pattern Recogn. **35**(12), 2695–2704 (2002)

6. Ha, J., Phillips, I.T., Haralick, R.M.: Document page decomposition using bounding boxes of connected components of black pixels. In: Proceedings of SPIE - The International Society for Optical Engineering, pp. 140–151 (1995)

7. Sauvola, J., Pietikainen, M.: Page segmentation and classification using fast feature extraction and connectivity analysis. In: 3rd International Conference on Document Analysis and Recognition, pp. 1127–1131. IEEE (1995)

8. Etemad, K., Doermann, D., Chellappa, R.: Multiscale segmentation of unstructured document pages using soft decision integration. IEEE Trans. Pattern Anal. Mach. Intell. **19**(1), 92–96 (1997)

9. He, K., Gkioxari, G., Dollr, P., Girshick, R.: Mask R-CNN. In: IEEE International Conference on Computer Vision, pp. 2961–2969 (2017)

10. Ren, S., He, K., Girshick, R., Sun, J.: Faster R-CNN: towards real-time object detection with region proposal networks. In: Advances in Neural Information Processing Systems, pp. 91–99 (2015)

11. Liu, W., et al.: SSD: single shot multibox detector. In: Leibe, B., Matas, J., Sebe, N., Welling, M. (eds.) ECCV 2016. LNCS, vol. 9905, pp. 21–37. Springer, Cham (2016). https://doi.org/10.1007/978-3-319-46448-0_2

12. Gao, L., Yi, X., Jiang, Z., Hao, L., Tang, Z.: ICDAR 2017 competition on page object detection. In: 14th IAPR International Conference on Document Analysis and Recognition, pp. 1417–1422. IEEE (2017)

13. Kieninger, T., Dengel, A.: Table recognition and labeling using intrinsic layout features. In: Singh, S. (ed.) International Conference on Advances in Pattern Recognition, pp. 307–316. Springer, London (1999). https://doi.org/10.1007/978-1-4471-0833-7_31

14. Kieninger, T., Dengel, A.: Applying the T-RECS table recognition system to the business letter domain. In: 6th International Conference on Document Analysis and Recognition, pp. 518–522. IEEE (2001)

15. Cesarini, F., Marinai, S., Sarti, L., Soda, G.: Trainable table location in document images. In: International Conference on Pattern Recognition, pp. 236–240. IEEE (2002)

16. Gatos, B., Danatsas, D., Pratikakis, I., Perantonis, S.J.: Automatic table detection in document images. In: Singh, S., Singh, M., Apte, C., Perner, P. (eds.) ICAPR 2005. LNCS, vol. 3686, pp. 609–618. Springer, Heidelberg (2005). https://doi.org/10.1007/11551188_67

17. Girshick, R., Donahue, J., Darrell, T., Malik, J.: Rich feature hierarchies for accurate object detection and semantic segmentation. In: IEEE Conference on Computer Vision and Pattern Recognition, pp. 580–587. IEEE Computer Society (2014)

18. He, K., Zhang, X., Ren, S., Sun, J.: Spatial pyramid pooling in deep convolutional networks for visual recognition. IEEE Trans. Pattern Anal. Mach. Intell. **37**(9), 1904–1916 (2014)

19. Girshick, R.: Fast R-CNN. In: IEEE International Conference on Computer Vision, pp. 1440–1448 (2015)
20. Vo, N.D., Nguyen, K., Nguyen, T.V., Nguyen, K.: Ensemble of deep object detectors for page object detection. In: 12th International Conference on Ubiquitous Information Management and Communication, p. 11. ACM (2018)
21. Tychsen-Smith, L., Petersson, L.: DeNet: scalable real-time object detection with directed sparse sampling. In: IEEE International Conference on Computer Vision (ICCV), pp. 428–436. IEEE Computer Society (2017)
22. Wang, X., Chen, K., Huang, Z., Yao, C., Liu, W.: Point linking network for object detection. arXiv preprint arXiv:1706.03646 (2017)
23. Lyu, P., Yao, C., Wu, W., Yan, S., Bai, X.: Multi-oriented scene text detection via corner localization and region segmentation. In: IEEE Conference on Computer Vision and Pattern Recognition, pp. 7553–7563 (2018)
24. Law, H., Deng, J.: CornerNet: detecting objects as paired keypoints. In: European Conference on Computer Vision (ECCV), pp. 734–750 (2018)

Dictionary Learning and Confidence Map Estimation-Based Tracker for Robot-Assisted Therapy System

Xiaolong Zhou[1,2(✉)], Sixian Chan[2], Junwei Li[3], Shengyong Chen[2,4], and Honghai Liu[5]

[1] Quzhou University, Quzhou 324000, China
xlvision@hotmail.com
[2] Zhejiang University of Technology, Hangzhou 310023, China
[3] Huawei Technologies Co., Ltd., Hangzhou 310023, China
[4] Tianjin University of Technology, Tianjin 300384, China
[5] University of Portsmouth, Portsmouth PO1 2UP, UK

Abstract. In this paper, we propose a new tracker based on dictionary learning and confidence map estimation for a robot-assisted therapy system. We first over-segment the image into superpixel patches, and then employ color and depth cues to estimate the object confidence of each superpixel patch. We build two Bag-of-Word (BoW) models from initial frames to encode foreground/background appearance, and compute object confidence at superpixel level using BoW model in both foreground and background. We further refine target confidence by depth-based statistical features to mitigate noise interference and the uncertainty of visual cues. We derive the global confidence of each target candidate at bag level, and incorporate the confidence estimations to determine the posterior probability of each candidate within the Bayesian framework. Experimental results demonstrate the superior performance of the proposed method, especially in long-term tracking and occlusion handling.

Keywords: Object tracking · RGB-D · Bag-of-Word · Occlusion handling

1 Introduction

Tracking and analyzing the behavior of the patients, in particular to track the objects in interaction plays a significant role in a Robot-Assisted Therapy (RAT) system. Although many excellent tracking methods have been proposed, issues of robustness and reliability make these methods unsuitable for real-world situations. One main cause of failing tracking is the degradation of the tracking model, where the accumulation of inaccurate tracking results and corresponding model update over a period of time may cause focus to drift from the subject.

Object tracking has witnessed great advance in both generative and discriminative branches [1]. One of the advantages of generative model is that the method models target appearance without large number of training samples, however, it cannot separate target effectively from clutter background, occlusion, and long-term period. Discriminative tracking methods [2–5] achieve superior performance both in success

© Springer Nature Switzerland AG 2019
Z. Lin et al. (Eds.): PRCV 2019, LNCS 11857, pp. 147–159, 2019.
https://doi.org/10.1007/978-3-030-31654-9_13

and precision rate thanks to the combination of robust feature representation, discriminative classifier and the exploit of background and foreground information. However, these methods cannot well handle clutter background and sudden target appearance variation problems. Recently, trackers proposed by combining Convolutional Neural Network (CNN) and Discriminative Correlation Filter (DCF) achieve state-of-the-art performance due to the representation of deep feature and the computational efficiency of DCF. For instance, one or multiple layer deep features have been employed to train the DCF in frequency domain and thus can get good performance [6]. Tao et al. [7] employ two Siamese CNN to learn a generic matching function for tracking task to handle appearance variation and lacking of training samples. David et al. [8] propose to learn a regression function by CNN from large annotated video sequence, which achieves a very high tracking speed (more than 100FPS). In recent years, superpixel-based tracking methods [9–11] have attracted extensive attentions due to high accuracy and robustness. Yang et al. [9] compute a target-background confidence map using discriminative appearance model based on superpixels, and obtain the best candidate by maximizing a posterior estimate. In [10], a Dynamic Graph-based Tracker (DGT) is built to model the superpixel interactions, the tracking problem is then posed as a matching problem between the target graph and the candidate graph. In [11], tracking method based on Bag-of-Word (BoW) model is proposed to estimate target confidence, however, the method cannot handle the image patches with similar appearance to both background and foreground, which make tracker prone to degradation over-time and not appropriate for long-term tracking.

The aforementioned trackers either suffer from lacking background information supervision, computational burden, or cannot handle noisy patch interference, which are inappropriate for accurate real-world tracking. To meet the goal of long-term robust target tracking for the RAT system, this paper proposes a discriminative model-based tracking method to achieve robust and accurate tracking even for long-term period by fusing color and depth information to estimate target confidence.

2 Proposed Tracking Method

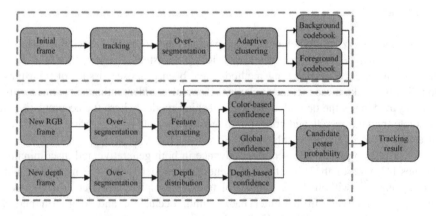

Fig. 1. Pipeline of the proposed tracking method.

The architecture of the proposed tracking method is illustrated in Fig. 1. The target object and background patches are over-segmented into superpixel collections, and then an adaptive AP is employed to select discriminative superpixel patches as background/foreground codebook. When a new frame arrives, we derive the posterior probability of each target candidate from three aspects within the Bayesian framework. To overcome model degradation over time, we propose a new update strategy based on the inspiration that the best appearance model could minimize the reconstruction error of current target.

2.1 Superpixel Appearance and BoW Model Construction

To compute the confidence of each superpixel, we construct foreground and background discriminative appearance model based on superpixel segmentation and BoW theory. Given the training image set $\{I_1, I_2, \ldots\ldots, I_k\}$, where k is number of training image, we first over-segment them into a set of superpixel patches using SLIC algorithm [12], and then the normalized color histogram f_i^k in the HSI space is extracted as an appearance representation descriptor, where i is superpixel index in I_k. HIS color histogram is employed because of its robustness in handling light changes and its discriminative ability in feature representation. Those superpixels inside the target area O_k are treated as positive training patches, while those outside the area of O_k but within $2 \times O_k$ are treated as negative training patches. The annular band can be expressed as S_k.

Given the feature set $\{f_i^k\}$ of target superpixel collection, the codebook of BoW model is generated by performing clustering, and cluster centers are used to initialize the codebook. In [11], the authors employ k-means algorithm to perform feature center selection. However, it needs to specify seed points manually. To remedy this, we utilize the Affinity Propagation (AP) clustering method [13] to determine the feature centers, which can facilitate two advantages: (1) it has the ability to determine the number of cluster centers automatically and (2) it is computation efficient. The input of AP is the affinity matrix of $S \subseteq R^{N \times N}$. Each data point of $S(i,j) = -\left\|f_i^K - f_j^k\right\|^2$ is defined as the negative Euclidean distance between f_i^k and f_j^k. By viewing each data point as a node in a network, the cluster centers and the corresponding exemplars are emerged by recursively transmit real-value distances along edges.

After the AP clustering, we can get two sets of codebook $F_m = \{F_1^F, F_2^F, \ldots, F_m^F\}$ and $B_n = \{F_1^B, F_2^B, \ldots, F_n^B\}$ corresponding to feature centers of background and foreground superpixel training sets, in which m and n denote the length of codebook, and the superscripts F and B correspond to foreground and background sets. The superpixels in O_k and S_k of each training samples are assigned to the nearest elements in F_m and B_n respectively, by minimizing Eqs. (1) and (2)

$$L_n^F = \arg\min_i \| f_n^k - F_i^F \|, f_n^k \in O_k \tag{1}$$

$$L_m^B = \arg\min_i \| f_m^k - F_i^B \|, f_m^k \in S_k \tag{2}$$

where f_n^k is the n-th superpixel feature vector of the k-th training image. L_n^F and L_m^B denote index of the n-th superpixel assigned to the word in codebook. Two histograms $H^F(I)$ and $H^B(I)$ are generated corresponding to the foreground and background bags, which indicate the occurrence frequency of each codeword in k training images. F_i^F and F_i^B denote the i-th codewords of foreground and background codebook, respectively.

2.2   Local Background-Foreground Confidence Estimation

One challenge to estimate the foreground and background confidence of each super-pixel is the interference of those superpixels which are inside the foreground rectangle patch but not belong to the target, which we name them as false-positive superpixels. So, the first step of our confidence estimation is to remove the impact of false-positive superpixels. For a test image I, we segment it into a set of superpixels $SP = \{sp(1), sp(2), \ldots, sp(k)\}$, and then compute two distances $\{d^F(i), d^B(i)\}$ between the i-th superpixel and the nearest codeword in F_n^F and F_m^B. Let $d^F(i, m)$ and $d^B(i, m)$ be the superpixel similarity to foreground and background codewords.

$$d^F(i, m) = \exp(- \parallel sp^k(i) - F_m^F \parallel_2^2) \tag{3}$$

$$d^B(i, n) = \exp(- \parallel sp^k(i) - F_n^B \parallel_2^2) \tag{4}$$

The similarity of $sp(k)$ to the nearest codeword is obtained by minimizing

$$d^F(i) = \min_m d^F(i, m), \text{ and } d^B(i) = \min_n d^B(i, n) \tag{5}$$

We define a false-positive superpixel based on rules in Eq. (6)

$$M(i) = \begin{cases} -1 & \text{if } d^F(i) \leq d^B(i) \\ 0 \text{ if } d^F(i) \geq & th^F, d^B(i) \geq th^B \\ 1 & \text{if } d^F(i) \geq d^B(i) \end{cases} \tag{6}$$

where th^F and th^B represent the outlier thresholds of foreground and background. If $M(i) = 0$, then the i-th superpixel is an ambiguity one, otherwise, it belongs to either foreground ($M(i) = 1$) or background ($M(i) = -1$). We assign foreground and background confidence of each superpixel based on the combination of bag similarity and superpixel distance. In Eq. (5), each superpixel in SP is assigned to the nearest codeword in codebook F_m and B_n. So, it is easy to compute bag histogram distribution of $B^F(I)$ and $B^B(I)$. Therefore, two bag similarities (see Eqs. (7) and (8)) can be determined.

$$S^F = \min_{l \in [1,k]} \{\exp(- \parallel B^F(I) - H_l^F \parallel)\} \tag{7}$$

$$S^B = \min_{l \in [1,k]} \{\exp(- \parallel B^B(I) - H_l^B \parallel)\} \tag{8}$$

where H_l^F and H_l^B denote background and foreground BoW histograms of the l-th positive and negative training sample. The two similarities indicate the target background confidence of a sample at bag level.

To further refine the confidence of each superpixel patch, a local confidence value $C(i) \in (0; 1)$ is assigned based on S^F and S^B. The value is computed as follows.

$$C(i) = M(i) * w(I) * \max\{d^F(i), d^B(i)\} \tag{9}$$

$$w(I) = \frac{S^F}{S^F + S^B} \tag{10}$$

where $w(I)$ denotes the weighting term of the sample image I belonging to target. The local confidence of $C(i)$ is determined jointly by $M(i)$, $w(I)$ and $max\{d^F(i), d^B(i)\}$. $M(i)$ is used to distinguish which category of the i-th superpixel belongs to. $w(I)$ corresponds to the weighting term of image I belonging to target, which is defined in Eq. (10). $max\{d^F(i), d^B(i)\}$ indicates the likelihood of the superpixel. It should be noted that the confidence of ambiguity superpixel patches is set to zero, which means that the local feature based on superpixel patch is not enough to estimate target-background confidence.

2.3 Depth-Based Confidence Estimation

For a superpixel patch which is difficult to estimate target confidence from appearance model, by incorporating the depth feature we can predict its category easily. However, only relying on the depth cue is still not enough to predict which category of a superpixel belongs to due to the fact that the depth is weak in encoding target texture feature. To remedy this, we employ both depth cue and appearance model to estimate the confidence of false-positive superpixel and refine the confidence of the other superpixels.

Instead of estimating superpixel confidence directly, we propose to use the aforementioned AP clustering result to compute the confidence of each cluster. Then the cluster center F_m^F and its member set $\{sp_m(k)\}$, where k is the superpixel index, correspond to their own image regions in training samples. Here, we compute two scores $R_{in}(i)$ and $R_{out}(i)$ for each cluster and its corresponding members. $R_{in}(i)$ denotes the area of the i-th cluster and its members overlapping the target area. $R_{out}(i)$ indicates the superpixel area out of the target region. The cluster confidence is defined as Eq. (11).

$$C_{clust}(i) = \frac{R_{in}(i) - R_{out}(i)}{R_{in}(i) + R_{out}(i)} \tag{11}$$

where $C_{clust}(i) \subseteq [-1, 1]$, higher value indicates that the superpixel clustering owns higher confidence belonging to target, otherwise, the clustering is more likely to belonging to background.

Then, we compute the depth mean and standard deviation of each cluster as the depth model to constraint the background and foreground confidence. Let

$$mean_m(i) = \frac{1}{k}\sum_{k=1}^{K} depth(sp(k)) \tag{12}$$

and

$$std_m(i) = \sqrt{\frac{1}{k}\sum_{k=1}^{K}(depth(k) - mean(i))^2} \tag{13}$$

be the depth mean and standard deviation of cluster F_M^F and the corresponding superpixel set $\{sp_m(k)\}$. Intuitively, for the superpixel patches belonging to the same clustering, their depth distribution should be uniform and the standard deviation is expected to be small. Although the depth feature of superpixel lacks discriminative capacity and semantic information to estimate confidence, it is an important cue to predict target confidence based on the prior knowledge of the homogeneity of the depth distribution and the continuity of depth changing.

The confidence value of each superpixel patch with depth constraint is defined as

$$C_{depth}(i) = w_{depth}(i, m) * C_{clust}(i) \tag{14}$$

$$w_{depth}(i, m) = \exp(-\lambda_d \times \frac{|depth(i) - mean_m(i)|}{std_m(i)}) \tag{15}$$

where $w_{depth}(i, m)$ is the constraint term and follows the Gaussian distribution. Greater distance to mean cluster depth indicates lower likelihood of the superpixel belonging to the foreground, the pairwise index of i and m means that the i-th superpixel is assigned to the m-th cluster by Eqs. (1) and (2).

2.4 Global Confidence Estimation

The previous appearance-based model and depth-based model are used to determine the confidence of a certain superpixel. Now we use bag similarity to compute global confidence of a test sample. When a target candidate arrives, we first segment it to a set of superpixels $sp(i), i \in \{1, 2, \ldots, N\}$, where N is the number of superpixels. Then, we assign each superpixel patch to the nearest codeword to compute two candidates' bags (codeword distribution) corresponding to background histogram $H_t^B(I)$ and foreground histogram $H_t^F(I)$. Two similarities $S^F(I)$ and $S^B(I)$ are employed to measure the candidate I belonging to background or foreground, and then they are considered to determine the global candidate confidence $C_{global}(I)$ jointly.

$$C_{global}(I) = \frac{S^F(I) - S^B(I)}{S^F(I) + S^B(I)} \tag{16}$$

$$S^F(I) = \exp(-\lambda_f \times \| H_t^F(I) - H^F(I) \|_2^2) \tag{17}$$

$$S^B(I) = \exp(-\lambda_b \times \| H_t^B(I) - H^B(I) \|_2^2) \tag{18}$$

The global confidence ranges from -1 to 1. When the similarity of candidate image becomes similar to the background model, its confidence value is close to -1, the confidence value is close to 1 if it is similar to the foreground model. Different from other global confidence estimation methods, two BoW models are used to estimate the target confidence, which is robust in dealing with the ambiguous candidates. In other words, when the candidate is close to both foreground and background models, its confidence of being the target is close to 0.

2.5 The Proposed Tracking Method

Given the target observation set $Y^t = \{y_1^t, y_2^t, \ldots, y_n^t\}$ at frame t, where y_n^t denotes the n-th observation of target at the t-th frame. We perform tracking by maximizing the posteriori probability in Eq. (19).

$$\hat{X}_t = \arg \max_{x_t^i} p(X_t^i | Y^t) \tag{19}$$

where X_t^i stands for the i-th target candidate state of frame t, and Y^t denotes the corresponding observation of X_t^i. In this paper, we define the target state as $X_t = \{X_t^c, X_t^{sx}, X_t^{sy}\}$, where X_t^c, X_t^{sx}, and X_t^{sy} represent the target center location, target scales in x-axis and y-axis, respectively. The posterior probability of the given observation set Y^t up to frame t is achieved by the Bayesian theorem recursively.

$$p(X_t | Y_t) \propto p(Y_t | X_t) \int p(X_t | X_{t-1}) p(X_{t-1} | Y_{t-1}) dX_{t-1} \tag{20}$$

where $p(Y_t | X_t)$ and $p(X_t | X_{t-1})$ denote the observation model and motion model respectively. The motion model indicates the relationship between target state and frames in time domain, and we assume that it follows the Gaussian distribution. Thus, the target state variation can be formulated as Eq. (21).

$$p(X_{t-1} | Y_{t-1}) = N(X_t; X_{t-1}, \Psi) \tag{21}$$

where Ψ is a diagonal covariance matrix, and the elements in Ψ denote the standard deviation of target state. The observation model is formulated based on the sum of appearance confidence in Eq. (9), depth confidence in Eq. (14) and the corresponding global target confidence at bag level in Eq. (16). When the target location of frame $t - 1$ has been determined, we select a rectangle R_t area around the previous target center as the searching space in the t-th test image. To reduce computation load, we only over-segment image into superpixels within R_t once. For each candidate target state in X_t^i, we assign the corresponding superpixel set to it, and then approximate the confidence based on the assigned superpixel collections.

$$p(Y_t|X_t) \propto C_{global}(I) + \sum_{i \in \Omega} (C(i) + C_{depth}(i)) \tag{22}$$

where Ω denotes the superpixel set when the target state is set to X_t. The state observation estimation is proportional to confidence sum in Eq. (22).

It is essential to update model effectively for capturing target appearance variation due to pose change, illumination change, and occlusion *et al*. In this paper, the words in codebook play an important role in encoding target appearance. So, the way to select and update discriminative words in both temporal and spatial domain is particular important. We assume that the best update strategy is to select words that can minimize the reconstruction error of the current target. Based on this inspiration, we propose a simple and effective sparse representation method to select the most discriminative words from the previous frames to estimate target state of current frame.

In order to effectively use the depth distribution to reduce the uncertainty of superpixel appearance, we update the mean and standard deviation of each cluster based on the depth distribution of the tracked target every frame. We use a temporal low-pass filtering method to accommodate target depth distribution variation.

$$mean_m^*(i) = (1 - \rho_1)mean_m(i) + mean_k(i) \tag{23}$$

$$std_m^*(i) = (1 - \rho_2)std_m(i) + std_k(i) \tag{24}$$

where $mean_k(i)$ and $std_k(i)$ denote the mean depth and standard deviation of the k-th frame target area.

3   Experimental Results and Analysis

Six challenging video sequences with RBG color channel and depth channel are captured by our RAT system, namely *Bear, Bear2, Wolf, Wolf2, Ballon, Dog*. Both the RGB channel and depth channel are recorded by a Kinect sensor and calibrated to the same coordinate system. We annotate the target bounding box manually by a rectangle in each image, and then the rectangle is projected to depth image as annotation. The annotation in RGB and depth channels is treated as groundtruth to evaluate the performance of our tracker. Each of the recorded video sequence contains at least one challenge such as occlusion, shape deformation, rotation, etc. The length of each video is 800, 952, 731, 1027, 1109 and 1210 frames, respectively.

We use SLIC algorithm to over-segment image in HSI color space and employ a KCF with HOG feature to track the initial four image frames (from the second to the fifth). A total of 5 frames are used to construct the BoW model. When performing AP clustering, we employ negative Euclidean distance as the real value information. The exemplar preference is set to 1.5 times of the average negative Euclidean distance. We update the codewords every 5 frames and update the depth model every frame.

3.1 Codewords Extracted by AP

To verify the impact of the number of codewords on appearance model, we implement varieties of F_m and B_m by setting different codeword numbers. The target and background appearances are encoded by codewords in F_m and B_m. We employ the AP method to select representative superpixel patches as feature centers adaptively, which overcomes the deficiency of generating seed points manually. However, another parameter, the number of codewords in F_m and B_m, is considered highly important. In AP cluster method, the number of clusters is influenced by a real value $s(k,k)$, which is referred as "preference" for each feature vector k. So, the feature vector with larger values of $s(k,k)$ is more likely to be chosen as a cluster center. As a priori knowledge, all the feature vectors are equally considered as cluster center candidates, and we set a common "preference" to each superpixel patch as initial state. The shared value can be varied to produce different numbers of clusters. Specifically, we will get a moderate number of clusters when set $s(k,k)$ to the median of input similarities. If the shared value is set to a smaller value than the median of input similarities, it would result in a smaller number of clusters.

Table 1. Analysis of AP preference on target appearance model in video sequence wolf

s(k,k)	Superpixel patch	AP clusters	AUC of success	AUC of precision
1.0	382	64	0.68	0.89
0.8	382	52	0.642	0.875
0.6	382	35	0.61	0.85
0.4	382	22	0.59	0.835
1.2	382	71	0.67	0.865
1.4	382	80	0.665	0.86
1.6	382	101	0.64	0.85

In Table 1, we build different target appearance codebooks by setting $s(k,k) = \{1.0, 0.8, 0.6, 0.4, 1.2, 1.4, 1.6\}$ in Wolf video sequence. $s(k,k) = 1.0$ denotes that we set the preference value to 1.0 times the median similarity. It can be seen that the AP cluster number increases with the value of $s(k,k)$. As $s(k,k)$ increases from 1 to 1.6, the number of clustering centers increases from 64 to 101, however, the AUC of success plot and precision plot are reduced by 5.8% and 4.4%, respectively. On the contrary, the cluster center number drops to 35 from 64 with respect to $s(k,k)$ varying from 1.0 to 0.4, while the corresponding tracking performance is reduced by about 13.2% (Success) and 6.2% (Precision). This indicates that the number of codewords plays an important role in appearance model. Too many codewords undermine the discriminative ability of the appearance model, while insufficient codewords is not robust to target appearance variation.

3.2   Effectiveness of the Background/Foreground Appearance Model

Contrary to existing target confidence map estimation methods, we propose to use background and foreground appearance model to perform confidence estimation jointly. We design the dual models mainly considering the disturbance of ambiguous superpixel patches. As a priori, when a superpixel is similar to both background and foreground, we consider it will undermine the model representative ability. Moreover, the confidence map based on these ambiguous superpixels is unreliable. Inspired by this observation, we propose to build a robust background-aware target appearance model.

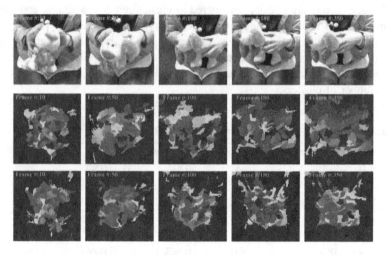

Fig. 2. Confidence estimation results between dual appearance model and target-based appearance model. The first row indicates the RGB image captured from the Kinect sensor. The second and the third rows indicate the corresponding confidence maps of a single appearance model (the second row) and a dual appearance model (the third row).

As shown in Fig. 2, the target appearance model based on background and foreground achieves excellent precision in predicting target confidence. From frame 10 to 350, the target experiences significant appearance variation (rotation and occlusion). The proposed dual model can identify ambiguous and noisy superpixel patches and then prevent them to participate in appearance mode building. On the other hand, the dual model selects the most discriminative superpixel automatically to encode target appearance, which is an effective method to prevent model degradation as well as keeps model robust to distractors. On the contrary, the confidence map in the second row of Fig. 2 is the result estimated from only target appearance model. In other words, we complete another appearance model with the same method to dual model, the main difference is that only target appearance (without considering background context) is used to compute the confidence map. The confidence map of the 100th frame has shown a significant deviation, with the increase in the number of frames, this error is gradually accumulated and results in model degradation. At frames 180 and 350, the confidence map from dual model still shows a high precision compared to the groundtruth in the first row. However, the confidence map corresponding to frames 180 and 350 in the second row starts to show large deviation and discontinuity, while the confidence margin between the background part and target becomes smaller.

3.3 Quantitative Analysis

We use two protocols to evaluate the tracking performance: area under curve (AUC) of one-pass evaluation (OPE) using success plot, and center location error (CLE). The success plot is used to measure the overlap rate between tracked bounding box and the grountruth on a sequence of video frames. The later metric denotes the distance between the tracked target center and groundtruth center.

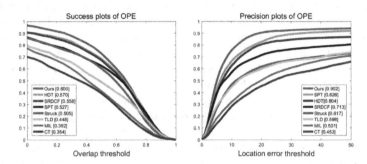

Fig. 3. Average success plot (left) and precision plot (right) of OPE on our own video sequences datasets.

We evaluate our tracker against 7 state-of-the-art trackers including SPT [9], HDT [14], CT [15], MIL [16], TLD [4], Struck [17], and SRDCF [18]. Among them, the SPT tracker is a superpixel-based tracking method, the SRDCF is a state-of-the-art KCF-based tracking method, the HDT is a hierarchical convolutional neural network and correlation filter based method, and the other trackers are selected due to their excellent performance in OTB benchmark. The quantitative evaluation results between the proposed tracker and the state-of-the-art trackers are show in Fig. 3. The success plot shows that our tracker outperforms all of the other trackers with a large margin. Comparing with the second-best tracker SRDCF and the third best tracker HDT, the proposed tracking method obtains the AUC of 0.652 and improves the performance of SRDCF and HDT by about 12% and 16%, respectively. Both the proposed tracker and SPT tracker make use of superpixel confidence to track object, however, our method shows an obvious improvement in terms of the both success and precision. As to center location error, our method is still superior to the rest trackers. Table 2 summarizes the average CLE of each tracker. The results demonstrate that the proposed tracker achieves the best performance with the minimum average CLE on all video sequences.

Table 2. Quantitative comparison of average CLE

Sequence	Ours	SPT	HDT	CT	MIL	TLD	Struck	SRDCF
Bear	4.2	5.9	7.8	7.9	8.6	6.9	7.2	7.2
Bear2	3.8	4.1	4.4	5.0	4.2	7.2	5.8	25.9
Wolf	4.6	9.7	6.9	8.0	7.4	60.8	7.6	11.2
Wolf2	3.7	7.7	5.4	5.9	6.1	4.3	9.5	4.8
Ballon	6.3	9.5	8.5	6.9	9.2	11.1	11.3	9.0
Dog	3.5	7.6	6.0	11.1	9.1	8.9	8.4	8.8

4   Conclusion

In this paper, we have presented a novel object tracking method using RGB and depth images from the Kinect sensor for a RAT system. We trained two BoW models to encode the target background appearance, and combined depth distribution to refine tracking result. To achieve accurate and long-term tracking, we computed two target confidence maps based on color and depth information at superpixel level, and computed a global confidence of each target candidate using codewords. Furthermore, our tracking method was equipped with a sparse representation-based discriminative online update strategy to handle with target appearance variation and occlusion. Experiments on six video sequences have showed that the proposed tracking method outperformed the state-of-the-art tracking methods in both success and precision plots. Moreover, our method can prevent tracking model degradation effectively which is suitable for long-term tracking and real-world application.

Acknowledgement. This work was supported by National Key R&D Program of China (2018YFB1305200), National Natural Science Foundation of China (61876168, U1509207, 61733011, 51575338), and Zhejiang Provincial Natural Science Foundation of China (LY18F030020).

References

1. Li, X., Hu, W., Shen, C., Zhang, Z., Dick, A., Hengel, A.V.D.: A survey of appearance models in visual object tracking. ACM Trans. Intell. Syst. Technol. **4**(4), 1–48 (2013)
2. Zhou, X., Li, J., Chen, S., Cai, H., Liu, H.: Multiple perspective object tracking via context-aware correlation filter. IEEE Access **6**(1), 43262–43273 (2018)
3. Zhou, X., Li, Y., He, B., Bai, T.: GM-PHD-based multi-target visual tracking using entropy distribution and game theory. IEEE Trans. Industr. Inf. **10**(2), 1064–1076 (2014)
4. Kalal, Z., Matas, J., Mikolajczyk, K.: P-n learning: bootstrapping binary classifiers by structural constraints. In: IEEE Conference on Computer Vision and Pattern Recognition, San Francisco, USA, pp. 49–56. IEEE Press (2010)
5. Chan, S., Zhou, X., Li, J., Chen, S.: Adaptive compressive tracking based on locality sensitive histograms. Pattern Recogn. **72**, 517–531 (2017)
6. Henriques, J.F., Caseiro, R., Martins, P., Batista, J.: High-speed tracking with kernelized correlation filters. IEEE Trans. Pattern Anal. Mach. Intell. **37**(3), 583–596 (2015)

7. Tao, R., Gavves, E., Smeulders, A.W.: Siamese instance search for tracking. In: Proceedings of the IEEE Conference on Computer Vision and Pattern Recognition, Las Vegas, USA, pp. 1420–1429. IEEE Press (2016)
8. Held, D., Thrun, S., Savarese, S.: Learning to track at 100 FPS with deep regression networks. In: Leibe, B., Matas, J., Sebe, N., Welling, M. (eds.) ECCV 2016. LNCS, vol. 9905, pp. 749–765. Springer, Cham (2016). https://doi.org/10.1007/978-3-319-46448-0_45
9. Yang, F., Lu, H., Yang, M.-H.: Robust superpixel tracking. IEEE Trans. Image Process. **23**(4), 1639–1651 (2014)
10. Wen, L., Du, D., Lei, Z., Li, S. Z., Yang, M.-H.: Jots: joint online tracking and segmentation. In: Proceedings of the IEEE Conference on Computer Vision and Pattern Recognition, Boston, Massachusetts, pp. 2226–2234. IEEE Press (2015)
11. Fan, H., Xiang, J., Zhao, L.: Robust visual tracking via bag of superpixels. Multimedia Tools Appl. **75**(14), 8781–8798 (2016). https://doi.org/10.1007/s11042-015-2790-3
12. Achanta, R., Shaji, A., Smith, K., Lucchi, A., Fua, P., Süsstrunk, S.: SLIC superpixels compared to state-of-the-art superpixel methods. IEEE Trans. Pattern Anal. Mach. Intell. **34**(11), 2274–2282 (2012)
13. Frey, B.J., Dueck, D.: Clustering by passing messages between data points. Science **315**(5814), 972–976 (2007)
14. Qi, Y., Zhang, S., Qin, L., Yao, H., Huang, Q., Lim, J., Yang, M.-H.: Hedged deep tracking. In: Proceedings of the IEEE Conference on Computer Vision and Pattern Recognition, Las Vegas, USA, pp. 4303–4311. IEEE Press (2016)
15. Zhang, K., Zhang, L., Yang, M.-H.: Real-time compressive tracking. In: Fitzgibbon, A., Lazebnik, S., Perona, P., Sato, Y., Schmid, C. (eds.) ECCV 2012. LNCS, vol. 7574, pp. 864–877. Springer, Heidelberg (2012). https://doi.org/10.1007/978-3-642-33712-3_62
16. Babenko, B., Yang, M.-H., Belongie, S.: Robust object tracking with online multiple instance learning. IEEE Trans. Pattern Anal. Mach. Intell. **33**(8), 1619–1632 (2011)
17. Hare, S., Golodetz, S., Saffari, A., Vineet, V., Cheng, M.-M., Hicks, S.L., Torr, P.H.: Struck: structured output tracking with kernels. IEEE Trans. Pattern Anal. Mach. Intell. **38**(10), 2096–2109 (2016)
18. Danelljan, M., Hager, G., Shahbaz Khan, F., Felsberg, M.: Learning spatially regularized correlation filters for visual tracking. In: Proceedings of the IEEE International Conference on Computer Vision, Santiago, Chile, pp. 4310–4318. IEEE Press (2015)

Power Line Corridor LiDAR Point Cloud Segmentation Using Convolutional Neural Network

Jisheng Yang⬛, Zijun Huang, Maochun Huang, Xianxian Zeng, Dong Li$^{(\boxtimes)}$, and Yun Zhang

Guangdong University of Technology, Guangdong, China
dong.li@gdut.edu.cn

Abstract. Regular inspection is important for ensuring safe operation of the power lines. Point cloud segmentation is an efficient way to carry out these inspections. Most of the existing methods depend on priori knowledge from a paticular power line corridor, which is not applicable for other unknown power line corridors. To address this problem, we propose the first end-to-end deep learning based framework for power line corridor point cloud segmentation. Specifically, we design an effective channel presentation for Light Detection and Ranging (LiDAR) point clouds and adapt a general convolutional neural network as our basic network. To evaluate the effectiveness and efficiency of our method, we collect and label a dataset, which covers a 720,000 square meter area of power line corridors. To verify the generalization ability of our method, we also test it on KITTI dataset. Experiments shows that our method not only achieves high accuracy with fast runtime on power line corridor dataset, but also performs well on KITTI dataset.

Keywords: Power line inspection · Point cloud segmentation · Convolutional neural network

1 Introduction

Power line is considered as one of the most significant infrastructures, which requires regular inspection to ensure the safe operation of a power grid. Thus, power line components such as power lines and pylons need regular checking to diagnose faults, for example, mechanical damage. In addition, power lines' surrounding objects like trees also require regular inspection in case their branches get close or touch the power line, which will cause disaster. Therefore, it is necessary to develop an automatic method for detecting obstacles along power line corridors. Point cloud segmentation is an efficient approach to carry out power line inspection, which has received much attention [2–6,9].

The first author is a student.

© Springer Nature Switzerland AG 2019
Z. Lin et al. (Eds.): PRCV 2019, LNCS 11857, pp. 160–171, 2019.
https://doi.org/10.1007/978-3-030-31654-9_14

Developing efficient and robust LiDAR point cloud segmentation for power line corridor scene remains as a challenging task owing to the variability of power line corridors. More specifically, power line corridors have complicated terrains where steep slopes and flat grounds interlace, leading the challenge of recognizing objects from unseen and diverse geographical environments. In addition, LiDAR point clouds have variant attribute. Their LiDAR intensity distributions could change dramatically even though they are collected from the same areas, due to the difference of airborne laser scanner's fight height and atmosphere conditions.

Although researchers have explored point cloud segmentation on power line corridor scene, their works [2–4, 6, 9] depends on handcrafted features, which requires much priori knowledge. Therefore, developing a feasible approach that is able to handle the aforementioned challenges for point cloud segmentation on power line corridor scene remains to be unsolved. Recently, deep convolutional neural networks for point cloud segmentation [1, 7, 15] have been brought into being, but there is a lack of deep learning method for power line corridor point cloud segmentation. Due to this fact, we contribute a deep learning approach for segmenting point cloud on power line corridor scene.

In this paper, we propose an end-to-end pipeline for power line corridor point cloud segmentation. To be more specific, we design an effective channel presentation for LiDAR point cloud and utilize a current state-of-the-art network [1] as our basic network, which is further adapted to be suitable for our input and output channels. To evaluate the effectiveness and efficiency of our approach, we collect and label a large scale point cloud dataset on power line corridor scene to do experiments. To verify the generalization ability of our approach, we also implement it on KITTI dataset [16].

The key contributions of this paper are: (1) It is the first deep learning based approach for segmenting power line corridor point clouds; (2) We design an effective channel presentation for LiDAR point cloud, which is not only suitable for power line corridor scene, but also other scene.

2   Related Work

2.1   Object Segmentation on Power Line Corridor Scene

Methods for recognizing and extracting objects of power line corridor scene can be divided into two categories: (a) point cloud based methods [2–4]; (b) image based methods [5, 6, 9]. Previous methods primarily work on LiDAR point clouds and comprise multiple stages including calculating hand-crafted features for points, designing filters based on the features and extracting objects with the filters. [4] classifies ground and non-ground points by statistically analyzing the skewness and kurtosis of the LIDAR intensity data and detects power lines by employing Hough transfer after that. [2] calculates 21 features of points, and use them to train a decision tree based filter, which is used to segment points. [3] removes ground by applying elevation-difference and slope criteria and then use a combination of height and spacial-density filters to extract power lines. For the methods mentioned above, the selection of handcrafted features highly depends on priori knowledge from specific areas, which makes them hard to generalize and infeasible in practical applications. Recently, many researchers utilize unmanned aerial vehicle (UAV) images to carry out power line inspection [5,6,9]. [6] segments power line components with three steps. It first segments images with fully convolutional neural network, and then implements 3D reconstruction with the images to get a point cloud, and finally matches points from images to the point cloud. In this case, compounded errors are caused by multiple steps. [9] proposed a novel method to sidestep the 3D reconstruction. It first utilize UAV images and ground sample distance (GSP) to generate Epipolar images and then uses left and right Epipolar images to calculate the 3D vectors of power lines. This method extracts power lines in a single step and achieve high accuracy, but its performance is sensitive to the illumination and resolution of the images.

2.2   3D Point Cloud Semantic Segmentation

Previous methods depends on intrinsic [10,11] and extrinsic [12] hand-crafted features to address specific semantic segmentation tasks. Invariant descriptors make them hard to generalize. Later on, deep learning methods occurs and shows great generalization performance by taking the advantage of massive training data. Volumetric CNNs [13,14] are the pioneers to implement 3D convolutional neural network on voxelized point cloud inputs. But their power is limited by the sparsity of data presentation and huge computation cost. Recently, light convolutional neural networks [1,7,15] was developed, which achieve high efficiency by directly consuming point clouds. But these methods are far from mature and only work well on specific experimental dataset.

3   Method Description

3.1   Dataset Collection

Power Line Corridor Dataset. To the best of out knowledge, there is no official or public point cloud dataset on power line corridor scene. In order to conduct our study, we collect and label a large scale power line corridor dataset. The original point cloud data is obtained by airborne laser scanners. And we manually label the point clouds by a software named CloudCompare [19]. Points of the dataset are classified into nine categories – high-voltage iron pylon, columnar pylon, power line, lightening protection line, insulator, tree, ground, others and noise. Finally, we get a point cloud dataset with 16 files, which covers a 720,000 m^2 area of power line corridors in total, containing eight kinds of different pylons. In this dataset, there are variable terrains where steep slopes and flat grounds interlace with each other. In addition, the distributions of LiDAR intensity varies from one file to another, because flight height and atmosphere conditions could be different during each journey of the airborne laser scanner. In order to simplify the segmentation task but also take practical applications into consideration, in experiments, we rearrange our dataset into three categories– pylon, power line and others. Others category mainly contains trees and a small part of grounds. One example of the rearranged dataset is shown in Fig. 1.

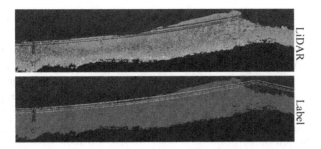

Fig. 1. Examples of LiDAR point cloud and segmentation label. LiDAR point cloud is at the top. The segmentation label is at the bottom. Polygons are denoted in blue, power lines in yellow and trees in red. (Color figure online)

KITTI Point Cloud Dataset. Initial data is from KITTI [16] Velodyne point clouds, which is a autonomous driving scene. However KITTI does not provide the point-wise labels. Due to the fact, we label the data by ourselves with the method described by [17]. Specifically, using the 3D bounding box labels from KITTI, all points within a 3D bounding box are considered belonging to an object. Corresponding label is then assigned to each point. With this method, we collected 7481 point clouds with point-wise labels.

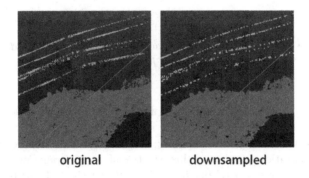

original   downsampled

Fig. 2. Visualization of the original and downsampled point cloud Examples. Original point cloud example is on the left. Downsampled point cloud example is on the right. (Color figure online)

3.2 Point Cloud Preprocessing

In order to feed point clouds into the CNN based model, we need to preprocess the point clouds into a series of groups that meets the need of CNN's input. In specific, point clouds are cut into several $W \times W$ m^2 square blocks with identical area. And then, N points are randomly sampled from each block. So points in each block are of size $N \times C$, where C represents channels. In this way, points in blocks are of the same size, so the CNN based model can directly consume them. When preprocessing power line corridor point cloud dataset, $W = 10, N = 4096$ is an appropriate choice. $W = 10$ is selected because blocks of such size are able to cover most areas of the components of interest like pylons and trees in the power line corridor. By statistics, pylons' widths are in range of 8–11 m and trees' are less than 6 m. $N = 4096$ is selected because downsampling point clouds to 40.96 points/m^2 not only still let point clouds completely describe the profiles of primary components in the power line corridors, as shown in Fig. 2, but also simplify computation.

3.3   An Effective Channel Presentation for LiDAR Points

Unlike [1,7,15] which try to explore more complicated and powerful network architectures, this paper aims to find an ideal channel presentation for LiDAR point clouds. The channel presentations p0–p4 that we will discuss are defined as follows:

$$p0 : X_c, Y_c, Z, I_N, X_n, Y_n, Z_n$$
$$p1 : X_c, Y_c, Z_l, I_N, X_n, Y_n, Z_n$$
$$p2 : X_c, Y_c, Z_l, I_{N2}, X_n, Y_n, Z_n$$
$$p3 : X_c, Y_c, Z_l, I_{N1}, X_n, Y_n, Z_n, I_{N2}$$

$$F_c = F - (F_{min\_of\_block} + block\_size/2)$$
$$F_N = F/255.0, \ F_{N1} = F/F_{max\_of\_block}, \ F_{N2} = F/F_{max\_of\_file}$$
$$F_n = F/F_{max\_of\_file}, \ F_l = F - F_{min\_of\_block}$$

where $F_{min\_of\_block}$ is the minimal value of feature F within a block; $F_{max\_of\_file}$ is the maximal value of feature F within the current point cloud file; digit 255.0 is the maximal value of LiDAR intensity; $block\_size$ is the width of the block.

Under presentation p0 that is directly transformed from PointNet's, pylon category cannot be recognized by the model unless weighted-loss is used during training. Note that only this experiment uses weighted-loss, the rest of experiments in this paper are done without weighted-loss. The result trained with weighted-loss under p0 is shown in Fig. 3a. As seen from the result, points on the flat region can be quite precisely recognized, however, points on the top of the slope are severely misclassified as pylons or power lines. From this phenomenon, it can be inferred that the model tends to classify points relying on global height information–altitude, causing points with the same altitude to gain the same classification labels. Hence, the model needs local height information to make prediction. From intuitional perspective, within a block, pylons should be higher than the ground or trees, and the power lines should locate in the upper part of pylons. In presentation p0, both feature 'Z' and 'Z_n' represent global height information. So we design p1 to replace the third feature 'Z' with

'$Z_l = Z - Z_{min\_of\_block}$', which represents information of local height. Now we get the first three coordinate features for local geometric information, and the last three coordinate features for global. With the new presentation p1, we obtain predicted result as shown in Fig. 3b. From the picture we see that pylon category is recognized and there are no longer a large amount of misclassified points at the top of the slope, which proves our new presentation more effective.

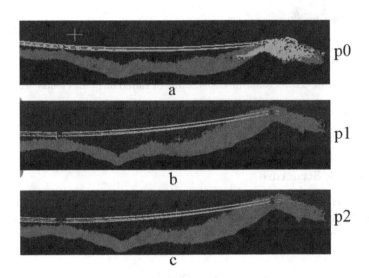

Fig. 3. Predicted results under different channel presentations. Figure 3a is the result under presentation p0. Figure 3b is the result under presentation p1. Figure 3c is the result under presentation p2. (Color figure online)

In addition, we notice that distributions of LiDAR intensity in different point cloud files of our power line corridor dataset are quite different, as shown in Fig. 4, and list different point clouds' maximal value of LiDAR intensity in Table 1. As mentioned above, presentation p1 normalize intensity with a fixed value 255.0. That is not optimal, because intensity features are more obvious if normalized intensity values have relatively bigger contrast among points. So we design p2 to normalize the intensity feature with the maximal intensity value of the current point cloud file rather than a fixed value. So the normalized 'I_N' is replaced with '$I_{N2} = I/I_{max\_of\_file}$'. Through this modification, we obtain further improvement in the predicted result as shown in Fig. 3c. Finally, following the concept of local and global features, the existing normalized intensity feature '$I_{N2} = I/I_{max\_of\_file}$' is regarded as a global feature and we design p3 by adding an extra feature '$I_{N1} = I/I_{max\_of\_block}$' as a local intensity feature. With presentation p3, we obtain the best performance among our experiments.

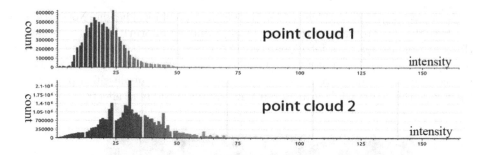

Fig. 4. Distribution of laser intensity for different point clouds

Table 1. Maximal intensity value of different point clouds

Point cloud index	1	2	3	4	5	6	7	8	9	10	11	12	13	14	15	16
Maximal intensity	147	100	101	206	100	163	236	166	249	120	101	150	100	112	126	101

3.4 Network Structure

Our deep learning based framework is shown in Fig. 5, which is adapted from
PointNet [1]. It is a simple but effective 3D semantic segmentation network that
directly consumes point clouds.

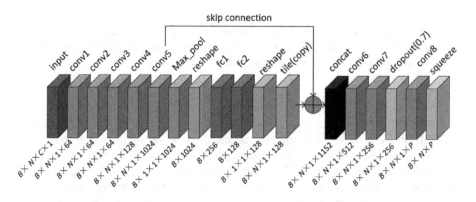

Fig. 5. Network architecture (Color figure online)

The input of the network is a $B \times N \times C \times 1$ tensor representing points within
a block as described in Sect. 3.2, where B is the batch size; N is the amount
of points sampled from a block; C represents channels, which is mentioned in
Sect. 3.3; and digit 1 is the expended dimension that helps to form the input
shape for a CNN. Conv1~conv5 layers implement point-wise convolutions, that
is to say each point is convolved independently. These five layers is used to
extract features from each point. Next, a symmetry function, max pooling is

applied to make the model invariant to input permutation, dealing with the unordered point clouds. Skip connection is then used to fuse local features from conv5 and global features from fc2. Fusing lower level and higher level features can effectively improve smoothness and detail of the segmentation output [8]. Finally, the model gets predicted classification for each point. In the last layer, P is the number of categories.

4 Experiments

The effectiveness and efficiency of our approach are evaluated on power line corridor dataset. In addition, the generalization ability of our approach is verified on KITTI dataset.

4.1 Evaluation Metrics

Our method's performance is evaluated on class-level. We compare predicted and ground-truth label values and calculate precision, recall and IoU (intersection over union) between them respectively. Among the three, IoU is the most important metric to estimate the performance of segmentation. So we mainly discuss IoU in this section. The evaluation metrics are defined as follows:

$$Precison_c = \frac{|P_c \cap G_c|}{|P_c|}, recall_c = \frac{|P_c \cap G_c|}{|G_c|}, IoU_c = \frac{|P_c \cap G_c|}{|P_c \cup G_c|} \qquad (1)$$

where P_c and G_c represent the predicted and ground truth point sets belonging to class c respectively, $| * |$ calculates the amount of points in the point set $*$.

4.2 Segmentation on Power Line Corridor Dataset

Settings. There are 16 large scale point cloud files in our dataset. Each of them covers an approximate area. One file is randomly chosen as validation set and the remaining 15 files are set as training set. In our split, validation set is ensured to be unseen during training. Note that our dataset is reorganized into three categories: pylon, power line and others. Others category mainly contains trees and grounds. In point cloud preprocessing procedure, point clouds are separated into 10×10 m^2 blocks and 4096 points are randomly sampled from each block as the inputs, as discussed in Sect. 3.2. And then, the network mentioned in Sect. 3.4 is trained without weighted-loss on a GTX 1070 GPU.

Results and Analysis. Experiments are implemented under different channel presentations that are discussed in Sect. 3.3. We compare our method with PointNet [1]. The results are summarized in Table 2. Note that results under p0 represent the results of PointNet.

Local height channel is critical. Point presentation of PointNet does not contain local height channel. As we can see, PointNet fails to recognize pylon category. In contrast, presentation p1 contains local height channel. Under p1, model

Table 2. Experiment Results under Different Point Channel Presentation. All values in the table are in percentages

	Pylon				Power line				Others			
	p0	p1	p2	p3	p0	p1	p2	p3	p0	p1	p2	p3
Precision	Nan	87.41	88.65	85.53	95.55	90.88	98.72	99.37	99.87	99.99	99.99	99.99
Recall	0	51.11	81.21	89.29	97.75	99.39	99.11	98.69	99.99	99.93	99.99	99.99
IoU	0	47.61	73.56	77.57	94.30	90.37	97.85	98.07	99.94	99.94	99.99	99.99

can segment pylon category with a relatively high IoU 47.61, which shows that local height channel is important and proves our channel presentation for LiDAR point cloud effective.

Appropriate normalization for LiDAR intensity is important. Presentation p1 normalizes intensity with a fixed value, while p2 normalizes intensity with a flexible value. This modification lets normalized intensity values have relatively bigger contrast among points, making points have more obvious intensity features. From the results, a relative 54.5% IoU improvement from presentation p1 to p2 in pylon category can be seen and IoUs of other categories also improve, which shows that normalizing features properly is vital. In addition, following the concept of local and global features, presentation p3 adds another normalized intensity feature as a local feature while regarding the original one as a global feature. Presentation p3 further improves the IoU in every category and it performs the best in our experiments.

Table 3. Statistics on our power line corridor dataset. All the values in this table are in percentages.

	Point percentage	Block percentage
Pylon	0.14	0.80
Power transmission line	4.15	25.89
Others	95.71	98.71

Note that recalls for both power line and others categories are near perfect, higher than 98%, which is desirable for power line inspection, as dangerous spots lie where trees are too close to power lines. However, even when using the most effective point presentation p3, recall for pylon is 89%, though high but relatively lower than other two categories. Lower performance on pylon category is attributed to two reasons: (a) Samples of different categories are unbalanced. Quantity characteristics of the power line corridor dataset is summarized in Table 3. Both point and block percentage on pylon category are much smaller than those on other two categories. Point percentage is defined as (number of points belonging to category c/number of all points); Block percentage is defined as (number of blocks containing category c points/number of all blocks). As a result, model does not 'see' enough samples of pylons so has lower performance of segmenting them; (b) As shown in Fig. 2, geometric structure of pylon is more complicated than those of other two categories and pylons have joint places with power lines and grounds, making it more difficult to segment.

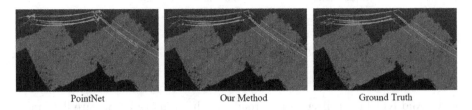

PointNet   Our Method   Ground Truth

Fig. 6. Visualization of PointNet's and our method's predicted results. (Color figure online)

A visualization of the segmentation results by our method, PointNet and ground truth label is shown in Fig. 6. Our method performs well on all categories while PointNet cannot recognize pylon category. On the whole, our predicted result is very close to the ground truth label. In addition, our model is efficient. On a GTX 1070 GPU, it only takes 0.93 ms to predict 1 m^2 data of our power line corridor dataset.

4.3   Segmentation on KITTI Point Cloud Dataset

Settings. KITTI point cloud dataset is randomly separated into a training set with 6481 frames and a validation set with 1000 frames. In addition, each point cloud is separated into 4×4 m^2 blocks. And 2048 points are randomly sampled from each block as the inputs. Reasons for the setting here is similar to those of the power line corridor dataset. Our method is implemented under our presentation p3 mentioned above, and PointNet [1] is under its original presentation p0. The model is trained on the same machine mentioned above.

Results and Analysis. To evaluate the generalization ability of our method, experiments on KITTI point cloud dataset are included. We compare our method with PointNet and SqueezeSeg [17]. SqueezeSeg is a leading segmentation algorithm on KITTI point cloud dataset. Experiment results on IoU are summarized in Table 4. Our method surpasses PointNet on all categories and is comparable with SqueezeSeg on car and pedestrian categories. IoU on car category from our method is even higher than that from SqueezeSeg without CRF. Consequently, our method not only has prominent performance on power line corridor dateset, but also generalizes well on KITTI dataset.

Note that PointNet's performance on KITTI is much better than that on Power Line Corridor Dataset. The difference is attributed to the following reason. PointNet was initially designed on S3DIS dataset [18], an indoor scene with

Table 4. Comparison with other methods on KITTI Dataset. Metric is IoU. All values in the table are in percentages

	Car	Pedestrian	Cyclist
SqueezeSeg	60.9	22.8	26.4
SqueezeSeg with CRF	64.6	21.8	25.1
PointNet	60.7	13.9	8.4
Our method	64.1	21.8	8.7

rooms. And KITTI is collected from roads. Both rooms and roads are flat landforms, which are different from power line corridor where steep slopes exist. In such conditions, the local height information referring to a block could be represented by global height referring to a file, so PointNet's channel presentation is effective on KITTI. This experiment also shows that our channel presentation is suitable for various terrains.

5   Conclusion

We propose the first deep learning based framework for power line corridor point cloud segmentation. In specific, we design an effective channel presentation for LiDAR point clouds and adapt a general convolutional neural network as our basic network. Compared to the existing works, our approach has three superiorities: (a) It does not rely on hand-crafted features which requires priori knowledge, but utilize a trainable deep learning model, which has strong generalization ability; (b) It does not use images but LiDAR data, so it is not sensitive to outer factors like illumination and thus more stable; (c) It finishes segmentation tasks within a single stage rather than multiple stages, so is able to leverage object context and get rid of propagated errors. In order to evaluate the effectiveness of our approach, we collect and label a large scale point cloud dataset of power line corridor scene to do experiments. To verify the generalization ability of our approach, we also test it on KITTI dataset. Experiments shows that our model can achieve very high segmentation accuracy with fast and stable runtime (0.93 $\pm$ 0.5 ms/m^2) on power line corridor dataset and generalize well on KITTI, which means that our approach is not only potential to meet the urgent need of automatically inspecting power lines but also is useful for other applications like autonomous driving.

References

1. Qi, C.R., et al.: PointNet: deep learning on point sets for 3D classification and segmentation. In: Proceedings of the IEEE Conference on Computer Vision and Pattern Recognition (2017)

2. Kim, H.B., Sohn, G.: 3D classification of power-line scene from airborne laser scanning data using random forests. Int. Arch. Photogramm. Remote Sens. **38**, 126–132 (2010)
3. Guan, H., et al.: Extraction of power-transmission lines from vehicle-borne LiDAR data. Int. J. Remote Sens. **37**(1), 229–247 (2016)
4. Liu, Y., et al.: Classification of airborne LiDAR intensity data using statistical analysis and hough transform with application to power line corridors. In: 2009 Digital Image Computing: Techniques and Applications. IEEE (2009)
5. Zhang, Y., et al.: UAV low altitude photogrammetry for power line inspection. ISPRS Int. J. Geo-Inf. **6**(1), 14 (2017)
6. Maurer, M., et al.: Automated inspection of power line corridors to measure vegetation undercut using UAV-based images. ISPRS Ann. Photogrammetry Remote Sens. Spat. Inf. Sci. **4** (2017)
7. Qi, C.R., et al.: PointNet++: deep hierarchical feature learning on point sets in a metric space. In: Advances in Neural Information Processing Systems (2017)
8. Long, J., Shelhamer, E., Darrell, T.: Fully convolutional networks for semantic segmentation. In: Proceedings of the IEEE Conference on Computer Vision and Pattern Recognition (2015)
9. Zhang, Y., et al.: Automatic power line inspection using UAV images. Remote Sens. **9**(8), 824 (2017)
10. Aubry, M., Schlickewei, U., Cremers, D.: The wave kernel signature: a quantum mechanical approach to shape analysis. In: 2011 IEEE International Conference on Computer Vision Workshops (ICCV Workshops). IEEE (2011)
11. Bronstein, M.M., Kokkinos, I.: Scale-invariant heat kernel signatures for non-rigid shape recognition. In: 2010 IEEE Computer Society Conference on Computer Vision and Pattern Recognition. IEEE (2010)
12. Rusu, R.B., et al.: Aligning point cloud views using persistent feature histograms. In: 2008 IEEE/RSJ International Conference on Intelligent Robots and Systems. IEEE (2008)
13. Maturana, D., Scherer, S.: VoxNet: a 3D convolutional neural network for real-time object recognition. In: 2015 IEEE/RSJ International Conference on Intelligent Robots and Systems (IROS). IEEE (2015)
14. Qi, C.R., et al.: Volumetric and multi-view CNNs for object classification on 3D data. In: Proceedings of the IEEE Conference on Computer Vision and Pattern Recognition (2016)
15. He, T., et al.: GeoNet: deep geodesic networks for point cloud analysis. arXiv preprint arXiv:1901.00680 (2019)
16. Geiger, A., Lenz, P., Urtasun, R.: Are we ready for autonomous driving? The KITTI Vision Benchmark Suite. In: Proceedings CVPR (2012)
17. Wu, B., et al.: SqueezeSeg: convolutional neural nets with recurrent CRF for real-time road-object segmentation from 3D LiDAR point cloud. In: 2018 IEEE International Conference on Robotics and Automation (ICRA). IEEE (2018)
18. Armeni, I., et al.: 3D semantic parsing of large-scale indoor spaces. In: Proceedings of the IEEE Conference on Computer Vision and Pattern Recognition (2016)
19. https://www.danielgm.net/cc/

Face Liveness Detection Based on Client Identity Using Siamese Network

Huiling Hao[1], Mingtao Pei[1], and Meng Zhao[2(✉)]

[1] Beijing Laboratory of Intelligent Information Technology, School of Computer Science, Beijing Institute of Technology, Beijing 100081, China
{haohuiling,peimt}@bit.edu.cn
[2] College of Electrical Engineering and Automation, Shandong University of Science and Technology, Qingdao 266590, China
zhaomeng@sdust.edu.cn

Abstract. Face liveness detection is an essential prerequisite for face recognition applications. Previous face liveness detection methods usually train a binary classifier to differentiate between a fake face and a real face before face recognition. The client identity information is not utilized in previous face liveness detection methods. However, in practical face recognition applications, face spoofing attacks are always aimed at a specific client, and the client identity information can provide useful clues for face liveness detection. In this paper, we propose a face liveness detection method based on the client identity using Siamese network. We detect face liveness after face recognition instead of before face recognition, that is, we detect face liveness with the client identity information. We train a Siamese network with image pairs. Each image pair consists of two real face images or one real and one fake face images. The face images in each pair come from a same client. Given a test face image, the face image is firstly recognized by face recognition system, then the real face image of the identified client is retrieved to help the face liveness detection. Experiment results demonstrate the effectiveness of our method.

Keywords: Face liveness detection · Client identity · Siamese network

1 Introduction

With the increasing deployment of face recognition in many applications such as intelligent entrance guard system, security surveillance and intelligent human machine interface, its security concern becomes increasingly important. Many face liveness detection methods are proposed [1–9].

Most previous face liveness detection methods train a binary classifier to differentiate between a fake face and a real face before face recognition. The client identity information is not utilized in previous face liveness detection methods. However, in practical face recognition applications, the real face images of the

Z. Lin et al. (Eds.): PRCV 2019, LNCS 11857, pp. 172–180, 2019.
https://doi.org/10.1007/978-3-030-31654-9_15

clients are available to the face recognition system, and face spoofing attacks are always aimed at a certain client. Therefore, the client identity information can provide useful clues for face liveness detection.

In this paper, we propose a face liveness detection method based on the client identity using Siamese network. We detect face liveness after face recognition instead of before face recognition, that is, we detect face liveness with the client identity information. In training stage, we collect face image pairs to train a Siamese network. Each image pair consists of two face images. The two face images can be a real face image and a fake face image, or two real face images. The two face images in each pair come from a same client. The trained Siamese network can classify the input image pair as "two real" or "one fake one real". In testing stage, the input test face image is first identified by a face recognizer and the identity information of the test face image is obtained. Then the real face image of the identified client is retrieved. The retrieved real face image and the test face image are classified by the trained Siamese network. If the Siamese network classify these two images as "two real", then the input test face image is a real face image, otherwise, it is a fake image.

The rest of this paper is organized as follows: Sect. 2 describes related works on face liveness detection. Section 3 demonstrates the details of our method. Section 4 shows the experimental results. And Sect. 5 concludes this paper.

2   Related Work

Existing face liveness detection methods can be categorized into three groups with respect to the clues used for liveness detection: motion-based methods, texture-based methods, and 3D shape-based methods.

Motion-based methods: Motion-based methods are mainly based on the fact that living face is dynamic. Given an image sequence, these methods attempt to capture facial response like eye blinking, mouth movement, and head pose, then exploit spatial and temporal features. Pan et al. [6] proposed a real-time face liveness detection method using an ordinary webcam by recognizing spontaneous eye-blinks. In this method, they constructed different stages of blinking action, and then used these as criterion to determine whether the eyes are open or closed. Bao et al. [7] proposed to detect face liveness based on the difference between the optical flow information real face and fake face. Singh et al. [23] distinguished fake faces from the real ones by detecting eye and mouth movements based on a haar classifier.

Texture-based methods: Texture-based methods use the texture distortions which are caused by secondary imaging to detect face liveness. On the basis of differences between live face image and forged face image in spectral composition, Li et al. [4] proposed a face living detection method using two-dimensional Fourier transform. In this method, they transformed face images into frequency domain to complete the classification. Dhrubajyoti et al. [5] distinguished the authenticity of face by analyzing the energy values in frequency domain. If the energy value of measured face is lower than the pre-set threshold, it's determined to be a fake face. Alotaibi et al. [24] employed the nonlinear diffusion to enhance edges in the input image, then used convolution neural networks to detect face liveness based on the enhanced edges.

3D shape-based methods: These methods are based on the fact that real face is 3-dimensional while fake face is usually 2-dimensional. However, these methods will fail when coping with 3D mask attacking, such as the 3D Mask Attack dataset (3DMAD) [25].

All of the above mentioned methods train a binary classifier to differentiate between a fake face and a real face before face recognition. Recently, some face liveness detection methods using client identity information are proposed. Ivana et al. [27] established two client-specific anti-spoofing systems by using the client's identity information, and the experiment results show better generalization ability in detecting spoofing attacks. Shervin et al. [28] proposed to use a pre-trained deep convolution neural networks to train a one-class client-specific classifications for face liveness detection. Different from these client specific methods, we use Siamese network, which can distinguish the input image pair as "two real" or "one fake one real", to detect spoofing attacks.

3   Proposed Method

3.1   Framework

In face spoofing attacks, attackers may spoof the face recognitions system with photo, video or even 3D mask. Whatever the spoofing method, the only goal of the attacker is to let the face recognition system believe that the attacker is a certain client of the system. Usually, the face recognition system does have the real face image of its clients.

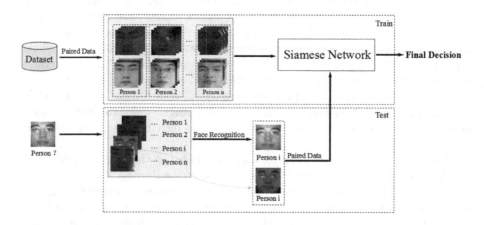

Fig. 1. The Framework of our method.

Based on the above observation, we propose a face liveness detection method based on the client identity. Figure 1 shows the framework of our method which contains two stages: offline training stage and online testing stage.

In the offline training stage, we collect face image pairs to train a Siamese network for the face liveness detection. Each image pair consists of two face images. The two face images can be a real face image and a fake face image, or two real face images. The two face images in each pair come from a same client. For an image pair, if its two face images are both real, it is a positive pair, otherwise, it is a negative pair. A Siamese network is trained on the positive and negative pairs. The trained Siamese network can classify the input image pair as "two real" or "one fake one real".

In testing stage, the input test face image is first identified by a face recognizer and the identity information of the test face image is obtained. Then the real face image of the identified client is retrieved. The retrieved real face image and the test face image form an image pair and are classified by the trained Siamese network. If the Siamese network classify these two images as "two real", then the input test face image is a real face image, otherwise, it is a fake image.

3.2 Siamese Network

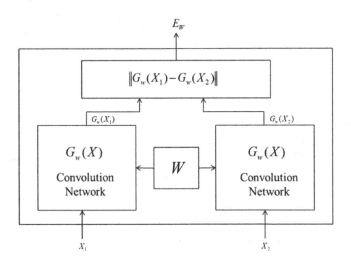

Fig. 2. Siamese architecture [11].

To utilize the client identity information for face liveness detection, we use the Siamese network, which is proposed in [10] and modified for face verification in [11,13]. Siamese Network is a class of neural network architectures that contain two or more subnetworks. The contained subnetworks may be identical or different. We use the Siamese network with two identical subnetworks. Figure 2 shows the architecture of the Siamese network. The two subnetworks are convolution networks. They have the same configuration with the same parameters and weights, and parameter updating is mirrored across both subnetworks.

The input of the Siamese network is an image pair (X_1, X_2). Then image features are extracted by the two identical convolution neural network as $G_w(X_1)$ and $G_w(X_2)$, respectively. The contrastive loss function [26] is employed to train the network and the equation of the contrastive loss function is shown on Eq. (1).

$$L = \frac{1}{2N} \sum_{n=1}^{N} yd^2 + (1 - y)max(m\,arg\,in - d, 0)^2 \qquad (1)$$

where $d = \|a_n - b_n\|_2$ is the Euclidean distance between two samples' features, y represents the label. In our case, $y = 1$ indicates that the two face images are both real face images, and $y = 0$ indicates that one of the two face images is a fake face image. *Margin* is the pre-set threshold.

This loss function encourages matching pairs (two real face images of a person) to be close together in feature space while pushing non-matching pairs (one real face image and one fake face image of a person) apart.

In our implementation, the two subnetworks are based on the wildly used AlexNet [12] architecture. We make some modifications on the AlexNet to fit our data. The details of the convolution neural network we used are shown in Fig. 3. There are five convolution layers and three pooling layers. We use it to extract hierarchical features through multi-layers' convolution and obtain invariance property through pooling layers' down-sampling operation.

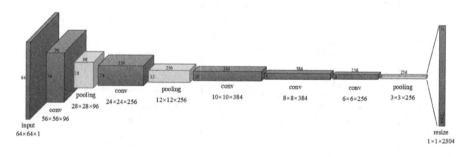

Fig. 3. The details of our convolution neural network.

4   Experiments

4.1   Datasets

To prove the effectiveness of our method, we conduct experiments on two public datasets: NUAA [14] and Replay-Attack [15].

NUAA is a publicly available dataset, which is provided by Nanjing University of Aeronautics and Astronautics, and is widely used for the evaluation of face liveness detection. The data set contains 12614 images of 15 different subjects, including both real and fake face images. The database is divided into a training set with a total of 3491 (real: 1,743/fake: 1,748) images and a test set with a total of 9123 (real: 3,362/fake: 5,761) images.

Replay-Attack is provided by IDIAP in 2012. It contains 1300 video clips of 50 different subjects. These video clips are divided into 300 real-access videos and 1000 spoofing attack videos. The dataset takes into consideration the different lighting conditions used in spoofing attacks. The Replay-Attack database consists of training set, development set and testing set.

To keep consistent to previous works, we use the half total error rate (HTER) as the metric in our experiments. The HTER is half of the sum of the false rejection rate (FRR) and false acceptance rate (FAR):

$$HTER = \frac{FRR + FAR}{2} \tag{2}$$

4.2   Results on NUAA

In NUAA, for each real face image in the training set, we randomly select a real face image of the same subject from the training set to form a positive pair, and randomly select a fake face image of the same subject to form a negative pair. In total, we construct 1743 positive pairs and 1743 negative pairs to train the Siamese network.

Table 1. Results on NUAA dataset.

Method	HTER (%)
LBP only [16]	5.45
LBP+Gabor+HOG [17]	3.95
LBP+Gabor+Pixcel [18]	2.45
Our method	**1.96**

In testing, for each image in the test set, we assume that the identity of the face in the test image is known (suppose the identity is p_i), we select one real face image of p_i from the training set, and form an image pair with the test image. The formed image pair is input to the trained Siamese network to justify whether the test image is real of fake. We compare our method with the LBP [16], LBP+Gabor+HOG [17] and LBP+Gabor+Pixcel [18]. Table 1 shows the comparison results of liveness detection on the NUAA dataset. We can see that our method performs better than the compared methods.

4.3 Results on Replay-Attack

For Replay-Attack dataset, we regard each video clip as a sequence of images. Similar to the NUAA dataset, we construct 14338 positive pairs and 14338 negative pairs to train the Siamese network. We compare our method with several state-of-art methods. Table 2 shows the comparison results of liveness detection on the Replay-Attack dataset.

Table 2. Results on Replay-Attack Dataset.

Method	HTER (%)
Fine-tuned VGG-Face [19]	4.30
DPCNN [19]	6.10
Boulkenafet et al. [20]	2.90
Boulkenafet et al. [21]	2.20
Moire pattern [22]	3.30
Patch-based CNN [2]	1.25
Depth-based CNN [2]	0.75
Patch and depth CNN [2]	0.72
Our method	**0.86**

We can see that our method achieves good performance on the Replay-Attack dataset. The depth-based CNN [2] and Patch and depth CNN [2] performs better than our method. The reason may be that these two methods use depth information in the face liveness detection.

5   Conclusion

In this paper, we propose a face liveness detection method based on the client identity information using Siamese network. Different from most of previous methods, we do the face liveness detection after face recognition. Therefore, the client identity information and the real face image of the client can be used to help the face liveness detection.

The drawback of our method is that when the face recognition fails, that is, when the client identity is not correct, the performance of face liveness detection will drop dramatically. However, as spoofing attack usually aims to pretend to be certain client to cheat the face recognition system, when the face recognition fails, the spoofing attack will also fail. In our future work, we will investigate how to use the client identity information to detect spoofing attack in videos.

Acknowledgement. This research was supported by China Postdoctoral Science Foundation Grant (2018M642680).

References

1. Lei, L., Xia, Z., Li, L., Jiang, X., Roli, F.: Face anti-spoofing via hybrid convolutional neural network. In: 2017 International Conference on the Frontiers and Advances in Data Science (FADS) (2017)
2. Atoum, Y., Liu, Y., Jourabloo, A., Liu, X.: Face anti-spoofing using patch and depth-based CNNs. In: IEEE International Joint Conference on Biometrics (2018)
3. Anjos, A., Marcel, S.: Counter-measures to photo attacks in face recognition: a public database and a baseline. In: International Joint Conference on Biometrics (2011)
4. Li, J., Wang, Y., Tan, T., Jain, A.K.: Live face detection based on the analysis of fourier spectra. Proc. SPIE **5404**, 296–303 (2004)
5. Das, D., Chakraborty, S.: Face liveness detection based on frequency and microtexture analysis. In: International Conference on Advances in Engineering & Technology Research (2015)
6. Gang, P., Lin, S., Wu, Z., Lao, S.: Eyeblink-based anti-spoofing in face recognition from a generic webcamera. In: IEEE International Conference on Computer Vision (2007)
7. Wei, B., Hong, L., Nan, L., Wei, J.: A liveness detection method for face recognition based on optical flow field. In: International Conference on Image Analysis & Signal Processing (2009)
8. Benlamoudi, A., Samai, D., Ouafi, A., Bekhouche, S.E., Talebahmed, A., Hadid, A.: Face spoofing detection using local binary patterns and fisher score, pp. 1–5 (2015)
9. Schwartz, W.R., Rocha, A., Pedrini, H.: Face spoofing detection through partial least squares and low-level descriptors. In: International Joint Conference on Biometrics (2011)
10. Bromley, J., Guyon, I., Lecun, Y., Säckinger, E., Shah, R.: Signatureverification using a "siamese" time delay neural network. Int. J. Pattern Recogn. Artif. Intell. **7**(04), 669–688 (1993)
11. Chopra, S., Hadsell, R., Lecun, Y.: Learning a similarity metric discriminatively, with application to face verification, vol. 1, pp. 539–546 (2005)
12. Krizhevsky, A., Sutskever, I., Hinton, G.E.: ImageNet classification with deep convolutional neural networks. In: Neural Information Processing Systems vol. 141, no. (5), pp. 1097–1105 (2012)
13. Bukovcikova, Z., Sopiak, D., Oravec, M., Pavlovicova, J.: Face verification using convolutional neural networks with Siamese architecture, pp. 205–208 (2017)
14. Tan, X., Li, Y., Liu, J., Jiang, L.: Face liveness detection from a single image with sparse low rank bilinear discriminative model. In: Daniilidis, K., Maragos, P., Paragios, N. (eds.) ECCV 2010. LNCS, vol. 6316, pp. 504–517. Springer, Heidelberg (2010). https://doi.org/10.1007/978-3-642-15567-3_37
15. Chingovska, I., Anjos, A., Marcel, S.: On the effectiveness of local binary patterns in face anti-spoofing, pp. 1–7 (2012)
16. Maatta, J., Hadid, A., Pietikainen, M.: Face spoofing detection from single images using micro-texture analysis. Int. J. Cent. Bank., 1–7 (2011)
17. Maatta, J., Hadid, A., Pietikainen, M.: Face spoofing detection from single images using texture and local shape analysis. IET Biometrics **1**(1), 3–10 (2012)
18. Yuan, H., Li, S., Deng, H.: 2D face spoofing detection method based on multi-feature fusion. Comput. Appl. Softw. (2017)

19. Li, L., Feng, X., Boulkenafet, Z., Xia, Z., Li, M., Hadid, A.: An original face anti-spoofing approach using partial convolutional neural network, pp. 1–6 (2016)

20. Boulkenafet, Z., Komulainen, J., Hadid, A.: Face anti-spoofing based on color texture analysis. In: International Conference on Image Processing, pp. 2636–2640 (2015)

21. Boulkenafet, Z., Komulainen, J., Hadid, A.: Face antispoofing using speeded-up robust features and fisher vector encoding. IEEE Signal Process. Lett. **24**, 141–145 (2017)

22. Patel, K., Han, H., Jain, A.K., Ott, G.: Live face video vs. spoof face video: use of moiré patterns to detect replay video attacks, pp. 98–105 (2015)

23. Singh, A.K., Joshi, P., Nandi, G.C.: Face recognition with liveness detection using eye and mouth movement. In: 2014 International Conference on Signal Propagation and Computer Technology (ICSPCT 2014), pp. 592–597. IEEE (2014)

24. Alotaibi, A., Mahmood, A.: Deep face liveness detection based on nonlinear diffusion using convolution neural network. Signal Image Video Process. **11**(4), 713–720 (2017)

25. Erdogmus, N., Marcel, S.: Spoofing 2D face recognition systems with 3D masks, pp. 1–8 (2013)

26. Hadsell, R., Chopra, S., Lecun, Y.: Dimensionality reduction by learning an invariant mapping, vol. 2, pp. 1735–1742 (2006)

27. Chingovska, I., Anjos, A.R.D.: On the use of client identity information for face antispoofing. IEEE Trans. Inf. Forensics Secur. **10**(4), 787–796 (2017)

28. Arashloo, S.R., Kittler, J.: Client-specific anomaly detection for face presentation attack detection (2018)

Learning Weighted Video Segments for Temporal Action Localization

Che Sun, Hao Song, Xinxiao Wu$^{(\boxtimes)}$, and Yunde Jia

Beijing Laboratory of Intelligent Information Technology, School of Computer
Science, Beijing Institute of Technology, Beijing 100081, China
{sunche,songhao,wuxinxiao,jiayunde}@bit.edu.cn

Abstract. This paper proposes a novel approach of learning weighted
video segments via supervised temporal attention for action localization
in untrimmed videos. The learned segment weights represent informativeness of video segments to recognize actions and benefit inferring the
boundaries to temporally localize actions. We build a Supervised Temporal Attention Network (STAN) to dynamically learn the weights of
video segments, and generate descriptive and discriminative video representations. We use a proposal generator and a classifier to estimate
the boundaries of actions and classify the classes of actions, respectively.
Extensive experiments are conducted on two public benchmarks THU-
MOS2014 and ActivityNet1.3. The results demonstrate that our approach achieves substantially better performance than the state-of-the-art
methods, verifying the effectiveness of learning weighted video segments.

Keywords: Temporal action localization · Weighted video segments ·
Attention mechanism

1 Introduction

Temporal action localization in untrimmed videos aims to analyze whether a
specific action occurs in videos and determine the temporal boundaries (the
start time and the end time) of the action simultaneously. There has been much
work on temporal action localization in untrimmed videos [24,26,27], but it
still remains challenging due to the cluttered background, large variances of
appearance and motion, and low resolution. Moreover, the same action may
occur several times in a video and the durations of action instances with the
same class may vary from a few seconds to a few minutes, which further makes
it extremely difficult to localize actions in untrimmed videos.

To tackle these problems, many deep methods have been proposed and
achieved remarkable progress in temporal action localization, owing to the great
success of deep learning on various visual tasks [6,13], especially on video analysis [23,25]. Some of the prominent methods [21,27] resort to sliding windows to
produce temporal boundaries of actions and many other methods [8,26] generate proposals as candidate action instances for localization. These deep methods

© Springer Nature Switzerland AG 2019
Z. Lin et al. (Eds.): PRCV 2019, LNCS 11857, pp. 181–192, 2019.
https://doi.org/10.1007/978-3-030-31654-9_16

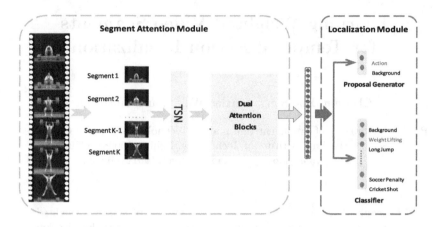

Fig. 1. The architecture of our method.

equally treat each video segment within the sliding windows or proposals and directly combine the video segments for temporal action localization. In practice, different segments embody diverse information in a video. Some segments present intrinsic motion and appearance of an action, which will play a vital role on action localization. Taking the triple jump action as an example, the segment of jumping action is obviously more important than other segments to localize the triple jump in a video, since the jumping motion reflects the essence characteristics of the triple jump. Therefore, it is necessary to learn weighted video segments to represent the intrinsic motion and appearance information.

In this paper, we propose a novel approach of learning weighted video segments via supervised temporal attention for action localization in untrimmed videos. The learned weights represent the importance of the corresponding video segments on recognizing actions and further benefit predicting temporal boundaries to localize actions. We build a Supervised Temporal Attention Network (STAN) that has two modules: segment attention module and localization module. The segment attention module is designed to dynamically learn the weights of video segments with supervised attention mechanism. With the learned weights, the segments are fed into a Long Short Term Memory (LSTM) model to capture the temporal relationships between them. Through the segment attention module, the STAN learns weighted video segments and generates video representation with superior descriptive and discriminative ability. Besides, the localization module is designed to classify the action classes and determine the temporal action boundaries, including a proposal generator and a classifier. The proposal generator is used to identify the input video as either background proposal or action proposal, and the classifier is used to classify the action classes of the identified action proposal. At last, a Non-Maximum Suppression (NMS) method is employed to remove the videos with small classification scores and produce the temporal boundaries of action instances. Figure 1 shows the detailed architecture of STAN.

Overall, the main contributions of our work are: (1) We propose a novel approach for temporal action localization by learning weighted video segments in untrimmed videos. The learned segment weights represent informativeness of video segments on recognizing actions and further benefit inferring the boundaries for temporally localizing actions. (2) We build a Supervised Temporal Attention Network (STAN) to dynamically learn the weights of video segments via a supervised attention mechanism. (3) Experiments on two public datasets comprehensively verify the superior performance of our approach compared with the state-of-the-art methods.

2   Related Work

Early methods of temporal action localization use the sliding windows to sample candidate video segments with multiple temporal scales, and then adopt classifiers to classify the segments. Wang et al. [24] extracted the deep feature of each frame and designed a system based on the iDT. They also used a postprocessing method to boost the localization performance. Shou et al. [21] built a three-stage framework for temporal action localization with an overlap loss function. Zhao et al. [27] used a structured temporal pyramid to model the temporal structure of each action instance. They utilized the context information of an action instance to produce informative features for temporal action localization. Different from these methods, our method generates action proposals by dynamically learning the weights of video segments for temporal action localization.

Much recent work tries to extract action proposals from the video and then classify the proposals into action classes. Gao et al. [8] used a cascaded boundary regression model to produce class-agnostic proposals and detect specific actions with the proposals. Xu et al. [26] applied the region-based method to temporal action localization and learned candidate temporal regions containing actions. Chao et al. [4] improved receptive field alignment to exploit the temporal context of actions for generating proposals and classifying actions. Different from these methods, we propose a supervised attention network to generate action proposals from the candidate video segments produced by sliding windows.

3   The Architecture

3.1   Segment Attention Module

Inspired by the attention mechanism [16,18], we introduce the attention mechanism to learn video segment weights. We assign each segment a weight to represent its contribution and build a segment attention module to compute the weight of each segment. In the segment attention module, we design dual attention blocks where one is to learn the universal video segments measurement and the other is to learn the context-aware video segments measurement, as shown in Fig. 2. Furthermore, we add a supervised constraint to the second attention block to eliminate the influence of background segments.

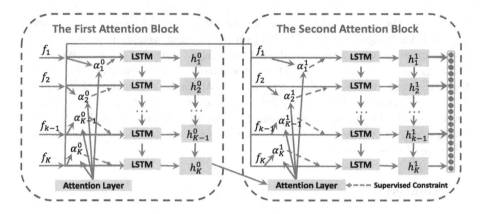

Fig. 2. The architecture of the dual attention blocks.

The First Attention Block. Given an input video v and its action class label y, the video v is split into K non-overlap segments, denoted by $\{s_1, s_2, \cdots, s_K\}$. Let $\{\mathbf{f}_1, \mathbf{f}_2, \cdots, \mathbf{f}_K\}$ be the feature vectors of the segments and $\{\alpha_1^0, \alpha_2^0, \cdots, \alpha_K^0\}$ be the weights of the segments. We build an internal layer that filters the feature vectors $\{\mathbf{f}_1, \mathbf{f}_2, \cdots, \mathbf{f}_K\}$ by taking the inner product to obtain the corresponding encodings $\{\mathbf{e}_1, \mathbf{e}_2, \cdots, \mathbf{e}_K\}$:

$$\mathbf{e}_t = \mathbf{u}^{0\top} \cdot \mathbf{f}_t, \tag{1}$$

where $\mathbf{u}^0$ is the parameter of the attention layer with the same size of the feature vectors. Then, $\{\mathbf{e}_1, \mathbf{e}_2, \cdots, \mathbf{e}_K\}$ are passed to a softmax operator to calculate the positive weights $\{\alpha_t^0\}$ with the constraint of $\sum_{t=1}^{K} \alpha_t^0 = 1$:

$$\alpha_t^0 = \frac{\exp(\mathbf{e}_t)}{\sum_{j=1}^{K} \exp(\mathbf{e}_j)}. \tag{2}$$

Different from the existing attention models [26,27] that use average pooling or concatenation operation, we aggregate the weighted segments using a LSTM model to generate the video representations by capturing temporal information. The LSTM has a cell state controlled by three gates, which decides how much information should be let through. In our work, the weighted segments are calculated as $\mathbf{x}_t = \alpha_t^0 * \mathbf{f}_t$, which are treated as the inputs of the LSTM model. We calculate the last hidden state $\mathbf{h}_K^0$ as the feature representation of the input video by

$$\mathbf{h}_K^0 = LSTM(\alpha_t^0 * \mathbf{f}_t). \tag{3}$$

The Second Attention Block. In the first attention block, the process of calculating attention weights α_t does not take the context information into consideration. Intuitively, weighting a video segment can benefit from other segments, where the segments are often correlated but temporally very separated. Thus, we introduce the second attention block to select context-aware segments that are more discriminative.

Let $\mathbf{u}^0$ be the first internal state in the first attention layer, and $\mathbf{h}_K^0$ be the learned feature representation, where $\mathbf{h}_K^0$ is the last hidden state of the LSTM model. The second internal state $\mathbf{u}^1$ is calculated by a transfer layer with the input $\mathbf{h}_K^0$:

$$\mathbf{u}^1 = \tanh(\mathbf{W}^1 \mathbf{h}_K^0 + \mathbf{b}^1), \tag{4}$$

where $\mathbf{W}^1$ and $\mathbf{b}^1$ are the weight matrix and the bias vectors of the neurons, respectively. $\tanh(x) = \frac{e^x - e^{-x}}{e^x + e^{-x}}$ imposes the hyperbolic tangent nonlinearity. We use another LSTM model to generate the last hidden $\mathbf{h}_K^1$, which will be the final representation generated by $\mathbf{u}^1$ reusing Eqs. (1), (2) and (3).

The Supervised Constraint. The dual attention blocks capture the important segments of an input video, but the background segments in the sliding window are non-negligible noises. The background segments usually have unique features that may get a higher attention weight under the traditional unsupervised learning method, but they contain less action information in essence. In order to eliminate this noise, we impose a supervised constraint to filter out the background segments and retain the meaningful action segments. According to the ground-truth action boundaries, we assign an actionness label to each segment as the supervised information to guide the learning of segment weights. The actionness label represents whether the segment contains an action frame or not. In practice, we relax the supervised constraint in the learning progress to fully exploit the ability of the attention mechanism. We use a multi-class loss function as the supervised constraint to train the attention module, as discussed in Sect. 3.3.

3.2   Localization Module

The localization module aims to infer the action boundaries and complete action classification, including a proposal generator and a classifier. The proposal generator generates video proposals that contain action instances. The classifier classifies the generated video proposal into a specific class.

Proposal Generator. Given an input video v, its representation $\mathbf{h}_K$ is learned via the attention module in Sect. 3.1, given by $\mathbf{h}_K^{pro} = \text{Attention}(v)$. $\mathbf{h}_K^{pro}$ is then fed into the proposal generator to compute a binary score p_{pro} and a relative offset $\{s_i, e_i\}$. p_{pro} shows that the corresponding proposal is an action or background, i.e., $p_{pro} = 1$ for an action and $p_{pro} = 0$ for background. If the proposal is an action (i.e., $p_{pro} = 1$), $\{s_i, e_i\}$ is the start and end offset of the action segment in the input video. We use two fully connected layers to construct the proposal generator. The training samples are selected using the following strategy. For the untrimmed videos, we only select the segments from the ground truth as positive samples. The negative samples consist of background segments that are randomly sampled from the background videos. The temporal Intersection-over-Union (tIoU) between the training video and its groundtruth is the main criterion: (1) if the tIoU of the video is larger than 0.7, a positive label is assigned according to its action class; (2) if the tIoU of the video is smaller than 0.3, we treat the video as background. We train the proposal generator with a positive/negative ratio of 1:1.

Classifier. After eliminating background videos using the proposal generator, we train the classifier for $N + 1$ classes, containing N action classes and background class. Similar to the proposal generator, the classifier consists of two separate fully connected layers to output action scores p_{cls} and the relative offset $\{s_i, e_i\}$. Both the proposal generator and the classifier are built on the segment attention module with the same structure but non-shared parameters. For training the classifier, we follow the similar training dataset construction strategy to the proposal generator. The differences are: (1) we explicitly set the action class label $y \in \{1, 2, \cdots, N\}$ when assigning a label for the positive training sample; (2) we train the classifier with a positive/negative ratio of 1:3.

3.3 Objective Function

The objective function of our network includes three parts: the classification loss, the regression loss, and the supervised attention loss. We use the softmax cross-entropy loss function for classification and the smooth L1 loss function [9] for regression.

We treat the supervised attention learning as a multi-class classification task, and use the sigmoid cross-entropy loss to constrain the attention module.

The classification loss is given by

$$L_{cls} = \frac{1}{N_t} \sum_i -y_i \ln(p_i), \tag{5}$$

where y_i is the one-hot encoding label of the action class, N_t stands for batch size, and p_i is the prediction score calculated by the proposal generator or classifier after the softmax layer.

The regression loss is formulated as

$$L_{reg} = \frac{1}{N_{pos}} \sum_i l_i^* (\|s_i - s_i^*\|_1^{smooth} + \|e_i - e_i^*\|_1^{smooth}), \tag{6}$$

where N_{pos} stands for the number of positive samples in a batch. s_i and e_i are the predicted start and end offset, respectively. s_i^* and e_i^* are the groundtruth start and end offset, respectively. $\| \cdot \|_1^{smooth}$ represents the smooth L1 loss function. l_i^* is the actionness label, i.e., $l_i^* = 1$ for positive samples, and $l_i^* = 0$ for negative samples.

The supervised attention loss is expressed as

$$L_{sat} = \frac{1}{N_{pos}} \sum_i \frac{1}{N_{seg}} \sum_j l_i^* \left[y_{ij}^s \ln \frac{1}{1 + \exp(-\log \mathbf{e}_{ij})} \right. \tag{7}$$
$$\left. + (1 - y_{ij}^s) \ln \frac{\exp(-\log \mathbf{e}_{ij})}{1 + \exp(-\log \mathbf{e}_{ij})} \right],$$

where N_{seg} stands for the number of segments in each video. y_{ij}^s is the label of the j-th segment in the i-th training sample. If the j-th segment contains any action frames, y_{ij}^s is set to 1; otherwise, y_{ij}^s is set to 0. $\mathbf{e}_{ij}$ represents the attention encoding of the j-th segment in the i-th training sample. The attention encoding $\{\mathbf{e}_1, \mathbf{e}_2, \ldots, \mathbf{e}_K\}$ is calculated by Eq. (1). The supervised attention loss is utilized to force the attention encoding to contain more actionness information.

The overall objective function is defined as

$$L = L_{cls} + \lambda_1 L_{reg} + \lambda_2 L_{sat}, \tag{8}$$

where λ_1 and λ_2 are the trade-off parameters, and λ_1 is set to 1. As for λ_2, we set an initial value of λ_2 to 0.95 and then decreases its value with iterations to relax the constraint. We find that the best models are obtained when λ_2 is multiplied by 0.95 after 1 K iterations.

4   Experiment

4.1   Datasets

To evaluate the effectiveness of our method, we conduct experiments on two challenging datasets: THUMOS2014 [10] and ActivityNet1.3 [7]. On the THU-MOS2014 dataset, we use the temporal annotated untrimmed videos in validation and test subsets for training and testing, respectively. On the ActivityNet1.3 dataset, we use the training set to train the STAN and the validation dataset for testing.

4.2   Evaluation Metric

We adopt the conventional evaluation strategy in THUMOS Challenge to calculate the temporal Intersection over Union (tIoU). A prediction is marked as correct only when it has a correct action class prediction and has tIoU with the groundtruth than a threshold. We report the mean Average Precision (mAP) at different tIoU thresholds as the evaluation metric.

4.3   Experiment Setup

Implementation Details. We split the video into short segments with equal temporal length. The length of segments is set to 15 frames for the THUMOS2014 dataset and 75 frames for the ActivityNet1.3 dataset. The segment scales are set to [1, 2, 3, 4, 5, 6, 8, 11, 16, 24, 32] on the THUMOS2014 dataset and [1, 2, 3, 4, 5, 6, 8, 10, 12, 14, 16, 20, 24, 28, 32, 40, 56, 64] on the ActivityNet1.3 dataset. The overlap segment of sliding windows with different scales is set to [0, 1, 2, 3, 4, 5, 6, 8, 12, 16, 24] and [0.6, 1, 2, 3, 4, 5, 7, 8, 10, 12, 14, 16, 20, 24, 28, 32, 40, 48, 56] on the THUMOS2014 and ActivityNet1.3 datasets, respectively.

We extract the appearance and motion features of the short segments using the Temporal Segment Network (TSN) [25]. In our work, the TSN model is trained by the ActivityNet1.3 dataset under the experiment setup in [25]. We follow the operation in [15] and extract the 400-dimensional feature vectors from the trained TSN per five frames. We cascade the TSN features of every 5 frames in each segment as the appearance and motion representation. All the segment features are normalized using L2-normalization. Then, we reduce the TSN feature vector dimension to 1024 by a fully connected layer. In the first attention block, the attention weight α_i^0 is calculated from a 1024×1 fully connection layer followed by a soft-max layer. Then α_i^0 is dot-multiplied by the i-th segment. The dimension of the hidden state in the LSTM model is set to 1024. In the second attention block, the attention weight α_i^1 is the output of the LSTM model of the first attention block followed by a soft-max layer. The dimension of the hidden state in the LSTM model of the second attention block is also set to 1024.

Post-processing. We use the proposal generator to remove the background videos and adjust the boundary of positives samples. These positives proposals may highly overlap with each other, so we adopt a soft Non-Maximum Suppression (soft-NMS) [1] method to eliminate highly overlapping. The soft-NMS threshold is set to 0.8 for the ActivityNet1.3 dataset and 0.65 for the THUMOS2014 dataset. We keep the top 300 proposals after the soft-NMS for action classification. Subsequently, the classifier accepts these processed proposals to produce the prediction scores and refine the temporal boundaries of the action instances again. At last, we conduct Greedy Non-Maximum Suppression (NMS) to remove redundant localization results and set the overlap threshold of NMS to $\alpha - 0.1$ in this paper, where α is the overlap threshold in evaluation.

4.4   Results on the THUMOS2014 Dataset

MAP Results. We report the comparison results between our method and the state-of-the-art methods in Table 1. From Table 1, we observe that: (1) STAN outperforms other methods especially when α is greater than 0.3, which demonstrates that our method localizes the action boundaries with higher accuracy in more difficult situations. (2) Our STAN outperforms the RNN based methods [2,19], since STAN effectively couples the attention mechanism and the LSTM model in a dual attention block, which learns the weighted video segments for temporal modeling of the entire video to further enhance the action localization. (3) Our method also works better than the methods [8,12] that use average pooling or concatenation operations to generate final video representations. This verifies that our method can generate more descriptive and discriminative video representations by learning weighted video segments.

Table 1. Results on the THUMOS2014 dataset with varied tIoU threshold α. We use the mean Average Precision (mAP) (%) as the localization results. The highest two scores are highlighted in bold and italic, respectively.

	α				
	0.1	0.2	0.3	0.4	0.5
The handcrafted features					
Karaman *et al.* [11]	1.5	0.9	0.5	0.3	0.2
Wang *et al.* [24]	19.2	17.8	14.6	12.1	8.5
Oneata *et al.* [17]	38.6	36.2	28.8	21.8	14.3
Heilbron *et al.* [3]	36.1	32.9	25.7	18.2	13.5
Deep neural networks					
Shou *et al.* [21]	47.7	43.5	36.3	28.7	19.0
Lin *et al.* [14]	50.1	47.8	43.0	35.0	24.6
Shou *et al.* [20]	–	–	40.1	29.4	23.3
Buch *et al.* [2]	–	–	45.7	–	29.2
Xu *et al.* [26]	54.5	51.5	44.8	35.6	28.9
Zhao *et al.* [27]	**66.0**	**59.4**	**51.9**	41.0	29.8
Gao *et al.* [8]	*60.1*	*56.7*	50.1	41.3	31.0
Qiu *et al.* [19]	–	–	48.2	*42.4*	*34.2*
Kong *et al.* [12]	54.7	53.0	48.5	41.3	32.5
STAN (ours)	56.1	54.3	*50.7*	**43.2**	**35.4**

Qualitative Results. Fig. 3 shows some examples of the prediction results on the THUMOS2014 dataset. Each prediction duration with the highest classification score is associated with the nearest ground truth annotation. In the "BasketballDunk" and "CricketShot" examples, our method localizes the action instance in the video accurately. In the "HighJump" example, the prediction start is a little earlier than the ground truth, because it is difficult to determine the boundary between the preparation and the start of "HighJump".

4.5 Results on ActivityNet Dataset

We also compare the STAN with the existing methods on the ActivityNet1.3 dataset. From Table 2, we find that our method works worse than [20], because [20] uses per-frame classifier to generate proposals with random temporal scales at each position, which may generate more accurate action candidates for temporal action localization than the segment based methods. Nevertheless, our method yields a higher mAP at a threshold of 0.95 than [20], which indicates that our method locates the action boundaries more accurately especially on the more difficult scenarios. Compared with the method [5], our approach yields comparable results, which demonstrates the effectiveness of learning weighted video segments for temporal action localization.

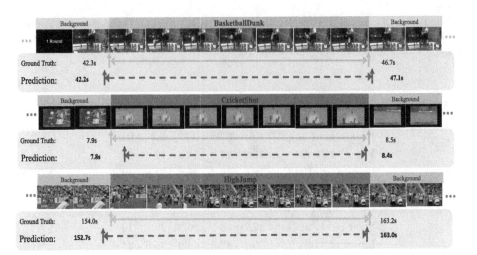

Fig. 3. The prediction results on the THUMOS2014 test dataset.

Table 2. Temporal action localization results (mAP) (%) on the ActivityNet1.3 dataset. The highest two scores are highlighted in bold and italic, respectively.

Model	$\alpha = 0.5$	$\alpha = 0.75$	$\alpha = 0.95$	Average
Singh *et al.* [22]	34.5	–	–	–
Shou *et al.* [20]	**45.3**	**26.0**	0.2	**23.8**
Xu *et al.* [26]	26.8	–	–	12.7
Dai *et al.* [5]	*36.4*	*21.1*	**3.9**	–
STAN (ours)	32.3	19.5	*1.7*	*17.2*

5   Conclusion

We have presented a novel end-to-end trainable Supervised Temporal Network (STAN) to learn weighted video segments for temporal action localization in untrimmed videos. With the supervision of actionness information, the segment attention module can dynamically learn the weights of video segments to represent their contributions to the action localization and further boost the localization performance. Extensive experiments on two public datasets of THUMOS2014 and ActivityNet1.3 show the superior performance of the STAN on temporally localizing actions in untrimmed videos. As we believe that STAN is a general solution for capturing the intrinsic motion and appearance information in videos, we are going to apply it in other video analysis tasks.

Acknowledgements. This work was supported in part by the Natural Science Foundation of China (NSFC) under grants No. 61673062.

References

1. Bodla, N., Singh, B., Chellappa, R., Davis, L.S.: Soft-NMS-improving object detection with one line of code. In: Proceedings of the IEEE International Conference on Computer Vision, pp. 5561–5569 (2017)
2. Buch, S., Escorcia, V., Ghanem, B., Fei-Fei, L., Niebles, J.C.: End-to-end, single-stream temporal action detection in untrimmed videos. In: Proceedings of the British Machine Vision Conference (BMVC), vol. 1, p. 2 (2017)
3. Caba Heilbron, F., Carlos Niebles, J., Ghanem, B.: Fast temporal activity proposals for efficient detection of human actions in untrimmed videos. In: Proceedings of the IEEE Conference on Computer Vision and Pattern Recognition, pp. 1914–1923 (2016)
4. Chao, Y.W., Vijayanarasimhan, S., Seybold, B., Ross, D.A., Deng, J., Sukthankar, R.: Rethinking the faster R-CNN architecture for temporal action localization. In: Proceedings of the IEEE Conference on Computer Vision and Pattern Recognition, pp. 1130–1139 (2018)
5. Dai, X., Singh, B., Zhang, G., Davis, L.S., Chen, Y.Q.: Temporal context network for activity localization in videos. In: 2017 IEEE International Conference on Computer Vision (ICCV), pp. 5727–5736. IEEE (2017)
6. Das, A., Agrawal, H., Zitnick, L., Parikh, D., Batra, D.: Human attention in visual question answering: do humans and deep networks look at the same regions? Comput. Vis. Image Underst. **163**, 90–100 (2017)
7. Caba Heilbron, F., Escorcia, V., Ghanem, B., Niebles, J.C.: Activitynet: a large-scale video benchmark for human activity understanding. In: Proceedings of the IEEE Conference on Computer Vision and Pattern Recognition, pp. 961–970 (2015)
8. Gao, J., Yang, Z., Nevatia, R.: Cascaded boundary regression for temporal action detection. In: British Machine Vision Conference (2017)
9. Girshick, R.: Fast R-CNN. In: IEEE International Conference on Computer Vision, pp. 1440–1448 (2015)
10. Jiang, Y.G., et al.: THUMOS challenge: action recognition with a large number of classes (2014). http://crcv.ucf.edu/THUMOS14/
11. Karaman, S., Seidenari, L., Del Bimbo, A.: Fast saliency based pooling offisher encoded dense trajectories, vol. 1 (2014)
12. Kong, W., Li, N., Liu, S., Li, T., Li, G.: BLP-boundary likelihood pinpointing networks for accurate temporal action localization. arXiv preprint arXiv:1811.02189 (2018)
13. Krizhevsky, A., Sutskever, I., Hinton, G.E.: Imagenet classification with deep convolutional neural networks. In: Advances in Neural Information Processing Systems, pp. 1097–1105 (2012)
14. Lin, T., Zhao, X., Shou, Z.: Single shot temporal action detection. In: Proceedings of the 2017 ACM on Multimedia Conference, pp. 988–996. ACM (2017)
15. Lin, T., Zhao, X., Su, H., Wang, C., Yang, M.: BSN: boundary sensitive network for temporal action proposal generation. In: Proceedings of the European Conference on Computer Vision (ECCV), pp. 3–19 (2018)
16. Mnih, V., Heess, N., Graves, A., et al.: Recurrent models of visual attention. In: Advances in Neural Information Processing Systems, pp. 2204–2212 (2014)
17. Oneata, D., Verbeek, J., Schmid, C.: The LEAR submission at Thumos 2014. In: Computer Vision and Pattern Recognition [cs.CV] (2014)
18. Qin, Y., Song, D., Chen, H., Cheng, W., Jiang, G., Cottrell, G.W.: A dual-stage attention-based recurrent neural network for time series prediction. In: Proceedings

of the Twenty-Sixth International Joint Conference on Artificial Intelligence, IJCAI 2017, Melbourne, Australia, 19–25 August 2017, pp. 2627–2633 (2017)

19. Qiu, H., Zheng, Y., Ye, H., Lu, Y., Wang, F., He, L.: Precise temporal action localization by evolving temporal proposals. In: Proceedings of the 2018 ACM on International Conference on Multimedia Retrieval, pp. 388–396. ACM (2018)

20. Shou, Z., Chan, J., Zareian, A., Miyazawa, K., Chang, S.F.: CDC: convolutional-deconvolutional networks for precise temporal action localization in untrimmed videos. In: 2017 IEEE Conference on Computer Vision and Pattern Recognition (CVPR), pp. 1417–1426. IEEE (2017)

21. Shou, Z., Wang, D., Chang, S.F.: Temporal action localization in untrimmed videos via multi-stage CNNs. In: Proceedings of the IEEE Conference on Computer Vision and Pattern Recognition, pp. 1049–1058 (2016)

22. Singh, G., Cuzzolin, F.: Untrimmed video classification for activity detection: submission to activitynet challenge. arXiv preprint arXiv:1607.01979 (2016)

23. Tran, D., Bourdev, L., Fergus, R., Torresani, L., Paluri, M.: Learning spatiotemporal features with 3D convolutional networks. In: Proceedings of the IEEE International Conference on Computer Vision, pp. 4489–4497 (2015)

24. Wang, L., Qiao, Y., Tang, X.: Action recognition and detection by combining motion and appearance features. THUMOS14 Action Recogn. Challenge 1, 2 (2014)

25. Wang, L., et al.: Temporal segment networks: towards good practices for deep action recognition. In: Leibe, B., Matas, J., Sebe, N., Welling, M. (eds.) ECCV 2016. LNCS, vol. 9912, pp. 20–36. Springer, Cham (2016). https://doi.org/10.1007/978-3-319-46484-8_2

26. Xu, H., Das, A., Saenko, K.: R-C3D: region convolutional 3D network for temporal activity detection. In: The IEEE International Conference on Computer Vision (ICCV), vol. 6, p. 8 (2017)

27. Zhao, Y., Xiong, Y., Wang, L., Wu, Z., Lin, D., Tang, X.: Temporal action detection with structured segment networks. arXiv preprint arXiv:1704.06228 (2017)

REAPS: Towards Better Recognition of Fine-Grained Images by Region Attending and Part Sequencing

Peng Zhang[1], Xinyu Zhu[2], Zhanzhan Cheng[1(✉)], Shuigeng Zhou[2], and Yi Niu[1]

[1] Hikvision Research Institute, Hangzhou, China
{zhangpeng23,chengzhanzhan,niuyi}@hikvision.com
[2] Fudan University, Shanghai, China
{16210720101,sgzhou}@fudan.edu.cn

Abstract. Fine-grained image recognition has been a hot research topic in computer vision due to its various applications. The-state-of-the-art is the part/region-based approaches that first localize discriminative parts/regions, and then learn their fine-grained features. However, these approaches have some inherent drawbacks: (1) the discriminative feature representation of an object is prone to be disturbed by complicated background; (2) it is unreasonable and inflexible to fix the number of salient parts, because the intended parts may be unavailable under certain circumstances due to occlusion or incompleteness, and (3) the spatial correlation among different salient parts has not been thoroughly exploited (if not completely neglected). To overcome these drawbacks, in this paper we propose a new, simple yet robust method by building part sequence model on the attended object region. Concretely, we first try to alleviate the background effect by using a region attention mechanism to generate the attended region from the original image. Then, instead of localizing different salient parts and extracting their features separately, we learn the part representation implicitly by applying a mapping function on the serialized features of the object. Finally, we combine the region attending network and the part sequence learning network into a unified framework that can be trained end-to-end with only image-level labels. Our extensive experiments on three fine-grained benchmarks show that the proposed method achieves the state of the art performance.

Keywords: Fine grained · Region attending · Part sequencing

1 Introduction

Fine-grained image recognition has attracted much research interest of the computer vision community [1–3,35], which tries to distinguish sub-ordinate categories such as car models [18], bird species [4,14,29], dog breeds [16] and flower categories [26] etc. Though much effort [9,14,15,23,30,39] has been devoted to solving this problem, recognizing fine-grained images is still a challenging task due to their relatively small inter-class difference and large intra-class variation.

© Springer Nature Switzerland AG 2019
Z. Lin et al. (Eds.): PRCV 2019, LNCS 11857, pp. 193–204, 2019.
https://doi.org/10.1007/978-3-030-31654-9_17

Roughly speaking, there are two kinds of popular frameworks for handling fine-grained categorization: *key region localization and amplification* (*abbr.* RLA) and *discriminative part learning* (*abbr.* PL). In general, RLA tries to attend and amplify the key region for capturing detailed visual representation while avoiding background disturbance. On the other hand, PL usually first localizes discriminative parts via some sophisticated part selection mechanisms such as part attentions [9,32,39] and convolutional responses [33,38], and then extracts the visual representations of the selected parts by using multiple independent feature extractors. Figure 1(a) and (b) illustrate these two frameworks. Though previous studies proved their effectiveness, they have several inherent drawbacks. For example, RLA-based methods may miss some salient parts when progressively attending the key region, as shown in Fig. 2(a). PL-based methods usually fix the number of salient parts to be extracted, which is unreasonable and inflexible because in certain scenarios some of the intended parts may be unavailable due to image occlusion and incompleteness, as shown in Fig. 2(b). Furthermore, learning independent extractor for each salient part neglects the spatial correlation among these different parts, which should be useful for image recognition if properly exploited.

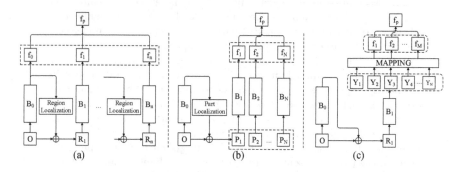

Fig. 1. An illustrative comparison between our framework and two popular existing fine-grained recognition frameworks. (a), (b) and (c) represent RLA, PL and our proposed framework respectively. O, P_i, R_i and B_i correspond to the original image, a selected part, an attended region and a backbone network respectively. $\oplus$ represents the operation of crop and zoom in.

These drawbacks mentioned above motivate us to develop a new method for fine-grained image recognition by simultaneously taking region attending and part sequence learning into consideration. We call the new method **REAPS** —— an abbreviation of **RE**gion **A**ttending and **P**art **S**equence learning. The framework of REAPS is shown in Fig. 1(c), and its detailed architecture is illustrated in Fig. 3, which consists of two major components:

Region Attending Network (RAN): Inspired by previous works [9,12], we apply the class activation mapping (CAM) mechanism [40] to constructing the region attending network for generating the region attention. The attended

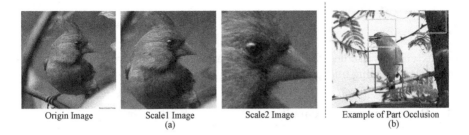

Origin Image   Scale1 Image   Scale2 Image   Example of Part Occlusion
                       (a)   (b)

Fig. 2. Drawbacks of the RLA and PL frameworks. (a) RLA focuses on a detailed region progressively, while neglecting some other salient parts (the feet and wings of the bird disappear in scale1 and scale2 images). (b) PL detects a fixed number of preset parts and may get into trouble when some intended parts miss or be occluded (the back of the bird cannot be seen). [Best viewed in color] (Color figure online)

region cropped and amplified from the origin image are fed into the part sequence-learning network (PSN). RAN can effectively depress the impact of the background noise, while PSN can depict the detailed visual features well.

Part Sequence-Learning Network (PSN): As mentioned above, the traditional part-based methods usually fix the number of parts and the representation of each part is explicitly learned by independent extractors. So we call them 'hard-part'-based methods. In addition to the drawbacks we previously mentioned, 'hard-part'-based methods adopt independent feature extractor (*e.g.* VGG19) for each part, which incurs high computational cost. In order to overcome the above drawbacks, we propose the 'soft-part' concept, which is implemented by mapping the serialized visual features into a group of implicit discriminative part representation and capturing the spatial correlation among different salient parts simultaneously.

In REAPS, we integrate the region attending network and the part sequence learning network into a unified framework, which can be trained end-to-end with only image-level annotations.

Our contributions are as follows: (1) We propose the novel 'soft-part' concept, and implement this concept by designing a part sequence learning network (PSN), which learns implicit discriminative part representation and captures the spatial context simultaneously. (2) We apply the region attending network to localizing the object region and alleviating the interference of complicated background to fine feature representation. (3) We integrate the region attending network and the part sequence learning network into a unified framework, and train it end-to-end without any part-level annotation. (4) We conduct extensive experiments on three challenging datasets (Stanford Cars, FGVC-Aircraft and CUB Birds), which demonstrate the superiority of our method over the existing ones.

2   Related Work

Fine-grained recognition (or categorization) is a challenging problem that has been extensively studied. Related works can be grouped in two dimensions: representation learning and part localization.

2.1   Representation Learning

Discriminative representation learning is crucial for fine-grained recognition. Thanks to their strong encoding capability, most existing fine-grained recognition algorithms [8,9,25,39] employ deep convolutional networks for feature representation, which have achieved much better performance than traditional descriptors and hand-crafted features [27,36].

To better handle the subtle inter-class difference and large intra-class variation in fine-grained recognition tasks, [21] proposes a bilinear structure to model second-order interactions of local convolutional features in a translationally invariant manner. This idea was later extended by [20] and other variants [10,17]for better recognition performance. Recently, [5,8] further exploit higher-order integration of convolutional activations that can yield more discriminative representation, and achieve impressive performance.

Besides, some approaches (e.g. [28,37]) try to learn more robust representations via distance metric learning. [38] unifies deep CNN features with spatially weighted Fisher vectors to capture important details and eliminate background disturbance. [25] incorporates deep CNNs into a generic boosting framework to combine the strength of multiple weaker learners, which improves the classification accuracy of a single model and simplifies the network design.

2.2   Part Localization

Previous works have studied the localization impact of discriminative parts on capturing subtle visual difference. Early part-based approaches rely on extra annotations of bounding boxes or part landmarks to localize pre-defined semantic parts. [11,22] assume that annotations are available in both training and testing. Some later works [14,18,19] use annotations only in training. However, the cost-prohibitive manually-labeled annotations prevent the application of these algorithms to large-scale real problems. Therefore, most of recent works focus on weakly-supervised task-driven part localization with only category labels. Attention-based models have been widely used to automatically discover salient parts. [33] proposes a two-level attention model, where one object-level filter-net selects relevant patches for a certain object, another part-level domain-net localizes discriminative parts. Since deep filter responses from CNNs are able to significantly and consistently respond to specific visual patterns, [38] proposes to learn part detectors by picking distinctive filters, while [30] identifies discriminative regions according to channel activations. [15] takes one step further and

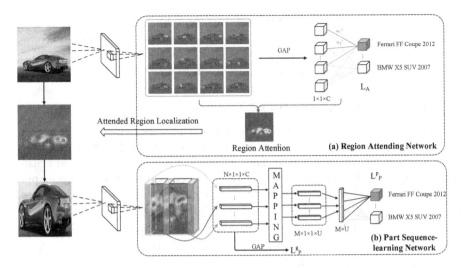

Fig. 3. The REAPS architecture. The region attending network (RAN) takes an original image as input and produces the region attention by weighting the last convolutional feature maps with the parameters of softmax layer. The attended region is cropped out and zoomed in, and fed into the part sequence learning network (PSN) where part representation is learned in an implicit way by applying the mapping function on the serialized features. The whole network can be trained end-to-end under the supervision of three softmax loss functions in Eq. (5). [Best viewed in color] (Color figure online)

proposes a spatial transform module based on the differentiable attention mechanism, which enables CNN to learn better invariance to classification and all kinds of warping.

The latest works use hidden filter responses of deep CNNs as part detectors. [23] proposes a fully convolutional attention network to optimally glimpse local discriminative regions by reinforcement learning. [9] introduces a recurrent attention convolutional neural network (RA-CNN) that recursively learns discriminative region attention from coarse to fine by an attention proposal network. [39] develops a multi-attention convolutional neural network (MA-CNN) that generates multiple part attentions by clustering, weighting and pooling from spatially-correlated channels, and achieves the state-of-art performance.

3 The REAPS Method

3.1 Overview

The architecture of our REAPS method is shown in Fig. 3, which consists of two major components: a *region attending network* (RAN) and a *part sequence learning network* (PSN). RAN leverages deep convolutional responses to generate the discriminative region attention. Then the attended region is cropped out and zoomed in as the input of PSN. While in PSN, the deep visual features are extracted by a backbone network and further serialized to a sequence of vectors, each of which describes a rectangle region in the raw image. A mapping function is learned to map the sequence of vectors to discriminative part representation.

3.2   Region Attending Network

The RAN is based on a standard classification network, where global average pooling is applied on the last convolutional feature maps, followed by a Soft-maxLoss layer. Given an input image $\mathcal{I}$, we can get its last convolutional feature maps, denoted as $\mathcal{F}$. In order to eliminate the background disturbance, we apply the CAM [40] mechanism to generating the region attention in a "self-guided" way. Concretely, let $f_{(x,y)}^k$ denote the activation value of unit k at (x,y) in $\mathcal{F}$, the global average pooling (*abbr.* GAP) can be represented as $\mathcal{P}_k = \sum_{x,y} f_{(x,y)}^k$. For a specific class c, the probability yielding c is $\sum_k W_{k,c}\mathcal{P}_k$, where $W_{k,c}$ is the weight of the last inner-product layer and can be learned under the supervision of SoftmaxLoss $\mathcal{L}_A$. $W_{k,c}$ also acts as the weight indicating the importance of unit k for class c. Therefore, we can compute the region attention of c at (x,y) by

$$RA_{x,y}^c = \sum_k W_k^c f_{(x,y)}^k. \tag{1}$$

Since each unit k responds to a certain type visual pattern (*e.g.* circle), the region attention can represent all the discriminative visual patterns at different locations by conducting weighted-sum over all units. Furthermore, we locate the attended region of class c by

$$AR^c = f_+(BB_\tau(RA^c), \mathcal{I}), \tag{2}$$

where BB_τ is the operation of calculating rectangular bounding box over the binary mask based on the preset threshold τ, and f_+ represents the operation of crop and zoom in.

3.3   Part Sequence Modeling

Let $X \in \mathbb{R}^{(H \times W \times C)}$ denote the deep representation through the deep convolutional neural network (the backbone network in Fig. 3), where H, W and C respectively refer to the height, width and the number of channels of X. Instead of localizing a fixed number of parts and extracting their representation separately, we learn the part representation in a soft way. Concretely, we evenly decompose X into a sequence of N vectors by

$$Y = [Y_1, Y_2, ..., Y_N] = seq(X), \tag{3}$$

where $Y_i \in \mathbb{R}^{(1 \times C)}$ describes a rectangle region in the raw image and seq can be the pooling operation with kernel size of $[H \times \frac{W}{N}]$. We abstract the sequence of visual feature vectors into M implicit parts with the learned mapping function

$$P_P = [P_1, P_2, ..., P_M] \simeq mapping(Y), \tag{4}$$

where $M \leq N$ refers to the rough number of learnt discriminative parts.

The mapping function here should keep the discriminative features and depress the useless ones. Several sequence learning techniques meet this requirement, *e.g.* the recurrent neural networks (GRU [6] and LSTM [13]) and attention-based sequence models [7,34]. Attention-based models can fulfill the mapping from a source sequence of length N to a target sequence of length M. With sequential labels, they can effectively learn the alignment between labels and their corresponding salient representation of features [7,34]. Recurrent neural networks (GRU [6] and LSTM [13] can strengthen the sequence representation with the sequence length being unchanged. In our case, classification is performed in a weakly-supervised way and the only available supervision information is the image-level category, thus we apply a bi-directional LSTM on the sequenced vectors and concatenate all the hidden states as the part representation $P_P \in \mathbb{R}^{(N \times U)}$, followed by a fully connected layer and a SoftmaxLoss $\mathcal{L}_P^p$.

To accelerate the training process, another SoftmaxLoss $\mathcal{L}_P^g$ is attached to the global representation $P_g \in \mathbb{R}^C$ of the backbone network of PSN.

3.4 Training and Joint Representation

Instead of alternative optimization, REAPS can be trained end-to-end straightforwardly by

$$\mathcal{L} = \lambda_1 \mathcal{L}_A + \lambda_2 \mathcal{L}_P^g + \lambda_3 \mathcal{L}_P^p, \tag{5}$$

where $\lambda_j (j = 1, 2, 3)$ is the corresponding loss weight. Once the training process converges, the joint representation F of the input image $\mathcal{I}$ can be represented by a set of descriptors, followed by a fully-connected layer with softmax function for final classification:

$$F = \{A_g, P_g, P_p\}, \tag{6}$$

where $A_g \in \mathbb{R}^C$ denotes the global representations of the backbone network of RAN.

4 Performance Evaluation

4.1 Datasets and Implementation Details

We conduct extensive experiments on three benchmark datasets, including Stanford Cars [18], FGVC-aircraft [24] and CUB-200-2011 [29], which are widely used to evaluate fine-grained image recognition. Table 1 shows the detailed statistics of the three datasets.

For fair comparison, all compared methods employ similar backbone network. Specifically, we start with the 19-layer VGGNets pre-trained on ImageNet and fine-tune it on the three fine-grained datasets. The parameters of RAN and PSN are initialized with the same pre-trained model. Input images and the cropped attended regions are both resized to 448×448, where high resolution highlights

Table 1. Statistics of the fine-grained benchmark datasets used in this paper.

Dataset	Category	Training	Testing
Stanford Cars [18]	196	8,144	8,041
FGVC-aircraft [24]	100	6,667	3,333
CUB-200-2011 [29]	200	5,994	5,794

details and benefits recognition. We use SGD with momentum 0.9 to minimize the loss function $\mathcal{L}$ in Eq. (5), where λ_1, λ_2, and λ_3 are all set to 1. The threshold τ in Eq. (2) is set to 0.1. Following the common practice of learning rate decaying schedule, the initial learning rate is set to 0.001 and multiplied by 0.1 every 60 epoches.

4.2 Experiment and Analysis

Effectiveness of Region Attending Network. We first visualize some results of our CAM-based region attending network in Fig. 4 for qualitative analysis. We can see that the discriminative regions of the input images are highlighted. The attended regions that are cropped from the raw images and then amplified preserve the object-level structure, eliminate background interference and enrich local visual details. We evaluate the effectiveness of RAN in terms of the single scale classification accuracy. In Table 2, we compare the result of our PSN *without* part modeling branch with that of two other attention based approaches. To be fair, we select the *single-attention* based performance from FCAN [23], and *the second scale* result from RA-CNN [9]. RA-CNN [9] is the most relevant work to ours considering the region attention concept and the way to use it. We can see that our method outperforms FCAN [23] with a clear margin (7.1% relative gain) and RA-CNN [9] with 1.3% accuracy improvement.

Effectiveness of Part Branch in PSN. As pointed out in Sect. 3.3, we take a bi-directional LSTM as the mapping function to map the serialized features to discriminative part representation. To evaluate its effectiveness, we present the classification results of two models: *PSN wo/w part*, which are the classification accuracy based on the P_g *without/ with* the part modeling branch. The results are shown in Table 2. We can see that the model adopting part sequence modeling branch achieves a relative performance gain of 1.0%. Some illustrations are given in Fig. 5. It can be observed that the part branch encourages a more compact distribution on the feature maps, further enhances the crucial part areas and depresses the unless ones.

Fine-Grained Categorization. We compare our REAPS framework with several existing methods and the results are summarized in Table 3. Our method achieves better performance than those [4,18,30–32] using ground-truth bounding boxes or part annotations during training or testing time on three datasets. Compared

Table 2. Performance comparison of attention localization on the Stanford Cars dataset.

Approach	Accuracy
FCAN (single-attention) [23]	84.2
RA-CNN (scale 2) [9]	90.0
PSN *wo part*	91.3
PSN	92.3

(a) Stanford Cars   (b) FGVC-aircraft   (c) CUB-200-2011

Fig. 4. Region attention localization results of RAN for some examples from (a) Stanford Cars, (b) FGVC-aircraft, and (c) CUB-200-2011. Pictures from left to right in (a–c) are the raw image, the attention mask with bounding box indicating the area of top attention response, and the cropped object-level region respectively.

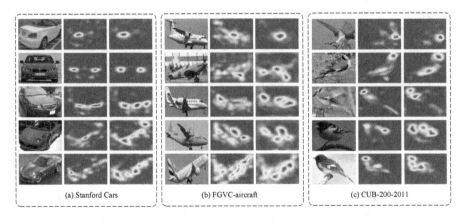

(a) Stanford Cars   (b) FGVC-aircraft   (c) CUB-200-2011

Fig. 5. Visualization of feature maps for some examples from (a) Stanford Cars, (b) FGVC Aircraft, (c) CUB-200-2011. Pictures from left to right in (a–c) are the raw image, the feature map generated by PSN *without* part branch and the feature map generated by PSN *with* part branch, respectively.

with BCNN-based methods [8,20,25] our method obtains comparable or even better performance due to accurate attention localization and part sequence modeling. To further enhance the capacity of REAPS, as RA-CNN [9] does, we incorporate one more PSN into our framework, and the 2nd PSN is based on the attended region of the 1st PSN. We call the resulting network REAPS+. Note that, REAPS+ obtains the best performance on three datasets. Especially on FGVC Aircraft dataset, our proposed REAPS+ obtains the best accuracy of 92.6%, surpassing state-of-the-art MA-CNN [39] by a relative 2.7% gain. The significant improvement suggests that the proposed part sequence modeling network works as expected to leverage spatial information of parts, and does even better when the objects to be recognized have strong sequential structures.

Table 3. Performance comparison on the Stanford Cars, FGVC Aircraft and CUB-200-2011 datasets. *(*)* indicates whether bounding box or part annotation is used in training.

Approach	Stanford Cars	FGVC Aircraft	CUB200-2011
PA-CNN [18]	92.8 (*)	–	82.8 (*)
MDTP [31]	92.5 (*)	88.4 (*)	–
MG-CNN [30]	–	86.6 (*)	83.0 (*)
PN-CNN [4]	–	–	85.4 (*)
Mask-CNN [32]	–	–	85.4 (*)
STNs [15]	–	–	84.1
FCAN [23]	91.5	–	84.3
PDFR [38]	–	–	84.5
Improved B-CNN [20]	92.0	88.5	85.8
BoostCNN [25]	92.1	88.5	86.2
KP [8]	92.4	86.9	86.2
RA-CNN(scale 1+2+3) [9]	92.5	–	85.3
MA-CNN [39]	92.8	89.9	**86.5**
REAPS *wo PSN*	92.0	89.8	81.3
REAPS	**93.1**	**91.8**	86.0
REAPS+	**93.5**	**92.6**	**86.8**

5   Conclusion

In this paper, we propose a novel framework REAPS for fine-grained recognition, which consists of a region attending network and a part sequence-learning network. The proposed framework does not need bounding box/part annotations for training and can be trained end-to-end. We conduct extensive experiments on three fine-grained benchmark datasets, and the experimental results show that REAPS outperforms the existing methods.

References

1. Angelova, A., Zhu, S.: Efficient object detection and segmentation for fine-grained recognition. In: CVPR, pp. 811–818 (2013)
2. Berg, T., Belhumeur, P.N.: POOF: part-based one-vs.-one features for fine-grained categorization, face verification, and attribute estimation. In: CVPR, pp. 955–962 (2013)
3. Berg, T., Liu, J., Lee, S.W., Alexander, M.L., Jacobs, D.W., Belhumeur, P.N.: Birdsnap: large-scale fine-grained visual categorization of birds. In: CVPR, pp. 2019–2026 (2014)
4. Branson, S., Horn, G.V., Belongie, S.J., Perona, P.: Bird species categorization using pose normalized deep convolutional nets. CoRR abs/1406.2952 (2014)
5. Cai, S., Zuo, W., Zhang, L.: Higher-order integration of hierarchical convolutional activations for fine-grained visual categorization. In: CVPR, pp. 511–520 (2017)
6. Cho, K., van Merrienboer, B., Bahdanau, D., Bengio, Y.: On the properties of neural machine translation: encoder-decoder approaches. In: EMNLP, pp. 103–111 (2014)
7. Cho, K., et al.: Learning phrase representations using RNN encoder-decoder for statistical machine translation. In: EMNLP, pp. 1724–1734 (2014)
8. Cui, Y., Zhou, F., Wang, J., Liu, X., Lin, Y., Belongie, S.J.: Kernel pooling for convolutional neural networks. In: CVPR, pp. 3049–3058 (2017)
9. Fu, J., Zheng, H., Mei, T.: Look closer to see better: recurrent attention convolutional neural network for fine-grained image recognition. In: CVPR, pp. 4476–4484 (2017)
10. Gao, Y., Beijbom, O., Zhang, N., Darrell, T.: Compact bilinear pooling. In: CVPR, pp. 317–326 (2016)
11. Gavves, E., Fernando, B., Snoek, C.G.M., Smeulders, A.W.M., Tuytelaars, T.: Fine-grained categorization by alignments. In: ICCV, pp. 1713–1720 (2013)
12. He, X., Peng, Y., Zhao, J.: Fast fine-grained image classification via weakly supervised discriminative localization. IEEE Trans. Circuits Syst. Video Technol. **29**(5), 1394–1407 (2019)
13. Hochreiter, S., Schmidhuber, J.: Long short-term memory. Neural Comput. **9**(8), 1735–1780 (1997)
14. Huang, S., Xu, Z., Tao, D., Zhang, Y.: Part-stacked CNN for fine-grained visual categorization. In: CVPR, pp. 1173–1182 (2016)
15. Jaderberg, M., Simonyan, K., Zisserman, A., Kavukcuoglu, K.: Spatial transformer networks. In: NIPS, pp. 2017–2025 (2015)
16. Khosla, A., Jayadevaprakash, N., Yao, B., Li, F.F.: Novel dataset for fine-grained image categorization: stanford dogs. In: CVPR Workshop on FGVC, vol. 2 (2011)
17. Kong, S., Fowlkes, C.C.: Low-rank bilinear pooling for fine-grained classification. In: CVPR, pp. 7025–7034 (2017)
18. Krause, J., Jin, H., Yang, J., Li, F.: Fine-grained recognition without part annotations. In: CVPR, pp. 5546–5555 (2015)
19. Lin, D., Shen, X., Lu, C., Jia, J.: Deep LAC: deep localization, alignment and classification for fine-grained recognition. In: CVPR, pp. 1666–1674 (2015)
20. Lin, T., Maji, S.: Improved bilinear pooling with CNNs. In: BMVC (2017)
21. Lin, T., Roy Chowdhury, A., Maji, S.: Bilinear CNN models for fine-grained visual recognition. In: ICCV, pp. 1449–1457 (2015)
22. Liu, J., Kanazawa, A., Jacobs, D.W., Belhumeur, P.N.: Dog breed classification using part localization. In: ECCV, pp. 172–185 (2012)

23. Liu, X., Xia, T., Wang, J., Lin, Y.: Fully convolutional attention localization networks: efficient attention localization for fine-grained recognition. CoRR abs/1603.06765 (2016)
24. Maji, S., Rahtu, E., Kannala, J., Blaschko, M.B., Vedaldi, A.: Fine-Grained Visual Classification of Aircraft. HAL - INRIA (2013)
25. Moghimi, M., Belongie, S.J., Saberian, M.J., Yang, J., Vasconcelos, N., Li, L.: Boosted convolutional neural networks. In: BMVC (2016)
26. Nilsback, M., Zisserman, A.: Automated flower classification over a large number of classes. In: Sixth Indian Conference on Computer Vision, Graphics & Image Processing, Bhubaneswar, India, pp. 722–729 (2008)
27. Perronnin, F., Sánchez, J., Mensink, T.: Improving the Fisher Kernel for large-scale image classification. In: Daniilidis, K., Maragos, P., Paragios, N. (eds.) ECCV 2010. LNCS, vol. 6314, pp. 143–156. Springer, Heidelberg (2010). https://doi.org/10.1007/978-3-642-15561-1_11
28. Qian, Q., Jin, R., Zhu, S., Lin, Y.: Fine-grained visual categorization via multi-stage metric learning. In: CVPR, pp. 3716–3724 (2015)
29. Wah, C., Branson, S., Welinder, P., Perona, P., Belongie, S.: The Caltech-UCSD Birds-200-2011 Dataset. Technical report CNS-TR-2011-001, California Institute of Technology (2011)
30. Wang, D., Shen, Z., Shao, J., Zhang, W., Xue, X., Zhang, Z.: Multiple granularity descriptors for fine-grained categorization. In: ICCV, pp. 2399–2406 (2015)
31. Wang, Y., Choi, J., Morariu, V.I., Davis, L.S.: Mining discriminative triplets of patches for fine-grained classification. In: CVPR, pp. 1163–1172 (2016)
32. Wei, X., Xie, C., Wu, J., Shen, C.: Mask-CNN: localizing parts and selecting descriptors for fine-grained bird species categorization. Pattern Recogn. **76**, 704–714 (2018)
33. Xiao, T., Xu, Y., Yang, K., Zhang, J., Peng, Y., Zhang, Z.: The application of two-level attention models in deep convolutional neural network for fine-grained image classification. In: CVPR, pp. 842–850 (2015)
34. Xu, K., et al.: Show, attend and tell: neural image caption generation with visual attention. In: ICML, pp. 2048–2057 (2015)
35. Zhang, N., Farrell, R., Darrell, T.: Pose pooling kernels for sub-category recognition. In: CVPR, pp. 3665–3672 (2012)
36. Zhang, N., Farrell, R., Iandola, F.N., Darrell, T.: Deformable part descriptors for fine-grained recognition and attribute prediction. In: ICCV, pp. 729–736 (2013)
37. Zhang, X., Zhou, F., Lin, Y., Zhang, S.: Embedding label structures for fine-grained feature representation. In: CVPR, pp. 1114–1123 (2016)
38. Zhang, X., Xiong, H., Zhou, W., Lin, W., Tian, Q.: Picking deep filter responses for fine-grained image recognition. In: CVPR, pp. 1134–1142 (2016)
39. Zheng, H., Fu, J., Mei, T., Luo, J.: Learning multi-attention convolutional neural network for fine-grained image recognition. In: ICCV, pp. 5219–5227 (2017)
40. Zhou, B., Khosla, A., Lapedriza, À., Oliva, A., Torralba, A.: Learning deep features for discriminative localization. In: CVPR, pp. 2921–2929 (2016)

Weakly-Supervised Action Recognition and Localization via Knowledge Transfer

Haichao Shi[1,2], Xiaoyu Zhang[1(✉)], and Changsheng Li[3]

[1] Institute of Information Engineering, Chinese Academy of Sciences, Beijing, China
[2] School of Cyber Security, University of Chinese Academy of Sciences,
Beijing, China
{shihaichao,zhangxiaoyu}@iie.ac.cn
[3] University of Electronic Science and Technology of China, Chengdu, China
lichangsheng@uestc.edu.cn

Abstract. Action recognition and localization has attracted much attention in the past decade. However, a challenging problem is that it typically requires large-scale temporal annotations of action instances for training models in untrimmed video scenarios, which is not practical in many real-world applications. To alleviate the problem, we propose a novel weakly-supervised action recognition framework for untrimmed videos to use only video-level annotations to transfer information from publicly available trimmed videos to assist in model learning, namely KTUntrimmedNet. A two-stage method is designed to guarantee an effective transfer strategy: Firstly, the trimmed and untrimmed videos are clustered to find similar classes between them, so as to avoid negative information transfer from trimmed data. Secondly, we design an invariant module to find common features between trimmed videos and untrimmed videos for improving the performance. Extensive experiments on the standard benchmark datasets, THUMOS14 and ActivityNet1.3, clearly demonstrate the efficacy of our proposed method when compared with the existing state-of-the-arts.

Keywords: Action recognition · Action localization · Knowledge transfer

1 Introduction

Action recognition and localization tasks have attracted more and more attention in the academic and industry communities [6,18,21]. Given a video, the goal of action recognition is to predict one action category for the video. Therefore, action recognition is usually cast as a multi-class classification problem. Action localization is devoted to localizing precise activity intervals in untrimmed videos. In order to learn robust models, mainstream approaches usually assume videos are trimmed and require ground-truth annotations of each video frame,

---

The first author is student.

© Springer Nature Switzerland AG 2019
Z. Lin et al. (Eds.): PRCV 2019, LNCS 11857, pp. 205–216, 2019.
https://doi.org/10.1007/978-3-030-31654-9_18

which is quite costly and time-consuming. In this paper, given only video-level annotations, we focus on learning a weakly supervised model to simultaneously locate action frames as well as recognize actions in untrimmed videos.

To date, many action recognition approaches have been proposed in the past decade [18,20]. For instance, earlier methods like Improved Dense Trajectory (iDT) algorithm [20], which effectively fuses hand-crafted HOF, MBH and HOG features. Recently, deep learning have been applied to the task of action recognition. Two-stream network [15] learns both appearance and motion information by operating the network on single frame and stacked optical flow, respectively. C3D network [18] utilizes 3D convolutional kernel to capture both spatial and temporal information directly from raw videos. In addition, RNN methods [3,12] are also widely used to improve the performance of action recognition. However, as aforementioned, the cost of trimming videos for training is extremely high. Moreover, these approaches originally designed for trimmed videos can not be directly applied to untrimmed videos.

With the development of machine learning, learning methods have been widely studied in the computer vision fields [29–39], such as deep learning, transfer learning, ensemble learning and so on. Among these methods, transfer learning aims to take advantage of useful knowledge gained from source datasets to the target dataset, such that the performance of the model can be improved, and the cost of annotating data is extremely reduced as well. So far, transfer learning has been widely studied for various image analysis tasks, such as image classification [13], style transfer [7], to name a few. In the meanwhile, existing works [9,10,19] mainly focus on improving the domain adaptability of deep neural networks. Recently, there appears several works [8,17] to generalize the discriminative ability across different datasets by increasing the cross-domain training datasets with the style transfer methods. One example is that Zhong et al. [28] smooth style disparities across the cameras with style transfer model and label smooth regularization. Given that the ability of transfer learning technologies about relieving the domain shift between different datasets, we can train a model by leveraging publicly available external annotated data to alleviate the problem of lacking of annotated data.

In light of this, we propose a novel weakly supervised learning framework, namely KTUntrimmedNet, to localize the temporal action intervals in untrimmed videos using only video-level annotations. An overview of our algorithm is shown in Fig. 1. Our method can not only capture common features between trimmed and untrimmed video datasets, but also learn action patterns more accurately. Specifically, we first jointly encode trimmed video and untrimmed video into a high-dimensional space, where the videos are clustered into several classes. After that, an invariant module is designed to find common features between trimmed videos and untrimmed videos for knowledge transfer. Finally, a decoder is used to reconstruct the video features for information preservation. Our method is based on an encoder-decoder architecture.

The main contributions of our work are summarized as follows:

- We propose a novel weakly supervised learning framework to localize temporal action instances based on knowledge transfer for untrimmed videos. To the

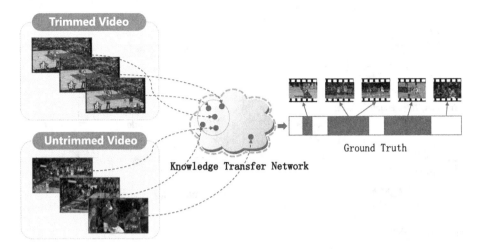

Fig. 1. Overview of our proposed approach. Firstly, the trimmed videos and untrimmed videos are mapped into a high dimensional space to extract similar classes between trimmed videos and untrimmed videos by clustering. The videos of the similar classes are used to train our model. Then we extract the common features of trimmed and untrimmed videos via knowledge transfer. The Knowledge Transfer Network is based on encoder-decoder.

best of our knowledge, this is the first work to leverage transfer learning for weakly supervised action localization.
- An invariant module is designed to extract common features between trimmed videos and untrimmed videos. And a decoder is presented to keep the information preserved for further improving the performance.
- Extensive experiments demonstrate that our method achieves significantly improvements, compared with the state-of-the-art weakly supervised action localization methods.

The rest of this paper is organized as follows. We describe the details of our model in the second section. In the third section, we present the analysis of our experimental results and conclude this paper in the fourth section.

2   Proposed Method

In this section, we present the proposed KTUntrimmedNet in detail, which consists of three modules, i.e. encoder, decoder and invariant module. The overall framework of our method is shown in Fig. 2.

2.1   Suppressing Negative Information Transfer

Most of methods on knowledge transfer have been proposed for transferring knowledge from a labeled source domain to a label-scarce target domain. Nevertheless, negative transfer occurs when learning in one dataset, which would

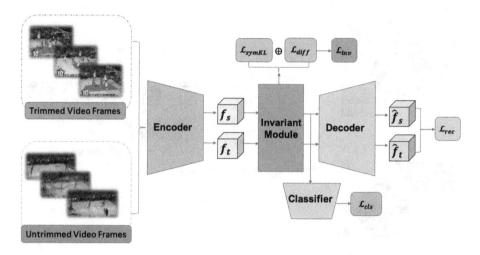

Fig. 2. The architecture of our Knowledge Transfer Network (KTUntrimmedNet). Our model is a typical encoder-decoder architecture. In the architecture of encoder-decoder, we design an invariant module to learn common features through an symmetric Kullback-Leibler divergence and a difference loss. A decoder is also incorporated into the whole framework as a regularization term to preserve the video information for further improving the performance.

bring in negative impact on the target model. The main reason for this issue is that knowledge is transferred from totally irrelevant or noisy data. Moreover, the imbalance of class distribution might lead to misunderstanding on the task of knowledge transfer. Thus, how to dig out common features between trimmed video and untrimmed video is a key factor to avoid negative information transfer.

In practice, there are often different categories between trimmed and untrimmed datasets, which we call them 'open set'. In the meantime, if the classes of trimmed and untrimmed datasets are completely the same, we call it 'closed set'. Intuitively, the problem of open set can be simplified down to a two-stage operation: The first step is to turn on an open set problem to a closed set one, and the second step is to tackle the issue of domain shift in the shared classes of two domains. For the sake of weakly supervised action localization, we can make good use of available trimmed action instances to learn a robust model for untrimmed videos by knowledge transfer.

To do this, we design a method which is aimed to find common classes from different datasets for useful information transfer. Specifically, we first map both trimmed data and untrimmed data into a high dimensional feature space, thus we can distinguish relevant data from irrelevant data by clustering, and pick up those useful samples for model training. Let $f(\boldsymbol{x})$ denote the distribution of trimmed video domain, and let $g(\boldsymbol{y})$ denote the distribution of untrimmed video domain. Then the mapped trimmed and untrimmed video domain can be represented as $f(x_1, x_2, ..., x_m)_{\mathcal{H}}$ and $g(y_1, y_2, ..., y_n)_{\mathcal{H}}$, respectively, where $\mathcal{H}$ represents the Reproducing Kernel Hilbert Space (RKHS). m and n denote the number of training instances of trimmed video and untrimmed video, respectively. Through clustering (we use k-means in our experiment) the two distributions into the RKHS, we can obtain the 'distance' between the two distributions. Here we denote the kernel function as $k(\cdot)$, and the kernel inner product is expressed as follows,

$$k(f, g) = < k(f, \cdot), k(g, \cdot) > = < \Phi(f(\boldsymbol{x})), \Phi(g(\boldsymbol{y})) >_{\mathcal{H}}, \tag{1}$$

where $\Phi(\cdot)$ represents a high-dimensional feature representation of videos.

2.2 Parameter Shared Feature Extraction

Each input sample pair that is fed into our KTUtrimmedNet consists of one single untrimmed video with a similar trimmed video. Following some state-of-the-art style transfer networks like AdaIN [4], which have proved to be effective on relieving domain shift in unsupervised scenario, we use a parameter shared architecture as the feature extractor, and apply it to extract features f_s and f_t for representing the trimmed video features and untrimmed video features, respectively. Note that this backbone network consists of two data streams: one spatial stream coming from RGB images and one temporal stream coming from optical flow, so as to capture the spatial-temporal information. In addition, we use ResNet101 as the two-stream architecture, where the network is pretrained on ImageNet for the 1000-class classification task.

2.3 Invariant Feature Learning

As we know, larger learning rate and faster convergence speed are always adopted to reduce the internal covariance shift when training convolutional neural networks (CNNs). Existing feature normalization methods, such as batch normalization, employ the mean and variance of each mini-batch during training. Although the global statistical information have preserved the discriminative information between individual samples, it could make the network more vulnerable to external factor like appearance, size, etc. In a nutshell, it's a key challenging problem on cross-domain network training. To find common features from trimmed and untrimmed videos, we design an invariant module to divide the feature set into two parts: common feature subset and private feature subset. Finally, we utilize batch-normalization to assist in the learning of invariant features.

Feature divergence caused by appearance variance often appears in the shallow parts of the CNNs. In contrast, the feature is highly discriminative on video content in deep layers. In this module, our KTUntrimmedNet is aimed to avoid negative impacts caused by illumination or object appearance, size, etc. After feature extraction, video features through the invariant feature learning module can reduce the video content variance at a deep insight. What's more, considering the video information integrity, we also combine the global statistics with the action instance statistics.

Formally, we define the invariant feature learning loss as follows, which consists of two parts: the KL-divergence loss is employed to measure the distance between features from the trimmed video features and untrimmed video features. Furthermore, in order to ensure the dataset-invariant, we introduce the difference loss $\mathcal{L}_{diff}$ to encourage the orthogonality between the two kind of features:

$$\mathcal{L}_{inv} = \mathcal{L}_{symKL} + \mathcal{L}_{diff} \tag{2}$$

where $\mathcal{L}_{symKL}$ is the *Symmetric-KL*-divergence loss, which can be defined as follows:

$$\mathcal{L}_{symKL} = \frac{1}{N} \sum_{i=1}^{N} (KL(F_s||F_t) + KL(F_t||F_s)) \tag{3}$$

where F_s and F_t represent the distribution of trimmed video domain and untrimmed video domain. $\mathcal{L}_{diff}$ is the difference loss, which is defined as follows:

$$\mathcal{L}_{diff} = ||\boldsymbol{f}_s - \boldsymbol{f}_t||_F^2 \tag{4}$$

where $\boldsymbol{f}_s$ and $\boldsymbol{f}_t$ are the feature representations, respectively. $||\cdot||_F^2$ denotes the square Frobenius norm.

In addition, we also use a classification loss to make the learnt features more discriminative. In this paper, we employ cross-entropy loss as the loss function as:

$$\mathcal{L}_{cls} = -\sum_{i=1}^{N_s} y_i^s log\hat{y}_i^s - \sum_{j=1}^{N_t} y_j^t log\hat{y}_j^t \tag{5}$$

where $\hat{y}_i^s$ represents the prediction of the i-th trimmed video, $\hat{y}_j^t$ denotes the j-th untrimmed video. N_s and N_t are the number of frames of trimmed videos and untrimmed videos, respectively.

Table 1. The comparison results of action recognition with different modalities on THUMOS14 and ActivityNet1.3. Note that 'Two-Stream' represents we use the original two-stream architecture to conduct experiments, '*' represents the KTUntrimmedNet without invariant loss, while the other means KTUntrimmedNet with invariant loss.

	THUMOS14			ActivityNet1.3		
	RGB	Optical flow	Two-stream	RGB	Optical flow	Two-stream
Two-stream	67.9%	71.3%	72.9%	71.3%	73.5%	79.3%
KTUntrimmedNet*	70.4%	76.0%	82.3%	77.8%	80.1%	86.2%
KTUntrimmedNet	73.1%	78.2%	86.5%	80.3%	85.6%	91.3%

Table 2. The comparison of KTUntrimmedNet with other state-of-the-art methods on THUMOS14 dataset for action recognition.

Method	THUMOS14
Wang et al. [20]	63.1%
Simonyan et al. [15]	66.1%
Zhang et al. [26]	61.5%
Jain et al. [5]	71.6%
Wang et al. [21] (3 seg)	78.5%
Wang et al. [22] (hard)	81.2%
Wang et al. [22] (soft)	82.2%
KTUntrimmedNet	86.5%

Table 3. Comparison of our algorithm with other recent techniques on the THU-MOS14 testing set. These methods are divided into two categories according to their supervision.

Supervision	Method	AP@IoU				
		0.1	0.2	0.3	0.4	0.5
Full	Shou et al. [14]	47.7	43.5	36.3	28.7	19.0
	Yeung et al. [24]	48.9	44.0	36.0	26.4	17.1
	Alwassel et al. [1]	49.6	44.3	38.1	28.4	19.8
	Yuan et al. [25]	51.4	42.6	33.6	26.1	18.8
	Xu et al. [23]	54.5	51.5	44.8	35.6	28.9
	Chao et al. [2]	54.5	51.5	44.8	35.6	28.9
	Zhao et al. [27]	66.0	59.4	51.9	41.0	29.8
Weak	Singh et al. [16]	36.4	27.8	19.5	12.7	6.8
	Wang et al. [22]	44.4	37.7	28.2	21.1	13.7
	Nguyen et al. [11]	45.3	38.8	31.1	23.5	16.2
	KTUntrimmedNet	**47.3**	**41.7**	**31.9**	**23.2**	**13.8**

2.4   Reconstruction Regularized Feature Learning

In order to make the learnt feature more representative, we use the decoder to reconstruct and recover the original inputs including trimmed videos and untrimmed videos. Actually, the reconstruction can be regarded as a regularization term to help to learn representative features. The loss function is defined as

$$\mathcal{L}_{rec} = \sum_{i=1}^{N_s} ||f_i^s - \hat{f}_i^s||_2^2 + \sum_{i=1}^{N_t} ||f_i^t - \hat{f}_i^t||_2^2 \qquad (6)$$

where f_i^s and f_i^t represent the features output by the invariant module. $\hat{f}_i^s$ and $\hat{f}_i^t$ represent the reconstruction features.

2.5 Overall Network and Training Scheme

To summarize, the total loss can be defined as follows:

$$\mathcal{L} = \mathcal{L}_{cls} + \alpha\mathcal{L}_{inv} + \beta\mathcal{L}_{rec} \tag{7}$$

where α and β are hyper-parameters that control the varying of the total loss.

We use the PyTorch library to train our KTUntrimmedNet. Besides, we choose the Two-Stream CNNs as our base architecture for feature extraction on RGB and optical flow streams, respectively. We utilize the ResNet101 pretained on ImageNet so as to encode the video features. The input of the encoder is resized with 224 × 224. The input to the spatial stream is one RGB frame and the temporal stream takes 5-frame stacks of TV-$L1$ optical flow. Our model is optimized with the mini-batch stochastic gradient descent algorithm. The batchsize is set to 256 and the momentum is set to 0.9. We set the initial learning rate to 0.0001 for the spatial stream and 0.0005 for the temporal stream. Both of them are decreased every 6,000 iterations by a factor of 10. We also utilize the dropout ratios set to 0.8 and common data augmentation techniques including center cropping, normalization and so on.

3 Experiments

We evaluate the performance of our proposed method, which is applied to action recognition and weakly supervised temporal action detection. We conduct the experiments at first, and then we compare and analysis the performance of our method with state-of-the-arts.

3.1 Dataset and Setup

We evaluate our experiments on two standard benchmark datasets, THUMOS14 and ActivityNet1.3. THUMOS14 contains three parts, training data, validation data and testing data, which have 101 classes in all. The validation data contains 1,010 untrimmed videos and the testing data contains 1,574 untrimmed videos. Among these videos, only 200 videos of validation data and 213 videos of testing data have temporal annotations belonging to 20 categories. Thus we train our model using the 200 untrimmed videos without using the temporal annotations and test our model on the 213 videos.

The ActivityNet dataset is recently introduced to be used in action recognition and temporal action localization. It contains a huge number of natural videos including various human activities, which consists of 10,024 videos for training, 4,926 videos for validation, and 5,044 videos for testing, with 200 activity classes. We use training data for training our model and validation data for testing. It should be noted that these two datasets both have temporal annotations of action positions, while we do not use these temporal annotations when training KTUntrimmedNet.

Besides, we also leverage the external trimmed video dataset, namely UCF101, which consists of 101 action classes and 9,965 videos for training and 3,355 for testing, which are all independent action instances of trimmed videos. Since our ultimate goal is to find the same class training data in different datasets to avoid the negative impacts on illumination or appearance. We only take the training set into account for knowledge transfer, which is in opposite of the untrimmed video dataset in terms of distribution.

3.2   Evaluation on Action Recognition

In this subsection, we mainly turn to the investigation of KTUntrimmedNet on the problem of action recognition and weakly supervised action localization on THUMOS14 and ActivityNet1.3 datasets.

Effectiveness of Invariant Module. We examine the effectiveness of instance-level domain-adaptation in KTUntrimmedNets for learning from untrimmed videos. The numerical results are summarized in Table 1. From these results, we can see that our KTUntrimmedNet equipped with the invariant loss outperforms KTUntrimmedNet without invariant loss.

Comparison with the State-of-the-Arts. After validating the effectiveness of KTUntrimmedNet on action recognition, we now make comparison with other state-of-the-art methods on those two challenging datasets. For the evaluation of THUMOS14, we use the paired datasets including the validation data of THUMOS14 and the paired part of training data of UCF101, to learn the KTUntrimmedNet. While on the dataset of ActivityNet, we also combine the training videos with UCF101 to pair the training list and report the performance on validation set. It is worth noting that KTUntrimmedNets only uses weak supervision information, which contains only labels of videos.

Table 1 shows the comparison results on different modalities for action recognition on THUMOS14 and ActivityNet1.3 datasets, respectively. Note that, our KTUntrimmedNet only utilizes weak supervision and have obtained better performance than those methods which are strong supervised. The fact is that KTUntrimmedNet can utilize the abundant context information in untrimmed videos rather than only depending on the segments. We also compare with several previous successful action recognition methods and perform action recognition and localization tasks respectively on THUMOS14 and ActivityNet1.3 datasets. As shown in Table 2, the numerical results are summarized with the other state-of-the-art methods for action recognition. Besides, KTUntrimmedNet has also achieved the recognition accuracy of 91.3% on ActivityNet1.3 dataset, which can be baseline in the future work. We can see that our KTUntrimmedNets outperforms all these methods. From the results we can see that our best performance is 4.3% above that of other methods on THUMOS14 dataset.

3.3 Evaluation on Weakly Supervised Action Localization

In the meantime, our KTUntrimmedNet can also conduct action localization tasks. Here we conduct action localization based on the action recognition scores. For each frame, we can obtain a recognition score, and can determine whether it is an action or background based on a certain threshold. According to each score, the video frames can be divided into several segments. Based on these segments, we generate the temporal proposals to be classified. Finally, we perform non-maximum suppression among temporal proposals of each class independently to remove highly overlapped detections.

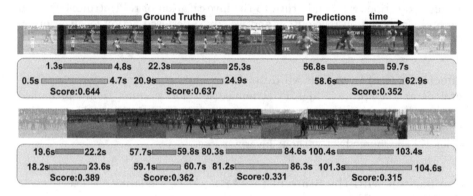

Fig. 3. Qualitative results on THUMOS14. The horizontal axis in the plots denote the timestamps (in seconds).

Quantitative Results. We perform the action localization tasks on THUMOS14 dataset based on the standard intersection over union (IoU) criteria. As shown in Table 3, the results of our algorithm is compared with other recent techniques on THUMOS14 testing set. As can be seen in the table, the KTUntrimmedNet has achieved good performance compared with some weakly supervised methods even with some fully supervised methods.

Qualitative Results. We also visualize the examples on the THUMOS14 dataset, which are presented in Fig. 3. The KTUntrimmedNet can not only identify the action intervals annotated by the dataset, it can also identify the other activity instances without annotations.

4 Conclusions

In this paper, we propose a novel weakly-supervised action recognition and detection architecture on untrimmed videos called KTUntrimmedNet, which can learn action categories for untrimmed videos directly. As demonstrated on two challenging datasets of untrimmed videos, our KTUntrimmedNet performs better performance for action recognition and temporal action detection.

Acknowledgements. This work was supported by the National Natural Science Foundation of China (Grant 61871378), and the Open Project Program of National Laboratory of Pattern Recognition (Grant 201800018).

References

1. Alwassel, H., Heilbron, F.C., Ghanem, B.: Action search: learning to search for human activities in untrimmed videos. CoRR abs/1706.04269 (2017)
2. Chao, Y., Vijayanarasimhan, S., Seybold, B., Ross, D.A., Deng, J., Sukthankar, R.: Rethinking the faster R-CNN architecture for temporal action localization. CoRR abs/1804.07667 (2018)
3. Girshick, R.B.: Fast R-CNN. In: ICCV, pp. 1440–1448 (2015)
4. Huang, X., Belongie, S.: Arbitrary style transfer in real-time with adaptive instance normalization. In: ICLR, pp. 1510–1519 (2017)
5. Jain, M., van Gemert, J.C., Snoek, C.G.M.: What do 15, 000 object categories tell us about classifying and localizing actions? In: CVPR, pp. 46–55 (2015)
6. Karpathy, A., Toderici, G., Shetty, S., Leung, T., Sukthankar, R., Li, F.: Large-scale video classification with convolutional neural networks. In: CVPR, pp. 1725–1732 (2014)
7. Li, X., Liu, S., Kautz, J., Yang, M.: Learning linear transformations for fast arbitrary style transfer. CoRR abs/1808.04537 (2018)
8. Li, Y., Yang, F., Liu, Y., Yeh, Y., Du, X., Wang, Y.F.: Adaptation and reidentification network: an unsupervised deep transfer learning approach to person reidentification. CoRR abs/1804.09347 (2018)
9. Long, M., Cao, Y., Wang, J., Jordan, M.I.: Learning transferable features with deep adaptation networks. In: ICML, pp. 97–105 (2015)
10. Long, M., Zhu, H., Wang, J., Jordan, M.I.: Deep transfer learning with joint adaptation networks. In: ICML, pp. 2208–2217 (2017)
11. Nguyen, P., Liu, T., Prasad, G., Han, B.: Weakly supervised action localization by sparse temporal pooling network. In: CVPR (2018)
12. Ren, S., He, K., Girshick, R.B., Sun, J.: Faster R-CNN: towards real-time object detection with region proposal networks. In: NIPS, pp. 91–99 (2015)
13. Shi, Q., Du, B., Zhang, L.: Domain adaptation for remote sensing image classification: a low-rank reconstruction and instance weighting label propagation inspired algorithm. IEEE Trans. Geosci. Remote Sens. **53**(10), 5677–5689 (2015)
14. Shou, Z., Wang, D., Chang, S.: Temporal action localization in untrimmed videos via multi-stage CNNs. In: CVPR, pp. 1049–1058 (2016)
15. Simonyan, K., Zisserman, A.: Two-stream convolutional networks for action recognition in videos. In: NIPS, pp. 568–576 (2014)
16. Singh, K.K., Lee, Y.J.: Hide-and-seek: forcing a network to be meticulous for weakly-supervised object and action localization. In: ICCV, pp. 3544–3553 (2017)
17. Sultani, W., Saleemi, I.: Human action recognition across datasets by foreground-weighted histogram decomposition. In: CVPR, pp. 764–771 (2014)
18. Tran, D., Bourdev, L.D., Fergus, R., Torresani, L., Paluri, M.: Learning spatiotemporal features with 3D convolutional networks. In: ICCV, pp. 4489–4497 (2015)
19. Venkateswara, H., Chakraborty, S., Panchanathan, S.: Deep learning systems for domain adaptation in computer vision: learning transferable feature representations. IEEE Signal Process. Mag. **34**(6), 117–129 (2017)
20. Wang, H., Schmid, C.: Action recognition with improved trajectories. In: ICCV, pp. 3551–3558 (2013)

21. Wang, L., et al.: Temporal segment networks: towards good practices for deep action recognition. In: Leibe, B., Matas, J., Sebe, N., Welling, M. (eds.) ECCV 2016. LNCS, vol. 9912, pp. 20–36. Springer, Cham (2016). https://doi.org/10.1007/978-3-319-46484-8_2

22. Wang, L., Xiong, Y., Lin, D., Gool, L.V.: Untrimmednets for weakly supervised action recognition and detection. In: CVPR, pp. 6402–6411 (2017)

23. Xu, H., Das, A., Saenko, K.: R-C3D: region convolutional 3D network for temporal activity detection. In: ICCV, pp. 5794–5803 (2017)

24. Yeung, S., Russakovsky, O., Mori, G., Fei-Fei, L.: End-to-end learning of action detection from frame glimpses in videos. In: CVPR, pp. 2678–2687 (2016)

25. Yuan, J., Ni, B., Yang, X., Kassim, A.A.: Temporal action localization with pyramid of score distribution features. In: CVPR, pp. 3093–3102 (2016)

26. Zhang, B., Wang, L., Wang, Z., Qiao, Y., Wang, H.: Real-time action recognition with enhanced motion vector CNNs. In: CVPR, pp. 2718–2726 (2016)

27. Zhao, Y., Xiong, Y., Wang, L., Wu, Z., Tang, X., Lin, D.: Temporal action detection with structured segment networks. In: ICCV, pp. 2933–2942 (2017)

28. Zhong, Z., Zheng, L., Zheng, Z., Li, S., Yang, Y.: Camera style adaptation for person re-identification. CoRR abs/1711.10295 (2017)

29. Zhang, X., Shi, H., Zhu, X., Li, P.: Active semi-supervised learning based on self-expressive correlation with generative adversarial networks. Neurocomputing 345, 103–113 (2019). https://doi.org/10.1016/j.neucom.2019.01.083

30. Zhang, X.: Simultaneous optimization for robust correlation estimation in partially observed social network. Neurocomputing 205, 455–462 (2016)

31. Zhang, X., Wang, S., Yun, X.: Bidirectional active learning: a two-way exploration into unlabeled and labeled dataset. IEEE Trans. Neural Netw. Learn. Syst. 26(12), 3034–3044 (2015)

32. Zhang, X., Wang, S., Zhu, X., Yun, X., Wu, G., Wang, Y.: Update vs. upgrade: modeling with indeterminate multi-class active learning. Neurocomputing 162, 163–170 (2015)

33. Zhang, X.: Interactive patent classification based on multi-classifier fusion and active learning. Neurocomputing 127, 200–205 (2014)

34. Zhang, X., Shi, H., Li, C., Zheng, K., Zhu, X., Duan, L.: Learning transferable self-attentive representations for action recognition in untrimmed videos with weak supervision. In: Proceedings of the 33rd AAAI Conference on Artificial Intelligence, pp. 1–8 (2019)

35. Liu, Y., Zhang, X., Zhu, X., Guan, Q., Zhao, X.: ListNet-based object proposals ranking. Neurocomputing 267, 182–194 (2017)

36. Shi, H., Dong, J., Wang, W., Qian, Y., Zhang, X.: SSGAN: secure steganography based on generative adversarial networks. In: Zeng, B., Huang, Q., El Saddik, A., Li, H., Jiang, S., Fan, X. (eds.) PCM 2017. LNCS, vol. 10735, pp. 534–544. Springer, Cham (2018). https://doi.org/10.1007/978-3-319-77380-3_51

37. Zhu, X., Zhang, X., Zhang, X., Xue, Z., Wang, L.: A novel framework for semantic segmentation with generative adversarial network. J. Vis. Commun. Image Represent. (JVCI) 58, 532–543 (2019)

38. Zhang, X., Xu, C., Cheng, J., Lu, H., Ma, S.: Effective annotation and search for video blogs with integration of context and content analysis. IEEE Trans. Multimedia (TMM) 11(2), 272–285 (2009)

39. Zhu, X., Li, Z., Zhang, X., Li, C., Liu, Y., Xue, Z.: Residual invertible spatiotemporal network for video super-resolution. In: Proceedings of the 33rd AAAI Conference on Artificial Intelligence, pp. 1–8 (2019)

Visual Tracking with Levy Flight Grasshopper Optimization Algorithm

Huanlong Zhang[1(✉)], Zeng Gao[1], Jie Zhang[1], and Guanglu Yang[2]

[1] College of Electric and Information Engineering,
Zhengzhou University of Light Industry, Zhengzhou, China
zzuli407@163.com
[2] Nanyang Cigarette Factory, China Tobacco Henan Industrial Co., Ltd.,
Nanyang, China

Abstract. Grasshopper optimization algorithm (GOA) is a new meta-heuristic optimization algorithm that it simulates behavior of grasshopper swarms in nature. In this paper, a tracking framework called improved levy flight grasshopper optimization algorithm (LGOA) tracker is proposed. The levy flight can increase the diversity of population, prevent premature convergence and enhance the capability of jumping out of local optimal optima, thus improving the tracking accuracy. In addition, GOA has been applied to visual tracking for the first time as far as we know. Finally, compared with other optimization-based trackers, experimental results show that our tracker has obvious advantages.

Keywords: Visual tracking · Grasshopper Optimization Algorithm · Levy flight · Local optimal

1 Introduction

Visual tracking is one of the most important tasks in computer vision and has been applied in many applications such as video surveillance, autonomous driving, human-computer interaction and so on [1,2]. Although significant progress has been achieved in the past decades, there still remain many challenges because of several tracking obstacles such as motion blur, deformations, illumination change, fast motions and so on. In recent years, we pay much attention to the visual tracking [3–5].

Essentially speaking, visual tracking can be reduced to a search task and formulated as an optimization problem. For obtaining a more intelligent searching mechanism to solve visual tracking, researchers have focused much attention on swarm optimization because of its robustness and flexibility. Gao et al. introduced some new meta-heuristic optimization algorithms (including firefly algorithm (FA) [6], cuckoo search (CS) [7], bat algorithm (BA) [8]) into visual tracking. These methods utilized optimization algorithm as a search strategy

Supported by the National Natural Science Foundation of China (No.61873246).

Z. Lin et al. (Eds.): PRCV 2019, LNCS 11857, pp. 217–227, 2019.
https://doi.org/10.1007/978-3-030-31654-9_19

to find targets, which outperformed the other trackers in accuracy and speed. Xu et al. [9] proposed a visual tracking framework based on differential evolution algorithm. The approach combined the improved differential evolution (DE) and structural similarity index (SSIM) to a visual tracking framework, which achieved better tracking performance than other trackers. Zhang et al. [10] proposed a sequential particle swarm optimization (PSO) based visual tracking, which was integrated sequential information into PSO method to form a robust tracking framework. The tracker got better performance, especially for arbitrary motion and large appearance changes. Chen et al. [11] proposed a Euclid distance based hybrid quantum particle swarm optimization (HQPSO). This method overcame the loss of population diversity in the later stage of PSO, which improved tracking efficiency and decrease detection time cost compared with mean shift algorithm. Nguyen et al. [12] presented a modified bacterial foraging optimization (m-BFO) algorithm, which was introduced into real-time tracking with changes. Hao et al. [13] proposed a particle filtering algorithm based on ant colony optimization (ACO), which enhanced the performance of particle filter with small sample set. The approach effectively improved the efficiency of visual tracking. Ljouad et al. [14] presented the hybrid kalman CS tracker, a new tracking approach, using a modified CS algorithm combined with the kalman filter. The proposed approach had better performance than PSO based tracker. In addition, Zhang et al. [15] presented a comparison of swarm optimization based abrupt motion tracking methods and analyzed each tracker qualitatively and quantitatively.

Recently, Saremi et al. [16] presented a novel nature-inspired algorithms called grasshopper optimization algorithm (GOA). The algorithm had been applied in lots of fields successfully due to its good robustness and fast convergence ability [17,18]. However, the GOA can not always achieve global search very well, so sometimes it may fall into local optimum. To overcome this drawback, some improved methods were proposed [19,20].

In this paper, levy flight first is introduced into GOA to update grasshoppers' location, which increase diversity of grasshoppers and ensure global optimum. Secondly, visual tracking is regarded to be a process of searching for target by various grasshoppers in video sequential. Thus, a new LGOA-based tracker is designed to obtain a better tracking performance by enhancing and balancing the exploration and exploitation efficiently. Finally, experimental results demonstrate the LGOA-based tracker shows better performance than other optimization-based trackers.

2 Grasshopper Optimization Algorithm and Levy Flight

2.1 Grasshopper Optimization Algorithm (GOA)

GOA is a nature-inspired algorithm which mimics the idealized swarming behavior of grasshopper insects in nature [16]. There are two types of swarming behaviour found in grasshoppers, namely nymph and adulthood phases. In the nymph phase, the main characteristics of grasshopper move slowly and with small steps (local search). In the adulthood phase, grasshoppers migrate a long range and abrupt movement in a swarm (global search).

In the GOA, suppose there are N grasshoppers in the swarm. The d–dimensional location of the $i-th$ grasshopper is $X_i^d(i = 1, 2, \cdots, N)$, the swarming behavior of grasshoppers can be written as:

$$X_i^d(t+1) = c \left(\sum_{j=1 \neq i}^{N} c \frac{ub_d - lb_d}{2} s(|X_j^d(t) - X_i^d(t)|) \frac{X_j(t) - X_i(t)}{d_{ij}} \right) + \hat{T}_d(t) \quad (1)$$

where ub_d is the upper bound, lb_d is lower bound in the d–dimension, t is the current iteration, $d_{ij} = |X_j(t) - X_i(t)|$ is the distance between the $i-th$ grasshopper and the $j-th$ grasshopper, $\hat{T}_d(t)$ represents the $d-th$ dimension location of the target grasshopper (best solution found so far), $s(\cdot)$ is a function of social forces strength, and the parameter c is shrinking factor to balance exploration and exploitation. The parameter c is updated to reduce exploration (global search) and increase exploitation (local search) proportional to the number of iteration. The function $s(\cdot)$ and the parameter c are calculated by following equation:

$$s(r) = f e^{\frac{-r}{l}} - e^{-r} \quad (2)$$

$$c = c_{\max} - \frac{t(c_{\max} - c_{\min})}{T} \quad (3)$$

where f indicates the intensity of attraction, l is the attractive length scale, t is the current iteration, T is the maximum number of iterations, $c_{\max}$ is the maximum value and $c_{\min}$ is the minimum value. In this work, we set $c_{\max} = 1$ and $c_{\min} = 0.00004$.

2.2   Levy Flight

The levy flight [21] is a random walk in which every step are derived from levy stable distribution. Numerous studies have shown that the behavior of many animals and insects is a classic feature of levy flight [22, 23]. The motion trajectory combines the short distance search and the occasional long distance search. The step length s of the levy flight can be calculated using mathematically model:

$$s = \frac{\mu}{|\nu|^{1/\beta}} \quad (4)$$

where $\beta = 1.5$ is referred to as levy index, $\mu = N(0, \sigma_\mu^2)$ and $\nu = N(0, \sigma_\nu^2)$ are drawn from normal distributions, i.e:

$$\begin{cases} \sigma_\mu = \left[\frac{\Gamma(1+\beta) \times \sin(\pi \times \beta/2)}{\Gamma(1+\beta/2) \times \beta \times 2^{(\beta-1)/2}} \right]^{1/\beta} \\ \sigma_\nu = 1 \end{cases} \quad (5)$$

where $\Gamma(\cdot)$ is the Gamma function.

3 The Improved GOA with Levy Flight

3.1 Motive

The standard GOA adopts linearly adaptive strategy on c to balance exploration and exploitation, but it has some drawbacks. Once this strategy falls into local optimum in the early stage of search, it will be difficult to escape and find the optimal solution in the later stage of search. Therefore, GOA should be improved, which can explore the search place efficiently and overcome the local optima.

3.2 The Proposed Method (LGOA)

For the local best trap, this paper proposes an improved levy flight grasshopper optimization algorithm (LGOA). Levy flight is an effective method to prevent from the premature convergence due to its long jump property. Therefore, levy flight is introduced into GOA to increase diversity of grasshoppers and ensure global optimum. The mathematical model is as follows.

$$X_i^d(t+1) = X_i^d(t) + \alpha \oplus Levy(\lambda) \tag{6}$$

where $X_i^d(t)$ represents the d–dimension location of the $i-th$ grasshopper, $\alpha > 0$ is the step size related to the scale of the problems. In most cases, we can use $\alpha = 0$. λ is levy distribution parameter and the product $\oplus$ means entrywise multiplication. The random step length $Levy(\lambda)$ is generated in Eq. (7).

$$Levy(\lambda) = \frac{a\mu}{|v|^{1/\beta}}(T_d(t) - X_i^t) \tag{7}$$

where a is a constant and sets to 0.5. μ and ν are drawn from normal distributions as shown in Eq. (5), $T_d(t)$ represents the d–dimension location of the target grasshopper (best solution found so far).

Levy flight can significantly improve the exploratory performance of GOA and achieve local minima avoidance. In addition, the LGOA can not only further search locally, but also increase the diversity of population.

4 LGOA-Based Tracking System

Suppose there is target (food) being searched in the image (state space) and a group of target candidates (grasshoppers) are randomly generated in the image. The purpose of LGOA tracker is to find the "best" target candidate using the proposed algorithm. The LGOA-based tracking framework is shown in Fig. 1.

As shown in Fig. 1, the target is marked by the user in the first frame and the state vector is initialized. The state vector is defined as $X = [x, y, s]$ in this work, where $[x, y]$ represents the target's location in pixel coordinates and s shows the scale parameter. Then, a dynamic model generates new target candidates and predicts the target's location in the next frame. Next, a similarity measurement

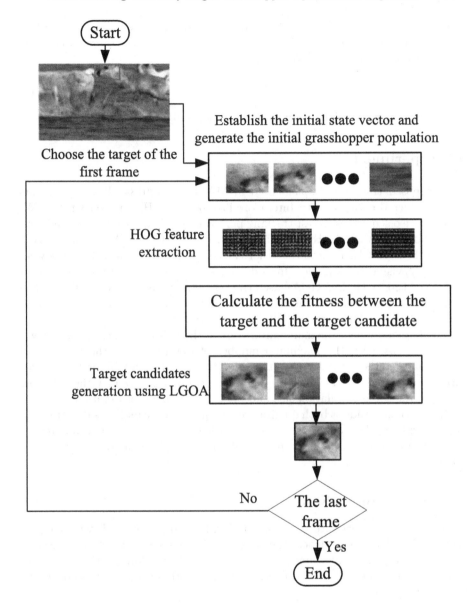

Fig. 1. The LGOA-based tracking framework

is used to calculate the similarity between the target and the target candidates. Finally, the LGOA is adopted to select the "best" target candidate.

In the LGOA tracker, correlation coefficient is utilized to measure the similarity and is defined as:

$$\rho(X,Y) = \frac{cov(X,Y)}{\sqrt{D(X)}\sqrt{D(Y)}} \tag{8}$$

where $cov(\cdot)$ shows covariance, $D(\cdot)$ denotes the variance, X and Y are the Histogram of Oriented Gradient (HOG) feature of the target and target candidates respectively. The object function is defined as follows:

$$E = 2 + 2 * \rho(X, Y) \tag{9}$$

The fitness value affects how to update the random walk of grasshoppers.

5   Experiments

The proposed tracker is implemented in MATLAB R2018a. The experiments were conducted on a PC with Intel Core i5-7500 3.40 GHz and 8 GB RAM. We select 8 video sequences to test tracking performance. These video sequences are: FISH, MAN, JUMPING, HUMAN7, DEER, FACE2, COUPLE and MHYANG. Among them, FACE2 is our own. Other video sequences are available on the website http://visual-tracking.net. In addition, we compared the proposed tracker with 4 trackers (including GOA-based tracker, ALO-based tracker (ant lion optimization, ALO), CS-based tracker and PSO-based tracker). To make a fair comparison, the same target model (HOG) and parameters were used.

As aforementioned, the main parameters in the LGOA tracker are as follows: population size (N), the maximum number of iterations (T), the intensity of attraction (f), the attractive length scale (l) and shrinking factor (c). In this experiment, $N = 100$, $T = 300$, $f = 0.5$, $l = 1.5$ and $c \in [0, 1]$. Other trackers maintain the same population size and maximum number of iterations.

In addition, we adopt both qualitative and quantitative methods to test tracking performance. For quantitative analysis, the tracking results are evaluated by using distance precision (DP), center location error (CLE) and overlap precision (OP)[24].

5.1   Qualitative Analysis

We quantitatively evaluate the 6 selected video sequences as shown in Fig. 2. For the FISH video sequence, the target undergoes seriously blurred because there is camera shake at frames #0058 and #0312. In addition, the brightness is dimmed at frame #0178. However, the target motion is relatively smooth. All trackers perform well.

In MAN video sequence, the target undergoes a process from dark to bright. All trackers can track the target successfully before the frame #0015. The ALO-based tracker and CS-based tracker lost the target unfortunately before the frame #0032. However, other trackers can capture targets and our trackers obtain the better tracking results.

JUMPING video sequence has been seriously blurred because of the camera shaking. Obviously, GOA-based tracker, ALO-based tracker and PSO-based tracker lose the target unfortunately at frame #0262. Our tracker obtains the best performance.

(a) FISH video sequence

(b) MAN video sequence

(c) JUMPING video sequence

(d) HUMAN7 video sequence

(e) DEER video sequence

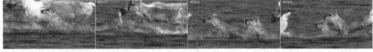

(f) FACE2 video sequence

(g) COUPLE video sequence

(h) MHYANG video sequence

——— LGOA ——— ALO ----- PSO
——— GOA ·········· CS

Fig. 2. A visualization of tracking results

HUMAN7 video sequence is obviously seen that the target is covered by trees shadow several times at frames #0090, #0168 and #0208. In addition, the target undergoes fast motion at frame #0168 with camera drastic camera shaking. All trackers are failure except for GOA-based tracker and our tracker. LGOA-based tracker have the superior results compared with GOA-based tracker.

For the DEER video sequence, it is very clear that the target experiences the fast motion, motion blur and multiple similar targets. All trackers can track targets successfully except for ALO-based tracker. Our tracker obtains the best performance compared with other trackers.

In FACE2 video sequence there has fast motion and slight illumination changing, our tracker and GOA-based tracker perform better and other trackers all failed at frames #0268 and #0308.

For COUPLE video sequence, the target experiences fast motion and background clutter. At the frame #0039, ALO-based tracker and PSO-based tracker loss the target, GOA-based tracker deviates the target. Although ALO-based tracker and PSO-based tracker restore the target at frame #0063 frames, they don't complete the whole video sequence. Our tracker tracked the whole video sequence successfully.

MHYANG video sequence has the larger illumination changing at frame #0378. GOA-based tracker and PSO-based tracker deviate the target, while CS-based tracker and our tracker perform very well.

5.2   Quantitative Analysis

In order to clearly analyse the tracking performance of different tracking methods, we utilized data to show the tracking results. Tables 1 and 2 list a per-sequence comparison of our tracker to GOA-based tacker, ALO-based tracker, CS-based tracker and PSO-based tracker, while Table 1 is concerned with average overlap rate and Table 2 refers to average center error rate. In addition, Fig. 3 reports DP and OP of 6 different video sequences.

It is obviously seen in Tables 1 and 2 and Fig. 3 that LGOA-based tracker performs much better than other trackers. Note that although the LGOA tracker has better performance in the JUMPING and HUMAN7 sequences, OP's data results are still very low because there is no scale change.

5.3   The Time Complexity

To analyze the time complexity, we calculated the average running time of five trackers on 8 video sequences. The average running time of LGOA, GOA, ALO, CS and PSO tracker is 16.2 s, 16.0 s, 10 s, 15.75 s and 13.1 s, respectively. As we all know, motion model, population size and maximum number of iterations are the three vital factors for the efficiency of the swarm optimization algorithm. LGOA, GOA and CS trackers run roughly the same time. The population size $n = 150$ and the maximum number of iterations $T = 500$ are generally required for ALO tracker to track the target successfully. In this case, the average running time of ALO tracker is 19.2 s, and PSO tracker is 21.8 s. Considering the above, our tracker shows better performance than other trackers.

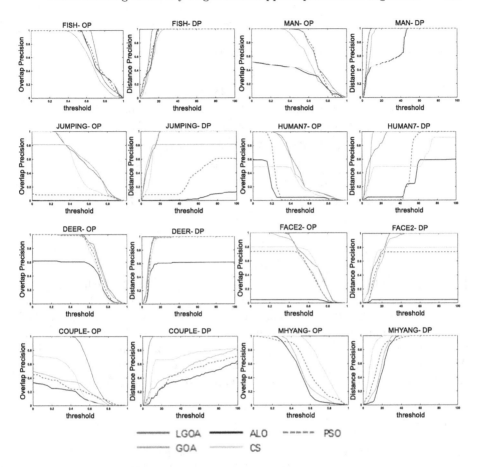

Fig. 3. The average precision of success plots

Table 1. Average overlap rate

Sequence	LGOA	GOA	ALO	CS	PSO
FISH	0.76	0.66	0.73	0.73	0.74
MAN	0.71	0.63	0.34	0.36	0.70
JUMPING	0.59	0.54	0.01	0.49	0.08
HUMAN7	0.48	0.46	0.14	0.26	0.23
DEER	0.74	0.72	0.45	0.68	0.69
FACE2	0.65	0.59	0.04	0.59	0.49
COUPLE	0.62	0.25	0.15	033	0.22
MHYANG	0.75	0.54	0.49	0.75	0.60

Table 2. Average center error rate

Sequence	LGOA	GOA	ALO	CS	PSO
FISH	8.54	12.17	10.38	10.80	9.77
MAN	4.35	6.79	23.15	22.56	4.48
JUMPING	8.44	36.21	126.73	10.80	85.62
HUMAN7	9.33	7.58	81.77	43.15	50.65
DEER	6.74	7.39	99.76	9.47	8.17
FACE2	13.36	17.62	308.51	54.43	135.19
COUPLE	4.32	51.75	76.93	37.87	63.27
MHYANG	7.27	17.68	20.30	7.27	14.77

6 Conclusion

In this paper, visual tracking is regarded to be a process of searching for target using various grasshoppers in sequential images. Therefore, a LGOA-based tracking framework is designed. The approach enables the GOA to jump out of the local optimum by levy flight, improving tracking accuracy. The experimental results show that the LGOA-based tracker outperforms GOA-based tracker, ALO-based tracker, CS-based tracker and PSO-based tracker. In the future, choosing the very strong deep features is expected in the LGOA-based tracker.

References

1. Haritaoglu, I., Harwood, D., Davis, L.S.: W4: real-time surveillance of people and their activities. IEEE Trans. Pattern Anal. Mach. Intell. **22**(8), 809–830 (2002)
2. Prisacariu, V.A., Reid, I., Prisacariu, V.A., et al.: 3D hand tracking for human computer interaction. Image Vis. Comput. **30**(3), 236–250 (2012)
3. Zhou, T., Liu, F., Bhaskar, H., et al.: Online discriminative dictionary learning for robust object tracking. Neurocomputing **275**(31), 1801–1812 (2018)
4. Zhang, H., Wang, Y., Luo, L., et al.: SIFT flow for abrupt motion tracking via adaptive samples selection with sparse representation. Neurocomputing **249**(2), 253–265 (2017)
5. Zhang, H., Zhang, X., Wang, Y., et al.: Extended cuckoo search-based kernel correlation filter for abrupt motion tracking. IET Comput. Vision **12**(6), 763–769 (2018)
6. Gao, M., He, X., Luo, D., et al.: Object tracking using firefly algorithm. IET Comput. Vision **7**(4), 227–237 (2013)
7. Gao, M., Yin, L., Zou, G., et al.: Visual tracking method based on cuckoo search algorithm. Opt. Eng. **54**(7), 073105 (2015)
8. Gao, M., Shen, J., Yin, L., et al.: A novel visual tracking method using bat algorithm. Neurocomputing **177**, 612–619 (2016)
9. Xu, F., Hu, H., Wang, C., et al.: A visual tracking framework based on differential evolution algorithm. In: Seventh International Conference on Information Science & Technology (2017)

10. Zhang, X., Hu, W., Maybank, S., et al.: Sequential particle swarm optimization for visual tracking. In: 2008 IEEE Conference on Computer Vision and Pattern Recognition, pp. 1–8. IEEE (2008)
11. Chen, J., Zhen, Y., Yang, D., et al.: Fast moving object tracking algorithm based on hybrid quantum PSO. WSEAS Trans. Comput. **12**, 375–383 (2013)
12. Nguyen, H., Bhanu, B.: Real-time pedestrian tracking with bacterial foraging optimization. In: 2012 IEEE Ninth International Conference on Advanced Video and Signal-Based Surveillance (AVSS), pp. 37–42. IEEE (2012)
13. Hao, Z., Zhang, X., Yu, P., et al.: Video object tracing based on particle filter with ant colony optimization. In: 2010 2nd International Conference on Advanced Computer Control (ICACC), vol. 3, pp. 232–236. IEEE (2010)
14. Ljouad, T., Amine, A., Rziza, M.: A hybrid mobile object tracker based on the modified cuckoo search algorithm and the Kalman filter. Pattern Recogn. **47**, 3597–3613 (2014)
15. Zhang, H., Zhang, X., Wang, Y., et al.: An experimental comparison of swarm optimization based abrupt motion tracking methods. IEEE Access **6**, 75383–75394 (2018)
16. Saremi, S., Mirjalili, S., Lewis, A.: Grasshopper optimisation algorithm: theory and application. Adv. Eng. Softw. **105**, 30–47 (2017)
17. Mirjalili, S.Z., Mirjalili, S., Saremi, S., et al.: Grasshopper optimization algorithm for multi-objective optimization problems. Appl. Intell. **48**(4), 805–820 (2018)
18. Liu, J., Wang, A., Qu, Y., et al.: Coordinated operation of multi-integrated energy system based on linear weighted sum and grasshopper optimization algorithm. IEEE Access **6**, 42186–42195 (2018)
19. Wu, J., Wang, H., Li, N., et al.: Distributed trajectory optimization for multiple solar-powered UAVs target tracking in urban environment by adaptive grasshopper optimisation algorithm. Aerosp. Sci. Technol. **70**, 497–510 (2017). S1270963817303930
20. Arora, S., Anand, P.: Chaotic grasshopper optimization algorithm for global optimization. Neural Comput. Appl. **31**, 1–21 (2018)
21. Yang, X.S., Deb, S.: Cuckoo search via levy flights. In: 2009 World Congress on Nature & Biologically Inspired Computing (NaBIC). IEEE (2009)
22. Mercadier, N., Guerin, W., Chevrollier, M., et al.: Levy flights of photons in hot atomic vapours. Nat. Phys. **5**(8), 602–605 (2012)
23. Schreier, A.L., Grove, M.: Ranging patterns of hamadryas baboons: random walk analyses. Anim. Behav. **80**(1), 75–87 (2010)
24. Wu, Y., Lim, J., Yang, M.: Online object tracking: a benchmark. In: 2013 IEEE Conference on Computer Vision and Pattern Recognition. IEEE Computer Society (2013)

Exploring Context Information for Accurate and Fast Object Detection

Zhenjun Shi, Xiaoqi Li, and Bin Zhang$^{(\boxtimes)}$

Beijing University of Posts and Telecommunications, Beijing 100876, China
{2013210668,clorislee,bluezb}@bupt.edu.cn

Abstract. Current top-performing object detectors depend on deep CNN backbones, such as ResNet-101 and InceptionNet, benefiting from their powerful feature representations but suffering from high computational costs. Conversely, some lightweight model based detectors can run at real time speed, while their performance is inferior to those equipped with powerful backbone network. In this paper, we propose an effective yet efficient one-stage detector. The proposed detector inherits the architecture of SSD and introduces two novel modules, Feature Enhancement Module (FEM) and Feature Fusion Module (FFM). The FEM could strengthen features by increasing the size of receptive field and introducing more context, while The FFM could enhance the shallow part of the detector by fusing two adjacent feature maps. To evaluate their effectiveness, experiments are conducted on two major benchmarks. Experimental results demonstrate that the proposed detector performs much better than the original SSD, without losing real-time processing speed.

Keywords: Real-time detector · Feature Enhancement Module (FEM) · Feature Fusion Module (FFM)

1 Introduction

Object detection serves as a prerequisite for a broad set of downstream vision applications, such as instance segmentation, human skeleton, face recognition and high-level object-based reasoning. Object detection combines both object classification and object localization. In recent years, Region-based Convolutional Neural Networks (R-CNN) [1], along with its representative updated descendants, e.g. Fast R-CNN [2] and Faster R-CNN [3], have persistently promoted the performance of object detection on major challenges and benchmarks, such as Pascal VOC [4] and MS COCO [5]. In region-based methods, object detection is formulated as a multi-task learning problem: (1) distinguish foreground object proposals from background and assign them with proper class labels; (2) regress a set of coefficients which localize the object. It is generally accepted that in these methods, CNN representation plays a crucial role, and the learned feature is expected to deliver a high discriminative power encoding object characteristics. A number of very recent efforts [6,7] have confirmed that

© Springer Nature Switzerland AG 2019
Z. Lin et al. (Eds.): PRCV 2019, LNCS 11857, pp. 228–238, 2019.
https://doi.org/10.1007/978-3-030-31654-9_20

robust feature is a key to improve the detector performance. The above methods reach better performance, however, they often suffer from a low inference speed.

To accelerate detection, a single-stage framework is investigated, where the phase of object proposal generation is discarded. The single-stage detectors tend to sacrifice accuracies, with a clear drop relative to state-of-art two stage solutions [8]. YOLO [9] and SSD [10] are two representative single-stage detectors. YOLO adopts a relative simple architecture thus very efficient, but cannot deal with dense objects or objects with large scale variants. As for SSD, it could detect objects with different size from multi-scale feature maps. Moreover, SSD uses anchor strategy to detect dense objects. Therefore, it achieves a pretty detection performance. In addition, SSD can achieve real-time speed on graphics processing unit (GPU). Due to the above advantages, SSD becomes a very practical object detector in industry, which has been widely used for many tasks. More recently, Deconvolutional SSD (DSSD) [11] and RetinaNet [8] substantially ameliorate the accuracy scores. Unfortunately, their speed is limited by the heavy computational costs from deep backbone model.

According to the discussion above, to build an effective yet efficient detector, a reasonable alternative is to enhance feature representation of the lightweight backbone network. In this paper, we propose Feature Enhancement Module (FEM), which enhances the robustness of feature maps.

There are several typical works exploring the feature pyramid representations for object detection. The Single Shot Detector (SSD) is one of the first attempts on using such technique in ConvNets. However, its performance on small objects is not good. The major reason is that it uses shallow feature map to detect small objects, which does not contain rich high-level semantic information thus not discriminative enough for classification. To overcome the disadvantage of SSD and make the networks more robust to object scales, we introduce Feature Fusion Module (FFM), which combines low-resolution and semantically-strong features with high-resolution and semantically-weak features.

We assemble the FEM module and the FFM module to SSD, a real-time approach with a lightweight backbone, and construct an advanced single-stage detector. The experiment results on Pascal VOC and MS COCO shows that our detector performs with higher detection accuracy than the Original SSD, while keeping the real-time speed.

Our main contributions can be summarized as follows:
1. We propose the Feature Enhancement Module which uses large convolutional kernel, aiming to enhance feature representation.
2. We introduce the Feature Fusion Module which enhances the low-level feature maps by combines high-level and semantically-strong features with low-level feature maps.
3. We assemble the above two modules to SSD, the detector shows significant performance gain while still keeping the computational cost under control.

2   Related Work

Two-Stage Detector: RCNN straightforwardly combines the steps of cropping box proposals like Selective Search [12] and classifying them through a CNN model, yielding a significant accuracy gain compared to traditional methods, which opens the deep learning era in object detection. Its descendants update the two-stage framework and achieve dominant performance.

Single-Stage Detector: The most representative single-stage detectors are YOLO and SSD. They predict confidences and locations for multiple objects based on the whole feature map. Recent more advanced single-stage detectors perform much better detection whose scores are comparable to two-stage methods.

Feature Pyramid: To make the detection more reliable, researchers usually adopt multi-scale representations [13]. Clearly, image pyramid methods are very time-consuming as they need to compute the features on each of image scale independently. Recently, a number of approaches improve the detection performance by combining predictions from different layers from a single CNN. For instance, ION [14] combines features from different layers before making predictions. SSD spreads out default boxes of different scales to multiple layers of different resolutions within a single CNN. So far, the SSD framework is a desired choice for object detection satisfying the speed-vs-accuracy trade-off.

Here, we briefly review the widely used single-stage detector SSD, which is the basis of our proposed detector.

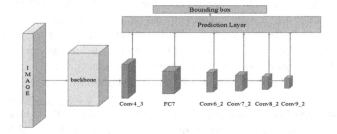

Fig. 1. Architecture of SSD with input-size 300 × 300.

As illustrated in Fig. 1, SSD is a fully convolutional network with a feature pyramid structure. The backbone-inside layer Conv4_3 is adopted for detecting objects of smallest size, the deeper layers are used to detect relative bigger objects. The range of the anchor size corresponding to each feature map is determined according to the object scale distributions on the training dataset. For anchor matching, it begins by matching each ground truth box to the default box with the best jaccard overlap, then match default boxes to any ground truth with jaccard overlap higher than a threshold. In this work, we attempt to improve SSD by assemble Feature Enhancement Module and Feature Fusion Module to it.

3   Method

In this section, we introduce our FEM and FFM components and describe the architecture of our detector.

3.1   Feature Enhancement Module

As mentioned in the Introduction section, object detection implies two challenges: classification and localization. However, the requirements of classification and localization problems are naturally contradictory. For classification, models are required invariant to transformation on the inputs. While for localization, models need to be transformation-sensitive because localization depends on the position of inputs.

In the physical world visual objects occur in particular environments and usually coexist with other related objects, and there is strong psychological evidence [15] that context plays an essential role in human object recognition. It is recognized that proper modeling of context helps object detection and recognition [16, 17].

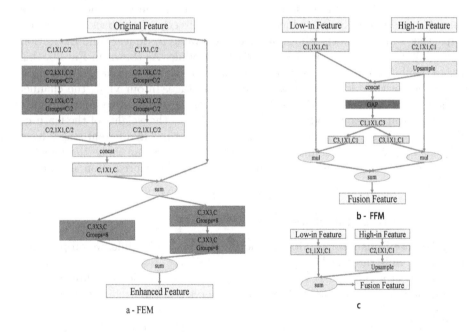

Fig. 2. Architecture of FEM, FFM and another simple fusion block. 'concat' means concatenate, 'sum' means element-wise addition, 'mul' means element-wise multiplication, 'GAP' means global average pooling, 'c1, k x k, c2' means k x k Convolution with input channel c1 and output channel c2.

Based on above observation, we introduce our Feature Enhancement Module. The structure of FEM is shown in Fig. 2a, which consists one Feature Enhancement block and one Refinement block. In the Feature Enhancement Block, there are two similar branches. We first use 1 * 1 Conv to reduce the number of channels, then use k * k Conv to model more context followed by 1 * 1 Conv for learning more non-linear relations. Meanwhile, we factorize the k * k Conv into a 1 * k and a k * 1 Conv layer for keeping receptive field as well as saving the inference time of the module. In the Refinement block, there are two branches, one branch consists two Conv layers, the other one consists one Conv layer. The two branches of the refinement block have different scales of receptive field; thus the fusion feature map is more robust. The FEM is designed to introduce more context information and enhance the feature maps. The module is motivated from some existing works, such as Inception module [18] and Xception module [19].

In our proposed detector, the backbone model can be divided into multiple stages according to the size of the feature maps. In the lower stage, the network encodes finer spatial information, however, it has poor semantic consistency because of its small receptive field and without the guidance of spatial context. While in the high stage, it has strong semantic consistency due to large receptive view, however, the prediction is spatially coarse. Overall, the lower stage makes more accurate spatial predictions, while the higher stage gives more accurate semantic predictions. SSD produces predictions directly on the backbone feature maps, thus suffers from the above problem. Motivated by Squeeze and Excitation network [20], we propose our Feature Fusion Module. As shown in Fig. 2b, this design combines the feature of adjacent stages to compute a channel attention vector for both the lower stage and the higher stage. In our view, the channel attention vector can select the features with more discriminative information.

Our Feature Fusion Module is designed to change the weights of the features on two adjacent stages. As mentioned above, the features in different stages have different degrees of discrimination. With the design, we can make the network to obtain more discriminative information to make the prediction intra-class consistent.

3.2   Network Architecture

With Feature Enhancement Module and Feature Fusion Module, we propose our detector as illustrated in Fig. 3.

Our detector assembles two Feature Enhancement Modules and three Feature Fusion Modules into original SSD and We preserve the SSD architecture as much as possible.

We use exactly the same backbone network as in SSD. It is a VGG16 [21] pre-trained on ILSVRC CLS-LOC dataset [22]. Though many lightweight networks (e.g. MobileNet [23] and ShuffleNet [24] and their descendants) have be proposed, we use this architecture for convenient direct comparison to the original SSD.

In the original SSD, the base architecture is followed by some convolutional layers to form a series of feature maps with consecutively decreasing spatial resolutions. Boxes regression and classification are produces directly on these feature maps. However, their learned features of the shallow stages are not good for the latter recognition process. In this paper, we use our proposed FFM to combine advantages from the original features [25].

Our Feature Enhancement Module and Feature Fusion Module could also be placed at other candidate positions. Considering the tradeoff between the improved accuracy and slower test speed, we have experimented and select the version shown in Fig. 3 finally.

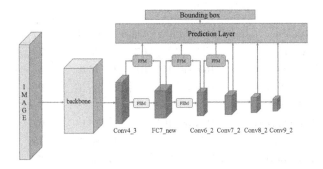

Fig. 3. The Pipeline of our detector with input size of 300×300. The green blocks represent the output feature maps of corresponding layers. (Color figure online)

4   Experiments

The experiments are conducted on Pascal VOC and MSCOCO datasets, which have 20 and 80 object categories respectively. The metric to evaluate detection performance is the meaning Average Precision (mAP) among all categories.

4.1   Implementation Details

We implement our detector with Pytorch. Our training strategies mostly follow SSD, including data augmentation, hard negative mining, criterion function and so on. In our experiments, we change our learning rate scheduling for better convergence. All new convolutional layers are initialized with the MSRA method [26].

4.2   Pascal VOC

In these experiments, we use the union of 2007 trainval set and 2012 trainval set to train our model and report results on 2007 test set. We set the batch size at 32 and the learning rate at 4e−3, and we use a "warmup" strategy to avoid some problems. We chose SGD [27] with a weight decay of 0.0005 and a momentum of 0.9 as our optimizer. The total number of training epoch is 270 and the learning rate is divided by 10 at 150, 200 and 250 epochs.

Table 1 shows the comparison between our results and some other ones on the VOC2017 test set. For fair comparison, we reimplement SSD and compute its inference time on our machine. For both the input size of 300×300 and 512×512, the improvement of our detector is significant, even better than two-stage detectors, while still running at a high speed.

Table 1. Comparison of detection methods on Pascal VOC 2007 test set. SSD and our detector are tested on our machine (GTX 1080), other methods are tested on GTX Titan X.

Method	Backbone	Data	mAP (%)	FPS
Faster [3]	VGG16	07+12	73.2	7
Faster++ [13]	ResNet-101	07+12	76.4	5
R-FCN [28]	ResNet-101	07+12	80.5	9
SSD300 [10]	VGG16	07+12	77.2	72♯
DSSD321 [11]	ResNet-101	07+12	78.6	9.5
RefineDet320 [30]	VGG16	07+12	80.0	40
Ours300	**VGG16**	**07+12**	**80.3**	**50**
SSD512 [10]	VGG16	07+12	79.8	30♯
DSSD513 [11]	ResNet-101	07+12	81.5	5.5
RefineDet512 [30]	VGG16	07+12	81.8	24
Ours512	**VGG16**	**07+12**	**82.3**	**26**

Table 2. Ablation study on Pascal VOC 2007 test set. In these experiments, we set $k = 7$ for Feature Enhancement Module

	SSD				Ours
More Prior			✓	✓	✓
FEM		✓	✓	✓	✓
Simple Fusion				✓	
FFM					✓
mAP (%)	77.2	79.0	79.2	80.0	80.3

4.3 Ablation Study

To evaluate the contribution of different components of our detector, we conduct ablation studies on Pascal VOC dataset. It should be pointed out that, the results are obtained on Pascal VOC 2007 test set to save time.

Feature Enhancement Module: To evaluate the effect of FEM, we assemble two FEMs into original SSD, we can see that the result is improved to 79.0%, delivering a gain of 1.8%, which shows the effectiveness of the added two FEMs.

More Prior: The original SSD associates only 4 default boxes at the smallest feature map. However, Hu [28] claims that low level features are critical to detecting small objects. We put 6 default boxes at the smallest feature map, and our detector obtains a gain of 0.2%.

Feature Fusion Module: To evaluate the effect of FFM, we choose a simple fusion block (the inner architecture is shown in Fig. 2c) as comparison, assembling the two kinds of modules at the same positions shown in Fig. 3. The last three columns of Table 2 illustrate that our FFM has a higher promotion.

Kernel size for FEM: We also investigate the impact of the kernel size k in FEM. The result is 80.3% at k = 7 and when we decrease the kernel size to 5, the result is 80.15%.

4.4   MS COCO

To further validate the proposed detector, we carry out experiments on the MS COCO dataset. In these experiments, we use the union of 80k training images and a 35 K subset of validation images (trainval35k) for training and set the batch size at 32. We keep the training strategies used in original SSD and still apply the "warmup" technique. We set the learning rate at 2e−3 and decrease it at 80, 100 and 120 epochs by the factor of 10, and end up at 130. Note that objects in MS COCO are smaller than those in Pascal VOC, so we decrease the size of anchor boxes following SSD.

Table 3. Detection performance on the COCO test-dev 2015. SSD and our detector are tested on our machine.

Method	Backbone	Time (ms)	Avg. Precision, IoU			Avg. Precision, Area		
			0.5:0.95	0.5	0.75	S	M	L
Faster [3]	VGG	147	24.2	45.3	23.5	7.7	26.4	37.1
Faster++ [13]	ResNet-101	3360	34.9	55.7	37.4	15.6	38.7	50.9
R-FCN [28]	ResNet-101	110	29.9	51.9	–	10.8	32.8	45.0
SSD300 [10]	VGG	18♮	25.1	43.1	25.8	–	–	–
SSD512 [10]	VGG	40♮	28.8	48.5	30.3	–	–	–
DSSD321 [11]	ResNet-101	–	28.0	46.1	29.2	7.4	28.1	47.6
DSSD513 [11]	ResNet-101	–	33.2	53.3	35.2	13.0	35.4	51.1
RefineDet320 [30]	VGG	–	29.4	49.2	31.3	10.0	32.0	44.4
RefineDet512 [30]	VGG	–	33.0	54.5	35.5	16.3	36.3	44.3
RetinaNet500 [8]	ResNet101-FPN	90	34.4	53.1	36.8	14.7	38.5	49.1
RetinaNet800 [8]	ResNet101-FPN	198	39.1	59.1	42.3	21.8	42.7	50.2
Ours300	VGG	27	30.2	49.5	31.7	12.0	32.6	45.9
Ours512	VGG	50	34.0	55.5	36.2	17.3	37.1	47.2

Fig. 4. Qualitative detection examples on VOC 2007 test set with SSD300 and Ours-300 models. For each pair, the left is the result of SSD and right is the result of ours. We show detections with scores higher than 0.6. Each color corresponds to a category in the image.

With the standard COCO evaluation metric, SSD300 scores 25.1% AP, and our model improves it to 30.2% AP, which is on par with DSSD with ResNet-101 backbone.

Regarding the bigger model, our detector with the input size of 512×512 achieves 34.0% AP on the test-dev set, which surpasses the baseline score of SSD512 and DSSD512 with a large margin. Considering small objects, the performance of our detector rises obviously. From this Table 3, it can be seen that our detector has a good speed-vs-accuracy trade-off (Fig. 4).

5   Conclusion

In this paper, we propose an effective single-stage detector based on SSD and two novel Modules. Experimental results on Pascal VOC and MS COCO reveal that our detector has significantly outperformed the original SSD, especially for detecting small objects, and it still retains the high speed of single-stage detector. Additionally, the FEM and FFM module are generic and impose few constraints on the network architecture. Due to the computational resource limit, we do not conduct experiments on other backbone networks and leave it for a further research.

References

1. Girshick, R., Donahue, J., Darrelland, T., Malik, J.: Rich feature hierarchies for object detection and semantic segmentation (2014)
2. Girshick, R.: Fast R-CNN. Comput. Sci. (2015)
3. Ren, S., He, K., Girshick, R., Sun, J.: Faster R-CNN: towards real-time object detection with region proposal networks. IEEE Trans. Pattern Anal. Mach. Intell. **39**(6), 1137–1149 (2017)
4. Everingham, M.: The pascal visual object classes challenge, (VOC) results. Int. J. Comput. Vis. **111**(1), 98–136 (2007). Lecture Notes in Computer Science
5. Lin, T.Y., et al.: Microsoft COCO: Common objects in context (2014)
6. He, K., Georgia, G., Piotr, D., Ross, G.: Mask R-CNN. IEEE Trans. Pattern Anal. Mach. Intell. **99**, 1–1 (2017)
7. Huang, J., et al.: Speed/accuracy trade-offs for modern convolutional object detectors (2016)
8. Lin, T.Y., Goyal, P., Girshick, R., He, K., Dollár, P.: Focal loss for dense object detection. IEEE Trans. Pattern Anal. Mach. Intell. **99**, 2999–3007 (2017)
9. Redmon, J., Divvala, S., Girshick, R., Farhadi, A.: You only look once: Unified, real-time object detection (2015)
10. Liu, W., et al.: SSD: single shot MultiBox detector. In: Leibe, B., Matas, J., Sebe, N., Welling, M. (eds.) ECCV 2016. LNCS, vol. 9905, pp. 21–37. Springer, Cham (2016). https://doi.org/10.1007/978-3-319-46448-0_2
11. Fu, C.Y., Liu, W., Ranga, A., Tyagi, A., Berg, A.: DSSD: deconvolutional single shot detector (2017)
12. Uijlings, J.R.R., van de Sande, K.E.A., et al.: Selective search for object recognition. Int. J. Comput. Vis. **104**(2), 154–171 (2013)
13. He, K., Zhang, X., Ren, S., Sun, J.: Deep residual learning for image recognition (2015)
14. Bell, S., Zitnick, C.L., Bala, K., Girshick, R.: Inside-outside net: detecting objects in context with skip pooling and recurrent neural networks. In: IEEE Conference on Computer Vision and Pattern Recognition (2016)
15. Atsumi, M.: Learning Probabilistic Semantic Network of Object-Oriented Action and Activity (2014)
16. Chen, L.C., Papandreou, G., Kokkinos, I., Murphy, K., Yuille, A.L.: Semantic image segmentation with deep convolutional nets and fully connected CRFs. Comput. Sci. **4**, 357–361 (2014)
17. Chen, L.C., Papandreou, G., Kokkinos, I., Murphy, K., Yuille, A.L.: Deeplab: semantic image segmentation with deep convolutional nets, atrous convolution, and fully connected CRFs. IEEE Trans. Pattern Anal. Mach. Intell. **40**(4), 834–848 (2018)
18. Szegedy, C., Vanhoucke, V., Ioffe, S., Shlens, J., Wojna, Z.: Rethinking the inception architecture for computer vision (2015)
19. Chollet, F.: Xception: deep learning with depthwise separable convolutions. In: IEEE Conference on Computer Vision and Pattern Recognition (2017)
20. Hu, J., Shen, L., Albanie, S., Sun, G., Wu, E.: Squeeze-and-excitation networks. **PP**(99), 1 (2017)
21. Simonyan, K., Vedaldi, K., Zisserman, A.: Deep fisher networks for large-scale image classification. In: International Conference on Neural Information Processing Systems (2013)

22. Russakovsky, O., et al.: Imagenet large scale visual recognition challenge. Int. J. Comput. Vis. **115**(3), 211–252 (2015)
23. Howard, A.G., et al.: MobileNets: efficient convolutional neural networks for mobile vision applications (2017)
24. Zhang, X., Zhou, X., Lin, M., Sun, J.: ShuffleNet: an extremely efficient convolutional neural network for mobile devices (2017)
25. Ronneberger, O., Fischer, P., Brox, T.: U-Net: convolutional networks for biomedical image segmentation (2015)
26. He, K., Zhang, X., Ren, S., Jian, S.: Delving deep into rectifiers: surpassing human-level performance on imagenet classification (2015)
27. Krizhevsky, A., Sutskever, A., Hinton, G.: Imagenet classification with deep convolutional neural networks. In: International Conference on Neural Information Processing Systems (2012)
28. Hu, P., Ramanan, D.: Finding tiny faces. In: Computer Vision and Pattern Recognition (2017)

A Novel Method for Thermal Image Based Electrical-Equipment Detection

Futian Wang[1,2], Songjian Hua[1], Xiao Wang[1], Zhengzheng Tu[1], Cheng Zhang[1],
and Jin Tang[1(✉)]

[1] School of Computer Science and Technology, Anhui University, Hefei 230601, China
{wft,cheng.zhang,tj}@ahu.edu.cn,hsj928@foxmail.com,
wangxiaocvpr@foxmail.com,zhengzhengahu@163.com
[2] Key Lab of Industrial Image Processing and Analysis of Anhui Province,
Hefei 230601, China

Abstract. An accurate and reliable thermal image based electrical-equipment detection is critical in smart power grids such as automatic defect diagnosis. However, few works have provided solutions to the task. To solve the problem, in this paper, we propose a new task named thermal image based electrical-equipment detection which includes two contributions. First, we have created a large-scale thermal electrical-equipment benchmark from 5558 thermal images which were taken during electrical-equipment inspection in reality. Second, we used the self-attention mechanism to get better detection performance. We have made some improvements based on Dual Attention Network (DANet) and applied it to further improve feature representation, we named our method Channel-Position Dual Attention Network (CPDANet). The experiment results show that our novel method can improve the mean Average Precision (mAP) from Faster R-CNN's 89.9% to 91.4%.

Keywords: Object detection · Benchmark dataset · Self-attention

1 Introduction

In this paper, we propose a new visual task named thermal image based electrical-equipment detection. Object detection is a fundamental and challenging problem in the computer vision community, whose goal is to identify all objects of interest in an image and determine their location and size. Thermal image based electrical-equipment detection is a important sub-task of object detection, it also is a critical component of smart power grids. Typically, at present, in the process of defect diagnosis, a equipment need to be manually marked, and then judging whether the equipment is defective according to the temperature information. Therefore, accurate detection of each type of electrical-equipment is the premise of automatic defect diagnosis. That is the equipment can be automatically marked and calculated relative temperature information, automatic defect diagnosis of the equipment can be achieved. Once a equipment

© Springer Nature Switzerland AG 2019
Z. Lin et al. (Eds.): PRCV 2019, LNCS 11857, pp. 239–250, 2019.
https://doi.org/10.1007/978-3-030-31654-9_21

is detected to be defective, the workers can timely repair the defect and avoid economic losses and changes in life, which significantly improve efficiency and safety of power grids. Sample detections over test set are illustrated in Fig. 1.

Fig. 1. Sample detections over the test set.

Traditional object detection methods are based on handcrafted features and easily stagnates their performance. Recently, with the development of deep learning, these problems existing in traditonal methods have been solved. Deep learning methods have shown superior performance for many tasks including object detection. Convolutional neural networks (CNNs) as one particular variant of deep neural networks, have shown their superiorities for many tasks including detection. PASCAL VOC [2] and ImageNet ILSVRC [19] are widely used to evaluate detection performance.

Object detection research has reached a very high level, such as vehicle detection [29], traffic-sign detection [30], pedestrian detection [14], face detection [23], person head detection [26], and so on. However, there is little research on thermal image based electrical-equipment detection. To solve this problem, we have created a realistic thermal electrical-equipment benchmark. Images in benchmark cover large variations in defect types (such as normal and defective, there are three criterias to judge whether the equipment is defective, temperature difference, relative temperature difference and hot spot temperature), season conditions (the change of season will cause the change of air temperature and also affect temperature of equipments, which will affect visual effect of images) and diurnal conditions (diurnal variations also will cause the change of air temperature and affect temperature of equipments).

Particularly, we analyzed our dataset and found that the dataset has one characteristic: there is a strong correlation between different equipments, i.e. the appearance of a equipment is often accompanied by the appearance of one or more other specific kinds of equipments. So, capturing contextual dependencies and integrating local features with their global dependencies by self-attention mechanism is a good way to get better detection performance. However, most methods do not focus on this.

To address above problem, we have made some improvements based on DANet [3], and applied it to integrate local features with their global dependencies, this have resulted in the better detection performance. The framework is illustrated in Fig. 4.

The primary contributions of this paper are as follows.

- We have created a new, realistic thermal electrical-equipment benchmark. The electrical-equipments in our benchmark cover real-world conditions which are large variations in such aspects as defect types, season conditions and diurnal conditions, examples of occlusion and incomplete equipment are also included. Our benchmark is annotated with a bounding box for each electrical-equipment, as well as giving it's class label. We call this benchmark TEED001. This benchmark will be open to public later.
- We have made some improvements based on DANet [3] and proposed CPDANet and applied it to further improve feature representation. The experiment results show that improvements can improve detection performance and robust.

The rest of the paper is organized as follows: related work are given in Sect. 2. In Sect. 3 we discuss details of our benchmark, while the approach we proposed presented in Sect. 4. We give experimental results in Sect. 5 and conclusions and future works in Sect. 6.

2 Related Work

According to the relevance to our work, we review related works following two research lines, i.e., Object Detection by CNNs and Attention modules.

2.1 Object Detection by CNNs

The CNNs was initially rekindled by the use of image classification in [10], and adapted to object detection quickly. It is observed in OverFeat [20] that the use of a convolutional network in the sliding window fashion is inherently efficient in nature by Sermanet et al., because many calculation can be reused in the overlapping region.

For using CNNs to object detection, another widely used strategy is to calculate some generic object proposals firstly and then classify only on these candidates. The first to use this strategy is R-CNN [5], but the following two reasons lead to the slow speed of it. First, it is costly to generate object proposals which is category-independent. Generating 1000 proposals for the Pascal VOC 2007 images, Selective search [24] need about 3 s, EdgeBoxes approach [31] which is more efficient still need about 0.3 s. Second, since each candidate proposal applies the deep convolution network, which increases the time cost. To improve efficiency, He et al. proposed spatial pyramid pooling network (SPP-Net) [6], which increases the speed of the R-CNN by about 100 times.

Then, based on R-CNN, Girshick et al. proposed Fast R-CNN [4], which didn't uses the SVM classifier used in R-CNN, but uses a softmax layer above the network instead. Because of ignoring object proposal time, Fast R-CNN processing one image takes 0.3 s. In order to overcome the bottleneck in the object proposal step, in Faster R-CNN [18], Ren et al. proposed region proposal networks (RPNs) which use convolutional feature maps to generate object proposals. This allows the object proposal generator to share full-image convolutional features with the detection network.

Compared with the two-stage detection framework mentioned above, the one-stage detection framework has more advantages in speed, such as SSD [15] and YOLO [16]. Liu et al. proposed Single Shot MultiBox Detector (SSD) [15] in 2016. SSD is based on VGG-16 [22] backbone network, and it is ends with extra convolutional layers. In the same year, Redmon et al. proposed You Only Look Once: Unified, Real-Time Object Detection (YOLO) [16], which frame object detection as a regression problem to spatially separated bounding boxes and associated class probabilities.

2.2 Attention Modules

Vaswani et al. proposed Attention is all you need [25] in 2017, which is the first work to propose the self-attention mechanism and apply it in machine translation. After this, attention mechanism have been widely applied in the field of Natural Language Processing (NLP). Attention modules can model long-range dependencies and directly draw global dependencies of inputs. Such a mechanism is dispensed with recurrence and convolutions entirely, which improves the parallelism and efficiency of model training. This attention mechanism has been extended in many NLP applications, such as natural language inference [21], text representation [11], sentence embedding [13] and so on.

Meanwhile, attention mechanism is also widely used in the field of computer vision. For example, the work Relation networks for object detection [8] proposed by Huet et al. in 2018. They proposed an object relation module to model the relationships among a set of objects, which improves object recognition. Self-attention generative adversarial networks [28] was proposed by Zhang et al. in 2018 for better image generation, because it introduces self-attention modules, which can efficiently find global dependencies within internal representations. Fu et al. proposed Dual Attention Network for Scene Segmentation [3] in 2018, this paper captures rich contextual dependencies based on the self-attention mechanism and proposes DANet adaptively integrate local features with their global dependencies and contributes to more precise segmentation results.

3 Benchmark

This section will introduce the details of the newly created benchmark dataset, called TEED001 in this paper, including dataset collection, annotation, statistics and baseline approaches.

3.1   Data Collection

It is a popular method to generate image datasets by downloading Internet images retrieved by search engines using keywords, many widely used datasets have been generated in this way, such as ImageNet ILSVRC [19] and Microsoft COCO [12]. However, there are few images of real-world thermal electrical-equipment on the Internet, even if they exist, the electrical-equipments are incidental: such images will not be tagged with the names of any equipments. Such an approach can't be used here. So, ideal way to generate images dataset is to collect useful thermal electrical-equipment images from lots of real world images taken during equipment inspection in reality by FLIR, DALI and FLUKE thermal imager.

3.2   Data Annotation

After collecting images, the next step is to annotate these images by hand. Our image dataset contains three regions of the power system: substation, transmission line and distribution line. A substation is an electrical system with high-voltage capacity. In order to transport the power from the power plant to a remote place, the voltage must be increased to become a high-voltage power, next the voltage should be lowered as the user requires. Normally, substations mainly include Step-up Type Substation and Step-down Substation, and so on. Transmission line uses a transformer to boost the electric energy generated by the generator, and then accesses the transmission line through a control device such as a circuit breaker. Distribution line refers to the line that sends power from the Step-down Substation to the Distribution Transformer or sends the power of the Distribution Substation to the power unit. During electrical-equipment annotation, we recorded the bounding box and class label. Equipment annotation case is similar to Fig. 1.

3.3   Data Statistics

After random selection, our new benchmark has 5558 images, These iamges contains 21 classes, 11180 electrical-equipment instances in total. There is an imbalance between different classes of electrical-equipment in our benchmark. Because some electrical-equipments are just rarely used. Instances per class are given in Fig. 2; most instances appear in relatively few classes. The image sizes (in pixels) of the electrical-equipments is given in Fig. 3; note that large electrical-equipments are most common, because in the actual shooting process, the lens will be zoomed.

   In summary, the benchmark we created provides detailed annotation for each equipment: it's bounding box and class label. All images in this benchmark have resolution 640 × 480. And cover large variations in temperature conditions. It will hopefully provide a suitable basis for research into detecting thermal electrical-equipment. We created the benchmark for this purpose.

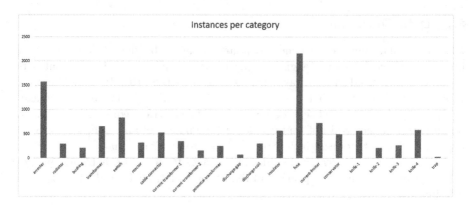

Fig. 2. Number of instances in each class.

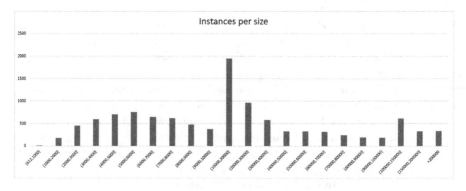

Fig. 3. Number of instances of each size.

3.4   Baseline Approaches

In order to verify the validity of our dataset, we have selected several advanced detectors available as baseline approaches for evaluation, which include Fast R-CNN [4], YOLOv2 [17], SSD [15], R-FCN [1], Faster R-CNN [18]. We experimented on these advanced baseline approaches and their mAP reached 79.9%, 81.7%, 89.7%, 89.1% and 89.9% respectively. The detail of results are shown in Table 1.

4   Proposed Approach

Both SE-Net [9] and CBAM [27] proposed channel attention and spatial attention, but they are implemented differently, and the way to get the final feature representation is also different. In addition, Dual Attention Network for Scene Segmentation [3] learned from two approaches above and proposed DANet. Based on the superiorities of the three approaches, we propose our own network architecture CPDANet. We use channel attention and position attention of DANet to get final feature representation. The architecture is shown in Fig. 4.

The implementation details of channel attention module and position attention module refer to Dual Attention Network for Scene Segmentation [3]. The structure of channel attention module is illustrated in Fig. 4(A). The structure of position attention module is illustrated in Fig. 4(B). In [3], channel attention module and position attention module are in parallel. Original features $A \in \mathbb{R}^{C \times H \times W}$ is used as input of channel attention and position attention, then fusing the outputs of the two attention branches in the way of element-wise summation to get the final feature maps.

In CPDANet, we don't fuse the outputs of the two attention branches in the way of element-wise summation used in Dual Attention Network for Scene Segmentation [3], we adapt a serial structure. We use CBAM [27] as reference. Firstly, we input the features $A \in \mathbb{R}^{C \times H \times W}$ obtained by ResNet-101 [7] into channel attention, and obtain the final output of channel attention module $E \in \mathbb{R}^{C \times H \times W}$. The final features E of each channel is a weighted sum of the features of all channels and original features, which models the long-range semantic dependencies between feature maps. It emphasizes class-dependent feature maps and helps to boost feature discriminability. Then we input E to position attention module, and obtain the final output $F \in \mathbb{R}^{C \times H \times W}$ of CPDANet as follows:

$$F_j = \alpha \sum_{i=1}^{N}(s_{ji}D_i) + E_j \tag{1}$$

where s_{ji} measures the ith position's impact on j^{th} position, α is initialized to 0 and gradually learned and assigned to a greater weight [28]. The Eq. (1) show that the resulting features F at each position is a weighted sum of the features at all positions and the output of channel attention module. Therefore, it has a global contextual view and selectively aggregates contexts according to the position attention map.

In summary, CPDANet can capture rich contextual dependencies which can get the better detection performance. The results of the two methods are shown in Table 1 (Faster R-CNN+DANet and Faster R-CNN+CPDANet). We can get that our method is more advantageous.

Particularly, we reverse the order of channel attention and position attention and input the features obtained by ResNet-101 [7] into position attention and get the output $E' \in \mathbb{R}^{C \times H \times W}$ firstly, then use E' as the input of channel attention, and finally get the further improved feature representation through channel attention, it's named P-C Dual Attention Network (PCDANet). The final output $F' \in \mathbb{R}^{C \times H \times W}$ as follows:

$$F'_j = \beta \sum_{i=1}^{C}(x_{ji}E'_i) + E'_j \tag{2}$$

where x_{ji} measures the ith channel's impact on the jth channel, β is initialized to 0, and gradually learned and assigned to a greater weight. However, we got

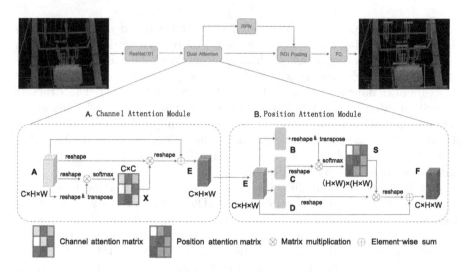

Fig. 4. Overall framework. And the details of channel attention module and position attention module are illustrated in (A) and (B).

a very poor detection performance in this method. The experimental results are shown in Table 1 (Faster R-CNN+PCDANet).

5   Experimental Results

We carry out comprehensive experiments on TEED001 dataset for evaluating the proposed method. Experimental results demonstrate that the proposed method achieves state-of-the-art performance on our dataset. Next, the detailed experimental process will be introduced.

5.1   Dataset and Evaluation Metrics

Dataset: Our algorithm is evaluated on our own dataset: TEED001. We separated TEED001 into a training set and a testing set. Training set contains 4448 images, and testing set contains 1110 images with about 4:1 ratio to give the deep learning methods plenty of training samples.

Evaluation Metrics: There are many evaluation metrics for object detection: accuracy, confusion matrix, precision and recall, Average Precision (AP), mAP etc. In this paper, we adopt mAP, which is the most widely used evaluation metric. And it is the average of multiple categories of AP, it's value must be in the [0, 1] interval, the larger the better.

5.2   Implementation Details

We implemented our method based on Pytorch. We employed the most commonly used learning rate policy, i.e., every time reach a certain number of iterations, we multiplied the current learning rate by the learning rate decay. The learning rate is initialized to 0.001, learning rate decay is set to 0.1. In addition, momentum and weight decay coefficients are set to 0.9 and 0.0001 respectively, batchsize is set to 2 for our dataset. Furthermore, all the parameter settings are available in the source code to be released for accessible reproducible research. Particularly, in our experimental evaluations of our neural network, both training and testing were done on a Linux PC with an Intel(R) Core(TM) i7-7700K 4.2 GHz CPU with 32 GB RAM, one NVIDIA GeForcd Gtx 1080 GPU and 8 GB memory.

5.3   Ablation Study

We employ our method on the top of the dilation network to capture long-range dependencies for getting better detection performance. In order to verify the effectiveness of our proposed method, we conducted the experiments as follow.

Firstly, we employed CPDANet after feature extraction to further improve feature representation. The experimental results are shown in Table 1. The data show that CPDANet can indeed further improve the detection performance compared to Faster R-CNN. Secondly, we used the DANet to further improve feature representation, the experimental results show that although mAP has also been improved to a certain extent, there is still a certain gap between the 0.8% improvement in the experiment used DANet and the 1.5% improvement in the experiment used CPDANet. The experiment proves that our improvements on DANet is positive. Then, we used only channel attention module, and only position attention module to further improve feature representation respectively. Only position attention module improved mAP by 1.1%, which is not as good as the experiment used CPDANet, even only channel attention module reduced mAP by 0.4%. Finally, we used PCDANet to get feature representation and reduced mAP by 3%. The experimental results prove that the dual attention mechanism is necessary. In summary, our method has got the best performance in all the comparative experiments.

5.4   Comparison with State-of-the-Art

We further compare our method with selected advanced baseline approaches on the TEED001 dataset. We evaluated 5 detectors on our dataset, including Fast R-CNN [4], YOLOv2 [17], SSD [15], R-FCN [1], Faster R-CNN [18]. And all detectors achieved the best results as shown in Table 1. Compared with the above mentioned methods, our method has great advantage in mAP and improve mAP by 11.5%, 9.7%, 1.7%, 2.3% and 1.5% respectively. Apart from the advantages of the overall framework, the biggest advantage is feature representation in our method integrate local features with their global dependencies.

Table 1. mAP on the TEED001 test dataset produced by all experiments. (All class names use abbreviations. Comparison of abbreviations and full names of all classes is illustrated in Table 2)

Methods	mAP	ar	ra	bu	tr	sw	re	cc	ct1	ct2	in
Fast R-CNN	79.9	69.9	99.1	72.4	89.0	90.6	75.2	70.7	80.4	73.1	61.6
Faster R-CNN	89.9	80.7	100.0	81.6	90.6	90.8	90.7	78.4	90.9	90.9	78.9
R-FCN	89.1	88.5	99.8	87.8	89.6	90.0	87.7	77.6	91.3	93.7	85.2
SSD300	89.7	84.6	100.0	74.6	90.8	90.3	92.8	67.3	90.4	89.7	87.9
YOLOv2	81.7	71.0	100.0	79.0	90.7	90.4	81.5	63.5	90.6	90.6	81.1
Faster R-CNN+DANet	90.7	80.8	100.0	80.9	89.2	90.8	90.9	81.0	90.8	90.6	80.3
Faster R-CNN+only Channel Attention	88.5	80.5	100.0	81.4	90.0	89.7	88.6	80.2	90.9	90.6	79.2
Faster R-CNN+only Position Attention	91.0	80.5	100.0	90.1	89.9	90.7	90.9	80.7	90.7	90.6	80.8
Faster R-CNN+PCDANet	86.9	78.7	100.0	80.8	89.5	89.9	90.2	77.9	90.6	90.3	80.4
Faster R-CNN+CPDANet(ours)	91.4	87.8	100.0	89.5	90.2	90.6	89.5	79.2	90.7	90.9	81.0

Methods	mAP	pt	dg	dc	fu	co	cl	k1	k2	k3	k4	ta
Fast R-CNN	79.9	100.0	44.9	42.7	80.3	90.7	81.2	90.0	90.9	80.9	81.4	72.7
Faster R-CNN	89.9	100.0	90.9	81.1	88.5	90.9	90.6	90.6	90.9	100.0	89.8	100.0
R-FCN	89.1	100.0	48.1	88.9	89.0	90.7	90.0	90.9	92.3	100.0	90.6	100.0
SSD300	89.7	100.0	98.2	82.9	87.3	90.4	85.3	90.6	90.9	99.8	90.6	100.0
YOLOv2	81.7	99.8	67.3	70.5	79.4	90.3	86.7	89.4	95.3	90.9	89.7	18.2
Faster R-CNN+DANet	90.7	100.0	100.0	90.2	88.1	89.9	90.6	90.4	90.2	100.0	90.0	100.0
Faster R-CNN+only Channel Attention	88.5	100.0	75.5	90.1	79.2	90.6	81.5	90.5	90.9	100.0	89.2	100.0
Faster R-CNN+only Position Attention	91.0	100.0	97.2	89.7	88.2	90.8	90.7	90.2	90.5	100.0	89.3	100.0
Faster R-CNN+PCDANet	86.9	100.0	53.2	80.8	80.2	81.7	90.8	90.5	90.9	100.0	89.6	100.0
Faster R-CNN+CPDANet(ours)	91.4	100.0	100.0	89.6	86.9	90.9	90.3	90.2	90.3	100.0	90.7	100.0

Table 2. Comparison of abbreviations and full names of all classes.

Abbreviations	ar	ra	bu	tr	sw	re	cc	ct1
Full names	arrester	radiator	bushing	transformer	switch	reactor	cable-connector	current-transformer-1
Abbreviations	ct2	in	pt	dg	dc			
Full names	current-transformer-2	insulator	potential-transformer	discharge-gap	discharge-coil			
Abbreviations	fu	co	cl	k1	k2	k3	k4	ta
Full names	fuse	conservator	current-limiter	knife-1	knife-2	knife-3	knife-4	trap

6   Conclusions and Future Works

In this paper, we have created a new benchmark for thermal image based electrical-equipment detection. And this is a leading work to propose this type of benchmark. We tested multiple baseline approaches with good experimental results. In addition, we proposed CPDANet based on the Dual Attention Network and applied it to further improve feature representation. The further improved feature map has gotten better detection performance.

In the future, we plan to add more images to those classes that have fewer images and study pixel-level segmentation of electrical-equipment based on the results of object detection, both of which can improve the accuracy of electrical-equipment defect detection.

Acknowledgment. This work was partly supported by the National Natural Science Foundation of China (Grant Nos. 61602006, 61872005), Anhui Provincial Natural Science Foundation (No. 1908085MF206).

References

1. Dai, J., Li, Y., He, K., Sun, J.: R-FCN: object detection via region-based fully convolutional networks. In: Advances in Neural Information Processing Systems, pp. 379–387 (2016)
2. Everingham, M., Van Gool, L., Williams, C.K., Winn, J., Zisserman, A.: The pascal visual object classes (VOC) challenge. Int. J. Comput. Vision **88**(2), 303–338 (2010)
3. Fu, J., Liu, J., Tian, H., Fang, Z., Lu, H.: Dual attention network for scene segmentation. arXiv preprint arXiv:1809.02983 (2018)
4. Girshick, R.: Fast R-CNN. In: Proceedings of the IEEE International Conference on Computer Vision, pp. 1440–1448 (2015)
5. Girshick, R., Donahue, J., Darrell, T., Malik, J.: Rich feature hierarchies for accurate object detection and semantic segmentation. In: Proceedings of the IEEE Conference on Computer Vision and Pattern Recognition, pp. 580–587 (2014)
6. He, K., Zhang, X., Ren, S., Sun, J.: Spatial pyramid pooling in deep convolutional networks for visual recognition. In: Fleet, D., Pajdla, T., Schiele, B., Tuytelaars, T. (eds.) ECCV 2014. LNCS, vol. 8691, pp. 346–361. Springer, Cham (2014). https://doi.org/10.1007/978-3-319-10578-9_23
7. He, K., Zhang, X., Ren, S., Sun, J.: Deep residual learning for image recognition. In: Computer Vision and Pattern Recognition, pp. 770–778 (2016)
8. Hu, H., Gu, J., Zhang, Z., Dai, J., Wei, Y.: Relation networks for object detection. In: Proceedings of the IEEE Conference on Computer Vision and Pattern Recognition, pp. 3588–3597 (2018)
9. Hu, J., Shen, L., Sun, G.: Squeeze-and-excitation networks. arXiv preprint arXiv:1709.01507 7 (2017)
10. Krizhevsky, A., Sutskever, I., Hinton, G.E.: ImageNet classification with deep convolutional neural networks. In: Advances in Neural Information Processing Systems, pp. 1097–1105 (2012)
11. Lin, G., Shen, C., Van Den Hengel, A., Reid, I.: Efficient piecewise training of deep structured models for semantic segmentation. In: Proceedings of the IEEE Conference on Computer Vision and Pattern Recognition, pp. 3194–3203 (2016)
12. Lin, T.-Y., et al.: Microsoft COCO: common objects in context. In: Fleet, D., Pajdla, T., Schiele, B., Tuytelaars, T. (eds.) ECCV 2014. LNCS, vol. 8693, pp. 740–755. Springer, Cham (2014). https://doi.org/10.1007/978-3-319-10602-1_48
13. Lin, Z., et al.: A structured self-attentive sentence embedding. arXiv preprint arXiv:1703.03130 (2017)
14. Liu, J., Zhang, S., Wang, S., Metaxas, D.N.: Multispectral deep neural networks for pedestrian detection. arXiv preprint arXiv:1611.02644 (2016)
15. Liu, W., et al.: SSD: single shot MultiBox detector. In: Leibe, B., Matas, J., Sebe, N., Welling, M. (eds.) ECCV 2016. LNCS, vol. 9905, pp. 21–37. Springer, Cham (2016). https://doi.org/10.1007/978-3-319-46448-0_2
16. Redmon, J., Divvala, S., Girshick, R., Farhadi, A.: You only look once: unified, real-time object detection. In: Proceedings of the IEEE Conference on Computer Vision and Pattern Recognition, pp. 779–788 (2016)
17. Redmon, J., Farhadi, A.: Yolo9000: better, faster, stronger. arXiv preprint (2017)
18. Ren, S., He, K., Girshick, R., Sun, J.: Faster R-CNN: towards real-time object detection with region proposal networks. IEEE Trans. Pattern Anal. Mach. Intell. **6**, 1137–1149 (2017)
19. Russakovsky, O., et al.: Imagenet large scale visual recognition challenge. Int. J. Comput. Vision **115**(3), 211–252 (2015)

20. Sermanet, P., Eigen, D., Zhang, X., Mathieu, M., Fergus, R., LeCun, Y.: Overfeat: Integrated recognition, localization and detection using convolutional networks. arXiv preprint arXiv:1312.6229 (2013)

21. Shen, T., Zhou, T., Long, G., Jiang, J., Pan, S., Zhang, C.: DiSAN: directional self-attention network for RNN/CNN-free language understanding. In: Thirty-Second AAAI Conference on Artificial Intelligence (2018)

22. Simonyan, K., Zisserman, A.: Very deep convolutional networks for large-scale image recognition. arXiv preprint arXiv:1409.1556 (2014)

23. Song, G., Liu, Y., Jiang, M., Wang, Y., Yan, J., Leng, B.: Beyond trade-off: accelerate FCN-based face detector with higher accuracy. In: Proceedings of the IEEE Conference on Computer Vision and Pattern Recognition, pp. 7756–7764 (2018)

24. Uijlings, J.R., Van De Sande, K.E., Gevers, T., Smeulders, A.W.: Selective search for object recognition. Int. J. Comput. Vision **104**(2), 154–171 (2013)

25. Vaswani, A., et al.: Attention is all you need. In: Advances in Neural Information Processing Systems, pp. 5998–6008 (2017)

26. Vu, T.H., Osokin, A., Laptev, I.: Context-aware CNNs for person head detection. In: Proceedings of the IEEE International Conference on Computer Vision, pp. 2893–2901 (2015)

27. Woo, S., Park, J., Lee, J.-Y., Kweon, I.S.: CBAM: convolutional block attention module. In: Ferrari, V., Hebert, M., Sminchisescu, C., Weiss, Y. (eds.) ECCV 2018. LNCS, vol. 11211, pp. 3–19. Springer, Cham (2018). https://doi.org/10.1007/978-3-030-01234-2_1

28. Zhang, H., Goodfellow, I., Metaxas, D., Odena, A.: Self-attention generative adversarial networks. arXiv preprint arXiv:1805.08318 (2018)

29. Zhou, Y., Liu, L., Shao, L., Mellor, M.: DAVE: a unified framework for fast vehicle detection and annotation. In: Leibe, B., Matas, J., Sebe, N., Welling, M. (eds.) ECCV 2016. LNCS, vol. 9906, pp. 278–293. Springer, Cham (2016). https://doi.org/10.1007/978-3-319-46475-6_18

30. Zhu, Z., Liang, D., Zhang, S., Huang, X., Li, B., Hu, S.: Traffic-sign detection and classification in the wild. In: Proceedings of the IEEE Conference on Computer Vision and Pattern Recognition, pp. 2110–2118 (2016)

31. Zitnick, C.L., Dollár, P.: Edge boxes: locating object proposals from edges. In: Fleet, D., Pajdla, T., Schiele, B., Tuytelaars, T. (eds.) ECCV 2014. LNCS, vol. 8693, pp. 391–405. Springer, Cham (2014). https://doi.org/10.1007/978-3-319-10602-1_26

State Detection of Electrical Equipment Based on Infrared Thermal Imaging Technology

Hejin Yuan[1]([⊠]), Xiuxin Chen[1], Yu Wang[2], and Ming Su[2]

[1] North China Electric Power University, Beijing, Hebei, China
651344234@qq.com
[2] Baoding Vocational and Technical College, Baoding, Hebei, China

Abstract. With the increasing demand of power supply reliability for electrical equipment in power grid and the continuous development of infrared thermal imaging technology, infrared thermal imaging technology has been widely used in electrical equipment detection. Using infrared instruments to detect and diagnose thermal fault of electrical equipment has become one of the mainstream methods of electric equipment inspection. However, at present, fault detection relies heavily on personnel's experience and has low detection efficiency. In order to improve the intelligent level of power system and solve the problem of accurate detection of thermal faults of electrical equipment in substations, this paper applies Faster RCNN algorithm to infrared detection to realize automatic detection of electrical equipment faults. The average recognition accuracy of equipment can reach more than 85%, which has good effect.

Keywords: Electrical equipment · Infrared detection · Faster RCNN

1 Introduction

The purpose of power equipment condition monitoring is to use effective detection means and analysis and diagnosis technology to grasp the operation status of equipment timely and accurately, and to ensure the safe, reliable and economic operation of equipment. The core of condition monitoring is the determination of equipment status. The equipment status data are obtained by means of inspection, test, live detection and on-line monitoring. The location, degree of hazards and trend of equipment hidden dangers are evaluated and evaluated, so that the maintenance plan can be formulated reasonably [1]. Infrared thermal image detection technology is an effective means to monitor the thermal state of electrical equipment. It can use infrared imager to transform the infrared radiation of electrical equipment into infrared image. Through the analysis of infrared image, the possible fault of the equipment can be determined. It can inspect the electrical equipment online to ensure that the equipment can complete the diagnosis without power failure and shutdown. At the same time, it has non-contact characteristics, which can ensure the safety of operators to a large extent. These characteristics of infrared thermal image detection technology just meet the requirements of power system fault diagnosis, so it is widely used in the operation and maintenance of power system transmission and transformation equipment, and has a significant role in the early detection of electrical equipment faults [2–4].

© Springer Nature Switzerland AG 2019
Z. Lin et al. (Eds.): PRCV 2019, LNCS 11857, pp. 251–260, 2019.
https://doi.org/10.1007/978-3-030-31654-9_22

With the continuous development of artificial intelligence technology and the continuous improvement of intelligent substation construction, the use of intelligent inspection robots and unmanned aerial vehicles has become one of the mainstream methods of power equipment inspection. By observing the collected infrared images, the inspectors can clearly distinguish the temperature changes inside the electrical equipment, so as to know whether the electrical equipment fails or not, and find out the equipment components that fail, and repair and maintain them in time. But because there are many kinds of electrical devices when intelligent robots or UAVs take images, different devices and even different parts of the same device have their own criteria, which makes it more difficult to detect the state of the equipment. In this paper, Faster RCNN is introduced into the infrared detection of electrical equipment, and the algorithm is improved. It can realize the accurate location and recognition of multiple electrical equipment in the image, lay the foundation for subsequent fault diagnosis, and improve the operation efficiency and detection accuracy of the diagnosis system.

2   Design of Infrared State Detection Scheme

In the past, most of the thermal condition monitoring of substation equipment based on infrared thermal imaging detection technology relied on manual analysis of infrared images, so as to diagnose the thermal fault of electrical equipment. This detection method requires higher experience and professional knowledge of operators, and at the same time, manual detection method is inefficient and error-prone [5–8]. With the development of artificial intelligence, more and more substations use intelligent inspection robots and unmanned aerial vehicles for equipment inspection. The degree of intelligence is getting higher and higher, which greatly reduces human and material resources. But there are many devices in the infrared image collected by this way, which makes it more difficult to diagnose the equipment. Therefore, this paper uses Faster RCNN algorithm to analyze the infrared image, which can determine the equipment category and locate the various equipment areas in the image accurately, and lay a foundation for equipment fault diagnosis.

2.1   Infrared State Detection Method

Infrared thermal imaging detection and judgment methods mainly include surface temperature judgment method (absolute temperature judgment method), comparative judgment method of the same kind, relative temperature difference judgment method, image feature judgment method, file analysis judgment method and real-time analysis judgment method. These six infrared detection and judgment methods are not single application. In practical application, two or more methods need to be combined and analyzed. In this paper, surface temperature judgment method, relative temperature difference judgment method and image feature judgment method are selected to carry out the analysis and diagnosis of electrical equipment.

Surface Temperature Judgment Method: Mainly applicable to current-induced heating and electromagnetic heating equipment. According to the measured surface temperature of the equipment, the temperature and temperature rise limits of various components, materials and insulating media of the high-voltage switchgear and control equipment in GB/T11022 are analyzed and judged in combination with the environmental and climatic conditions and load magnitude.

Relative Temperature Difference Judgment Method: Mainly applicable to current-induced heating equipment. Especially for small load current heating equipment, the leakage rate of small load defects can be reduced by using relative temperature difference judgment method.

Image feature judgment method: It is mainly suitable for voltage heating equipment. According to the thermal image of the normal and abnormal state of the same kind of equipment, judge whether the equipment is normal or not. Attention should be paid to excluding the influence of various interference factors on the image as far as possible. When necessary, comprehensive judgment should be made based on the results of electrical test or chemical analysis.

2.2   Overview of Faster RCNN

Faster RCNN is another work of Ross Girshick team, the leader in target detection field, after RCNN [9], fast RCNN [10]. It is the first real end-to-end deep learning detection algorithm. The detection speed of simple network is 17 fps, and the accuracy of PASCAL VOC is 59.9%, while that of complex network is 5 fps, the accuracy is 78.8%.

The idea of Faster RCNN is to integrate the four basic steps of target detection (region proposal, feature extraction, classification and regression) into a deep network framework. All calculations are completed in GPU without repetition, which greatly improves the speed of operation. A comparison of algorithm evolution is shown in Fig. 1.

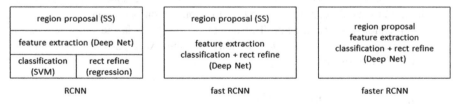

Fig. 1. Evolution of target detection algorithms.

The overall framework of Faster RCNN is divided into the following four parts. The network structure is shown in Fig. 2.

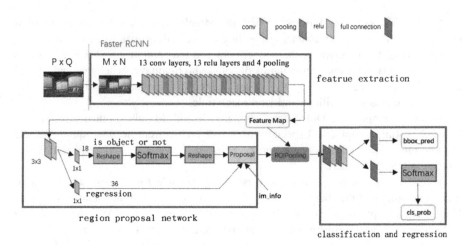

Fig. 2. Faster RCNN overall structure.

(1) CONV layers. The main function of this part is to extract the feature map of the input image. The input image is the whole picture, and the output image is the extracted feature map. In this paper, VGG16 network structure is used to extract image feature map, which is shared for subsequent RPN layer and full connection layer.

(2) Regional Proposal Networks. RPN network is mainly used to generate region suggestions. Firstly, a group of candidate regions (anchors) are generated, then they are cut and filtered, and then the candidate regions are judged to be foreground or background by Softmax classifier. At the same time, another branch makes border regression to modify the candidate regions to form more accurate proposals [11–17].

(3) ROI Pooling. The main function of this layer is to convert input of different sizes into output of fixed length. Fixed-size feature maps are obtained from the last layer of proposals and VGG16 generated by RPN. After entering, target recognition and location can be achieved by full-connection operation.

(4) Classification and Regression. The output of this layer is the ultimate goal. It outputs the classes of candidate regions and the exact positions of candidate regions in the image.

2.3   Improvement of Faster RCNN

In practical application, the whole equipment is easy to distinguish because of its appearance. However, some specific parts of different equipment (such as porcelain bottles, sleeves, wiring heads, etc.) are similar in shape, and it is difficult to distinguish them in infrared images. Therefore, recognition errors will inevitably occur, and the error rate is relatively high. Because the candidate boxes obtained by Faster RCNN are independent of each other, they can't modify the equipment category, which will lead to the subsequent diagnosis will be analyzed and diagnosed according to the type of model identification errors, thus making the diagnosis results wrong and increasing the workload of the relevant personnel.

Based on this, this paper proposes to improve the Faster RCNN. In the original algorithm classification step, it adds the equipment location category correction function, which can correct the wrong equipment location and improve the recognition accuracy of the equipment location. At the same time, the CNN for fault diagnosis based on image features is integrated into Faster RCNN, which can give the preliminary diagnosis results of the equipment, and then combined with the surface temperature judgment method and the relative temperature difference judgment method to realize the detailed diagnosis of electrical equipment. The network structure of the improved algorithm is shown in Fig. 3.

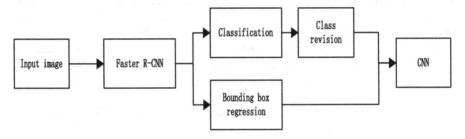

Fig. 3. Improves the structure of Faster RCNN.

The main idea of category revision is to mark the equipment in the way of "equipment + equipment parts". It not only marks the whole equipment, but also marks the specific parts of the equipment. In the test step, all the candidate boxes identified in the infrared image are divided into two categories: equipment and location. Then, the equipment category is corrected by using the idea of NMS (Non-Maximum Suppression). The specific steps are as follows:

(1) A and B represent the collection of equipment and equipment parts respectively. Sort all candidate boxes in A and B by size.
(2) The Overlapping area ratio (OAR) is calculated by traversing the candidate box (B_i) in B and comparing it with the candidate box in A: OAR = area of overlap area/area of B_i, and then comparing it with the set threshold of 0.8. If the OAR is greater than 0.8, the B_i candidate box is considered to belong to the whole device, and the B_i candidate box is classified. Adding an array index ensures that subsequent traversals are no longer accessed, reducing computation and processing time.
    If the OAR is less than 0.8, the B_i candidate box is not considered to belong to the overall device, and the next candidate box is not processed.
(3) Repeat operations (1) and (2) until all candidate boxes are modified.

2.4   CNN

Convolutional neural network (CNN) is an efficient recognition algorithm widely used in pattern recognition, image processing and other fields in recent years. Unlike traditional neural networks, the neurons in each layer of the network are not fully connected, but partially connected. Its weight sharing network structure reduces the complexity of network model and the number of weights. The network avoids the complex pre-processing of the image, can input the original image directly, avoids the complex feature extraction and data reconstruction process in traditional recognition algorithm, and has good abstraction ability.

Temperature is the most important diagnostic basis in condition detection and fault diagnosis of electrical equipment, and the direct expression of temperature in infrared image is the gray value of the image. CNN can extract and analyze the gray image of infrared image very well. It plays a very important role in condition detection and fault diagnosis of electrical equipment. By comparing the maximum gray value with the average gray value of the equipment area identified by Faster RCNN, the operation state of the electrical equipment can be preliminarily determined. If the difference between the maximum gray value and the average gray value exceeds a certain proportion, the abnormal condition of the equipment in this area can be determined, and the more accurate quasi-segment results can be obtained by combining the surface temperature judgment method and the relative temperature difference judgment method.

The complete flow of electrical equipment condition detection and fault diagnosis is shown in Fig. 4.

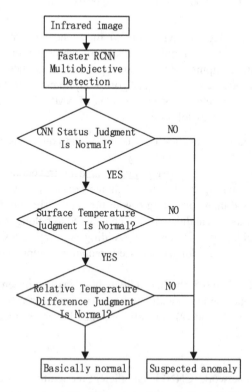

Fig. 4. Complete process of condition detection and fault diagnosis for electrical equipment.

3   Experiments

The experiment selected 16581 infrared images with good quality as training samples, and used PASCAL VOC2007 format data set to iterate the algorithm 70,000 iterations, with a learning rate of 0.001. In the training process of the algorithm, the first 100 score

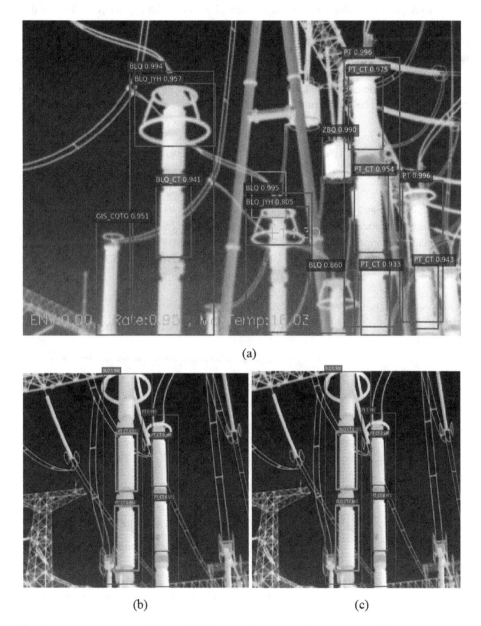

(a)

(b)   (c)

Fig. 5. (a) is the result of Faster RCNN algorithm recognizing correctly, (b) is the result of Faster RCNN algorithm recognizing errors, (c) is the result of improved Faster RCNN algorithm.

predictions are selected for each infrared image by non-maximum suppression (NMS) operation with a threshold of 0.5. At this time, all predictions are independent and unrelated. In the process of algorithm testing, a kind of inclusion relationship between equipment and equipment parts is established by category correction function, which improves the accuracy of equipment parts classification.

The experiment selected 761 infrared images from the same station and 846 infrared images from other stations as test samples to test the application effect of the algorithm, and counted the recognition rate and accuracy of the equipment. The author chooses arresters, voltage transformers, current transformers and circuit breakers with a large number of samples to illustrate the application effect of the algorithm (Fig. 5).

The experimental results show that Faster RCNN algorithm has good application effect in infrared detection of electrical equipment and high recognition accuracy of equipment. As can be seen from (a), Faster RCNN can accurately identify most of the

Table 1. Accuracy of algorithm recognition.

Electrical equipment	Faster RCNN		Improved Faster RCNN	
	Same station	Different station	Same station	Different station
Lightning arrester	84.7%	77.9%	95.4%	85.9%
Voltage transformer	74.5%	68.4%	93.2%	87.6%
Current transformer	79.3%	70.8%	90.1%	86.3%
Circuit breaker	81.3%	73.4%	91.2%	85.7%

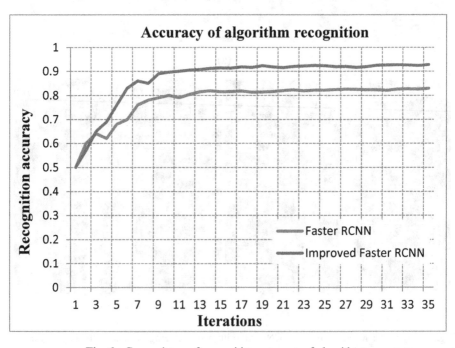

Fig. 6. Comparisons of recognition accuracy of algorithms.

devices and their parts in infrared images. By comparing (b) (c) two graphs, it can be seen that the improved Faster RCNN algorithm can modify the type of equipment and further improve the accuracy of electrical equipment identification.

Aiming at the situation of equipment location recognition error, this paper improves the algorithm, and counts the recognition effect of more than 1000 pictures from the same station and different stations. The result of equipment identification is shown in Table 1.

From the data in Table 1 and the curve in Fig. 6, it can be seen that the recognition accuracy of the improved Faster RCNN algorithm is much higher than that of the original Faster RCNN algorithm, about 10% higher than that of the original Faster RCNN algorithm. In addition, because the voltage level of different stations is different, the appearance of the equipment is also different, resulting in the same station identification accuracy will be a little higher than different stations.

4   Conclusion

The normal operation of high-voltage electrical equipment is related to the normal development of the national economy. Ensuring its efficient and sustainable operation is an effective means to promote rapid economic development. Infrared detection technology has been widely recognized and applied in the diagnosis of high-voltage electrical equipment. The application of infrared detection technology has a direct impact on the fault monitoring of high-voltage electrical equipment. In this paper, Faster RCNN, a target detection algorithm, is applied to infrared detection of electrical equipment and improved. Good detection results and accuracy are obtained. But there are also some problems. The improved algorithm modifies the category names of the parts it contains by the whole device. Therefore, once the overall identification of the equipment is wrong, the parts of the equipment will be modified with the error, and the algorithm will continue to be studied and improved to further improve the recognition rate and accuracy of electrical equipment.

References

1. Zhang, X., Tang, Z., Fei, X., et al.: Power apparatus state detection and diagnosis based on infrared thermal imaging technology. J. State Grid Technol. College **20**(05), 6–9 (2017)
2. Zeng, K.: The Research on Infrared On-line Monitoring System of High Voltage Distribution Equipment. Nanchang University (2018)
3. Kang, L.: Substation equipment fault diagnosis based on infrared image processing. North China Electric Power University (2016)
4. Ning, T.: Application Research of Infrared Temperature Diagnosis Technique in QingYuan Distribution Network. Jilin University (2017)
5. He, J., Li, T.: Infrared detection method and application of power equipment defect. Techn. Autom. Appl. **37**(10), 97–100 + 104 (2018)
6. Zhong, Y., Zhou, G.: Discussion on infrared detection and diagnosis and optimization of temperature measurement of electrical equipment in the substation. Electric. Eng. **01**, 104–106 (2018)

7. Chen, M.: A Study on Fault Diagnosis for Electrical Equipment Based on Infrared Thermography. Huazhong University of Science and Technology (2016)
8. Song, S.: The Research of Infrared Diagnosis for High Voltage Electric Equipment. Huazhong University of Science and Technology (2016)
9. Girshick, R., et al.: Rich feature hierarchies for accurate object detection and semantic segmentation. In: Proceedings of the IEEE Conference on Computer Vision and Pattern Recognition (2014)
10. Girshick, R.: Fast R-CNN. In: Proceedings of the IEEE International Conference on Computer Vision (2015)
11. Ren, S., et al.: Faster R-CNN: towards real-time object detection with regional proposal networks. In: Advances in Neural Information Processing Systems (2015)
12. Lin, T., et al.: Pose detection in complex classroom environment based on improved Faster R-CNN. IET Image Proc. 13(3), 451 (2019)
13. Li, C.Y., Song, D., Tong, R.F., Tang, M.: Illumination-aware faster R-CNN for robust multispectral pedestrian detection. Pattern Recogn. 85, 161–171 (2019)
14. Yang, Q.M., Xiao, D.Q., Lin, S.C.: Feeding behavior recognition for group-housed pigs with the Faster R-CNN. Comput. Electron. Agric. 155, 453–460 (2018)
15. Liu, Z., Wang, H.: Automatic detection of transformer components in inspection images based on improved faster R-CNN. Energies 11(12), 3496 (2018)
16. Huang, J., Shi, Y., Gao, Y.: Multi-scale faster-RCNN algorithm for small object detection. Comput. Res. Dev. 56(02), 319–327 (2019)
17. Simonyan, K., Zisserman, A.: Very deep convolutional networks for large-scale image recognition. In: International Conference on Learning Representations (ICLR) (2015)

Attention Based Convolutional Recurrent Neural Network for Environmental Sound Classification

Zhichao Zhang, Shugong Xu[✉], Tianhao Qiao, Shunqing Zhang, and Shan Cao

Shanghai Institute for Advanced Communication and Data Science, Shanghai University, Shanghai 200444, China
{zhichaozhang,shugong,qiaotianhao,shunqing,cshan}@shu.edu.cn

Abstract. Environmental sound classification (ESC) is a challenging problem due to the complexity of sounds. The ESC performance is heavily dependent on the effectiveness of representative features extracted from the environmental sounds. However, ESC often suffers from the semantically irrelevant frames and silent frames. In order to deal with this, we employ a frame-level attention model to focus on the semantically relevant frames and salient frames. Specifically, we first propose an convolutional recurrent neural network to learn spectro-temporal features and temporal correlations. Then, we extend our convolutional RNN model with a frame-level attention mechanism to learn discriminative feature representations for ESC. Experiments were conducted on ESC-50 and ESC-10 datasets. Experimental results demonstrated the effectiveness of the proposed method and achieved the state-of-the-art performance in terms of classification accuracy.

Keywords: Environmental sound classification · Convolutional recurrent neural network · Attention mechanism

1 Introduction

Environmental sound classification (ESC) is an important branch of sound recognition and is widely applied in surveillance [17], home automation [22], scene analysis [4] and machine hearing [13].

Thus far, a variety of signal processing and machine learning techniques have been applied for ESC, including dictionary learning [7], matrix factorization [5], gaussian mixture model (GMM) [8] and recently, deep neural networks [19,27]. For traditional machine learning classifiers, selecting proper features is key to effective performance. For instance, audio signals have been traditionally characterized by Mel-frequency cepstral coefficients (MFCCs) as features and classified using a GMM classifier.

In recent years, deep neural networks (DNNs) have shown outstanding performance in feature extraction for ESC. Compared to hand-crafted feature, DNNs

© Springer Nature Switzerland AG 2019
Z. Lin et al. (Eds.): PRCV 2019, LNCS 11857, pp. 261–271, 2019.
https://doi.org/10.1007/978-3-030-31654-9_23

have the ability to extract discriminative feature representations from large quantities of training data and generalize well on unseen data. McLoughlin et al. [14] proposed a deep belief network to extract high-level feature representations from magnitude spectrum which yielded better results than the traditional methods. Piczak [15] first evaluated the potential of convolutional neural network (CNN) in classifying short audio clips of environmental sounds and showed excellent performance on several public datasets. Takahashi et al. [20] created a three-channel feature as the input to a CNN by combining log mel spectrogram and its delta and delta-delta information in a manner similar to the RGB input of image. In order to model the sequential dynamics of environmental sound signals, Vu et al. [24] applied a recurrent neural network (RNN) to learn temporal relationships. Moreover, there is a growing trend to combine CNN and RNN models into a single architecture. Bae et al. [2] proposed to train the RNN and CNN in parallel in order to learn sequential correlation and local spectro-temporal information.

In addition, attention mechanism-based models have shown outstanding performance in learning relevant feature representations for sequence data [6]. Recently, attention mechanism-based RNNs have been successfully applied to a wide variety of tasks, including speech recognition [6], machine translation [3] and document classification [25]. In principle, attention mechanism-based RNNs are well suited to ESC tasks. First, environmental sound is essentially the sequence data which contains correlation information between adjacent frames. Second, not all frame-level features contribute equally to the representations of environmental sounds. Usually, in public ESC datasets, signals contains many periods of silence, with only a few intermittent frames associated with the sound class. Thus, it is important to select semantically relevant frames for specific class. Similar to attention mechanism-based RNN, we can also compute the frame-level attention map from CNN features, focusing on the semantically relevant frames. In the field of ESC, several works [9,11,12,18] have studied the effectiveness of attention mechanisms and have obtained promising results in several datasets. Different from previous works, we explored both the performance of frame-level attention mechanism for CNN layers and RNN layers.

In this paper, we propose an attention mechanism-based convolutional RNN architecture (ACRNN) in order to focus on semantically relevant frames and produce discriminative features for ESC. The main contributions of this paper are summarized as follows.

- To deal with silent frames and semantically irrelevant frames, We employ an attention model to automatically focus on the semantically relevant frames and produce discriminative features for ESC. We explore both the performance of frame-level attention mechanism for CNN layers and RNN layers.
- To analyze temporal relations, We propose a novel convolutional RNN model which first uses CNN to extract high level feature representations and then inputs the features to bidirectional GRUs. We combine the convolutional RNN and attention model in a unified architecture.

– To indicate the effectiveness of the proposed method and achieve current state-of-the-art performance, we conduct experiments on ESC-10 and ESC-50 datasets.

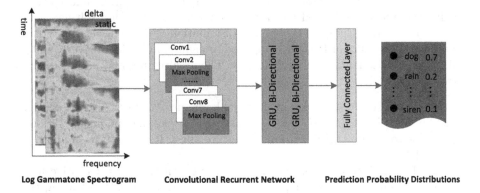

Fig. 1. Architecture of convolutional recurrent neural network for environmental sound classification

2   Methods

In this section, we introduce the proposed method for ESC. First, we generate Log Gammatone spetrogram (Log-GTs) features from environmental sounds as the input of ACRNN, as shown in Fig. 1. Then, we introduce the architecture of ACRNN, which combines convolutional RNN and a frame-level attention mechanism. For the architecture of convolutional RNN and attention mechanism, we will give a detailed description, respectively. Finally, the data augmentation methods we used are introduced.

2.1   Feature Extraction and Preprocessing

Given a signal, We first use short-time Fourier Transform (STFT) with hamming window size of 23 ms (1024 samples at 44.1 kHz) and 50% overlap to extract the energy spectrogram. Then, we apply a 128-band Gammatone filter bank [23] to the energy spectrogram and the resulting spectrogram is converted into logarithmic scale. In order to make efficient use of limited data, the spectrogram is split into 128 frames (approximately 1.5 s in length) with 50% overlap. The delta information of the original spectrogram is calculated, which is the first temporal derivative of the static spectrogram. Afterwards, we concatenate the log gammatone spectrogram and its delta information to a 3-D feature representation $X \in R^{128 \times 128 \times 2}$ (Log-GTs) as the input of the network.

2.2 Architecture of Convolutional RNN

In this section, we propose an convolutional RNN to analyze Log-GTs for ESC. We first use CNN to learn high level feature representations on the Log-GTs. Then, the CNN-learned features are fed into bidirectional gated recurrent unit (GRU) layers which are used to learn the temporal correlation information. Finally, these features are fed into a fully connected layer with a softmax activation function to output the probability distribution of different classes. In this paper, the convolutional RNN is comprised of eight convolutional layers (l_1–l_8) and two bidirectional GRU layers (l_9–l_{10}). The architecture and parameters of network are as follows:

- l_1–l_2: The first two stacked convolutional layers use 32 filters with a receptive field of (3,5) and stride of (1, 1). This is followed by a max-pooling with a (4, 3) stride to reduce the dimensions of feature maps. ReLU activation function is used.
- l_3–l_4: The next two convolutional layers use 64 filters with a receptive field of (3, 1) and stride of (1, 1), and is used to learn local patterns along the frequency dimension. This is followed by a max-pooling with a (4, 1) stride. ReLU activation function is used.
- l_5–l_6: The following pair of convolutional layers uses 128 filters with a receptive field of (1, 5) and stride of (1, 1), and is used to learn local patterns along the time dimension. This is followed by a max-pooling with a (1, 3) stride. ReLU activation function is used.
- l_7–l_8: The subsequent two convolutional layers use 256 filters with a receptive field of (3, 3) and stride of (1, 1) to learn joint time-frequency characteristics. This is followed by a max-pooling of a (2, 2) stride. ReLU activation function is used.
- l_9–l_{10}: Two bidirectional GRU layers with 256 cells are used for temporal summarization, and tanh activation function is used. Dropout with probability of 0.5 is used for each GRU layer to avoid overfitting.

Batch normalization [10] is applied to the output of the convolutional layers to speed up training. L2-regularization is applied to the weights of each layer with a coefficient 0.0001.

2.3 Frame-Level Attention Mechanism

Not all frame-level features contribute equally to representations of environmental sounds. As shown in Fig. 2, except for the semantically relevant frames ($f1$), the features usually contain silent or noisy frames ($f2$), which reduce the robustness of model and increase misclassification. Hence, we apply frame-level attention mechanisms to focus on the parts that are most vital to the meaning of the sound and to produce discriminative representations for ESC. In this paper, we employ attention mechanism for CNN layers and RNN layers, respectively.

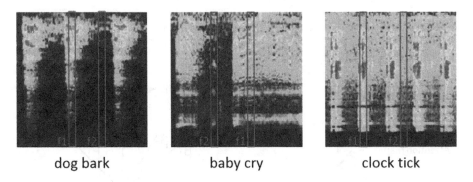

| dog bark | baby cry | clock tick |

Fig. 2. Visualization of Log-GTs of different classes with semantically relevant frame ($f1$) and silent or noisy frame ($f2$). From left to right, the class is *dog bark*, *baby cry* and *clock tick*.

Attention for CNN Layers: As shown in Fig. 3(a), given CNN features $M \in R^{F \times T \times C}$, we first use a 3×3 convolution filter to learn a hidden representation. This is followed by a average-pool with $(F, 1)$ size in order to reduce the frequency dimension to one. Then, we use softmax function to form a normalized attention map $A \in R^{1 \times T \times 1}$, which holds the frame-level attention weights for CNN features. With attention map A, the attention weighted CNN features are obtained as

$$M' = M \cdot A \tag{1}$$

The attention is applied by multiplying the attention vector A to each feature vector of M along frequency dimension and channel dimension.

Attention for RNN Layers: As shown in Fig. 3(b), we first feed the GRU output $h_t = [\overrightarrow{h_t}, \overleftarrow{h_t}]$ through a one-layer MLP to obtain a hidden representation of h_t, then we calculate the normalized importance weight β_t by a softmax function (2). After that, we compute the feature vector v through a weighted sum of the frame-level convolutional RNN features based on the weights (3). The feature vector v is forwarded into the fully connected layer for final classification.

$$\beta_t = \frac{exp(W * h_t)}{\sum_{t=1}^{T} exp(W * h_t)} \tag{2}$$

$$v = \sum_{t=1}^{T} \beta_t h_t \tag{3}$$

2.4   Data Augmentation

Limited data easily leads model towards overfitting. In this paper, we use time stretch with a factor randomly selected from [0.8, 1.3] and pitch shift with a

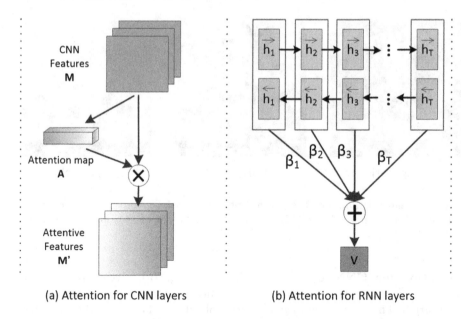

(a) Attention for CNN layers   (b) Attention for RNN layers

Fig. 3. Frame-level attention for (a) CNN layers and (b) RNN layers. For CNN layers, we use frame-level attention to obtain attention map, which is multiplied in frame-wise of CNN features, resulting the attention weighted features. For RNN layers, we utilize frame-level attention to obtain attention weights, which is multiplied in frame-wise of input features. Then, we aggregate these attention weighted representations to form a feature vector, which can be seen as a high-level representation of a sound like "dog bark".

factor randomly selected from $[-3.5, 3.5]$ to increase raw training data size. In addition, an efficient mixup [26] augmentation method is used to construct virtual training data and extend the training distribution. In mixup, a feature and a target $(\hat{\mathbf{x}}, \hat{\mathbf{y}})$ are generated by mixing two feature-target examples, which are determined by

$$\begin{cases} \hat{\mathbf{x}} = \lambda x_i + (1 - \lambda)x_j \\ \hat{\mathbf{y}} = \lambda y_i + (1 - \lambda)y_j \end{cases} \tag{4}$$

where x_i and x_j are two features randomly selected from the training Log-GTs, and y_i and y_j are their one-hot labels. The mix factor λ is decided by a hyper-parameter α and $\lambda \sim \text{Beta}(\alpha, \alpha)$.

3   Experiments and Results

3.1   Experiment Setup

To evaluate the performance of our proposed methods, we carry out experiments on two publicly available datasets: ESC-50 and ESC-10 [16]. ESC-50 is a collection of 2000 environmental recordings containing 50 classes in 5 major categories, including *animals, natural soundscapes and water sounds, human non-speech sounds, interior/domestic sounds,* and *exterior/urban noises.* All audio samples are 5 s in duration with a 44.1 kHz sampling frequency. ESC-10 is a subset of 10 classes (400 samples) selected from the ESC-50 dataset (*dog bark, rain, sea waves, baby cry, clock tick, person sneeze, helicopter, chainsaw, rooster, fire crackling*).

In this paper, we use a sampling rate of 44.1 kHz for all samples in order to use rich high-frequency information. For training, all models optimize cross-entropy loss using mini-batch stochastic gradient descent with Nesterov momentum of 0.9. Each batch consists of 64 segments randomly selected from the training set without repetition. All models are trained for 300 epochs by beginning with an initial learning rate of 0.01, and then divided the learning rate by 10 every 100 epochs. We initialize the network weights to zero mean Gaussian noise with a standard deviation of 0.05. In the test phase, we evaluate the whole sample prediction with the highest average prediction probability of each segment. Both the training and testing features are normalized by the global mean and standard deviation of the training set. All models are trained using Keras library with TensorFlow backend on a Nvidia P100 GPU with 12 GB memory.

3.2   Experiment Results

Table 1. Comparison of ACRNN and existing methods. We perform 5-fold cross validation (CV) by using the official fold settings. The average results of CV are recorded.

Model	ESC-10	ESC-50
PiczakCNN [15]	80.5%	64.9%
SoundNet [1]	92.1%	74.2%
WaveMsNet [28]	93.7%	79.1%
EnvNet-v2 [21]	91.4%	84.9%
Multi-Stream CNN [12]	93.7%	83.5%
ACRNN	**93.7%**	**86.1%**

We compare our model with existing networks reported as PiczakCNN [15], SoundNet [1], WaveMsNet [28], EnvNet-v2 [21] and Multi-Stream CNN [12]. According to [15], PiczakCNN consists of two convolutional layers and three fully connected layers. The input features of CNN are generated by combining log mel spectrogram and its delta information. We refer PiczakCNN as a baseline method.

The results are summarized in Table 1. We see that ACRNN outperforms PiczakCNN and obtains an absolute improvement of 13.2% and 21.2% on ESC-10 and ESC-50 datasets, respectively. Then, we compare our model with several state-of-the-art methods: SoundNet8 [1], WaveMsNet [28], EnvNet-v2 [21] and Multi-Stream CNN [12]. We observe that on both ESC-10 and ESC-50 datasets, ACRNN obtains the highest classification accuracy. Note that WaveMsNet [28] and Multi-Stream CNN [12] achieve same classification accuracy as ACRNN on ESC-10 but using feature fusion (raw data and spectrogram features), whereas ACRNN only utilizes spectrogram features.

In Fig. 4, we provide the confusion matrix generated by ACRNN for ESC-50 dataset. We see that most classes achieve higher accuracy than 80%(32/40). Particularly, *Church bells* obtains a 100% recognition rate. However, we observe that only 52.5%(21/40) *Helicopter* samples are correctly recognized, with 17.5%(7/40) samples misclassified as *Airplane*. We attribute this mistakes to the similar characteristics between the two environmental sounds.

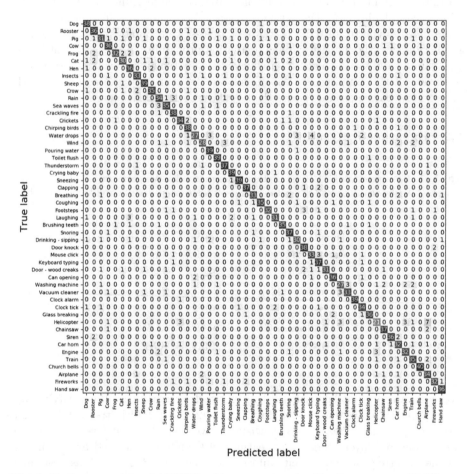

Fig. 4. Confusion matrix of ACRNN with an average classification accuracy 86.1% on ESC-50 dataset.

3.3   Effects of Attention Mechanism

Table 2. Classification accuracy of proposed convolutional RNN with and without the attention mechanism. 'augment' denotes a combination of time stretch, pitch shift and mixup.

Model settings	ESC-10	ESC-50
Convolutional RNN	89.2%	79.9%
Convolutional RNN-attention	91.7%	81.3%
Convolutional RNN-augment	93.0%	84.6%
Convolutional RNN-attention-augment	**93.7%**	**86.1%**

To investigate the effects of the attention mechanism, we compare the results of proposed convolutional RNN with and without the attention mechanism. In Table 2, the results show that the attention mechanism delivers a significantly improved accuracy even when we use a data augmentation scheme. In addition, data augmentation boasts an improvement of 2.0% and 4.8% on ESC-10 and ESC-50 datasets, respectively.

3.4   Where to Apply Attention

Table 3. Classification accuracy of applying the attention mechanism to the output of different layers of the proposed convolutional RNN.

Model settings	ESC-10	ESC-50
No attention	93.0%	84.6%
Attention at l_2	93.5%	85.2%
Attention at l_4	92.7%	83.8%
Attention at l_6	92.7%	84.4%
Attention at l_8	92.5%	84.9%
Attention at l_{10}	**93.7%**	**86.1%**

In this section, we investigate the classification performance when applying frame-level attention mechanism to the different layers of CNN and RNN. As shown in Table 3, we obtained the highest classification accuracy and boosted an absolutely improvement of 0.7% and 1.5% when applying the attention mechanism at l_{10} on both ESC-10 and ESC-50 datasets, respectively. On the ESC-50 dataset, the classification accuracy obtained a slight improvement when the attention mechanism was applied at l_2 and l_8, while for other CNN layers, the classification accuracy decreased. On the ESC-10 dataset, we obtained an improvement of 0.5% when only applying attention at l_2 for CNN layers. Furthermore, we found that on both ESC-10 and ESC-50 datasets, the classification accuracy is improved than standard convolutional RNN when applying attention at l_2 for CNN layers.

4   Conclusion

In this paper, we proposed an attention mechanism-based convolutional recurrent neural network (ACRNN) for ESC. We explored the frame-level attention mechanism and gave a detailed description for CNN layers and RNN layers, respectively. Experimental results on ESC-10 and ESC-50 datasets demonstrated the effectiveness of the proposed method and achieved state-of-the-art performance in terms of classification accuracy. In addition, we compared the classification accuracy when applying different layers, including CNN layers and RNN layers. The experimental results showed that applying attention for RNN layers obtained highest accuracy. However, we found when applying attention for CNN layers, the performance is not always improved. We plan to explore this in our future work.

References

1. Aytar, Y., Vondrick, C., Torralba, A.: SoundNet: learning sound representations from unlabeled video. In: Proceedings of the International Conference on Neural Information Processing Systems, pp. 892–900 (2016)
2. Bae, S.H., Choi, I., Kim, N.S.: Acoustic scene classification using parallel combination of LSTM and CNN. DCASE 2016 Challenge, Technical report (2016)
3. Bahdanau, D., Cho, K., Bengio, Y.: Neural machine translation by jointly learning to align and translate. arXiv preprint arXiv:1409.0473 (2014)
4. Barchiesi, D., Giannoulis, D., Stowell, D., Plumbley, M.D.: Acoustic scene classification: classifying environments from the sounds they produce. IEEE Signal Process. Mag. **32**(3), 16–34 (2015)
5. Bisot, V., Serizel, R., Essid, S., Richard, G.: Feature learning with matrix factorization applied to acoustic scene classification. IEEE/ACM Trans. Audio Speech Lang. Process. **25**(6), 1216–1229 (2017)
6. Chorowski, J.K., Bahdanau, D., Serdyuk, D., Cho, K., Bengio, Y.: Attention-based models for speech recognition. In: Proceedings of the International Conference on Neural Information Processing Systems, pp. 577–585 (2015)
7. Chu, S., Narayanan, S., Kuo, C.C.J.: Environmental sound recognition with time-frequency audio features. IEEE Trans. Audio Speech Language Process. **17**(6), 1142–1158 (2009)
8. Dhanalakshmi, P., Palanivel, S., Ramalingam, V.: Classification of audio signals using AANN and GMM. Appl. Soft Comput. **11**(1), 716–723 (2011)
9. Guo, J., Xu, N., Li, L.J., Alwan, A.: Attention based CLDNNs for short-duration acoustic scene classification. In: Proceedings of the Interspeech, pp. 469–473 (2017)
10. Ioffe, S., Szegedy, C.: Batch normalization: accelerating deep network training by reducing internal covariate shift. arXiv preprint arXiv:1502.03167 (2015)

11. Jun, W., Shengchen, L.: Self-attention mechanism based system for DCASE2018 challenge task1 and task4. DCASE 2018 Challenge, Technical report (2018)
12. Li, X., Chebiyyam, V., Kirchhoff, K.: Multi-stream network with temporal attention for environmental sound classification. arXiv preprint arXiv:1901.08608 (2019)
13. Lyon, R.F.: Machine hearing: an emerging field [exploratory dsp]. IEEE Signal Process. Mag. **27**(5), 131–139 (2010)
14. McLoughlin, I., Zhang, H., Xie, Z., Song, Y., Xiao, W.: Robust sound event classification using deep neural networks. IEEE/ACM Trans. Audio Speech Lang. Process. **23**(3), 540–552 (2015)
15. Piczak, K.J.: Environmental sound classification with convolutional neural networks. In: Proceedings of the 25th International Workshop Machine Learning Signal Processing, pp. 1–6 (2015)
16. Piczak, K.J.: ESC: dataset for environmental sound classification. In: Proceedings of the 23rd ACM International Conference Multimedia, pp. 1015–1018 (2015)
17. Radhakrishnan, R., Divakaran, A., Smaragdis, A.: Audio analysis for surveillance applications. In: Proceedings of the IEEE Workshop on Applications of Signal Processing to Audio and Acoustics, pp. 158–161 (2005)
18. Ren, Z., et. al.: Attention-based convolutional neural networks for acoustic scene classification. DCASE2018 Challenge, Technical report (2018)
19. Salamon, J., Bello, J.P.: Deep convolutional neural networks and data augmentation for environmental sound classification. IEEE Signal Process. Lett. **24**(3), 279–283 (2017)
20. Takahashi, N., Gygli, M., Pfister, B., Van Gool, L.: Deep convolutional neural networks and data augmentation for acoustic event detection. arXiv preprint arXiv:1604.07160 (2016)
21. Tokozume, Y., Ushiku, Y., Harada, T.: Learning from between-class examples for deep sound recognition. arXiv preprint arXiv:1711.10282 (2017)
22. Vacher, M., Serignat, J.F., Chaillol, S.: Sound classification in a smart room environment: an approach using GMM and HMM methods. In: Proceedings of the 4th IEEE Conference on Speech Technique, Human-Computer Dialogue, vol. 1, pp. 135–146 (2007)
23. Valero, X., Alias, F.: Gammatone cepstral coefficients: biologically inspired features for non-speech audio classification. IEEE Trans. Multimed. **14**(6), 1684–1689 (2012)
24. Vu, T.H., Wang, J.C.: Acoustic scene and event recognition using recurrent neural networks. DCASE 2016 Challenge, Technical report (2016)
25. Yang, Z., Yang, D., Dyer, C., He, X., Smola, A., Hovy, E.: Hierarchical attention networks for document classification. In: Proceedings of the NAACL-HLT, pp. 1480–1489 (2016)
26. Zhang, H., Cisse, M., Dauphin, Y.N., Lopez-Paz, D.: Mixup: beyond empirical risk minimization. arXiv preprint arXiv:1710.09412 (2017)
27. Zhang, Z., Xu, S., Cao, S., Zhang, S.: Deep convolutional neural network with mixup for environmental sound classification. In: Proceedings of the Chinese Conference on Pattern Recognition Computer Vision, pp. 356–367 (2018)
28. Zhu, B., Wang, C., Liu, F., Lei, J., Lu, Z., Peng, Y.: Learning environmental sounds with multi-scale convolutional neural network. arXiv preprint arXiv:1803.10219 (2018)

Salient Object Detection via Light-Weight Multi-path Refinement Networks

Kang Ma, Jun Feng, Tuo Zhang, Rui Wang, and Qirong Bu[✉]

Northwestern University, Xi'an, Shaanxi, China
boqirong@nwu.edu.cn

Abstract. Recently, deep learning-based saliency detection has achieved fantastic performance over conventional works. However, repeated subsampling operations in deep CNNs lead to difficulties for full resolution prediction and accurate prediction at boundaries of salient regions. In this paper, we use Light-Weight Multi-Path Refinement Networks (RefineNet) for image saliency detection task, an encoder-decoder architecture that explicitly exploits all the information available along the down-sampling process to enable full resolution prediction using long-range residual connections. The squeeze and excitation residual network (SE-ResNet) is adopted as our baseline network to better extract multi-level and multi-scale feature maps according to the resolutions. Furthermore, we proposed our end-to-end network architecture and reduced the parameters by more than 50% while maintaining the same performance. We carry out comprehensive experiments and set new state-of-the-art results on four public datasets. By contrast, our method is highly competitive.

Keywords: Saliency detection · RefineNet · SE-ResNet · Multi-level

1 Introduction

Faced with various natural scenes, the human visual system can quickly lock the differentiable and attractive targets using its powerful information processing capabilities. By simulating the human visual attention mechanism, saliency detection aims to dig out the most attractive objects in natural images. As an important part in computer vision and image processing, saliency detection has been applied to a wide range of tasks, such as image retrieval [1], video saliency detection [2], action recognition [3], image segmentation [4], etc.

In a variety of computer vision tasks, convolutional neural networks (CNNs) [6] have successfully broken the limits of traditional hand-crafted features. The emergence of fully convolutional neural networks (FCNs) [5] have further boosted the development of these research areas [7]. However, it is difficult for a network to learn saliency at boundaries of salient regions. This is because pixels around the boundaries are centered at similar receptive fields, while the network is trained to discriminate binary labels. We argue that features from all levels are helpful for saliency detection.

Student as the first author.

© Springer Nature Switzerland AG 2019
Z. Lin et al. (Eds.): PRCV 2019, LNCS 11857, pp. 272–283, 2019.
https://doi.org/10.1007/978-3-030-31654-9_24

High-level semantic features help the category recognition of image regions, while low-level visual features help to generate sharp, detailed boundaries for high-resolution prediction. Thus, how to design an effective deep learning based saliency detection model with the ability to effectively exploit middle layer features is the focus of consideration.

Based on the above observations, an end-to-end light-weight multi-path refinement network (RefineNet) [17, 18] has been used to achieve our goal of full resolution saliency detection. And the squeeze-and-excitation-residual network (SE-ResNet) [16, 19] is adopted as our baseline network to better dig out fine details and potential cues. Our main contributions are as follows:

1. A novel end-to-end saliency detection model is proposed, which is based on multi-level and multi-scale feature extraction and multi-path refinement.
2. We proposed new RefineNet components and ultimately reduced the parameters by more than 50% on the premise of maintaining the same performance.
3. Compared with other sixteen state-of-the-art approaches, comprehensive evaluations on four benchmark datasets quantitatively and qualitatively demonstrate the superior performance of our proposed method.

2 Related Work

CNNs have become the most successful methods for saliency detection in recent years, which include region-based methods and pixel-based methods [8–11]. By using superpixels [13, 14] to learn the correlation between pixels, the classification accuracy of pixels at the boundary is greatly improved. However, such methods tend to develop a region-level network for superpixels, which leads to more complex network structure and more network parameters. Wang et al. [12] extend a super-pixel-based guided filter to be a layer in the network which has a simple structure and is trained end-to-end. And dilation convolution is used in [12] which has a significant cost in memory. In practice, dilation convolution methods usually have a resolution prediction of no more than 1/8 size of the original rather than 1/4. Li et al. [20] paid more attention to channel-wise feature responses and proposed an end-to-end deep learning-based saliency detection method which was based on SE-ResNet. This is a very advanced saliency detection method based on deep learning.

In the field of semantic segmentation, Lin et al. [17] proposed a means to enjoy both the memory and computational benefits, while still able to produce effective and efficient high-resolution segmentation prediction. The individual components of RefineNet employ residual connections following the identity mapping mindset, which allows for effective end-to-end training. Further, the author introduce chained residual pooling, which captures rich background context in an efficient manner. This has great reference significance in image saliency detection. In this paper, we apply the network idea belonging to semantic segmentation to the saliency detection task and optimize the network parameters refer to [18]. Finally, we get good results.

3 Proposed Method

In this section, we will introduce our work from such three aspects as multi-level and multi-scale feature extraction, multi-path refinement and lightweight network.

3.1 Multi-level and Multi-scale Feature Extraction

As pointed out in most previous works, features from all levels are helpful for saliency detection. Coarse high-level semantic features help the category recognition of image regions, while finer-grained low-level visual features help to generate sharp, detailed boundaries for high-resolution prediction. A good salient object detection network should be deep enough such that multi-level and multi-scale features can be learned to optimize the boundary information. ResNeXt [21] presents a simple highly modularized network architecture for image classification, and SE-ResNeXt can explicitly model the inter dependencies between channels of convolutional features to improve the representational power of a network.

In terms of the above observations, SE-ResNet50 and SE-ResNeXt154 were used as backbone respectively, which are pre-trained on the ImageNet 2012 dataset. A unit of SE-ResNeXt154 with cardinality set to 64 is shown in Fig. 1. We divided the pre-trained network into 6 parts, which are shown in Fig. 2(a). We extracted the feature maps of Block1, Block3, Block4, Block5 and Block6 according to the resolutions, and their sizes are 1/2, 1/4, 1/8, 1/16 and 1/32 of the input images respectively.

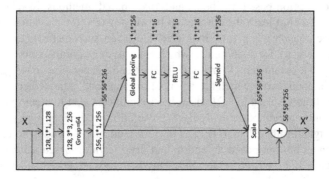

Fig. 1. A unit of SE-ResNeXt154 with cardinality = 64.

3.2 Multi-path Refinement and Feature Fusion

We aimed to fuse multi-level and multi-scale features to generate full resolution saliency feature maps in this section.

After the above process in Sect. 3.1, we got five levels of feature maps according to the resolutions, and employ a 5-cascaded architecture with 5 RefineNet units, as shown in Fig. 2(a). Each RefineNet unit includes new residual Conv unit (NRCU) block, new multi-resolution fusion (NMRF) block and new chained residual pooling (NCRP) block, as shown in Fig. 2(b–d). These components are able to refine the coarse high-level semantic features by exploiting low-level visual features.

We denote RefineNet-m as the RefineNet block that connects to the output of Block-m. In the multi-path overview shown in Fig. 2(a), there is only one input for RefineNet-6, and RefineNet-6 fine tuning the pre-trained SE-ResNeXt154 weights. And the outputs of RefineNet-6 and Block5 are fed to RefineNet-5. RefineNet-5 will use the low-level features from Block5 to refine the high-level feature maps output by RefineNet-6 in the previous stage. Similarly, RefineNet-4, RefineNet-3 and RefineNet-1 repeat this stage-wise refinement.

Finally, the high-resolution feature maps output by RefineNet-1 are fed to a dense soft-max layer and then up-sampled to full resolution using bilinear interpolation.

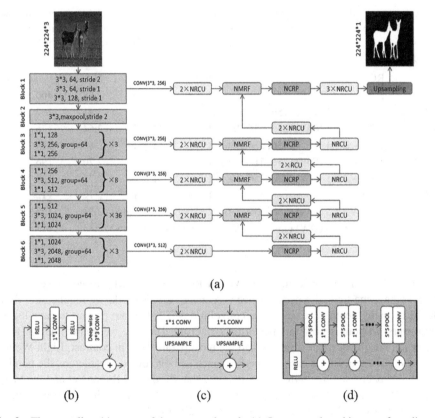

(a)

(b)   (c)   (d)

Fig. 2. The overall architecture of the proposed work. (a) Our network architecture for saliency detection; (b) New Residual Conv Units block; (c) New Multi-resolution Fusion block; (d) New Chained Residual Pooling block.

3.3   Light-Weight Network

RefineNet has the ability to produce high-resolution prediction but is difficult to train due to many parameters introduced by the decoder. We used ResNet50 as the backbone, train on the MSRA10K dataset using different blocks and observe the MAE metrics on the validation set, as shown in Table 1. It is necessary to note that 3 * 3 (dw) is depth-wise separable convolutions [22], and we omit the RELU activation function (RCU blocks) and pooling layers (MRF blocks and CRP blocks).

We replace the 3 * 3 convolutions in the MRF blocks and CRP blocks with 1 * 1 convolutions by referring to the Light-Weight RefineNet [18]. In practice, each SE-ResneXt154 output is passed through one 3 * 3 convolutional layer to adapt the dimensionality, which we call channel conv units (CCU) blocks. We found that replacing the 3 * 3 convolutions with 1 * 1 convolutions in CCU blocks will cause more performance degradation than MRF blocks and CRP blocks. Thus, we choose to keep CCU blocks for better performance.

Table 1. The result of some combinations of different blocks on a validation set (red, blue, green and orange texts respectively indicate the combinations of different blocks in the proposed method, original RefineNet, Light Weight RefineNet (with RCU) and Light Weight RefineNet (without RCU).

CCU	RCU	MRF	CRP	MAE, %	Params, M
3 * 3	**3 * 3 – 3 * 3 (256, 256)**	**3 * 3**	**3 * 3**	**2.58**	**406**
3 * 3	1 * 1 – 3 * 3–1 * 1 (256, 256, 256)	1 * 1	1 * 1	2.61	267
3 * 3	**1 * 1 – 3 * 3 (DW) (256, 256, 256)**	**1 * 1**	**1 * 1**	**2.64**	**175**
1 * 1	**1 * 1 – 3 * 3–1 * 1 (256, 256, 256)**	**1 * 1**	**1 * 1**	**2.68**	**219**
3 * 3	1 * 1 – 3 * 3 (DW) (256, 512, 256)	1 * 1	1 * 1	2.70	196
1 * 1	1 * 1 – 3 * 3 (DW) (256, 256, 256)	1 * 1	1 * 1	2.71	127
1 * 1	–	**1 * 1**	**1 * 1**	**2.72**	**112**
3 * 3	1 * 1 – 3 * 3 (DW) (256, 256, 256)	3 * 3 (dw)	3 * 3 (dw)	2.79	175
3 * 3 (dw)	1 * 1 – 3 * 3 (DW) (256, 256, 256)	3 * 3 (dw)	3 * 3 (dw)	2.83	128

RCU blocks is removed in Light-Weight RefineNet in order to get fewer parameters, at the same time, the performance is reduced. In this work, we retained the RCU blocks by using depth-wise separable convolutions [22] that are proven to save lots of parameters without sacrificing performance. From Table 1, we found that original RefineNet has the best performance and the most parameters. In contrast, Light Weight RefineNet (without RCU) has poor performance and the fewest parameters, the number of which is decreased by 294M compared with that of original RefineNet and the MAE value is increased by 0.14, while the number of the parameters of the proposed method is decreased by 231M compared with that of original RefineNet and the MAE value is only increased by 0.06. In other words, under the same condition of reducing more than 200M parameters, the increase of MAE value is less than half of that of Light Weight RefineNet (without RCU). On the other hand, compared with Light Weight RefineNet (with RCU), our method is better in both performance and parameter value.

The MAE value of the second combination is the closest to original RefineNet, but we think the performance of our proposed method is almost the same with significantly fewer parameters. In the fifth combination, the Inverted residuals structure proposed in

MobileNet-v2 [26] was used. However, the performance of the model decreased after the number of channels and model parameters were increased. In the eighth and ninth, we used depth-wise separable convolutions in CCU blocks, MRF blocks and CRP blocks, however, it's not as good as the 1 * 1 convolutions. Therefore, considering both performance and model parameters, we believe that the proposed method is the best in these methods.

The architecture of RefineNet is flexible. We can also choose our own combination according to the requirements in practical application. Finally, proposed new residual conv units block (NRCU), new multi-resolution fusion block (NMRF) and new chained residual pooling block (NCRP), as shown in Fig. 2(b–d).

3.4 Implementation Details

In this work, SE-ResNet50 and SE-ResNeXt154 are adopted as our baseline networks, which are pre-trained on the ImageNet 2012 dataset. And then we trained the entire network end-to-end with MSRA10K dataset [24], which contains 10000 scene images with single salient object. During training, we scale both training images and ground truths to 224 * 224. The final network is trained with Mean Square Error (MSE) loss for 200 epochs. We use Adam [25] with an initial learning rate of 1e−5 to update the weights. The learning rate is reduced when validation performance stops improving. We implement the network with PyTorch framework. All experiments are performed with NVIDIA GeForce RTX 2080Ti GPU, 3.6 GHz CPU, and 32G RAM.

4 Experiments

4.1 Datasets

We evaluate the performance of the proposed method on four benchmark datasets. The SED2 [26] is composed of 100 images with two salient objects. The ECSSD [27] contains 1000 images with complex content. The HKU-IS [9] contains 4447 images with multiple objects. The THUR [28] has 6232 images collected from Flickr with 5 topics: "Butterfly", "Coffee Mug", "Dog Jump", "Giraffe" and "Plane".

4.2 Evaluation Metrics

Three metrics are used for quantitative performance comparison and analysis, including Precision-Recall (PR) curve, Mean Absolute Error (MAE), and ω-Fβ [29]. S is used to indicate the saliency map and G signifies the ground truth in the datasets. Let saliency value be in the range [0, 255]. And then, we vary the threshold from 0 to 255 to segment the saliency map S, thus the corresponding binary map M is obtained. The precision and recall can be pair-wise computed to form the PR curve:

$$\Pr ecision = \frac{|M \cap G|}{|M|}, \mathrm{Re}call = \frac{|M \cap G|}{|G|} \tag{1}$$

where |*| represents the nonzero value of a binary image. MAE is defined as the mean absolute error between the normalized saliency map S and the ground truth G. With saliency map value varying in [0, 1] and ground-truth value varying in {0, 1}:

$$MAE = \frac{1}{W \times H} \sum_{x=1}^{W} \sum_{y=1}^{H} |S(x,y) - G(x,y)| \qquad (2)$$

where W and H indicate the width and height of the image, respectively. However, the above evaluation criteria may be not reliable due to the curve interpolation defect and equal importance assignment to all errors. Therefore, we choose ω-Fβ criterion proposed in [29] to overcome the above-mentioned defects. The ω-Fβ criterion is computed in the following:

$$F_\beta^\omega = (1 + \beta^2) \frac{\Pr ecision^\omega \cdot Recall^\omega}{\beta^2 \cdot \Pr ecision^\omega + Recall^\omega} \qquad (3)$$

where the weight ω and β were provided by authors with the default setting [29].

4.3 Performance Comparison

We compare our proposed method with other sixteen state-of-the-art approaches including seven deep CNNs based methods (CHFR [20], Amulet, DHSNet, DSMT, MDF, RFCN, KSR) and 9 conventional methods (DRFI, DSR, GMR, HDCT, MC, RBD, RC, MBD, SMD) on four benchmark datasets. The experimental results of PR curve, ω-Fβ value and MAE value are shown in Fig. 3(a), and (b), respectively.

It is necessary to note that Ours represents the proposed method using the SE-Resnet50 as the backbone and Ours+ represents the proposed method using the SE-ResneXt154 as the backbone.

It can be seen that deep learning based methods achieve much better performance than traditional methods. Compared with the existing state-of-the-art methods, our method achieves better performance where both precision and recall are high (top-right region of the P-R curve). Good segmentation results are usually generated using a threshold within this range. As shown in Fig. 3(b), the proposed method can achieve better adaptive-threshold segmentation performance than other methods.

We also found that the method Ours achieves better performance than Ours+ on the SED2 dataset, as shown in the third column of Fig. 3(a), Ours has higher precision, recall and the value of ω-Fβ, at the same time, has lower MAE value. This is because our training set MSRA10K is a single salient object dataset, but the SED2 is composed of only 100 images with two salient objects. They have different annotation standards and the number of images in SED2 dataset is so small that the experimental results were accidental.

ECSSD   HKU-IS   SED2   THUR15K

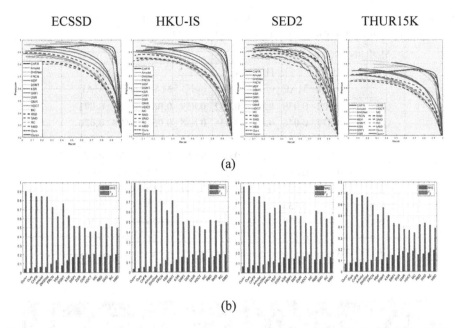

(a)

(b)

Fig. 3. Results of all test approaches on four standard benchmark datasets, i.e. ECSSD, HKU-IS, SED2 and THUR15K. (a) presents the PR curves, (b) presents the ω-Fβ and MAE of different saliency detection method on different test datasets.

Comparisons of MAE and ω-Fβ are shown in Table 2. Our model achieves the best performance on four datasets. Among these models, the recent state-of-the-art method CHFR is built on the SE-Resnet50, which is the same setting as the method Ours. However, it should be pointed out that CHFR is different from the method proposed by us (trained on the MSRA10K dataset). It was trained on the MSRA10K dataset and OMRON dataset. In spite of this, our proposed method still achieves better results.

Some qualitative comparisons are shown in Fig. 4. Our model is able to produce saliency maps that highlight salient regions accurately and uniformly. As can be seen from the first row and the fifth row of Fig. 4 respectively, our method can better detect the highly difficult boundaries of salient regions of rhino horn and dogleg.

Table 2. The ω-Fβ and MAE of different saliency detection method on different test datasets (red, green and blue texts respectively indicate rank 1, 2, and 3).

Methods	Datasets							
	ECSSD		HKU-IS		SED2		THUR15K	
	ω-Fβ	MAE	ω-Fβ	MAE	ω-Fβ	MAE	ω-Fβ	MAE
Ours+	**0.902**	**0.039**	**0.885**	**0.032**	**0.859**	**0.064**	**0.709**	**0.071**
Ours	**0.879**	**0.046**	**0.866**	**0.036**	**0.868**	**0.054**	**0.688**	**0.076**
CHFR	0.842	**0.056**	**0.820**	**0.047**	0.756	0.074	0.658	0.083
Amulet	**0.844**	0.061	0.810	0.053	**0.763**	**0.069**	**0.678**	**0.079**
DHSNet	0.839	0.059	0.814	0.050	0.709	0.078	0.666	0.079
RFCN	0.726	0.095	0.705	0.078	0.597	0.110	0.591	0.098
MDF	0.622	0.135	0.613	0.113	0.646	0.113	0.509	0.125
DSMT	0.763	0.079	0.712	0.076	0.673	0.099	0.569	0.107
KSR	0.629	0.133	0.583	0.119	0.518	0.151	0.499	0.122
DRFI	0.519	0.170	0.497	0.145	0.576	0.137	0.431	0.145

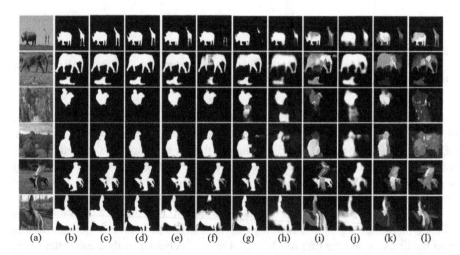

Fig. 4. Visual Comparisons of different saliency detection approaches in various challenging scenarios. The first two rows are images with multiple disconnected objects, the third and the forth rows are images with complex background and the last two rows are images with multiple connected objects. (a) Original images, (b) Ground truths, (c) Ours+, (d) Ours, (e) CHFR, (f) Amulet, (g) DHSNet, (h) RFCN, (i) MDF, (j) DSMT, (k) KSR, (l) DRFI.

4.4   Performance Comparison

We show the heat map of saliency detection results in Fig. 5. They are single object image, multiple objects image, low-contrast image and complex content image, respectively. Our model is able to produce heat maps and saliency maps that highlight salient regions accurately and uniformly.

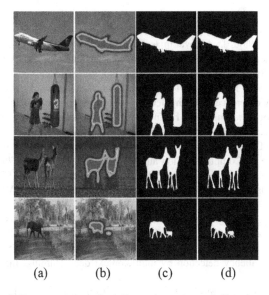

(a)   (b)   (c)   (d)

Fig. 5. Examples of the proposed method Ours+ in various challenging scenarios. (a) Input. (b) Heat maps. (c) Saliency maps. (d) Ground-truth.

5   Conclusion

In this paper, an end-to-end light-weight multi-path refinement network has been proposed to detect salient objects. SE-ResNet50 and SE-ResNeXt154 are used as backbones to extract multi-level and multi-scale feature maps according to the resolutions. Then, we fuse coarse high-level semantic features with finer-grained low-level features to generate full resolution saliency feature maps. Furthermore, we reduced the parameters by more than 50% on the premise of maintaining the same performance. Experiments on four benchmark datasets demonstrate that the proposed network can detect salient objects effectively and efficiently.

Acknowledgement. This work is supported by Shaanxi international science and technology cooperation and exchange program of china (2017KW-010), Scientific Research Project of Shaanxi Education Department of China (15JK1689).

References

1. Hussain, C.A., Rao, D.V., Masthani, S.A.: Robust pre-processing technique based on saliency detection for content based image retrieval systems. Procedia Comput. Sci. **85**, 571–580 (2016)
2. Chen, C., Shuai, L., Wang, Y., et al.: Video saliency detection via spatial-temporal fusion and low-rank coherency diffusion. IEEE Trans. Image Process. A Publ. IEEE Signal Process **26**(7), 3156–3170 (2017)

3. Wang, X., Qi, C., Lin, F.: Combined trajectories for action recognition based on saliency detection and motion boundary. Signal Process, Image Commun. **57**, 91–102 (2017)

4. Liu, W., Xue, Q., Zhou, J.: A novel image segmentation algorithm based on visual saliency detection and integrated feature extraction. In: International Conference on Communication and Electronics Systems. IEEE (2017)

5. Long, J., Shelhamer, E., Darrell, T.: Fully convolutional networks for semantic segmentation. In: IEEE Conference on Computer Vision Pattern Recognition, pp. 3431–3440 (2015)

6. LeCun, Y., Bottou, L., Bengio, Y., Haffner, P.: Gradient-based learning applied to document recognition. Proc. IEEE **86**(11), 2278–2324 (1998)

7. Liu, N., Han, J.: Dhsnet: deep hierarchical saliency network for salient object detection. In: IEEE Conference on Computer Vision and Pattern Recognition, pp. 678–686 (2016)

8. Li, G., Yu, Y.: Deep contrast learning for salient object detection. In: CVPR, pp. 478–487

9. Li, G., Yu, Y.: Visual saliency based on multiscale deep features. In: CVPR, pp. 5455–5463 (2015)

10. Tang, Y., Wu, X.: Saliency detection via combining region-level and pixel-level predictions with CNNs. In: Leibe, B., Matas, J., Sebe, N., Welling, M. (eds.) ECCV 2016. LNCS, vol. 9912, pp. 809–825. Springer, Cham (2016). https://doi.org/10.1007/978-3-319-46484-8_49

11. Zhao, R., et al.: Saliency detection by multi-context deep learning. In: CVPR, pp. 1265–1274. IEEE (2015)

12. Hu, P., Shuai, B., et al.: Deep level sets for salient object detection. In: CVPR, pp. 2300–2309. IEEE (2017)

13. Malik, J.: Learning a classification model for segmentation. In: ICCV, vol. 1, pp. 10–17 (2003)

14. Achanta, R., Shaji, A., Smith, K., et al.: SLIC superpixels compared to state-of-the-art superpixel methods. IEEE Trans. Pattern Anal. Mach. Intell. **34**(11), 2274–2282 (2012)

15. He, K., Sun, J., Tang, X.: Guided image filtering. IEEE Trans. Softw. Eng. **35**(6), 1397–1409 (2013)

16. Hu, J., Shen, L., Sun, G.: Squeeze-and-excitation networks. In CVPR, arXiv:1709.01507 (2017)

17. Lin, G., Milan, A., Shen, C., et al.: RefineNet: multi-path refinement networks for high-resolution semantic segmentation, pp. 1925–1934 (2016)

18. Nekrasov, V., Shen, C., Reid, I.: Light-weight RefineNet for real-time semantic segmentation. In: BMVC, arXiv:1810.03272 (2018)

19. Roy, A.G., Navab, N., Wachinger, C.: Concurrent Spatial and channel 'squeeze & excitation' in fully convolutional networks. In: Frangi, A., Schnabel, J., Davatzikos, C., Alberola-López, C., Fichtinger, G. (eds.) MICCAI 2018. LNCS, vol. 11070, pp. 421–429. Springer, Cham (2018). https://doi.org/10.1007/978-3-030-00928-1_48

20. Cuiping, L., Zhenxue, C., Jonathan, W.Q.M., et al.: Deep saliency detection via channel-wise hierarchical feature responses. Neurocomputing **322**, 80–92 (2018)

21. Xie, S., Girshick, R., Dollár, Piotr, et al.: Aggregated residual transformations for deep neural networks. In: CVPR, vol. 1, pp. 5987–5995 (2017)

22. Chollet, F.: Xception: Deep learning with depthwise separable convolutions. In: CVPR, arXiv:1610.02357 (2017)

23. Sandler, M., Howard, A.G., Zhu, M., et al.: Inverted residuals and linear bottlenecks: mobile networks for classification, detection and segmentation. arXiv:1801.04381 (2018)

24. Cheng, M.-M., Mitra, N.J., Huang, X., Torr, P.H., Hu, S.-M.: Global contrast based salient region detection. IEEE Trans. PAMI **37**(3), 569–582 (2015)

25. Kingma, D., Ba, J.: Adam: a method for stochastic optimization, arXiv:1412.6980 (2014)
26. Alpert, S., Galun, M., Brandt, A., Basri, R.: Image segmentation by probabilistic bottom-up aggregation and cue integration. IEEE Trans. on PAMI **34**(2), 315–327 (2012)
27. Yan, Q., Xu, L., Shi, J., Jia, J.: Hierarchical saliency detection. In: CVPR, pp. 1155–1162 (2013)
28. Cheng, M.-M., Mitra, N.J., Huang, X., Hu, S.-M.: Salientshape: group saliency in image collections. Vis. Comput. **30**(4), 443–453 (2014)
29. Margolin, R., Zelnik-Manor, L., Tal, A.: How to evaluate foreground maps? In: CVPR (2014)

Visual Object Tracking via an Improved Lightweight Siamese Network

Mingyang Liu[1], Qing Lei[1], Li Yu[1], Yun Gao[1,2(✉)],
and Xuejie Zhang[1]

[1] School of Information Science and Engineering, Yunnan University,
Kunming 650504, China
gausegao@163.com
[2] Kunming Institute of Physical, Kunming 650223, China

Abstract. Object tracking has recently raised a great research interest, and many Siamese network-based trackers have achieved the state-of-the-art performances. However, by analyzing their network structure, it can be found that those feature extraction modules still use AlexNet or its variants. Compared with some recent lightweight networks, there is still much room for improvement in accuracy. In this paper, we proposed an improved lightweight Siamese network, which combine the MobileNetV2 and SiamRPN. By utilizing strategy of the improved network which expanding the feature channels at first then compressing it, more feature information of object can be obtained for object tracking and the accuracy of the tracking algorithm can be effectively improved. We demonstrate the tracking performance of the proposed algorithm on OTB-100 dataset, and the proposed algorithm has a better performance in AUC and accuracy than some state-of-the-art trackers, with a 0.646 AUC and a 0.877 precision.

Keywords: Object tracking · Siamese network · MobileNetV2 · Lightweight network

1 Introduction

Visual tracking uses bounding box to track the target we are interested in, and provides an important basis for the video sequences analysis and understanding. However, the trackers can be easily distracted by the movement of targeted and surrounding objects in real scenarios, such as illumination changes and occlusion issues, it makes tracker face the bag challenge in accuracy [4, 6].

At present stage, visual tracking algorithms can be roughly divided into two branches. The first branch is correlation filter based tracking, which trains a regressor by exploiting the properties of circular correlation and performing operations in the Fourier domain, such as KCF [8], ECO [4]. However, these trackers have great limitations in real scenarios. KCF obtains excellent real-time performance while accuracy is

---

The first author is a graduate student of Yunnan University.

© Springer Nature Switzerland AG 2019
Z. Lin et al. (Eds.): PRCV 2019, LNCS 11857, pp. 284–294, 2019.
https://doi.org/10.1007/978-3-030-31654-9_25

hard to guarantee. ECO has high accuracy but is hard to use in real scenarios due to the high computational cost. Another branch is based on Siamese network [3], such as CFNet [19], SiamRPN [10]. CFNet introduces correlation filter as a layer to the template branch of Siamese network, and lighten the network layer of the Siamese network to improve the accuracy and real-time performance. However, the accuracy still cannot match the excellent Correlation filter-based (CF-based) tracking algorithms. SiamRPN combines Siamese network backbone and region proposal subnetwork (RPN) [15], which has good performance in speed and accuracy. However, if we analyze the network structure of SiamRPN, we will easily find this tracker is still using SiamFC [1] feature extraction module AlexNet [9]. Compare with the lightweight network proposed in recent years, such as MobileNetV2 [17], there is still much room for improvement in accuracy.

In this paper, we proposed an improved lightweight Siamese network combining the MobileNetV2 with SiamRPN. We train our tracker end-to-end with ILSVRC dataset [16] and Youtube-BB dataset [14]. Finally, we evaluate the proposed lightweight Siamese network in OTB-100 and OTB-50 datasets [22]. Figure 1 shows the tracking results of the proposed tracking algorithm with some state-of-the-art Siamese network-based tracking algorithms. The proposed algorithm delivers the state-of-the-art performance.

The rest of this paper is organized as follows. Related works are introduced in Sect. 2. The proposed architecture is described in Sect. 3. While Sect. 4 presents the experimental results and Sect. 5 concludes this paper.

2 Related Works

In this section, we briefly introduce the development of visual tracking algorithms in recent years, with a specially focus on the Siamese network-based trackers.

ours   SiamRPN   SiamFC

Fig. 1. Siamese network-based tracking results in OTB-100.

Under the rapid construction of a large number of new benchmark datasets, we have witnessed the rapid development of visual tracking over the last decade. The standardized benchmarks [22] provide fair testbeds for comparisons with different algorithms. With these advancements, numerous tracking algorithms have been proposed. The seminal work by Bolme *et al.* [2] introduces the Convolution Theorem from the signal-processing field into visual tracking and transforms the object template-matching problem into a correlation operation in the frequency domain. With this seminal work, a large number of CF-based tracking algorithms are proposed with the high speed. In addition, those trackers have good performance when using suitable features (e.g. HOG, CN) [8]. When using deep feature in CF-based tracking algorithms while the accuracy has been greatly improved and obtained the state-of-the-art accuracy in popular tracking benchmarks. However, when tracker with deep feature updates the model, it will bring significant computational cost to hinder the speed and reduce the real-time performance of the algorithm [4, 6].

In order to break through the non-real-time problems in CF-based tracking algorithms, many seminal works are unfolding. Among those works, SiamFC made a huge contribution. The goal of SiamFC is to find the potential area of the targeted objects in the following frames by comparing with the template images. In this approach, the tracker does not need to perform the online parameter update, which greatly improve the real-time performance of the algorithm. Since the advent of this algorithm, there have been many derivative algorithms. Among them, SA-Siam [7] implements a two-branch Siamese network with one branch for semantic and the other for appearance. RASNet [21] introduces three different attention mechanisms to enhance the performance. In addition, SiamRPN integrates the RPN as the backend to improve the performance in speed. However, if we analyze the network structure of those algorithms, we will easily find those trackers are still using the AlexNet as the feature extraction module. SiamVGG [11] further improved the performance in accuracy by replacing the AlexNet with VGG-16, which can reach 50 FPS on a GTX 1080Ti with a very deep network. Although VGG [18] can obtain the better performance in extracting the underlying semantic features for the targeted objects, it is still difficult to reproduce those experimental performances in real scenarios, where the operating conditions of the algorithm become harsh.

3   Improved Lightweight Siamese Network

The main idea of our design is to deploy a stronger lightweight network to combine with the advantages of using the SiamRPN. In this section, we describe the proposed network architecture and the corresponding training methods.

3.1   Network Architecture

Following the idea from the SiamRPN, we choose the MobileNetV2 as the feature extraction module. (Its strong ability has shown in other tasks, e.g., ImageNet classification [16], COCO object detection [13]) We also follow the base design strategy from SiamRPN and use it as our baseline design for further comparison.

We first introduce SiamRPN [10], which is based on the Siamese network. The Siamese network-based tracking algorithms formulate visual tracking as a cross-correlation problem and learn a tracking similarity map from deep models with a Siamese network structure, one branch for learning the feature presentation of the target denotes as z, and the other one for the search area denotes as x. This process can be defined as $f(z; x)$ in Eq. 1. In Eq. (1), $\varphi()$ represents a convolutional embedding function, $*$ represents convolution operation, and b represents the bias.

$$f(z; x) = \varphi(z) * \varphi(x) + b \tag{1}$$

Next, let us briefly introduce the RPN [15]. The region proposal subnetwork has two branches, one for scores map denotes as $A^{cls}_{w \times h \times 2k}$ and the other for region difference map denotes as $A^{reg}_{w \times h \times 4k}$. Then can define the tracking process as Eq. (2)

$$\begin{aligned} A^{cls}_{w \times h \times 2k} &= [\varphi(x)]_{cls} * [\varphi(z)]_{cls} \\ A^{reg}_{w \times h \times 4k} &= [\varphi(x)]_{reg} * [\varphi(z)]_{reg} \end{aligned} \tag{2}$$

where (w, h, k) indicates the width, height and ratios of anchor of the output channel. This method is still used in our method. However, in order to better fit MobileNetV2 as feature extraction module, we have to redesign the (w, h, k). After many experiments, we finally adopted the $15 \times 15 \times 5$ channel structure.

Figure 2 shows the whole network structure of our proposed network with two inputs (z for template image and x for detection image) and two outputs (scores map and region difference map). The scores map indicates the similarity information between the current detection image and template image. The region difference map indicates the distance between anchor and proposal ground truth.

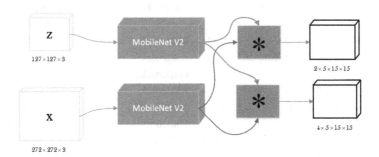

Fig. 2. Architecture of the proposed network combining with MobileNetV2 based SiamRPN.

In the process of screening networks as feature extraction modules, we find an interesting phenomenon. Most networks compress feature map channels with a 1 * 1 CONVlayer [12] and finally the feature map channels are expanded back through the 1 * 1 CONVlayer. However, in visual tracking, trackers only can get the target feature map of the first frame which mean only can get sparse features of target. If this feature map passes the compression operation, the sparse features will further dilution.

It has been a pursued goal for object tracking how to learn more about the first frame target, which coincides with the strategy of MobileNetV2. MobileNetV2 abandons the strategy of most networks which compressing the feature channels at first and then expanding them, and adopts the opposite strategy which expanding the feature channels at first and then compressing them. This opposite strategy can get more features by increasing the number of channels and effectively improve the accuracy of the tracking algorithm. The above process can be denoted as $F(x)$ in Eq. (3)

$$F(x) = \sum_{i=1}^{n} (A_i \circ N \circ B_i)(x) \tag{3}$$

where A is a linear transformation, N is a non-linear per-channel transformation, and B is again a linear transformation to the output domain. Via the feature extraction of MobileNetV2, our proposed algorithm can be summarized as Eq. (4)

$$\begin{aligned} A_{w \times h \times 2k}^{cls} &= [F(x)]_{cls} * [F(z)]_{cls} \\ A_{w \times h \times 4k}^{reg} &= [F(x)]_{reg} * [F(z)]_{reg} \end{aligned} \tag{4}$$

Network Configuration. The proposed network combine MobileNetV2 with SiamRPN through a large number of 1 * 1 CONVlayers. Its network configuration is list in Table 1.

Table 1. The configuration of the improved lightweight Siamese network. Where *bottleneck* $= A_i \circ N \circ B_i$, c_k and r_k represent the two-channel feature maps of the template branch output, and c_i and r_i represent the feature maps of the detection frame. t, c, n and s represent the expansion factor, output channels, repeat times and strides

tem_Imput	det_Imput	chan.	Operator	t	c	n	s
127 × 127	272 × 272	×3	conv2d	–	32	1	2
64 × 64	136 × 136	×32	bottleneck	1	16	1	1
64 × 64	136 × 136	×16	bottleneck	6	24	2	2
32 × 32	68 × 68	×24	bottleneck	6	32	3	2
16 × 16	34 × 34	×32	bottleneck	6	64	4	2
8 × 8	17 × 17	×64	bottleneck	6	96	3	1
8 × 8	17 × 17	×96	bottleneck	6	160	3	2
4 × 4	9 × 9	×160	bottleneck	6	320	1	1
4 × 4	9 × 9	×320	conv2d 1 × 1		1280	1	1
4 × 4	9 × 9	×1280	Resize				

c_k	r_k	c_i	r_i		tem	det				
8 × 8	8 × 8	18 × 18	18 × 18	×320	Conv 5 × 5	Conv 1 × 1				
4 × 4	4 × 4	18 × 18	18 × 18	×512	Conv 1 × 1	Conv 1 × 1				

3.2   Network Training

During the training phase, sample pairs are picked from ILSVRC with a random interval and from Youtube-BB continuously. The template patch and detection patch can be extracted from two random frames of a same video. We train the lightweight network end-to-end via Stochasic Gradiant Descent (SGD) after pretraining Mobile-NetV2 with ImageNet.

Image Pairs. First, let us talk about how we handle image pairs. when denoting the size of target bounding box as (w, h), we crop the template patch center at the historical frame with size A^2 which is defined as Eq. (5)

$$(w + p) \times (h + p) = A^2 \tag{5}$$

where $p = (w + h)/2$. Then the template patch is resized to 127 * 127. In the same way, the detection patch is cropped on the current frame with $2A' * 2A'$ where A' is determined by the previous frame, and then it is resized to 272 * 272.

Anchor. We adopted the anchor ratios are $[0.33, 0.66, 1, 1.5, 3]$. In order to balance the positive and negative samples, we only select the top 16 IOU of the target bounding box with anchors as positive samples while we randomly selected 48 anchors with IOU below 0.3 as negative samples, and the remaining anchors are not involved in training.

4   Experiments

In this section, we demonstrate the tracking performance of our proposed network in OTB-50 and OTB-100 datasets, and compare our tracker with the state-of-the-art trackers. Our model is implemented based on PyTorch framework, and it is trained on in Linux server with Intel E5-2609, 64G RAM, and NVIDIA GTX 1080Ti GPU. The tracker runs on a PC with Intel i7-7700HQ, 16 GB RAM, and NVIDIA GTX 1060 GPU.

4.1   Quantitative Assessment

We evaluate the proposed algorithm in OTB-100 and OTB-50 datasets. The one-pass evaluation (OPE) is employed to compare different trackers, based on two metrics: precision and success plot. The precision plot shows the percentage of frames that the tracking results are within 20 pixels from the target. The success plot shows the ratios of successful frames when the threshold varies from 0 to 1, where a successful frame means its overlap is larger than given threshold. The area under curve (AUC) of success plot is used to rank tracking algorithm.

The OTB-50 dataset is one of the most widely used dataset in visual tracking and contains 50 image sequences with various challenging factors while the OTB-100 dataset extends OTB-50 and contain 100 videos with 11 different challenges, such as abrupt motion, illumination variation, scale variation and motion blurring. Using those datasets, we compare the proposed algorithm with 7 state-of-the-art trackers including ECO-HC [4], DeepSRDCF [5], DeepLMCF [20], SiamFC, SiamFC-3 s [1], and SiamRPN [10], CFNet [19].

Figure 3 reports the precision and success plots of different trackers based on the two metrics: AUC and distance precision score at the threshold on 20 pixels. Among all compared trackers. the proposed algorithm obtains the best performance, which achieves the 90.9% distance precision rate at the threshold of 20 pixels and a 66.8% AUC score in OTB-50 while achieves the 87.7% distance precision rate at the threshold of 20 pixels and a 64.6% AUC score in OTB-100. Compared with our baseline algorithm selected, our algorithm has improved the results of precision by 2% respectively.

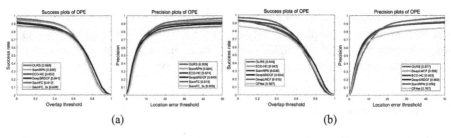

(a)   (b)

Fig. 3. The distance precision score at the threshold on 20 pixels and the AUC score of different trackers on the OTB-50 datasets (a) and OTB-100 (b).

4.2 Qualitative Analysis

We note that it is very useful to evaluate the performance of trackers in various challenges. The OTB-100 dataset is divided into 11 challenges, each of which corresponds to a challenging factor (e.g., illumination, motion and occlusion). Figure 4 illustrates the overlap success plots of the 6 algorithms on 6 challenges. We can see that our tracker achieves the best performance in all these challenges. Specially, the proposed algorithm improves the baseline SiamRPN by 5.1%, 6.1% in the challenges of background clutter and out of view, respectively.

More qualitative results for OTB sequences are shown in Fig. 5. From Video frame in Fig. 5, we can see the *MotorRolling* sequence with background clutter challenge, the matrix sequence with illumination variation challenge, the *DragonBaby* sequence with motion blur challenge, the Liquor and Coke sequence with occlusion challenge, the

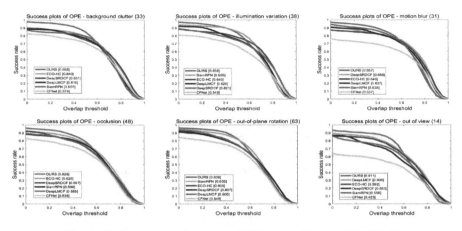

Fig. 4. Performance evaluation on 6 different challenges of OTB-100.

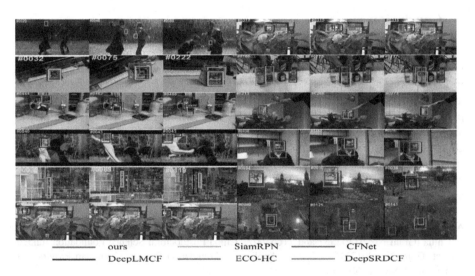

Fig. 5. OTB-100 video sequence results with 11 challenges: scale variation (SV), occlusion (OCC), illumination variation (IV), motion blur (MB), deformation (DEF), fast motion (FM), out-of-plane rotation (OPR), background clutter (BC), out of view (OV), in-plane rotation (IPR) and low resolution (LR).

FleetFace sequence with out-of-plane rotation challenge, the tiger sequence with out of view challenge, *etc.* From the results in those sequences, our proposed algorithm has better tracking performance than all compared trackers. More detail performance illustration in Table 2.

Table 2. Performance of 5 algorithms in 11 challenges of OTB-100. bold and italic represent 1st and 2nd.

Challenge	Ours	SiamRPN	ECO-HC	DeepSRDCF	DeepLMCF
IV	**0.658**	*0.655*	0.640	0.621	0.625
OPR	**0.636**	*0.633*	0.608	0.607	0.605
SV	**0.637**	*0.625*	0.614	0.609	0.591
OCC	**0.628**	0.590	*0.626*	0.597	0.585
DEF	*0.613*	**0.623**	0.592	0.560	0.559
MB	**0.657**	0.635	0.640	*0.656*	0.637
FM	*0.632*	0.611	**0.634**	0.629	0.604
IPR	*0.616*	**0.633**	0.581	0.589	0.596
OV	**0.611**	0.550	0.592	0.553	*0.608*
BC	**0.658**	0.607	*0.640*	0.631	0.615
LR	0.594	*0.601*	0.564	0.474	**0.651**

5   Conclusion

In this paper, we propose a lightweight Siamese network combining the lightweight network and SiamRPN, which is trained end-to-end offline with large-scale image pairs from ILSVRC and YoutubeBB. By modifying the network from the baseline SiamRPN algorithm, our proposed algorithm can deliver significant improvements of tracking performance with the AUC. And our proposed algorithm can be reduplicated easily, and especially it can be deployed onto Internet of Things (IoT) devices with limited computation and memory resources because of its compact network structure and small-scale parameters. Experiments showed that our algorithm can outperform several existing trackers in OTB-50 and OTB-100 datasets. In addition, our algorithm can reach real-time performance for most of the real-time applications.

Acknowledgement. This work was supported in part by National Natural Science Foundation of China (Grant No. 61802337 and 11663007), China Postdoctoral Science Foundation funded project (Grant No. 2017M623323XB); Application Foundation Project of Yunnan Province of China (Grant No. 2016FB103)

References

1. Bertinetto, L., Valmadre, J., Henriques, J.F., Vedaldi, A., Torr, P.H.: Fully-convolutional siamese networks for object tracking. In: Hua, G., Jégou, H. (eds.) ECCV 2016. LNCS, vol. 9914, pp. 850–865. Springer, Cham (2016). https://doi.org/10.1007/978-3-319-48881-3_56
2. Bolme, D.S., Beveridge, J.R., Draper, B.A., Lui, Y.M.: Visual object tracking using adaptive correlation filters. In: 2010 IEEE Computer Society Conference on Computer Vision and Pattern Recognition, pp. 2544–2550. IEEE (2010)
3. Chopra, S., Hadsell, R., LeCun, Y., et al.: Learning a similarity metric discriminatively, with application to face verifcation. In: CVPR (1), pp. 539–546 (2005)

4. Danelljan, M., Bhat, G., Shahbaz Khan, F., Felsberg, M.: ECO: efficient convolution operators for tracking. In: Proceedings of the IEEE Conference on Computer Vision and Pattern Recognition, pp. 6638–6646 (2017)
5. Danelljan, M., Hager, G., Shahbaz Khan, F., Felsberg, M.: Convolutional features for correlation filter based visual tracking. In: Proceedings of the IEEE International Conference on Computer Vision Workshops, pp. 58–66 (2015)
6. Danelljan, M., Robinson, A., Khan, F.S., Felsberg, M.: Beyond correlation filters: Learning continuous convolution operators for visual tracking. In: Leibe, B., Matas, J., Sebe, N., Welling, M. (eds.) ECCV 2016. LNCS, vol. 9909, pp. 472–488. Springer, Cham (2016). https://doi.org/10.1007/978-3-319-46454-1_29
7. He, A., Luo, C., Tian, X., Zeng, W.: A twofold siamese network for real-time object tracking. In: Proceedings of the IEEE Conference on Computer Vision and Pattern Recognition, pp. 4834–4843 (2018)
8. Henriques, J.F., Caseiro, R., Martins, P., Batista, J.: High-speed tracking with kernelized correlation filters. IEEE Trans. Pattern Anal. Mach. Intell. 37(3), 583–596 (2015)
9. Krizhevsky, A., Sutskever, I., Hinton, G.E.: ImageNet classification with deep convolutional neural networks. In: Pereira, F., Burges, C.J.C., Bottou, L., Weinberger, K.Q. (eds.) Advances in Neural Information Processing Systems 25, pp. 1097–1105. Curran Associates, Inc. (2012)
10. Li, B., Yan, J., Wu, W., Zhu, Z., Hu, X.: High performance visual tracking with siamese region proposal network. In: Proceedings of the IEEE Conference on Computer Vision and Pattern Recognition, pp. 8971–8980 (2018)
11. Li, Y., Zhang, X.: SiamVGG: Visual tracking using deeper siamese networks. arXiv preprint arXiv:1902.02804 (2019)
12. Lin, M., Chen, Q., Yan, S.: Network in network. arXiv preprint arXiv:1312.4400(2013)
13. Lin, T.Y., et al.: Microsoft COCO: common objects in context. In: Fleet, D., Pajdla, T., Schiele, B., Tuytelaars, T. (eds.) ECCV 2014. LNCS, vol. 8693, pp. 740–755. Springer, Cham (2014). https://doi.org/10.1007/978-3-319-10602-1_48
14. Real, E., Shlens, J., Mazzocchi, S., Pan, X., Vanhoucke, V.: YouTube-BoundingBoxes: a large high-precision human-annotated data set for object detection in video. In: Proceedings of the IEEE Conference on Computer Vision and Pattern Recognition, pp. 5296–5305 (2017)
15. Ren, S., He, K., Girshick, R., Sun, J.: Faster R-CNN: towards real-time object detection with region proposal networks. In: Advances in Neural Information Processing Systems, pp. 91–99 (2015)
16. Russakovsky, O., et al.: Imagenet large scale visual recognition challenge. Int. J. Comput. Vision 115(3), 211–252 (2015)
17. Sandler, M., Howard, A., Zhu, M., Zhmoginov, A., Chen, L.C.: MobileNetV2: inverted residuals and linear bottlenecks. In: Proceedings of the IEEE Conference on Computer Vision and Pattern Recognition, pp. 4510–4520 (2018)
18. Simonyan, K., Zisserman, A.: Very deep convolutional networks for large-scale image recognition. arXiv preprint arXiv:1409.1556 (2014)
19. Valmadre, J., Bertinetto, L., Henriques, J., Vedaldi, A., Torr, P.H.: End-to-end representation learning for correlation filter based tracking. In: Proceedings of the IEEE Conference on Computer Vision and Pattern Recognition, pp. 2805–2813 (2017)
20. Wang, M., Liu, Y., Huang, Z.: Large margin object tracking with circulant feature maps. In: Proceedings of the IEEE Conference on Computer Vision and Pattern Recognition, pp. 4021–4029 (2017)

21. Wang, Q., Teng, Z., Xing, J., Gao, J., Hu, W., Maybank, S.: Learning attentions: residual attentional siamese network for high performance online visual tracking. In: Proceedings of the IEEE Conference on Computer Vision and Pattern Recognition, pp. 4854–4863 (2018)
22. Wu, Y., Lim, J., Yang, M.H.: Online object tracking: a benchmark. In: Proceedings of the IEEE Conference on Computer Vision and Pattern Recognition, pp. 2411–2418 (2013)

A Simple and Robust Attentional Encoder-Decoder Model for License Plate Recognition

Linjiang Zhang[1,2]([✉]), Peng Wang[1,2], Fan Dang[1,2], and Shaojie Zhang[1,2]

[1] School of Computer Science, Northwestern Polytechnical University, Xi'an, China
{zhanglinjiang,dangfan,shaojiezhang}@mail.nwpu.edu.cn
peng.wang@nwpu.edu.cn
[2] National Engineering Laboratory for Integrated Aero-Space-Ground-Ocean Big Data Application Technology, Xi'an, China

Abstract. Recognizing car license plates in natural scene images is an important yet challenging task in intelligent transport systems. Most of current methods perform well for license plates collected under constrained conditions [1], e.g., from a single region with specific patterns or shot in front-view with nearly horizontal position. In this work, we propose a simple yet robust approach for license plate recognition under complex conditions. It is composed of an off-the-shelf Xception module and 2-dimension attention based image to sequence learning framework. Despite its simplicity, the proposed model can recognize license plates under various scenarios, including license plates captured in dark or strong lighting conditions, from different regions, oriented, distorted, or even blurred. A CycleGAN based method is employed to generate synthetic license plate images with different province characters and under various situations (shadow, darkness, glare, etc.), which enriches the training data largely and improves the recognition capability greatly. The proposed model achieves state-of-the-art recognition performance on various datasets, which demonstrates its effectiveness and robustness.

Keywords: License plate recognition · Attention · Generative adversarial networks

1 Introduction

License plate recognition in complex scenarios is a challenging and significant task, which is widely used in the highway vehicle management, electronic toll collection (ETC) system and road monitoring. Although the recognition accuracy on standard license plates is acceptable, license plate recognition in complex environment is still unreliable, especially for images photographed in dark, glare, rainy, snowy, tilted or blurred scenarios as shown in Fig. 1. Besides, license plates are often dirty or bent, which makes the recognition become more difficult.

The first author is a student. This work is supported in part by the National Natural Science Foundation of China (No. 61876152).

Z. Lin et al. (Eds.): PRCV 2019, LNCS 11857, pp. 295–307, 2019.
https://doi.org/10.1007/978-3-030-31654-9_26

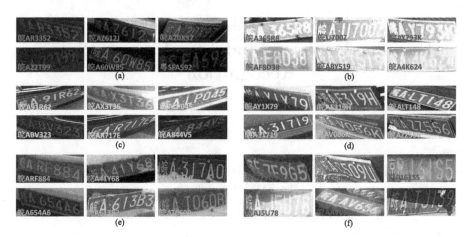

Fig. 1. Some successfully recognized images in testing datasets. (a) Illuminations on the LP area are dark; (b) Extremely bright or uneven; (c) Great horizontal tilt degree; (d) Great vertical tilt degree; (e) Image taken on a snowy or rainy day; (f) The most challenging images.

At present, the common methods for complex license plate recognition are to extract feature maps via CNNs, and then use Connectionist Temporal Classification (CTC) [2], number classifiers [3] or OCR [4] directly. These methods perform well for regular license plates (e.g., nearly horizontal). When the license plate images are tilting or bending, an extra rectification step is required before recognition.

This paper tackles the task of license plate recognition and proposes a robust and highly accurate method which can handle both regular and challenging cases effectively. It is composed of a 24-layers lightweight Xception for feature extraction and a 2D-attention based decoding module for sequence generation. With 2D-attention, the proposed module is capable of attending to the corresponding characters on license plates in decoding process, regardless of the appearance of license plate patterns. Our recognition model is very concise, but is capable of recognizing both regular and irregular license plates in various scenarios. It gives significant improvements on recognition accuracy (nearly 5%), compared with other state-of-the-art algorithms.

It is difficult to collect license plates from different provinces across a country. Therefore, many license plate datasets are collected from one city, which will cause deviations to the training and test results. Xu *et al.* [3] introduced a license plate dataset **CCPD** which contains about 290 K real world license plate images of various complex situations in 2018, as shown in Fig. 1. However, since more than 95% of the images are photographed in the same city, the first two digits in license plates are mostly the same, which will result in that the model is only workable in this city and cannot be used nationwide. Considering the advantage of GAN in image generation, we employ it here to generate different kinds of license plate images, which may contain shadows, be in dark or strong lighting conditions, and include various provinces characters. The synthetic license plates in cluttered conditions are suitable for training high-performance recognizers.

It should be noted that this work aims to handle license plate recognition. In order to get license plate bounding boxes, YOLOv2 [5] is adopted here firstly in consideration of its good detection performance. The main contributions of this paper can be summarized as the follows:

1. We designed a concise and robust method for license plate recognition in natural scene images. It is made up of a tailored Xception module and a 2-dimension attention based image to sequence learning module. The Xception model is tailored modified, with only half parameter size in comparison with the original one. The whole model can be trained end-to-end without pre-training.
2. We optimized the recognition framework by simply using a 2D attention mechanism. It is able to extract local features for individual characters in a weakly supervised manner, without character level annotations needed. Compared to existing license plate recognition approaches, our method does not need an extra module to handle the irregularity of license plates or segment each character for recognition.
3. Some ideas were proposed based on CycleGAN so as to synthesize license plates under various scenarios, including adding shadows, glare or darkness, perspective transformation, etc. With this engine we can generate license plate images from different regions/provinces, and get sufficient training data easily to train our model.

2   Related Work

In this section, we present a concise introduction to the previous works on license plate recognition, light-weight convolutional neural networks and generative adversarial networks.

2.1   License Plate Recognition

Existing methods on license plate recognition can be divided into two categories: Segmentation based [4,6–8] and Non-segmentation based methods [2,3,9,10]. The segmentation based methods generally segment the license plate into characters and then recognize individual characters by OCR models [4]. However, this kind of method relies heavily on the segmentation performance. They are very susceptible to the environment, including strong or weak lighting, bad weather, blurring, etc., and will result in a low recognition accuracy for complicated license plates. Recent methods are mostly segmentation free. For example, Li et al. [2] proposed to extract the region features through CNNs and encode the sequential features with Bidirectional RNNs (BRNNs) and CTC. RPnet proposed by Xu et al. [3] combines ROI features extracted from different layers and feeds them to subsequent Classifiers for recognition. However, both methods perform badly for challenging scenarios and oriented LPs.

2.2 Light-Weight Convolutional Neural Networks

In today's research, there is a tendency of adopting formidable neural networks to extract feature maps such as ResNet, VGG or DenseNet. However, license plate recognition is highly demanding on speed. Therefore, lightweight networks are usually a better choice to improve recognition efficiency, such as MobileNet, ShuffleNet and Xception [11], etc. In this work, we reconstructed a CNN model based on Xception, with a parameter size almost half of the original one.

2.3 Generative Adversarial Networks

With the invention of the Generative Adversarial Networks (GANs) [12], many improved models have emerged, such as Deep Convolutional Generative Adversarial Networks (DCGANs) [13], Conditional GAN [14], Wasserstein GANs (WGAN) [15] etc. Zhu *et al.* [16] proposed the Cycle-Consistent Adversarial Networks (CycleGAN), which learns the mapping between an input image and an output image using a training set of unaligned image pairs. In order to migrate the style of one image set to another one, cycle consistency loss is introduced. Based on this, we propose an improved algorithm to generate synthetic license plate images in more complex environments, which improves the accuracy of license plate recognition furthermore.

3 Methodology

We introduce our proposed model in this section. As presented in Fig. 2, the whole recognition model consists of two main parts: a lightweight Xception for feature extraction as image encoder and a 2D-attention based model for sequence decoder.

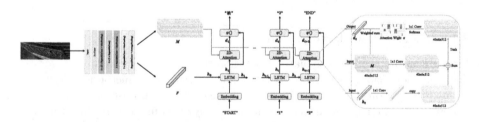

Fig. 2. Overview of the proposed architecture for complex scenarios LP recognition.

3.1 The Convolutional Image Encoder

The redesigned 24-layers Xception is inspired by the original Xception [11] framework, with the designed specifications as presented in Fig. 3. The convolutional parts of our model are based entirely on depthwise separable convolution layers that usually implements channel-wise spatial convolution and 1×1 convolution. The 24 convolutional layers are structured into 9 modules, all of which have linear residual connections around them, except for the first and the last modules.

The input image firstly goes through the entry flow, then through the middle flow which is repeated four times, and finally through the exit flow. Note that all convolutional and separable convolution layers are followed by batch normalization (not shown in the image). In the exit flow, we extract a middle feature map as context for attention network (denoted as M of size $40 \times 6 \times 512$) and a 512-dimensional final feature vector as the holistic feature (denoted as F of size $40 \times 6 \times 512$).

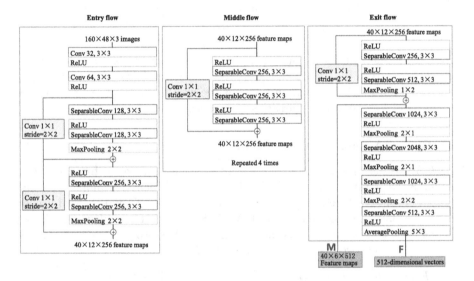

Fig. 3. The redesigned Xception architecture. "Conv" stands for Convolutional layers, with output channels and kernel size presented. The stride and padding for convolutional layers are all set to "1", no padding for Max-pooling layers.

3.2 The Recurrent Sequence Decoder

CNN-RNN is widely used in translation, image caption, scene text recognition tasks. Here we extend it to license plate recognition. With a two-dimensional attention mechanism integrated, there is no need to make any corrections for irregular license plate images or segment each character. The proposed attention-based model can handle images in complex scenarios.

The final feature vector F is fed into an LSTM with 2 layers and 512 hidden states at time step 0. Then a "BEGIN" token is input into the model at time step 1. From time step 2, the output of previous time step is fed into LSTM until the "END" token received. The inputs of LSTM are represented by one-hot vectors with linear transformation and the ground-truth characters are used as input during training time. A single LSTM cell can be expressed as:

$$h_{t+1} = f(h_t, x_t) = f(h_t, \varphi(h_t, d_t)) \tag{1}$$

where h_t is the current hidden state and d_t is the output of 2D-attention. f represents the LSTM operation and φ is a linear transformation. 2D-attention mechanism can be formulated as follows:

$$g_{ij} = \tanh(W_m M_{ij} + W_h h_t) \tag{2}$$

$$\alpha_{ij} = \text{softmax}(W_g \cdot g_{ij}) \tag{3}$$

$$d_t = \sum_{i,j}^{H,W} \alpha_{ij} M_{ij} \tag{4}$$

where M_{ij} is the feature vector at position i, j in M and h_t is the hidden state at time step t. W_m, W_h, W_g are linear transformation weights to be learned; α_{ij} is the attention weight at location i, j; d_t is the weighted sum of image features, i.e., the local feature of the characters to be decoded at current time step t.

3.3 CycleGAN for LP Generation

CycleGAN is an approach for learning to translate an image from a source domain X to a target domain Y in the absence of paired examples. In our work, we record the fake image generated by OpenCV as X, and the real license plate image as Y. The standard CycleGAN is composed of two adversarial losses and one cycle consistency loss as shown in Eq. 5. It has two generators: $G : X \rightarrow Y, F : Y \rightarrow X$ and two discriminators D_X and D_Y.

$$L(G, F, D_X, D_Y) = L_{GAN}(G, D_Y, X, Y) + L_{GAN}(F, D_X, Y, X) + \lambda L_{cyc}(G, F) \tag{5}$$

where

$$L_{cyc}(G, F) = E_{x \sim p_{data}(x)}[\|F(G(x)) - x\|_1] + E_{y \sim p_{data}(y)}[\|G(F(y)) - y\|_1] \tag{6}$$

What we need is a mapping from synthesized data to real data, that is $G(x)$ by adding noises on the fake images and making it similar to the real license plates. $F(G(X))$ can be regarded as adding some noises on X and then subtracting these noises, while $G(F(x))$ is the opposite process. As we know, it is easier to add some noises on the image and then subtract this noise. On the contrary, it is more difficult to reduce the noises firstly and then add the noises. Because even if the same noise is added, the position added is different from the original image, which will make the loss increase. Therefore, we design a new loss as denoted in Eq. 7 which discards the second cycle consistency loss, since $F(Y), G(F(Y)), F(G(X))$ are useless for us. The new CycleGAN model is shown in Fig. 4.

$$L_{cyc-new}(G, F) = E_{x \sim p_{data}(x)}[\|F(G(x)) - x\|_1] \tag{7}$$

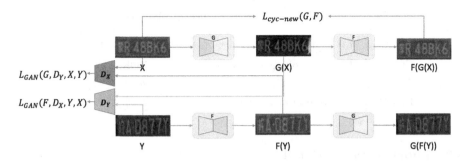

Fig. 4. The architecture of the CycleGAN model.

4   Experiments

In this section, we conduct extensive experiments to compare our license plate recognition model with state-of-the-art recognition methods. To demonstrate the effectiveness of the proposed model, experiments and comparisons are performed on three different license plate datasets.

4.1   Datasets

CCPD [3] is the largest publicly available License Plate (LP) dataset that provides over 290k unique Chinese LP images with detailed annotations. The dataset is separated into different groups according to the difficulty of identification, the illuminations on LP area, the distance from the license plate when photographing, the degree of horizontal tilt and vertical tilt, and the weather (rainy, snowy or fog). Each category includes 10k to 20k images. CCPD-base consists of approximately 200k different images. For fair comparison, CCPD-base is equally divided into two parts according to the dataset provider's division, The first half is the default training set and the other half is the test set. The other subdatasets (CCPD-DB, CCPD-FN, CCPD-Rotate, CCPD-Weather, CCPD-Challenge) are also used for test.

AOLP [17] database consists of 2049 images of Taiwan license plate. This dataset is categorized into three subsets according to different levels of difficulty and photographing conditions: Access Control (AC), Traffic Law Enforcement (LE) and Road Patrol (RP). Since we do not have any other images with Taiwan license plate, we use any two of these subsets as training sets and the remaining one as testing set.

PKUData [18] is issued by Yuan et al., which provides 2253 images for license plate detection. The license plate labels are not annotated and we labeled by ourselves.

Some more information about these datases is summarized in Table 1.

Table 1. The evaluated datasets for license plate recognition.

Database	LP angle	Vehicle dist	Images	Region
CCPD	Frontal + oblique	Near, medium, far	180K	Anhui
AOLP	Frontal + oblique	Near	2049	Taiwan
PKUData	Mostly frontal	Far	2253	Anhui

4.2 Implementation Details

In this work, we mainly focus on license plate recognition. In order to get the license plate bounding boxes, YOLOv2 [5] is adopted and trained on half of the CCPD dataset without structure modification. We set the IOU threshold to 0.5, and achieve a result of precision $= 99.5\%$ and recall $= 99.6\%$. An LP recognition is correct if and only if the IoU is greater than 0.5 and all characters in the LP number are correctly recognized, including the Chinese character.

LP Recognition Network. The recognition network is trained with cross-entropy loss and ADAM optimizer without any pre-training. In the training process, we adopt a batch size of 24 and a learning rate of 1e−3 initially. The learning rate is multiplied by 0.9 every 12000 iterations until it reaches to 10^{-5}. The heights of input images in a batch is fixed, while the width is calculated according to the aspect ratio of original images. All the experiments are conducted on a NVIDIA GTX1080ti GPU with 11 GB memory.

CycleGAN Training. To train the CycleGAN model, we further marked the CCPD data according to the situation of photographing. It is divided into night-time, strong illumination, and long shooting distance, close-up shooting. According to each specific situation, 800 real license plate images are taken as the Y set. We use OpenCV to generate the same number of fake license plates as the X set. All the images are resized to 256×256 without image cropping. The model is trained with a learning rate of 0.0002 and no more than 20 epochs.

4.3 CycleGAN Generation Results

The generated license plate images by CycleGAN are presented in Fig. 5. As we mentioned before, there is no dataset available currently with license plates all over the country. The number of challenging images is also limited which makes the existing models cannot handle difficult situations like blurring, dark, shadow, etc. Hence, we trained a CycleGAN model which can augment available datasets by adding various effects. In our experiment, we generate 40000 bright ones, 40000 dark ones, 50000 with perspective transformation and 10000 with shadow effect. As shown in Fig. 5, the generated license plate images can simulate various real world situations.

Fig. 5. Data Augmentation (a) Original LPs generated by OpenCV; (b) Bright LPs by CycleGAN; (c) Dark LPs by CycleGAN; (d) Shadowed LPs by OpenCV.

4.4 Recognition Results on CCPD

CCPD is a dataset with Chinese license plates. For fair comparison with other methods, YOLOv2 is adopted firstly to get license plate bounding boxes.

Table 2. LP recognition accuracy (percentage) on each testing set (Number of images in parentheses), AP means average accuracy. We achieved the highest recognition accuracy compared with other algorithms, especially in the datasets of rotate, weather and challenge.

| Model | AP | Base | DB | FN | Rotate | Tilt | Weather | Challenge |
Number		(100k)	(20k)	(20k)	(10k)	(10k)	(10k)	(10k)
Wang et al. [19]	58.9	69.7	67.2	69.7	0.1	3.1	52.3	30.9
Ren et al. [20]	92.8	97.2	94.4	90.9	82.9	87.3	85.5	76.3
Liu et al. [21]	95.2	98.3	96.6	95.9	88.4	91.5	87.3	83.8
Joseph et al. [5]	93.7	98.1	96.0	88.2	84.5	88.5	87.0	80.5
Li et al. [9]	94.4	97.8	94.8	94.5	87.9	92.1	86.8	81.2
Xu et al. [3]	95.5	98.5	96.9	94.3	90.8	92.5	87.9	85.1
Ours (only real data)	98.4	99.6	98.4	98.5	96.3	97.7	98.4	88.2
Ours (Add synthetic data)	**98.8**	**99.8**	**98.9**	**98.7**	**98.1**	**98.8**	**98.5**	**89.5**

As shown in Table 2, we achieved the highest recognition accuracy in all the test subsets, compared with other algorithms. The improvement is even obvious on challenging datasets, such as CCPD-Rotate, CCPD-Weather, CCPD-Challenge. To be specific, our method increases about 10% and 6% respectively on the Weather and Rotate datasets. However, our model speed is 40 FPS which is slower than RPnet [3] (86 FPS), mainly because LSTM is serial computing. We leave the computation acceleration as our future work. And the FPS (40 images per second) of our model contains the time of YOLOv2 detection (17.02 ms per image) and LPR recognition (7.94 ms per image).

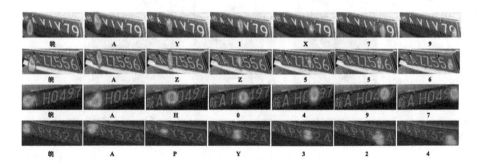

Fig. 6. Visualization of 2D attention weights at each decoding timestep. Results indicate that 2D-attention model can even handle extremely tilted LPs

We visualize the 2D attention heat maps when decoding each character in Fig. 6. The result shows that our 2D attention model can localize feature area corresponding to each character to be decoded. Experimental results show that 2D-attention can even handle extremely tilted images.

We try to replace bounding boxes detected by YOLOv2 with ground truth bounding boxes. The experimental results are shown in Table 3. To our surprise, the accuracy rate does not drop too much. The main reason is that attention mechanism does not heavily depend on the accurate bounding boxes, which also shows the robustness of our algorithm.

Table 3. Performance with different bounding boxes. With different bounding boxes, the recognition results are not much different, which indicates that the 2D-attention model is not highly dependent on the detection.

Bounding box	Base	DB	FN	Rotate	Tilt	Weather	Challenge
Detection	99.8	98.9	98.7	98.1	98.8	98.5	89.5
Ground truth	**99.8**	**99.4**	**99.3**	**98.2**	**98.9**	**98.6**	**89.8**

Table 4. Performance with different CNN channels.

CNN channels	Base	DB	FN	Rotate	Tilt	Weather	Challenge
128	99.7	98.0	98.1	96.1	97.7	98.1	86.3
256	99.7	98.4	98.4	97.1	98.3	98.2	87.9
512	**99.8**	**98.9**	**98.7**	**98.1**	**98.8**	**98.5**	**89.5**
1024	99.3	97.1	97.1	94.2	96.4	97.4	83.4

In order to analyze the impact of different CNN parameters on recognition performance, we experimented with different CNN channels and all training data and testing data are identical. The results are shown in the following Table 4. These results show that simple recognition tasks rely more on low or middle level convolution features and original detailed representation in images.

4.5   Recognition Results on AOLP

In this section, we compare our model with other state-of-the-art methods on AOLP dataset, which is divided into three subsets. We use any two of them as the training set, and the remaining one is used as the test set. For example, the license plates from the AC and LE subsets are used for training YOLOv2 and recognition model, and then RP is adopted to test performance. Since Taiwan license plates are not common, only perspective transformation is adopted during training time for data augmentation. The results in Table 5 show that our approach performs better than other methods on all three subsets, which proves the robustness of our approach. In particular, our method gives accuracy increases of 0.6% on AC subset, 0.5% on LE subset and 0.8% on RP subset. Note that RP subsets are mainly oriented or distorted license plates. The remarkable improvement demonstrates the effectiveness of our model in recognizing irregular license plates.

Table 5. The recognition accuracy (percentage) on each testing set of AOLP. Our approach performs better than other methods on all three subsets, Wu et al. [22] uses six different data augmentation methods. However, we only use perspective transformation.

Model	AC	LE	RP
Number	(681)	(757)	(611)
Li et al. [2]	94.9	94.2	88.4
Li et al. [9]	95.3	96.6	83.7
Wu et al. [22]	96.6	97.8	91.0
Ours	**97.2**	**98.3**	**91.8**

4.6   Recognition Results on PKUData

For PKUData, we use three-fifths for training and the remaining two-fifths for test. The recognition results are shown in Table 6. When we take the Chinese character into consideration, our algorithm significantly outperforms previous method by 7%. It should be note that most license plate recognition models cannot handle Chinese characters [9,23]. In contrast, with the modified Cycle-GAN model for realistic synthetic data generation, our model can recognize both Alphanum and Chinese characters, and hence can be used to handle license plates from various regions/provinces.

Table 6. The recognition accuracy (ACC) and recognition accuracy without Chinese character (ACC w/o CC) on PKUData. For ACC w/o CC, the recognition is considered to be correct if all the characters except the first one (Chinese character) are correctly recognized.

Model	PKUData	
Number	2253	
Criterion	ACC	ACC w/o CC
Xu *et al.* [3]	77.6	78.4
Ours	**84.3**	**86.5**

5   Conclusion

In this paper, we present a lightweight and robust framework for license plate recognition. The proposed framework is built upon a Xception module for feature extraction, and a 2D-attention based module for sequence decoding. Our experimental results indicate that the proposed model performs well for both regular and irregular license plate images without any extra rectification or segmentation work needed. In addition, CycleGAN is tailored here to generate sufficient number of synthetic images with real-world condition, which contributes a lot to the recognition ability of our model.

As to future works, the proposed framework can be improved in several measures. First of all, we plan to use parallelized networks instead of LSTMs to accelerate recognition speed. Secondly, the Xception can be replaced by a more lightweight network without performance dropping. Last but not least, Cycle-GAN does not handle the details well in the license plate generation, especially in the display of letters and Chinese characters. Attention mechanism may be integrated into CycleGAN, which will facilitate the generation of more realistic scene images.

References

1. Gruzdev, A., Zherzdev, S.: LPRNet: license plate recognition via deep neural networks. arXiv preprint arXiv:1806.10447 (2018)
2. Li, H., Shen, C.: Reading car license plates using deep convolutional neural networks and LSTMs. arXiv preprint arXiv:1601.05610 (2016)
3. Xu, Z., Yang, W., Meng, A., Lu, N., Huang, H., Ying, C., Huang, L.: Towards end-to-end license plate detection and recognition: a large dataset and baseline. In: Ferrari, V., Hebert, M., Sminchisescu, C., Weiss, Y. (eds.) ECCV 2018. LNCS, vol. 11217, pp. 261–277. Springer, Cham (2018). https://doi.org/10.1007/978-3-030-01261-8_16
4. Silva, S.M., Jung, C.R.: License plate detection and recognition in unconstrained scenarios. In: Ferrari, V., Hebert, M., Sminchisescu, C., Weiss, Y. (eds.) ECCV 2018. LNCS, vol. 11216, pp. 593–609. Springer, Cham (2018). https://doi.org/10.1007/978-3-030-01258-8_36

5. Redmon, J., Farhadi, A.: Yolo9000: better, faster, stronger. In: Proceedings of the IEEE Conference on Computer Vision and Pattern Recognition, pp. 7263–7271 (2017)
6. Gou, C., Wang, K., Yao, Y., Li, Z.: Vehicle license plate recognition based on extremal regions and restricted Boltzmann machines. IEEE Trans. Intell. Transp. Syst. **17**(4), 1096–1107 (2015)
7. Guo, J.-M., Liu, Y.-F.: License plate localization and character segmentation with feedback self-learning and hybrid binarization techniques. IEEE Trans. Veh. Technol. **57**(3), 1417–1424 (2008)
8. Gonçalves, G.R., da Silva, S.P.G., Menotti, D., Schwartz, W.R.: Benchmark for license plate character segmentation. J. Electron. Imaging **25**(5), 053034 (2016)
9. Li, H., Wang, P., Shen, C.: Towards end-to-end car license plates detection and recognition with deep neural networks. corr abs/1709.08828 (2017)
10. Duan, S., Hu, W., Li, R., Li, W., Sun, S.: Attention enhanced ConvNet-RNN for Chinese vehicle license plate recognition. In: Chinese Conference on Pattern Recognition and Computer Vision (PRCV) (2018)
11. Chollet, F.: Xception: deep learning with depthwise separable convolutions. In: Proceedings of the IEEE Conference on Computer Vision and Pattern Recognition, pp. 1251–1258 (2017)
12. Goodfellow, I., et al.: Generative adversarial nets. In: Advances in Neural Information Processing Systems, pp. 2672–2680 (2014)
13. Radford, A., Metz, L., Chintala, S.: Unsupervised representation learning with deep convolutional generative adversarial networks. arXiv preprint arXiv:1511.06434 (2015)
14. Mirza, M., Osindero, S.: Conditional generative adversarial nets. arXiv preprint arXiv:1411.1784 (2014)
15. Arjovsky, M., Chintala, S., Bottou, L.: Wasserstein gan. arXiv preprint arXiv:1701.07875 (2017)
16. Zhu, J.-Y., Park, T., Isola, P., Efros, A.A.: Unpaired image-to-image translation using cycle-consistent adversarial networks. In: Proceedings of the IEEE International Conference on Computer Vision, pp. 2223–2232 (2017)
17. Hsu, G.-S., Chen, J.-C., Chung, Y.-Z.: Application-oriented license plate recognition. IEEE Trans. Veh. Technol. **62**(2), 552–561 (2012)
18. Yuan, Y., Zou, W., Zhao, Y., Wang, X., Xuefeng, H., Komodakis, N.: A robust and efficient approach to license plate detection. IEEE Trans. Image Process. **26**(3), 1102–1114 (2016)
19. Wang, S.-Z., Lee, H.-J.: A cascade framework for a real-time statistical plate recognition system. IEEE Trans. Inf. Forensics Secur. **2**(2), 267–282 (2007)
20. Ren, S., He, K., Girshick, R., Sun, J.: Faster R-CNN: towards real-time object detection with region proposal networks. In: Advances in Neural Information Processing Systems, pp. 91–99 (2015)
21. Liu, W., et al.: SSD: single shot MultiBox detector. In: Leibe, B., Matas, J., Sebe, N., Welling, M. (eds.) ECCV 2016. LNCS, vol. 9905, pp. 21–37. Springer, Cham (2016). https://doi.org/10.1007/978-3-319-46448-0_2
22. Wu, C., Xu, S., Song, G., Zhang, S.: How many labeled license plates are needed? In: Lai, J.-H., et al. (eds.) PRCV 2018. LNCS, vol. 11259, pp. 334–346. Springer, Cham (2018). https://doi.org/10.1007/978-3-030-03341-5_28
23. Masood, S.Z., Shu, G., Dehghan, A., Ortiz, E.G.: License plate detection and recognition using deeply learned convolutional neural networks. arXiv preprint arXiv:1703.07330 (2017)

Semi-supervised Deep Neural Networks for Object Detection in Video Surveillance Systems

Jinshan Chen[1], Yujun Liu[1], Kaiming Ding[1], Shimin Li[1], Songxin Cai[1], Jinhe Su[1], Zongyue Wang[1], and Guorong Cai[1,2(✉)]

[1] Computer Engineering College, Jimei University, Xiamen 360121, China
guorongcai.jmu@gmail.com
[2] Fujian Collaborative Innovation Center for Big Data Applications in Governments, Fuzhou 350003, China

Abstract. Moving object detection under video surveillance systems is a critical task for many computer vision applications. That being said, extracting object from real-world surveillance video is still a challenging task, since various appearances and shapes, and light condition are all unsolved problems. Exploiting contexts from adjacent frames is believed to be valuable for tackling these challenges in surveillance video and is far from development. In this paper, we introduce a novel one-stage approach, named SDNN, to detect objects with multiple successive frames in videos. Specifically, the network fuses the context information of multiple frames, and combines predictions from multi-scale feature maps at different layers. The multi-frame feature fusion scheme enable the training process follows an end-to-end fashion. Experimental results conducted on surveillance video dataset show that the proposed SDNN achieved state-of-the-art results. *The source code is available at* https://github.com/jmuyjl/SDNN.

Keywords: Object detection · Semi-supervised · Context · Multi feature fusion · One stage

1 Introduction

Object detection in the video surveillance systems has achieved remarkable success in recent years. Object detection is a hot research area in computer vision community, since the results can be easily applicated in intelligent cities, intelligent transportation, and other fields. The purpose of object detection under the video surveillance system is to find out the objects of interest in the videos, including the location of the objects and their corresponding categories, such

---

The first author is a student. This work is supported by the National Natural Science Foundation of China under Grant No. 61702251, the Key Technical Project of Fujian Province under Grant No. 2017H6015.

Z. Lin et al. (Eds.): PRCV 2019, LNCS 11857, pp. 308–321, 2019.
https://doi.org/10.1007/978-3-030-31654-9_27

as pedestrian, rider, motorcycle, and so on. Nevertheless, there are many uncertain factors in the detection process. For example, objects always have different appearances, shapes and postures. Meanwhile, some interference such as illumination and occlusion, may increase the difficulty of detection. Therefore, object detection under video surveillance systems is a non-trivial and challenging task.

Previously object detection algorithms were mainly relied on hand-crafted features and the sliding window paradigm [1], such as VJ face detector [2] and HOG human detection [3], etc. Typical scheme is to slide a window on the image with specified step size. Then each window is judged whether the current window contains an instance of the target object or not. However, this is computationally expensive and performs poorly in most cases. In ImageNet 2012 [4] classification task, convolutional neural network made a breakthrough. Since then, object detection has entered a new era with deep learning architecture.

In real-world applications, object detection from video has widely used in intelligent surveillance scenarios. In the background of video-based object detection task, the appearance, shape, scale and other attributes of objects may change with the movement of the instance. Therefore, the single-frame detection may have many missed detection targets. Nevertheless, these missed detection targets may be included in the adjacent frame. Our approach is inspired by the assumption. Since adjacent frame provides objects motion and spatial information, which are useful for the detection of target frames. Therefore, exploiting contexts from adjacent frames can be taken into consideration.

Although object detection based on deep learning model has achieved state-of-the-art results, most methods are based on supervised learning. This means that training a model requires large amounts of annotated training data. Simultaneously, labeling large amounts of dataset is expensive, cumbersome, and inflexible. In fact, semi-supervised [5] learning is a very natural approach to solve this problem. It uses small amount of labeled data and a large amount of unlabeled data for training deep neural network. The benefit of this strategy is to use unlabeled data to improve the generalization ability and the robustness of extracted features.

2   Related Work

Recently, great break through has been made in object detection using deep convolutional networks [6–8]. Mainstream detectors can be roughly categorized into two main types of pipelines, namely, two-stage approaches and one-stage approaches.

Two-Stage Approaches. In this scheme, the object detection task is divided into two stages. The first stage generates a sparse set of region proposals by Region Proposal Network (RPN) or Select Search [9]. The second stage is to refine and to classify region proposals. Typical two-stage approaches are R-CNN [10] such as Fast R-CNN [11], Faster R-CNN [12] and the Feature Pyramid Networks (FPN) [13].

One-Stage Approaches. This scheme removes the region proposals extraction process, then directly classifying and regressing the locations of objects in a single network. Generally speaking, one-stage scheme is more efficient than two-stage methods. However, the accuracy may be lower than two-stage algorithms. Mainstream one-stage schemes including YOLOv3 [14], SSD [15] and RetinaNet [16], etc.

Anchor-Free Approaches. Recently, a novel strategy that does not require the generation of anchors, has attracted the attention of researchers. Typical algorithm such as CornerNet [17] regresses the bounding as a pair of keypoints. Anchor-free approaches transform object detection problem into keypoint regression, which achieved better performance in terms of speed and accuracy.

Video Object Detection. Compared to image detection, object detection for video usually joins temporal context. The method of combining optical flow is one of the most representative detection methods. The purpose is to extract features by keyframes then propagate the keyframe features to non-key frames through optical flow, such as DFF [18]. Usually those algorithms have a good performance in high speed, where the accuracy is unpromising.

The Semi-supervised Deep Neural Network (SDNN) proposed in this paper belongs to one-stage detector and can be trained end-to-end. In addition, in order to ensure the accuracy of the object detection at various shapes, the network fuses the context [19–21] information of the feature maps at different resolutions. Then the tasks of classification and regression are performed in multiple scales. The experimental results show that SDNN achieve state-of-the-art detection performance in a semi-supervised setting.

3   The Proposed Context-Based Object Detection Framework

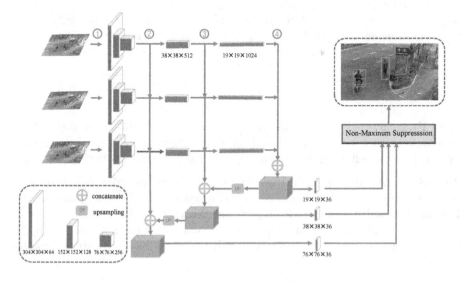

Fig. 1. Architecture of SDNN

Figure 1 gives an overview of the proposed SDNN. Note that three successive frames are used as the input, where only the center frame has annotated objects. Consequently, three pipelines are employed to obtain the feature maps of different scales. Moreover, we concatenate the last three layers of feature maps for classification and regression. Finally, Non-Maximum Suppression (NMS) is used to remove duplicate proposals.

Input Layer. As mentioned before, three successive frames have been selected to be the input of our network. Therefore, the network has three branches. It is worth noting that only the central one has label information, while the previous and the latter frames are unlabeled data, namely, the whole process is semi-supervised. In the proposed framework, it is possible to make full use of the context information of moving objects, such as contour, position, etc.

Backbone. We adopt a fully convolutional network that similar to Darknet-53 with no pooling layer structure. The reason is that pooling layer may lose significant feature information in the process of dimension reduction. Therefore, we set stride of $(2, 2)$ to achieve downsampling. Our convolution module consists of a convolution layer, a Batch Normalization (BN) layer and a Leaky Rectified Linear Unit (LReLU) layer. In the proposed framework, the Convolution + BN + LReLU (CBL) is a generic module. After the CBL module, the residual module is constructed by shortcut module. The advantage of this scheme is to avoid the notorious problem of vanishing/exploding gradients. The input of the whole network is $608 \times 608 \times 3$, where the three-output scale are respectively as 19×19, 38×38, and 76×76.

Context-Based Feature Fusion. In order to obtain high-level semantic features, our network adopts the context feature fusion scheme. The feature maps from different resolutions are acquired via downsampling, and the number of channels are increased after the concatenation. For example, the feature maps of size 19×19 are upsampling to 38×38 after step 4, then these maps are concatenated with the feature map of size 38×38 in the previous layer. In a similar manner, feature maps of 38×38 will be concatenated with 76×76 after upsampling. The concatenation scheme can fuse the features that extracted by three branches from different resolutions.

Bounding Boxes. Multi-scale feature maps obtained from the context feature fusion layer, are respectively with resolutions of 19×19, 38×38, and 76×76. We then generate the proposals with different resolutions. We generate 3 bounding boxes per cell, then the feature map has $19 \times 19 \times 3$ bounding boxes. Each bounding box needs to predict the coordinates (x, y), the size w and h, the confidence, and 7 classes in the dataset. Therefore, the number of channels of the above scales is $36(3 \times (4 + 1 + 7))$. Similarly, the remainder two feature maps generate three bounding boxes for each cell. As a consequent, the network returns 22743 bounding boxes. Instead of using SoftMax to predict object categories, we use logistic regression to predict output tensor. The advantage is that we can deal with overlapping multi-label problems.

4   Loss Function

Loss function is a prominent component in deep neural networks. In the task of object detection, the principle of loss function should be designed to optimize object localization and classification. Therefore, the loss function of our network contains three components, respectively as regression loss, confidence loss, and classification loss, given as the following equation.

$$Loss = \lambda_{coord} L_{reg} + L_{confidence} + L_{cls} \tag{1}$$

where λ_{coord} indicates the weight attached to regression loss. Typically, we found that $\lambda_{coord} = 5$ gives a promising trade-off between recall and precision.

4.1   Regression Loss

The first component is the predicted bounding boxes loss. The coordinates of bounding boxes are defined by 4 values, including the center coordinates (x, y) and the size parameters w, h. The location and the size are trained with a binary Cross Entropy (CE) and Sum-Square Error (SSE) loss:

$$L_{reg} = \sum_{l=1}^{L} \sum_{i=0}^{S_l^2} \sum_{j=0}^{B} \tau_{ij}^{obj} \cdot CE[(x_i, y_i), (\hat{x}_i, \hat{y}_i)] + \sum_{l=1}^{L} \sum_{i=0}^{S_l^2} \sum_{j=0}^{B} \tau_{ij}^{obj} \cdot SSE[(\sqrt{w_i}, \sqrt{h_i}), (\sqrt{\hat{w}_i}, \sqrt{\hat{h}_i})] \tag{2}$$

where CE indicates the center coordinates (x, y) loss, SSE represents the loss of the size of the bounding box. $l = 1, 2...L$, representing the number of feature maps at different scales. For example, as shown in Fig. 1, $L = 3$ since the size of feature maps are respectively with 19×19, 38×38, and 76×76, S_l^2 represents the number of cells in the feature map. B is the number of bounding boxes that predicted in each cell. The value of τ_{ij}^{obj} is 0 or 1, which indicates whether there is an object in the cell or not. In addition, $(\hat{x}, \hat{y}, \hat{w}, \hat{h})$ is a regressed bounding box, where (x, y, w, h) is ground truth label. In summary, the loss function combines the information of each bounding box from each feature map at different resolutions.

4.2   Confidence Loss

Confidence loss reflects the extent of how a proposal can be an object. The value of confidence usually ranges from 0 to 1. Note that there are two cases in our method. The first is the loss of the foreground object in the bounding box, and the second is the loss when the foreground object is not included in the bounding box. The details are shown in Eqs. (3) and (4)

$$L_{object} = \sum_{l=1}^{L} \sum_{i=0}^{S_l^2} \sum_{j=0}^{B} \tau_{ij}^{obj} \cdot CE(C_i, \hat{C}_i) \tag{3}$$

$$L_{noobj} = \lambda_{noobj} \sum_{l=1}^{L} \sum_{i=0}^{S_l^2} \sum_{j=0}^{B} \tau_{ij}^{noobj} \cdot CE(C_i, \hat{C}_i) \qquad (4)$$

$$L_{confidence} = L_{noobj} + L_{object} \qquad (5)$$

where C denotes the confidence score, $\hat{C}$ is the Intersection over Union (IoU) of the prediction bounding box and ground truth. In the session of experiments, we set the threshold of IoU = 0.5 and $\lambda_{noobj} = 0.5$, which are recommended by [12].

4.3   Classification Loss

The last component is used to represent the classification loss, where τ_{ij}^{obj} determines whether the center of the object falls in the ith cell. If a cell contains the center of an object, it is responsible for predicting the class probability of the object. c represents class information, $\hat{p}_i$ represents the predicted score for each box.

$$L_{cls} = \sum_{l=1}^{L} \sum_{i=0}^{S_l^2} \tau_i^{obj} \sum_{c \in classes} CE(p_i(c), \hat{p}_i(c)) \qquad (6)$$

5   Experiments

5.1   Dataset

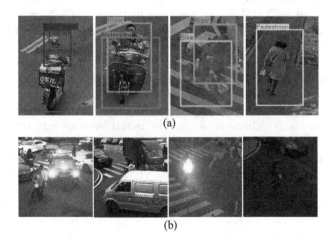

(a)

(b)

Fig. 2. (a) Categories in RIDER and (b) Complex scene of RIDER dataset (Color figure online)

Due to the limitations of previous dataset, we construct a new dataset called RIDER to evaluate our method. The dataset is derived from video surveillance in real-world scenarios, covering day-time, nightfall-time and rainy days. We extracted three consecutive frames of the original video based on the annotation information of RIDER dataset. Only the images belonging to RIDER dataset are labeled, and the other two are unlabeled. To sum up, our RIDER-context is made up of 13659 training sets and 1518 test sets. The RIDER dataset consists 7 categories, *Pedestrian, Rider, Electromobile, Bike, Helmet, Motorbike* and *Rider_trunc*. These categories are selected since they have a significant impact on Two-wheel vehicle monitoring system management. There are 15177 labeled images, including 13659 images for training and 1518 images for testing. As shown in Fig. 2, the labeled *Rider* (green rectangles) is characterized by a person driving a two-wheeled vehicle and the entire body is visible; *Rider_trunc* (purple rectangles) is characterized by people driving a two-wheeled vehicle but only part of body is visible; *Electromobile* (red rectangles) is characterized by a smaller size than the *Motorbike*, and the tire part is similar to a *Bike*; *Motorbike* (cyan rectangles) is characterized by its larger size and resemblance to the ship type; *Bike* (blue rectangles) is characterized by a simple structure and a narrow width; *Helmet* (pink rectangles) is a safety hat, which is elliptical; *Pedestrian* (yellow rectangles) is characterized by person walking on the road.

5.2   Baseline and Implementation Details

In order to verify the effectiveness of the proposed algorithm, we selected the mainstream methods, including Faster R-CNN [12], RetinaNet [16], YOLOv3 [14] and SSD [15] as the baseline. In Faster R-CNN, we use the pre-trained VGG16 model on ImageNet as the backbone network. The learning rate is 0.001, dimension of input image is $600 \times 1000 \times 3$. The training batch of Faster R-CNN is set to be 1. In YOLOv3, we use Darknet-53 as the backbone network. The initial learning rate is 0.001, the dimension of input image is $608 \times 608 \times 3$, the training batch is set to be 64, and the gradient descent momentum is 0.9. RetinaNet uses the Keras framework to implement the Resnet-50 model pre-trained on ImageNet as the backbone network. The initial learning rate is 0.00001, the dimension of input image is $600 \times 1000 \times 3$, and the training batch is set to be 1. The gradient descent momentum is 0.9. Last but not the least, SSD is implemented using the PyTorch framework. The VGG16 is also used as the backbone network. The dimension of input image is $300 \times 300 \times 3$, the initial learning rate is 0.0005, and the training batch is set to be 32. In the proposed SDNN, we use Darknet-53 as the backbone network. The initial learning rate is 0.001, the dimension of input image is $608 \times 608 \times 3$, the training batch is set to be 64. For all methods, the training and the testing process are conducted on NVIDIA 1080Ti (11 GB Memory), CUDA 9.0 and cuDNN 7.1.4.

5.3 Overall Accuracy Evaluation

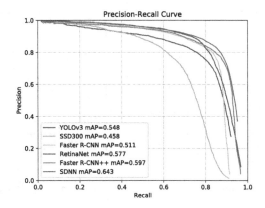

Fig. 3. Precision-Recall curves of the six algorithms

As shown in Fig. 3, the proposed SDNN achieved the best performance, considering the value mAP. The main reason is that we adopt semi-supervised learning with context information. Moreover, the fusion of multi-scale feature maps also plays an important role in the pipelines. The APs for each category are given in Table 1, note that our algorithm has achieved the best performance in the categories of *Pedestrian*, *Bike*, *Motorbike*, and *Rider_trunc*. However, there are still some categories that are not as good as the mainstream algorithms, such as *Rider* and *Electromobile*, and *Helmet*.

Table 1. The mAP and the AP on RIDER dataset based on different methods

Method	mAP	Pedestrian	Rider	Electromobile	Bike	Helmet	Motorbike	Rider_trunc
SSD [15]	0.458	0.673	0.763	0.826	0.467	0.118	0.189	0.174
YOLOv3 [14]	0.548	0.766	0.811	0.851	0.456	0.360	0.201	0.402
Faster R-CNN [12]	0.511	0.848	0.839	0.874	0.628	0.000	0.045	0.344
Faster R-CNN++	0.597	0.837	0.846	0.869	0.595	**0.449**	0.083	0.499
RetinaNet [16]	0.577	0.872	**0.872**	**0.917**	0.474	0.393	0.029	0.484
SDNN	**0.643**	**0.879**	0.801	0.877	**0.687**	0.400	**0.312**	**0.546**

5.4   The Evaluation on Different Categories

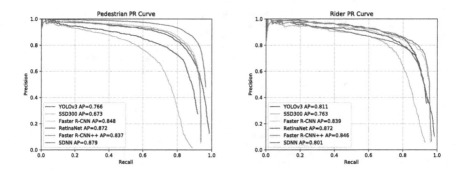

Fig. 4. The average precision on *Pedestrian* and *Rider*

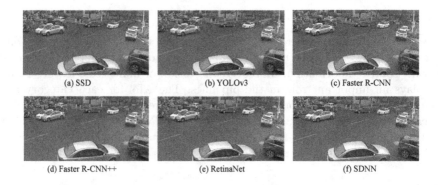

Fig. 5. The detection results on the position of *Rider*

In the first experiment, we will analyze the results of *Pedestrian*. Figure 4 shows the accuracy of each algorithm on the *Pedestrian*. Intuitively, our algorithm is significantly better than other algorithms. The second experiment was conducted on *Rider*. It is a challenging task since there are abundant *Rider* objects under video surveillance. Figure 5 shows the detection results of each algorithm on *Rider*. In this situation, SSD failed to detect the riders, which may be the IoU between prediction boxes and ground truth less than 0.5. The rest of the baselines are able to extract several bounding boxes. However, some methods such as YOLOv3 generates some false positives. On the other hand, Faster R-CNN, Faster R-CNN++ and RetinaNet all exist some missed objects. Figure 5(f) indicates that SDNN achieved better results on small and dense objects.

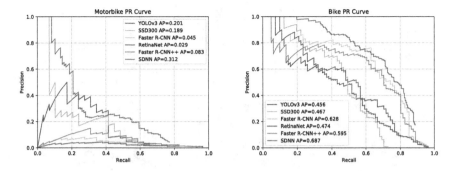

Fig. 6. The average precision on *Motorbike* and *Bike*

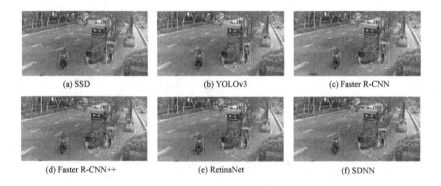

Fig. 7. The detection results on the position of *Motorbike*.

The third experiments including the categories of *Motorbike* and *Bike*. As shown in Fig. 6, SDNN significantly outperforms the rest methods. In Fig. 7, we select one typical image to show the detection results of each algorithm from *Motorbike*. Note that only the SDNN successfully extract motorbikes, without generating any false positive. The main reason may be that SDNN combines the features of the context, which has global information from time series, thus can distinguish slight difference in each category. Figure 8 shows the results of each algorithm on typical image including *Bike*. Note that SSD has poor detection results, which misses a large number of objects. The results of RetinaNet are similar to SSD. Also, there are some missing objects in YOLOv3 and Faster R-CNN. Fortunately, SDNN has the best results in this frame. Using the context information, the detector can extract object information well in the case of large differences between angular.

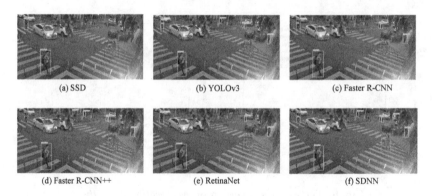

(a) SSD   (b) YOLOv3   (c) Faster R-CNN

(d) Faster R-CNN++   (e) RetinaNet   (f) SDNN

Fig. 8. The detection results on the position of *Bike*.

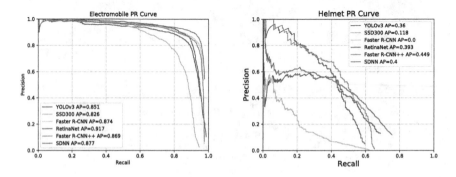

Fig. 9. The average precision on *Electromobile* and *Helmet*.

Figure 9 shows the P-R curves for the two categories of *Electromobile* and *Helmet*. Noteworthy that SDNN has no obvious advantages in both categories. However, the precision of the SDNN is higher than other methods when recall >0.6. Figure 10 shows the typical results of all methods for the two categories. As for *Electromobile*, YOLOv3 produce false detection, which regards *Electromobile* as *Motorbike*. The rest of four methods have missed detection. The SDNN succeed in detecting all electromobiles in Fig. 10(f). As for *Helmet*, the size are all very small, also the color and shape are variant. As a result, SSD, Faster R-CNN, RetinaNet are all failed to detect *Helmet*. It is worth noting that Faster R-CNN++ and YOLOv3 have a promising performance on small object detection. Fortunately, our SDNN can correctly extract the categories of *Electromobile* and *Helmet*. We can draw a conclusion that the multi-scale feature maps and context fusion can improve the accuracy of small and variant objects.

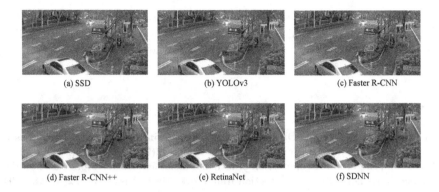

| (a) SSD | (b) YOLOv3 | (c) Faster R-CNN |
| (d) Faster R-CNN++ | (e) RetinaNet | (f) SDNN |

Fig. 10. The detection results on the position of *Electromobile* and *Helmet*.

5.5 Run Time Evaluation

We present the inference speed of SDNN and the state-of-the-art methods in Table 2. Since Faster R-CNN is a two-stage framework that generates a set of proposals based on the RPN, the run time is the slowest with 298 ms per image. On the other hand, RetinaNet uses the deep residual network ResNet as backbone network, the run time of a single image reaches 150 ms. Although the SSD is a one-stage framework, it uses multi-scale testing which generates a large number of boxes on the feature map for each scale, makes the run time reaches 116 ms for each image. It is noteworthy that YOLOv3 is one-stage detector and does not need to generate proposals. Therefore, YOLOv3 is faster than other methods. Last but not the least, the proposed SDNN with three frames as input takes about the same run time with YOLOv3.

Table 2. Run time comparison

Method	Average runtime (ms)
Faster R-CNN [12]	298
SSD300 [15]	116
YOLOv3 [14]	51
RetinaNet [16]	150
Ours	66

6 Conclusions

In this paper, we proposed a semi-supervised one-stage object detection framework based three successive frames in video surveillance systems. On the basis of Darknet, we conduct a multi-scale feature fusion scheme to improve the efficiency of detecting process. Experimental results on the RIDER dataset demonstrated that the proposed SDNN outperforms state-of-the-art methods, considering the mAP of all category. This high-performance detector can be effectively applied to security system. We believe that these promising results pave the way to numerous extensions.

References

1. Felzenszwalb, P.F., et al.: Object detection with discriminatively trained part based models. IEEE Trans. Pattern Anal. Mach. Intell. **32**(9), 1627–1645 (2010)
2. Castrilln, M., et al.: A comparison of face and facial feature detectors based on the Viola–Jones general object detection framework. Mach. Vis. Appl. **22**(3), 481–494 (2011)
3. Pang, Y., et al.: Efficient HOG human detection. Signal Process. **91**(4), 773–781 (2011)
4. Krizhevsky, A., Sutskever, I., Hinton, G.E.: Imagenet classification with deep convolutional neural networks. In: Advances in Neural Information Processing Systems (2012)
5. Papandreou, G., et al.: Weakly-and semi-supervised learning of a deep convolutional network for semantic image segmentation. In: Proceedings of the IEEE International Conference on Computer Vision (2015)
6. Lin, T.-Y., et al.: Microsoft COCO: common objects in context. In: Fleet, D., Pajdla, T., Schiele, B., Tuytelaars, T. (eds.) ECCV 2014. LNCS, vol. 8693, pp. 740–755. Springer, Cham (2014). https://doi.org/10.1007/978-3-319-10602-1_48
7. Everingham, M., et al.: The pascal visual object classes challenge: a retrospective. Int. J. Comput. Vis. **111**(1), 98–136 (2015)
8. Deng, J., et al.: Imagenet: a large-scale hierarchical image database. In: 2009 IEEE Conference on Computer Vision and Pattern Recognition. IEEE (2009)
9. Uijlings, J.R.R., et al.: Selective search for object recognition. Int. J. Comput. Vis. **104**(2), 154–171 (2013)
10. Girshick, R., et al.: Rich feature hierarchies for accurate object detection and semantic segmentation. In: Proceedings of the IEEE Conference on Computer Vision and Pattern Recognition (2014)
11. Girshick, R.: Fast R-CNN. In: Proceedings of the IEEE International Conference on Computer Vision (2015)
12. Ren, S., et al.: Faster R-CNN: towards real-time object detection with region proposal networks. In: Advances in Neural Information Processing Systems (2015)
13. Lin, T.-Y., et al.: Feature pyramid networks for object detection. In: Proceedings of the IEEE Conference on Computer Vision and Pattern Recognition (2017)
14. Redmon, J., Farhadi, A.: Yolov3: an incremental improvement. arXiv preprint arXiv:1804.02767 (2018)
15. Liu, W., et al.: SSD: single shot MultiBox detector. In: Leibe, B., Matas, J., Sebe, N., Welling, M. (eds.) ECCV 2016. LNCS, vol. 9905, pp. 21–37. Springer, Cham (2016). https://doi.org/10.1007/978-3-319-46448-0_2
16. Lin, T.-Y., et al.: Focal loss for dense object detection. In: Proceedings of the IEEE International Conference on Computer Vision (2017)
17. Law, H., Deng, J.: CornerNet: detecting objects as paired keypoints. In: Proceedings of the European Conference on Computer Vision (ECCV) (2018)
18. Liu, X., et al.: DFF, a heterodimeric protein that functions downstream of caspase-3 to trigger DNA fragmentation during apoptosis. Cell **89**(2), 175–184 (1997)

19. Mottaghi, R., et al.: The role of context for object detection and semantic segmentation in the wild. In: Proceedings of the IEEE Conference on Computer Vision and Pattern Recognition (2014)
20. Torralba, A., et al.: Context-based vision system for place and object recognition (2003)
21. Tu, Z.: Auto-context and its application to high-level vision tasks. In: 2008 IEEE Conference on Computer Vision and Pattern Recognition. IEEE (2008)

Machine Learning

YNBIRDS: A System for Fine-Grained Bird Image Recognition

Yili Zhao[✉] and Hua Zhou

School of Big Data and Intelligent Engineering, Southwest Forestry University,
Kunming 650224, China
ylzhao@swfu.edu.cn

Abstract. Fine-grained bird image recognition is a challenging computer vision problem, due to the small inter-class variations caused by highly similar subordinate categories, and the large intra-class variations in poses, scales and rotations. This paper proposes a deep convolution neural networks collaborated with semantic parts detection. The model consists of two modules, one module is a parts detector network, and another module is a three-stream classification network based on deep residual networks. In the meantime, a new bird images dataset was collected and labeled to facility the research of fine-grained bird image recognition. Experiment results on two challenging fine-grained bird species categorization datasets illustrate the proposed model has higher part detection and image classification accuracy comparing with state-of-the-arts fine-grained bird image recognition approaches. Based on the proposed model, we have designed an intelligent system which can recognize fine-grained bird image interactively and accurately.

Keywords: Fine-grained image recognition · Semantic parts detection · Convolutional neural networks

1 Introduction

Fine-grained recognition tasks such as identifying the species of a bird, have been popular in computer vision. Since the categories are all similar to each other, different categories can only be distinguished by slight and subtle differences, which makes fine-grained recognition a challenging problem. Compared to the general object recognition tasks, fine-grained recognition benefits more from learning critical parts of the objects, which helps discriminate different subclasses and align objects of the same class.

In order to recognize fine-grained images correctly, it is usually necessary for the observer to have some domain knowledge. As shown in Fig. 1, Narcissus Flycatcher and Yellow-rumped Flycatcher, both belong to the same Muscicapidae family and Ficedula genus, and the distinguishing features between them are mainly in the difference of eyebrow color.

Supported by NSFC 61662072.

(a) Narcissus Flycatcher   (b) Yellow-rumped Flycatcher

Fig. 1. Narcissus Flycatcher and Yellow-rumped Flycatcher recognition.

In this paper, we propose a three-stream model with joint semantic parts detection for fine-grained bird image recognition. We only require the part annotations and image-level labels during the training time. Given the part annotations, by treating part localization as a three-class detection task, we leverage SSD [11] to detect bird object, head and torso in the testing time for localizing semantic parts in a bird image. Based on these semantic parts, a three-stream convolutional neural networks is built for joint training and aggregating the object-level and part-level features simultaneously. The architecture of the proposed three-stream model is shown in Fig. 2. In each stream of model, we utilize the deep residual networks [6] as baseline model. After that, the feature vectors of these three streams are concatenated, and then a classification (fc+softmax) layer is added for end-to-end joint training.

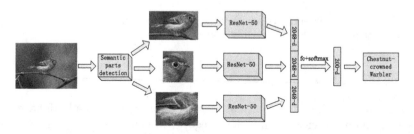

Fig. 2. Architecture of the proposed three-stream model. The three streams correspond to the object, head and torso respectively.

We validate the proposed three-stream model on the YUB and CUB datasets, in which we achieved 96.2% and 87.4% classification accuracy respectively. We also get accurate part localization (92.4% for head and 95.5% for torso). The key advantages and major contributions of the proposed model are:

1. We collected and labeled a new dataset for fine-grained bird image recognition. To the best of our knowledge, this is the first Chinese bird images dataset.

2. We present a novel and efficient part-based three-stream model for fine-grained recognition. Comparing with state-of-the-art methods, this model achieves 96.2% and 87.4% classification accuracy on the YUB and CUB datasets, respectively.
3. Based on this model, we developed YNBIRDS, a system for fine-grained bird image recognition. The system is available at http://ynbirds.swfu.edu.cn/.

2 Related Work

Fine-grained recognition is a challenging problem and has recently emerged as a hot topic in the computer vision. During the past few years, a number of effective fine-grained recognition methods have been developed in the literature. At present, according to the amount of supervised information used, we can roughly categorize these methods into two groups: strong supervised learning based model and weak supervised learning based model.

The methods in first group attempted to learn a more discriminative feature representation by integrating semantic parts bounding boxes, segmentation masks or semantic key points for classifying fine-grained bird image. Part R-CNN [23] firstly uses selective search [18] to generate candidate boxes in a bird image, then uses R-CNN [5] to localize three parts and geometric constraints to restrict the generated bounding boxes. The detected image patches are used as input to fine-tune the pre-trained convolutional neural networks. Finally, support vector machine is used to classify the extracted features. Pose normalized deep convolutional networks [1] firstly uses deformable part model to calculate bounding boxes at object level and part level through feature points, and aligns image patches at semantic part level. Secondly, convolution features of different layers in CNNs are extracted and cascaded as the representation of the whole image, and SVM is used for classification. Deep LAC [9] includes three components: semantic parts localization, alignment and classification. Among them, semantic parts localization is accomplished by directly regressing bounding boxes; then semantic parts are aligned by template matching, and localization, alignment and classification are connected through value link function for end-to-end training. SPDA-CNN [22] consists of convolution-shared semantic parts detection sub-net and parts abstraction and classification sub-net. In order to detect more small-scale semantic parts, it uses k-nearest neighbor to generate multiple candidate boxes and Fast R-CNN [4] to generate the final bounding box of semantic parts. Meanwhile, the parts abstraction and classification sub-nets of SPDA-CNN introduce semantic part RoI pooling layer, part-based fully connected layer and concatenation fully connected layer to perform end-to-end training. PS-CNN [7] uses fully convolutional networks [12] to locate the key points of semantic parts in a bird image, then uses two networks to process the object and semantic parts, and finally uses three sub-networks composed of fully connection layers as feature classifiers. PS-CNN pays more attention to the interpretability of the model. Mask-CNN [20] also uses fully convolutional networks to learn the segmentation mask of semantic parts, and combines the masks of two semantic parts to form object mask. Then three sub-networks are trained for classification based on object and part patches. In each sub-network, key convolution features of CNNs are filtered by using masks of semantic parts. Finally, the remaining features are averaged and pooled, and concatenated as the feature representation of the whole image.

The classification models based on strong supervised learning can achieve satisfactory classification accuracy, but the annotation of semantic parts, such as bounding boxes or key points, should be provided in the training process. In contrast, models based on weak supervised learning only use image-level annotation in model training. Bilinear-CNN [10] consists of a quadruple $B = (f_A, f_B, P, C)$, where f_A and f_B are feature functions, P is a pooling function, and C is a classification function. The output of these two feature functions can be aggregated by bilinear operation to obtain the final feature description. Attention-CNN [21] focuses on recognizing object and parts through attention mechanism. Firstly, it generates a large number of candidate regions from the input image and filters these regions and retains candidate regions mainly containing foreground objects. Secondly, a CNNs is trained to classify object-level images. Thirdly, features are extracted from candidate regions and spectral clustering of these features is used to obtain different clusters. Each cluster can be regarded as a local part. Constellation-CNN [15,16] visualizes the convolution features extracted by CNNs, and finds that some regions with strong response correspond to some potential local key points in the input image. Then, the local region features are extracted and classified according to these key points. SWFV-CNN [24] constructs complex features by selecting filters in CNNs. Firstly, it uses the selectivity of CNNs to mine the filter sensitive to some modes. Thus, a weakly supervised semantic parts detector is obtained, which is used as the initial value to train a more discriminant parts detection model. Secondly, deep convolutional features are extracted from image patches, and are pooled by space-weighted Fisher vector to get the final feature description. RA-CNN [3] proposes a novel recurrent attention convolutional neural network for fine-grained recognition without bounding box/part annotations. It recursively learns discriminative region attention and region-based feature representation in a mutually reinforced manner.

Compared with the fine-grained recognition model based on strong supervised learning, the best fine-grained recognition model based on weak supervised learning still has a certain gap in classification accuracy. However, the fine-grained recognition model based on weak supervised learning does not need labeling information of semantic parts, so it has unique advantages in network training.

3   Fine-Grained Bird Image Recognition

In this section, we present the proposed three-stream fine-grained image recognition model. Firstly, we discuss why the head and torso are selected as discriminative parts and why SSD [11] is used as the object/part detector. Then, based

Fig. 3. The YUB dataset.

on these bounding boxes, the three-stream model is built for joint training and capturing both object-level and part-level information.

3.1   Dataset

Compared with the dataset of general classification tasks, the fine-grained image dataset is more difficult to acquire, and requires professional domain knowledge to perform data collection and labeling. Currently, the canonical bird images dataset widely used in fine-grained image recognition research field is the CUB dataset [19], which contains 200 different categories of North American birds with a total of 11,788 bird images; among them, the training set includes 5,594 images and the test set includes 5,794 images. This dataset provides 15 keypoints and 1 bounding box for each image.

China is rich in wild bird resources, especially Yunnan Province is known as the "plant kingdom" and "animal kingdom". There are more than 1,300 wild birds totally in China, and there are more than 800 species in Yunnan Province, and it accounts for 60% of the total number of wild birds in China. The author collected 200 species of birds from wild birds in Yunnan Province for fine-grained bird recognition research, and this dataset contains 60 high-quality images in each class, and there are 12,000 images totally. This dataset is named YUB.

In order to compare with the CUB dataset, the YUB dataset was splitted in the same way as the CUB dataset. That is, 30 images were selected randomly from each class as training images, and the remaining 30 images as test images. Therefore, the training set or test set of the YUB dataset contains 6,000 bird images. In addition to the class labels, every image in the YUB dataset provides bounding boxes for the bird object, head and torso. The image mosaic by randomly selecting an image from 200 classes from the YUB dataset is illustrated as Fig. 3.

3.2 Discriminative Parts Selection

Since the differences between different bird species are mainly in the details of the local parts, the selection of the key parts is especially important for fine-grained bird image recognition. When CNNs is used to classify a bird image, the features extracted through the convolutional layers will lose position information after passing through the fully connected layers. However, the internal attention mechanism of CNNs can implicitly select the discriminative region of the bird image. Zhou *et al.* [25] proposed a method for discriminative localization based on weak supervised learning. Their method can locate the discriminative region of the image with only the image class label. For a given image, let $f_k(x, y)$ represent the activation value of the unit k in the last convolutional layer of the CNNs at the spatial position (x, y). For unit k, the output of the global average pooling layer is $F_k = \sum_{x,y} f_k(x, y)$. For a given class c, the input to the softmax classifier is $S_c = \sum_k w_k^c F_k$, where w_k^c is the weight corresponding to class c for unit k. The weight coefficient w_k^c can be considered as the importance of F_k for class c. Therefore, the input to the softmax classifier for class c is:

$$S_c = \sum_k w_k^c \sum_{x,y} f_k(x, y) = \sum_{x,y} \sum_k w_k^c f_k(x, y) \tag{1}$$

The class activation map M_c for class c can be defined as:

$$M_c(x, y) = \sum_k w_k^c f_k(x, y) \tag{2}$$

Thus the input to the softmax classifier can be represented as:

$$S_c = \sum_{x,y} M_c(x, y) \tag{3}$$

where M_c represents the importance of the activation at the spatial grid location (x, y) for CNNs to classify the image into class c.

In order to generate class activation maps, for AlexNet [8] and VGGNet [17], the fully connected layer before the last output layer of the network needs to be deleted and replaced with the global average pooling layer. However, removing the full connection layer will impact classification performance for the network. We select ResNet [6] as the main network architecture for fine-grained recognition of bird image, while ResNet uses global average pooling layer, so class activation maps can be generated without affecting the classification accuracy. Based on ResNet, the class activation map on the YUB dataset was computed to visualize the discriminative parts of the bird image. Figures 4, 5 and 6 show the and their corresponding discriminative parts. It can be seen that when using CNNs to classify the bird image, the most discriminating parts are head and torso of the bird. Therefore, we use these two semantic parts plus the bird object itself as the semantic parts for the fine-grained bird image recognition.

Fig. 4. Grey throated Babbler and its heatmap.

Fig. 5. Himalayan Bluetail and its heatmap.

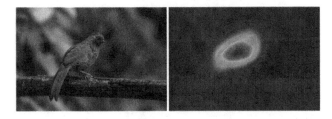

Fig. 6. Chestnut crowned Laughingthrush and its heatmap.

3.3   Discriminative Parts Detection

Currently, object detection based on deep learning is mainly divided into two categories: one is two-stage algorithm which includes candidate regions generation and classification, such as Faster R-CNN [14] and R-FCN [2]; The other is one-stage algorithm which generates the bounding box directly, such as YOLO [13] and SSD [11]. In order to select a suitable object detection algorithm as the discriminative semantic parts detector, we use PCP (percentage of correctly estimated body parts) based on IoU = 0.7 (intersection over union) as the semantic parts detector benchmark. The different object detection models are quantitatively evaluated on the YUB and CUB datasets. The results are shown in Tables 1 and 2. It can be seen that SSD has higher average detection accuracy for three semantic parts. Table 3 shows semantic parts detection results of single image by four detectors. It can be seen that SSD and YOLO have faster detection time compared with Faster R-CNN and R-FCN. Considering the semantic parts detection accuracy and time, this paper chooses SSD as the object detector for semantic parts.

Table 1. Parts detection on the YUB dataset

Method	Bird	Head	Torso
Faster R-CNN	98.6%	91.8%	94.7%
R-FCN	98.5%	94.2%	94.6%
YOLO	93.2%	79.4%	89.5%
SSD	98.2%	93.4%	95.1%

Table 2. Parts detection on the CUB dataset

Method	Bird	Head	Torso
Faster R-CNN	95.1%	76.2%	79.8%
R-FCN	95.2%	77.4%	80.9%
YOLO	76.3%	59.2%	60.1%
SSD	95.7%	78.9%	82.9%

Table 3. Parts detection time comparison

Method	Time
Faster R-CNN	111 ms
R-FCN	82 ms
YOLO	20 ms
SSD	21 ms

3.4   Model Training and Testing

After obtaining the object and part bounding boxes, we build a three-stream CNNs for joint training. The overall architecture of the proposed model is presented in Fig. 2. We take the head image stream as an example to illustrate the pipeline of each stream in the model.

The input of the head stream are the cropped head patch resized with 224×224. The resized patch is fed into a convolutional neural networks. Specifically, we use ResNet-50 pretrained on ImageNet as the baseline model. We obtain a $7 \times 7 \times 2048$ activation tensor in layer $res5c$ if the input image is 224×224. Then, a global average pooling layer $pool5$ with kernel size 7×7 to pool them into a 2048-d feature vector. After that, we concatenate them with object feature vector and torso feature vector as the final representation of the input image. Thus the aggregated feature vector includes both the object-level and part-level cues. In the classification step, the last layer of this three-stream model is a 200-way classification (fc+softmax) layer for classification on the YUB and CUB datasets. The three-stream model is learned end-to-end, with the parameters of three CNNs learned simultaneously. During training, the parameters of the learned SSD detection network are fixed.

During inference, when facing with a testing image, the learned SSD parts detector firstly returns the corresponding predictions for both object, head and torso. Then, based on the predicted bounding boxes, the extracted object, head and torso image patches are regarded as the inputs for the object, head and torso streams in the model. At last, the three-stream feature vectors are aggregated following the strategy in the training stage, and then we can get the predicted label based on the final image representation.

Table 4. Semantic parts detection on the CUB dataset

Method	Head	Torso
Part R-CNN [23]	61.4%	70.7%
Deep LAC [9]	74.0%	96.0%
SPDA-CNN [22]	93.4%	94.9%
MASK-CNN [20]	84.6%	89.8%
Proposed	**92.4%**	**95.5%**

4 Experiments

The GPU used in this experiment is NVIDIA Quadro GP100, which has 16 GB memory. We also used CUDA 9.0 with cuDNN 7.3. The operating system is Ubuntu 16.04, and Caffe was used to train the network.

4.1 Semantic Parts Detection Comparison

The accuracy of the semantic parts detection of different methods on the CUB dataset is compared. When the IoU threshold is 0.5, the PCP results are shown in Table 4. It can be seen that the detection accuracy for bird head is 92.4%, and the detection accuracy for the bird torso is 95.5% respectively.

4.2 Classification Accuracy Comparison

In this section, we compare the proposed method with state-of-the-arts on the YUB and CUB datasets, respectively. The comparison results are shown in Table 5. Due to the precise detection of semantic parts and features of different semantic parts are aggregated, the classification accuracy of the proposed method on these two datasets are 96.2% and 87.4% respectively.

We also investigate what different streams contribute to the final recognition performance. Table 6 reports the classification accuracy of different streams on the YUB and CUB datasets. When it only has the bird stream, on the YUB dataset, the accuracy is 91.2%. By incorporating the head and torso stream,

Table 5. Classification accuracy on the YUB and CUB datasets

Method	YUB	CUB
SWFV-CNN [24]	80.3%	75.2%
Part R-CNN [23]	75.8%	70.7%
Deep LAC [9]	84.6%	80.3%
SPDA-CNN [22]	91.7%	85.1%
PS-CNN [7]	81.2%	76.2%
MASK-CNN [20]	93.4%	85.2%
Attention-CNN [21]	83.6%	77.9%
Bilinear-CNN [10]	91.3%	84.1%
Constellation-CNN [15]	89.7%	81.0%
Proposed	**96.2%**	**87.4%**

Table 6. Different streams classification comparison

Dataset	Bird	Head	Torso	Accuracy
YUB	✓			91.2%
YUB	✓	✓		94.4%
YUB	✓		✓	92.9%
YUB	✓	✓	✓	96.2%
CUB	✓			82.1%
CUB	✓	✓		85.8%
CUB	✓		✓	83.7%
CUB	✓	✓	✓	87.4%

the accuracy increases to 96.2%. After incorporating the head stream, the original bird stream can improve 3.2%. However, incorporating the torso stream, it just increases 1.7% accuracy. We can find the head stream could be more discriminative than the torso stream. This observation is consistent with the CUB dataset.

4.3   The YNBIRDS System

Based on the proposed model, we have developed YNBIRDS, an intelligent system for fine-grained bird image recognition. Users of this system can upload their photo and the system will return recognition results automatically. The results include kingdom, phylum, class, order, family, genus, species and geographical distribution of the bird. The system is available at http://ynbirds.swfu.edu.cn/.

5   Conclusion

This paper proposes a fine-grained bird images recognition system with joint semantic parts detection. After using the SSD-based detection network to locate the semantic parts of the bird image, the object-level and part-level features were encoded by the proposed three-stream model. A high-quality fine-grained bird images dataset was collected and labeled for the fine-grained recognition of bird images. Bird species classification and semantic parts detection accuracy are quantitatively compared on the YUB and CUB datasets with other state-of-the-art methods. The experimental results show that the model has high accuracy in both of semantic parts detection and fine-grained classification.

In the future, we plan to explore the parts detection problem in the weakly supervised setting, in which we only require the image-level labels. Thus, it will require far less labeling effort to achieve comparable classification accuracy. In addition, we are also interested in other research of the YUB dataset usage like instance segmentation.

References

1. Branson, S., Van Horn, G., Perona, P., Belongie, S.: Improved bird species recognition using pose normalized deep convolutional nets. In: Proceedings of the British Machine Vision Conference (BMVC), pp. 1–14. BMVA Press, Nottingham (2014)
2. Dai, J., Li, Y., He, K., Sun, J.: R-FCN: object detection via region-based fully convolutional networks. In: Proceedings of Advances in Neural Information Processing Systems (NIPS), pp. 379–387. Curran Associates, Barcelona (2016)
3. Fu, J., Zheng, H., Mei, T.: Look closer to see better: recurrent attention convolutional neural network for fine-grained image recognition. In: Proceedings of the IEEE Conference on Computer Vision and Pattern Recognition (CVPR), pp. 4438–4446. IEEE, Hawaii (2017)
4. Girshick, R.: Fast R-CNN. In: Proceedings of the IEEE International Conference on Computer Vision (ICCV), pp. 1440–1448. IEEE, Santiago (2015)
5. Girshick, R., Donahue, J., Darrell, T., Malik, J.: Rich feature hierarchies for accurate object detection and semantic segmentation. In: Proceedings of the IEEE Conference on Computer Vision and Pattern Recognition (CVPR), pp. 580–587. IEEE, Ohio (2014)
6. He, K., Zhang, X., Ren, S., Sun, J.: Deep residual learning for image recognition. In: Proceedings of the IEEE Conference on Computer Vision and Pattern Recognition (CVPR), pp. 770–778. IEEE, Las Vegas (2016)
7. Huang, S., Xu, Z., Tao, D., Zhang, Y.: Part-stacked CNN for fine-grained visual categorization. In: Proceedings of the IEEE Conference on Computer Vision and Pattern Recognition (CVPR), pp. 1173–1182. IEEE, Las Vegas (2016)
8. Krizhevsky, A., Sutskever, I., Hinton, G.E.: Imagenet classification with deep convolutional neural networks. In: Proceedings of Advances in Neural Information Processing Systems (NIPS), pp. 1097–1105. Curran Associates, Nevada (2012)
9. Lin, D., Shen, X., Lu, C., Jia, J.: Deep LAC: deep localization, alignment and classification for fine-grained recognition. In: Proceedings of the IEEE Conference on Computer Vision and Pattern Recognition (CVPR), pp. 1666–1674. IEEE, Boston (2015)

10. Lin, T.Y., RoyChowdhury, A., Maji, S.: Bilinear CNN models for fine-grained visual recognition. In: Proceedings of IEEE International Conference on Computer Vision (ICCV), pp. 1449–1457. IEEE, Santiago (2015)
11. Liu, W., et al.: SSD: single shot MultiBox detector. In: Leibe, B., Matas, J., Sebe, N., Welling, M. (eds.) ECCV 2016. LNCS, vol. 9905, pp. 21–37. Springer, Cham (2016). https://doi.org/10.1007/978-3-319-46448-0_2
12. Long, J., Shelhamer, E., Darrell, T.: Fully convolutional networks for semantic segmentation. In: Proceedings of the IEEE Conference on Computer Vision and Pattern Recognition (CVPR), pp. 3431–3440. IEEE, Boston (2015)
13. Redmon, J., Divvala, S., Girshick, R., Farhadi, A.: You only look once: Unified, real-time object detection. In: Proceedings of the IEEE Conference on Computer Vision and Pattern Recognition (CVPR), pp. 779–788. IEEE, Las Vegas (2016)
14. Ren, S., He, K., Girshick, R., Sun, J.: Faster R-CNN: towards real-time object detection with region proposal networks. IEEE Trans. Pattern Anal. Mach. Intell. (TPAMI) 39(6), 1137–1149 (2017)
15. Simon, M., Rodner, E.: Neural activation constellations: unsupervised part model discovery with convolutional networks. In: Proceedings of IEEE International Conference on Computer Vision (ICCV), pp. 1143–1151. IEEE, Santiago (2015)
16. Simon, M., Rodner, E., Denzler, J.: Part detector discovery in deep convolutional neural networks. In: Cremers, D., Reid, I., Saito, H., Yang, M.-H. (eds.) ACCV 2014. LNCS, vol. 9004, pp. 162–177. Springer, Cham (2015). https://doi.org/10.1007/978-3-319-16808-1_12
17. Simonyan, K., Zisserman, A.: Very deep convolutional networks for large-scale image recognition. CoRR abs/1409.1556 (2014). http://arxiv.org/abs/1409.1556
18. Uijlings, J.R., Sande, K.E., Gevers, T., Smeulders, A.W.: Selective search for object recognition. Int. J. Comput. Vis. (IJCV) 104(2), 154–171 (2013)
19. Wah, C., Branson, S., Welinder, P., Perona, P., Belongie, S.: The Caltech-UCSD Birds-200-2011 Dataset. Technical report CNS-TR-2011-001, California Institute of Technology (2011)
20. Wei, X.S., Xie, C.W., Wu, J.: Mask-CNN: localizing parts and selecting descriptors for fine-grained image recognition. Pattern Recogn. 76, 704–714 (2018)
21. Xiao, T., Xu, Y., Yang, K., Zhang, J., Peng, Y., Zhang, Z.: The application of two-level attention models in deep convolutional neural network for fine-grained image classification. In: Proceedings of IEEE Conference on Computer Vision and Pattern Recognition (CVPR), pp. 842–850. IEEE, Boston (2015)
22. Zhang, H., et al.: SPDA-CNN: unifying semantic part detection and abstraction for fine-grained recognition. In: Proceedings of the IEEE Conference on Computer Vision and Pattern Recognition (CVPR), pp. 1143–1152. IEEE, Las Vegas (2016)
23. Zhang, N., Donahue, J., Girshick, R., Darrell, T.: Part-based R-CNNs for fine-grained category detection. In: Fleet, D., Pajdla, T., Schiele, B., Tuytelaars, T. (eds.) ECCV 2014. LNCS, vol. 8689, pp. 834–849. Springer, Cham (2014). https://doi.org/10.1007/978-3-319-10590-1_54
24. Zhang, X., Xiong, H., Zhou, W., Lin, W., Tian, Q.: Picking deep filter responses for fine-grained image recognition. In: Proceedings of the IEEE Conference on Computer Vision and Pattern Recognition (CVPR), pp. 1134–1142. IEEE, Las Vegas (2016)
25. Zhou, B., Khosla, A., Lapedriza, A., Oliva, A., Torralba, A.: Learning deep features for discriminative localization. In: Proceedings of the IEEE Conference on Computer Vision and Pattern Recognition (CVPR), pp. 2921–2929. IEEE, Las Vegas (2016)

Quadratic Approximation Greedy Pursuit for Cardinality-Constrained Sparse Learning

Fanfan Ji$^{(\boxtimes)}$, Hui Shuai, and Xiao-Tong Yuan

Jiangsu Key Laboratory of Big Data Analysis Technology, School of Automation, Nanjing University of Information Science and Technology, Nanjing 210044, China
Jiff1995@nuist.edu.cn

Abstract. An efficient sparse model is very significant to handle the highly or super-highly dimensional data. The optimization algorithms in solving the sparsity constraint problem have been progressively improved. In this paper, we propose a new quadratic approximation greedy pursuit algorithm (QAGP) for ℓ_0-constrained minimization with linear models. Our method first constructs an upper bound to the linear model at each iteration once the cost function of the model is L-Smooth, then we apply greedy pursuit to search the feasible solution of the upper bound. Compared to the Newton-type methods, our method does not need to calculate the Hessian matrix. We analyze the convergence of our method and verify the efficiency of it in sparse logistic regression and sparse L_2-SVMs tasks on synthetic and real datasets. The results demonstrate that the performance of our method is superior to other methods.

Keywords: Sparse model · Optimization algorithms · QAGP · Linear model · L-Smooth

1 Introduction

Billions of data is generated every day, which sources from videos, images, texts to electronic and neuroscience data. Mining the valuable information from the high-dimensional data is a hot topic for sparsity models, which is very challenging because of the statistical and computational perspectives. Estimating of linear model parameters with sparse structure is usually cast as an optimization problem which can be formulated as:

$$\min_{w \in \mathbb{R}^p} F(x^\top w) = \frac{1}{n} \sum_{i=1}^{n} f(x_i^\top w), \text{ s.t. } \|w\|_0 \leq k, \tag{1}$$

Fanfan Ji is currently working toward the Master degree in the School of Automation, Nanjing University of Information Science and Technology.

where $f(x_i^\top w)$ is a convex and smooth loss function of the linear model (e.g. linear regression, logistic regression, support vector machine (SVM), etc). $\|w\|_0$ denotes the number of nonzero entries in w. Because of the cardinality constraint on independent variable w, the problem (1) is not only non-convex, but also NP-hard in general [14]. Thus, it is impractical to solve this problem unless to seek an approximate solution.

1.1 Related Work

If the models are the least square regression models, the solution to the problem (1) will be very important in the area of Compression Sensing (CS) [8]. A large amount of efficient algorithms have been proposed. Iterative Hard Thresholding (IHT) [5], which performed hard thresholding on the variables iteratively to find the optimal solutions. Many existing literatures have applied the IHT algorithm in their work and make excellent results. Needell et al. [15] proposed Compressive Sampling Matching Pursuit (CoSaMP), whose basic idea was that firstly finding an approximate feasible domain and then finding the best vector fits the measurement in this domain. Foucart [9] proposed an iterative algorithm by combining the IHT algorithm and the CoSaMP algorithm to find sparse solutions under certain conditions, which is called Hard Thresholding Pursuit. Many existing literatures have applied the IHT algorithm in their work and make excellent results. Yuan et al. [17,19] performed hard thresholding on the parameters after the parameters were updated at each iteration. Applying a special way of sampling, Zhou et al. [21] proposed an HSG-HT and applied the heavy ball acceleration technique to improve the convergence rates. Based on the Stochastic Variance Reduces Gradient (SVRG) [10], Li et al. [13] performed the hard thresholding operation on the parameters, which achieved a better iteration complexity for high-dimensional sparse estimation and a more efficient result. The several above algorithms all utilize the gradient information which is called first-order information. Several literatures introduced second-order information together with iterative IHT in their algorithms. In contrast, second-order algorithms can achieve faster convergence rates than first-order algorithms. Yuan et al. [18] proposed Newton Greedy Pursuit (NTGP) method, which was a quadratic approximation greedy selection method for sparity-constrained algorithms, whose main idea was to construct a proximate objective function based on the second-order Taylor expansion and applied IHT on the parameters at each iteration. Although NTGP can achieve sound result, the huge calculation of Hessian matrix is inevitable. Combining the idea of Lissa [1] and IHT, Chen and Gu [7] proposed a method that used an unbiased stochastic Hessian estimator for the inverse Hessian matrix, which can significantly reduce the calculation.

Inspired by the efficiency of NTGP method, we propose a new quadratic approximation greedy pursuit method (QAGP) in this paper. We find a new way to approach the Hessian matrix and provide the theoretical analysis to prove the feasibility. If the loss function of a linear model is L-Smooth, the second derivative of the loss function will have an upper bound. Under this prerequisite, we can construct a square matrix to replace the Hessian matrix and the square matrix is related to the data samples. We approximate the quadratic term bases on the square matrix. Then we propose an iterative method to find the optimal parameters of the approximation. Like the above methods, the IHT method is also applied in our algorithm to solve the ℓ_0-constraint problem.

1.2 Contributions and Organization

Our contributions of this paper are summarized as follows: (i) We propose a new algorithm (QAGP) that can be applied to linear model, and we also give a simple convergence analysis for our method. (ii) Our method does not need to calculate the Hessian matrix, which is more practical in computation complexity compared with other second-order methods. What's more, our method can be performed to some linear models that have complicated Hessian matrix or have no Hessian matrix. (iii) As the experiments results show, our proposed algorithm outperforms the first-order algorithms and has the best performance in some cases. (iv) Our algorithm can reach an acceptable point faster than other methods. Therefore, under the circumstance when high precision is unnecessary, the proposed method is more practical.

The arrangement of the following part of the paper is as follows: In Sect. 2, we give an introduction to our method and compare our method with NTGP/QNTGP. Then we show the results of the application of our method to the spare logistic regression and spare L_2-SVMs in Sect. 3. Finally, we conclude our article in Sect. 4.

Notation. We set $w \in \mathbb{R}^d$ as the parameter vector and $k \in N$ is a positive integer denotes the sparsity. We define $X \in \mathbb{R}^{d \times n}$ is the data samples where n and d denote the number of samples and features, $x \in \mathbb{R}^d$ is one feature sample and y is the label of the sample. Finally, I represents the identity matrix of compatible size.

2 The Proposed Algorithm

In this section, we start briefly by showing the derivation process of QAGP, then we introduce our method to solve the sparse constraint problem. Next we will describe the convergence of the method. At last, we will analyse the difference between QAGP and NTGP/QNTGP.

2.1 The New Quadratic Greedy Pursuit Algorithm

Definition 1(L-Smooth). Suppose that f satisfies that

$$f(\beta) \leq f(\hat{\beta}) + \nabla f(\hat{\beta})(\beta - \hat{\beta}) + \frac{L}{2}\|\beta - \hat{\beta}\|^2.$$

Then we say that f is L-Smooth.

Our method derives from the classical constrained Newton method [3]. The constrained Newton method minimizes a convex and linear objective f at each iteration:

$$\min_{w} F(x^\top w), \text{ s.t. } \|w\|_0 \leq k, \tag{2}$$

where $F(x^\top w) = \frac{1}{n}\sum_{i=1}^{n} f(x_i^\top w)$. Suppose f is L-Smooth, we can get that

$$f(x_i^\top w) \leq f(x_i^\top w^{(t)}) + \nabla f(x_i^\top w^{(t)})^\top (x_i^\top w - x_i^\top w^{(t)})$$
$$+ \frac{L}{2}(x_i^\top w - x_i^\top w^{(t)})^\top (x_i^\top w - x_i^\top w^{(t)}), \tag{3}$$

where $\nabla f(x_i^\top w^{(t)})$ is the gradient of f with $x^\top w$ at t-th iteration. Next we let $Q_i(w; w^{(t)})$ be a function with parameter vector w and $w^{(t)}$,

$$Q_i(w; w^{(t)}) = f(x_i^\top w^{(t)}) + \nabla f(x_i^\top w^{(t)})^\top x_i^\top (w - w^{(t)})$$
$$+ \frac{L}{2}(w - w^{(t)})^\top A_i (w - w^{(t)}), \tag{4}$$

where $L \in \mathbb{R}$ is a scalar, and we set $A_i = x_i x_i^\top \in \mathbb{R}^{d \times d}, A = \frac{1}{n}\sum_{i=1}^{n} A_i = \frac{1}{n}XX^\top$ is a square matrix which only relates to the data sample. In conclusion, we can get that

$$F(x^\top w) = \frac{1}{n}\sum_{i=1}^{n} f(x_i^\top w) \leq \frac{1}{n}\sum_{i=1}^{n} Q_i(w; w^{(t)}) = Q(w; w^{(t)}). \tag{5}$$

Thus, we can minimize the objective function f through seeking the optimal solution $\tilde{w}$ to its upper bound Q.

We present the global architecture of our method in Algorithm 1.

Algorithm 1: Quadratic Approximation Greedy Pursuit(QAGP).

Input: sparsity k
Output: $w^{(t)}$
Initialization: $w^{(0)}$ with $\|w^{(0)}\|_0 \leq k$;
for $t = 1, 2, ...,$ **do**

Find any $w^{(t)}$ with $\|w^{(t)}\|_0 \leq k$ such that for all $\bar{\theta}$ with $\|\bar{\theta}\|_0 \leq k$,

$$Q(w^{(t)}; w^{(t-1)}) \leq Q(\bar{\theta}; w^{(t-1)}) + \epsilon. \tag{6}$$

where $\epsilon \geq 0$ controls the precision of solution.

2.2 The ℓ_0-Constrained Model

In order to solve the problem (6) at t-th iteration, which can be modeled as:

$$\min_{w} Q(w; w^{(t-1)}), \text{ s.t. } \|w\|_0 \leq k, \tag{7}$$

which is a typical CS problem [8]. We have mentioned many proposed algorithms in the previous part of this paper. Here we resort the IHT [5] method. The procedure of the algorithm is shown in Algorithm 2.

The step 1 is a normal gradient descent procedure and the η is the step size. The Step 2 is a hard thresholding operation and the operator $supp(\theta, k)$ is defined as follows:

$$supp(\theta, k) = \begin{cases} \theta_i, & \text{if } abs(\theta_i) \text{ is in the top } k \text{ (in magnitude) entries,} \\ 0, & \text{otherwise.} \end{cases}$$

The last step is a procedure of fine tuning actually. We tune nonzero entries of the parameters actually and we utilize the line search to find the optimal solution.

Algorithm 2: IHT for solving the problem(7)

Input: The cost function Q, the sparsity k
Output: The optimal value w
Initialization: $w^{(0)} = w^{(t)}$
for $\tau = 1, 2, ...,$ **do**
  Step1:Compute the gradient descent:
  $\tilde{w}^{(\tau)} = w^{(\tau-1)} - \eta\nabla Q(w; w^{(\tau-1)})$,
  Step2:Perform hard thresholding operation on $\tilde{w}^{(\tau)}$:
  $T^\tau = supp(\tilde{w}^{(\tau)}, k)$,
  Step3: Minimizer over the support:
  $w^{(\tau)} = \arg\min_{supp(w) \subseteq T^\tau} Q(w; w^{(\tau-1)})$.

2.3 Comparison with NTGP/QNTGP Method

NTGP/QNTGP [18] are Newton-type greedy selection methods to solve ℓ_0-constrained minimization problems which also derives from constrained Newton method [3]. The central of these methods are that constructing a quadratic approximation to the objective function f at each iteration by the second-order Taylor expansion:

$$\begin{aligned} Q_{(Q)NTGP}(w; w^{(t)}) = f(w^{(t)}) + \nabla f(w^{(t)})^\top (w - w^{(t)}) \\ + \frac{1}{2}(w - w^{(t)})^\top H(w - w^{(t)}), \end{aligned} \tag{8}$$

where $\nabla f(w^{(t)})$ is the gradient of function f at $w^{(t)}$. H is the quadratic entries, $H_{NTGP} = \nabla^2 f(w^{(t)})$ and H_{QNTGP} is an approximation of $\nabla^2 f(w^{(t)})$ that constructed according to L-BFGS rules [6].

While the approximation of our method is that:

$$Q_{QAGP}(w; w^{(t)}) = \frac{1}{n} \sum_{i=1}^{n} [f(x_i^\top w^{(t)}) + \nabla f(x_i^\top w^{(t)})^\top x_i^\top (w - w^{(t)})$$

$$+ \frac{L}{2}(w - w^{(t)})^\top A_i(w - w^{(t)})]. \tag{9}$$

Compare (8) and (9), the main difference between this two methods is the quadratic entries. We can take sparse logistic regression and sparse L_2-SVMs as examples.

Sparse Logistic Regression: The sparse logistic regression is a very common linear regression analysis model and is widely applied in pattern recognition and machine learning [4]. In this model, we let $x \in R^d$ be a random feature vector, $\bar{w} \in R^d$ be the parameter vector, and $y \in \{-1, 1\}$ be its associated random binary label generates randomly according to Bernoulli distribution:

$$\mathbb{P}(y|x; \bar{w}) = \frac{\exp(2yx^\top \bar{w})}{1 + \exp(2yx^\top \bar{w})}. \tag{10}$$

Given a set of n independently drawn data samples $\{(x_i, y_i)\}_{i=1}^{n}$, logistic regression learns the optimal w by minimizing the loss function:

$$l(w) := \frac{1}{n} \sum_{i=1}^{n} \log(1 + \exp(-2y_i x_i^\top w)). \tag{11}$$

In practical scenes, the ℓ_2-regularization is usually joint with the cost function [2], together with the ℓ_0-constraint, the cost function conventionally used in high-dimensional analysis is:

$$\min_w f(w) = l(w) + \frac{\lambda}{2}\|w\|_2^2, \text{ s.t. } \|w\|_0 \le k, \tag{12}$$

where $\lambda > 0$ is the user-defined regularization penalty. Obviously $f(w)$ is in accordance with the criterion of strong convexity, thus it has unique minimum. The ℓ_0-constraint enforces sparse solution.

To apply NTGP, we need to calculate the $\nabla f(w^{(t)})$ and the $\nabla^2 f(w^{(t)})$. If the expression of the sigmoid function is $\sigma(z) = 1/(1 + exp(-z))$, we can get that $\nabla f(w) = \frac{-2}{n} \sum_{i=1}^{n} y_i(1 - \sigma(2y_i x_i^\top w))x_i + \lambda w$ and $\nabla^2 f(w) = \frac{4}{n} \sum_{i=1}^{n} \sigma(2y_i x_i^\top w)(1 - \sigma(2y_i x_i^\top w))x_i x_i^\top + \lambda I$. While applying QAGP in sparse logistic regression model, we need to access the product of $\nabla f(x_i^\top w)$ and the feature vector x_i, and the square matrix $A = \frac{1}{n} \sum_{i=1}^{n} x_i x_i^\top$. It is easy to compute the entries: $\nabla f(x_i^\top w)x_i = \frac{-2}{n} \sum_{i=1}^{n} y_i(1 - \sigma(-2y_i x_i^\top w))^\top x_i + \lambda w$, and we set $L \in (0, 1]$. In summary, our method consists a simpler quadratic entry, which only relates to the data samples and saves a large amount of calculation.

Sparse L_2-SVMs: SVMs are supervised learning models that widely applied for classification and regression analysis. The cost function of SVMs can be described as follows:

$$\min_w f(w) = \frac{1}{2n} \sum_{i=0}^{n} (\max\{0, 1 - y_i x_i^\top w\})^2 + \frac{\lambda}{2} \|w\|_2^2, \text{ s.t. } \|w\|_0 \le k, \qquad (13)$$

where $\frac{\lambda}{2}\|w\|_2^2$ is the regularization. For L_2-SVMs, $f(w)$ is λ-strongly convex and the ℓ_0-constraint enforces the sparse solution. Because the special structure of the loss function, $f(w)$ is not second-order smooth and thus the NTGP algorithm cannot be applied directly. Alternatively, Yuan et al. [18] propose QNTGP that adopting L-BFGS method to construct the Hessian matrix [6], which is a little complicated. However, our method does not need to calculate the Hessian matrix, which can save lots of sources.

2.4 Convergence Analysis

In this section, we describe briefly the convergence of our method. Considering at t-th iteration, we get the optimal solution $w^{(t)}$, which is:

$$w^{(t)} = \arg\min_w Q(w; w^{(t-1)}),$$

so we can get that

$$Q(w^{(t)}; w^{(t-1)}) \le Q(w^{(t-1)}; w^{(t-1)}) = f(w^{(t-1)}) \le Q(w^{(t-1)}; w^{(t-2)}). \quad (14)$$

Thus, we can get that $Q(w; w^{(t-1)})$ is monotone decreasing. From Sect. 2 we get that the f is L-Smooth, so we can conclude that:

$$Q(w; w^{(t)}) \ge \min_w f(w).$$

In summary, we can conclude that $Q(w, w^{(t)})$ is convergent. We plot the logistic regression model value curve, which is shown in Fig. 1(a).

3 Experiments

To prove the theoretical results and opinions in Sect. 4, we conduct experiments on two models: Sparse Logistic Regression and Sparse L_2-SVMs. All the experiments are implemented in Matlab 2017b running on a desktop with i7-4790 CPU @3.60 GHz and 20 GB RAM.

3.1 Datasets

In this section, we show the datasets we employed in the experiments.

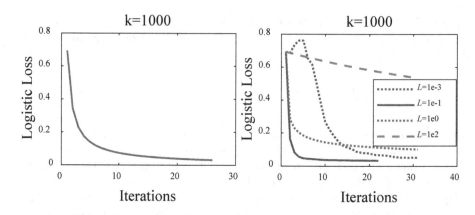

Fig. 1. The sparse logistic regression on synthetic data with the sparsity of 1000: **(a)** The value curves vs iterations (left). **(b)** The value curves vs various L values (right).

Synthetic Data: We generate the data sample x that subject to the normal distribution. The sparse parameter vector $\bar{w}$ is a d dimensional vector. The data labels $y \in \{-1, 1\}$ are generated randomly according to Bernoulli distribution:

$$\mathbb{P}(y = 1|x; \bar{w}) = \frac{\exp(2x^\top \bar{w})}{1 + \exp(2x^\top \bar{w})}, \tag{15}$$

In synthetic data experiment, we generate 4 groups of data: (i) $n = 2,000, d = 5,000$ and $k = 1,500$; (ii) $n = 4,800, d = 8,000$ and $k = 1,500$; (iii) $n = 3,000, d = 10,000$ and $k = 5,000$; (iv) $n = 6,000, d = 15,000$ and $d = 3,000$. We train the sparse logistic regression model with the synthetic data.

RCV1 Data: Reuters Corpus Volume I (RCV1) is an archive of over 800,000 manually categorized newswire stories recently made available by Reuters, Ltd [12]. This dataset contains 47,236 features, 20,242 training samples and 677,399 testing samples. We use all the training instances for the training step and 20,000 training instances for the testing progress. The dataset is applied to the sparse logistic regression.

20Newsgroups Data: The 20 Newsgroups data is a collection of approximately 20,000 newsgroup documents, partitioned nearly across 20 different newsgroups [11]. This dataset has become a popular dataset in many machine learning experiments. The dataset contains 10,000 training instances with 1,355,191 features and 9,996 testing instances. We perform L_2-SVMs model on this dataset with the corresponding number of training and testing.

3.2   Baseline Methods

We compare our algorithm with the following sparsity constraint optimization algorithms.

NTGP/QNTGP: These two Newton-type greedy selection methods [18] have solved the sparsity constraint problem by constructing a second-order Taylor expansion to approximate the objective function at each iteration. We compare our method with NTGP for the Logistic Regression model and QNTGP method for the L_2-SVMs model.

FoBa: The greedy algorithm combines the forward and backward selection to investigate the problems of learning sparse representations [20]. We compare our algorithm with the method in the synthetic data and real data experiments.

FCFGS: The authors [16] propose a forward greedy selection method that sparsify a given estimate of the objective function through the trade-off between sparsity and accuracy. We compare our method with this method on synthetic data ans 20Newgroup data.

GraHTP: The algorithm is to perform the hard thresholding operation in each gradient descent iteration [19]. We compare our method with this method on both synthetic and real data.

3.3   The Parameters Setting

In this section, we show the setting of two parameters: the coefficient L and the coefficient of the loss function regularization λ. We uniformly set $\lambda = 10^{-5}$ in sparse logistic regression and $\lambda = 10^{-4}$ in sparse L_2-SVMs experiments according to [18]. We need to tune the L in different models and various sparsity. If the value of L is too small, the loss will be unstable even oscillating and if the value is too large, the loss will decline slowly (as shown in Fig. 1b). In our experiments, we tune L until we achieve the sound result. For sparse logistic regression on the synthetic data, we set $L \in [0.08, 0.25]$ with the various sparsity, and on the RCV1 data we set $L \in [0.09, 0.3]$ while $k = [100 : 100 : 1,000]$. For L_2-SVMs regression on 20newsgroup, we set $L \in [0.35, 0.55]$ while $k = [1,000 : 1,000 : 10,000]$. Meanwhile, the max value of τ in the Algorithm 2 needs to be tuned as well.

3.4   The Results

In this section, we show the experiments results of our proposed algorithm applied to sparse logistic regression and sparse L_2-SVMs tasks.

The Experiments on the Synthetic Data

As introduced in Sect. 3.1, we apply our algorithm to the sparse logistic regression model on the synthetic datasets. As shown in Fig. 2, we generate four groups of synthetic datasets with the various sizes and depict the loss along with the CPU time under the different sparsity conditions. We can see that our algorithm outperforms the other methods.

The Experiments on RCV1

We further apply our method to sparse logistic regression on RCV1. The results are shown in Fig. 3. Two pictures at the top are the CPU time the algorithms cost and the classification error verse the sparsity ranging from 100 to 1,000. The two pictures at the bottom are the curve of empirical logistic loss versus the iterations of algorithms with the sparsity of 500 and 1000. It can be seen that

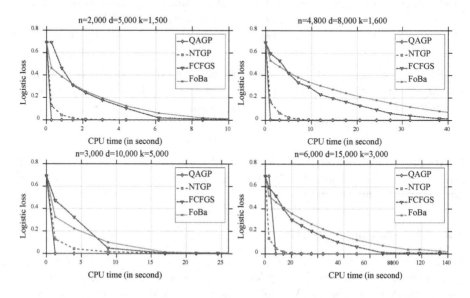

Fig. 2. The sparse logistic regression experiments on synthetic data

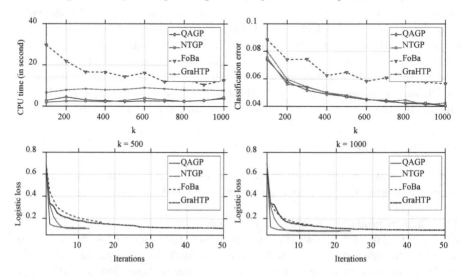

Fig. 3. The sparse logistic regression experiments on RCV1.

our algorithm is comparable in testing performance with NTGP and GraHTP. Meanwhile, our method cost the equivalent time with NTGP. We can also see that our algorithm can search the optimal point faster than other methods. So if the precision criterion of the task is not too hard, our algorithm will be quite outstanding.

The Experiments on 20Newsgroups
In this experiment, we evaluate the performance of our algorithm for sparse L_2-SVMs on 20Newsgroups data. We first compare our method with other methods in three terms: the cpu time, the objective loss and the classification error. We also plot curves of logistic loss values verse numbers of functions. Figure 4 shows that our method QAGP is as competitive as QNTGP in all the terms and our method can achieve sound result in each term.

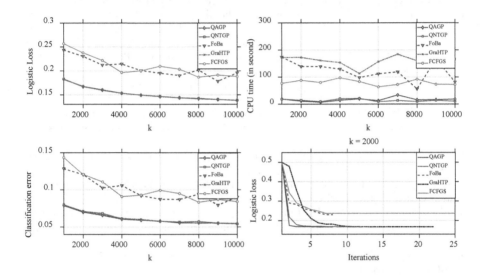

Fig. 4. The sparse L_2-SVMs experiments on 20Newsgroups.

4   Conclusion

In this paper, we propose a new quadratic approximation greedy pursuit method (QAGP) for sparsity-constrained optimization with linear models. Our main idea is that if the linear model is L-Smooth, we can construct a special approximation to the model function at each iteration. Then we can utilize the greedy search to find the optimal solution of the approximation at each iteration. We demonstrate the advantages of our algorithm over some classical first-order algorithms and the (Q)NTGP method when applied to sparse logistic regression and sparse L_2-SVMs model. The results of experiments show that our method is more efficient than the other algorithms. We conclude that our method is a better alternative for solving the sparsity-constrained problems with linear models.

Acknowledgements. This work was supported by the National Natural Science Foundation of China under Grant Numbers: 61876090.

References

1. Agarwal, N., Bullins, B., Hazan, E.: Second-order stochastic optimization in linear time. Statistics **1050**, 15 (2016)
2. Bahmani, S., Raj, B., Boufounos, P.T.: Greedy sparsity-constrained optimization. J. Mach. Learn. Res. **14**, 807–841 (2013)
3. Bertsekas, D.P.: Nonlinear programming. J. Oper. Res. Soc. **48**(3), 334 (1997)
4. Bishop, C.M.: Pattern Recognition and Machine Learning. Springer, Cham (2006)
5. Blumensath, T., Davies, M.E.: Iterative hard thresholding for compressed sensing. Appl. Comput. Harmonic Anal. **27**(3), 265–274 (2009)
6. Byrd, R.H., Lu, P., Nocedal, J., Zhu, C.: A limited memory algorithm for bound constrained optimization. SIAM J. Sci. Comput. **16**(5), 1190–1208 (1995)
7. Chen, J., Gu, Q.: Fast newton hard thresholding pursuit for sparsity constrained nonconvex optimization. In: Proceedings of the 23rd ACM SIGKDD International Conference on Knowledge Discovery and Data Mining, pp. 757–766. ACM (2017)
8. Donoho, D.L., et al.: Compressed sensing. IEEE Trans. Inf. Theory **52**(4), 1289–1306 (2006)
9. Foucart, S.: Hard thresholding pursuit: an algorithm for compressive sensing. SIAM J. Numer. Anal. **49**(6), 2543–2563 (2011)
10. Johnson, R., Zhang, T.: Accelerating stochastic gradient descent using predictive variance reduction. In: Advances in Neural Information Processing Systems, pp. 315–323 (2013)
11. Lang, K.: Newsweeder: learning to filter netnews. In: Machine Learning Proceedings 1995, pp. 331–339. Elsevier (1995)
12. Lewis, D.D., Yang, Y., Rose, T.G., Li, F.: RCV1: a new benchmark collection for text categorization research. J. Mach. Learn. Res. **5**, 361–397 (2004)
13. Li, X., Zhao, T., Arora, R., Liu, H., Haupt, J.: Stochastic variance reduced optimization for nonconvex sparse learning. In: International Conference on Machine Learning, pp. 917–925 (2016)
14. Natarajan, B.K.: Sparse approximate solutions to linear systems. SIAM J. Comput. **24**(2), 227–234 (1995)
15. Needell, D., Tropp, J.A.: CoSaMP: iterative signal recovery from incomplete and inaccurate samples. Appl. Comput. Harmonic Anal. **26**(3), 301–321 (2009)
16. Shalev-Shwartz, S., Srebro, N., Zhang, T.: Trading accuracy for sparsity in optimization problems with sparsity constraints. SIAM J. Optim. **20**(6), 2807–2832 (2010)
17. Yuan, X.T., Li, P., Zhang, T.: Gradient hard thresholding pursuit. J. Mach. Learn. Res. **18**, 1–43 (2018)
18. Yuan, X.T., Liu, Q.: Newton-type greedy selection methods for ℓ_0-constrained minimization. IEEE Trans. Pattern Anal. Mach. Intell. **39**(12), 2437–2450 (2017)
19. Yuan, X., Li, P., Zhang, T.: Gradient hard thresholding pursuit for sparsity-constrained optimization. In: International Conference on Machine Learning, pp. 127–135 (2014)
20. Zhang, T.: Adaptive forward-backward greedy algorithm for sparse learning with linear models. In: Advances in Neural Information Processing Systems, pp. 1921–1928 (2009)
21. Zhou, P., Yuan, X., Feng, J.: Efficient stochastic gradient hard thresholding. In: Advances in Neural Information Processing Systems, pp. 1988–1997 (2018)

Iterative Discriminative Domain Adaptation

Xiaofu Wu$^{(\boxtimes)}$, Jiahui Fu, Suofei Zhang, and Quan Zhou

Nanjing University of Posts and Telecommunications, Nanjing, China
{xfuwu,1017010637,zhangsuofei,quan.zhou}@njupt.edu.cn

Abstract. A popular formulation of domain adaptation (DA) is to simultaneously minimize the source risk and the cross-domain discrepancy between the source domain $\mathcal{D}_s$ and target domain $\mathcal{D}_t$. However, this is believed to be suboptimal since the shared feature, which is indistinguishable by a domain classifier, could be far from optimum for the purpose of classification. In this paper, we propose an iterative DA framework for directly optimizing the classification error, which provides DA solutions to both unsupervised and semi-supervised scenarios. Instead of directly attacking $\mathcal{D}_s \rightarrow \mathcal{D}_t$, we employ an iterative self-training approach of $\mathcal{D}_s + \mathcal{D}_t^{l-1} \rightarrow \mathcal{D}_t^l$ for progressively-labelling of $\mathcal{D}_t$ with the aim of $\lim_{l \rightarrow \infty} \mathcal{D}_t^l \approx \mathcal{D}_t$. For unsupervised DA, it performs comparable to the state-of-the-art DA methods. In particular, it performs the best among various unsupervised DA methods for the very difficult task MNIST $\rightarrow$ SVHN. By employing a few labeled samples in the target domain, we show that it can achieve significantly improved performance. For MNIST $\rightarrow$ SVHN, the use of 60 labeled samples from SVHN is able to improve the accuracy margin about $+10\%$ over the state-or-the-art unsupervised DA method. For a comparison with semi-supervised learning methods, it achieves the accuracy margin about $+30\%$ over Mean Teacher with 60 labeled samples in SVHN.

Keywords: Domain adaptation · Unsupervised · Semi-supervised

1 Introduction

Deep learning has brought impressive advances to the state-of-the-art across a wide variety of machine-learning tasks and applications. The success of deep learning depends heavily on the large-scale fully-labeled datasets and the development of easily trainable deep neural architectures under the back-propagation algorithm, such as convolutional neural networks (CNNs) and their variants [7,8]. In practical applications, a new target task and its dataset (target domain) may be similar to a known source task and its fully-labeled dataset (source domain). However, the difference between the source and target domains is often not negligible, which makes the previously trained model not work well for the new task.

© Springer Nature Switzerland AG 2019
Z. Lin et al. (Eds.): PRCV 2019, LNCS 11857, pp. 349–360, 2019.
https://doi.org/10.1007/978-3-030-31654-9_30

This is known as domain-shift [6]. As the cost of massive labelling is often expensive, it is very attractive for the target task to exploit any existing fully-labeled source dataset and adapt the trained model to the target domain.

This domain adaptation (DA) approach is aiming to learn a discriminative classifier in the presence of a shift between the source and target domains [2,3]. In order to mitigate the harmful effects of domain shift, a common idea is to learn deep-neural-network based transformations that map both domains into a common feature space. This can be achieved by optimizing the representation to minimize some measure of domain shift, typically defined as the distance between the source and target domain distributions or its degraded form, such as Maximum Mean Discrepancy (MMD) [11,20] or correlation distance [19]. The MMD metric is computed between features extracted from sets of samples from each domain. The domain confusion network by [20] has an MMD loss at a single layer in the CNN architecture while [11] proposed the deep adaptation network that has MMD losses at multiple layers.

With the invention of generative adversarial networks [5], various adversarial methods have been proposed for the purpose of unsupervised DA, where the domain discrepancy distance is believed to be minimized through an adversarial objective with respect to a binary domain discriminator. The domain-invariant features could be extracted whenever this domain discriminator cannot distinguish between the distributions of the source and target domain examples [2,4].

2   Related Works

This paper is closely related to self-training, and its adapted methods for unsupervised DA. Self-training can be regarded as a special form of expectation-maximization algorithm [14]. As a semi-supervised learning method, self-training takes an iterative learning process, which starts with a few labeled for training a classifier and then this trained classifier is further employed to predict the labels for unlabeled samples. Among all predicted labels, the most confident labels are selected as "true" labels (often called pseudo-labels) and these pseudo-labeled samples are then regarded as labeled in the following training process. This learning process repeated. A detailed survey of semi-supervised learning techniques can be found in [23].

The idea of self-training was also employed for unsupervised DA. Among various issues, how to generate high confident pseudo-labels for unlabeled target samples is key to the success of unsupervised DA methods [10,16,18]. The cyclic consistency was employed for ensuring the label consistency between two domains and the structured consistency was used for in-domain label transduction [18]. In [16], a novel asymmetric tri-training (TRIPPLE) method was proposed for unsupervised DA, where discriminative representations were obtained by utilizing pseudo-labels assigned to unlabeled target samples. With three classifiers, two networks assign pseudo-labels to unlabeled target samples and the remaining network learns from them. Tri-training can be regarded as the extension of the co-training method [22] for domain-adaptation.

Following the work of [16], we make several contributions in this paper:

1. Instead of directly transferring from source domain to target domain, we present a novel viewpoint of transferring from the joint source-target domain to target domain and show its power for both unsupervised and semi-supervised DA tasks.
2. We propose a self-training-based iterative discriminative domain adaptation (IDDA) method as depicted in Fig. 1, which is simpler than TRIPPLE and employs only two classifiers with shared subnetwork for progressively-labelling of target samples. As an iterative learning process, it often starts with a few labeled target samples, along with fully-labeled source samples for training a source classifier and then this trained source classifier is further employed to predict the labels for target samples. The pseudo-labeled target samples with high confidence are added into the labeled dataset and further employed to train a target classifier. This process iterates for minimizing the target classification error.
3. The proposed IDDA provides DA solutions to both unsupervised and semi-supervised scenarios. It performs very competitive among existing unsupervised DA methods and we show it performs the best for MNIST → SVHN. For semi-supervised scenarios, we also compare IDDA with the state-of-the-art semi-supervised learning method and shows the performance advantage when the number of labeled samples is very limited.

3   Iterative Discriminative Domain Adaptation

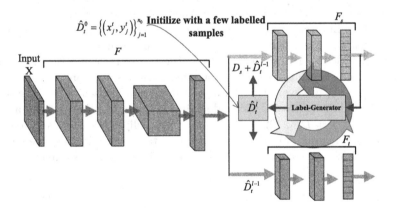

Fig. 1. Iterative discriminative domain adaptation.

In unsupervised DA, we are given a source domain $\mathcal{D}_s = \{(x_i^s; y_i^s)\}_{i=1}^{n_s}$ of n_s labeled examples and a target domain $\mathcal{D}_t = \{x_j^t\}_{j=1}^{n_t}$ of n_t unlabeled examples. The source domain and target domain are sampled from joint distributions $P(x^s; y^s)$ and $Q(x^t; y^t)$ respectively, while the identically independently distributed (IID) assumption is violated as $P \neq Q$.

For unsupervised DA, the goal is to design a deep network $y = G(x)$ which formally reduces the shifts in the joint distributions across domains, such that the target risk $\epsilon_t(G) = \mathbb{E}_{(x^t;y^t)\sim Q}[G(x^t) \neq y^t]$ can be minimized by jointly minimizing the source risk $\epsilon_s(G) = \mathbb{E}_{(x^s;y^s)\sim P}[G(x^s) \neq y^s]$ and the cross-domain discrepancy $D(P;Q)$. It is often assumed that there exists a feature extraction function, which maps an input x to $\mathbf{f} = F(x)$. Noting that F is a subnetwork of G. It means that $G(x) = F_c(F(x)) = F_c \circ F(x)$, where F_c is a classifier. The potential problem of this formulation is that the common feature extractor F obtained by minimizing both the source risk and cross-domain discrepancy may not be optimal for the purpose of classification in the target domain.

To circumvent this potential problem, we propose an iterative discriminative domain adaptation approach as shown in Fig. 1. Instead of minimizing the cross-domain discrepancy, we aim to directly minimize the target classification error by using a self-training approach. In general, there are two parallel networks with a shared sub-network F. The features generated by F are followed by two independent classifier, F_s and F_t, for two parallel networks, G_s and G_t, where $G_s = F_s(F(x))$ denotes a source-aggressive network and $G_t = F_t(F(x))$ a target-specific network.

3.1 General Idea: From $\mathcal{D}_s \rightarrow \mathcal{D}_t$ to $\mathcal{D}_s + \mathcal{D}_t^{l-1} \rightarrow \mathcal{D}_t^l$ ($\lim_{l\to\infty} \mathcal{D}_t^l \approx \mathcal{D}_t$)

For DA, the traditional wisdom is to train a neural network with shared features between the source and target domains. The output features should be not discriminative in domains whenever input samples are switched from source domain to target domain. There are two main methods for deciding if the extracted features are domain-discriminative, one is measured by the distance between two distributions, and the other is done by adversarial learning.

A popular idea for many existing DA methods is to recognize the distinguishable difference between two separate domains, namely, source an target domains. In this paper, we, however, consider a joint domain approach, where the source domain $\mathcal{D}_s$ and an aggressive target domain $\mathcal{D}_t^{l-1}$ join together to form a single joint domain $\mathcal{D}_J = \mathcal{D}_s + \mathcal{D}_t^{l-1}$. If $\mathcal{D}_t^{l-1} = \mathcal{D}_t$ is fully labeled, it is straightforward to train a neural network for classification task by minimizing the negative log-likelihood of the ground truth class for each joint domain sample:

$$\min_{F,F_s} \mathcal{L}_{\text{task}}(\mathcal{D}_s + \mathcal{D}_t) = \mathbb{E}_{(x,y)\sim(1-\lambda)P+\lambda Q}\left\{-\sum_{k=1}^{K} \mathbb{1}[k = y] \log G_s(\mathbf{x})\right\}, \quad (1)$$

where $\lambda = \frac{|\mathcal{D}_t|}{|\mathcal{D}_t|+|\mathcal{D}_s|} = \frac{n_t}{n_t+n_s}$.

With this supervised joint-domain training approach, the trained neural network is expected to work well for any of domain-specific ($\mathcal{D}_s$ or $\mathcal{D}_t$) classification task. *By training two deep neural networks with the same architecture over $\mathcal{D}_J$ and D_t, respectively, we got almost the same test accuracy over D_t for two independently-trained networks in experiments.* With this joint-training approach, the common features generated by F (as shown in Fig. 1) has the following desirable properties:

1. They are shared between both domains $\mathcal{D}_s$ and $\mathcal{D}_t$, which should be not distinguishable by a binary domain-classifier.
2. They are discriminative in classes since the learning process is directly optimized for the purpose of classification, while many existing domain-adaptation approaches do not consider task-specific decision boundaries between classes [17].

For the classification task in the target domain, one may expect better performance if the neural network is only trained within the target domain by minimizing the negative log-likelihood of the ground truth class for each target domain sample:

$$\min_{F,F_t} \mathcal{L}_{\text{task}}(\mathcal{D}_t) = \mathbb{E}_{(x^t,y^t)\sim Q} \left\{ -\sum_{k=1}^{K} \mathbb{1}[k = y^t] \log G_t(\mathbf{x}^t) \right\}. \tag{2}$$

As both tasks (1) and (2) are involved with the input samples from the target domain, it is reasonable to decompose the source net as $G_s = F_s \circ F$ and the target net as $G_t = F_t \circ F$, where F denotes the shared sub-network between G_s and G_t. This shared architecture is plotted in Fig. 1, which was extensively reported in [4,16].

For domain-adaptation applications, the target domain is often unlabeled or weakly-labeled. This makes the target task (2) impossible for supervised training. To circumvent this problem, [16] proposed an asymmetric tri-training approach, where the target domain is progressively pseudo-labeled.

Following the idea in [16], we propose a simpler iterative discriminative domain-adaptation approach by solving the following optimization problems at each iteration:

$$\min_{F,F_s} \mathcal{L}_{\text{task}} \left(\mathcal{D}_s + \hat{\mathcal{D}}_t^{l-1} \right) = \mathbb{E}_{(x,y)\sim(1-\lambda_l)P+\lambda_l \hat{Q}_l} \left\{ -\sum_{k=1}^{K} \mathbb{1}[k = y] \log F_s(F(x)) \right\}$$
$$+ \beta \cdot \ell_{\log} \left(\mathbb{E}_{x\sim P} \left\{ F(x) J F^T(x) \right\}, \mathbb{E}_{x\sim Q} \left\{ F(x) J F^T(x) \right\} \right), \tag{3}$$

$$\hat{\mathcal{D}}_t^l \leftarrow \text{Labelling}(\mathcal{D}_t, G_s = F_s \circ F, n_l), \tag{4}$$

$$\min_{F,F_t} \mathcal{L}_{\text{task}}(\hat{\mathcal{D}}_t^l) = \mathbb{E}_{(x^t,y^t)\sim\hat{Q}_l} \left\{ -\sum_{k=1}^{K} \mathbb{1}[k = y_t] \log F_t(F(x^t)) \right\}. \tag{5}$$

Noting that $\lambda_0 = 0$ for unsupervised DA and it takes a very small value for semi-supervised DA, and it monotonically increases whenever the algorithm proceeds with iterations ($l = 0, 1 \cdots, L - 1$). If $\lim_{l\to\infty} \hat{\mathcal{D}}_t^l \approx \mathcal{D}_t$, this iterative learning method is expected to achieve the excellent classification performance since the "fully-labeled" target dataset is employed to train the classifier after a number of iterations.

The labelling process, namely, Labelling($\mathcal{D}_t, G_s = F_s \circ F, n_l$), is explained in detail in what follows.

4 Progressive Label Generation and Its Possible Limitation

4.1 Progressive Label Generation

With each unlabeled image $x^t \in \mathcal{D}_t$ as input, we can perform the inference over the network G_s to obtain the softmax prediction $G_s(x^t) = F_s(F(x^t)) \triangleq [\sigma_1(x^t), \cdots, \sigma_K(x^t)]^T$. The inferred class for x^t is taken as $\hat{y}^t = \arg\max_k \sigma_k(x^t)$. With this manner, a trained network G_s can generate a pseudo-label for each sample $x^t \in \mathcal{D}_t$ to form a pseudo-labeled pair $(x^t, \hat{y}^t)$. Hence, the target domain could be pseudo-labeled and its labelling accuracy is determined by the trained network $G_s = F_s \circ F$.

The labelling reliability could be measured by computing the entropy

$$\mathcal{I}(x^t) = -\sum_{k=1}^{K} \sigma_k(x^t) \log \sigma_k(x^t), \tag{6}$$

Since the cross-entropy loss is employed for supervised learning, it is well expected that for the correct classification of a test image x^t, $\mathcal{I}(x^t)$ could take a small value, at least with high probability. By setting a threshold $\mathcal{I}_0$, one can partition $\mathcal{D}_t$ into two disjoint set, $\mathcal{D}_t = \mathcal{D}_t^{\geq} \bigcup \mathcal{D}_t^{<}$, where

$$\mathcal{D}_t^{<} = \left\{ x^t : \mathcal{I}(x^t) < \mathcal{I}_0, x^t \in \mathcal{D}_t \right\}. \tag{7}$$

By carefully controlling the threshold value of $\mathcal{I}_0$, a partially-pseudo-labelling target domain $\hat{\mathcal{D}}_t^l$ can be obtained as $\hat{\mathcal{D}}_t^l \leftarrow \mathcal{D}_t^{<}$. This is in effect equivalent to Entropy Regularization [10].

Progressive Growth of Labeled Samples. To further prevent the overfitting to pseudo-labels, we resample the candidate for labeling samples in each step as did in [1,16]. We set the number of the initial candidates as n_0, which typically takes the value of 5,000. We gradually increase the number of the candidates $n_l = l/P \cdot n$, where P typically takes an integer value between 1 and 100, n denotes the number of all target samples and l denotes the number of steps, and we set the maximum number of pseudo-labeled candidates as $n_{\lim}$. With resampling, $\hat{\mathcal{D}}_t^l$ is replaced by

$$\hat{\mathcal{D}}_t^l \leftarrow \mathcal{D}_t^{<}(n_l) \triangleq \left\{ x^t : \mathcal{I}(x^t) < \mathcal{I}_0, x^t \in \mathcal{D}_t(n_l) \right\}, \tag{8}$$

where $\mathcal{D}_t(n_l)$ denotes the sequentially-selected subset of $\mathcal{D}_t$ with $n_l \leq n$ samples.

With the update of sub-networks F and F_s, this labelling processed can be progressively implemented. Hopefully, the cardinality of $\mathcal{D}_t^{l+1}$ increases progressively and at the same time its labelling accuracy would be maintained.

Dynamic Threshold. Instead of keep the threshold value of $\mathcal{I}_0$ constant over iterations, we employ a dynamic threshold value for each iteration l, namely, $\mathcal{I}_0^l$. To reduce the labelling error probability in $\hat{\mathcal{D}}_t^l$, it is often required that

$$\mathcal{I}_0^l \leq \mathcal{I}_0^{l+1}, \forall l = 0, 1, \cdots .$$

In experiments, we observe that when the fully-labeled target samples (x^t, y^t) are input to train the target net $(F \rightarrow F_t)$, the entropy of the outputs at the soft-max layer (6) is exponentially-decreased as the iteration proceeds. Hence, we propose an exponentially-decreased threshold value of l with the form of

$$\mathcal{I}_0^l = 2^{-l} a + b. \tag{9}$$

From Unsupervised Domain Adaptation to Semi-supervised Domain Adaptation. With unsupervised DA, the above progressive labelling process can be implemented simply with the initial labelling of $\hat{\mathcal{D}}_t^0 = \Phi$ since there is no any labelling information available for the target domain. By performing an iterative domain adaptation as shown in Fig. 1, the partially-pseudo-labelling target domain at phase l, $\hat{\mathcal{D}}_t^l = \{(x^t, \hat{y}^t)\}$, can be progressively updated as

$$\hat{\mathcal{D}}_t^0 \rightarrow \hat{\mathcal{D}}_t^1 \rightarrow \cdots \rightarrow \hat{\mathcal{D}}_t^{L-1}.$$

For each partially-pseudo-labelling target domain $\hat{\mathcal{D}}_t^l$, we are often interested in two metrics, one is labelling accuracy $\mathcal{A}(\hat{\mathcal{D}}_t^l) \triangleq \Pr\left[(x^t, \hat{y}^t) = (x^t, y^t), \forall x^t \in \hat{\mathcal{D}}_t^l\right]$, and the other is its cardinality $|\hat{\mathcal{D}}_t^l|$.

For supervised learning, it is clear that its classification accuracy could not be better than the accuracy of labelling dataset if it contains labelling errors. Therefore, we often require a high accuracy metric for $\hat{\mathcal{D}}_t^l$. It is, however, very difficult to obtain a non-empty $\hat{\mathcal{D}}_t^0$ at the initial phase $(l = 0)$ for unsupervised DA. This was proved to be the case when we want to transfer from MNIST to SVHN. By adjusting the threshold $\mathcal{I}_0$, we found that $\mathcal{A}(\hat{\mathcal{D}}_t^l)$ is almost always smaller than 90%.

Although there exists various methods to improve the performance of domain-adaptation, extended experiments show that it is very difficult to get a high value of $\mathcal{A}(\hat{\mathcal{D}}_t^l)$ even if we reduce its cardinality below 1000. For example, the asymmetric tri-training approach [16] does fail to do this.

A possible way out is to give up completely unsupervised transferring, but introduce some labeled samples in the target domain, where the number of labeled samples should be as few as possible for controlling the labelling cost. Hopefully, only a very few number of labeled samples are enough for warming up the transferring training process under the framework of Fig. 1.

On the Choice of Target Samples for Initial Labelling. Let n_0 denote the number of labeled samples in the target domain for the semi-supervised DA. From both theoretical and practical points of view, it is of interest to discuss how to choose n_0 target samples for boosting the training performance. In general, one should choose those target samples, which have "maximum" domain-shift against the fully-labeled source samples. However, an exact formulation of this idea is not straightforward. Even this is possible, we doubt that it may be computationally-intensive, since the source domain is required to be enumerated for computing the *pair-wise* domain shift. We thus resort to a simple and straightforward method as what follows.

Assume that the network G_s has been trained with fully-labeled dataset $\mathcal{D}_s$. By inputting to the trained network G_s with the samples from $\mathcal{D}_t$, one can locate n_0 samples by sorting the values of $\mathcal{I}(x^t)$ (6). As this may still be computationally-intensive, we simply employ a threshold $\mathcal{I}_h$ to find enough candidates $\mathcal{L} = \{x_t : \mathcal{I}(x^t) \geq \mathcal{I}_h, x_t \in \mathcal{D}_t\}$ ($|\mathcal{L}| \geq n_0$) and randomly select n_0 samples among $\mathcal{L}$ in experiments.

4.2 Training Procedure

Algorithm 1. Iterative Discriminative Domain Adaptation (Semi-supervised or Unsupervised)

Require: $\mathcal{D}_s = \{(x_i^s; y_i^s)\}_{i=1}^{n_s}, \mathcal{D}_t = \{x_j^t\}_{j=1}^{n_t}, I(\text{number of training iterations}), B(\text{batch-size})$

1: Training Phase Initialization: $l \leftarrow 0$.

2: Training the network G_s with $\mathcal{D}_s$: $\min_{F,F_s} \mathcal{L}_{\text{task}}(\mathcal{D}_s, G_s = F_s \circ F, B, I)$
3: Training the network G_t with $\mathcal{D}_s$: $\min_{F,F_t} \mathcal{L}_{\text{task}}(\mathcal{D}_s, G_t = F_t \circ F, B, I)$
4: Label Initialization: $\hat{\mathcal{D}}_t \leftarrow \{(x_j^t; y_j^t)\}_{j=1}^{n_0}$ **[Semi-supervised]** or $\hat{\mathcal{D}}_t \leftarrow \mathcal{D}_t^{<}$ **[Unsupervised]**
5: **for** $l = 1$ to $L - 1$ **do**
6:     Training the network G_s with $\mathcal{D}_s + \hat{\mathcal{D}}_t$: $\min_{F,F_s} \mathcal{L}_{\text{task}}(\mathcal{D}_s + \hat{\mathcal{D}}_t, G_s = F_s \circ F, B, I)$

7:     Training the network G_t with $\hat{\mathcal{D}}_t$: $\min_{F,F_t} \mathcal{L}_{\text{task}}(\hat{\mathcal{D}}_t, G_t = F_t \circ F, B, I)$
8:     $n_l = \min\left\{\max\{\frac{l+1}{P} \times n_t, n_0^{\min}\}, n_{\lim}\right\}$
9:     Label generation: $\hat{\mathcal{D}}_t = \text{Labelling}(\mathcal{D}_t, G_s = F_s \circ F, \mathcal{I}_0^l, n_l)$
10: **end for**

The entire procedure of training the network is shown in Algorithm 1. First, the entire network is trained with the source training set $\mathcal{D}_s$. Then, pseudo-labels are generated according to the labelling mechanism discussed previously. These pseudo-labeled target samples are joined with the source samples for further training the source network, while the target-specific network is trained only on target samples and discriminative representations could be learned. As the learning proceeds, F will learn target-discriminative representations, resulting in an improvement in accuracy in both F_s and F_t. This cycle will gradually enhance the accuracy in the target domain.

5   Experiments

We run the adaptation experiments on the digits datasets. We focus on the two digits datasets, MNIST [9] and SVHN [13], with particular emphasis on the task of MNIST $\rightarrow$ SVHN.

We employed the CNN architecture used in [4,16]. IDDA employs an exponentially decreased threshold value of $\mathcal{I}_0^l = 2^{-l}a + b$, where l is the iteration number.

In experiments, we employ $(a, b) = (0.1, 0.01), (0.2, 0.04), (0.2, 0.02), (0.2, 0.02)$ for IDDA + 0 (unsupervised), IDDA + 60, IDDA + 80, IDDA + 100, respectively.

To limit the number of pseudo-labeled samples, a progressive growth of $n_l = \min\left\{\max\left\{\frac{l+1}{P} \times n_t, n_0^{\min}\right\}, n_{\lim}\right\}$ over training phase is employed. In experiments, $n_{\lim}$ is set to 60000, and P is set to 30, 15, 25, 25 for IDDA + 0, IDDA + 60, IDDA + 80, IDDA + 100, respectively. The number of training iterations is set to $I = 30$ for each training phase.

5.1   Joint-Training vs. Separate Training

With fully-supervised joint-domain training, we do experiments to evaluate the potential performance gap between joint-domain training and separate-domain training. By training the network G_s over $\mathcal{D}_J = \mathcal{D}_s + \mathcal{D}_t$ and $\mathcal{D}_t$, independently, we evaluate the test accuracy over $\mathcal{D}_t$. With $\mathcal{D}_s = $ MNIST and $\mathcal{D}_t = $ SVHN, we obtain the test accuracy of 0.937, 0.938 (over the test set of $\mathcal{D}_t$) for the joint training and separate training, respectively. This reveals that with the supervised joint-training approach, the trained neural network is expected to work well for any of domain-specific classification task.

5.2   Unsupervised IDDA

Table 1. Unsupervised domain-adaptation (measured as accuracy %)

Methods	MNIST SVHN	SVHN MNIST	SYN DIGITS SVHN	MNIST MNIST-M	SYN SIGNS GTSRB
DAAN ([4])	35.7	71.1	90.3	81.5	88.7
ADDA ([21])	–	76.0	–	–	–
kNN-Ad ([18])	40.3	78.8	–	86.7	–
CORAL ([19])	–	90.2	–	–	–
MECA ([12])	–	95.2	90.3	–	–
TRIPPLE ([16])	48.4 ± 3.0	85.0	92.9	94.0	96.2
Ours (average)	50.1 ± 3.8	94.1 ± 3.7	92.0 ± 1.2	97.1 ± 0.2	97.9 ± 0.6
Ours (max)	**52.6**	**97.4**	**93.2**	**97.3**	**98.3**

Table 1 reports the comparison of our method and baselines in the unsupervised scenario. For SVHN → MNIST, IDDA performs very close to MECA. It achieves the average classification accuracy of 93.8% and the best accuracy of 96.2% among 10 trials. For MNIST → SVHN, IDDA performs the best among various baseline methods with the average accuracy of 50.9% and the best accuracy of 56.0% among 10 trials. By running TRIPPLE (available at https://github. com/ksaito-ut/atda) for 10 trials, it achieved the average accuracy of 48.4% [1]. Our method improves the accuracy about +2% for this transferring scenario. Visualization of features in the last pooling layer is shown in Fig. 3. We can observe that the target samples are more dispersed when adaptation is achieved and the proposed method performs better than TRIPPLE.

5.3   Semi-supervised IDDA

We evaluate our method for MNIST → SVHN, which is compared to Mean Teacher for semi-supervised learning over SVHN. The test classification errors with 60, 80, 100 labeled samples in the target SVHN are shown in Table 2. For Mean Teacher, we run the code (available at https://github.com/CuriousAI/ mean-teacher) with its default setting for training with 100000 steps. When the number of labeled samples is very limited, the proposed IDDA significantly outperforms Mean Teacher. With 60 labeled samples, IDDA achieves the accuracy margin about +30% over Mean Teacher. Mean Teacher, however, can improve the performance more quickly when the number of labeled samples increases.

5.4   Ablation Study

In the ablation study, we focus on the task of MNIST → SVHN.

Dynamic Threshold vs Constant Threshold. We show in Fig. 2 the performance comparison in the test accuracy for the use of dynamic threshold vs. const threshold over different training phase. Two constant threshold strategies, namely, $\mathcal{I}_0^l = 0.14$ and $\mathcal{I}_0^l = 0.04$, are employed. Remembering that the dynamic threshold method use $\mathcal{I}_0^l = 2^{-l} \times 0.2 + 0.04$, which takes a value between 0.04 and 0.14. Clearly, the use of dynamic thresholds over different training phases show its performance advantage.

Choice of Initial Labeled Samples for Semi-supervised IDDA. We employ two methods for the choice of n_0 target samples for initial labelling, one is to randomly select n_0 target samples, and the other is to employ a threshold $\mathcal{I}_h$ to find enough candidates $\mathcal{L} = \{x_t : \mathcal{I}(x^t) \geq \mathcal{I}_h, x_t \in \mathcal{D}_t\}$ ($|\mathcal{L}| \geq n_0$) and randomly select n_0 samples among $\mathcal{L}$. For IDDA + 60 ($n_0 = 60$), the later method provides +2% improvement in average on the test accuracy (61.2% vs. 63.5%).

---

[1] In [16], the authors reported the accuracy of just one trial and the accuracy was 52.8%.

Table 2. Semi-supervised learning (%)

Methods	60	80	100
Mean teacher	29.7	40.5	54.2
IDDA	**61.4** ± 3.3	**67.4** ± 2.0	**68.7** ± 2.1

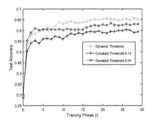

Fig. 2. Dynamic threshold vs. constant threshold for IDDA + 60

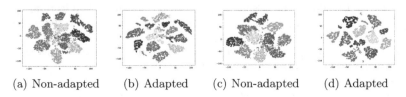

(a) Non-adapted   (b) Adapted   (c) Non-adapted   (d) Adapted

Fig. 3. t-SNE feature visualization of TRIPPLE and IDDA features on the SVHN → MNIST task. Features visualized from the first dense layer of our Target Classifier.(a), (c) The case where we only use source samples for training. (b), (d) The case of adaptation by TRIPPLE and our method. Obviously, the target samples are more dispersed through adaptation in our method.

6   Conclusion

In this paper, we have proposed an iterative discriminative domain adaptation framework, which provides a unified solution to both unsupervised and semi-supervised scenarios. Instead of minimizing the cross-domain discrepancy, it employs a joint-domain approach for directly minimizing the target classification error. The proposed method performs very competitive for unsupervised DA. It is yet simple and can be efficiently implemented. For some semi-supervised scenarios, it achieves better performance than the state-of-the-art semi-supervised learning method. Since IDDA and Mean Teacher have different mechanisms for exploiting the labeled samples in the target domain, their combination may yield even better targets. This deserves further exploitation.

References

1. Tarvainen, A., Valpola, H.: Mean teachers are better role models: weight-averaged consistency targets improve semi-supervised deep learning results. In: NIPS (2017)
2. Bousmalis, K., Trigeorgis, G., Silberman, N., Krishnan, D., Erhan, D.: Domain separation networks. In: NIPS (2016)
3. Chen, M., Weinberger, K.Q., Blitzer, J.: Co-training for domain adaptation. In: NIPS (2011)
4. Ganin, Y., Lempitsky, V.: Unsupervised domain adaptation by backpropagation. In: ICML (2015)

5. Goodfellow, I., et al.: Generative adversarial nets. In: NIPS (2014)
6. Gretton, A., Smola, A., Huang, J., Borgwardt, K.M., Schölkopf, B.: Covariate shift and local learning by distribution matching. In: Quiñonero-Candela, J., Sugiyama, M., Schwaighofer, A., Lawrence, N.D. (eds.) Dataset Shift in Machine Learning, pp. 131–160. MIT Press, Cambridge (2009)
7. He, K., Zhang, X., Ren, S., Sun, J.: Deep residual learning for image recognition. In: CVPR (2016)
8. Huang, G., Liu, Z., van der Maaten, L., Weinberger, K.Q.: Densely connected convolutional networks. In: CVPR (2017)
9. LeCun, Y., Bottou, L., Bengio, Y., Haffner, P.: Gradient-based learning applied to document recognition. Proc. IEEE 86(11), 2278–2324 (1998)
10. Lee, D.-H.: Pseudo-label: the simple and efficient semi-supervised learning method for deep neural networks. In: ICML Workshop on Challenges in Representation Learning (2013)
11. Long, M., Cao, Y., Wang, J., Jordan, M.I.: Learning transferable features with deep adaptation networks. In: ICML (2015)
12. Morerio, P., Cavazza, J., Murino, V.: Minimal-entropy correlation allignment for unsupervised deep domain adaptation. In: ICLR (2018)
13. Netzer, Y., Wang, T., Coates, A., Bissacco, A., Wu, B., Ng, A.Y.: Reading digits in natural images with unsupervised feature learning. In: NIPS (2011)
14. Nigam, K., Mccallum, A.K., Thrun, S., Mitchell, T.: Text classification from labeled and unlabeled documents using EM. Mach. Learn. 39, 103–104 (2000)
15. Rohrbach, M., Ebert, S., Schiele, B.: Transfer learning in a transductive setting. In: NIPS (2013)
16. Saito, K., Ushiku, Y., Harada, T.: Asymmetric tri-training for unsupervised domain adaptation. In: ICML (2017)
17. Saito, K., Watanabe, K., Ushiku, Y., Harada, T.: Maximum classifier discrepancy for unsupervised domain adaptation. In: CVPR (2018)
18. Sener, O., Song, H.O., Saxena, A., Savarese, S.: Learning transferrable representations for unsupervised domain adaptation. In: NIPS (2016)
19. Sun, B., Saenko, K.: Deep CORAL: correlation alignment for deep domain adaptation. In: ICCV Workshop on Transferring and Adapting Source Knowledge in Computer Vision (2016)
20. Tzeng, E., Hoffman, J., Zhang, N., Saenko, K.: Deep domain confusion: maximizing for domain invariance. arXiv:1412.3474 (2014)
21. Tzeng, E., Hoffman, J., Saenko, K., Darrell, T.: Adversarial discriminative domain adaptation. In: CVPR (2017)
22. Zhou, Z.-H., Li, M.: Tri-training: exploiting unlabeled data using three classifiers. TKDE 17(11), 1529–1541 (2005)
23. Zhu, X.: Semi-supervised learning literature survey. Technical report, University of Wisconsin-Madison (2008)

Common Structured Low-Rank Matrix Recovery for Cross-View Classification

Zihan Long[2], Jiamiao Xu[2], Fangzhao Wang[2], Chuanwu Yang[2], and Xinge You[1,2(✉)]

[1] Research Institute of Huazhong, University of Science and Technology in Shenzhen, Shenzhen, China
youxg@mail.hust.edu.cn
[2] Huazhong University of Science and Technology, Wuhan 430074, China

Abstract. Low-rank multi-view subspace learning (LMvSL) has been an essential solution to the problem of cross-view classification. Despite the promising performance on real applications, it still remains challenging to classify objects when there is a large discrepancy between gallery data and probe data. In this paper, we propose a Common Structured Low-rank Matrix Recovery (CSLMR) algorithm to elegantly handle view discrepancy and discriminancy simultaneously. Specifically, our CSLMR incorporates common representation constraint and structured regularization into the fundamental model of LMvSL to learn a discriminant latent subspace. Furthermore, an efficient optimization method is developed and the complexity analysis of CSLMR is presented for completeness. Experimental results on CMU PIE dataset demonstrate the superiority of our CSLMR.

Keywords: Low-rank representation · Multi-view learning · Subspace learning · Cross-view classification

1 Introduction

Objects captured with different sensors or at different viewpoints generate multi-view data [6,14]. For example, faces can be observed by visual light cameras, near-infrared cameras or artists, resulting in visual light images, near-infrared images or sketches, respectively. Moreover, a face can also be taken from diverse viewpoints, leading to multi-pose face photos. Due to the underlying complementarity and commonness among multi-view data, two research subjects come to public attention including multi-view fusion [21] and cross-view classification [16,18], where the former aims to learn a latent intact space by integrating information, whereas the latter intends to find a common subspace by extracting view-variance features. This work focuses on the latter.

Cross-view classification is aim at performing classification when gallery and probe data are from different views. However, it is not meaningful to directly

---

The first author is a student.

Z. Lin et al. (Eds.): PRCV 2019, LNCS 11857, pp. 361–372, 2019.
https://doi.org/10.1007/978-3-030-31654-9_31

match samples from diverse views due to the distribution difference among views. Many work in recent years has been done to handle this problem. Among all approaches, multi-view subspace learning (MvSL) [1,5,7,16] based approaches are the most well-known methods that endeavor to project data into a common subspace by multiple mapping functions, one for each view, in which the view discrepancy is removed. Despite their empirical success, this kind of methods cannot be used when the view-related information of test samples is not provided in advance.

To circumvent this drawback, low-rank multi-view subspace learning (LMvSL) was thereafter presented. Different from MvSL based approaches, it intends to learn a common mapping function shared by all views. One of the most typical LMvSL based algorithm is the Low-rank Common Subspace (LRCS) [2] that attempts to discover the shared information among multi-view data by view-specific projections. Although LRCS is of great significance in this area, its performance is limited in real applications by reason of the neglect of supervised information. For this reason, Supervised Regularization based Robust Subspace (SRRS) [10], Robust Multi-view Subspace Learning (RMSL) [3] and Collective Low-rank Subspace (CLRS) [4] were later proposed by taking into consideration discriminant information under the framework of graph embedding. It is worth noting that, benefiting from the consideration of view-variance and class structures, RMSL can learn a more discriminant subspace compared with SRRS and CLRS. The above methods learn view-invariance features via low-rank representation (LRR) [12,13]. However, LRR cannot reach this target especially when the view gap is large. To cope with this scenario, Low-rank Discriminant Embedding (LRDE) [8] was proposed by further establishing the relations among inter-view within-class samples. Despite its satisfactory performance, one should note that the graph for criteria A is not precise due to the inaccurate similarity measurements between heterogeneous samples [16,18].

This work aims to more perfectly deal with this scenario when the discrepancy among views is large. Different from aforementioned methods that either only rely on the efficacy of LRR or build relations among heterogeneous samples in a brute force manner, motivated with [18], we develop a common representation constraint to handle view discrepancy. Furthermore, inspired by block-diagonal representation [19,20], we design a structured regularization to learn multiple block-diagonal representation for multi-view data, which thus improves discriminancy.

The remainder of this paper is arranged as follows. Section 2 describes our CSLMR, its optimization and complexity analysis in detail, and experiments to demonstrate the effectiveness are conducted in Sect. 3. Finally, Sect. 4 concludes this paper.

2   Common Structured Low-Rank Matrix Recovery

In this section, we first elaborate on the motivation and general idea of our CSLMR. Furthermore, an efficient optimization and its computational complexity for CSLMR are presented.

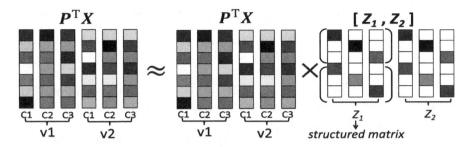

Fig. 1. An overview of our CSLMR. The given two-view data is from three classes. Squares stand for features and white square denotes the value of feature is zero. We have $Z_1 = Z_2$ when common representation constraint is employed, and a multiple block-diagonal representation (also term it structured matrix) Z_1 is learned when structured regularization is imposed on Z_1.

2.1   Common Structured Low-Rank Matrix Recovery

Suppose that we are given a training set with m objects, where each object is captured with n sensors or at n viewpoints, leading to n samples $\{x_1^i, \ldots, x_n^i\}$ for each object o^i. Here, $\{x_1^i, \ldots, x_n^i\}$ are also known as paired samples [14,16] with respect to object o^i. We then obtain a n-view dataset $X = [X_1, X_2, \ldots, X_n]$, where $X_v = [X_{v_1}, \cdots, X_{vC}] \in \mathcal{R}^{D \times m}$ is the data matrix from the v-th view, D is the feature dimensionality and $X_{v_c} \in \mathcal{R}^{D \times n_c}$ stands for all samples from the c-th class under the v-th view. LMvSL based approaches intend to project multi-view data into a d-dimensional subspace via a common projection P. Its fundamental framework can be formulated as:

$$\min \|Z\|_* + \lambda_1 \|E\|_{2,1}$$
$$s.t. \quad P^{\mathrm{T}} X = P^{\mathrm{T}} X Z + E, \quad P^{\mathrm{T}} P = \mathrm{I}, \tag{1}$$

where $Z = [Z_1, \ldots, Z_n] \in \mathcal{R}^{mn \times mn}$ is the low-rank representation of $P^{\mathrm{T}} X$ and $Z_v \in \mathcal{R}^{mn \times m}$ denotes the representation of $P^{\mathrm{T}} X_v$. Furthermore, E in Eq. (1) is used to model outliers [12]. $\lambda_1 > 0$ is a balanced parameter. Despite its elegant flexibility, one should note that most LMvSL based methods cannot effectively remove view discrepancy among data.

The state-of-the-art multi-view subspace learning (MvSL) based methods for cross-view classification [16,18] have indicated that the proper utilization of paired samples helps to mitigate the discrepancy. To this end, we develop a common representation constraint and integrate it into Eq. (1):

$$\min \|Z_1\|_* + \lambda_1 \|E\|_{2,1}$$
$$s.t. \quad P^{\mathrm{T}} X = P^{\mathrm{T}} X Z_1 D + E, \quad P^{\mathrm{T}} P = \mathrm{I_d}, \tag{2}$$

where I_d is an d-dimensional identity matrix and $D \in \mathcal{R}^{m \times mn}$ is defined as:

$$D = \left(\overbrace{I_m, ..., I_m}^{n} \right). \tag{3}$$

It is worth noting that we have $Z_1 = Z_2 = \cdots = Z_n$ after solving problem (2). Hence, paired samples present the same representation vector, which thus results in the mitigation of view discrepancy.

Moreover, block-diagonal representation learning has shown great potential in improving discriminability [19,20]. To this end, we extend this idea to multi-view scenario and develop a structured regularization to learn a multiple block-diagonal representation for multi-view data:

$$\min \|Z_1\|_* + \lambda_1 \|E\|_{2,1} + \lambda_2 \|M \circ Z_1\|_F^2$$
$$s.t. \quad P^T X = P^T X Z_1 D + E, \quad P^T P = I_d, \tag{4}$$

where $\lambda_2 > 0$ is a trade-off parameter and $M \in \mathcal{R}^{mn \times m}$ is defined as:

$$M = G - H,$$
$$G = \begin{pmatrix} e_m e_m^T \\ \vdots \\ e_m e_m^T \end{pmatrix}, \quad H = \begin{pmatrix} Y \\ \vdots \\ Y \end{pmatrix},$$
$$Y = \begin{pmatrix} e_{n_1} e_{n_1}^T & \cdots & 0 \\ \vdots & \ddots & \vdots \\ 0 & \cdots & e_{n_C} e_{n_C}^T \end{pmatrix}, \tag{5}$$

where e_m is a m-dimensional column vector with all elements equal to one, and n_c ($c \in \{1, \cdots, C\}$) is the number of samples from the c-th class. Obviously, a multiple block-diagonal representation (structured matrix) is learned by optimizing Eq. (4). To make readers easier to follow, an overview of our CSLMR is shown in Fig. 1.

2.2   Solution to CSLMR

To optimize Z_1 for ease, a relax variable J_1 is introduced and Eq. (4) can be reformulated as:

$$\min_{J_1, E, P, Z_1} \|J_1\|_* + \lambda_1 \|E\|_{2,1} + \lambda_2 \|M \circ Z_1\|_F^2$$
$$s.t. \quad P^T X = P^T X Z_1 D + E, \quad J_1 = Z_1. \tag{6}$$

Then, by introducing the Lagrange multipliers $Y_1 \in \mathcal{R}^{d \times nm}$ and $Y_2 \in \mathcal{R}^{nm \times m}$, we have the augmented Lagrangian function as below:

$$\|J_1\|_* + \lambda_1 \|E\|_{2,1} + \lambda_2 \|M \circ Z_1\|_F^2$$
$$+ \text{tr}\left(Y_1^T \left(P^T X - P^T X Z_1 D - E\right)\right) + \text{tr}\left(Y_2^T (Z_1 - J_1)\right)$$
$$+ \frac{\mu}{2} \left(\left\|P^T X - P^T X Z_1 D - E\right\|_F^2 + \|Z_1 - J_1\|_F^2 \right) \tag{7}$$

where $\mu > 0$ is a penalty parameter.

Same as [4,9], our CSLMR algorithm can be optimized by alternately updating J_1, E, P and Z_1 in Eq. (7). It is worth noting that other variables are regarded as known variables with values in the t-th iteration when one variable is optimized in the $(t+1)$-th iteration. Here, we optimize variables in the $(t+1)$-th iteration as follows.

Updating J_1:

$$J_{1,t+1} = \arg\min \frac{1}{\mu_t} \|J_1\|_* + \frac{1}{2} \left\| J_1 - \left(Z_{1,t} + \frac{Y_{2,t}}{\mu_t} \right) \right\|_F^2. \tag{8}$$

From [11], Eq. (8) can be optimized by

$$J_{1,t+1} = U S_\epsilon [S] V^{\mathrm{T}}, \tag{9}$$

where $U S V^{\mathrm{T}}$ is the singular value decomposition (SVD) of $\left(Z_{1,t} + \frac{Y_{2,t}}{\mu_t} \right)$, and soft thresholding operator $S_\epsilon [S]$ is defined as:

$$S_\epsilon [S_{ij}] = \begin{cases} S_{ij} - \epsilon, & S_{ij} > \epsilon, \\ S_{ij} + \epsilon, & S_{ij} < -\epsilon, \\ 0, & \text{otherwise}. \end{cases} \tag{10}$$

where $\epsilon > 0$ and S_{ij} is the i-th row j-th column element of S.
Updating E:

$$E_{t+1} = \arg\min \frac{\lambda_1}{\mu_t} \|E\|_{2,1} + \frac{1}{2} \left\| E - \left(P_t^{\mathrm{T}} X - P_t^{\mathrm{T}} X Z_{1,t} D + \frac{Y_{1,t}}{\mu_t} \right) \right\|_F^2, \tag{11}$$

Eq. (11) can be optimized by shrinkage operate [17].
Updating P

$$P_{t+1} = \left((X - X Z_{1,t} D)(X - X Z_{1,t} D)^{\mathrm{T}} \right)^{-1} \left((X - X Z_{1,t} D) \left(E_t^{\mathrm{T}} - \frac{Y_{1,t}^{\mathrm{T}}}{\mu_t} \right) \right) \tag{12}$$

Updating Z_1:

$$Z_{1,t+1} = \arg\min \lambda_2 \|M \circ Z_1\|_F^2 + \mathrm{tr}\left(Y_{1,t}^{\mathrm{T}} \left(P_t^{\mathrm{T}} X - P_t^{\mathrm{T}} X Z_1 D - E_t \right) \right)$$
$$+ \mathrm{tr}\left(Y_{2,t}^{\mathrm{T}} (Z_1 - J_{1,t}) \right) + \frac{\mu}{2} \left(\left\| P_t^{\mathrm{T}} X - P_t^{\mathrm{T}} X Z_1 D - E_t \right\|_F^2 + \|Z_1 - J_{1,t}\|_F^2 \right). \tag{13}$$

To facilitate optimization, Eq. (13) can be translated to

$$Z_{1,t+1} = \arg\min \lambda_2 \|Z_1 - R\|_F^2 + \mathrm{tr}\left(Y_{1,t}^{\mathrm{T}} \left(P_t^{\mathrm{T}} X - P_t^{\mathrm{T}} X Z_{1,t} D - E_t \right) \right)$$
$$+ \mathrm{tr}\left(Y_{2,t}^{\mathrm{T}} (Z_{1,t} - J_{1,t}) \right) + \frac{\mu}{2} \left(\left\| P_t^{\mathrm{T}} X - P_t^{\mathrm{T}} X Z_{1,t} D - E_t \right\|_F^2 + \|Z_{1,t} - J_{1,t}\|_F^2 \right), \tag{14}$$

where R is defined as:

$$R = H \circ Z_{1,t} \tag{15}$$

Then, the matrix Z_1 can be updated as follows:

$$
\begin{aligned}
Z_{1,t+1} &= T_1^{-1} T_2, \\
T_1 &= \left(\frac{2\lambda_2}{\mu_t} + n X^{\mathrm{T}} P_t P_t^{\mathrm{T}} X + I \right), \\
T_2 &= \left(X^{\mathrm{T}} P_t \left(P_t^{\mathrm{T}} X - E_t \right) D^{\mathrm{T}} + J_{1,t} + \frac{1}{\mu_t} \left(2R + X^{\mathrm{T}} P Y_{1,t} D^{\mathrm{T}} - Y_{2,t} \right) \right).
\end{aligned}
\tag{16}
$$

Finally, Lagrange multipliers and penalty parameter are updated as below:

$$
\begin{aligned}
Y_{1,t+1} &= Y_{1,t} + \mu_t \left(P_{t+1}^{\mathrm{T}} X - P_{t+1}^{\mathrm{T}} X Z_{1,t+1} D - E_{t+1} \right), \\
Y_{2,t+1} &= Y_{2,t} + \mu_t \left(Z_{1,t+1} - J_{1,t+1} \right), \\
\mu_{t+1} &= \min \left(\rho \mu_t, \mu_{max} \right),
\end{aligned}
\tag{17}
$$

where constants ρ and μ_{max} are determined by cross validation.

2.3 Complexity Analysis

In this section, we analyze the computational complexity of CSLMR in one iteration for simplicity. Obviously, according to the optimization in Sect. 2.2, the computational cost of CSLMR mainly comes from the updating of J_1, E, P and Z_1. From Eqs. (9) and (10), the complexity of J_1 is approximately $\mathcal{O}\left(m^3 n\right)$. From Eq. (11), the computational complexity of E is close to $\mathcal{O}\left(m^2 nD + mnDd\right)$. The main cost of P and Z_1 is from matrix multiplication and matrix inverse. Hence, from Eqs. (12) and (16), the computational cost of P and Z_1 is approximately $\mathcal{O}\left(m^2 nD + mnD^2 + D^3\right)$ and $\mathcal{O}\left(m^2 n^2 d + mnDd + m^3 n^3\right)$ considering that $D > d$ satisfies. Furthermore, we have $m > D$ and $m > n$ in practice. The complexity of CSLMR in one iteration is $\mathcal{O}\left(m^3 n^3\right)$.

3 Experiments

In this section, the performance of CSLMR is qualitatively and quantitatively evaluated on the CMU Pose, Illumination, and Expression database (CMU PIE), where this benchmark dataset is commonly used to perform face recognition across pose. To sufficiently demonstrate the efficacy of our CSLMR, the state-of-the-art LMvSL based methods are chosen for comparison, including SRRS [10], LRCS [2], RMSL [3], LRDE [9] and CLRS [4] (Table 1).

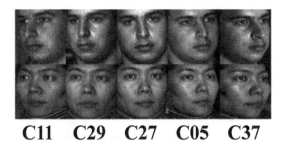

C11   C29   C27   C05   C37

Fig. 2. Exemplar subjects from CMU PIE.

Table 1. Comparison results (%) of LMvSL based approaches. The best two results are marked with bold and italic.

Methods	SRRS	LRCS	RMSL	LRDE	CLRS	CSLMR
Case 1	74.3 ± 6.5	74.0 ± 6.7	75.7 ± 7.7	*81.1 ± 5.9*	75.1 ± 6.2	**88.7 ± 3.2**
Case 2	66.8 ± 4.3	66.1 ± 4.4	68.0 ± 4.7	*74.1 ± 6.4*	67.3 ± 4.3	**78.1 ± 4.1**
Case 3	69.0 ± 5.2	68.9 ± 5.5	70.7 ± 4.4	*84.0 ± 4.9*	69.1 ± 5.4	**89.6 ± 2.8**
Case 4	56.2 ± 3.4	56.3 ± 3.1	57.9 ± 3.2	*70.3 ± 5.6*	56.7 ± 3.8	**76.9 ± 3.1**
Case 5	59.4 ± 3.3	58.1 ± 3.8	62.0 ± 3.0	*79.5 ± 5.0*	60.0 ± 3.3	**82.8 ± 2.3**

3.1 Superiority of Our CSLMR

We present the evaluation of LMvSL based approaches in a subset of CMU PIE, where this set contains 1,360 images of 68 persons under 5 near frontal poses, i.e., C37, C05, C27, C29, C11 (see Fig. 2). In our experiments, 5 poses are specially combined to construct multiple cases, namely case 1: {C27, C29}, case 2: {C27, C11}, case 3: {C05, C27, C29}, case 4: {C37, C27, C11} and case 5: {C37, C05, C27, C29, C11}. Experiments in each case are conducted 10 times by randomly dividing the face subset into training, validation and testing sets at a ratio of 40 : 14 : 14. Same as [7,16], Principal Component Analysis (PCA) [15] is used for dimensionality reduction. Validation set is used to determine hyperparameters in the training phase and pairwise manner is adopted to evaluate algorithms during the test period. All the classification accuracy in 5 cases of face subset, obtained by our CSLMR and the recent LMvSL based methods, is summarized in Table 3.

As can be seen, the performance of LRCS ranks the lowest in almost all cases among LMvSL based methods as expected. Due to the consideration of supervised information, SRRS and CLRS perform better than LRCS. RMSL further improves the cross-view classification performance by taking into consideration class structure and view-variance structure. On the other hand, LRDE outperforms RMSL with a large improvement. One possible reason is that criteria A (see reference [9] for more details) can more effectively remove the discrepancy among views compared with low-rank constraint. Moreover, our CSLMR consistently

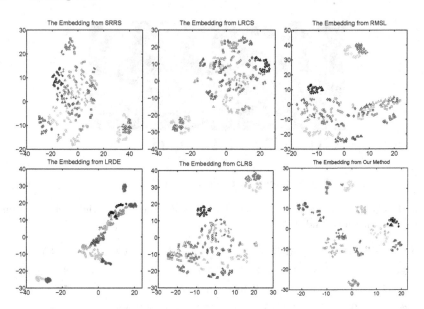

Fig. 3. The 2D subspace from LMvSL based methods in case 5. Colors and markers denote classes and views, respectively. (Color figure online)

achieves the best results in all cases with a large gain owing to the mitigation of discrepancy by common representation constraint and the improvement of discriminancy by structured regularization. To make the comparison more intuitive, we further visualize the results of all methods in case 5 and present them in Fig. 3. It is obvious that compared with other competitors, within-class samples from all views are united and between-class samples are more thoroughly separated in the subspace generated by our method. This indicates that the view discrepancy is removed and the discriminancy is enhanced for our CSLMR.

To deeply analyze the effectiveness of our method, we present all pairwise accuracy of LMvSL based counterparts in case 5 in Table 2. As expected, our CSLMR outperforms other comparative approaches in almost all scenario. Specifically, the more significant advantage appears when the divergence between gallery and probe data is large, such as gallery-probe: C37-C11, C05-C11 and C27-C37 and so on. The indicates that the common representation constraint did help to reduce view discrepancy. Furthermore, our method achieves the best results when gallery and probe data are from the same view. This implies that the structured regularization has the ability to effectively improve discriminability.

We finally present the training time of all methods in all cases of face subset to evaluate the computational complexity of the proposed CSLMR. As can be seen, although the time complexity of all competing methods is in the same time order, the advantage of our CSLMR becomes more obvious with the increase of the number of views. The reason is that the size of representation matrix in Eq. (4) for CSLMR is smaller than competitors in Eq. (1).

Table 2. Pairwise accuracy (%) of LMvSL based approaches in case 5 of face subset.

Gallery	Probe	SRRS	LRCS	RMSL	LRDE	CLRS	CSLMR
C37	C37	98.4	95.1	*100.0*	99.1	99.5	**100.0**
	C05	69.3	71.6	69.5	84.1	*84.6*	**85.4**
	C27	30.5	29.1	37.7	**68.2**	50.4	*66.1*
	C29	28.6	29.8	30.4	**63.0**	38.0	*61.4*
	C11	29.8	28.0	32.5	*61.6*	33.2	**66.4**
C05	C37	83.2	80.5	*84.1*	78.4	69.3	**92.7**
	C05	87.9	85.7	99.8	*100.0*	92.9	**100.0**
	C27	63.0	60.0	67.3	*83.4*	76.3	**86.6**
	C29	47.3	47.7	49.6	*75.2*	39.6	**82.1**
	C11	45.9	43.2	45.7	*65.7*	26.4	**82.3**
C27	C37	50.2	49.3	48.0	*66.1*	28.9	**78.8**
	C05	72.3	70.4	74.3	*85.7*	63.8	**85.9**
	C27	85.0	81.4	89.1	*97.1*	88.9	**99.1**
	C29	64.1	62.3	66.6	*79.5*	47.5	**82.3**
	C11	50.1	49.1	52.1	*67.5*	31.1	**77.9**
C29	C37	38.2	37.5	37.3	*64.5*	28.0	**68.2**
	C05	43.8	42.5	46.4	*79.8*	47.0	**81.6**
	C27	49.1	45.5	48.8	**85.5**	64.8	*75.5*
	C29	91.6	89.6	*98.9*	98.8	94.3	**99.6**
	C11	85.9	83.6	85.5	*89.8*	84.8	**95.2**
C11	C37	34.8	33.9	37.0	63.8	**70.5**	*62.7*
	C05	27.7	29.6	31.8	*70.5*	48.0	**73.4**
	C27	32.5	34.1	38.0	**75.9**	50.4	*69.5*
	C29	84.3	82.1	82.9	*91.4*	88.9	**96.6**
	C11	91.8	89.3	96.6	*98.0*	94.3	**100.0**
Average		59.4	58.1	62.0	*79.7*	60.0	**82.2**

Table 3. Training time of 10 iterations. **Bold** denotes the best result.

Methods	SRRS	LRCS	RMSL	LRDE	CLRS	CSLMR
Case 1	54	48	113	47	99	**32**
Case 2	54	48	116	47	99	**32**
Case 3	113	87	214	87	195	**52**
Case 4	112	87	215	87	195	**52**
Case 5	503	202	398	203	468	**103**

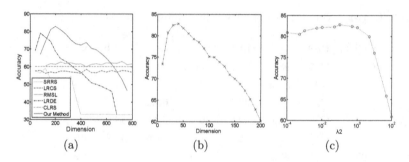

Fig. 4. Classification accuracy in case 5 of face subset. (a) Classification accuracy of different algorithms with diverse PCA dimensions. (b) Classification accuracy of our CSLMR on diverse dimensionality subspace. (c) Classification accuracy of our CSLMR with diverse λ_2.

3.2 Property Analysis

In the last experiments, we first analyze the impact of PCA dimensionality, subspace dimensionality and the hyper-parameter λ_2 on the performance of CSLMR. It is worth mentioning that the influence of λ_1 is neglect, since the SVD is not converged when λ_1 is not unreasonable. The change trend of performance is clearly shown in Fig. 4. As shown in (a), despite the sensitivity of our method to PCA dimensions, it maintains superiority over a wide range. Moreover, our CSLMR prefers a low-dimensional subspace generated by PCA. Similarly, as shown in (b), the performance of CSLMR dramatically changes with subspace dimensionality. We suggest using cross validation to determine its value in real applications. On the other hand, the proposed CSLMR achieves a high accuracy when $\lambda_2 \in [10^{-2}, 1]$. We finally show the change trend of accuracy with different iterations in Fig. 5. Obviously, the performance of CSLMR reaches its maximum after a certain number of iterations. This indicates the fast convergence of the optimization method to CSLMR.

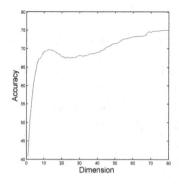

Fig. 5. Classification accuracy in case 5 of face subset with the increment of iterations.

4 Conclusion

In this paper, we proposed a novel CSLMR algorithm for cross-view classification by incorporating common representation constraint and structured regularization into the basic LMvSL based model. Experimental results demonstrate that our method can effectively remove the view discrepancy and learn a more discriminant common subspace, thus boosting the cross-view classification performance. From the in-depth analysis, we can find that paired samples are required for our model. Hence, we are interested in developing a new version of our model to handle incomplete-view data.

Acknowledgments. This work was supported partially by the Key Science and Technology of Shenzhen (JCYJ20180305180637611), the Shenzhen Research Council (JCYJ20180305180804836 and JSGG20180507182030600), the Key Science and Technology Innovation Program of Hubei Province (2017AAA017), the Natural Science Foundation of Hubei Province (2018CFB691), the Special Projects for Technology Innovation of Hubei Province (2018ACA135), the National Natural Science Foundation of China (61571205 and 61772220) and the key research and development program of China (2016YFE0121200).

References

1. Cao, G., Iosifidis, A., Chen, K., Gabbouj, M.: Generalized multi-view embedding for visual recognition and cross-modal retrieval. IEEE Trans. Cybern. **48**(9), 2542–2555 (2018)
2. Ding, Z., Fu, Y.: Low-rank common subspace for multi-view learning. In: 2014 IEEE International Conference on Data Mining (ICDM), pp. 110–119. IEEE (2014)
3. Ding, Z., Fu, Y.: Robust multi-view subspace learning through dual low-rank decompositions. In: Proceedings of the Thirtieth AAAI Conference on Artificial Intelligence, AAAI 2016, pp. 1181–1187 (2016)
4. Ding, Z., Fu, Y.: Robust multiview data analysis through collective low-rank subspace. IEEE Trans. Neural Netw. Learn. Syst. **29**(5), 1986–1997 (2018)
5. Hotelling, H.: Relations between two sets of variates. Biometrika **28**(3/4), 321–377 (1936)
6. Kan, M., Shan, S., Zhang, H., Lao, S., Chen, X.: Multi-view discriminant analysis. In: Fitzgibbon, A., Lazebnik, S., Perona, P., Sato, Y., Schmid, C. (eds.) ECCV 2012. LNCS, vol. 7572, pp. 808–821. Springer, Heidelberg (2012). https://doi.org/10.1007/978-3-642-33718-5_58
7. Kan, M., Shan, S., Zhang, H., Lao, S., Chen, X.: Multi-view discriminant analysis. IEEE Trans. Pattern Anal. Mach. Intell. **38**(1), 188–194 (2016)
8. Li, J., Wu, Y., Zhao, J., Lu, K.: Low-rank discriminant embedding for multiview learning. IEEE Trans. Cybern. **47**(11), 3516–3529 (2017)
9. Li, J., Wu, Y., Zhao, J., Lu, K.: Low-rank discriminant embedding for multiview learning. IEEE Trans. Cybern. (2016)
10. Li, S., Fu, Y.: Robust subspace discovery through supervised low-rank constraints. In: Proceedings of the 2014 SIAM International Conference on Data Mining, pp. 163–171. SIAM (2014)
11. Lin, Z., Chen, M., Ma, Y.: The augmented lagrange multiplier method for exact recovery of corrupted low-rank matrices. arXiv preprint arXiv:1009.5055 (2010)

12. Liu, G., Lin, Z., Yan, S., Sun, J., Yu, Y., Ma, Y.: Robust recovery of subspace structures by low-rank representation. IEEE Trans. Pattern Anal. Mach. Intell. **35**(1), 171–184 (2013)
13. Liu, G., Lin, Z., Yu, Y.: Robust subspace segmentation by low-rank representation. In: Proceedings of the 27th International Conference on Machine Learning (ICML-10), pp. 663–670 (2010)
14. Sharma, A., Kumar, A., Daume, H., Jacobs, D.W.: Generalized multiview analysis: a discriminative latent space. In: 2012 IEEE Conference on Computer Vision and Pattern Recognition (CVPR), pp. 2160–2167. IEEE (2012)
15. Turk, M., Pentland, A.: Eigenfaces for recognition. J. Cogn. Neurosci. **3**(1), 71–86 (1991)
16. Xu, J., Yu, S., You, X., Leng, M., Jing, X.Y., Chen, C.: Multi-view hybrid embedding: a divide-and-conquer approach. arXiv preprint arXiv:1804.07237 (2018)
17. Yang, J., Yin, W., Zhang, Y., Wang, Y.: A fast algorithm for edge-preserving variational multichannel image restoration. SIAM J. Imaging Sci. **2**(2), 569–592 (2009)
18. You, X., Xu, J., Yuan, W., Jing, X.Y., Tao, D., Zhang, T.: Multi-view common component discriminant analysis for cross-view classification. Pattern Recogn. (2019)
19. Zhang, Y., Jiang, Z., Davis, L.S.: Learning structured low-rank representations for image classification. In: Proceedings of the IEEE Conference on Computer Vision and Pattern Recognition, pp. 676–683 (2013)
20. Zhang, Z., Xu, Y., Shao, L., Yang, J.: Discriminative block-diagonal representation learning for image recognition. IEEE Trans. Neural Netw. Learn. Syst. **29**(7), 3111–3125 (2018)
21. Zhao, Y., et al.: Multi-view manifold learning with locality alignment. Pattern Recogn. **78**, 154–166 (2018)

Pruning Convolutional Neural Networks via Stochastic Gradient Hard Thresholding

Xin Yang$^{(\boxtimes)}$, Haiwei Lu, Hui Shuai, and Xiao-Tong Yuan

Jiangsu Key Laboratory of Big Data Analysis Technology, School of Automation,
Nanjing University of Information Science and Technology, Nanjing 210044, China
favorxin@163.com

Abstract. In this paper, we introduce an iterative filter pruning method to compress deep convolutional neural networks. Different from many existing network compression methods which fall into the training-pruning-fine-tuning framework, we propose a new hybrid stochastic gradient hard thresholding algorithm (AHSG-HT) for adaptive structured pruning. Our approach trains the original network from scratch and continually prunes the "unimportant" filters by setting their values to zero in order to let algorithm automatically select filters. After training, we adopt physically pruning method to discard the filters with zero weights. Finally, we reconstruct the network and obtain a compact network without fine-tuning which also has a comparable performance. We conduct several experiments using ResNet on CIFAR-10 and CIFAR-100. Our approach achieves 92.40% accuracy on ResNet-56 with 63% reduction in parameters and FLOPs. The accuracy of CIFAR-10 on Resnet-110 with 20% pruning rate can reach up to 94.09%, which exceeds the baseline accuracy of the full network without pruning.

Keywords: Convolutional neural network · Hybrid stochastic gradient hard thresholding algorithm · Iterative filter pruning

1 Introduction

The success of deep CNNs is usually accompanied by over-parameters and high computational costs, and the deeper networks have more resource costs. However, the numbers of parameters, which often exceed 100 million, deter many practical applications (especially those based on portable devices) from carrying out. Taking the classic VGG-16 as an example, it has a significant number of parameters which reach up to 130 million, and takes up more than 500 MB storage space. Moreover, it needs 30.9 billion float point operations (FLOPs) to just

---

Xin Yang is currently working toward the Master degree in the School of Automation, Nanjing University of Information Science and Technology.

© Springer Nature Switzerland AG 2019
Z. Lin et al. (Eds.): PRCV 2019, LNCS 11857, pp. 373–385, 2019.
https://doi.org/10.1007/978-3-030-31654-9_32

complete the recognition task of an image. The mentioned aspects are seriously restricting the deployment of CNNs in real-world applications.

In recent years, network compression and acceleration in deep CNNs gradually become a hot topic in the field of deep learning. Many researchers have proposed various novel algorithms, which can reduce the complexity as much as possible while pursuing high accuracy of the model in order to achieve a balance between performance and overhead. Overall, most of the compression algorithms aim to transform a large and complex pre-trained model to an efficient and compact network. According to the damaged degree of pre-trained network architectures, we divide the compression algorithms into two distinct parts. One part is the unstructured compression, which contains low-rank approximation [2,20], weight pruning [5,6,23], parameter quantization [5,21] and binary network [19]. The above algorithms are conducted to reduce the network size as much as possible, and thus could greatly transform the architecture of the pre-trained network. The other part is structured compression, which will not destroy the original architecture. It mainly includes knowledge distillation [10,16], compact convolutional filters [1] and filter pruning [8,9,13-15,17]. Structured compression only discards the "unimportant" layers or filters of the original network, then we can obtain the final efficient small network which ideally adapts to the existing deep learning libraries (i.e., Pytorch) [18].

In this paper, we propose an iterative filter pruning approach, which completes the pruning process through hybrid stochastic gradient hard thresholding algorithm (AHSG-HT) [24]. The flowchart of the proposed method is shown in Fig. 1. Inspired by soft filter pruning [8], we adopt AHSG-HT algorithm as the optimizer and prune the filters by hard thresholding [4,22] operation. In the optimizer, we measure the weights of filters with hard thresholding and select the filters with small weights to set zero values. As the epochs increase, the filters' weight parameters are updated with the samples and gradients, that means these filters with zero value weight are not constant and can be continually updating. As for how to define the filters is "important", we find that preserving filters with larger weights normally have a better impact on the final performance.

We prune ResNet [7] on several benchmark datasets shows that we have the following advantages: (1) We implement the automatic structured pruning method which allows the algorithm to select the "important" filters. It can be also understood as filter search or a guide to neural architecture search. (2) Our approach employs iterative filter pruning in the iteration progress that results in saving the time of fine-tuning and retraining. The proposed algorithm can provide convergence guarantees and enhance performance while using the pre-trained network. (3) Not only that, we can obtain compact ResNet with up to 39% parameters and FLOPs reduction at the cost of a few accuracies or even better performance with 27% parameters and FLOPs reduction while compared with the baseline.

The remainder of this paper is organized as follows. In Sect. 2, we introduce some relevant work and concrete pruning strategies. Section 3 gives the details of the proposed iterative pruning filters algorithm. Some contrast experiments using

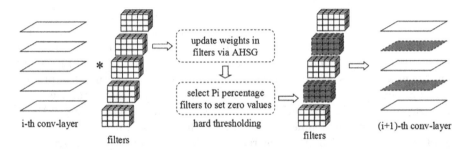

Fig. 1. Pruning filters at each convolutional layer and influence on the next layer. We use an orange dashed block to represent a pruned filter and parallelogram to indicate a feature map which is generated from different mini-batch sizes data. The network's weights are updated via AHSG while the filters' weights need to carry on the hard thresholding operation. We use hard thresholding to select the "unimportant" filters, which is conducted by computing the weights of filters and sort them. If we set the "unimportant" filters to zero, the corresponding orange feature maps in (i+1)th convolutional layer will be influenced. Moreover, we repeatedly judge the importance of each layer's filters to prune and affect the output. After iterative pruning, we realize automatically selecting the useful filters to preserve and the useless filters to prune. (Color figure online)

several benchmark datasets on ResNet are shown in Sect. 4. Section 5 concludes this paper.

2   Related Work

In recent years, the success of deep convolutional networks is accompanied by the increasing demand for computing resources. Network size, storage cost, and FLOPs are the main constraints which hinder the application in the mobile devices. Many researchers proposed various compression algorithms in terms of the above problems. We divide related work into the following two aspects.

Unstructured Compression. Han et al. [6] propose a three-step weight pruning method. First, it learns which weight connections are "important" through normal training, and then prunes the "unimportant" weights. Finally, they retrain the pruned network and fine-tune the remaining sparse connections. [5] is mainly about quantization which also adopts the above weight pruning method. After weight pruning, they quantize the weights to enforce weight sharing, then apply Huffman coding to quantized weights for further compression. Jin et al. [11] preserve the most prominent weight parameters and zero the others. For a better balance of performance and network size, they fine-tune the preserved weight parameters. Although the pruned network has considerable performance and compression rate, the pruned network is unstructured and the pruned connections are discontinuous. The random sparse network can achieve the theoretical acceleration effect only by a special library or even specialized hardware devices. Thus the generality of the pruned network is greatly restricted.

Structured Compression. Li et al. [13] present a filter pruning method by removing the whole filters together with their connecting feature maps which are identified as "unimportant". This approach considers that the convolutional layer should be pruned, and they use ℓ_1-norm to select "unimportant" filters and prune them as well as related feature maps. Finally, they fine-tune the pruned network as the same as conventional methods. He et al. [9] use an iterative two-step method to prune channels in each layer. The first step is using LASSO regression to select the channels and maintain the representative channels. The second step is using the remaining representative channels to reconstruct the original output of the layer which is trying to keep the output of feature maps after pruning the same as before by using linear least squares. Liu et al. [14] take the scaling factor of the network BN layer as an important factor that decides which corresponding channels will be pruned. They impose L1 regularization on the important factor that can identify insignificant channels and automatically prune corresponding specific channels. He et al. [8] propose a soft filter pruning method which allows the pruned filters to update during the training procedure instead of directly pruning. They use the ℓ_2-norm to evaluate the importance of each filter and set the value of filters with the small ℓ_2-norm to zero. After iterating, they delete the pruned filters and obtain the compressed network. Soft filter pruning trains the network from scratch without the fine-tuning process. Liu et al. [15] compare six state-of-the-art pruning algorithms and considers that training an over-parameterized network is not necessary to obtain an efficient final network. They also use various contrast experiments to demonstrate that most pruning algorithms can be regarded to perform network architecture search.

Our work also adopts structured compression, which use AHSG-HT algorithm to select "unimportant" filters and set them to zero that the values of filters can be updated in the training process. We iteratively prune the filters in each optimizer step till the final epoch. Our algorithm doesn't need the fine-tuning process, which results in the saving of fine-tuning time. After iterative pruning, we physically prune the filters with zero values and reconstruct the network. Finally, a compact and efficient network is obtained.

3   Methodology

In this section, we aim to provide a simple way to achieve filter pruning in deep CNNs. We first introduce the efficient stochastic gradient hard thresholding method. Moreover, we explain how the algorithm iteratively prunes filters in the training process and describe the final physical pruning procedure to obtain a compact network.

3.1   Hybrid Stochastic Hard Thresholding

Let us consider the following optimization problem which is used in high-dimensional statistical estimation:

$$\min_{x} f(x) = \frac{1}{n} \sum_{i=1}^{n} f_i(x), \tag{1}$$

where $f_i(x)$ is the i-th sample's individual loss. A plain gradient descent hard thresholding iteration as follows:

$$x^{t+1} = \Phi_k(x^t - \eta \nabla f(x^t)), \tag{2}$$

where Φ_k is the hard thresholding operation which keeps the largest k entries in magnitude for vector $(x^t - \eta \nabla f(x^t))$ and sets the other entries to zero values, η is the learning rate. For pruning filters, we determine whether the weights in the filters need to be pruned or not with ℓ_1-norm. In practice, we define ℓ_1-norm: $\| x \|_1 \doteq \Sigma_j | x_j |$.

The above is normal gradient descent hard thresholding, but we adopt an efficient approach. The hybrid stochastic gradient descent hard thresholding (AHSG-HT) [24] method can iteratively and randomly extract gradually increasing the mini-batch size from whole data for gradient estimation. It randomly selects s_t samples S_t from all data and evaluates the average gradient

$$g^t = \frac{1}{s_t} \sum_{i_t \in S_t} \nabla f_{i_t}(x^t). \tag{3}$$

For variable update x^{t+1}, they use the average gradient g^t with a hard thresholding step. Hybrid stochastic gradient descent hard thresholding has the following variable update form:

$$x^{t+1} = \Phi_k(x^t - \eta g^t). \tag{4}$$

For further acceleration, AHSG-HT adds a momentum $\nu > 0$ based on the variant $(x^t - x^{t-1})$ and forms the following formulation:

$$x^{t+1} = \Phi_k(x^t - \eta g^t + \nu(x^t - x^{t-1})). \tag{5}$$

3.2   AHSG-HT Filter Pruning

Pruning is considered as a fast and effective compression method. According to the standard of pruning, we can divide the pruning into serval kinds, e.g., weight-level, filter-level, and even layer-level. Filter-level pruning methods [9,13,14,17] propose a lot of pruning criterions based channels and filters. They usually prune an over-parameterized network to obtain a compact network and fine-tune the pruned model to achieve similar or better performance. Those algorithms directly discard the whole filters or channels and do not affect the network's architecture. Considering the application of pruning methods, we adopt filter-level pruning to achieve a compact and efficient network.

In Algorithm 1, our approach uses iterative hard thresholding operation to select "unimportant" filters and prune them in the training procedure. We judge the filters less useful and set the whole filter to zero after the optimizer update parameters in each epoch. Inspired by [8], we can also allow the pruned filters to update during the epoch. Thus we can maximize the network's capacity which can rival the original network's performance. We update parameters as normal, but the difference is that we use the hard thresholding operation to prune filters at each step of optimizer instead of pruning filters after every epoch. In other words, we use the pruning operation more frequently than [8]. We obtain a sparse network which has a certain number of filters with zero weights after the final epoch. Finally, we reconstruct the sparse network to a compact network.

Algorithm 1: Convolutional Neural Networks Pruning via AHSG-HT.

Input: Initial network parameters $x = \{x_c, x_b, x_f\}$, convolutional layers' parameters x_c, convolutional layers' filter parameters x_{filter}, BN layers' parameters x_b, fully connected layers' parameters x_f, sample index set $S = \{1, \cdots, n\}$, pruning rate P_i, learning rate η, momentum strength ν, mini-batch sizes $\{s_t\}$, increasing step size δ, max mini-batch sizes$\{s_{tmax}\}$, convolutional layers' numbers L, filter numbers ℓ.

Output: The compact network and its architecture.

1   **for** $epoch = 1, 2, \cdots, epoch_{max}$ **do**
2   **for** $step = 1, 2, \cdots, step_{max}$ **do**
3   **if** $s_t \leq s_{tmax}$ **then**
4   Uniformly randomly select s_t sample S_t from S;
5         $s_t = s_t + \delta$
6   **else**
7   Uniformly randomly select s_{tmax} sample S_t from S;
8   **end**
9   Compute the approximate gradient $g^t = \frac{1}{s_t} \sum_{i_t \in S_t} \nabla f_{i_t}(x^t)$;
10   Update $x^{t+1} = \{x_c^{t+1}, x_b^{t+1}, x_f^{t+1}\}$: $\overline{x}^{t+1} = x^{t+1} - \eta g^t + \nu(x^t - x^{t-1})$;
11   **for** $i = 1, 2, \cdots, L$ **do**
12        $\|\overline{x}_{c_i}^{t+1}\|_1 = \{\|x_{filter_1}\|_1, \|x_{filter_2}\|_1, \cdots, \|x_{filter_\ell}\|_1\}$;
13        $x_{c_i}^{t+1} = \Phi_{1-P_i}(\overline{x}_{c_i}^{t+1})$; / sort $\|\overline{x}_{c_i}^{t+1}\|_1$, preserve $\lfloor (1 - P_i) \cdot \ell \rfloor$ largest filters and set $\lfloor P_i \cdot \ell \rfloor$ filters to zero. / ($\lfloor * \rfloor$ is integral function)
14   **end**
15      $x^{t+1} = \{x_c^{t+1}, \overline{x}_b^{t+1}, \overline{x}_f^{t+1}\}$;
16   **end**
17 **end**
18 Physically discarding the filters with P_i percentage zero values and reconstructing the network to obtain the compact network and sparse parameters.

Training Network with AHSG-HT Algorithm. The CNNs (convolutional neural networks) constantly extract features from local features to global features through filters one by one. Thus CNNs can carry out image classification, object detection, action recognition, and many others. If we prune the filters in the convolutional layers with a suitable rate, it will improve accuracy or even promote generalization ability. AHSG-HT filter pruning method prunes the original network from scratch, and we use hard thresholding operation at a very early time. If the pruning rate is too high, some important information will be lost in the early iterations, which will affect the final performance. Therefore, the trade-off between accuracy and pruning rate is crucial. Compared with hard pruning, our approach can recover some important information and improve the final accuracy. We use hard thresholding to evaluate the importance of each filter. In deep CNNs, the filters in the convolutional layer are four-dimensional tensors in the optimizer step. We adopt Φ_{P_i} to calculate the sums of absolute weight values in each filter and sort the filters. Pruning rate P_i is used to constrain the small values in filters, and we prune P_i percent of the filters in the optimizer step. Normally, the final performance of a network can be affected more when the larger sum of absolute values is pruned. Certainly, it will have an obvious influence on the final accuracy if we prune the filter with bigger values. Furthermore, we prune the selected filters and allow weights in filters to update while the different batch-size data are fed into as an input. Thus we realize the automatic pruning by pruning the selected filters in the optimizer step. Repeat the above work until epochs are over and finally we obtain a network with a certain number of filters with zero values.

Physically Pruning Filters. In the above training network procedure, we prune the filters by setting the selected filters to zero instead of discarding the whole filters. After training the original network from scratch, an efficient network with the "important" filters is gained. Then we physically prune the obtained network by discarding P_i percent of the filters with zero values. We reconstruct the network and transfer the "important" filters to the new reconstructed network. Thus the new network has similar or even better performance and a more compact architecture compared with the original network. From our experiments, it improves accuracy about 0.4% on ResNet-110 for 27% reduction in parameters and 28% reduction in FLOPs without fine-tuning. The pruning procedure can be regarded as the criterion of filter selecting or advantage of architecture search.

4 Experiments

We conduct experiments to evaluate AHSG-HT algorithm on two benchmark datasets, i.e. CIFAR-10 [12] and CIFAR-100 [12]. We implement our pruning algorithm to accelerate ResNet [7] on Cifar-10, Cifar-100. We use Pytorch [18] to carry out our AHSG-HT algorithm in deep CNNs' compression. Our pruning work is conducted in the optimizer step while we train deep CNNs from scratch with setting the "unimportant" filters to zero. Moreover, we iteratively update the weights in the filters in the optimizer step. Our work repeats the pruning operation in order that the training itself can automatically select the "unimportant" filters to prune. We compare several advanced methods and set up two comparative experiments according to different mini-batch sizes. To verify whether the hybrid mini-batch size is efficient, We fix mini-batch size to 64 and 128.

4.1 Datasets and Experimental Setting

CIFAR. CIFAR-10 consists of 60000 color images, which are 32×32 resolution and divided into 10 categories which include 6000 images. There are 50000 images for training and 10000 images for testing. CIFAR-100 is similar to CIFAR-10, except that it has 100 classes and each class contains 600 images. Each class has 500 training images and 100 testing images.

Hyperparameters. We randomly select images to arrange into training batches with different sizes. Generally speaking, the mini-batch size is gradually increasing to a stable mini-batch size. Considering the running time of going through the whole data, we set the mini-batch size to increase from 64 to 128 by step size 4. We adopt a learning rate η which gradually decreases and a constant momentum strength $\nu = 0.1$ for the basic setting while training the network from scratch. For fine-tuning, we use a stable learning rate $1e^{-3}$ and fine-tune 20 epochs for CIFAR-10 and CIFAR-100.

4.2 ResNet on CIFAR-10

We prune ResNet-20, 32, 56 and 110 based on CIFAR-10 dataset by using our AHSG-HT algorithm. We adopt various pruning rates to pursue the balance of compression rate and performance. Moreover, a quantitative comparison of several pruning methods using lower pruning rates is listed in Table 1. We set the same compression rate with soft filter pruning and compare the accuracy. So we can obtain the same FLOPs reduction with the same compression rate. Li et al. [13] believe that it is sensitive to prune some special layers on ResNet (layer 20, 38 and 54 for ResNet-56, layer 36, 38 and 74 for ResNet-100). They skip these layers and prune other layers with 10% filters as pruned-A method. Our method directly sets all selected filters to zero and physically prunes a certain compression rate filters at the last step. We achieve better performance without fine-tuning than [13] with fine-tuning. Soft filter pruning often performs well in low compression rates, but our method is comparable or even better at pruning 10% and 20% filters. Furthermore, hybrid mini-batch size often performs better than fixed mini-batch size. Our accuracy can reach up to 94.17% on ResNet-110 which exceeds the baseline accuracy about 0.5%.

The following Table 2 is a comparison of various pruning methods with high compression rates which normally exceed 30%. Higher compression rate usually results in accuracy's decline which is more obvious in small network structures. For both ResNet-20 and ResNet-32, our approach is better than soft filter pruning with 30% compression rate. We have higher accuracy when both of the three methods prune 30% filters without fine-tuning. On ResNet-56, we fine-tune the pruned network with high compression rate and find that we also have the best performance in those methods. Moreover, our approach exceeds channel pruning [9] when we prune 50% filters which is the same as [9]. For ResNet-110, we can obtain almost the same performance as soft filter pruning with fine-tuning while we didn't fine-tune and better performance than the other methods.

Table 1. Performance comparison of pruning ResNet on CIFAR-10 with a lower pruning rate of filters. In Method column, we use percentage after methods to represent the compression rate. And in Fine-tune column, we use "no" to express pruning algorithm without fine-tuning and "yes" to with fine-tuning. ASG-HT-64 and ASG-HT-128 represent method with fixed batch size 64 and 128. The Pruned FLOPs is the percentage which is the new network's FLOPs divided by old network's FLOPs.

Depth	Method	Baseline Acc (%)	Pruned Acc (%)	Fine-tune	Pruned FLOPs (%)
20	SFP [8] (10%)	92.20	**92.24**	no	15.24
	ASG-HT-64 (10%)	92.20	92.12	no	15.24
	ASG-HT-128 (10%)	92.20	92.03	no	15.24
	AHSG-HT (10%)	92.20	92.22	No	15.24
	LCCL [3]	91.53	91.43	no	20.3
	SFP [8] (20%)	92.20	91.20	no	29.31
	ASG-HT-64 (20%)	92.20	91.36	no	29.31
	ASG-HT-128 (20%)	92.20	91.53	no	29.31
	AHSG-HT (20%)	92.20	**91.57**	no	29.31
32	SFP [8] (10%)	92.63	93.22	no	14.93
	ASG-HT-64 (10%)	92.63	93.02	no	14.93
	ASG-HT-128 (10%)	92.63	92.98	no	14.93
	AHSG-HT (10%)	92.63	**93.28**	no	14.93
	SFP [8] (20%)	92.63	92.63	no	28.77
	ASG-HT-64 (20%)	92.63	92.56	no	28.77
	ASG-HT-128 (20%)	92.63	92.82	no	28.77
	AHSG-HT (20%)	92.63	**92.97**	no	28.77
56	L1-pruning-A [13]	93.04	93.10	yes	10.40
	SFP [8] (10%)	93.59	93.89	no	14.74
	ASG-HT-64 (10%)	93.59	93.57	no	14.74
	ASG-HT-128 (10%)	93.59	93.63	no	14.74
	AHSG-HT (10%)	93.59	**93.97**	no	14.74
	SFP [8] (20%)	93.59	93.47	no	28.42
	ASG-HT-64 (20%)	93.59	93.07	no	28.42
	ASG-HT-128 (20%)	93.59	93.60	no	28.42
	AHSG-HT (20%)	93.59	**93.64**	no	28.42
110	L1-pruning-A [13]	93.53	93.55	yes	15.90
	SFP [8] (10%)	93.68	93.83	no	14.62
	ASG-HT-64 (10%)	93.68	93.72	no	14.62
	ASG-HT-128 (10%)	93.68	94.09	no	14.62
	AHSG-HT (10%)	93.68	**94.17**	no	14.62
	SFP [8] (20%)	93.68	93.93	no	28.21
	ASG-HT-64 (20%)	93.68	93.93	no	28.21
	ASG-HT-128 (20%)	93.68	94.04	no	28.21
	AHSG-HT (20%)	93.68	**94.09**	no	28.21

Table 2. Performance comparison of pruning ResNet on CIFAR-10 with a higher pruning rate of filters.

Depth	Method	Baseline Acc (%)	Pruned Acc (%)	Fine-tune	Pruned FLOPs (%)
20	SFP [8](30%)	92.20	90.83	no	42.22
	ASG-HT-64 (30%)	92.20	91.03	no	42.22
	ASG-HT-128 (30%)	92.20	91.15	no	42.22
	AHSG-HT (30%)	92.20	**91.25**	no	42.22
32	SFP [8](30%)	92.63	92.08	no	41.51
	ASG-HT-64 (30%)	92.63	92.09	no	41.51
	ASG-HT-128 (30%)	92.63	91.78	no	41.51
	AHSG-HT (30%)	92.63	**92.20**	no	41.51
56	LCCL [3]	92.33	90.74	no	31.2
	SFP [8](30%)	93.59	93.10	no	41.06
	SFP [8](30%)	93.59	93.78	yes	41.06
	ASG-HT-64 (30%)	93.59	93.30	no	41.06
	ASG-HT-128 (30%)	93.59	93.08	no	41.06
	AHSG-HT (30%)	93.59	93.27	no	41.06
	AHSG-HT (30%)	93.59	**93.83**	yes	41.06
	SFP [8] (40%)	93.59	92.26	no	52.63
	SFP [8] (40%)	93.59	93.35	yes	52.63
	ASG-HT-64 (40%)	93.59	92.66	no	52.63
	ASG-HT-128 (40%)	93.59	92.25	no	52.63
	AHSG-HT (40%)	93.59	92.69	no	52.63
	AHSG-HT (40%)	93.59	**93.61**	yes	52.63
	Channel-pruning [9]	92.63	91.80	yes	50.0
	ASG-HT-64 (50%)	93.59	91.41	no	63.16
	ASG-HT-128 (50%)	93.59	92.02	no	63.16
	AHSG-HT (50%)	93.59	92.24	no	63.16
	AHSG-HT (50%)	93.59	**92.40**	yes	63.16
110	L1-pruning-B [13]	93.53	93.30	yes	38.6
	LCCL [3]	93.63	93.44	no	34.2
	SFP [8] (30%)	93.68	93.38	no	40.78
	SFP [8] (30%)	93.68	93.86	yes	40.78
	ASG-HT-64 (30%)	93.68	93.19	no	40.78
	ASG-HT-128 (30%)	93.68	93.52	no	40.78
	AHSG-HT (30%)	93.68	93.83	no	40.78
	AHSG-HT (30%)	93.68	**94.01**	yes	40.78

4.3   ResNet on CIFAR-100

We conduct the CIFAR-100 experiments on ResNet and compare the accuracy with fixed mini-batch size's and baseline. There are few experiments accelerating ResNet on CIFAR-100. Therefore, we mainly compare with the original accuracy. We find that accuracy's reduction appears a relationship with the improvement of dataset's complexity. It seems that every additional 10% rate will be accompanied by one point accuracy's decline, which is shown in Table 3.

Table 3. Pruning ResNet on CIFAR-100 with several pruning rates of filters. The "Drop Acc" represents the dropped accuracy percentage after pruning.

Depth	Method	Baseline Acc (%)	Pruned Acc (%)	Drop Acc (%)	Pruned FLOPs (%)
20	ASG-HT-64 (10%)	68.64	68.00	0.64	20.3
	ASG-HT-128 (10%)		67.46	1.18	
	AHSG-HT (10%)		**68.03**	0.72	
	ASG-HT-64 (20%)	68.64	67.00	1.64	29.3
	ASG-HT-128 (20%)		66.37	2.27	
	AHSG-HT (20%)		**67.08**	1.56	
	ASG-HT-64 (30%)	68.64	65.51	3.13	42.2
	ASG-HT-128 (30%)		65.15	3.49	
	AHSG-HT (30%)		65.74	2.90	
	AHSG-HT (30% fine-tune)		**66.38**	2.26	
56	ASG-HT-64 (10%)	72.89	**72.44**	0.45	20.3
	ASG-HT-128 (10%)		72.07	0.82	
	AHSG-HT (10%)		72.33	0.56	
	ASG-HT-64 (20%)	72.89	71.54	1.35	29.3
	ASG-HT-128 (20%)		71.32	1.57	
	AHSG-HT (20%)		**71.56**	1.33	
	ASG-HT-64 (30%)	72.89	70.47	2.42	42.2
	ASG-HT-128 (30%)		70.02	2.87	
	AHSG-HT (30%)		70.46	2.43	
	AHSG-HT (30% fine-tune)		**71.33**	1.56	
110	ASG-HT-64 (10%)	74.46	**73.99**	0.47	20.3
	ASG-HT-128 (10%)		73.49	0.97	
	AHSG-HT (10%)		73.65	0.81	
	ASG-HT-64 (20%)	74.46	72.01	2.45	29.3
	ASG-HT-128 (20%)		72.33	2.13	
	AHSG-HT (20%)		**72.74**	1.72	
	ASG-HT-64 (30%)	74.46	71.49	2.97	42.2
	ASG-HT-128 (30%)		72.11	2.35	
	AHSG-HT (30%)		72.27	2.19	
	AHSG-HT (30% fine-tune)		**73.09**	1.37	

In consideration of 30% compression rate, we fine-tune the pruned network to pursue higher accuracy. For pruning 30% filters on ResNet-20, the fine-tuning process makes the pruned network perform well as the network with 20% compression rate. What's more, fine-tuning performs better in larger models like ResNet-56 and ResNet-110 with 30% compression rate, which can compare with the networks with 10% compression rate. It can be seen that method with hybrid mini-batch size has a better performance than methods with fixed mini-batch size by dropped accuracy.

5   Conclusion

In this paper, we propose an efficient stochastic gradient hard thresholding pruning method to compress convolutional neural networks' (CNNs) size while preserving the outstanding performance as much as possible. Our method has better performance with higher compression rate compared with other relevant methods. We implement the pruning method with two steps: (1) Optimizer set the "unimportant" filters to zero in order to architecture with zero filters in each iteration; (2) Prune the architecture by discarding the filters with zero values. We finally obtain a compact and efficient network, and achieve 40% reduction in parameters and 42% reduction in FLOPs on ResNet based on CIFAR-10 and CIFAR-100, but the accuracy is still comparable to the baseline and the state-of-the-art methods.

Acknowledgements. This work was supported by the National Natural Science Foundation of China under Grant Numbers: 61876090.

References

1. Cohen, T., Welling, M.: Group equivariant convolutional networks. In: International Conference on Machine Learning, pp. 2990–2999 (2016)
2. Denton, E.L., Zaremba, W., Bruna, J., LeCun, Y., Fergus, R.: Exploiting linear structure within convolutional networks for efficient evaluation. In: Advances in Neural Information Processing Systems, pp. 1269–1277 (2014)
3. Dong, X., Huang, J., Yang, Y., Yan, S.: More is less: a more complicated network with less inference complexity. In: Proceedings of the IEEE Conference on Computer Vision and Pattern Recognition, pp. 5840–5848 (2017)
4. Foucart, S.: Hard thresholding pursuit: an algorithm for compressive sensing. SIAM J. Numer. Anal. **49**(6), 2543–2563 (2011)
5. Han, S., Mao, H., Dally, W.J.: Deep compression: Compressing deep neural networks with pruning, trained quantization and huffman coding. arXiv preprint arXiv:1510.00149 (2015)
6. Han, S., Pool, J., Tran, J., Dally, W.: Learning both weights and connections for efficient neural network. In: Advances in Neural Information Processing Systems, pp. 1135–1143 (2015)
7. He, K., Zhang, X., Ren, S., Sun, J.: Deep residual learning for image recognition. In: Proceedings of the IEEE Conference on Computer Vision and Pattern Recognition, pp. 770–778 (2016)
8. He, Y., Kang, G., Dong, X., Fu, Y., Yang, Y.: Soft filter pruning for accelerating deep convolutional neural networks. arXiv preprint arXiv:1808.06866 (2018)
9. He, Y., Zhang, X., Sun, J.: Channel pruning for accelerating very deep neural networks. In: Proceedings of the IEEE International Conference on Computer Vision, pp. 1389–1397 (2017)
10. Hinton, G., Vinyals, O., Dean, J.: Distilling the knowledge in a neural network. arXiv preprint arXiv:1503.02531 (2015)
11. Jin, X., Yuan, X., Feng, J., Yan, S.: Training skinny deep neural networks with iterative hard thresholding methods. arXiv preprint arXiv:1607.05423 (2016)
12. Krizhevsky, A., Hinton, G.: Learning multiple layers of features from tiny images. Technical report, Citeseer (2009)
13. Li, H., Kadav, A., Durdanovic, I., Samet, H., Graf, H.P.: Pruning filters for efficient convnets. arXiv preprint arXiv:1608.08710 (2016)
14. Liu, Z., Li, J., Shen, Z., Huang, G., Yan, S., Zhang, C.: Learning efficient convolutional networks through network slimming. In: Proceedings of the IEEE International Conference on Computer Vision, pp. 2736–2744 (2017)
15. Liu, Z., Sun, M., Zhou, T., Huang, G., Darrell, T.: Rethinking the value of network pruning. arXiv preprint arXiv:1810.05270 (2018)

16. Luo, P., Zhu, Z., Liu, Z., Wang, X., Tang, X.: Face model compression by distilling knowledge from neurons. In: Thirtieth AAAI Conference on Artificial Intelligence (2016)
17. Molchanov, P., Tyree, S., Karras, T., Aila, T., Kautz, J.: Pruning convolutional neural networks for resource efficient inference. arXiv preprint arXiv:1611.06440 (2016)
18. Paszke, A., et al.: Automatic differentiation in pytorch (2017)
19. Rastegari, M., Ordonez, V., Redmon, J., Farhadi, A.: XNOR-Net: imagenet classification using binary convolutional neural networks. In: Leibe, B., Matas, J., Sebe, N., Welling, M. (eds.) ECCV 2016. LNCS, vol. 9908, pp. 525–542. Springer, Cham (2016). https://doi.org/10.1007/978-3-319-46493-0_32
20. Sindhwani, V., Sainath, T., Kumar, S.: Structured transforms for small-footprint deep learning. In: Advances in Neural Information Processing Systems, pp. 3088–3096 (2015)
21. Wu, J., Leng, C., Wang, Y., Hu, Q., Cheng, J.: Quantized convolutional neural networks for mobile devices. In: Proceedings of the IEEE Conference on Computer Vision and Pattern Recognition, pp. 4820–4828 (2016)
22. Yuan, X.T., Li, P., Zhang, T.: Gradient hard thresholding pursuit (2018)
23. Zhang, T., et al.: A systematic DNN weight pruning framework using alternating direction method of multipliers. In: Ferrari, V., Hebert, M., Sminchisescu, C., Weiss, Y. (eds.) ECCV 2018. LNCS, vol. 11212, pp. 191–207. Springer, Cham (2018). https://doi.org/10.1007/978-3-030-01237-3_12
24. Zhou, P., Yuan, X., Feng, J.: Efficient stochastic gradient hard thresholding. In: Advances in Neural Information Processing Systems, pp. 1988–1997 (2018)

Channel and Constraint Compensation for Generative Adversarial Networks

Wei Wang, Haifeng Hu, and Dihu Chen[✉]

School of Electronic and Information Technology, Sun Yat-sen University,
Guangzhou 510006, China
stscdh@mail.sysu.edu.cn

Abstract. In this paper, we propose channel and constraint compensation mechanism applied in Generative Adversarial Networks (GANs) to help distribution fitting and improve the visual quality of generated samples. The proposed channel compensation focuses on specific feature-related regions by weighting the channel of conv-layer feature maps, so specific feature modes of data distribution can be compensated and irrelevant features can also be decayed. By combining the Jensen-Shannon (JS) divergence and Wasserstein distance (WD) into a well-designed objective function, the constraint compensation can impose more useful constraints upon the generator to diversify the estimated density in capturing multi-modes. Extensive experiments are conducted on synthetic 2D data and real-world datasets (CIFAR-10, STL-10, CelaBa). The qualitative and quantitative comparisons against baselines demonstrate the effectiveness and superiority of our method.

Keywords: Generative Adversarial Networks · Visual quality · Distribution fitting

1 Introduction

Image synthesis is an important problem in computer vision. So far, Generative Adversarial Networks [1] have achieved great success in many fields [9–12], especially image generation. By a two-player minimax game between a generator G and a discriminator D, the generate network can be trained to fit the distribution of real data. One of the basic problems in image generation for Generative Adversarial Networks [1] is the poor visual quality of the generated samples [2–4]. Two significant reasons should be taken into account. One is the feature loss and dissipation in the process of feature mapping from low dimensional subspaces to high dimensional subspaces by the convolution operation [5–7]. As a result, the feature modes captured by the generative network fail to fit the distribution of real data. The other is the lack of effective constraints applied

---

Wei Wang is currently pursuing the M.S. degree at Sun Yat-sen University.

© Springer Nature Switzerland AG 2019
Z. Lin et al. (Eds.): PRCV 2019, LNCS 11857, pp. 386–397, 2019.
https://doi.org/10.1007/978-3-030-31654-9_33

to the generator [5,6,8]. It means that, during the two-player minimax game, not enough high-level constraint can be used to guide the generator towards probable configurations of abstract real data distribution.

Many methods have been proposed to address the above issues. One way is to utilize complicated convolutional networks that improves the efficiency of feature mapping. Instead of hoping each few stacked layers directly fit a desired underlying mapping, the Resnet [26] explicitly let these layers fit a residual mapping by using a shortcut connections. Furthermore, by concatenating feature-maps learned by different layers, DenseNets [27] exploits the potential of the network through feature reuse. Although the performance of convolutional network has been improved a lot, the cost in computation is expensive. And some works focus on the optimizing loss functions. WGAN [5] and WGAN-GP [6] introduce Wasserstein distance with a gradient penalty instead of regular KL divergence or JS divergence to train the model, achieving some positive effects. MGAN [13] simultaneously trains a set of generators with the proposed objective function that the mixture of these generators' distributions would approximate the real data distribution, whilst encouraging them to specialize in different data modes. Although MGAN [13] can improve the visual quality of generated samples efficiently, the computational cost is expensive. By adopting the least squares loss function for the discriminator, LSGAN can overcome the vanishing gradient problem during the learning process. What inspires us greatly is the D2GAN [14], by combining the KL and reverse KL divergences into a novel objective function, D2GAN [14] builds the complementary statistical properties from these divergences, which helps to capture multi-modes. Since D2GAN [14] has to equilibrate the effects of both KL and reverse KL, the visual quality of generated samples can't be increased by a large margin. Some novel training skills also have achieved great success. The SNGAN [15] can stabilize the training of GANs with little increase in computation by applying spectral normalization to the discriminator. In addition, some novel structures have also been proposed, DFM [8] uses a denoising autoencoder to propose high-level targets for the generator, and it can overcome shortcomings of the original GANs by directing the generator towards probable configurations of abstract discriminator features. Although improvement has been achieved, the details of samples tend to show poor. Lately, the applying of attention framework has been widely used in image processing [24,25]. The Self-attention GANs [16] can model long range, multi-level dependencies across image regions by calculating response at a channel as a weighted sum of the features at all channels. In this way, details can be generated using cues from all feature locations at the price of little increase in computation.

To address the challenge, we propose novel channel compensation mechanism and constraint compensation mechanism to help distribution fitting and improve the visual quality of generated samples. In signal transmission field, compensation module is often employed to compensate for the decayed frequency, where some important frequencies can be strengthened and some irrelevant noise can be decayed. The problem of feature lost or decay also exists in traditional Convolutional Neural Network (CNN) in the process of feature mapping [5–7]. The abstract representation of features can be treated as special signals. Each filter can be viewed as a feature mode detector, and each channel of a feature map is a response activation of the corresponding convolutional filter. When the generator wants to generate images of particular attributes to fool the discriminator, contextual information at different channels should be collected. However, the features in different channels have different focuses and should not be treated equally. Therefore, applying a compensation mechanism in channels can be regarded as a process of compensating important attributes and decaying irrelevant ones instead of considering each channel equally. Besides, Classical GANs models often employ the Jensen-Shannon (JS) divergence or the Wasserstein distance (WD) divergence to measure the distance of different data distributions, however, each of which has its superiority or weakness [6,14,17]. Visual quality can be achieved by minimizing JS divergence or reverse Kullback-Leibler (KL) divergence, whereas it may cause the problem of mode collapse [3,4,6]. The WD divergence introduces weights clipping to enforce the k-Lipschitz constraint and overcome training instability, however, weight clipping often fails to capture higher moments of real data distribution [6]. In this paper, we propose constraint compensation which is able to combine JS and WD into a well-designed loss function. By building a complementary relationship, more effective constraints can be imposed on the generate network to help capture feature modes and fit distribution.

We conduct extensive experiments on one synthetic dataset and three real-world widely adopted datasets CIFAR-10 [18], STL-10 [19], CeleBa [20]. The results show the validity of the proposed mechanisms on helping distribution fitting and improving the visual quality of generated samples. In a word, the major contributions of this paper are as follow: (i) A novel channel compensation module embedded into classical GANs to compensate important features and help improve the visual quality of generated samples. (ii) A well-designed loss function combined JS divergence and WD distance to impose more effective constraints on the generator. (iii) Extensive experiments are conducted out to verify the validity of the proposed method.

2   Channel Compensation Mechanism and Constraint Compensation Mechanism

In this section, we first present a general framework of our compensation network embedded into GANs that aggregates these two compensations together. Then we introduce in detail the two compensation mechanisms respectively.

2.1   Overview

As is shown in Fig. 1, the basic framework consists of a generator G, two discriminators D_1 and D_2. The channel compensation module CN is embedded in convolutional layer both generated network and discriminate network to make up for the important feature modes in feature mapping. The output samples generated by G are transferred into D_1 and D_2 simultaneously. Although D_1 and D_2 share the same architecture of network, the difference is that JS divergence and WD divergence are applied in D_1 and D_2 respectively.

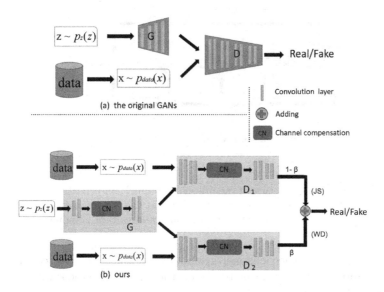

Fig. 1. The comparison of the original GANs and our proposed Channel and Constraint Compensation GANs. The channel compensation network (CN) is embedded into the middle convolutional layer in both generator and discriminator. In addition, two discriminators that share the same architecture are used to build a complementary adversarial loss. z denotes input noise and x denotes real image.

2.2   Channel Compensation Module

Channel compensation can be viewed as the process of selecting specific attributes and decaying irrelevant ones on the demand of the samples to better fool the discriminator. To achieve this, the compensation module (CN) is embedded into convolutional networks to process the abstract features in channels.

As shown in Fig. 2, the original input feature maps $x \in R^{W \times H \times C}$ are first transformed into two feature spaces h and f. By flattening the width and height of the original x and transposing operation, we get $f(x) = [f_1, f_2, ..., f_c]$ where $f_i \in R^{W \times H}$ represents the i-th channel of the feature map x, and C is the total number of channels. Meanwhile, by a convolutional operation, we get $h(x) = W_h \times x$, where $h(x) \in R^{W \times H \times \overline{C}}$. h(x) can be viewed as a representation of region feature and can be trained to self-adaption choose certain attributes. The shape of filter we choose is relatively larger 5×5 because more widely dependence can be modeled across regions to help build weights for compensation. Then by performing a matrix multiplication between f(x) and the flattening of h(x), the

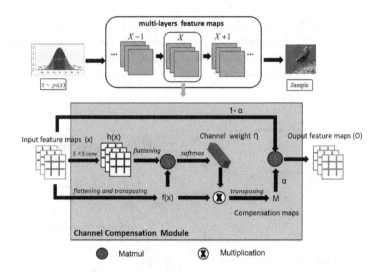

Fig. 2. The detailed architecture of the proposed channel compensation network (CN). Given the input feature maps, the model can output the corresponding compensation maps to make up for the modes of data distribution in feature mapping.

correlation degree of each channel attends to specific attribute can be built. Then, we apply a softmax layer to obtain the channel compensation weighs η which can be represented by

$$\eta_i = \frac{exp(h(x) * f(x_i))}{\sum\limits_{i=1}^{C} exp(h(x) * f(x_i))}, \tag{1}$$

where η_i can be viewed as the correlation degree of the i-th channel and the specific attribute h(x). In the above formulation, $W_h \in R^{C \times \overline{C}}$ are the learned weight matrices. We use $\overline{C} = 1$ in our experiments. Finally, the output compensation maps are $M \in R^{W \times H \times C}$, where

$$tranposing(M) = \sum\limits_{i=1}^{C} [f(x_i) \times \eta_i]. \tag{2}$$

In addition, we further multiply compensation maps by a scale parameter α and add back to the input feature maps x, so a complementary relationship can be modeled. Therefore, the final output is given by,

$$o = \alpha M + (1 - \alpha)x. \tag{3}$$

The α is initialized as 0, which can progressively increase the weights and complexity to stabilize the training. In all experiments, the proposed channel compensation module has been applied to both generator and discriminator, which are trained to minimizing JS and WD adversarial loss in D_1 and D_2 respectively.

2.3   Constraint Compensation Module

As shown in Fig. 1, D_1 and D_2 are used to build JS adversarial loss [10] $V_1(G, D_1)$ and WD adversarial loss [5] $V_2(G, D_2)$ respectively.

$$V_1(G, D_1) = \min_G \max_{D_1} E_{x \sim P_{data}(x)}[log D_1(x)]$$
$$+ E_{z \sim P_z(z)}[log(1 - G(z))]. \tag{4}$$

$$V_2(G, D_2) = \min_G \max_{D_2} E_{x \sim P_{data}(x)}[-D_2(x)]$$
$$+ E_{x \sim P_z(z)}[D_2(G(z))]. \tag{5}$$

By modeling a complementary relationship between them, more useful constraints can be imposed on generate network to help fit distribution and capture feature modes of real data. These high-level constraints can direct the generator towards probable configurations of abstract discriminator features, as a result, high-visual quality samples can be generated to better fool the discriminator. A scale parameter β is introduced to balance the effects of the two adversarial loss and stable the training network. Therefore, the final adversarial loss can be represented by

$$V(G, D_1, D_2) = \min_G \max_{D_1 D_2}[(1 - \beta)V_1 + \beta V_2], \tag{6}$$

where the β is initialised as 0.5 in our experiments.

3   Experiments

In the following, experiments are carried out to investigate the validity of our proposed compensation methods. Firstly, we conduct experiments on 2D synthetic data [14] to evaluate the learning behaviors of our proposed mechanism in helping distribution fitting, then we present experimental results using specific values to analyze the effectiveness of our proposed compensation mechanism on improving the visual quality of generated images quantitatively. Lastly, we show some randomly generated samples to give a qualitative analysis.

DataSets: Three widely-adopted datasets are used: CIFAR-10 [18], STL-10 [19], and CeleBa [20]. CIFAR-10 [18] is a well-studied dataset of 50,000 32×32 training images of 10 classes: airplane, automobile, bird, cat, deer, dog, frog, horse, ship, and truck. STL-10 [19], a subset of ImageNet, contains about 100,000 unlabeled 96×96 images, which is more diverse than CIFAR-10. CeleBa [20] is a large-scale face attributes dataset with more than 200K celebrity images, each with 40 attribute annotations which cover large pose variations and background clutter. In order to facilitate fair comparison with the baselines, the STL-10 images are resized from 96×96 to 32×32 and the CeleBa images are center cropped to 64×64 and 128×128 in our experiments.

Evaluation Metric: By computing the KL divergence between the conditional class distribution and the marginal class distribution, the inception score (IS) [21]

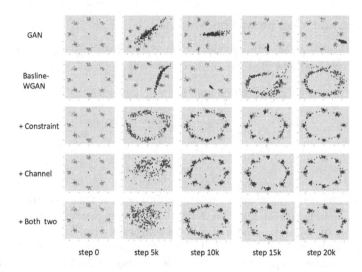

Fig. 3. The comparison of standard GANs and our compensation network on the 2D synthetic dataset of 8 Gaussians. Data sampled from the true mixture are red, and the data generated by the generative model are blue. (Color figure online)

is widely used as an assessment for sample quality from a labeled dataset. Fréchet inception distance (FID) [22] is often employed for quantitative evaluation on image quality by measuring the Wasserstein-2 distance between the generated images and the real images in the feature space of an Inception-v3 network. The higher the IS is or the lower the FID is, the better the visual quality the samples have. We show the best values after 200K iterations training on CIFAR-10 [18] and STL-10 [19] datasets, and after 20 epochs training on CeleBa [20] dataset.

Model Architecture: The generator and discriminator we used in our model originated from the DCGAN-based network [10]. The complementary loss functions we employed are traditional DCGAN [10] adversarial loss and WGAN [5] adversarial loss.

3.1   2D Synthetic Data

In this section, we use the experimental design proposed in D2GAN [14] to prove the ability of our method in helping fit distribution. To be specific, our training data is sampled from a 2D mixture of eight isotropic Gaussian distributions and arranged in a circle of zero centroids and a radius of 2.0. The aim of using such low variance mixture components is to create a low-density area and separate the modes. The basic architecture: a generator with two fully connected hidden layers of leakyRelu activations, two discriminators with one hidden layer of ReLU activations and channel compensation module with one fully connected hidden layer. Figure 3 shows the evolution of 256 samples generated by our model and baselines over time with a learning rate of 0.0002.

Table 1. Inception Score (IS) and Fréchet Inception Distance (FID)

Evaluation metric	IS		FID	
Dataset	CIFAR-10	STL-10	CIFAR-10	CeleBa
Real data	11.24 ± 0.16	26.08 ± 0.26	7.80	~
Baseline DCGAN [10]	7.25 ± 0.09	7.86 ± 0.11	28.29	14.04
+Self-attention [16]	7.35 ± 0.04	7.88 ± 0.03	27.5	12.34
+Channel Compensation	**7.5 ± 0.06**	**8.19 ± 0.08**	**25.8**	**11.98**
Baseline WGAN [5]	7.24 ± 0.06	7.88 ± 0.11	26.15	14.87
+Self-attention [16]	7.3 ± 0.1	7.92 ± 0.07	27.33	14.99
+Channel Compensation	**7.4 ± 0.08**	**8.1 ± 0.01**	**25.76**	**12.79**
+Constraint Compensation	**7.38 ± 0.08**	**7.95 ± 0.09**	**22.64**	**13.20**
+Both	**7.68 ± 0.06**	**8.4 ± 0.04**	**22.58**	**11.31**
Baseline LSGAN [23]	5.92 ± 0.03	6.07 ± 0.04	49.02	14.96
+Channel Compensation	**6.26 ± 0.07**	**6.33 ± 0.07**	**43.1**	**12.05**

It can be seen in Fig. 3 that, after increasing numbers of training steps, the regular GAN [1] converges to only a single separate feature mode, which is called mode collapse. As a contrast, the baseline-WGAN [5] can disperse widely after 10k iteration, however, it fails to capture specific feature mode. When adding channel compensation mechanism or constraint compensation mechanism, the samples generated by WGAN [5] can quickly spread out and converge to multiple modes of the real data and distribute around all eight mixture components, which demonstrates the good ability to fit the multi-modal structure of the target data distribution. Meanwhile, when used both two compensation mechanisms, the data modes captured by WGAN [5] are more concentrated and accurate, which shows a well complementary relationship between the two mechanisms.

3.2   Quantitative Analysis: IS and FID

In this section, we report the IS and FID results obtained, which are shown in Table 1. From the results, we can see that the baseline models can improve a lot when added our proposed compensation model. Furthermore, The best result is achieved when aggregated them together, which verifies the great effects of our proposed method on improving the visual quality of generated samples. Compared with some popular GANs variants implemented in different optimization methods [16,23], our mechanism also shows superiority to them. Baseline DCGAN and baseline WGAN are used to build a constraint complementary relationship in our experiments. We also show some training curves in Fig. 4 to display the training details.

3.3   Qualitative Analysis of Generated Samples

Next, we show several samples randomly generated by our proposed model trained on three datasets (CIFAR-10 [18], STL-10 [19], CeleBa [20]). It can be

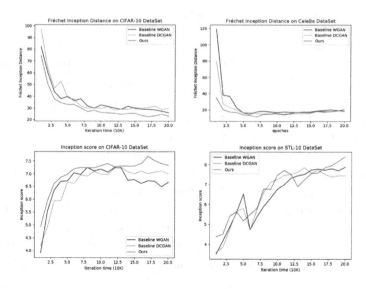

Fig. 4. Some training curves for baseline models and our model.

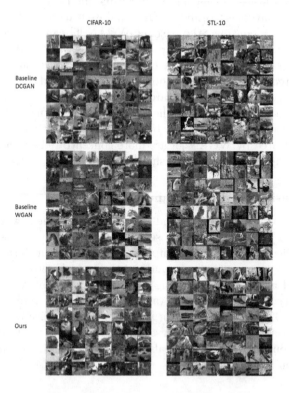

Fig. 5. The comparison of randomly generated samples after 200k iterations training on CIFAR-10 and STL-10 datasets.

seen in Fig. 5 that, on CIFAR-10 [18] and STL-10 [19], the samples generated by baselines are blurry and hard to be classified. However, when added channel compensation module or constraint compensation module, the profile of generated images are more recognizable which contain a wide range of objects such as trucks, ships, etc. Fig. 6 shows the generated samples (128×128) trained on CeleBa [20] dataset, from which we can see our model can achieve higher visual quality with fine details compared with baselines. This verifies the great effect of our proposed mechanism on improving the visual quality of generated samples.

Fig. 6. The comparison of randomly generated samples after 20 epoches training on CelebA dataset

4   Conclusion

In this paper, we propose channel compensation and constraint compensation mechanisms applied in classical GANs model to help distribution fitting and improve the visual quality of generated samples. The experiments on a 2D mixture of eight isotropic Gaussian distributions shows the preeminent ability of our mechanism in helping fit data distribution. The improvement in IS and FID confirms the effectiveness of our proposed method in improving visual quality and the generated samples also present high visual quality with fine details.

Acknowledgment. This work was supported in part by the National Natural Science Foundation of China (61673402, 61273270, 60802069), the Natural Science Foundation of Guangdong Province (2017A030311029, 2016B010123005, 2017B090909005), the Science and Technology Program of Guangzhou of China (201704020180, 201604020024), and the Fundamental Research Funds for the Central Universities of China.

References

1. Goodfellow, I., et al.: Generative adversarial nets. In: Advances in 27th Neural Information Processing Systems (NIPS), Canada, pp. 2672–2680 (2014)

2. Berthelot, D., Schumm, T., Metz, L.: Began: Boundary equilibrium generative adversarial networks. arXiv preprint arXiv:1703.10717 (2017)
3. Fedus, W., Rosca, M., Lakshminarayanan, B., Dai, A.M., Mohamed, S., Goodfelblow, I.: Many paths to equilibrium: GANs do not need to decrease adivergence at every step, arXiv preprint arXiv:1710.08446 (2017)
4. Kodali, N., Abernethy, J., Hays, J., Kira, Z.: On convergence and stability of GANs, arXiv preprint arXiv:1705.07215 (2017)
5. Arjovsky, M., Chintala, S., Bottou, L.: Wasserstein GAN, arXiv preprint arXiv:1701.07875 (2017)
6. Gulrajani, I., Ahmed, F., Arjovsky, M., Dubmoulin, V., Courville, A.: Improved training of wasserstein GANs, arXiv preprint arXiv:1704.00028 (2017)
7. He, K., Zhang, X., Ren, S., Sun, J.: Deep residual learning for image recognition. In: Computer Vision and Pattern Recognition, Boston, Massachusetts (2015)
8. Warde-Farley, D., Bengio, Y.: Improving generative adversarial networks with denoising feature matching. In: The 5th International Conference on Learning Representations. Toulon, France (2017)
9. Denton, E.L., Chintala, S., Fergus, R.: Deep generative image models using a laplacian pyramid of adversarial networks. In: Advances in 28th Neural Information Processing Systems. Montreal, Canada (2015)
10. Radford, A., Metz, L., Chintala, S.: Unsupervised representation learning with deep convolutional generative adversarial networks. In: The 4th International Conference on Learning Representations. San Juan, Puerto Rico (2016)
11. Zhang, H., et al.: StackGAN++: realistic image synthesis with stacked generative adversarial networks. In: Computer Vision and Pattern Recognition (2018)
12. Karras, T., Aila, T., Laine, S., Lehtinen, J.: Progressive growing of GANs for improved quality, stability, and variation. In: The 6th International Conference on Learning Representations. Vancouver, Canada (2018)
13. Hoang, Q., Nguyen, T.D., Le, T., Phung, D.: Multi-Generator Generative Adversarial Nets, arXiv preprint arXiv:1708.02556 (2017)
14. Nguyen, T.D., Le, T., Vu, H., Phung, D.: Dual discriminator generative adversarial nets. In: The 31th Conference on Neural Information Processing Systems, State of California, America (2017)
15. Miyato, T., Kataoka, T., Koyama, M., Yoshida, Y.: Spectral normalization for generative adversarial networks. In: The 6th International Conference on Learning Representations. Vancouver, Canada (2018)
16. Zhang, H., Goodfellow, I., Metaxas, D., Odena, A.: Self-Attention Generative Adversarial Networks, arXiv preprint arXiv:1805.08318 (2018)
17. Bang, D., Shim, H.: Improved training of generative adversarial networks using representative features. In: The 36th International Conference on Machine Learning. Long Beach, California (2018)
18. Krizhevsky, A., Hinton, G.: Learning multiple layers of features from tiny images (2009)
19. Coates, A., Lee, H., Ng, A.Y.: An analysis of single-layer networks in unsupervised feature learning. In: Proceedings of the Thirteenth International Conference on Artificial Intelligence and Statistics (AISTATS 2011) (2011)
20. Liu, Z., Luo, P., Wang, X., Tang, X.: Deep learning face attributes in the wild. In: Proceedings of the IEEE International Conference on Computer Vision, pp. 3730–3738 (2015)
21. Salimans, T., Goodfellow, I., Zaremba, W., Cheung, V., Radford, A., Chen, X.: Improved techniques for training GANs. In: Advances in Neural Information Processing Systems, pp. 2234–2242 (2016)

22. Heusel, M., Ramsauer, H., Unterthiner, T., Nessler, B., Hochreiter, S.: GANs trained by a two time-scale update rule converge to a local nash equilibrium. In: The 31th Conference on Neural Information Processing Systems, pp. 6629–6640 (2017)
23. Mao, X., Li, Q., Xie, H., Lau, R.Y., Wang, Z., Smolley, S.P.: Least squares generative adversarial networks. In: The IEEE International Conference on Computer Vision (2017)
24. Fu, J., et al.: Dual attention network for scene segmentation. In: Computer Vision and Pattern Recognition, Long Beach, CA (2019)
25. Chen, L., Zhang, H., Xiao, J., Nie, L., Shao, J., Chua, T.S.: SCA-CNN: spatial and channel-wise attention in convolutional networks for image captioning. In: Computer Vision and Pattern Recognition. Honolulu, Hawaii (2017)
26. He, K., Zhang, X., Ren, S., Sun, J.: Deep residual learning for image recognition. In: Computer Vision and Pattern Recognition, Las Vegas, Nevada (2016)
27. Huang, G., Liu, Z., van der Maaten, L., Weinberger, K.Q.: Densely connected convolutional networks. In: Computer Vision and Pattern Recognition, Honolulu, Hawaii (2017)

Faster Real-Time Face Alignment Method on CPU

Pengfei Duan[1], Xin Ning[1,2(✉)], Yuan Shi[1], Shaolin Zhang[1],
and Weijun Li[1,2]

[1] Cognitive Computing Technology Joint Laboratory, Wave Group,
Beijing 100083, China
[2] Laboratory of Artificial Neural Networks and High-Speed Circuits, Institute
of Semiconductors, Chinese Academy of Sciences, Beijing 100083, China
ningxin@semi.ac.cn

Abstract. Face alignment for facial images captured in-the-wild is a challenging and important problem. In this work, we introduced a two-stage face alignment method in order to solve the problem of the normal face alignment method running slowly on the CPU. Using the residual error between ground truth and mean shape as a training label makes the network easier to converge. The joint input of heatmap and original data in the second stage deepens the feature learning of these landmarks, making the minimal network also has suitable performance. The convolution and pooling structure allow the network to be faster and have good learning ability. The test results on open datasets show that our method has a significant improvement in processing performance with real-time CPU speed of 1100 fps while maintaining high accuracy.

Keywords: Residual label · Heatmap · Real-time · Global pooling

1 Introduction

Face alignment, which refers to facial landmark detection in this work, serves as a key step for many face applications, e.g., face recognition [18, 25], as well as face verification [19]. As such, it is imperative to improve the accuracy of the face alignment algorithm.

Before the deep learning method was proposed, most of the face alignment methods were based on traditional machine learning methods [3, 4, 6, 8, 13, 14, 16, 23]. This type of method is basically faster and has better precision. For instance, Ren et al. [6] proposed a method called learning binary features (LBF), which using a locality principle for feature extraction [6], realized 300 fps on a mobile phone. Zhu et al. [8] presented a new framework of face alignment based on coarse-to-fine shape searching (CFSS) method, which can prevent falling into local optimum and improve the robustness in coping with large pose variations. Xiong et al. [4] presented supervised descent method (SDM) to solve the optimization problem of nonlinear least squares. Cao et al. [3] presented an explicit shape regression approach (ESR), which learns a vectorial regression function to infer a set of facial landmarks from the image and minimize the alignment errors over the training data.

Z. Lin et al. (Eds.): PRCV 2019, LNCS 11857, pp. 398–408, 2019.
https://doi.org/10.1007/978-3-030-31654-9_34

In recent years, state-of-the-art performance of face alignment has been achieved with deep learning methods [9, 10, 17, 21, 25]. Among them, some papers realize real-time on Graphics Processing Unit (GPU). For example, Bhagavatula et al. [1] proposed a real-time face alignment method using a 3D space conversion network in unrestricted posture, which achieved state-of-art of 3D face alignment at that time. Tang et al. [2] enhanced the real-time face alignment algorithm by tracking algorithm, and Liu et al. [24] proposed a dense face alignment method (DeFA) based on face contour and scale-invariant feature transform (SIFT) method to enhance the fitting effect of face landmarks. Kowalski et al. [10] proposed a multi-stage regression deep alignment network (DAN) containing multi-type feature training and achieved the current optimal results. Sun et al. [3] designed an explicit shape regression (ESR) method based on correlation, which able to learn accurate models from mass training data in short time. Xiao et al. [5] proposed a recurrent attentive-refinement network for face landmarks location (RAR) and used LSTM model for estimating reliability at each recursive stage. Wu et al. [9] proposed that face shape boundary information should be added to the face alignment network (LAB), and optimal location accuracy has been achieved through the joint learning of three parts: the heatmap generation network of face landmarks, the face boundary discrimination network, and the face landmark regression network.

Most of the face alignment methods introduced in recent years focus on improving the accuracy of the algorithm. However, these methods also bring some problems, such as having a large model, being time-consuming, presenting slow calculation.

For these reasons, we propose a real-time face alignment method on CPU. This method can achieve 1100 fps processing speed in i5-CPU computing environment. At the same time, it also has good performance on ARM processor chips. The algorithm also maintains good positioning accuracy, allowing it to be better used for the actual deployment of a low-power consumption mobile platform.

To summarize, the two main contributions of this work are as follows:

- The residual error between ground truth and mean shape is used as the training label, and joint heatmap and original map as input of second-stage deepens the feature learning of the landmarks.
- A two-stage face alignment network is proposed using convolution and global pooling structure with real-time CPU speed of 1100 fps.

This paper is divided into four parts. The first part is a brief introduction of the related technology and structure of the paper. The second part is the method and technology proposed. The third part presents the comparative and validation experiment. The last part consists of the summary and conclusion.

2 Proposed Method

2.1 Data Fusion with Heatmap

The first stage of the network learns the residual values between ground truth and mean shape. In the second stage of training, the network needs to generate the heatmap of the landmarks. A landmark heatmap is an image with high intensity values around landmark locations where intensity decreases with distance from the nearest landmark. The generation of the heatmap depends on the prediction value generated in the first stage, and the generation of the prime value of the heatmap is derived from Eq. (1) in transform layer.

$$H(x,y) = \frac{1}{1 + \min_{s_i \in pre1} \|(x,y) - s_i\|} \tag{1}$$

Where $H(x, y)$ denotes the pixel value of the generated heatmap, while S_i denotes the coordinates of the predicted landmarks obtained in the first stage. The heatmap values are calculated in a circle of radius 8 around each landmark. The closer the coordinates of the heatmap value are to landmarks, the closer the pixel value is to 1. On the contrary, the farther the coordinates are to the landmarks, the pixel value is to 0. The generated heatmap is shown in Fig. 1.

Fig. 1. Data & Heatmap

2.2 Proposed Network

For mobile devices and low-power devices, hardware computing power is low, and GPU real-time is difficult to apply in practice, so solving the real-time of CPU is a key problem. In this paper, we build a two-stage network and use the convolution add global pooling structure to preserve the features of each convolution layer. Finally, we fuse the features to make the network learn more extensive features (Table 1 and Fig. 2).

2.3 Training Label with Residual

Using the landmark label provided by the original data set, the mean shape of the entire data set is calculated as the initial standard landmark, which is typically an average face shape placed in the bounding box returned by the face detector [3, 4, 6, 15], and the residual error between the mean shape and ground truth is used as the label of the training network.

The formulas for calculating the training labels in the first and second stages are as follows. The training of the network in the second stage is based on the first stage of training. In the second stage, the training label is the residual error between the ground truth and the predicted value of the first stage, as shown in Eq. (3).

Table 1. Parameters of the proposed network. The format according to height*width*depth, stride.

Name	Shape-in	Shape-out	Kernel
Conv1_1	112*112*1	56*56*16	3*3*1,2
Conv1_2	56*56*16	28*28*32	3*3*16,2
Pool1_2	28*28*32	14*14*32	2*2*32,2
Conv1_2.1	14*14*32	7*7*128	3*3*32,2
Pool1_2.1	7*7*128	1*1*128	global_pool
Conv1_3	14*14*32	7*7*128	3*3*32,2
Pool1_3	7*7*128	4*4*128	2*2*128,2
Conv1_3.1	4*4*128	2*2*128	3*3*128,2
Pool1_3.1	2*2*128	1*1*128	global_pool
Conv1_4	4*4*128	2*2*128	3*3*128,2
Pool1_4.1	2*2*128	1*1*128	global_pool
Concat	1*1*128*3	1*1*384	–
Fc_1	1*1*384	1*136	–
Transform	1*136	112*112*1	–
Concat	112*112*1*2	112*112*2	–
Conv2_1	112*112*2	56*56*8	3*3*2,2
Pool2_1	56*56*8	28*28*8	3*3*8,2
Conv2_2	28*28*8	28*28*16	3*3*8,1
Pool2_2	28*28*16	14*14*16	3*3*16,2
Conv2_2.1	14*14*16	14*14*64	3*3*16,1
Pool2_2.1	14*14*64	1*1*64	global_pool
Conv2_3	14*14*16	7*7*64	3*3*16,2
Pool2_3	7*7*64	3*3*64	3*3*64,2
Conv2_3.1	3*3*64	3*3*64	3*3*64,1
Pool2_3.1	3*3*64	1*1*64	global_pool
Conv2_4	3*3*64	2*2*64	3*3*64,2
Pool2_4.1	2*2*64	1*1*64	global_pool
Concat	1*1*64*3	1*1*192	–
Fc_2	1*1*192	1*136	–

$$res1 = S_{gt} - S_{meanshape} \qquad (2)$$

$$res2 = S_{gt} - S_{pre1} \qquad (3)$$

where S_{gt} is a vector of ground truth landmark locations, $S_{meanshape}$ is a vector of standard landmark locations, and S_{pre1} is a vector of predicted landmark locations after stage1 (Fig. 3).

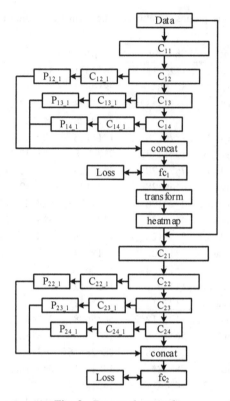

Fig. 2. Proposed network

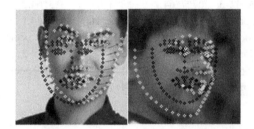

Fig. 3. Image of residual regression

3 Experiments

Error Measures: The mean distance between the predicted landmarks and the ground truth landmarks are divided by the inter-pupil distance (the distance between the eye centers) [8, 12, 20]. In this paper, we present our results using this measure.

The formula for calculating the normalized root-mean-square error (NRMSE) of the model is shown as follows:

$$NRMSE = \frac{\sum_{i=1}^{L} \left\| p_i^{pre} - p_i^{gt} \right\|_2}{\left\| p_{leye} - p_{reye} \right\|_2} \quad (4)$$

where P_i^{pre} and P_i^{gt} accordingly denote the i-th landmark coordinates of the predicted and ground-truth facial landmark positions. P_{leye} and P_{reye} denote the pupil locations of the left eye and the right eye, respectively. Finally, we averaged the NRMSEs for all testing face samples in our experiments as the averaged error comparisons for evaluation.

Datasets: We evaluated our method on two challenging datasets including 300W [12] and COFW [26].

300W [12] Dataset: 300W is a widely used open benchmark data set. We use all the training samples about 3148 images as the training data and perform testing on full set (689 images). Full set is composed of common subset (554 images) and challenging subsets (135 images).

COFW [26] Dataset: COFW consists of 1345 and 507 images for training and testing, respectively. Each COFW image originally has 29 manually annotated landmarks. We use the test data which has been re-annotated by [27], in this way, we can compare with the previous methods easily.

All training images are cropped and resized to 112×112 according to provided bounding boxes. The face detected in the image is cut by rotation, zoom, mirror, and so on. The original image is expanded to 20 pictures of different shapes as the training set of the face alignment network. The images generated by rotation, zoom, and mirror operations contain more pose angles and face sizes. Therefore, the network was trained with this data and used Euclidean Loss, so it is more robust to the location of the face detection box, so even if the location of the face detection box appears to have a certain deviation or the detection box is small, the location of the landmarks of the face returned by the network is still accurate.

3.1   Comparison with Different Training Labels and Networks

The models are evaluated on a 3.10 GHz Intel Core i5-4440 CPU. In this paper, the training data of the network is enhanced by data enhancement method to obtain more training data with different poses and face sizes. The input graph of the network is the expanded data of the original image data after face detection and rotation, scaling, and translation operations. After expansion, the data size is 112×112, the data preprocessing method consists of subtracting the mean value 127.5 and multiplying the scaling factor size by 0.0078125. The batch size of the network training is 32, the learning rate is set to 0.0001, and the weight attenuation is set to 0.0005. The test data set is 300W and COFW_68, and Ours model test use the same face detection algorithm. The test results are shown in Tables 2 and 3, the number of frames processed per second is represented by fps.

Model Description:

(1) **One_stage** is a model that was trained using one stage network.
(2) **Without_conv_pool** is a model that was trained using two stages network without convolution and global pooling structure.
(3) **Ours_res** is a model that was trained using two stages network with convolution and global pooling structure.
(4) **Ours_gt** is a model that was trained also using two stages network with convolution and global pooling structure but using different training label.

The first three models mentioned above were trained using the residual error between ground truth and mean shape as label, while the last model directly takes the real ground truth landmark of the image as the training label.

Table 2. Comparing the results of different training methods (300W_Fullset)

Methods	NRMSE	Time (ms)	FPS
One_stage	9.73	0.4	2500
Without_conv_pool	7.17	0.7	1400
Ours_gt	8.26	0.9	1100
Ours_res	**6.25**	**0.9**	**1100**

Table 3. Comparing the results of different training methods (COFW_68)

Methods	NRMSE	Time (ms)	FPS
One_stage	9.79	0.4	2500
Without_conv_pool	7.44	0.7	1400
Ours_gt	8.51	0.9	1100
Ours_res	**6.41**	**0.9**	**1100**

Tables show that the test results of single-stage network training model are much worse, because the single-stage network is shallow and it is very difficult for the network to learn very fine features in one stage, so the multi-stage cascaded network will have better accuracy. When there is no convolution and global pooling structure, the time is reduced by 22%, but the accuracy is also reduced by 14%.

From the comparison of tables, we can see that the model using residual as label has better test performance. The reason for this may be that the network using ground truth as the label needs to initialize from 0, and then learns the coordinates of the specific landmarks. This is more difficult for the network to learn. Directly learning the residual error between ground truth and mean shape is equivalent to giving the network an initial value of a standard landmark. The initial value of the network is closer to the true value, and the network converges more easily.

3.2   Comparison with Existing Approaches

Facial face alignment algorithm is more so a preprocessing step in face recognition and person-to-person comparison than it is used in special scenes such as special facial features calibration. Since too long of time-consumption will directly affect the user experience of the product, a practical and feasible algorithm is the key to solving the problem.

From the comparison results in Table 4, our method has obvious advantages in accuracy and time compared with the traditional algorithm. Compared with traditional methods, such as LBF, SDM, and ESR, our proposed method achieved 2:17% and 92:66% improvement in terms of mean error and time, respectively. Our method produces a significant time reduction of over 66% in comparison to the traditional methods. Although the loss of precision has dropped by 0.49, the algorithm running time is reduced by nearly 40 times compared with the traditional algorithm of CFSS.

Compared with the new deep learning methods proposed in recent years, such as DAN, LAB, and TCDCN [27], our proposed method achieved 3000:1800% improvement in time and only lost a slight amount of precision, as shown from the results in Table 5. As can be seen from the predicted results in Fig. 4, our method also shows good performance for images with yaw angle in [60°, 90°].

Table 4. Compared test error (300W_Fullset)

Methods	NRMSE	Time (ms)	FPS
ESR [3]	7.58	8.3	120
SDM [4]	7.52	14.2	70
LBF [6]	6.32	3.1	320
CFSS [8]	5.76	40	25
DAN_menpo [10]	5.27	150	6
LAB [9]	4.12	1500	0.6
Ours_res	**6.25**	**0.9**	**1100**

Table 5. Compared test error (COFW_68)

Methods	NRMSE	Time (ms)	FPS
HPM [27]	6.72	3000	0.3
RCPR [26]	8.76	66	15
TCDCN [28]	7.66	18	55
CFSS [8]	6.28	40	25
LAB [9]	4.62	1500	0.6
Ours_res	**6.41**	**0.9**	**1100**

Although the accuracy of the proposed method is lower than that of the latest deep learning method, the processing speed of the proposed method is greatly improved, meeting the needs of practical application.

3.3 Results

Fig. 4. Results of predicted landmarks

4 Conclusion

We have presented a novel real-time and high-precision face alignment method. The network is advantageous over the conventional cascaded approach in that it is both faster and learns more fully. Convolution and pooling structure in the network can better preserve different features. The resulting method is highly accurate, efficient, and can be used in real time applications such as face tracking. The next stage of work will be devoted to improving the accuracy of face alignment while maintaining the performance of the algorithm. Furthermore, it also shows considerable performance on other databases.

References

1. Bhagavatula, C., Zhu, C., Luu, K., Savvides, M.: Faster Than Real-time Facial Alignment: A 3D Spatial Transformer Network Approach in Unconstrained Poses. arXiv:1707.05653 [cs] (2017)
2. Tang, F., Zhang, J., Feng, Y., Guan, Q., Zhou, X.: Real-time face alignment enhancement by tracking. In: 2016 IEEE International Conference on Robotics and Biomimetics (ROBIO), pp. 1011–1016. IEEE, Qingdao (2016). https://doi.org/10.1109/ROBIO.2016.7866457
3. Cao, X., Wei, Y., Wen, F., Sun, J.: Face alignment by explicit shape regression. Int. J. Comput. Vis. **60**(2), 135–164 (2014)
4. Xiong, X., De la Torre, F.: Supervised descent method and its applications to face alignment. In: 2013 IEEE Conference on Computer Vision and Pattern Recognition, pp. 532–539. IEEE, Portland (2013). https://doi.org/10.1109/CVPR.2013.75
5. Xiao, S., Feng, J., Xing, J., Lai, H., Yan, S., Kassim, A.: Robust facial landmark detection via recurrent attentive-refinement networks. In: Leibe, B., Matas, J., Sebe, N., Welling, M. (eds.) ECCV 2016. LNCS, vol. 9905, pp. 57–72. Springer, Cham (2016). https://doi.org/10.1007/978-3-319-46448-0_4
6. Ren, S., Cao, X., Wei, Y., Sun, J.: Face alignment at 3000 FPS via regressing local binary features. In: 2014 IEEE Conference on Computer Vision and Pattern Recognition, pp. 1685–1692. IEEE, Columbus (2014). https://doi.org/10.1109/CVPR.2014.218
7. Lee, D., Park, H., Yoo, C.D.: Face alignment using cascade Gaussian process regression trees. In: 2015 IEEE Conference on Computer Vision and Pattern Recognition (CVPR), pp. 4204–4212. IEEE, Boston (2015). https://doi.org/10.1109/CVPR.2015.7299048
8. Zhu, S., Li, C., Loy, C.C., Tang, X.: Face alignment by coarse-to-fine shape searching. In: 2015 IEEE Conference on Computer Vision and Pattern Recognition (CVPR), pp. 4998–5006. IEEE, Boston (2015). https://doi.org/10.1109/CVPR.2015.7299134
9. Wu, W., Qian, C., Yang, S., Wang, Q., Cai, Y., Zhou, Q.: Look at Boundary: A Boundary-Aware Face Alignment Algorithm. arXiv:1805.10483 [cs] (2018)
10. Kowalski, M., Naruniec, J., Trzcinski, T.: Deep Alignment Network: A convolutional neural network for robust face alignment. arXiv:1706.01789 [cs] (2017)
11. Milborrow, S., Nicolls, F.: Locating facial features with an extended active shape model. In: Forsyth, D., Torr, P., Zisserman, A. (eds.) ECCV 2008. LNCS, vol. 5305, pp. 504–513. Springer, Heidelberg (2008). https://doi.org/10.1007/978-3-540-88693-8_37
12. Sagonas, C., Tzimiropoulos, G., Zafeiriou, S., Pantic, M.: 300 faces in-the-wild challenge: the first facial landmark localization challenge. In: 2013 IEEE International Conference on Computer Vision Workshops, pp. 397–403. IEEE, Sydney (2013). https://doi.org/10.1109/ICCVW.2013.59
13. Saragih, J., Goecke, R.: A nonlinear discriminative approach to AAM fitting. In: 2007 IEEE 11th International Conference on Computer Vision, pp. 1–8. IEEE, Rio de Janeiro (2007). https://doi.org/10.1109/ICCV.2007.4409106
14. Saragih, J.M., Lucey, S., Cohn, J.F.: Deformable model fitting by regularized landmark mean-shift. Int. J. Comput. Vis. **91**, 200–215 (2011). https://doi.org/10.1007/s11263-010-0380-4
15. Yang, S., Luo, P., Loy, C.C., Tang, X.: From Facial Parts Responses to Face Detection: A Deep Learning Approach. arXiv:1509.06451 [cs] (2015)
16. Smith, B.M., Zhang, L.: Collaborative facial landmark localization for transferring annotations across datasets. In: Fleet, D., Pajdla, T., Schiele, B., Tuytelaars, T. (eds.) ECCV 2014. LNCS, vol. 8694, pp. 78–93. Springer, Cham (2014). https://doi.org/10.1007/978-3-319-10599-4_6

17. Sun, Y., Wang, X., Tang, X.: Deep convolutional network cascade for facial point detection. In: 2013 IEEE Conference on Computer Vision and Pattern Recognition, pp. 3476–3483. IEEE, Portland (2013). https://doi.org/10.1109/CVPR.2013.446

18. Sun, Y., Wang, X., Tang, X.: Deep learning face representation from predicting 10,000 classes. In: 2014 IEEE Conference on Computer Vision and Pattern Recognition, pp. 1891–1898. IEEE, Columbus (2014). https://doi.org/10.1109/CVPR.2014.244

19. Sun, Y., Wang, X., Tang, X.: Hybrid deep learning for face verification. In: TPAMI (2016)

20. Trigeorgis, G., Snape, P., Nicolaou, M.A., Antonakos, E., Zafeiriou, S.: Mnemonic descent method: a recurrent process applied for end-to-end face alignment. In: 2016 IEEE Conference on Computer Vision and Pattern Recognition (CVPR), pp. 4177–4187. IEEE, Las Vegas (2016). https://doi.org/10.1109/CVPR.2016.453

21. Wu, W., Yang, S.: Leveraging intra and inter-dataset variations for robust face alignment. In: 2017 IEEE Conference on Computer Vision and Pattern Recognition Workshops (CVPRW), pp. 2096–2105. IEEE, Honolulu (2017). https://doi.org/10.1109/CVPRW.2017.261

22. Wu, Y., Gou, C., Ji, Q.: Simultaneous facial landmark detection, pose and deformation estimation under facial occlusion. In: 2017 IEEE Conference on Computer Vision and Pattern Recognition (CVPR), pp. 5719–5728. IEEE, Honolulu (2017). https://doi.org/10.1109/CVPR.2017.606

23. Zhu, S., Li, C., Loy, C.C., Tang, X.: Unconstrained face alignment via cascaded compositional learning. In: 2016 IEEE Conference on Computer Vision and Pattern Recognition (CVPR), pp. 3409–3417. IEEE, Las Vegas (2016). https://doi.org/10.1109/CVPR.2016.371

24. Liu, Y., Jourabloo, A., Ren, W., Liu, X.: Dense face alignment. In: 2017 IEEE International Conference on Computer Vision Workshops (ICCVW), pp. 1619–1628. IEEE, Venice (2017). https://doi.org/10.1109/ICCVW.2017.190

25. Zhu, Z., Luo, P., Wang, X., Tang, X.: Deep learning identity-preserving face space. In: ICCV (2013)

26. Burgos-Artizzu, X.P., Perona, P., Dollar, P.: Robust face landmark estimation under occlusion. In: 2013 IEEE International Conference on Computer Vision, pp. 1513–1520. IEEE, Sydney (2013). https://doi.org/10.1109/ICCV.2013.191

27. Ghiasi, G., Fowlkes, C.C.: Occlusion coherence: localizing occluded faces with a hierarchical deformable part model. In: 2014 IEEE Conference on Computer Vision and Pattern Recognition, pp. 1899–1906. IEEE, Columbus (2014). https://doi.org/10.1109/CVPR.2014.306

28. Zhang, Z., Luo, P., Loy, C.C., Tang, X.: Learning deep representation for face alignment with auxiliary attributes. IEEE Trans. Pattern Anal. Mach. Intell. **38**, 918–930 (2016). https://doi.org/10.1109/TPAMI.2015.2469286

A Siamese Pedestrian Alignment Network for Person Re-identification

Yi Zheng[1,2], Yong Zhou[1,2(✉)] [iD], Jiaqi Zhao[1,2] [iD], Meng Jian[3], Rui Yao[1,2] [iD], Bing Liu[1,2], and Xuning Liu[1,2]

[1] School of Computer Science and Technology, China University of Mining and Technology, Xuzhou 221116, China
yzhou@cumt.edu.cn
[2] Engineering Research Center of Mine Digitization of the Ministry of Education of the People's Republic of China, Xuzhou 221116, China
[3] Faculty of Information Technology, Beijing University of Technology, Beijing 100124, China

Abstract. Deep learning methods show strong ability in extracting high-level features for images in the field of person re-identification. The produced features help inherently distinguish pedestrian identities in images. However, on deep learning models over-fitting and discriminative ability of the learnt features are still challenges for person re-identification. To alleviate model over-fitting and further enhance the discriminative ability of the learnt features, we propose siamese pedestrian alignment networks (SPAN) for person re-identification. SPAN employs two streams of PAN (pedestrian alignment networks) to increase the size of network inputs over limited training samples and effectively alleviate network over-fitting in learning. In addition, a verification loss is constructed between the two PANs to adjust the relative distance of two input pedestrians of the same or different identities in the learned feature space. Experimental verification is conducted on six large person re-identification datasets and the experimental results demonstrate the effectiveness of the proposed SPAN for person re-identification.

Keywords: Person re-identification · Deep learning · Neural network · Verification loss · Feature learning

1 Introduction

The goal of person re-identification is to find people with the same identity in pictures taken by different cameras. Usually, it is treated as the problem of image retrieval [33], i.e., searching for a specific person (query) in a large image pool (gallery) [32]. Recently, several convolutional neural networks (CNN) based deep learning methods have been developed to deal with person re-identification problem. Since 2014 [12], CNN-based deep learning methods have greatly improved

The first author of this paper is a full-time postgraduate student.

ⓒ Springer Nature Switzerland AG 2019
Z. Lin et al. (Eds.): PRCV 2019, LNCS 11857, pp. 409–420, 2019.
https://doi.org/10.1007/978-3-030-31654-9_35

the performance of person re-identification [33] due to its powerful discriminative learning on large-scale datasets.

Currently, deep learning based methods are widely used in computer vision and pattern recognition tasks. In these methods, we usually use feature vectors to represent samples. To describe the relationship between feature vectors and take advantage of this relationship, the distance between feature vectors becomes an important indicator to measure the similarity of feature vectors. The purpose of metric learning is to obtain a metric matrix that can effectively reflect the similarity between samples. In the feature space based on the metric matrix, the distribution of intra-class samples is more compact, while the distribution of inter-class samples is more sparse. Xing *et al.* [25] first proposed the metric learning method in 2003. They improved the results of the clustering algorithm by learning the distance metric between pairs of samples. Weinberger *et al.* [24] combined a meta sample with a similar sample and a dissimilar sample to learn a distance metric that enables the distance between similar samples to be greater than the distance between dissimilar samples. Davis *et al.* [4] proposed the Information Theoretical Metric Learning (ITML). They randomly chose sample pairs and constrains the distances by labels, and proposed a regularization method for metric matrices. Law *et al.* [11] proposed a distance metric learning framework which exploits distance constraints over up to four different examples. This comparison between pairs of samples is often used in the retrieval process.

The pedestrian alignment network (PAN) was proposed in [36] to deal with two types of detector errors in person re-identification caused by excessive background and part missing, which were introduced by automatic pedestrian detectors. PAN treats pedestrian alignment and re-identification tasks as two related issues. It finds an optimal affine transformation from a given pedestrian image without extra annotations. With affine transformation, the pedestrian in the image is aligned to avoid excessive background in person re-identification. The discriminative ability of learnt features could be highly improved with the alignment since the learned feature maps usually exhibit strong activations on human body rather than background [36]. However, the verification loss as a special characteristic of person re-identification is not taken into consideration.

By making use of the pairwise relationships in metric learning, we propose siamese pedestrian alignment network (SPAN) for person re-identification. As an extension of PAN, SPAN takes two streams of input and output constructing a verification network. The main contributions of this paper are summarized as follows:

- The proposed siamese PAN constructs a verification model by combining two streams of PANs for person re-identification, which alleviates the overfitting of PAN greatly by taking pairwise samples to increase the input size in training the siamese network.
- SPAN evolves a verification loss embedded between PAN streams, which introduced the metric learning mechanism to make the images belonging to the same identity get close and push away the image with different identities in the learnt feature space.

- The features learnt from SPAN was cascaded with features extracted from unaligned pedestrian for person retrial. The ensemble feature help improve the person re-identification performance dramatically.

The rest of this paper is organized as follows. Related works are reviewed and discussed in Sect. 2. Section 3 introduces the proposed method in detail and experimental results and comparisons are discussed in Sect. 4. The conclusions and further discussion are given in Sect. 5.

2 Related Work

2.1 Siamese-Based Methods

Currently, most deep learning based person re-identification methods are developed on the siamese model [7], which is fed with image pairs. Dong et al. [27] proposed deep metric learning method to investigate the part model for person re-identification. An input image was partitioned into three overlapping parts and then fed into three siamese CNNs for feature learning. A patch matching layer was designed to extract the result of patch displacement matrices in different horizontal stripes in [12]. The cross input neighborhood difference feature was proposed by Ahmed et al. [1], in which the features from one input image were compared to features in neighboring locations of the other image. Zeng et al. [29] proposed a person re-identification method based on Mahalanobis distance feature. The long short-term memory (LSTM) modules were incorporated into a siamese network for person re-identification in [21]. The discriminative feature learning ability was further enhanced by adopting LSTMs to process image parts sequentially. Siamese model only takes weak label of whether a pair of images is similar or not, while ignoring the given pedestrian labels. To make use of the pedestrian labels, Zheng et al. [34] proposed a discriminative siamese network combining both identification loss and verification loss in discriminative feature learning. It simultaneously learn discriminative and similarity metrics, which effectively improves pedestrian retrieval accuracy dramatically.

2.2 Pedestrian Alignment Network

Pedestrian alignment network (PAN) is able to simultaneously re-localize the person in a given image and categorize the person to one of pre-defined identities. The architecture of PAN is illustrated in Fig. 1. As shown in Fig. 1, PAN consists of a base branch and an alignment branch which includes grid network and ResNet blocks.

Both branches of PAN are classification networks to infer the identity of the input pedestrian images. The base branch performs to extract appearance features of the given image and provide corresponding information for the spatial localization of the person in the image. The alignment branch takes a similar neural network with base branch and further extracts features from the aligned feature maps produced by the grid network. The two branches work together by sequentially combining aligned features for person re-identification.

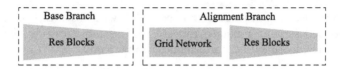

Fig. 1. The architecture of pedestrian alignment network. It consists of base branch and alignment branch.

3   Siamese Pedestrian Aligned Network

It is still far from satisfactory for PAN in pedestrian feature learning. As we observed, PAN is easily trapped into over-fitting with insufficient training data. In addition, pairwise verification is not taken into consideration, which reveals important clues for person re-identification. With these motivation, we scale up input size of PAN in SPAN by employing pairwise input images for the streams of PANs and embed a verification loss between the two streams to further leverage pairwise relationships in feature learning. The details of the proposed siamese PAN (SPAN) are illustrated in this Section.

3.1   Overview of SPAN

Since there are a large number of parameters in many deep learning models, a large number of labeled samples are needed for model training. However, it is hard to provide training samples of high quality for person re-identification. The siamese model [34] provides an effective way to make full use of the limited training samples by employing pairwise input and metric learning mechanism.

The architecture of the proposed SPAN is shown in Fig. 2. The SPAN consists of siamese base branch and siamese alignment branch. Both of them have two streams and the parameters are shared with each other. The input of the siamese base branch is a pair of pedestrian images with the same or different identities. The siamese base branch is constructed to learn high-level image features by minimizing both identification loss and verification loss. The input of the siamese alignment branch is a pair of pedestrian feature maps obtained from the based branch. The siamese alignment branch works to learn the location of pedestrians and extract discriminative features for further pedestrian retrieval. The ResNet-50 [5] is adopted as the base component of the two branches due to its excellent performance in feature learning, details of ResNet-50 can be seen in [36]. In addition, the verification loss, which bridges the two PAN streams for similarly metric learning, is embedded in both siamese based branch (SBB) and siamese alignment branch (SAB).

3.2   Siamese Base Branch

Besides the initial base branch of PAN, a square layer is further embedded to measure the difference between the high-level features f_a^1 and f_a^2 in the siamese

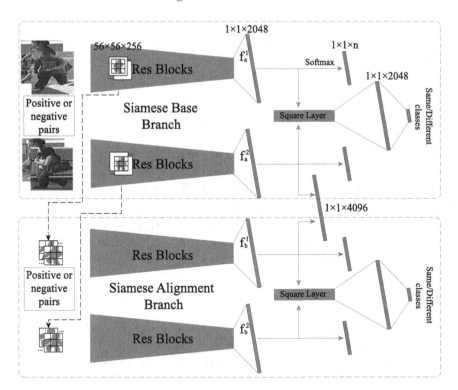

Fig. 2. The architecture of the SPAN model, which consists of the siamese base branch and siamese alignment networks. The output of the two branch is a $1 \times 1 \times 2048$ vector. In the retrieval phase, two 2048-dim vectors, i.e., f_b^1 and f_a^1 are concatenated to describe the input image.

base branch. A convolutional layer is built following the square layer as a verification module, which is constructed to evaluate whether the input pair of images belongs to the same or different identities. The high-level features learned by the additional convolutional layer act as a metric learning module, which forces the distance of pedestrians of the same identity as close as possible, and the distance between different pedestrians as far as possible in the feature space.

Identification: In SBB, the identification loss plays a key role in discriminative feature learning and pedestrian identification. Each stream of SBB contains five Res blocks [5] and they are pre-trained on ImageNet [10] to fine tune the Res blocks. By replacing the fully-connected layer with a convolutional layer and softmax unit [34], we could infer the multi-class probabilities as Eq. 1.

$$\hat{p^i} = softmax(\phi_b^I \circ f_b^i), i = 1, 2 \tag{1}$$

where, $\circ$ denotes the convolutional operation, f_b^i is a 2048-dim feature vector extracted by one stream of SBB, and ϕ_b^I denotes the parameters of the convolutional layer which connected to the output feature f_b^i. The cross-entropy loss of classification model is formulated as Eq. 2.

$$loss_{C-SBB}(f_b^i, \phi_b^i) = -\sum_{i=1}^{2}\sum_{k=1}^{K} p_k^i \log(\hat{p_k^i}) \tag{2}$$

where, K denotes the number of identity classes in the dataset, and the target class is represented by t. Only if $k = t$ then $p_k^i = 1$, otherwise $p_k^i = 0$, $\hat{p_k^i}$ is the probability of every class predicted by softmax function.

Verification: Depending on the relationship of the input image pair, we further add a verification module in the siamese base branch to adjust relative distances of pedestrian pair in the learnt feature space by a verification loss. Firstly, a 2048-dim tensor f_b^s is obtained by multiplying the difference between f_b^1 and f_b^2 element-wisely as Eq. 3.

$$f_b^s = (f_b^1 - f_b^2) \times (f_b^1 - f_b^2) \tag{3}$$

After the added convolutional layer and softmax output function, f_b^s is mapped to a 2-dim vector $(\hat{q_b^1}, \hat{q_b^2})$. Here $\hat{q_b^1} + \hat{q_b^2} = 1$, which represents the predicted probability whether the two input images belong to the same identity or not. The formulation is represented as Eq. 4.

$$\hat{q_b} = softmax(\phi_b^S \circ f_b^s), \tag{4}$$

where, ϕ_b^S denotes the parameters of the convolutional layer. The verification loss of SBB is denoted by Eq. 5.

$$loss_{V-SBB}(f_b^s, s, \phi_b^S) = -\sum_{i=1}^{2} q_b^i \log(\hat{q_b^i}), \tag{5}$$

where, p represents whether the inputted image pairs belong to the same class or not. If the input images belong to the same class, $q_b^1 = 1$ and $q_b^2 = 0$, otherwise $q_b^1 = 0$ and $q_b^2 = 1$.

3.3   Siamese Alignment Branch

Similar to the siamese base branch, each stream of siamese alignment branch is a categorization module for pedestrian identification, including a variation ResNet and a grid network which aligns the position of pedestrians in feature maps [36]. The identification loss of the SAB is constructed as Eqs. 6 and 7.

$$\hat{p^i} = softmax(\phi_a^I \circ f_a^i), i = 1, 2 \tag{6}$$

$$loss_{C-SAB}(f_a^i, t, \phi_a^I) = -\sum_{i=1}^{2}\sum_{k=1}^{K} p_k^i \log(\hat{p_k^i}) \tag{7}$$

where, f_a^i denotes the feature vector extracted by each stream of the siamese alignment branch. ϕ_a^I represents the parameters of the corresponding deep model.

A verification module is embedded in the SAB network which introduces the metric learning mechanization to optimize the pairwise relationships of images. The verification loss in alignment branch is represented by Eq. 9.

$$\hat{q}_a = softmax(\phi_a^S \circ f_a^s) \tag{8}$$

$$loss_{V-SAB}(f_a^s, s, \phi_a^S) = -\sum_{i=1}^{2} q_a^i \log(\hat{q}_a^i) \tag{9}$$

Here in Eqs. 8 and 9, f_a^s denotes the 2048-dim vector calculated by f_a^1 and f_a^2, ϕ_a^S represents the parameters of the added convolutional layer. Similarly, when giving images belong to the same class $q_a^1 = 1$ and $q_a^2 = 0$, otherwise $q_a^1 = 0, q_a^2 = 1$. The vector $(\hat{q}_a^1, \hat{q}_a^2)$ mapped by f_a^s represents the probability if the input images belong to the same class.

In summary, the target of the proposed siamese pedestrian alignment network is to perform aligned pedestrian feature learning by minimizing two cross-entropy losses of the siamese base branch and siamese alignment branch, as Eq. 10.

$$min(\lambda_1 loss_{C-SBB} + \lambda_2 loss_{V-SBB} + \lambda_3 loss_{C-SAB} + \lambda_4 loss_{V-SAB}), \tag{10}$$

here $\lambda_i, i = 1, 2, 3, 4$ represent the weight of each loss in the entire network respectively.

3.4   Feature Concatenation

In the testing phase, for an input pedestrian image x SPAN extracts two features of f_b and f_a by feeding the image to one stream of the SBB and SAB respectively. As the features of SBB and SAB tend to compensate with each other, we concatenate them together to jointly represent features of the image for pedestrian retrieval. After combining features of SBB and SAB, an l^2-normalization layer is performed to unify feature space as Eq. 11.

$$f = [|f_b|^T, |f_a|^T]^T *, \tag{11}$$

where, $*$ represents the operation of l^2-normalization.

4   Experimental Results

In this section, six large-scale datasets, i.e., Market-1501 [32], CUHK03 [37], DukeMTMC-reID [16], PKU-Reid [15], MSMT17 [23], Airport [9] are selected to evaluate the performance of the proposed method.

During the training process, our network needs to read at least two images belong to the same identity at the same time. If not, the network could not find vectors to push them together in the feature space. In Airport dataset, some pedestrian identities have only one image, in Market-1501 and MSMT17 dataset there are some identities just have two or three images. Therefore, we have expended these identities with fewer images in the datasets through random cropping. Also, random cropping can cause more serious part missing problems.

4.1   Implementation Details

All of the experiments were based on the MatConvnet [22] and were implemented on a graphics workstation with Intel core i7-8700k CPU, 32 GB memory and a Nvidia GTX 1080Ti. The maximum number of training epochs was set as 85 for the SBB, and the learning rate was set to 10^{-3} for the first 70 epochs then it turned to 10^{-4} for 10 epochs, and 10^{-5} was the learning rate for the last 5 epochs. The mini-batch stochastic gradient descent (SGD) was adapted to update the parameters of the whole network. For SBB, there are three objectives include identification loss and verification loss in our network. So we computed all the gradients produced by every objective respectively and gave them weight before we added them together to update the network. The identification loss $loss_{C-SBB}$ contain two objectives and the weight $\lambda_1 = 0.5$, the weight of verification loss $loss_{V-SBB}$ is $\lambda_2 = 1$.

The settings in SAB were similar to the SBB, except some differences such as the maximum number of training epochs, learning rates, and the objectives and their weights. We set the number of training epochs to 110 and the learning rate was 10^{-3}, 10^{-4}, 10^{-5} for 1st to 70th epochs, 71st to 90th epochs and 91st to 110th respectively. In SAB, there are five objectives, four of them belong to identification loss. We got our best result under the setting of $\lambda_3 = 0.5$ $\lambda_4 = 1$

The mean average precision (mAP) and the rank-1 accuracy are selected to evaluate the performance on these datasets.

4.2   Results

We compare the performance of the proposed model with PAN [36] and a siamese CNN (SCNN) network [34] which is based on ResNet-50. The results of three methods on six datasets are shown in Table 1.

According to [36], the PAN is used to reduce the problems of excessive background and part missing. These problems occur more frequently in pedestrian detectors than hand-drawn bounding boxes. So, the results obtained by CUHK03 (labeled), in which the detected boxes are cropped manually, the PAN does not make enough contributions to align the pedestrian, even may cause the part missing problem because of overcropping.

On Market-1501 and DukeMTMC-reID dataset, we compare SPAN with the state-of-the-art methods. The results are shown in Tables 2 and 3. With re-ranking step the mAP of SPAN reached to **76.54%** on Market-1501, which is better than most results in both published paper and arXiv paper. On DukeMTMC-reID dataset, we reached to a competitive result **mAP = 64.68%** after re-ranking. On CUHK03, the **mAP** had improved to **44.73%** for detected setting, and **48.62%** for labeled setting.

At present, the machine we are using for the experiments had met the out of memory error when performing the re-ranking [37] step on MSMT17 dataset because of the number of identities in the query is over 10,000, that is why we did not get result after re-ranking step on MSMT17 dataset.

Table 1. Comparison of different methods on six datasets. Rank-1 accuracy (%) and mAP(%) are shown in the table.

Dataset	Accuracy	SCNN	PAN	SPAN
Market1501	R-1	81.41	80.10	**85.58**
	mAP	62.55	58.93	**68.13**
DukeMTMC-reID	R-1	71.09	67.95	**73.42**
	mAP	51.14	48.69	**54.32**
CUHK03 (detected)	R-1	46.28	28.28	**47.42**
	mAP	42.01	26.65	**43.58**
CUHK03 (labeled)	R-1	**48.78**	29.35	48.21
	mAP	45.48	28.07	**46.15**
MSMT17	R-1	51.78	50.73	**52.81**
	mAP	26.96	24.93	**28.94**
Airport	R-1	15.15	8.92	**15.56**
	mAP	12.68	6.84	**13.77**
PKU-Reid	R-1	37.71	58.77	**63.51**
	mAP	33.97	42.75	**48.41**

Table 2. Comparision of the SPAN with start of the art methods of mAP (%) on Market-1501.**RR**:Re-Ranking [37]

Methods	mAP
PDF [19]	63.41
DSR [6]	64.25
GAN [35]	66.07
SSM [2]+RR	68.80
CamGAN [38]+RR	71.55
DaF [28]	72.42
JLML [13]+RR	72.9
HA-CNN [14]	75.7
SPAN	68.13
SPAN+RR	**76.54**

Table 3. Comparision of the SPAN with start of the art methods of mAP (%) on Market-1501.**RR**:Re-Ranking [37]

Methods	mAP
SVDNet [20]	56.8
dMpRL [8]	58.56
AACN [26]	59.25
CamGAN [38]	57.61
DPFL [3]	60.6
PSE [18]	62.0
ATWL [17]	63.40
HA-CNN [14]	63.8
SPAN	54.32
SPAN+RR	**64.68**

However, on PKU-Reid dataset we further improve our result **mAP = 70.27%** and **Rank-1 accuracy = 73.68%** after re-ranking step.

Otherwise, the mAP and Rank-1 accuracy of airport dataset were not improved when using re-ranking.

5   Conclusion

In this paper, we proposed siamese pedestrian alignment network (SPAN) for person re-identification. SPAN is devoted to alleviating the problem of overfitting and enhancing discriminative ability of the learnt features of PAN model. A verification loss was embedded between the two PAN streams to adjust the relative distance of the two pedestrians with the same or different identifies. The proposed model is able to improve the discriminative learning and similarity measurement at the same time by addressing the misalignment problem and the specifical problem of person re-identification. The effectiveness of the proposed method was verified on six large-scale person re-ID datasets. Experimental results shown that the proposed method outperforms PAN and siamese CNN greatly.

Re-ranking [37] is a very effective way to improve the results of re-identification. In [36], the result of PAN had improved from 63% to 76% on Market-1501 dataset. So we can also make SPAN get a better result by adding re-ranking steps.

However, the computation complexity of the proposed model did not take into consideration. In the future, we will focus on optimizing the structure of deep neural networks to reduce the computation complexity and improve its efficiency for person re-identification by using multi-objective learning methods [30,31].

Acknowledgments. This work was supported in part by the National Natural Science Foundation of China (No. 61572505, No. 61772530, No. U1610124, and No. 61806206), in part by the State's Key Project of Research and Development Plan of China (No. 2016YFC0600900), in part by the Six Talent Peaks Project in Jiangsu Province under Grant 2015-DZXX-010, under Grant 2018-XYDXX-044, in part by the Natural Science Foundation of Jiangsu Province (No. BK20171192, No. BK20180639), and in part by the China Postdoctoral Science Foundation (No. 2018M642359).

References

1. Ahmed, E., Jones, M., Marks, T.K.: An improved deep learning architecture for person re-identification. In: Computer Vision and Pattern Recognition, pp. 3908–3916 (2015)
2. Bai, S., Bai, X., Tian, Q.: Scalable person re-identification on supervised smoothed manifold. In: Proceedings of the IEEE Conference on Computer Vision and Pattern Recognition, pp. 2530–2539 (2017)
3. Chen, Y., Zhu, X., Gong, S.: Person re-identification by deep learning multi-scale representations. In: Proceedings of the IEEE International Conference on Computer Vision, pp. 2590–2600 (2017)
4. Davis, J.V., Kulis, B., Jain, P., Sra, S., Dhillon, I.S.: Information-theoretic metric learning. In: Proceedings of the 24th International Conference on Machine Learning, pp. 209–216. ACM (2007)
5. He, K., Zhang, X., Ren, S., Sun, J.: Deep residual learning for image recognition. In: Proceedings of the IEEE Conference on Computer Vision and Pattern Recognition, pp. 770–778 (2016)

6. He, L., Liang, J., Li, H., Sun, Z.: Deep spatial feature reconstruction for partial person re-identification: alignment-free approach. In: Proceedings of the IEEE Conference on Computer Vision and Pattern Recognition, pp. 7073–7082 (2018)
7. Hu, J., Lu, J., Tan, Y.P.: Discriminative deep metric learning for face verification in the wild. In: The IEEE Conference on Computer Vision and Pattern Recognition (CVPR), June 2014
8. Huang, Y., Xu, J., Wu, Q., Zheng, Z., Zhang, Z., Zhang, J.: Multi-pseudo regularized label for generated data in person re-identification. IEEE Trans. Image Process. **28**(3), 1391–1403 (2019)
9. Karanam, S., Gou, M., Wu, Z., Rates-Borras, A., Camps, O., Radke, R.J.: A systematic evaluation and benchmark for person re-identification: features, metrics, and datasets. arXiv preprint arXiv:1605.09653 (2016)
10. Krizhevsky, A., Sutskever, I., Hinton, G.E.: ImageNet classification with deep convolutional neural networks. In: Advances in Neural Information Processing Systems, pp. 1097–1105 (2012)
11. Law, M.T., Thome, N., Cord, M.: Learning a distance metric from relative comparisons between quadruplets of images. Int. J. Comput. Vision **121**(1), 65–94 (2017)
12. Li, W., Zhao, R., Xiao, T., Wang, X.: DeepReID: deep filter pairing neural network for person re-identification. In: Proceedings of the IEEE Conference on Computer Vision and Pattern Recognition, pp. 152–159 (2014)
13. Li, W., Zhu, X., Gong, S.: Person re-identification by deep joint learning of multi-loss classification. arXiv preprint arXiv:1705.04724 (2017)
14. Li, W., Zhu, X., Gong, S.: Harmonious attention network for person re-identification. In: Proceedings of the IEEE Conference on Computer Vision and Pattern Recognition, pp. 2285–2294 (2018)
15. Ma, L., Liu, H., Hu, L., Wang, C., Sun, Q.: Orientation driven bag of appearances for person re-identification. arXiv preprint arXiv:1605.02464 (2016)
16. Ristani, E., Solera, F., Zou, R., Cucchiara, R., Tomasi, C.: Performance measures and a data set for multi-target, multi-camera tracking. In: Hua, G., Jégou, H. (eds.) ECCV 2016. LNCS, vol. 9914, pp. 17–35. Springer, Cham (2016). https://doi.org/10.1007/978-3-319-48881-3_2
17. Ristani, E., Tomasi, C.: Features for multi-target multi-camera tracking and re-identification. In: Proceedings of the IEEE Conference on Computer Vision and Pattern Recognition, pp. 6036–6046 (2018)
18. Saquib Sarfraz, M., Schumann, A., Eberle, A., Stiefelhagen, R.: A pose-sensitive embedding for person re-identification with expanded cross neighborhood re-ranking. In: Proceedings of the IEEE Conference on Computer Vision and Pattern Recognition, pp. 420–429 (2018)
19. Su, C., Li, J., Zhang, S., Xing, J., Gao, W., Tian, Q.: Pose-driven deep convolutional model for person re-identification. In: Proceedings of the IEEE International Conference on Computer Vision, pp. 3960–3969 (2017)
20. Sun, Y., Zheng, L., Deng, W., Wang, S.: SVDNet for pedestrian retrieval. In: Proceedings of the IEEE International Conference on Computer Vision, pp. 3800–3808 (2017)
21. Varior, R.R., Shuai, B., Lu, J., Xu, D., Wang, G.: A siamese long short-term memory architecture for human re-identification. In: Leibe, B., Matas, J., Sebe, N., Welling, M. (eds.) ECCV 2016. LNCS, vol. 9911, pp. 135–153. Springer, Cham (2016). https://doi.org/10.1007/978-3-319-46478-7_9

22. Vedaldi, A., Lenc, K.: MatconvNet: convolutional neural networks for matlab. In: Proceedings of the 23rd ACM International Conference on Multimedia, pp. 689–692. ACM (2015)
23. Wei, L., Zhang, S., Gao, W., Tian, Q.: Person trasfer GAN to bridge domain gap for person re-identification. In: IEEE Conference on Computer Vision and Pattern Recognition (2018)
24. Weinberger, K.Q., Blitzer, J., Saul, L.K.: Distance metric learning for large margin nearest neighbor classification. In: Advances in Neural Information Processing Systems, pp. 1473–1480 (2006)
25. Xing, E.P., Jordan, M.I., Russell, S.J., Ng, A.Y.: Distance metric learning with application to clustering with side-information. In: Advances in Neural Information Processing Systems, pp. 521–528 (2003)
26. Xu, J., Zhao, R., Zhu, F., Wang, H., Ouyang, W.: Attention-aware compositional network for person re-identification. In: Proceedings of the IEEE Conference on Computer Vision and Pattern Recognition, pp. 2119–2128 (2018)
27. Yi, D., Lei, Z., Liao, S., Li, S.Z.: Deep metric learning for person re-identification. In: 2014 22nd International Conference on Pattern Recognition (ICPR), pp. 34–39. IEEE (2014)
28. Yu, R., Zhou, Z., Bai, S., Bai, X.: Divide and fuse: a re-ranking approach for person re-identification. arXiv preprint arXiv:1708.04169 (2017)
29. Zeng, M., Wu, Z., Tian, C., Zhang, L., Zhao, X.: Person re-identification based on a novel mahalanobis distance feature dominated kiss metric learning. Electron. Lett. **52**(14), 1223–1225 (2016)
30. Zhao, J., et al.: Multiobjective optimization of classifiers by means of 3D convex-hull-based evolutionary algorithms. Inf. Sci. **367–368**, 80–104 (2016)
31. Zhao, J., et al.: 3D fast convex-hull-based evolutionary multiobjective optimization algorithm. Appl. Soft Comput. **67**, 322–336 (2018)
32. Zheng, L., Shen, L., Tian, L., Wang, S., Wang, J., Tian, Q.: Scalable person re-identification: a benchmark. In: Proceedings of the IEEE International Conference on Computer Vision, pp. 1116–1124 (2015)
33. Zheng, L., Yang, Y., Hauptmann, A.G.: Person re-identification: past, present and future. arXiv preprint arXiv:1610.02984 (2016)
34. Zheng, Z., Zheng, L., Yang, Y.: A discriminatively learned CNN embedding for person reidentification. ACM Trans. Multimedia Comput. Commun. Appl. (TOMM) **14**(1), 13:1–13:20 (2017)
35. Zheng, Z., Zheng, L., Yang, Y.: Unlabeled samples generated by GAN improve the person re-identification baseline in vitro. arXiv preprint arXiv:1701.07717 3 (2017)
36. Zheng, Z., Zheng, L., Yang, Y.: Pedestrian alignment network for large-scale person re-identification. IEEE Trans. Circuits Syst. Video Technol. (2018)
37. Zhong, Z., Zheng, L., Cao, D., Li, S.: Re-ranking person re-identification with k-reciprocal encoding. In: 2017 IEEE Conference on Computer Vision and Pattern Recognition (CVPR), pp. 3652–3661. IEEE (2017)
38. Zhong, Z., Zheng, L., Zheng, Z., Li, S., Yang, Y.: Camera style adaptation for person re-identification. In: Proceedings of the IEEE Conference on Computer Vision and Pattern Recognition, pp. 5157–5166 (2018)

Training Low Bitwidth Model with Weight Normalization for Convolutional Neural Networks

Haoxin Fan[1,2], Jianjing An[1,2], and Dong Wang[1,2(✉)]

[1] Institute of Information Science, Beijing Jiaotong University, Beijing 100044, China
{17120306,16112065,wangdong}@bjtu.edu.cn
[2] Beijing Key Laboratory of Advanced Information Science and Network Technology, Beijing 100044, China

Abstract. Convolutional Neural Networks (CNNs) is now widely utilized in computer vision applications, including image classification, object detection and segmentation. However, high memory complexity and computation intensive have limited the deployment on low power embedded devices. We propose a method to train convolutional neural networks with low bitwidth by performing weight normalization. By normalization, the distribution of the weight can be narrowed, which enables the low bitwidth network to achieve a good trade-off between range and precision. Moreover, adding a scaling factor to the weight solves the problem of inadequate expressiveness at low bits, which further improves the performance of classification. The experiments on various datasets show that our method can achieve comparable prediction accuracy as that of full-precision models. To emphasize, the proposed scheme can quantize the network of AlexNet to 3-bit fixed point on ImageNet, and the accuracy of top-1 drop only by 1%.

Keywords: Network compression · Quantization · Convolutional neural networks

1 Introduction

These years, we have witnessed that deep convolution neural networks (DCNNs) is widely used in computer vision work, such as image classification, object detection and segmentation. The success of deep learning largely owes to the fast development of computing resources. However, most of the deep neural networks are trained on GPU or CPU because they need computational power and large amounts of memory. Some networks also have more parameters as they deepen. For example, the 16-layer VGG contains 528M parameters. Hence, high computational complexity and storage space hinder the promotion of deep neural network to some resource limited scenarios, especially for embedded and IoT systems.

© Springer Nature Switzerland AG 2019
Z. Lin et al. (Eds.): PRCV 2019, LNCS 11857, pp. 421–430, 2019.
https://doi.org/10.1007/978-3-030-31654-9_36

Much work has been done to reduce the model size and accelerate the inference of deep neural networks. Denil [1] pointed out that network workload has obvious redundancy, and suggested using the linear structure of the network to reduce the number of network parameters. This shows that the network model does not need full-precision representation to achieve high performance. If we use low bitwidth weight, the storage space will be greatly reduced. The low bitwidth fixed-point format can not only reduce the storage space, but also reduce the computational complexity. At present, 8-bit or 16-bit quantization is usually used to maintain the same accuracy as the original full-precision. When using lower bits to represent model weights, some methods work on small data sets, but for large data sets such as ImageNet, the quantized neural network will cause a greater loss of accuracy and can not complete tasks such as classification.

In this paper, a method of low bitwidth fixed point quantization based on weight normalization is proposed. During training, the weight distribution is limited by normalization and the weight is quantized to the low bitwidth fixed point representation to achieve the light-weight effect of convolutional neural network model. It effectively solves the issue that low bitwidth quantized neural network model can not achieve a good balance between quantization range and accuracy. By quantizing the weight into the low bitwidth, not only the storage size of the model can be saved more than 8×, but also the fixed-point format can be accelerated computation of the neural network on embedded devices such as FPGA. Experiments show that it not only is effective on small datasets, but also works on large datasets, i.e., ImageNet and the accuracy is only reduced by 1% compared to full-precision models.

2   Related Work

At present, many works for acceleration and compression of deep convolution neural networks (DCNNs) have been proposed, such as low rank decomposition of weight matrix [1,2], network pruning [3,4], weight quantization [5–7] and knowledge distillation [8,9]. The essence of weight quantization is to approximate some similar weights to the same numerical value. It is feasible because the neural network has a very high tolerance for low-precision weights, and extremely rough weights will not reduce the prediction accuracy.

Weight quantization can be divided into two categories: weight sharing and weight reduction. Weight sharing is a quantization method that approximately replaces some values with the same value, and then codes them. Deep Compression [3] clustered into several classes by K-means clustering algorithm, quantized these clustering centers, and then coded. Hashed-Net [10] uses hash coding to map the weight into the corresponding hash bucket. The parameters in the same bucket share the same value and then encode. Weight reduction is a method of approximating 32-bit floating-point with low bitwidth representation. In binary connect [5] and binary neural network [6,7], all of them are expressed by the two values. Although the storage space is saved 32×, the accuracy of recognition image classification has been greatly reduced. The proposed ternary neural network [11,12] can improve the binary network by quantizing the weights to –1,

0 and 1. But, it still can not meet the accuracy requirements of image classification. Dorefa-Net [13] sets weights, activations and gradients to low bitwidth. Although it can accelerate the training and testing process, the weights are quantized to non-zero values, ignoring the sparsity and redundancy of the neural network model. In Ristretto [14], the weight is quantized by approximating 32-bit floating-point networks by condensed dynamic fixed point models. From research [14], it is found that the neural network model can have a good classification performance with 8 bits. However, the accuracy drops sharply for lower bit widths, and model can not be improved by fine-tuning. Therefore, the low precision of neural network models still faces great challenges.

The method in this paper belongs to the latter. The 32-bit floating-point weights of the original model are approximated by low bitwidth fixed-point. The existence of zero can further compress the network model, and the fixed-point can be easily accelerated computation on the FPGA. Quantized to 4 bits on ImageNet, the network model is compressed 8×, and accuracy still only reduced 1% compared with the full-precision model.

3   Methods

In this section, we will first revisit the quantization of dynamic fixed point approximation in Ristretto [14]. Then we will elaborate the deficiencies of dynamic fixed point and our method in the subsequent sections.

3.1   Dynamic Fixed-Point Quantization Revisited

In Ristretto [14], the deep convolution neural network model is quantized from 32 bits floating-point to 8 bits fixed-point model. Because of the fractional position, the standard fixed-point format is extended to dynamic fixed-point, so that the weights can cover a wide dynamic range. In dynamic fixed-point, each number is represented as follows:

$$(-1)^s \cdot 2^{-FL} \sum_{i=0}^{BW-2} 2^i \cdot x_i \tag{1}$$

where x_i denotes the mantissa value, s denotes the sign bit, FL denotes the fractional length, and BW denotes the bit width.

The fractional length is chosen based upon the dynamic range of each number group. The integer length needs enough bits to avoid saturation according to the maximum value of a set of numbers. Therefore, for a given set of numbers, the required integer length is determined by the following formula:

$$IL = \lceil log_2(\max_s x + 1) \rceil \tag{2}$$

After determining the bit width, the quantized neural network model can be obtained by polling the maximum value of the weight of each layer and calculating its fractional length.

3.2 Weight Normalization

According to the dynamic fixed-point method proposed in [14], we find that the 8 bits dynamic fixed-point representation can maintain the same accuracy as the original full-precision. It is unable to obtain better quantization results with lower bitwidth. On the one hand, dynamic fixed point representation is greatly affected by boundary-value and quantitative interval. The larger the deviation between the boundary-value and the global distribution is, the larger the quantization interval will be under the same bit width. On the other hand, although these boundary-values far from the distribution are very rare, they are very important to the model. We can not simply approximate or discard these values. There is no good trade-off between range and precision as the bitwidth decreases. Consequently, direct quantization on pretrained model could not achieve low bitwidth while introducing little drop in accuracy. Considering that the quantized value should be close to the original value and not affected by some deviations from deviation values, we propose a fixed-point quantization method training low bitwidth with weight normalization in convolutional neural networks.

For the above problems, we propose a method based on weight normalization, and then quantize the normalized weights by using fixed-point low bitwidth representation. In this paper, the weight normalization is treated as follows:

$$r_o = \frac{tanh(r_i)}{max(|tanh(r_i)|)} \tag{3}$$

The weights are constrained to [−1,1] by normalization. Weight normalization has two purposes: one is to change the original distribution of weights, which can narrow the relative range. We use the formula (3) to normalize, which can make the distribution more uniform. Therefore, even if the bit width is low, the quantization interval remains very small; The other is that we don't need to search the fractional length, compared to dynamic fixed-point. By doing so, we can obtain a unified fixed-point format by weight normalization. the weight is represented by fixed point. Then, the weight is represented by fixed point. Considering the general case of bitwidth quantization as in [15], we define the weight quantization function is as follows:

$$r_o = f_w^k(r_i) = \frac{1}{2^{BW-1}} round(\frac{tanh(r_i)}{max(|tanh(r_i)|)} \cdot 2^{BW-1}) \tag{4}$$

where BW denotes quantization bitwidth. In addition, our method didn't suffer from such a problem which selecting the fractional lengths adapted to the individual channels.

3.3 Weight Scaling

Considering lower bitwidth, the quantized model has fewer number of weights, and the expression ability of the model is weak. In order to compensate for the deficiency of low bitwidth fixed-point quantization, we decided to add an additional scaling factor to increase the expression ability of the model. Approximating the full-precision floating-point W by this scaling factor α and low bit fixed-point W', we can get that $W \approx \alpha W'$. Then the L2 distance between the full precision weight and the quantized weight is minimized to obtain the optimal scaling factor:

$$\alpha^*, W'^* = argmin_{\alpha, W'} \|W - \alpha W'\|_2^2 \tag{5}$$

Expand the formula:

$$J(\alpha, W') = \sum_{i=0}^{n} (\alpha^2 (W_i')^2 - 2\alpha W_i W_i') + c \tag{6}$$

where c denotes a constant , W and W_i' respectively denotes the ith element of W and W'. Then we derive the upper formula with respect to α, then we command the derivative 0 and the optimal solution of formula, we got is as follows:

$$\alpha^* = \frac{\sum_{i=1}^{n} W_i'^* W_i'}{\sum_{i=1}^{n} (W_i'^*)^2} \tag{7}$$

where $W' = (-1)^s \cdot 2^{BW-2} \sum_{i=0}^{BW-2} 2^i \cdot x_i$. By doing this, we can make the quantized weights approximate the full-precision model better and have better model expression ability at low bitwidth. Therefore, the quantization model is similar to the accuracy of the full precision model.

3.4   Algorithmic Description

We give a training algorithm as Algorithm 1. The network is assumed to have a feed-forward linear topology, and there were omitted like batch normalization and pooling layers. When we are doing forward training, the original weight is copied to W_i^{copy}, and the quantized weight W_i^k is obtained by the above normalized fixed-point quantization. Then we use the quantized weight for forward training. In the backward, the original weight is restored and the unquantized weight W_i^{copy} is used to update the backward gradient. We train the network model from scratch, which can effectively quantize the weight to low bitwidth.

4   Experiment

In order to investigate the performance of these weight quantization methods, we conduct experiments on CIFAR-10 and ImageNet datasets. We use AlexNet variants of the network structure, which removes the LRN layer and adds batch normalization (BN layer) in each convolution layer. This kind of structure has been widely used in previous projects [13]. Dynamic [14] is the Sect. 3.1 method to quantize the weight. It only needs pretrained model, and then quantizes it into low bitwidth. Although this method can save time, it still has a great limitation on the bitwidth. The method in this paper adopts the strategy of training from scratch, and the weight distribution range is limited by normalizing the weight. Next, we compare our method with other different methods under low bitwidth.

Algorithm 1. Training a L-layer Net with k-bit weights. Weights are quantized according to Eqn.5.

Require: A minibatch of inputs and outputs a previous weights W, learning rate lr.

Output: A low bitwidth deep model M_{low}^k with weights being quantized into k bits.

{1. Forward propagation:}

1:for i = 1 to L do

2:    $W_i^{copy} = W_i$

3:    $W_i^k \leftarrow \frac{1}{2^{k-1}} round(\frac{tanh(W_i)}{max(|tanh(W_i)|)} \cdot 2^{k-1})$

4:    $a_i \leftarrow forward(a_{i-1}, W_i^k)$

5:end for

{2. Backward propagation:}

1:for i = L to 1 do

2:    $\triangle \omega \leftarrow backward(a_i, W_i^k)$

3:    $W_i^{t+1} \leftarrow update(W_i^{copy}, \triangle \omega, lr)$

4:end for

4.1   Results on CIFAR-10

CIFAR-10 is a 10-class dataset, which contains 32×32, 50000 training sets and 10000 test sets' images. We use ResNet-44 network structure to do the experiments. The results are shown in Table 1. It can be seen from the table that no matter what quantification method is used, the classification effect in 8-bit is better. As the bit decreases, the dynamic fixed-point quantization method loses its accuracy first. When the bitwidth is smaller, Dynamic [14] can no longer achieve a better trade-off between range and accuracy, which will result in a great loss of accuracy. WNQ (Weight Normailization Quantization) is normalized quantization of weights in Sect. 3.2, and WNQ+ is method of adding scaling factor to the normalized fixed-point type to increase the diversity of weights in Sect. 3.3 WNQ's results are drastically better than Dynamic at each bit.

Table 1. Error rate of full-precision and ResNet-44 on CIFAR-10.

Method	Full-precision	8 bits		4 bits		3 bits		2 bits	
		Error	Improve	Error	Improve	Error	Improve	Error	Improve
Dynamic	7.18%	6.43%	0.75%	7.73%	−0.55%	10.92%	−3.74%	76.17%	−68.99%
WNQ		6.42%	0.76%	6.92%	0.26%	7.70%	−0.52%	18.76%	−11.58%
WNQ+		6.39%	**0.79%**	6.85%	**0.33%**	6.97%	**0.21%**	8.56%	−1.38%

Comparing the results of Table 1, both the proposed WNQ and WNQ+ outperform Dynamic method, which validates the effectiveness of weight normalization quantization. In addition, we also can see that the result of WNQ+ by adding a scaling is significantly higher than WNQ, especially the accuracy of the two bits is increased by 10.2%. Because of the low-precision network limited representation capability, it can hardly achieve good accuracy. Adding a scale factor can improve this problem very well. Moreover, WNQ+ can improve the accuracy by 0.79%, 0.33% and 0.21% under 8-bit, 4-bit, 3-bit respectively with the full precision.

We expand our experiments (WNQ+) to ResNet-20 and VGG16 in Table 2. All models are trained from scratch. Our results show that the accuracy of 4 bits is improved by 0.78% on ResNet-20. Furthermore, that of ResNet-20 and VGG16 is only reduced by 0.04% and 0.78% under 3 bits. Obviously, even with low bits, our method can still maintain a good performance, and it applies to any network structure.

Table 2. Accuracy of low bitwidth model of WNQ+ on CIFAR-10.

Networks	Baseline	8 bits		4 bits		3 bits	
		Acc	Improve	Acc	Improve	Acc	Improve
ResNet-20	91.77%	92.77%	1.00%	92.55%	0.78%	91.73%	−0.04%
VGG16	94.12%	94.20%	0.08%	93.75%	−0.37%	93.34%	−0.78%

4.2 Results on ImageNet

The ILSVRC-12 dataset includes more than 1.2 million images and 50,000 validated images. We use AlexNet network structure to do experiments. In a first step, we use Ristretto [14] to progressively conduct the quantization from higher to low bitwidth. Figure 1 shows the effect of quantizing Alexnet to different bit widths. Fine-tuning was used for this experiment. The classification accuracy of a 8-bit dynamic fixed point network is comparable to the 32-bit FP baseline, but the accuracy drops sharply for lower bit widths. Sometimes it has never recovered even after exhaustive fine-tuning.

In a next step, we compare our method with other different methods under low bitwidth. The results are shown in Table 3. We can see that there is little difference performance in low bit on small data sets, but the number of bit width has a great impact on large data sets. In dynamic fixed-point method, the network accuracy of 4 bit is only 21.804%. Therefore, the low bit model can not be obtained directly from the pre-trained model. We also compare our method with Dorafe. Both of them adopt the strategy of training from scratch, and quantize while training. The performance of WNQ is similar to that of Dorefa, but WNQ+ is much better than that of the two. We can get low bitwidth model under 3 bits. In addition, Dorefa makes the weight quantize into low bit which is non-zero and 32 floating-point. Our method have the existence of zero, so that it can be combined with pruning to further compress the network. By QWN+, the accuracy of 3 bit only drop by 1%, and even that of 2 bit is less than 3%.

We adopt the strategy of training from scratch while quantizing, and get the low bitwidth quantization model of neural network. Figure 2 is the training curve of different quantization methods under 4 bit. We can see that Dorefa [13] and

Table 3. Top-1 validation accuracy of Alexnet on ImageNet.

Method	Baseline	8 bits	4 bits	3 bits	2 bits
Dynamic	57.309%	56.453%	21.804%	N/A	N/A
Dorefa		56.256%	54.874%	51.092%	45.138%
WNQ		55.346%	55.321%	53.024%	45.778%
WNQ+		**56.496%**	**56.786%**	**56.312%**	**53.662%**

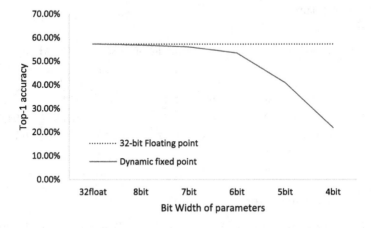

Fig. 1. Approximation of AlexNet with fine-tuning.

the other have similar training trends. Although the trend is the same as that of baseline, the accuracy of Dorefa [13] is always lower than that of baseline in different periods. WNQ+ is obviously better than the other two methods, similar to Baseline, and even better than baseline in the early stage to achieve better convergence. Compared with the full precision, this lower deep neural network model not only has similar effect, but also saves about 8 times the storage space.

Our method not only quantizes the network to 3 bits which keeps the accuracy loss to 1%, but also quantizes the weight to lower bits within a tolerable degradation, such as 2 bits. It proves that our method can be implemented on large datasets. And it also can combine be combined with pruning to further compress the network. This not just greatly reduces the storage space of the deep convolution neural network model, it even can accelerate the computation in embedded devices such as FPGA because of the fixed-point quantization value.

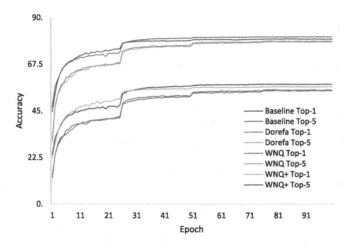

Fig. 2. Prediction accuracy of AlexNet variants on Validation Set of ImageNet indexed by epoch number under 4 bits.

5 Conclusion

In this paper, a method of fixed-point quantization based on weight normalization is proposed. Firstly, the weight is constrained to $[-1, 1]$ by normalizing, and then quantized it to low bitwidth fixed-point. Secondly, adding a scaling factor on the weights can better improve the expression ability of the model. The network can be quantized to 3 bits on the ImageNet dataset, and achieve the best performance and are within 1% of original network. Furthermore, a good accuracy can still be maintained even on 2 bits with the high tolerance for accuracy. It effectively solves the problem that the memory complexity and computation intensive of deep neural network in embedded devices such as FPGA. The model can be compressed more than 8× and accelerate the inference of deep neural networks. However, due to the limitation of fixed-point accuracy range, we will combine clustering coding and other methods to further optimize and further study the neural network model compression in the future work.

Acknowledgment. This work was supported by NNSF of China Grants No. 61574013, 61532005.

References

1. Denil, M., Shakibi, B., Dinh, L., de Freitas, N., et al.: Predicting parameters in deep learning. In: Advances in Neural Information Processing Systems, pp. 2148–2156 (2013)
2. Tai, C., Xiao, T., Zhang, Y., Wang, X., et al.: Convolutional neural networks with low-rank regularization. In: Proceedings of International Conference on Learning, Representations (2016)

3. Han, S., Mao, H., Dally, W.J.: Deep compression: compressing deep neural networks with pruning, trained quantization and huffman coding. arXiv preprint arXiv:1510.00149 (2015)

4. Molchanov, D., Ashukha, A., Vetrov, D.: Variational dropout sparsifies deep neural networks. In: International Conference on Machine Learning, pp. 2498–2507 (2017)

5. Courbariaux, M., Bengio, Y., David, J.P.: Binaryconnect: training deep neural networks with binary weights during propagations. In: Advances in Neural Information Processing Systems, pp. 3123–3131 (2015)

6. Courbariaux, M., Bengio, Y.: Binarynet: training deep neural networks with weights and activations constrained to +1 or −1. CoRR (2016)

7. Rastegari, M., Ordonez, V., Redmon, J., Farhadi, A.: Xnor-net: Imagenet classification using binary convolutional neural networks. arXiv preprint arXiv:1603.05279 (2016)

8. Buciluǎ, C., Caruana, R., Niculescu-Mizil, A.: Model compression. In: Proceedings of the 12th ACM/SIGKDD International Conference on Knowledge Discovery and Data Mining, KDD 2006, pp. 535–541. New York, NY, USA (2006)

9. Sau, B.B., Balasubramanian, V.N.: Deep Model Compression: Distilling Knowledge from Noisy Teachers (2016)

10. Hu, Q., Wang, P., Cheng, J.: From Hashing to CNNs: Training Binary Weight Networks via Hashing (2018)

11. Li, F., Liu, B.: Ternary weight networks. arXiv preprint arXiv:1605.04711 (2016)

12. Zhu, C., Han, S., Mao, H., Dally, W.J.: Trained ternary quantization. In: Proceedings of International Conference on Learning Representations (2017)

13. Zhou, S., Wu, Y., Ni, Z., Zhou, X., Wen, H., Zou, Y.: Dorefa-net: Training low bitwidth convolutional neural networks with low bitwidth gradients. arXiv preprint arXiv:1606.06160 (2016)

14. Gysel, P.: Ristretto: Hardware-Oriented Approximation of Convolutional Neural Networks (2016)

15. Zhuang, B., Shen, C., Tan, M., Liu, L., Reid, I.: Towards Effective Low-bitwidth Convolutional Neural Networks. arXiv preprint arXiv:1711.00205 (2017)

Virtual Adversarial Training on Graph Convolutional Networks in Node Classification

Ke Sun[1], Zhouchen Lin[2], Hantao Guo[1], and Zhanxing Zhu[1,3,4(✉)]

[1] Center for Data Science, Peking University, Beijing, China
{ajksunke,guohantao,zhanxing.zhu}@pku.edu.cn
[2] Key Laboratory of Machine Perception (MOE), School of EECS,
Peking University, Beijing, China
zlin@pku.edu.cn
[3] School of Mathematical Science, Peking University, Beijing, China
[4] Beijing Institute of Big Data Research (BIBDR), Beijing, China

Abstract. The effectiveness of Graph Convolutional Networks (GCNs) has been demonstrated in a wide range of graph-based machine learning tasks. However, the update of parameters in GCNs is only from labeled nodes, lacking the utilization of unlabeled data. In this paper, we apply Virtual Adversarial Training (VAT), an adversarial regularization method based on both labeled and unlabeled data, on the supervised loss of GCN to enhance its generalization performance. By imposing virtually adversarial smoothness on the posterior distribution in semi-supervised learning, VAT yields an improvement on the performance of GCNs. In addition, due to the difference of property in features, we perturb virtual adversarial perturbations on sparse and dense features, resulting in GCN Sparse VAT (GCNSVAT) and GCN Dense VAT (GCNDVAT) algorithms, respectively. Extensive experiments verify the effectiveness of our two methods across different training sizes. Our work paves the way towards better understanding the direction of improvement on GCNs in the future.

Keywords: Graph Convolutional Networks · Virtual Adversarial Training

1 Introduction

Recently, research of analyzing graphs with machine learning has received more and more attention, mainly focusing on node classification [8], link prediction [17] and clustering tasks [5]. Graph convolutions, as the transformation of traditional

---

The first author is a student.

© Springer Nature Switzerland AG 2019
Z. Lin et al. (Eds.): PRCV 2019, LNCS 11857, pp. 431–443, 2019.
https://doi.org/10.1007/978-3-030-31654-9_37

convolutions from Euclidean domain to non-Euclidean domain, have been leveraged to design Graph Neural Networks to deal with a wide range of graph-based machine learning tasks.

Graph Convolutional Networks (GCNs) [8] generalize convolutional neural networks (CNNs) to graph structured data from the perspective of spectral theory based on prior works [1,4]. It has been demonstrated that GCN and its variants [2,3,7,15] significantly outperform traditional multi-layer perceptron (MLP) models and prior graph embedding approaches [6,12,14].

However, there are still many deficits on GCNs, thus in this paper we propose to apply VAT on GCNs to tackle these drawbacks of GCNs. Particularly, we firstly highlight the importance of VAT on GCNs from the following aspects, which construct the motivation of our approaches.

Lacking the Leverage of Unlabeled Data for GCNs. The optimization of GCNs is solely based on the labeled nodes. Concretely speaking, GCNs directly distribute gradient information over the entire labeled set of nodes from the supervised loss. Due to the lack of loss on unlabeled data, the parameters that are not involved in the receptive field may not be updated [2], resulting in the inefficiency of information propagation of GCNs.

Effect of Regularization in Semi-supervised Learning. Regularization plays a crucial role in semi-supervised learning including graph-based learning tasks. On the one hand, by introducing regularization, a model can make full use of unlabeled data, thus enhancing the performance in semi-supervised learning. On the other hand, regularization can also be regarded as prior knowledge that can smooth the posterior output. For GCN model, a good regularization can not only leverage the unlabeled data to refine its optimization, but only benefit the performance of GCNs, resulting in a improved generalization performance.

Virtual Adversarial Regularization on GCNs. Virtual Adversarial Training (VAT) [11] smartly performs adversarial training without label information to impose a local smoothness on the classifier, which is especially beneficial to semi-supervised learning. In particular, VAT endeavors to smooth the model anisotropically in the direction in which the model is the most sensitive, i.e., the adversarial direction, to improve the generalization performance of a model. In addition, the existence of robustness issue in GCNs has been explored in recent works [18,19], allowing VAT on graph-based learning task.

Due to the fact that VAT has been successfully applied on semi-supervised image classification [11,16] and text classification [10], a natural question could be asked: *Can we utilize the efficacy of VAT to improve the performance of GCNs in semi-supervised node classification?*

Following this motivation, in our paper, we formally introduce VAT regularization on the original supervised loss of GCNs in semi-supervised node classification task. Concretely speaking, firstly, a detailed analysis of GCNs focusing on the first-order approximation of local spectral convolutions is provided to demystify how GCNs work in semi-supervised learning. Moreover, based on the motivation described above, we elaborate the process of applying VAT on GCNs in a theoretical way by additionally imposing virtual adversarial loss on the basic loss of GCNs, resulting in GCNVAT algorithm framework. Next, due to the sparse property of node features, in the realization of our method, we actually add virtual adversarial perturbations on sparse and dense features, respectively, and attain the GCNSVAT and GCNDVAT algorithms. Finally, in the experimental part, we demonstrate the effectiveness of the two approaches under different training sizes and refine a theoretical analysis on the sensitivity to the hyper-parameters on VAT, facilitating us to apply our approaches in real applications involving graph-based machine learning tasks. In summary, the contributions of the paper are listed below:

- To the best of our knowledge, we are the first to focus on applying better regularization on original GCN to refine its generalization performance.
- We are the first to successfully transfer the efficacy of Virtual Adversarial Training (VAT) to the semi-supervised node classification on graphs and point out the difference compared with image and text classification setting.
- We refine the sensitivity analysis of hyper-parameters in GCNSVAT and GCNDVAT algorithms, facilitating the deployment of our methods in real scenarios.

2   GCNs with Virtual Adversarial Training

In this section, we will elaborate how GCNs work in semi-supervised learning and how to utilize the virtual adversarial training to smooth the posterior distribution of GCNs.

2.1   Semi-supervised Classification with GCNs

Firstly, we denote a graph by $G = (V, E)$, where V is the vertex set and E is the edge set. X and A are the features and adjacent matrix of the graph, respectively and $D = \mathrm{diag}(d_1, d_2, \cdots, d_n)$ denotes the degree matrix of A, where $d_i = \sum_j a_{ij}$ is the degree of vertex i.

First-Order Approximation. GCNs are based on the graph spectral theory. For efficient computation, [4] approximate the spectral filter g_θ with Chebyshev polynomials up to K^{th} order:

$$g_{\theta'}(\Lambda) = \sum_{k=0}^{K-1} \theta'_k T_k(\Lambda), \tag{1}$$

where Λ is the eigenvalues matrix of normalized graph Laplacian $L = I_N - D^{-\frac{1}{2}} A D^{-\frac{1}{2}}$. T_k is the Chebyshev polynomials and θ'_k is a vector of Chebyshev coefficients. Further, [8] simplified this model by limiting $K = 1$ and then the first-order approximation of spectral graph convolution is defined as:

$$g_\theta \star x = \theta(I_N + D^{-\frac{1}{2}} A D^{-\frac{1}{2}})x, \tag{2}$$

where θ is the only Chebyshev coefficients left. Through the normalization trick, the final form of graph convolutional networks with two layers in GCNs [8] is:

$$Z = f(X, A) = \text{softmax}(\hat{A}\,\text{ReLU}(\hat{A}XW^{(0)})W^{(1)}), \qquad (3)$$

where $\hat{A} = \tilde{D}^{-\frac{1}{2}}\tilde{A}\tilde{D}^{-\frac{1}{2}}, \tilde{A} = A + I$. $\tilde{D}$ is the degree matrix of $\tilde{A}$. Z is the obtained embedding matrix from nodes, $W^{(0)}$ is the input-to-hidden weight matrix and $W^{(1)}$ is the hidden-to-output weight matrix.

Optimization. Finally, the loss function is defined as the cross entropy error over all labeled nodes:

$$\mathcal{L}_0 = -\sum_{l \in \mathcal{Y}_L} \sum_{f=1}^{F} Y_{lf} Z_{lf}, \qquad (4)$$

where $\mathcal{Y}_L$ is the set of node indices that have labels. In fact, the performance of GCNs heavily depends on the efficiency of this Laplacian Smoothing Convolutions, which has been demonstrated in [8,9]. Therefore, how to design a good regularization to smooth the posterior distribution of GCNs plays a crucial role for the improvement of performance for GCNs.

2.2   Virtual Adversarial Training in GCNs

Virtual Adversarial Training (VAT) [11] is a regularization method that trains the output distribution to be isotropically smooth around each input data point by selectively smoothing the model in its most anisotropic direction, namely adversarial direction. In this section, we apply VAT on GCNs to smooth the posterior distribution of GCNs.

Assumptions. Firstly, both VAT and GCNs mainly focus on semi-supervised setting, in which two assumptions should be implicitly met [16]:

– **Manifold Assumption.** The observed data x presented in high dimensional space is with high probability concentrated in the vicinity of some underlying manifold with much lower dimensional space.
– **Smoothness Assumption.** If two points $x_1, x_2 \in \mathcal{M}$ are close in manifold distance, then the conditional probability $p(y|x_1)$ and $p(y|x_2)$ should be similar. In other words, the true classifier, or the true condition distribution $p(y|x)$ varies smoothly along the underlying manifold $\mathcal{M}$.

In the node classification task, GCNs, which involve the graph embedding process, also implicitly conform to these assumptions. There is underlying manifold in the process of graph embedding and the conditional distribution of embedding vectors are expected to vary smoothly along the underlying manifold. In this way, we are capable of utilizing VAT to smooth the embedding of nodes in the adversarial direction to improve the generalization of GCNs.

Difference of VAT on Graph and Image, Text. Traditional VAT [11] is proposed on image classification while VAT on text classification [10] is applied on word embedding vectors of each word. For VAT on graphs, we simply apply VAT on the features of nodes for easy implementation. Additionally, another obvious difference lies in that the relation between each node is not independent for the node classification task compared with image and text classification. The classification result of each node not only depends on the feature itself but also the features of its neighbors, resulting in the *Propagation Effect* of perturbations on feature of each node. We use $\mathcal{D}_l$ and $\mathcal{D}_{ul}$ to denote dataset with labeled nodes and unlabeled nodes respectively. $\overline{x}$ represents features excluding feature x of current node.

Adversarial Training in GCNs. Here we formally define the adversarial training in GCNs, where adversarial perturbations are solely added on features of labeled nodes:

$$\min_{\theta} \max_{r, \|r\| \leq \epsilon} D\left[q(y|x_l, \overline{x}, A), p(y|x_l + r, \overline{x}, A; \theta)\right], \tag{5}$$

where $D[q, p]$ measures the divergence between two distributions q and p. $q(y|x_l, \overline{X}, A)$ is the true distribution of output labels, usually one hot vector $h(y; y_l)$ and $p(y|x_l + r, \overline{x}, A) = f(X, A)$ denotes the predicted distribution by GCNs. x_l represents the feature of current labeled node and r represents the adversarial perturbation on the feature x_l. When the true distribution is denoted by one hot vector $h(y; y_l)$, the perturbation r_{adv} in L_2 norm can be linearly approximated:

$$r_{\mathrm{adv}} \approx \epsilon \frac{g}{\|g\|_2}, \text{ where } g = \nabla_{x_l} D\left[h(y; y_l), p(y|x_l, \overline{x}, A; \theta)\right]. \tag{6}$$

Virtual Adversarial Loss. In order to utilize the unlabeled data, we are expected to evaluate the true conditional probability $q(y|x_l, \overline{x}, A)$. Therefore, we use the current estimate $p(y|x, \overline{x}, A; \hat{\theta})$ in place of $q(y|x, \overline{x}, A)$.

$$\min_{\theta} \max_{r, \|r\| \leq \epsilon} D\left[p(y|x, \overline{x}, A; \hat{\theta}), p(y|x + r, \overline{x}, A; \theta)\right] \tag{7}$$

Then virtual adversarial regularization is constructed from inner max loss:

$$\mathcal{R}_{\mathrm{vadv}}(x, \mathcal{D}_l, \mathcal{D}_{ul}, \theta) = \max_{r, \|r\| \leq \epsilon} D\left[p(y|x, \overline{x}, A; \hat{\theta}), p(y|x + r, \overline{x}, A; \theta)\right] \tag{8}$$

The final regularization term we propose in this study is the average of $\mathcal{R}_{\mathrm{vadv}}(x, \mathcal{D}_l, \mathcal{D}_{ul}, \theta)$ over all input nodes:

$$\mathbb{E}_{x \sim \mathcal{D}} \mathcal{R}_{\mathrm{vadv}} = \frac{1}{N_l + N_{ul}} \sum_{x \in \mathcal{D}_l, \mathcal{D}_{ul}} \mathcal{R}_{\mathrm{vadv}}(x, \mathcal{D}_l, \mathcal{D}_{ul}, \theta) \tag{9}$$

Virtual Adversarial Training. The full objective function is thus given by:

$$\min_{\theta} \mathcal{L}_0 + \alpha \mathbb{E}_{x \sim \mathcal{D}} \mathcal{R}_{\mathrm{vadv}}, \tag{10}$$

where $\mathcal{L}_0$ is constructed from labeled nodes in GCNs, α denotes the regularization coefficient and VAT regularization is crafted from both labeled and unlabeled nodes.

2.3   Fast Approximation of VAT in GCNs

The key of VAT in GCNs is the approximation of r_{vadv} where

$$r_{\text{vadv}} = \underset{r,\|r\|\le\epsilon}{\arg\max}\, D\left[p(y|x,\overline{x},A;\hat{\theta}), p(y|x+r,\overline{x},A;\hat{\theta})\right]. \tag{11}$$

Second-Order Approximation. Just like the situation in traditional VAT, the evaluation of GCNs with VAT cannot be performed with the linear approximation since first-order approximation equals zero [10]. Therefore, a second-order approximation is needed:

$$D(r,x,\overline{x},A;\hat{\theta}) \approx \frac{1}{2}r^T H(x,\overline{x},A;\hat{\theta})r, \tag{12}$$

where $H(x,\overline{x},A;\hat{\theta}) := \nabla_r^2 D(r,x,\overline{x},A;\hat{\theta})|_{r=0}$. Then the evaluation of r_{vadv} can be approximated by:

$$r_{\text{vadv}} \approx \arg\max_r\{r^T H(x,\hat{\theta})r;\ \|r\|_2 \le \epsilon\} = \overline{\epsilon u(x,\overline{x},A;\hat{\theta})}, \tag{13}$$

where $u(x,\overline{x},A;\hat{\theta})$ is the first dominant eigenvector of $H(x,\overline{x},A;\hat{\theta})$ with magnitude 1.

Power Iteration and Finite Difference Approximation. After power interation and finite difference approximation mentioned in [10], the final approximation of r_{vadv} is:

$$r_{\text{vadv}} \approx \epsilon\frac{g}{\|g\|_2}, \text{where } g = \nabla_r D\left[p(y|x,\overline{x},A;\hat{\theta}), p(y|x+r,\overline{x},A;\hat{\theta})\right]\Big|_{r=\xi d}. \tag{14}$$

3   Algorithm

In this section, we will elaborate our Graph Convolutional Networks with Virtual Adversarial Training (GCNVAT) Algorithm. Algorithm 1 summarizes the procedures of the computation of mini-batch SGD for GCNs with VAT algorithm.

Our GCNVAT Algorithm Framework is economical in computation since the derivative of the full objective function can be computed with at most three sets of propagation in total. Specifically speaking, firstly, by initializing the random unit vector $d^{(i)}$ in mini-batch and computing the gradient of divergence between predicted distribution of GCNs and that with the initial perturbation, we can evaluate the fast approximated r_{vadv}, which is involved in the first set of back propagation. Secondly, after the computation of r_{vadv}, we are able to compute the average virtual adversarial loss in the mini-batch and optimize this loss under fixed r_{vadv}, which incorporates the second set of back propagation. Finally, the third back propagation is related to the original supervised loss based on labeled nodes in GCNs. All in all, by this GCNs with VAT algorithm including three sets of back propagation, we are capable of imposing the local adversarial

---

Algorithm 1. Mini-batch SGD for GCNVAT Framework

Input: Features Matrix X, Adjacent Matrix A. Graph Convolution Network f_θ
Output: Graph Embedding $Z = f_\theta(X, A)$

1: Choose M samples of $x^{(i)}(i = 1, \ldots, M)$ from dataset $\mathcal{D}$ at random.
2: Compute the predicted distribution of current GCNs:

$$p(y|x_l, \overline{x}, A; \hat{\theta}) \leftarrow f_{\hat{\theta}}(X, A)$$

3: % **Step 1: Fast Approximation of** r_{vadv}
4: Generate a random unit vector $d^{(i)} \in R^I$ using an iid Gaussian distribution.
5: Calculate r_{vadv} via taking the gradient of D with respect to r on $r = \xi d^{(i)}$ on each input data point $x^{(i)}$:

$$g^{(i)} \leftarrow \nabla_r D \left[p(y|x^{(i)}, \overline{x}, A; \hat{\theta}), p(y|x^{(i)} + r, \overline{x}, A; \hat{\theta}) \right] \Big|_{r = \xi d^{(i)}}$$

6: Evaluation of r_{vadv}:

$$r_{\text{vadv}}^{(i)} \leftarrow \epsilon g^{(i)} / \|g^{(i)}\|_2$$

7: % **Step 2: Evaluation of Virtual Adversarial Loss**

$$\mathbb{E}_{x \sim \mathcal{D}} \mathcal{R}_{\text{vadv}} = \nabla_\theta \left(\frac{1}{M} \sum_{i=1}^{M} D \left[p(y|x^{(i)}; \hat{\theta}), p(y|x^{(i)} + r_{\text{vadv}}^{(i)}; \theta) \right] \right) \Big|_{\theta = \hat{\theta}}$$

8: % **Step 3: Virtual Adversarial Training**
9: Compute the supervised loss $\mathcal{L}_0$ of GCNs:

$$\mathcal{L}_0 = - \sum_{l \in \mathcal{Y}_L} \sum_{f=1}^{F} Y_{lf} Z_{lf}$$

10: Update θ by optimizing the full objective function $\mathcal{L}$:

$$\mathcal{L} = \mathcal{L}_0 + \alpha \mathbb{E}_{x \sim \mathcal{D}} \mathcal{R}_{\text{vadv}}$$

---

regularization on the original supervised loss of GCNs through smoothing the posterior distribution of the model in the most adversarial direction, thereby improving the generalization of original GCNs.

GCNSVAT and GCNDVAT. In the real scenarios, there are usually sparse features for each node especially for a large graph, which are involved in the computation of sparse tensor. In this case, in the implementation of our GCNVAT algorithm framework, we customize two similar GCNVAT methods for different properties of node features. For GCN Sparse VAT (GCNSVAT), we only apply virtual adversarial perturbations on the specific sparse elements in feature of each node, which may save much computation time especially for high-dimensional feature vectors. For GCN Dense VAT (GCNDVAT), we actually perturb each element in feature by transforming the sparse feature matrix to a dense one.

4   Experiments

In the experimental part, we conduct extensive experiments to demonstrate the effectiveness of our GCNSVAT and GCNDVAT algorithms. Firstly, we test the performance of both algorithms under different label rates compared with the original GCN. Then we make another comparison under the standard semi-supervised setting with other state-of-the-art approaches. Finally, a sensitivity analysis of hyper-parameters is provided for broad deployment of our method in real applications.

Experimental Setup. For the graph dataset, we select the three commonly used citation networks: CiteSeer, Cora and PubMed [13]. Dataset statistics are summarized in Table 1. For all methods involved in GCNs, we use the same hyper-parameters as in [8]: learning rate of 0.01, 0.5 dropout rate, 2 convolutional layers, and 16 hidden units without validation set for fair comparison. As for the hyper-parameters, we fix regularization coefficient $\alpha = 1.0$ and only change the perturbation magnitude ϵ to control the regularization effect under different training sizes, which is further discussed later in the sensitivity analysis part. All the results are the mean accuracy of 10 runs to avoid stochastic effect.

Table 1. Dataset statistics

Dataset	Nodes	Edges	Classes	Features	Label rate
CiteSeer	3327	4732	6	3703	3.6%
Cora	2708	5429	7	1433	5.2%
PubMed	19717	44338	3	500	0.3%

4.1   Effect Under Different Training Sizes

To verify the consistent effectiveness of our two methods on the improvement of generalization performance, we compare GCNSVAT and GCNDVAT algorithms with original GCN method [8] under different training sizes across the three datasets and the results can be observed in Fig. 1.

As illustrated in Fig. 1, GCNSVAT (the red line) and GCNDVAT (the blue line) outperform original GCN (the black line) consistently under all tested label rates. Actually, it is important to note that with the increasing of label rates, the regularization effect imposed by VAT on GCNs diminishes in both approaches since the improvement from regularization based on unlabeled data is decreasing. In other words, the superior performance of GCN with Virtual Adversarial Training are especially significant when there are few training sizes. Fortunately, in real scenarios, it is common to observe graphs with a small number of labeled nodes, thereby our algorithms are especially practical in these applications.

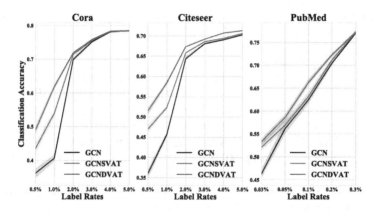

Fig. 1. Classification accuracies of GCNSVAT and GCNDVAT algorithms compared with GCN across three datasets. (Color figure online)

Choice of GCNSVAT and GCNDVAT. GCNDVAT performs consistently better in comparison with GCNSVAT even though GCNDVAT requires extra computation cost related to perturbations in the entire feature space. As for the reason, we argue that continuous perturbations in features facilitate the effect of VAT than discrete perturbations in sparse features. However, in the scenarios where the graph are large-scaled and their features are sparse, it is more appropriate to utilize GCNSVAT from the perspective of economical computation.

Table 2. Classification accuracies on Cora with different label rates. Numbers in bracket are the standard deviation of accuracies.

	Rates	0.5%	1%	2%	3%	4%	5%
Cora	GCN	36.2	40.6	69.0	75.2	78.2	78.4
		(0.11)	(0.08)	(0.05)	(0.03)	(0.1)	(0.01)
	GCN SVAT	43.6	53.9	71.4	75.6	78.3	78.5
		(0.10)	(0.08)	(0.05)	(0.02)	(0.01)	(0.01)
	GCN DVAT	**49.0**	**61.8**	**71.9**	**75.9**	**78.4**	**78.6**
		(0.10)	**(0.06)**	**(0.03)**	**(0.02)**	**(0.01)**	**(0.01)**

More specifically, we list the detailed performances of GCNSVAT and GCND-VAT compared with original GCN under different label rates, which are exhibited in Tables 2, 3 and 4, respectively. We report the mean accuracy of 10 runs. The results in tables provide a more sufficient evidence for the effectiveness of our two methods.

4.2 Effect on Standard Semi-supervised Learning

Apart from the experiments under different training sizes, we also test the performance of GCNSVAT and GCNDVAT algorithms in standard semi-supervised

Table 3. Classification accuracies on CiteSeer with different label rates. Numbers in bracket are the standard deviation of accuracies.

	Rates	0.5%	1%	2%	3%	4%	5%
CiteSeer	GCN	36.1 (0.09)	45.7 (0.04)	64.3 (0.04)	68.1 (0.02)	69.1 (0.01)	70.3 (0.01)
	GCN SVAT	47.0 (0.08)	52.4 (0.02)	65.8 (0.02)	68.6 (0.01)	69.5 (0.01)	70.7 (0.01)
	GCN DVAT	**51.5 (0.07)**	**58.5 (0.03)**	**67.4 (0.01)**	**69.2 (0.01)**	**70.8 (0.01)**	**71.3 (0.01)**

Table 4. Classification accuracies on PubMed with different label rates. Numbers in bracket are the standard deviation of accuracies.

	Rates	0.03%	0.05%	0.1%	0.2%	0.3%
PubMed	GCN	46.3 (0.08)	56.1 (0.10)	63.3 (0.06)	70.4 (0.04)	77.1 (0.02)
	GCN SVAT	52.1 ·(0.06)	56.9 (0.08)	63.5 (0.07)	71.2 (0.04)	77.2 (0.02)
	GCN DVAT	**53.3 (0.06)**	**58.6 (0.06)**	**66.3 (0.05)**	**72.2 (0.03)**	**77.3 (0.02)**

setting with standard label rates listed in Table 1. Particularly, we compare our methods with other state-of-the-art methods on the node classification task under standard label rate and the results of baselines are referred from [8].

From Table 5, it turns out that our GCNDVAT algorithm exhibits the state-of-the-art performance though the improvement are not apparent compared with that in few training sizes, while our GCNSVAT algorithm also shares a similar performance. Through the extensive experiments in semi-supervised learning, we demonstrate thoroughly that VAT suffices to improve the generalization performance of GCNs by additionally providing an adversarial regularization both in semi-supervised setting with few labeled nodes and standard semi-supervised setting.

Table 5. Accuracy under 20 labels per class across three datasets.

Method	CiteSeer	Cora	PubMed
ManiReg	60.1	59.5	70.7
SemiEmb	59.6	59.0	71.7
LP	45.3	68.0	63.0
DeepWalk	43.2	67.2	65.3
Planetoid	64.7	75.7	77.2
GCN	68.4	78.4	77.3
GCNSVAT	68.7	78.5	77.5
GCNDVAT	**69.3**	**78.6**	**77.6**

4.3   Sensitivity Analysis of Hyper-parameters

One of the notable advantage of VAT in GCNs is that there are just two scalar-valued hyper-parameters: (1) the perturbation magnitude ϵ that constraints the norm of adversarial perturbation and (2) the regularization coefficient α that controls the balance between supervised loss $\mathcal{L}_0$ and virtual adversarial loss $\mathbb{E}_{x \sim \mathcal{D}} \mathcal{R}_{\text{vadv}}$. We refine the analysis in original VAT [11] and theoretically demonstrate the total loss is more sensitive to ϵ rather than α in the regularization control of GCNs with VAT setting.

Consider the second approximation of virtual adversarial regularization:

$$
\begin{aligned}
\mathcal{R}_{\text{vadv}}(x, \mathcal{D}_l, \mathcal{D}_{ul}, \theta) &= \max_r \{ D(r, x, \overline{x}, A; \theta); \|r\|_2 \le \epsilon \} \\
&\approx \frac{1}{2} \epsilon^2 \lambda_1(x, \overline{x}, A; \theta),
\end{aligned}
\tag{15}
$$

where $\lambda_1(x, \overline{x}, A; \theta)$ is the dominant eigenvalue of Hessian matrix $H(x, \overline{x}, A; \theta)$ of D. Substituting this into the objective function, we obtain

$$
\begin{aligned}
\mathcal{L}_0 + \alpha \mathbb{E}_{x \sim \mathcal{D}} \mathcal{R}_{\text{vadv}} &= \mathcal{L}_0 + \alpha \frac{1}{N_l + N_{ul}} \sum_{x_* \in \mathcal{D}_l, \mathcal{D}_{ul}} \mathcal{R}_{\text{vadv}}(x, \mathcal{D}_l, \mathcal{D}_{ul}, \theta) \\
&\approx \mathcal{L}_0 + \frac{1}{2} \alpha \epsilon^2 \frac{1}{N_l + N_{ul}} \sum_{x_* \in \mathcal{D}_l, \mathcal{D}_{ul}} \lambda_1(x_*, \overline{x}, A; \theta).
\end{aligned}
\tag{16}
$$

Thus, the strength of regularization is approximately proportional to α and ϵ^2. In consideration of the regularization term is more sensitive to the change of ϵ, in our experiments we just tune the perturbation ϵ to control the regularization by fixing $\alpha = 1$ for both methods.

Further, we present the tendency between the selected optimal ϵ and label rates. As for the different label rates, it is natural to expect that GCNs with VAT under lower label rate requires larger VAT regularization, yielding the urge for larger optimal ϵ. We empirically verify this conclusion in Fig. 2.

From Fig. 2, it is easy to observe that with the increasing of label rates, there is a descending trend of optimal ϵ for both GCNSVAT and GCNDVAT across three datasets. It meets our expectation since large VAT regularization are more expected for GCNs under lower label rates to obtain the optimal generalization of GCNs. In addition, the optimal ϵ parameter in GCNSVAT under the same label rate tends to be higher than that in GCNDVAT, especially when the label rate is lower. The reason is obvious because GCNSVAT only applies perturbations on specific elements of sparse feature for each node, thus requiring larger perturbations on those features to get similar regularization effect compared with GCNDVAT.

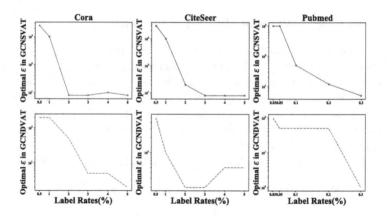

Fig. 2. Sensitivity analysis of epsilon ϵ on two methods.

5   Discussions and Conclusion

GCNs with Virtual Adversarial Training is established on the adversarial training on GCNs, which in our paper is simply constrained in the adversarial perturbations on the features of nodes. However, there may exists a better form of adversarial training in GCNs by additionally considering the change of sensitive edges with respects to the output performance. Therefore, incorporating a better form of Virtual Adversarial Training into graphs allows better improvement of generalization of GCNs. Besides, how to combine VAT with other form Graph Neural Networks especially in inductive setting, is also worthwhile to explore in the future.

In our paper, we impose VAT regularization on the original supervised loss of GCN to enhance its generalization in semi-supervised learning, resulting in GCNSVAT and GCNDVAT, whose perturbations are added in sparse and dense features, respectively. Particularly, we apply VAT on GCNs in a theoretical way by additionally imposing virtual adversarial loss on the basic supervised loss of GCNs. Then we empirically demonstrate the improvement caused by the VAT regularization under different training sizes across three datasets. Our endeavour validates that smoothing anisotropic direction on the posterior distribution of GCNs suffices to improve the performance of original GCN model.

References

1. Bruna, J., Zaremba, W., Szlam, A., LeCun, Y.: Spectral networks and locally connected networks on graphs. arXiv preprint arXiv:1312.6203 (2013)
2. Chen, J., Zhu, J.: Stochastic training of graph convolutional networks. arXiv preprint arXiv:1710.10568 (2017)
3. Dai, H., Kozareva, Z., Dai, B., Smola, A., Song, L.: Learning steady-states of iterative algorithms over graphs. In: International Conference on Machine Learning, pp. 1114–1122 (2018)

4. Defferrard, M., Bresson, X., Vandergheynst, P.: Convolutional neural networks on graphs with fast localized spectral filtering. In: Advances in Neural Information Processing Systems, pp. 3844–3852 (2016)
5. Fortunato, S.: Community detection in graphs. Phys. Rep. **486**(3–5), 75–174 (2010)
6. Grover, A., Leskovec, J.: node2vec: Scalable feature learning for networks. In: Proceedings of the 22nd ACM SIGKDD International Conference on Knowledge Discovery and Data Mining, pp. 855–864. ACM (2016)
7. Hamilton, W., Ying, Z., Leskovec, J.: Inductive representation learning on large graphs. In: Advances in Neural Information Processing Systems, pp. 1024–1034 (2017)
8. Kipf, T.N., Welling, M.: Semi-supervised classification with graph convolutional networks. arXiv preprint arXiv:1609.02907 (2016)
9. Li, Q., Han, Z., Wu, X.M.: Deeper insights into graph convolutional networks for semi-supervised learning. arXiv preprint arXiv:1801.07606 (2018)
10. Miyato, T., Dai, A.M., Goodfellow, I.: Adversarial training methods for semi-supervised text classification. arXiv preprint arXiv:1605.07725 (2016)
11. Miyato, T., Maeda, S.I., Ishii, S., Koyama, M.: Virtual adversarial training: a regularization method for supervised and semi-supervised learning. IEEE Trans. Pattern Anal. Mach. Intell. **41**(8), 1979–1993 (2018)
12. Perozzi, B., Al-Rfou, R., Skiena, S.: Deepwalk: online learning of social representations. In: Proceedings of the 20th ACM SIGKDD International Conference on Knowledge Discovery and Data Mining, pp. 701–710. ACM (2014)
13. Sen, P., Namata, G., Bilgic, M., Getoor, L., Galligher, B., Eliassi-Rad, T.: Collective classification in network data. AI Mag. **29**(3), 93 (2008)
14. Tang, J., Qu, M., Wang, M., Zhang, M., Yan, J., Mei, Q.: Line: large-scale information network embedding. In: Proceedings of the 24th International Conference on World Wide Web, pp. 1067–1077. International World Wide Web Conferences Steering Committee (2015)
15. Velickovic, P., Cucurull, G., Casanova, A., Romero, A., Lio, P., Bengio, Y.: Graph attention networks. arXiv preprint arXiv:1710.10903 1(2) (2017)
16. Yu, B., Wu, J., Zhu, Z.: Tangent-normal adversarial regularization for semi-supervised learning. arXiv preprint arXiv:1808.06088 (2018)
17. Zhu, J., Song, J., Chen, B.: Max-margin nonparametric latent feature models for link prediction. arXiv preprint arXiv:1602.07428 (2016)
18. Zügner, D., Akbarnejad, A., Günnemann, S.: Adversarial attacks on neural networks for graph data. In: Proceedings of the 24th ACM SIGKDD International Conference on Knowledge Discovery & Data Mining, pp. 2847–2856. ACM (2018)
19. Zügner, D., Günnemann, S.: Adversarial attacks on graph neural networks via meta learning (2018)

Brain Functional Connectivity Augmentation Method for Mental Disease Classification with Generative Adversarial Network

Qi Yao and Hu Lu[✉️] (iD)

School of Computer Science and Communication Engineering, Jiangsu University,
Zhenjiang 212200, China
luhu@ujs.edu.cn

Abstract. Functional magnetic resonance imaging (fMRI) plays a significant role in the study and analysis of brain cognitive function. In the existing fMRI classification research, because of the small number of trainable samples, it is easily over-fitted in the classification task. In this paper, we propose an improved deep learning generative adversarial network (GAN) to augment fMRI functional connectivity data. The network has the data augmentation ability using Wasserstein distance and double-class distance constraint to augment the data of subjects and control groups. Finally, the data generated by the GAN are used to improve the ability of the classifier. We investigated two brain disorders, attention deficit hyperactivity disorder (ADHD) and autism spectrum disorder (ASD), and evaluated the classification performance of the model in these two diseases. The results revealed that compared to existing classifiers, classification accuracy was greatly improved after data augmentation by the GAN. In addition, compared to several common deep network data generation methods, the performance of the proposed network is significantly better.

Keywords: Generative adversarial network · fMRI · Functional connectivity · Classification · Brain disorders

1 Introduction

The exact identification of neurological and psychiatric disorders is essential in the treatment and diagnosis of patients with brain disorders. With the development of brain imaging technology, such as functional magnetic resonance imaging (fMRI) and positron emission tomography (PET) (Sejnowski et al. 2014), many researchers have attempted to find specific biomarkers of neurological and psychiatric diseases by machine learning (Group et al. 2001). Resting fMRI (rs-fMRI) has attracted much attention. In the process of scanning, it does not require patients to accept stimuli or perform tasks, which eliminates the influence of some potential factors (Biswal et al. 1995).

© Springer Nature Switzerland AG 2019
Z. Lin et al. (Eds.): PRCV 2019, LNCS 11857, pp. 444–455, 2019.
https://doi.org/10.1007/978-3-030-31654-9_38

In recent few years, with the development of machine learning technology, an increasing number of researchers have begun to apply machine learning algorithms in the recognition and classification of neural and mental data. These methods have achieved remarkable results in their respective tasks (Heinsfeld et al. 2018). Although the size of neuroimaging data-sets is increasing, each data-set contains only a small number of high-dimensional samples compared with other machine learning tasks. Therefore, many of the existing machine learning methods used in neuroimaging classification inevitably encounter the problem of overfitting, whereby the classification effect is limited and difficult to generalize to unknown samples. The existing machine learning methods for neuroimaging data classification usually consist of unsupervised feature extraction and supervised classification (Suk et al. 2016; Vergun et al. 2016; Abraham et al. 2017; Biswal et al. 1995; Heinsfeld et al. 2018). These methods first use unsupervised dimensionality reduction methods (such as auto encoder (Heinsfeld et al. 2018), principal component analysis (Li et al. 2015)) to extract features, and transform high-dimensional data into low-dimensional patterns. Then supervised classifiers (such as support vector machine (Salvatore et al. 2015), neural network classifier (Heinsfeld et al. 2018)) are used to classify based on the extracted features. Although unsupervised training model is considered to reduce the risk of over-fitting, unsupervised feature extraction inevitably extracts some information unrelated to classification, ignoring the useful information for classification (Lin et al. 2016).

Recently, the rapid development of deep learning has provided new ideas in the field of medical imaging (Ge 2017; Wang et al. 2017). In order to solve the problem that the amount of data in neuroimaging is small and the problem that machine learning methods are easily over-fitted, we propose to augment the data using the Generative Adversarial Network (GAN) (Goodfellow et al. 2014). The GAN is an effective generation model, which has been widely used in the field of computer vision. In the field of medical imaging, the application of the GAN framework has achieved good results (Costa et al. 2017; Nie et al. 2017; Schlegl et al. 2017). In this paper, we study the functional connectivity network from fMRI data, and use the GAN to augment the data in order to improve classification accuracy. We propose an improved generating model based on the Wasserstein Generative Adversarial Network (WGAN) to augment brain functional connectivity.

In summary, our contributions are threefold:

1. A new loss function is proposed and a new model structure for generating adversarial network is proposed based on WGAN.
2. Functional connection data of fMRI images are generated and expanded by generating adversarial network. The generated data is used as training set to enhance the classification performance, and the performance evaluation is carried out on two common data sets.
3. We compare the experimental results on two functional connectivity datasets of brain disorders. We also demonstrate the performance of our approach compared to others classifiers and deep Learning Generators.

To the best of our knowledge, this study is the first to use the Generative Adversarial Network to generate fMRI functional connectivity data.

2   Related Work

2.1   Current Status of fMRI Classification

In recent years, an increasing number of researchers analyze fMRI data and classify neurological and psychiatric diseases using machine learning. Song et al. (2019) used community pattern features derived from resting-state fMRI and linear discriminant analysis (LDA) to classify persons with autism and normal individuals with relatively high accuracy. Koyamada et al. (2015) first used a deep neural network to investigate brain state from measurable brain activity. They trained a DNN consisted of two hidden layers and a softmax output layer, and divided the fMRI data from 499 subjects into seven categories. Compared to the previous supervised machine learning methods (such as linear regression and support vector machine), the deep learning model can get better results. In their experiments, the average accuracy was increased by about 3%. Santos et al. (2017) used deep belief networks and deep neural networks to classify cocaine addicts. Plis et al. (2014) classified psychiatric patients from four different locations using deep learning and T1-weighted structural magnetic resonance images. They trained a three-tier deep belief network, with 50 hidden units on the first and second tiers and 100 hidden units on the top tier. Compared to the 68% accuracy obtained from the original data using SVM, the 90% classification accuracy of the features extracted from the deep network is achieved, which indicates that deep learning has great potential in clinical brain imaging applications. Using unsupervised learning, Heinsfeld et al. (2018) applied auto encoder and deep learning in the classification of brain imaging data for autism, and obtained good classification results on multi-site Autism Brain Imaging Data Exchange datasets. They extracted features from brain functional connections using denoising auto encoder by unsupervised training, and then use deep learning for classification. Their classification accuracy of autism reached 70%, which exceeds the current highest level.

However, these methods inevitably encounter the problems of small amounts of data and easy over-fitting. In this paper, we use the GAN to augment the brain functional connection data, so as to improve the robustness of the classification network and classification accuracy.

2.2   Generative Adversarial Network for Medical Applications

Mahapatra et al. (2017) proposed an image super-resolution method using a GAN to input low-resolution fundus images to generate high-resolution super-resolution images. Zhang et al. (2017) used GAN for semi-supervise cardiac segmentation, and added unmarked medical image data to the training. Nie et al. (2017) estimated computed tomography (CT) images through magnetic resonance images using a GAN, which is of great importance for reducing the damage to the patient's body during CT scanning. Baumgartner et al. (2018) attempted to find the differences between mild cognitive impairment (MCI) and Alzheimer's (AD) on 3D MR images using WGAN, which is of great importance to the study of these two diseases.

2.3 Wasserstein Generative Adversarial Network

In the original GAN structure, generator G and discriminator D always compete with each other in a zero-sum game during the training process. The generator transforms the random noise into fake data approximating real data. The discriminator tries to learn the difference between the real and fake data and distinguish them. In the initial GAN, G and D are trained by Solving Minimax problems:

$$\min_G \max_D L_{GAN}(D, G) = \mathbb{E}_x[\log D(x)] + \mathbb{E}_z[\log(1 - D(G(z)))] \qquad (1)$$

The x is the distribution of real data and the z is the distribution of noise vector. Generator G maps the noise vector z to the simulated real sample, which is represented by $\overline{x}$. When D training is too good, the optimization of G will be equivalent to minimizing the Jensen Shannon (JS) divergence of $\overline{x}$ and x, which will cause the gradient on G to disappear and G will not be updated (Gulrajani et al. 2017).

Arjovsky and Bottou (2017) suggested the Wasserstein distance as a measure between generated data and real data and converted the classification task of the discriminator into a regression task. Since then, an improved WGAN gradient penalty scheme has been proposed to accelerate the convergence rate of the network. It obtains D and G by solving the following minimax problems:

$$\min_G \max_D L_{WGAN}(D, G) = -\mathbb{E}_x[D(x)] + \mathbb{E}_x[D(G(z))] + \lambda\mathbb{E}_{\hat{x}}[(\|\nabla\hat{x}D(\hat{x})\|_2 - 1)^2] \qquad (2)$$

The first two items are the estimates of Wasserstein distance, the last one is the penalty of the gradient, and λ is the weighted coefficient of the gradient penalty. During the training process, the other parameters are trained by fixing one of D and G.

3 Methods

Our goal is to design a mapping process G, which converts random noise Z into brain functional connectivity feature X:

$$G : Z \rightarrow X \qquad (3)$$

We divided the data into $Pd(x|c = 0)$ and $Pd(x|c = 1)$ for two categories of $c \in 0, 1$, in which $c = 1$ refers to the data of the experimental group with a certain brain disease and $c = 0$ refers to the data of the control group. The method proposed in this paper is divided into the following steps. In the first step, we train the generating model, and generate the experimental group and the control group separately. In the second step, the training set is augmented by the generated data, and then the augmented data is used to train the deep neural network as a classifier. We propose a WGAN-based generation adversarial model called WGAN-Classification (WGAN-C). The network structure is shown in Fig. 1. We will elaborate on the details of this process in the next part of this section.

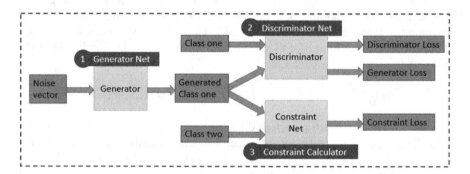

Fig. 1. The whole network consists of three parts: the generator maps the input noise vector to the pseudo-real brain function connection data, and the discriminator and constraint calculator get the final training loss through the pseudo-real data and the real data of two categories.

3.1   Preliminary Data Augmentation

GAN requires a lot of data for training. Adding noise to the input data can regularize the network weight (Bishop 1995). Random noise of range $(-\alpha, \alpha)$ is used to add noise to the disease data. According to our experiment, when α is 0.05, the classification result will not be affected. Because the tanh activation function is used in the output layer of the generator, we normalize the data by adding noise in the range of $(-1, 1)$. Finally, much more data than the original data set is obtained as training data for the network.

3.2   Loss Function

Although the conditional generation network can generate the experimental group and the control group at the same time, the generation quality cannot be guaranteed. In order to improve the quality of the generated data, we choose to generate a single category of brain functional connectivity features each time. One category of brain disease is used by a normal WGAN for generating the data of a single category. However, it only uses the data of a single category to train, and the amount of data is too small. To this end, we add a constraint function, so that another category of data can also play a role in training. We trained a DNN as a constraint calculator in advance and added it to the WGAN. During the training of the WGAN, the weight of the constraint calculator was frozen. The network structure of the constraint calculator is the same as that of the WGAN discriminator. The loss function of the constraint calculator is defined as:

$$L_{constraint}(z, x') = M[G(z)] - M(x') + \lambda_1[\|M(G(z))\|_2^2 + \|M(x')\|_2^2] \quad (4)$$

Where M represents the mapping output of the constraint calculator and x' represents the data distribution of the second category. The first two items represent the Wasserstein distance between the generated data distribution and the data distribution of the second category. Through this value, the difference between the generated data distribution and the data distribution of the second category can be expressed, which is called the distance between classes. The latter two terms represent the intra-class distance between the generated data distribution and the data distribution of the second category. λ_1 is a weighted parameter used to balance the two distances. In order to obtain the convergence of the constrained calculator, we limit the parameter range to $[-0.1, 0.1]$ when training the constrained calculator. By adding the distance constraint function of the two categories distributions, the generated network can more easily to generate high-quality data that can improve the classification effect. Combining $L_{constraint}$ and the loss of WGAN, we get the final loss function:

$$L = \min_G \max_D L_{WGAN}(D, G) + \lambda_2[L_{constraint}(G, x')] \quad (5)$$

Where λ_2 is a weighted parameter used to control the balance between the two losses. The recommended coefficients are $\lambda_1 = 10$ and $\lambda_2 = 0.01$.

3.3 Generating Network Structure

The proposed generation network structure is shown in Fig. 1. For convenience, we named the network WGAN-C. Given that the dimension of the brain functional connection data we use are about 1000 dimensions, we designed these three parts in the form of Fig. 2. In Fig. 2(a), in the generator section, we input noise vectors with uniform distributions of 100 dimensions and output vectors with the same dimensions as the disease data. The generator structure is composed of fully-connected multi-layer perceptrons, batch normalization is added between layers, the *leaky_relu* activation function is used in addition to the last layer, and the *tanh* activation function is used in the last layer. The network has two hidden layers, the size of which are set to 500-1000.

In Fig. 2(b), the discriminator and the constraint parts of the network use the same structure. We also set the network structure as a fully-connected multi-layer perceptron, deleting batch normalization between layers, using the *relu* activation function in addition to the last layer, and no activation function in the last layer. The network has two hidden layers, the size of which are set to 1000–500.

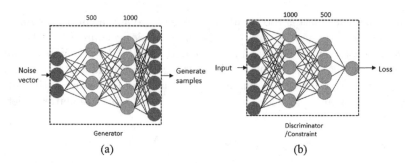

Fig. 2. Generator and discriminator/constraint structures. (a) Generator network structure, (b) Discriminator and constraint network structure.

3.4 Training

In order to optimize our network, we follow Gulrajani et al. (2017) and update the generator and discriminator of the network in an alternate manner. Unlike the conventional GAN, the WGAN needs to keep the discriminator close to optimal throughout the training process. Therefore, every time we update the generator, we update the discriminator five times. In addition, for the first 25 iterations and every 100th iteration, we update the generator once and the discriminator 100 times.

Using the above architecture, the batch training size is set to 60 on the Nvidia GTX 980ti GPU with 6 GB of memory. We used the ADAM optimizer to perform all of the steps in the experiment. The optimizer parameters were set to $\beta 1 = 0.5$, $\beta 2 = 0.9$, the learning rate of the generator and discriminator was set to 10^{-5}, and the learning rate of the classifier is set to 10^{-3}. In all experiments and evaluations, we used 5-folds cross-validation, and each fold used a different training set and test set. The whole process took about 20 h.

4 Experiments and Results

4.1 Data Set

The data used in this paper are from the public database provided by Zhao et al. (2019) including attention deficit hyperactivity disorder (ADHD), autism spectrum disorder (ASD) and other disease data. These data included disease subjects and matched healthy controls. We chose ADHD and ASD data as our experimental data due to the large amount of data on these two diseases. Data acquisition: https://github.com/xinyuzhao/identification-of-brain-based-disorders.git.

The specifications of the data-set are shown in Table 1. "Samples" is the number of disease samples and "Features" is the dimension of functional connection after preprocessing by data providers.

Table 1. fMRI dataset specification

Data	ADHD	ASD
Samples	487	454
Features	672	1722

4.2 Generation Experiment of Brain Functional Connection Data

WGAN-C was trained with preliminary augmented data by adding noise and the training data was expanded from 400 original samples to 20000 samples. The experiment used 5-fold cross-validation. The training set in each fold was strictly separated from the test set. In order to observe the generated data, a DNN classifier was used to classify the generated data in the training process. At this time, the training data of the classifier is a mixture of the generated data in the training process and another class of real samples. We recorded the changes in the accuracy of the WGAN-C generated data during the training process. Figure 3 is an augmentation of data-sets in one fold and a test of the classification effect using the augmented data-set.

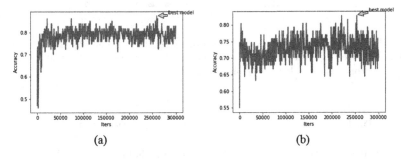

(a)   (b)

Fig. 3. Accuracy varies with using augmented datasets. (a) and (b) are the changes of classification accuracy when the experimental group and the control group were generated separately.

From the comparison of Fig. 3(a) and (b), we can see that the classification accuracy is higher when generating the experimental group separately compared to when generating the control group separately. We consider that the experimental group is closely related to the characteristics of the disease, and the generation of a diversified control group is a difficult task for the models.

4.3 Evaluation of Augmentation Effect of Generating Brain Functional Connection Data

We used the classification accuracy of the data augmented only by adding noise as our baseline, and compared this with the accuracy of the data augmented by our method. We call DNN-AUG the method of preliminary augmentation, and DNN-GAN the method of WGAN-C augmentation. We gradually added the training set and trained the DNN classifier before comparing the accuracy changes of the two augmented methods. The results are shown in Fig. 4.

As can be seen from Fig. 4, for our baseline blue line, the accuracy is saturated at 86% using only preliminary noise augmentation. The red line indicates that when using synthetic data to augment training data, the classification accuracy is improved to 90% and saturated. We recorded the optimal point under each fold and the results are displayed in Table 2.

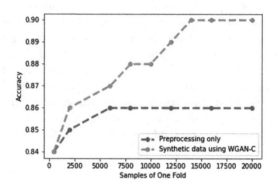

Fig. 4. Classification accuracy as the training set increases. The blue lines represents the effect of noise augmentation data, and the red lines represents the effect of WGAN-C augmentation data. (Color figure online)

Table 2. Classification accuracy of cross-validation with 5 folds

Data	Method	Fold-1	Fold-2	Fold-3	Fold-4	Fold-5	Ave
ADHD	DNN-AUG	0.862	0.92	0.88	0.84	0.86	0.872
	DNN-GAN	0.908	0.96	0.88	0.86	0.90	0.902
ASD	DNN-AUG	0.926	0.88	0.79	0.84	0.83	0.853
	DNN-GAN	0.963	0.92	0.82	0.84	0.85	0.879

As can be seen from Table 2, accuracies of 90.2% and 87.9% for the ADHD and ASD datasets, respectively, were obtained using our proposed WGAN-C augmentation method, while accuracies of 87.2% and 85.3% for the ADHD and ASD datasets, respectively, were obtained using only the random noise augmentation method. The result is about a 3% increase. The results show that the generated adversarial network provides a obvious improvement on the classification of brain functional connection data.

4.4   Performance Comparison of Different Classifiers

In order to evaluate the results obtained by our method, we compared the performance of the model with support vector machine (SVM), random forest (RF), and other classifiers using only the original data-set. All models were evaluated based on five-fold cross-validation. Table 3 displays a comparison of the classification results.

Table 3. Comparison of algorithms on ADHD and ASD datasets

Data/Method	ADHD	ASD
SVM	0.786	0.790
RF	0.688	0.660
KNN	0.702	0.672
WGAN-C + DNN	0.902	0.879

As can be seen from Table 3, the classification method using deep learning provides a obvious improvement in accuracy compared to the traditional machine learning method. Moreover, the data set augmented by the generated brain functional connectivity features also provides a obvious improvement in classification accuracy.

4.5   Performance Comparison of Different Deep Learning Generators

We compared the proposed WGAN-C generation method with several commonly used generation networks such as variational auto encoder (VAE) (Kingma and Welling 2013) and GAN. The comparison results are shown in Table 4.

Table 4. Comparisons of generating models

Data/Method	ADHD	ASD
VAE + DNN	0.87	0.85
GAN + DNN	0.87	0.85
WGAN + DNN	0.893	0.867
WGAN-C + DNN	0.902	0.879

As can be seen from Table 4, compared with other popular generators, the generated data in this paper is more conducive to improving classification performance. The generation quality of VAE and GAN is difficult to control. When adding the generated data to augment the data, the classification accuracy will be reduced.

5   Conclusion

In this paper, we have proposed a generation model, WGAN-C, for improving the classification accuracy of neurological diseases by augmenting the data of brain functional connectivity. Importantly, we have demonstrated the superiority of this method in the classification of attention deficit hyperactivity disorder (ADHD) and autism spectrum disorder (ASD). Compared with the ordinary DNN, this method provided an accuracy improvement of about 3%, which surpasses some existing classification methods. In the future, we plan to extend our work to the field of original fMRI medical images and use computer vision to classify fMRI data in order to improve the classification results.

Acknowledgments. This study was supported by the Postgraduate Research & Practice Innovation Program of Jiangsu Province (Project No. SJCX18_0741). Scientific Research Foundation for Advanced Talents of Jiangsu University (Project No. 14JDG040).

References

Abraham, A., et al.: Deriving reproducible biomarkers from multi-site restingstate data: an autism-based example. NeuroImage **147**, 736–745 (2017)

Arjovsky, M., Bottou, L.: Towards principled methods for training generative adversarial networks, 1050 (2017)

Baumgartner, C.F., Koch, L.M., Can Tezcan, K., Xi Ang, J., Konukoglu, E.: Visual feature attribution using Wasserstein GANs. In: Proceedings of the IEEE COnference on Computer Vision and Pattern Recognition, pp. 8309–8319 (2018)

Bishop, C.M.: Training with noise is equivalent to Tikhonov regularization. Neural Comput. **7**(1), 108–116 (1995)

Biswal, B., Zerrin Yetkin, F., Haughton, V.M., Hyde, J.S.: Functional connectivity in the motor cortex of resting human brain using echo-planar MRI. Magn. Reson. Med. **34**(4), 537–541 (1995)

Costa, P., Galdran, A., Meyer, M.I., Abramoff, M.D., Campilho, A.: Towards adversarial retinal image synthesis. IEEE Trans. Med. Imaging 1 (2017)

Ge, W.: A perspective on deep imaging. IEEE Access **4**(99), 8914–8924 (2017)

Goodfellow, I.J., et al.: Generative adversarial nets. In: International Conference on Neural Information Processing Systems (2014)

Biomarkers Definitions Working Group, Atkinson Jr, A.J., Colburn, W.A., DeGruttola, V.G., DeMets, D.L., Downing, G., et al.: Biomarkers and surrogate endpoints: preferred definitions and conceptual framework. Clin. Pharmacol. Ther. **69**(3), 89–95 (2001)

Gulrajani, I., Ahmed, F., Arjovsky, M., Dumoulin, V., Courville, A.: Improved training of Wasserstein GANs (2017)

Heinsfeld, A.S., Franco, A.R., Craddock, R.C., Buchweitz, A., Meneguzzi, F.: Identification of autism spectrum disorder using deep learning and the abide dataset. Neuroimage Clin. **17**(C), 16–23 (2018)

Kingma, D.P., Welling, M.: Auto-encoding variational bayes (2013). arXiv preprint arXiv:1312.6114

Koyamada, S., Shikauchi, Y., Nakae, K., Koyama, M., Ishii, S.: Deep learning of fMRI big data: a novel approach to subject-transfer decoding. Computer Science (2015)

Li, F., Tran, L., Thung, K.-H., Ji, S., Shen, D., Li, J.: A robust deep model for improved classification of AD/MCI patients. IEEE J. Biomed. Health Inform. **19**(5), 1610–1616 (2015)

Lin, Z., Yang, C., Zhu, Y., Duchi, J., Fu, Y., Wang, Y.: Simultaneous dimension reduction and adjustment for confounding variation. Proc. Nat. Acad. Sci. U.S.A. **113**(51), 14662–14667 (2016)

Mahapatra, D., Bozorgtabar, B., Hewavitharanage, S., Garnavi, R.: Image super resolution using generative adversarial networks and local saliency maps for retinal image analysis. In: International Conference on Medical Image Computing and Computer-assisted Intervention, pp. 382–390 (2017)

Nie, D., et al.: Medical image synthesis with context-aware generative adversarial networks. In: International Conference on Medical Image Computing and Computer-Assisted Intervention (2017)

Plis, S.M., et al.: Deep learning for neuroimaging: a validation study. Front. Neurosci. **8**(8), 229 (2014)

Salvatore, C., Cerasa, A., Battista, P., Gilardi, M.C., Quattrone, A., Castiglioni, I.: Magnetic resonance imaging biomarkers for the early diagnosis of Alzheimer's disease: a machine learning approach. Front. Neurosci. **9**, 307 (2015)

Santos, J.S., Savii, R.M., Ide, J.S., Li, C.-S.R., Quiles, M.G., Basgalupp, M.P.: Classification of cocaine dependents from fMRI data using cluster-based stratification and deep learning. In: International Conference on Computational Science and Its Applications, pp. 298–313 (2017)

Schlegl, T., Seebck, P., Waldstein, S.M., Schmidt-Erfurth, U., Langs, G.: Unsupervised anomaly detection with generative adversarial networks to guide marker discovery (2017)

Sejnowski, T.J., Churchland, P.S., Anthony, J., Movshon, J.A.: Putting big data to good use in neuroscience. Nat. Neurosci. **17**(11), 1440–1441 (2014)

Song, Y., Epalle, T.M., Lu, H.: Characterizing and predicting autism spectrum disorder by performing resting-state functional network community pattern analysis. Front. Hum. Neurosci. **13**, 203 (2019)

Suk, H.-I., Wee, C.-Y., Lee, S.-W., Shen, D.: State-space model with deep learning for functional dynamics estimation in resting-state fMRI. NeuroImage **129**, 292–307 (2016)

Vergun, S., et al.: Classification and extraction of resting state networks using healthy and epilepsy fMRI data. Front. Neurosci. **10**, 440 (2016)

Wang, G., Kalra, M., Orton, C.G.: Machine learning will transform radiology significantly within the next 5 years. Med. Phys. **44**(6), 2041–2044 (2017)

Zhang, Y., Yang, L., Chen, J., Fredericksen, M., Hughes, D.P., Chen, D.Z.: Deep adversarial networks for biomedical image segmentation utilizing unannotated images. In: International Conference on Medical Image Computing and Computer Assisted Intervention, pp. 408–416 (2017)

Zhao, X., Rangaprakash, D., Denney Jr., T.S., Katz, J.S., Dretsch, M.N., Deshpande, G.: Identifying neuropsychiatric disorders using unsupervised clustering methods: data and code. Data Brief **22**, 570–573 (2019)

Attention-Based Label Consistency for Semi-supervised Deep Learning

Jiaming Chen and Meng Yang[(✉)]

School of Data and Computer Science, Sun Yat-sen University, Guangzhou, China
chenjm26@mail2.sysu.edu.cn, yangm6@mail.sysu.edu.cn

Abstract. Semi-supervised deep learning, which aims to effectively use the available labeled and unlabeled data together to improve the accuracy of model, is a hot topic recently. In this paper, we propose a novel attention-based label consistency (ALC) model for semi-supervised deep learning. The relationships between different samples are well exploited by the proposed scheme of channel and sample attention, while the class estimations are required to be smooth for nearby unlabeled data. We have implemented the proposed ALC model in the framework of Π model and MeanTeacher, and the experimental results on three benchmark datasets, (e.g., Fashion-MNIST, CIFAR-10 and SVHN) clearly show the advantages of our proposed method.

Keywords: Semi-supervised learning · Deep neural network · Attention mechanism

1 Introduction

Deep Learning have achieved tremendous performance in various computer vision tasks. One of the major bottlenecks of deep learning [4,6,15] is how to obtain large-scale labeled datasets. Recent researches have paid increased efforts in developing semi-supervised deep learning for effectively employing the available labeled and unlabeled data together.

One intuitive way to use massive unlabeled data is to pre-train deep neural network models in an unsupervised way, and fine-tune the models on labeled data [1,3,19]. Although these methods have been able to simultaneously conduct both supervised and unsupervised learning, their goals are different. For instance, most of the information required for data reconstruction in unsupervised learning way are irrelevant for classification tasks of supervised learning.

Exploiting unlabeled data in the entire training process instead of just pre-training has been developed in recent works [8,12,13]. In Pseudo-Label [8], both the labeled and the unlabeled data are used to train the deep neural networks, with regarding the predicted class of unlabeled data as their labels. Rasmus et al. [12] trained deep neural network with all available data and avoided layer-wise pre-training by skipping connections from encoders to decoders. The Manifold Tangent Classifier (MTC) [13] trains contrastive auto-encoders (CAEs)

© Springer Nature Switzerland AG 2019
Z. Lin et al. (Eds.): PRCV 2019, LNCS 11857, pp. 456–467, 2019.
https://doi.org/10.1007/978-3-030-31654-9_39

approximately invariant to local perturbations along the manifold. And some works [2,14] combine the semi-supervised learning and Generative Adversarial Networks (GAN) by making the discriminator not only recognize real image or not but also recognize the class label of real and generated images. Although improvements have been reported by these methods, how to effectively explore the discrimination embedded in the unlabeled data is still an open question.

In recent years, consistency-based semi-supervised deep learning methods have achieved outstanding performances. Π model [7] and MeanTeacher [16] encourage the smoothness around the data points against the small perturbations imposed in the data. Another work, VAT [10], rewards the average of local distributional smoothness (LDS) over all the training samples and minimizes the KL-distance based measurement to enhance the model's robustness against perturbation. The idea behinds them is that a "good" classification model should give consistent predictions for the same data points under small perturbations. However, these methods only focus on the smoothness around each single point, while ignore the relationships between data points. Although SNTG [9] proposed a cluster-like regularization to enforce neighbors to be smooth, the distance of samples is designed too simply to handle the complex sample relationships well.

In this paper, we propose a novel attention-based label consistency (ALC) for semi-supervised deep learning, which fully utilizes the structural information among data points. In the proposed attention-based label consistency regularization, the similarity of different samples is described by using channel and sample attention, with which the label consistency of different samples is preserved. By enhancing the smoothness of label prediction among data, the network can be trained better and better for utilizing the structural information about data. Extensive experiments are conducted on three image datasets, with improved results reported compared to the state-of-the-art Π model [7] and MeanTeacher [16].

2   Related Work

In the past, many semi-supervised deep learning methods [7,8,10,16] have been developed. In this section, we focus on the closely related works, specifically, the network consistency loss in Π model [7] and MeanTeacher [16] and the attention scheme.

2.1   Network Consistency Loss

We consider the case that a data set A consist of limited labeled data and large-scale unlabeled data. The network function f, parameterized by $\boldsymbol{\theta}$, represents the prediction distribution. Thus network consistency loss in Π model [7] is defined as

$$l_{nc} = \sum_{j=1}^{|A|} ||f(\boldsymbol{x}_j, \boldsymbol{\theta}, \eta') - f(\boldsymbol{x}_j, \boldsymbol{\theta}, \eta)||^2 \tag{1}$$

where $x \in A$ and $|A|$ is the number of whole data set, η and η' are the different noise regularizations. This loss encourages the network function f to produce the similar predictions on the sample under different noise regularizations.

Tarvainen et al. [16] further improved Π model and proposed a better model, called teacher model, by averaging weight of (student) model every iteration:

$$\theta' = \alpha\theta' + (1 - \alpha)\theta \tag{2}$$

where θ' is the weights of teacher model and α is a hyperparameter. In Mean-Teacher [16], the network consistency loss, l_{nc}, takes the form as follow

$$l_{nc} = \sum_{j=1}^{|A|} ||f(x_j, \theta', \eta') - f(x_j, \theta, \eta)||^2 \tag{3}$$

where θ' and θ are the weights of teacher model and student model, respectively. And the teacher model is an average of consecutive student models via Eq. (2). MeanTeacher enables learning from unlabeled data through more accurate targets generated by teacher model $f(x_j, \theta', \eta')$.

2.2 Attention

Recently, attention mechanism has been successfully applied to various tasks, such as image classification [5,17], monocular depth prediction [21], and semantic segmentation. SENet [5] benefits from enhancing channel relationship through the squeeze-and Excitation block which adaptively recalibrates channel-wise features. Residual Attention Network [17] learns the attention-aware features by stacking attention modules. And the attention-aware features from different modules change adaptively as layers going deeper. Attention can be viewed as a tool to bias the allocation of available processing resources towards the most informative components of an input signal.

3   Method

The deep semi-supervised learning methods with network consistency loss, e.g. MeanTeacher [16], have achieved remarkable results in image classification. However, these methods only consider each data point alone, while ignore the relationships between data points. In order to fully utilize the structural information among data, we propose a novel method, attention-based label consistency (ALC) for semi-supervised deep learning, which can capture the relationships through the introduced attention mechanisms and the designed consistency regularization. Compared to SNTG [9], the proposed attention-based label consistency is a more flexible and powerful method to capture the information among training samples.

3.1   Model of Attention-Based Label Consistency

The framework of deep convolutional neural network for recognition tasks can divided into two parts: deep feature learning and classification loss. By directly using the deep feature learning part, we proposed a novel deep model, attention-based consistency (ALC), of which the loss function is

$$L = l_{sup} + w_1 l_{nc} + w_2 l_{alc} \tag{4}$$

where l_{alc} is the proposed attention-based label consistency regularization, l_{sup} and l_{nc} are the supervised classification loss and the network consistency loss, respectively. w_1 and w_2 are the weights to control the importance of l_{nc} and l_{alc}, respectively, where w_1 is set according to the previous methods, such as Π model and Meanteacher. The overview of the proposed ALC model is shown in Fig. 1. The proposed ALC model accepts the available labeled and unlabeled data together, where the supervised loss utilizes the labeled data only and the network consistency loss enhances the smoothness only for a single data point. The proposed attention-based label consistency regularization captures the relationships among data by attention mechanisms.

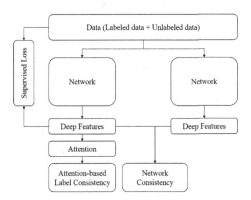

Fig. 1. Framework of the proposed attention-based label consistency (ALC) model.

Let x and $y \in \Re^{K \times 1}$ be learned deep convolutional feature in some iteration and an one-hot vector indicating the label of x, respectively. Given a data set A containing K classes, $L \subseteq A$ is the data set with known labels. Let $p(x, \theta)$ denote the output of multi-layer perception layer before the Softmax layer (denoted by $\sigma(\cdot)$) for the sample $x \in L$, and l_{sup} is defined as

$$l_{sup} = -\sum_{j=1}^{|L|} \sum_{i=1}^{K} y_{ji} \log \sigma(p(x_j, \theta))_i \tag{5}$$

where θ is the network parameter and $|L|$ is the number of labeled data. When the x_j belongs to k^{th} class, the $y_{jk} = 1$ and $y_{jl} = 0$ if $l \neq k$.

For the network consistency loss, Eq. (1) for Π model [7] and Eq. (3) for MeanTeacher [16] can be used in our proposed model of Eq. (4).

The structural information among data is introduced by the designed attention-based label consistency. More specifically, the relationships between different data points are described by attention schemes; while the labels of data points are regularized by the attention-based regularization.

3.2   Channel and Sample Attention

The inter-channel relationships of features embed an essential information, which benefits to make the network learn better feature representation. In this paper, the squeeze-and-excitation attention [5] is used to capture the channel attention.

$$U = MLP(AvgPool(\boldsymbol{X})) \tag{6}$$

where $\boldsymbol{X} = [\boldsymbol{X}_1, \boldsymbol{X}_2, ..., \boldsymbol{X}_B] \in R^{B \times H \times W \times C}$ is an input feature and B is the batch size and $\boldsymbol{U} = [\boldsymbol{u}_1, \boldsymbol{u}_2, ..., \boldsymbol{u}_B] \in R^{B \times C}$ is a matrix whose element $\boldsymbol{u}_i$ represents the channel excitation vector for $\boldsymbol{X}_i$. Then the feature $\boldsymbol{X}$ will be reweighted by the channel attention map $\boldsymbol{U}$

$$\hat{\boldsymbol{X}}_i = \boldsymbol{u}_i * \boldsymbol{X}_i \tag{7}$$

where $\hat{\boldsymbol{X}} = [\hat{\boldsymbol{X}}_1, \hat{\boldsymbol{X}}_2, ..., \hat{\boldsymbol{X}}_B]$ and Eq. (7) is a channel-wise multiplication between the feature $\boldsymbol{X}_i \in R^{H \times W \times C}$ and the vector $\boldsymbol{u}_i$. The flowchart of squeeze-and-excitation channel attention is shown in Fig. 2.

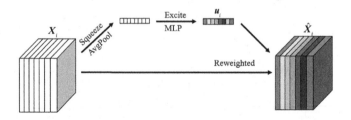

Fig. 2. Squeeze-and-excitation channel attention.

After channel attention, we conduct sample attention to measure the similarities between different samples, as shown in Fig. 3. By using both global-average-pooled and global-max-pooled features to capture the information simultaneously, we can generate two new feature representations $\bar{\boldsymbol{X}}$ and $\widetilde{\boldsymbol{X}}$ via

$$\bar{\boldsymbol{X}} = MLP(GAvgPool(\hat{\boldsymbol{X}})) \tag{8}$$

$$\widetilde{\boldsymbol{X}} = MLP(GMaxPool(\hat{\boldsymbol{X}})) \tag{9}$$

where MLP is the multi-layer perception layer, $GAvgPool$ and $GMaxPool$ represent global-average-pooling and global-max-pooling operations, which can gather different important image clues [18].

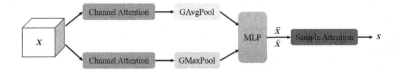

Fig. 3. Similarity measures.

For measuring the similarities of samples, we use a softmax normalization to compute the relationships among the features of $\bar{X}$ and $\widetilde{X}$

$$s_{ji} = \frac{exp(\widetilde{X}_i \cdot \bar{X}_j)}{\sum_{i=1}^{B} exp(\widetilde{X}_i \cdot \bar{X}_j)} \tag{10}$$

where s_{ji} measures the ith data point's impact on j^{th} data points. Here we compute the Eq. (10) across features of $\bar{X}$ and $\widetilde{X}$ in order to capture different image information more completely. The more similar feature representations of the two data points, the greater the correlation between them.

3.3 Attention-Based Label Consistency Regularization

The neighbor-similarity matrix S, whose element s_{ji} generated by attention mechanisms, actually builds a graph incorporating neighborhood information among data. It is quite reasonable that the samples close to each other should have similar labels. Thus the proposed attention-based label consistency is designed as

$$l_{alc} = \sum_{i,j} s_{ji} \|p(x_i, \theta) - p(x_j, \theta)\|_2^2 \tag{11}$$

where the x_i is the inputted labeled and unlabeled samples to the model and θ is the weights of network parameters. The objective function with adaptive neighborhood information s_{ji} incurs penalty if the neighboring feature representations are classified far apart. Therefore, minimizing it is an attempt to ensure that if the features are "close" then their predictions are close as well.

4 Network Optimization

In this section, we will present the optimization of attention-based label consistency, which can capture the neighborhood information adaptively by attention mechanisms. The attention mechanisms, implemented by fast vector or matrix operator in software toolkit, only cost ignorable computational burden. The overall framework of ALC model is shown in Algorithm 1.

Algorithm 1. The proposed framework of ALC model.

Input: Training Data set A.
Output: Network parameter θ
  1: Extract deep feature representations X.
  2: Feed $X \in R^{B \times H \times W \times C}$ into channel attention layer to generate the feature representation $\hat{X}$.
  3: Apply global-average-pooling and global-max-pooling operations on $\hat{X}$ to generate $\bar{X} \in R^{B \times C}$ and $\widetilde{X} \in R^{B \times C}$.
  4: Compute the neighbor-similarity matrix S via Eq (10).
  5: Evaluate Eq (11) with $S = \{s_{ij}\}$ and network predictions.
  6: Compute the network consistency l_{uc} via Eq.(1) or Eq.(3).
  7: Compute the supervised classification loss via Eq.(5).
  8: Compute the overall loss Eq.(4) and update the network parameter θ via mini-batch SGD.

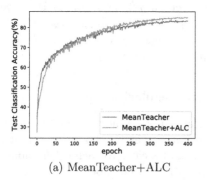 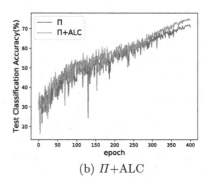

(a) MeanTeacher+ALC   (b) Π+ALC

Fig. 4. Test classification accuracy on CIFAR-10. (a) The blue line is the results of MeanTeachner and the orange one is MeanTeacher+ALC. (b) The blue line is results of Π and the orange one is Π+ALC. (Color figure online)

After computing the attention-based label consistency term, the optimization of the network can be conducted in the framework of existing deep models, such as Π model [7] and MeanTeacher [16].

By incorporating the attention-based label consistency via Eq. (11), the existing deep models can not only enhance the smoothness around each single data point, but also exploit the structural information among the data points. The Fig. 4 shows the results of ALC model on CIFAR-10 dataset. In Fig. 4, we can observe that the proposed regularization clearly improve the performances on both MeanTeacher and Π model. Although our model seems a bit worse than the consistency-based model (i.e. MeanTeacher or Π model) at the beginning, our model gradually overtakes the consistency-based model as the proposed regularization learns the structural information among data.

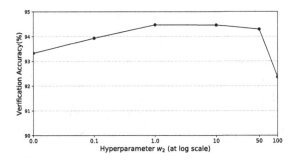

Fig. 5. The verification accuracy on different w_2 at log scale.

5   Experiment

In this section, we conduct some experiments on benchmark datasets, Fashion-MNIST [20], CIFAR-10 and SVHN [11], to evaluate the proposed method and then discuss the experimental results, which are averaged over 5 runs with different seeds for data splits.

We use the public codes[1] of MeanTeacher [16] and reimplement the Π model [7], and try our best to reproduce them. We use SGD with a mini-batch size of 100 and train the model 400 epochs. The learning rate, using a cosine annealing schedule, starts from 0.1 in initialization. Further, for comparison, we implement the Pseudo-Label [8] with the same 13-layer convolutional neural network in the same experimental setting to the original paper [8]. We also report the results of SNTG [9] by running the public code[2] for fair comparison. Following the public codes, the smoothing coefficient hyperparameter α of MeanTeacher is set 0.97 in all experiments and w_1 is set to $\{5.0, 100.0, 5.0\}$ on Fashion-MNIST, CIFAR-10 and SVHN, respectively.

5.1   Discussion of Key Parameters

Since w_1 has been used in previous models, we detail the setting of the other hyperparameter w_2 in Eq. (4) in the following. The hyperparameter w_2 weights to control the importance of the proposed l_{alc}. The validation set was used for evaluating the hyperparameter. The Fig. 5 shows the experiments on SVHN dataset with 1000 labeled data to investigate the influence of w_2 for our model. In this experiment, we fix $w_1 = 5.0$ and vary w_2 to learn different models whose verification accuracies on SVHN dataset are shown in Fig. 5. The results shows that the proposed regularization clearly improve the performance of model as the weight w_2 increases. The stable improving is observed across a wide range of w_2, which shows that the performance is not sensitive to the choice of w_2.

---

[1] https://github.com/CuriousAI/mean-teacher.
[2] https://github.com/xinmei9322/SNTG.

Table 1. Test classification rate % on Fashion-MNIST

Method	250	500
Supervised	77.64 ± 0.34	81.55 ± 0.47
Pseudo-Label	77.70 ± 0.68	81.75 ± 0.52
SNTG [9]	81.92 ± 0.27	84.40 ± 0.20
MeanTeacher [16]	78.61 ± 0.14	84.92 ± 0.21
MeanTeacher+ALC	80.14 ± 0.30	**85.43 ± 0.17**
Π model [7]	80.21 ± 0.60	83.26 ± 0.53
Π **model+ALC**	**82.59 ± 0.43**	**84.82 ± 0.40**

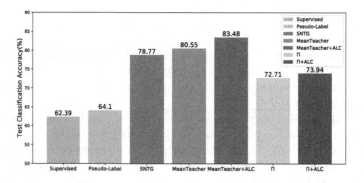

Fig. 6. Test classification accuracy on CIFAR-10 with 1000 labeled data.

5.2   Fashion-MNIST

Fashion-MNIST is comprise of 28×28 grayscale images of 70000 fashion products from 10 categories, with 7000 images per category. The training set has 60000 images and the test set has 10000 images. For experiment on Fashion-MNIST, we use the standard 10000 testing samples as a held out test set and all 60000 training samples as train set. We randomly select {25, 50} samples from each class in the train set as the labeled data. For Fashion-MNIST, we set $w_2 = 1.0$ in the experiments. The labeled batch size is set to 10. The results are shown in Table 1. In both 250-labels and 500-labels experiment on Fashion, the proposed method outperforms other method.

5.3   CIFAR-10

CIFAR-10 benchmark contains 32×32 pixel RGB images belonging to ten different classes. CIFAR-10 consists of 50000 training samples and 10000 test samples. For semi-supervised setting, we randomly select 100 samples from each class in the train set as the labeled data. Thus the size of labeled data set is 1000. For CIFAR-10, we set $w_2 = 100.0$ in the experiments and the labeled batch size is 30.

Table 2. Test classification rate % on SVHN

Method	250	350	500
Supervised	48.5 ± 0.31	58.32 ± 0.41	74.99 ± 0.57
Pseudo-Label	74.22 ± 0.80	81.71 ± 0.74	85.79 ± 0.43
SNTG [9]		93.14 ± 1.21	93.64 ± 0.77
MeanTeacher [16]	93.18 ± 0.46	94.55 ± 0.23	95.51 ± 0.12
MeanTeacher+ALC	**94.98 ± 0.34**	**95.70 ± 0.27**	**96.07 ± 0.21**
Π model [7]	91.41 ± 0.39	92.13 ± 0.31	92.86 ± 0.26
Π model+ALC	**93.14 ± 0.27**	93.47 ± 0.17	94.59 ± 0.11

The result is shown in Fig. 6, from which we can observe that the proposed regularization clearly improve the performances on both MeanTeacher and Π model. The MeanTeacher+ALC outperforms other methods in the experiment.

5.4 SVHN

Here we ran experiments using the Street View House Numbers (SVHN). SVHN contain 32×32 pixel RGB images belonging to ten different classes as CIFAR-10. In SVHN, each example is close-up of a house number, and the class represents the identity of the digit at the center of the image. The SVHN dataset contains of 73257 training samples and 26032 test samples. For semi-supervised setting, we randomly select {25, 50, 100} samples from each class in the train set as the labeled data. For SVHN, we set $w_2 = 1.0$ in the experiments and the labeled batch size is 3.

The results in Table 2 show the the significant improvements of the proposed method, e.g. from 91.41% to 93.14% and from 92.13% to 93.47% for Π model+ALC on SVHN with 250 and 350 labeled data, respectively. The proposed method outperforms other semi-supervised method clearly. And on 250-labels experiments, the SNTG can not get convergence, so we don't report it.

5.5 Ablation Study

In this experiment, we validate our proposed regularization with the ablation study on the attention mechanisms (sample/channel) and pooling methods (GMaxPool/GAvgPool). Table 3 lists the results on benchmarks of SVHN with 250 labeled samples and CIFAR-10 with 1000 labeled samples. We use MeanTeacher as baseline and analyze: (a) MeanTeacher with GMaxPool only. (b) MeanTeacher with GAvgPool only. (c) MeanTeacher with sample attention. (d) MeanTeacher with ALC. (e) MeanTeacher model. As shown in Table 3, the similarity of GMaxPool and GAvgPool features exploits more information than single pooling only. The sample attention improves MeanTeacher on both SVHN and CIFAR-10 experiments. For CIFAR-10, the complex samples benefit from inter-channel information captured by channel attention.

Table 3. Test classification rate % on ablation study

Method			SVHN	CIFAR-10
	GMaxPool	GAvgPool		
a	$\checkmark$		94.19 ± 0.11	82.24 ± 0.27
b		$\checkmark$	94.45 ± 0.25	82.81 ± 0.39
	Sample	Channel		
c	$\checkmark$		94.31 ± 0.24	82.22 ± 0.20
d	$\checkmark$	$\checkmark$	94.98 ± 0.34	83.48 ± 0.21
e			93.18 ± 0.46	80.55 ± 0.43

6   Conclusion

In this paper we propose a novel attention-based label consistency regularization term that can effectively exploit the relationships among the data to improve the model performance. Specifically the regularization term encourages the smoothness of label prediction among data by model the structural information. Moreover, the designed regularization captures the relationships among data through two attention mechanisms, channel attention and sample attention, which can model the structural information automatically through back-propagation algorithm. The experimental results on three benchmark datasets have shown that our method can improve the accuracy of image classification compared to recent semi-supervised deep learning models.

Acknowledgement. This work is partially supported by National Natural Science Foundation of China (Grant no. 61772568), the Guangzhou Science and Technology Program (Grant no. 201804010288), and the Fundamental Research Funds for the Central Universities (Grant no. 18lgzd15).

References

1. Dai, A.M., Le, Q.V.: Semi-supervised sequence learning. In: Advances in Neural Information Processing Systems, vol. 28, pp. 3079–3087. Curran Associates, Inc. (2015)
2. Dai, Z., Yang, Z., Yang, F., Cohen, W.W., Salakhutdinov, R.R.: Good semi-supervised learning that requires a bad GAN. In: Advances in Neural Information Processing Systems, vol. 30, pp. 6510–6520. Curran Associates, Inc. (2017)
3. Goodfellow, I.J., Mirza, M., Courville, A., Bengio, Y.: Multi-prediction deep Boltzmann machines. In: Proceedings of the 26th International Conference on Neural Information Processing Systems, NIPS 2013, vol. 1, pp. 548–556. Curran Associates Inc., USA (2013)
4. He, K., Zhang, X., Ren, S., Sun, J.: Deep residual learning for image recognition. In: The IEEE Conference on Computer Vision and Pattern Recognition (CVPR), June 2016

5. Hu, J., Shen, L., Sun, G.: Squeeze-and-excitation networks. In: The IEEE Conference on Computer Vision and Pattern Recognition (CVPR), June 2018
6. Krizhevsky, A., Sutskever, I., Hinton, G.E.: Imagenet classification with deep convolutional neural networks. In: Proceedings of the 25th International Conference on Neural Information Processing Systems, NIPS 2012, vol. 1, pp. 1097–1105. Curran Associates Inc., USA (2012)
7. Laine, S., Aila, T.: Temporal ensembling for semisupervised learning. In: Proceedings of ICLR (2017)
8. Lee, D.H.: Pseudo-label: the simple and efficient semi-supervised learning method for deep neural networks. In: ICML 2013 Workshop: Challenges in Representation Learning (WREPL), July 2013
9. Luo, Y., Zhu, J., Li, M., Ren, Y., Zhang, B.: Smooth neighbors on teacher graphs for semi-supervised learning. In: The IEEE Conference on Computer Vision and Pattern Recognition (CVPR), June 2018
10. Miyato, T., Maeda, S., Ishii, S., Koyama, M.: Virtual adversarial training: a regularization method for supervised and semi-supervised learning. IEEE Trans. Pattern Anal. Mach. Intell. **41**, 1979–1993 (2018)
11. Netzer, Y., Wang, T., Coates, A., Bissacco, A., Wu, B., Ng, A.Y.: Reading digits in natural images with unsupervised feature learning. In: NIPS Workshop on Deep Learning and Unsupervised Feature Learning (2011)
12. Rasmus, A., Valpola, H., Honkala, M., Berglund, M., Raiko, T.: Semi-supervised learning with ladder network. In: Advances in Neural Information Processing Systems, July 2015
13. Rifai, S., Dauphin, Y.N., Vincent, P., Bengio, Y., Muller, X.: The manifold tangent classifier. In: Proceedings of the 24th International Conference on Neural Information Processing Systems, NIPS 2011, pp. 2294–2302. Curran Associates Inc., USA (2011)
14. Salimans, T., et al.: Improved techniques for training GANs. In: Advances in Neural Information Processing Systems, vol. 29, pp. 2234–2242 (2016)
15. Szegedy, C., et al.: Going deeper with convolutions. In: The IEEE Conference on Computer Vision and Pattern Recognition (CVPR), June 2015
16. Tarvainen, A., Valpola, H.: Mean teachers are better role models: weight-averaged consistency targets improve semisupervised deep learning results. In: Advances in Neural Information Processing Systems, pp. 1195–1204 (2017)
17. Wang, F., et al.: Residual attention network for image classification. In: The IEEE Conference on Computer Vision and Pattern Recognition (CVPR), July 2017
18. Woo, S., Park, J., Lee, J.Y., So Kweon, I.: CBAM: convolutional block attention module. In: The European Conference on Computer Vision (ECCV), September 2018
19. Wu, H., Prasad, S.: Semi-supervised deep learning using pseudo labels for hyperspectral image classification. IEEE Trans. Image Process. **27**(3), 1259–1270 (2018)
20. Xiao, H., Rasul, K., Vollgraf, R.: Fashion-MNIST: a novel image dataset for benchmarking machine learning algorithms (2017)
21. Xu, D., Wang, W., Tang, H., Liu, H., Sebe, N., Ricci, E.: Structured attention guided convolutional neural fields for monocular depth estimation. In: The IEEE Conference on Computer Vision and Pattern Recognition (CVPR), June 2018

Semantic Reanalysis of Scene Words in Visual Question Answering

Shiling Jiang[1], Ming Ma[1], Jianming Wang[2,3], Jiayu Liang[1], Kunliang Liu[1], Yukuan Sun[2], Wei Deng[2], Siyu Ren[1], and Guanghao Jin[1,4(✉)]

[1] School of Computer Science and Technology, Tianjin Polytechnic University, Tianjin, China
jinguanghao@tjpu.edu.cn
[2] School of Electronics and Information Engineering, Tianjin Polytechnic University, Tianjin, China
[3] Tianjin International Joint Research and Development Center of Autonomous Intelligence Technology and Systems, Tianjin Polytechnic University, Tianjin, China
[4] Tianjin Key Laboratory of Autonomous Intelligence Technology and Systems, Tianjin Polytechnic University, Tianjin, China

Abstract. Visual Question Answering (VQA) is a joint task that aims to answer questions based on the given images. The correct analysis of multiple album aggregate issues to remain a key issue in the VQA case, especially when answering question from multiple albums, how to correctly understand album images and corresponding question is an urgent problem. Under the influence of multiple photo albums and the presence of scene words in the question, it may lead to understanding the wrong scene and outputting the wrong answer, resulting in a decrease in VQA performance. In order to solve this problem, this paper proposes a new image and sentence similarity matching model, which outputs the correct image representation by learning the semantic concept. Due to the scene word is not an entity, sometimes the information which the model extracted may be incorrect. Therefore, we can try to reanalyse the question in another different way and give the answer by the similarity between the question and the visual-text. Our model was tested on the MemexQA dataset. The experimental results show that our model not only produces meaningful text sentences to prove the correctness of the answer, but also improves the accuracy by nearly 10%.

Keywords: Visual question answering · Similarity match · Scene words · Computer vision · Natural language processing

The first author of this paper is a student. This work was supported by the National Natural Science Foundation of China (No. 61373104, No. 61405143); the Excellent Science and Technology Enterprise Specialist Project of Tianjin (No. 18JCTPJC59000) and the Tianjin Natural Science Foundation (No. 16JCYBJC42300).

Z. Lin et al. (Eds.): PRCV 2019, LNCS 11857, pp. 468–479, 2019.
https://doi.org/10.1007/978-3-030-31654-9_40

1   Introduction

Visual Question Answering (VQA) [1,14] is a successful direction of solving a problem using computer vision and natural language processing techniques: Giving a pair of images and a question, the model can answer questions based on clues found in image and questions. At present, many deep learning-based networks [4,5,13,15,20] have been developed. The initial VQA method uses CNN to extract features of images and applies RNN to analyze the question to obtain text features, and then passes two different modal features through simple element-wise, and combining them into the classifier to generate the answer. However, the model seems does not understand the image area of fine-grained level well, resulting in poor performance of VQA. In recent years, many methods have been proposed to solve this task, such as dynamic memory network [22] and spatial attention [11]. In general, the results of multiple choices are better than open results, and as expected, all methods perform much worse than humans.

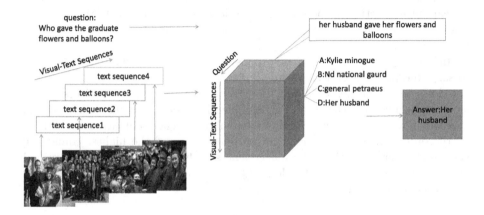

Fig. 1. The above image shows an example of the multiple-choice VQA, given a sequence of visual-text and the question, our model captures balloons and flowers, and according to the text we can find the appropriate information "her husband" and then give the correct answer. Red indicates the correct answer and green indicates the wrong answer. (Color figure online)

Since the work proposed by Ankit Kumar et al. [11], the dynamic memory network has played an important role in solving various problems of artificial intelligence. The framework consists of four modules: input module, question module, semantic memory module, and answer module. The model first computes the vector representation of the input and the question, and then selects the input related to the question by using the gating method according to the attention mechanism triggered by the question. Semantic memory module then iteratively generates memory in conjunction with related inputs and questions, generating a vector representation of the answer. Finally, the answer module combines the vector with the question vector to generate the final answer.

Based on the work of Ankit Kumar et al. [11], some revised modular networks is proposed. The results of these methods are superior to existing VQA methods. However, the analysis found that when the common sense reasoning of the background of the picture is wrong or the problem-focused object is too small or a high-level logical reasoning is required, the model often fails to give a correct prediction. To the best of our knowledge, all VQA methods use a single answer framework, which makes it difficult to output the correct answer. It is easy to make incorrect answers when the question contains scene words. Such as, "When did we last go to a wedding?" or "Where did we have the party". An example is shown in Fig. 1. For questions that come from large collections (multiple albums), which some of the keywords may have scene words, such as parties, weddings, etc. the machine sometimes misunderstands the meaning, which caused the corresponding picture could not be found, and gets the incorrect answer. If the answer is incorrect, we will reanalyze the other possible answers and choose the most likely correct answer in the second chance. We first answer the question through attention mechanisms. When a scene noun appears in a question, although the attention mechanism detects the target, a single object can not describe the scene, and the wrong description leads to an incorrect answer.

Inspired by this observation, we propose a sentence similarity matching model to solve the problem of scene words in the VQA task. When this picture may not describe the scene, you need to reconfirm whether all the objects in the picture may appear in the scene. For example, the wedding should include priests, churches, flowers and other wedding-related objects. Then semantically matching all the objects in the wedding with the questions, and the highest confidence value is the answer we want. The effectiveness of the proposed method is verified by experimental results. On the MemexQA dataset [8], our method is better than the state-of-the-art method.

2 Related Work

Visual Question Answering. Image-based question answering (QA) has received extensive attention in the field of computer vision. In the past few years, many Visual Question Answering (VQA) models have been proposed. All existing methods are (1) extracting accurate forms of visual features and text features, and (2) obtaining answers by algorithms that combine these features. There are two differences between the current work and the existing image-based QA: (1) Image-based QA is based on a single picture answering the question, and our work can handle general visual text sequences, one of which may have multiple albums and images. (2) The existing image-based QA methods mostly map a sequence with text into a context feature vector, and our work is to establish the correlation between the query and the text sequence data at each time. We conducted experiments on the MemexQA dataset [8]. At present, a lot of work has been done on the single image QA dataset [1,2,7], and significant progress has been made in answering questions about individual images. The baseline approach proposed in the VQA dataset to address this task uses a CNN-LSTM architecture that includes a convolutional neural network for extracting image features and an LSTM for question feature coding. It combines these two features to predict the final answer. In recent years, a lot of work has followed this principle and substantial improvements have been made in the baseline model. Among them, the attention mechanism [7,11,18,21,23,25] and the joint embedding of images and question representations [4] have been extensively studied. Attention mechanism learning focuses on the most discriminating sub-regions rather than the entire image, providing a degree of reasoning for the answers. Different attention methods, such as stacking attention [23] and common attention [13] at different levels of questions and images, continue to improve the performance of VQA tasks. Andreas et al. [2,6] proposed a neural module network consisting of a series of modules that perform independent operations to solve specific questions. Kim et al. [9] proposed the use of compact bilinear methods to fuse images and questions embedding, and combined with attention mechanisms to further improve performance.

However, the keywords of some questions may contain scene words. Generally speaking, the meaning of words is vague, which may lead to incorrect answers. Recent work has shown that depth models for these good performance can be achieved by using semantic matching. In order to solve this problem, we propose a semantic similarity model to eliminate semantic barriers to understanding scene words.

Semantic Similarity Matching Model. In the field of visual question answering, semantic understanding is a common linguistic phenomenon. If there are nouns that can be defined by a single object, such as scene words, we need to replace them with many objects to judge the semantic similarity between these objects and the question. To understand the correlation between the two statements well, it is important to introduce algorithms for semantic analysis, which can provide users with more accurate and valuable content. Because of the importance of semantic similarity [17] assessment in different applications, it was selected as the first task of SemEval in 2014, in which many researchers applied methods to tagged datasets containing sentence pairs that involved Synthetic knowledge [10]. These data competition methods use heterogeneous features, such as word similarity, sentence or phrase synthesis and external resources (such as WordNet [19]), and apply a variety of learning algorithms (such as SVM, k-nearest neighbors, and model collections). Another high-performance system, from Bjerva et al. [3] uses formal semantics and logical reasoning, combined with features derived from the popular word2vec neuro-language model of Mikolov et al. [16], using these word vectors as the only input to the model.

Recently, two neural network methods that are more similar to ours have achieved significant performance improvements. Kiros et al. [10] proposed the skip-thoughts model, which is an extension from word to sentence level. The model we propose also uses neural networks to represent sentences, and its input is a vector of words learned from a large corpus. Unlike the method of Kiros et al. [10], our representational learning objectives directly reflect the given semantic similarity label. Although the neural network mentioned above uses complex learners to predict semantic similarity from sentence representations, we impose a stronger requirement that the semantically structured [17] representation space should be learned so that simple metrics are sufficient to capture statement similarity.

Our method calculates the distance between two semantic vectors, which can be used to predict the semantic similarity of two sentences. The model is the input as the question and the text sequence, and the output is the similarity score of the input sentence (the score is 1–5) and The most similar statement is our answer.

3   Methods

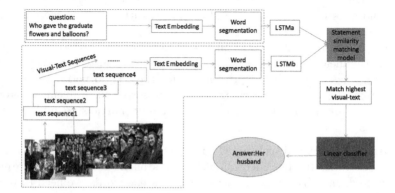

Fig. 2. Shows an overview of our model. For visual-text and question embedding, we first classify them, use our model to output the visual-text with the highest evaluation value, the final output layer for the multiple-choice classification, and the linear classifier to generate the final answer.

Our model consists of three main components: a question module, a visual-text module, and a module that outputs the highest confidence value as the final answer. An overview of our model is shown in Fig. 2.

3.1   Question Module

In the VQA system, there are pairs of questions and images $(Q; I)$, We use LSTM [5] to generate question features. This module embeds the question into the representation, which can then be queried from the input module. let $\{q_1, \ldots, q_N\} \subseteq \{Q\}$ represents the question of N words $Q \in Z^N$, where each word is an integer index in the vocabulary. Sentence word segmentation for each question$(I_1^{(a)}, \ldots, I_{Z_a}^{(a)})$. Z_a represents that each sentence has a different length, $I_i^{(a)}$ represents the word vector from the question, and pass the question to LSTMa.

3.2 Visual-Text Module

For the K-sequence of the visual-text sequence, $K = K_1, \ldots, K_T$, representing T words, Sentence word segmentation for each visual-text $(L_1^{(b)}, \ldots, L_{Z_b}^{(b)})$. Z_b represents that each sentence has a different length, $L_i^{(b)}$ represents the word vector from the visual-text, and pass the question to LSTMb. and the weight of the binding network is LSTMa = LSTMb, LSTMa and LSTMb update the hidden state at each sequence index by Eqs. (2)–(7). The final representation of the sentence is encoded by the model's last hidden state $g_T \in R^{drep}$. The RNN network is a standard feedforward neural network that has been adapted to accommodate sequence data, for sequence data $(y_1, \ldots, y_T)$, at each time $t \in 1, \ldots, T$, hidden state vector

$$g_t = sigmoid(W y_t + U g_{t-1}) \tag{1}$$

Similar to RNN, LSTM updates the hidden state representations in order, but these steps also depend on memory cells that contain four components (real-valued matrices), four components: a memory state d_t, and an output gate e_t (determining how memory states affect Memory unit), and an input (and forgotten) gate j_t (and h_t) that controls memory content and forgotten content based on each input and current state. The following is an update formula for LSTM [5] at each time $t \in \{1, \ldots, T\}$, the parameters are the weight matrix $W_j, W_h, W_d, W_e, V_j, V_h, V_d, V_e$, and the offset vector c_j, c_h, c_d, c_e:

$$j_t = sigmoid(W_j y_t + V_j g_{t-1} + c_j) \tag{2}$$

$$h_t = sigmoid(W_h y_t + V_h g_{t-1} + c_h) \tag{3}$$

$$\tilde{d}_t = tanh(W_d y_t + V_d g_{t-1} + c_d) \tag{4}$$

$$d_t = j_t \odot d_t + h_t \odot d_{t-1} \tag{5}$$

$$e_t = tanh(W_e y_t + V_e g_{t-1} + c_e) \tag{6}$$

$$g_t = e_t \odot tanh(d_t) \tag{7}$$

Given a pair of sentences, our method uses a predefined similarity function $g : R^{drep} \times R^{drep} \to R$ to LSTM. The similarity of the representation space is then used to infer the semantic similarity of the sentence. Therefore, the only error signal for backpropagation during training stems from the similarity between the sentence representations $g_{T_b}^a$ and $g_{T_b}^b$, and how this predictive similarity deviates from the basic factual relevance of artificial annotation. We use the similarity matching model to apply in the scene words in Fig. 3. We are limited to simple similarity functions:

$$f(g_{T_b}^a, g_{T_b}^b) = e^{-\|g_{T_b}^a - g_{T_b}^b\|_1} \in [0, 1] \tag{8}$$

Define a contextual visual text sequence for T examples, $I = \{I_i\}_1^T$, where I_t^{img} represents an image. I_t^{txt} is its corresponding text sentence, where its $j-th$

word is indexed by I_{tj}^{txt}. Next, the answer to the question is the integer $z \in [1, L]$ of the answer vocabulary of size L. Given a set of N questions and their context sequences, λ represents the parameters of the model, we have a model of maximum likelihood:

$$\underset{\lambda}{argmax} = \sum_{j=1}^{N} logP(z_j \mid Q_j, I_j; \lambda) \tag{9}$$

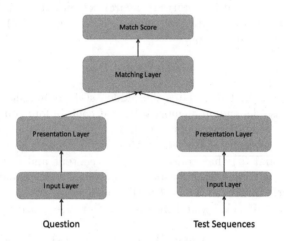

Fig. 3. Shows an overview of the statement similarity matching model. The word vector representing each input sentence is read using LSTM and its final hidden state is used as a vector representation for each sentence. The similarity between these semantics is then evaluated and the score is output.

4   Experiment

Our method is evaluated on the MemexQA dataset [8] and shows the accuracy comparison between our method and the state-of-the-art on the Memex QA dataset.

4.1   Dataset

The Memex QA dataset [8] consists of $20,860$ questions and approximately $13,591$ individual photos from 101 users. The model is trained on a set of 14,156 randomly selected QA pairs and tested on a set of 3,539 QA pairs. These personal photos record key moments in their lives, such as weddings, football matches, and friends gatherings. Each album and photo has comprehensive visual text information, including time, album title, picture description, and photo title. The MemexQA

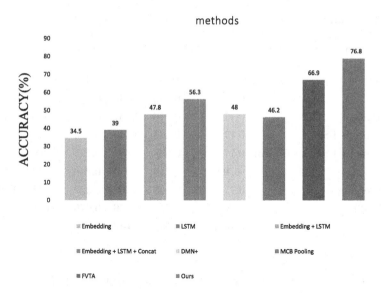

Fig. 4. The different methods of the question on the MemexQA dataset. The comparison of our method and other methods on the Memex QA dataset, the highest value is our method.

dataset [8] provides 4 answer options, each with only one correct answer. Some questions are about photos taken one day, for example, "Where did we party in May 2005?"; others are about all images, for example, "How many people were sitting around the table when I took an aerial shot?". A good VQA system not only has to give a clear answer, but also provides an image of real evidence or a piece of text that proves the reasoning process in the input sequence.

4.2 Evaluation

Our approach is based on the MemexQA dataset. Figure 4 shows the accuracy of our method and existing methods such as **DMN+** [22], **MCB** [4] on the MemexQA dataset. There are 3539 questions in MemexQA, and the questions and images are entered into the network, and the model gets 2366 correct answers on the first chance. For the wrong answer, enter the question again and use our method as the second chance to answer. Then our method can correct 353 answers in the 1173 answers to all errors in the first chance. The existing methods cannot correct the wrong answer for the second time because their models are trained by fixed structures. The results show that our method can correct the wrong answer in the second chance and achieve higher accuracy than the existing method. It shows that our method has better performance because it can solve the question where the scene words are not easy to explain with an object.

Table 1 shows the results of our method and the methods of the existing methods on different branches.

Table 1. Accuracy comparison of these branches on MemexQA dataset (higher is better). *When, Where, Who, How, What* means branches in Semantic scene function, and Overall means the task of counting numbers in MemexQA dataset.

Methods	How many	What	When	Where	Who	Overall
LSTM	0.758	0.340	0.336	0.332	0.348	0.390
Embedding	0.719	0.270	0.261	0.351	0.325	0.345
Embedding + LSTM	0.771	0.564	0.349	0.314	0.310	0.478
Embedding + LSTM + Concat	0.776	0.668	0.398	0.433	0.409	0.563
DMN+ [22]	0.792	0.616	0.346	0.248	0.224	0.480
MCB Pooling [4]	0.773	0.618	0.250	0.229	0.248	0.462
FTVA [12]	0.761	0.714	0.476	0.676	0.668	0.669
Ours	**0.804**	**0.801**	**0.660**	**0.760**	**0.776**	**0.768**

A large part of the existing solution is to embed images or video into space and use these embeddings to train the classification model. As we have seen, the proposed method is always superior to the baseline method and achieves the most advanced precision on the dataset. For qualitative comparison, we select some representative questions and answer the answers and retrieved images from our method and other methods in Fig. 5.

For some baseline models, **LSTM** represents the VQA model of LSTM in [15], where the question is embedded and the average image feature and average metadata embedded connections are sent to each LSTM unit. **Embedding** is similar to Logistic Regression. In addition to predicting answers from images, questions, and metadata, it also learns the embedding of embedded question and metadata. **Embedding + LSTM** utilizes word embedding and character embedding, as well as visual embedding, through LSTM encoding to obtain the final context representation. **Embedding + LSTM + Concat** connects the last LSTM output to produce the final output. **DMN+** [22] is a dynamic memory network that improves the Input Module, Attention mechanism, and Memory update mechanism. It solves the problem that the GRU in the DMN can only get the above information in the current sentence. Using the DMN+ network, each sentence and each picture representation in the dataset is taken as input. **Multimodal Compact Bilinear Pooling (MCB)** [4] effectively combines multimodal features to avoid high dimensional features. For VQA, an architecture using MCB twice is proposed, which is used to predict the attention of spatial features as image input, based on the verification result. **Focal Visual-Text Attention (FTVA)** [12] uses pre-trained GloVe word embedding. For image embedding, the pre-trained CNN model Inception-ResNet is used to extract features by connecting the output of the pool5 layer and the classification layer before softmax. Image features are compressed to 100 dimensions using a linear transformation, and a bidirectional LSTM is used for each modal to obtain a context representation.

Fig. 5. Qualitative comparison of our model and other models on the MemexQA dataset. For each question, we show the answer and the images of the highest weights. Arrange images from left to right based on all the photos in the album. The correct image and answer have a green border, and the incorrect answer is surrounded by red. (Color figure online)

Below are the implementation details of our approach. Each question is asked from a series of photos in the album. When there are a large number of scene words in the question, it is also important to understand the scene words [24]. To input the question and the visual-text, it is first necessary to segment the sentence, and convert it into a word vector corresponding to the pre-trained fixed dimension by means of a table-by-word. The two sentences are encoded to obtain the representation vector of the sentence, and input into the network in order [17], and finally the distance between the two obtained vectors is calculated. Since the model uses a scoring function, we use the output score range in (1–5). In order for our model to generalize beyond the limited vocabulary in the MemexQA dataset, we provide LSTM with input that can reflect the relationship between words, beyond the relationship that can be inferred from a few training set sentences. LSTM requires a large amount of data to achieve good generalization results due to a large number of parameters. So we use a lot of extra data to expand data. We use the 300-dimensional Word2vec word embedding [16] to prove that we can capture complex inter-word relationships.

5 Conclusions and Future Work

In this paper, we construct a model to solve the potential semantic information problem of scene words in VQA. When the first analysis of scene words is wrong, and there is another chance to reanalyse the scene word to get the answer. The modular framework we constructed is used to answer questions about visual text sequences, primarily using LSTM to learn semantic structured representation spaces so that simple metrics can capture sentence similarity. Our approach not only predicts the right answers, but also provides the right reasons to help users validate the results of the system. Since the ability to give a second answer is also important for human-computer interaction, AI machines can become smarter by a deep understanding of the meaning between the two semantics. This work shows that simple LSTM can model complex semantics by using synonym enhancement and pre-trained words embedding. Analysis of the learning model shows that different hidden units are used to encode different features of each sentence. Our work can make the application of semantic fuzziness in the communication process more flexible. In the future, it will play an important role in visual question answering including evaluation of semantic relevance, deployment in real-time applications, search engines and other examples.

References

1. Agrawal, A., et al.: VQA: visual question answering. Int. J. Comput. Vis. **123**(1), 4–31 (2017)
2. Andreas, J., Rohrbach, M., Darrell, T., Klein, D.: Neural module networks. In: Proceedings of the IEEE Conference on Computer Vision and Pattern Recognition, pp. 39–48 (2016)
3. Bjerva, J., Bos, J., Van der Goot, R., Nissim, M.: The meaning factory: formal semantics for recognizing textual entailment and determining semantic similarity. In: Proceedings of the 8th International Workshop on Semantic Evaluation (SemEval 2014), pp. 642–646 (2014)
4. Fukui, A., Park, D.H., Yang, D., Rohrbach, A., Darrell, T., Rohrbach, M.: Multimodal compact bilinear pooling for visual question answering and visual grounding. arXiv preprint arXiv:1606.01847 (2016)
5. Hochreiter, S., Schmidhuber, J.: Long short-term memory. Neural Comput. **9**(8), 1735–1780 (1997)
6. Hu, R., Andreas, J., Rohrbach, M., Darrell, T., Saenko, K.: Learning to reason: end-to-end module networks for visual question answering. In: Proceedings of the IEEE International Conference on Computer Vision, pp. 804–813 (2017)
7. Ilievski, I., Yan, S., Feng, J.: A focused dynamic attention model for visual question answering. arXiv preprint arXiv:1604.01485 (2016)
8. Jiang, L., Liang, J., Cao, L., Kalantidis, Y., Farfade, S., Hauptmann, A.: MemexQA: visual memex question answering. arXiv preprint arXiv:1708.01336 (2017)
9. Kim, J.H., On, K.W., Lim, W., Kim, J., Ha, J.W., Zhang, B.T.: Hadamard product for low-rank bilinear pooling. arXiv preprint arXiv:1610.04325 (2016)
10. Kiros, R., et al.: Skip-thought vectors. In: Advances in Neural Information Processing Systems, pp. 3294–3302 (2015)
11. Kumar, A., et al.: Ask me anything: dynamic memory networks for natural language processing. In: International Conference on Machine Learning, pp. 1378–1387 (2016)
12. Liang, J., Jiang, L., Cao, L., Li, L.J., Hauptmann, A.G.: Focal visual-text attention for visual question answering. In: Proceedings of the IEEE Conference on Computer Vision and Pattern Recognition, pp. 6135–6143 (2018)

13. Lu, J., Yang, J., Batra, D., Parikh, D.: Hierarchical question-image co-attention for visual question answering. In: Advances In Neural Information Processing Systems, pp. 289–297 (2016)
14. Ma, C., et al.: Visual question answering with memory-augmented networks. In: Proceedings of the IEEE Conference on Computer Vision and Pattern Recognition, pp. 6975–6984 (2018)
15. Malinowski, M., Rohrbach, M., Fritz, M.: Ask your neurons: a neural-based approach to answering questions about images. In: Proceedings of the IEEE International Conference on Computer Vision, pp. 1–9 (2015)
16. Mikolov, T., Sutskever, I., Chen, K., Corrado, G.S., Dean, J.: Distributed representations of words and phrases and their compositionality. In: Advances in Neural Information Processing Systems, pp. 3111–3119 (2013)
17. Mueller, J., Thyagarajan, A.: Siamese recurrent architectures for learning sentence similarity. In: Thirtieth AAAI Conference on Artificial Intelligence (2016)
18. Nguyen, D.K., Okatani, T.: Improved fusion of visual and language representations by dense symmetric co-attention for visual question answering. In: Proceedings of the IEEE Conference on Computer Vision and Pattern Recognition, pp. 6087–6096 (2018)
19. Sagala, T.W., Wati, T., Budi, N.F.A., Hidayanto, A.N., et al.: Analysis and implementation measurement of semantic similarity using content management information on wordnet. In: 2018 International Conference on Advanced Computer Science and Information Systems (ICACSIS), pp. 337–342. IEEE (2018)
20. Schwartz, I., Schwing, A., Hazan, T.: High-order attention models for visual question answering. In: Advances in Neural Information Processing Systems, pp. 3664–3674 (2017)
21. Shih, K.J., Singh, S., Hoiem, D.: Where to look: focus regions for visual question answering. In: Proceedings of the IEEE Conference on Computer Vision and Pattern Recognition, pp. 4613–4621 (2016)
22. Xiong, C., Merity, S., Socher, R.: Dynamic memory networks for visual and textual question answering. In: International Conference on Machine Learning, pp. 2397–2406 (2016)
23. Yang, Z., He, X., Gao, J., Deng, L., Smola, A.: Stacked attention networks for image question answering. In: Proceedings of the IEEE Conference on Computer Vision and Pattern Recognition, pp. 21–29 (2016)
24. Yoon, S., Kim, J.: Object-centric scene understanding for image memorability prediction. In: 2018 IEEE Conference on Multimedia Information Processing and Retrieval (MIPR), pp. 305–308. IEEE (2018)
25. Zhu, C., Zhao, Y., Huang, S., Tu, K., Ma, Y.: Structured attentions for visual question answering. In: Proceedings of the IEEE International Conference on Computer Vision, pp. 1291–1300 (2017)

A Dustbin Category Based Feedback Incremental Learning Strategy for Hierarchical Image Classification

Ying Chen, Wen Shen, Qianwen Li, and Zhihua Wei$^{(\boxtimes)}$

Department of Computer Science and Technology, Tongji University, Shanghai, China
{1833019,1810068,1730788,zhihua_wei}@tongji.edu.cn

Abstract. Hierarchical classification (HC) is an effective method to solve the problem of multi-class classification especially when the categories are organized hierarchically. However, HC models perform worse than flat classification (FC) models due to blocking, i.e. errors occur at the higher level will be propagated to the lower level. The first step in solving the blocking problem is to capture the blocked samples. In this paper, we present a novel HC model to capture the blocked samples by adding a virtual dustbin category for each middle-layer classifier, referred to as DBHC model. Furthermore, in order to improve the classification accuracy and accelerate the convergence process, we propose a feedback incremental learning (FIL) strategy to take into account the weights of samples, which can adjust the composition of training samples according to the test results of the previous training steps. Experiments on fashion image classification shows the superiority of the proposed model compared with several prior methods.

Keywords: Hierarchical classification · Blocking · Feedback incremental learning · Dustbin category

1 Introduction

With the development of deep learning, convolutional neural networks (CNN) [1] have shown superb capabilities for image classification tasks [2–4]. However, CNN wastes the hierarchical relationship between categories, while hierarchical classification (HC) [16,17,22] is an effective method when the categories are organized hierarchically. Over the years, HC has received extensive attention from researchers, and has been successfully used in various domains including computer vision [5], bioinformatics [6] and so on. Generally, HC use a simple-yet-effective top-down level-based strategy to classify images. Unfortunately, it may fails due to the blocking problem.

In the past few years, various approaches have been established to improve the HC performance. The early attempts were mainly working on the probabilities of the base classifiers, taking into account the horizontal or vertical

---

The first author is a student.

Z. Lin et al. (Eds.): PRCV 2019, LNCS 11857, pp. 480–491, 2019.
https://doi.org/10.1007/978-3-030-31654-9_41

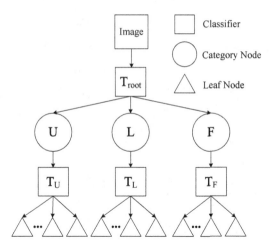

Fig. 1. Illustration of hierarchical classification. Take the first-level and second-level of DeepFashion as an example.

base classifiers' results, and help blocked samples return to the correct category. Greiner et al. proposed the top-down soft-decision approach as a possible solution to overcome blocking [7]. Dumais and Chen proposed the three-level category tree, taking into account the probability values generated by the two-layer classifier as a classification decision [8]. These methods provided the first insight into processing blocking. Follow the hierarchy modification based approaches, where blocking is resolved by changing the original hierarchy, methods such as Restricted Voting method (RVM) [9], Priori Knowledge Based Hierarchical Classification method (PKHC) [10] are proposed. Although many HC methods have been proposed in the past few years, these methods did not focus on capturing the blocked samples, and did not consider the weights of the samples.

In this paper, we present a novel HC model, which contributes to capturing blocked samples and then correcting them. We first add a virtual dustbin category for each middle-layer classifier, as Fig. 2 shows. The dustbin category is trained with samples that randomly selected from subclasses that are not part of the parent category. Our intuition is that, if a sample is assigned to the dustbin category, it means that the sample may not belong to the current parent category (because the dustbin category is trained with sample not belong to the current parent category). At this point, we think the sample may have been blocked. Furthermore, We apply a feedback incremental learning (FIL) strategy to DBHC model, referred to as FIL-DBHC model. The proposed strategy will automatically adjust the composition of training samples according to the test results of the previous training steps and encourage the model to be trained with samples that are easily misclassified.

Experiments results on the challenging fashion dataset demonstrate the superiority of the proposed DBHC model, and the FIL strategy is verified to be able to improve the classification accuracy and accelerate the convergence process.

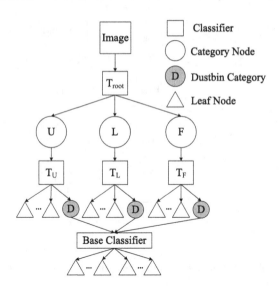

Fig. 2. Illustration of our proposed model. To capture the blocked samples, we add a dustbin category for each middle-layer classifier, which is trained with samples that randomly selected from subclasses that are not belong to the parent category. If the sample is assigned to the dustbin category, it indicates that the sample is blocked, then we will reclassify it.

Compared with several methods in literature, our model is more capable at handling the blocking problem. The main contributions of this study include:

(1) We propose a novel hierarchical classification model that captures blocking by introducing dustbin category into the classifier, effectively reducing blocking errors.
(2) Take into account the weights of samples, we propose a feedback incremental learning strategy which can automatically adjust the composition of training samples according to the previous prediction result. Experiments verify that the proposed method indeed improve the classification accuracy.

2   Related Work

2.1   Hierarchical Classification

The HC methods can be divided into two types: global classification methods and local classification methods. The top-down local hierarchical classification methods only use local hierarchical relationship information. Contrary to local classification, global classification methods learn a single complex model over all the nodes in the hierarchy, but are computationally more expensive. Several hierarchical classification methods have been proposed during the past decades. Koller et al. [11] proposed a conquer and divide method to solve the HC problem. After this, many methods have been developed to improve the HC for large datasets. Liu et al. [12] proposed a SVM based algorithm to improve the classification performance. Xue et al. [13] proposed a method of selecting a small number of nodes from the original hierarchy to construct a simplified classification hierarchy. However, the original HC model not performs well due to blocking. Greiner et al. [7] proposed the top-down soft-decision approach as a possible solution to overcome blocking. Dumais and Chen addressed the problem by introducing the three-level category tree [8]. These methods provided the first insight into processing blocking. In the past few years, Zhu et al. [14] reduced the blocking through a collaborative branch selection scheme. Naik et al. [15] propose a scalable data-driven based rewiring approach to modify the original hierarchy. Although these methods effectively address the blocking problem, they did not focus on capturing the blocked samples, and did not consider the weights of the samples. In this work, we present a novel HC model for blocking reduction problem and on this basis we propose our feedback incremental learning strategy to further improve the classification accuracy and make the convergence faster.

2.2 Fashion Image Classification

Recently, many research efforts have been invested to fashion image classification [18–21]. In particular, the development of deep learning provides more discriminative representation for fashion image classification. For example, Liu et al. [20] proposed FashionNet to learn clothing features by jointly predicting clothing attributes and landmarks. More contributive is that they introduced a large-scale clothes dataset DeepFashion, which contains over 800,000 fashion images. DeepFashion provides labels with a three-level category hierarchy. First level has 3 categories: "upper cloth", "lower cloth", and "full cloth". Second level has 50 categories, respectively belonging to one of three first level categories. Third level has 5620 categories, each category has a first-level label and a second-level label. Although these methods have achieved good recognition performance, they rarely use HC to classify images, even if some of them have realized that there are hierarchies in fashion images. In this work, we use deep learning models to train base classifiers of HC and do experiments on DeepFashion dataset. Our work makes up for the vacancy in using HC to classify fashion images.

3   Method

In this section, we elaborate the proposed models. First, we introduce the notation used in this paper. Then, we describe how dustbin category works. Finally, we introduce the feedback incremental learning strategy.

3.1   Notation

Let c_1, c_2,..., c_n denote the classification path from the root category c_1 to the leaf category c_n and τ_{c_1}, τ_{c_2},..., $\tau_{c_{n-1}}$ denote the corresponding classifier. The

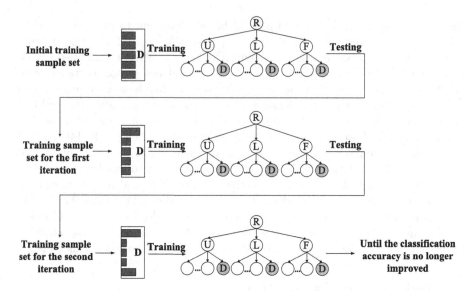

Fig. 3. Illustration of our proposed feedback incremental learning strategy. For each iteration, the composition of the training samples will be adjusted according to the test results of the previous training steps. If the sample is detected as BM, we will increase the importance of the sample. Otherwise, if the sample is detected as BC, we will reduce the importance of the sample. The model will stop training until the classification accuracy is no longer improved.

work domain of τ_{c_i}, denoted by $wd(\tau_{c_i})$, is the set of sub-node categories of τ_{c_i}. When the input image is misclassified by any of the subtree classifier τ_{c_1}, τ_{c_2},..., $\tau_{c_{n-1}}$, we say that the image is blocked.

3.2 Dustbin Category

As mentioned before, hierarchical classification not performed well due to blocking, reducing blocking is an effective way to improve the performance of hierarchical classification. To this end, we present our DBHC model to capture and then correct the blocked samples. Our proposed model add a virtual dustbin category for each middle-layer classifier, which is trained with samples that randomly selected from subclasses that are not belong to the parent class. If the sample is assigned to the node corresponding to the dustbin category, it indicates that the sample may not belong to the current parent category. According to the definition of blocking, the sample is likely to be blocked. In this way, each middle-layer classifier is capable of capturing blocked samples and then correcting them. Moreover, in order to prevent over-fitting, we add a regular term to the loss function

$$L(\lambda) = \frac{\lambda}{2N} \sum_{\omega} \omega^2 \tag{1}$$

where ω represents the weight of the neural network, N represents the number of training samples, $\lambda > 0$ represents the regularization parameter.

3.3   Feedback Incremental Learning

As stated before, the DBHC can effectively captures blocked samples and then correct them. However, during the training phase, DBHC model inevitably uses the samples that have been captured for training, which not only increase the training time, but also weak the generalization ability of the model. Therefore, we intuitively propose a feedback incremental learning (FIL) strategy, as shown in Fig. 3. Our proposed strategy mainly focuses on blocking samples that have not yet been captured. It can adjust composition of the training samples according to the test results of the previous training steps. In this way, the model tend to be trained with samples that are easily misclassified. Before introducing our proposed strategy, we first define two concepts: blocking correction and blocking misjudgment.

Definition 1. *If the sample is misclassified at the first level, but captured at the next level (classified as dustbin category), we call it blocking captured (BC).*

Definition 2. *If the sample is correctly classified at the first level, but misclassified as the dustbin category at the next level, we call it blocking misjudged (BM).*

At the beginning of training, we give each sample the same weight w, then we have

$$p = \frac{w_i}{\sum_{n=1}^{N} w_n} \tag{2}$$

where w represents the weight of the sample and p represents the probability of being selected as the training sample. Additionally, we let $0 < \alpha < 1$ denote the learning rate, which determine the change rate of w.

In the training phase, for each iteration, if the sample is determined as BM, we increase the importance of the sample and update the weight of the sample:

$$w_{new} = w_{old}/\alpha \tag{3}$$

Otherwise, if the sample is determined as blocking correction, we reduce the importance of the sample and let

$$w_{new} = \alpha * w_{old} \tag{4}$$

See Algorithm 1 for specific implementation.

4   Experiment

In this section, we experimentally validate the proposed method on public fashion image classification benchmark DeepFashion [20]. Extensive experiments on DeepFashion dataset demonstrate the superiority of our DBHC model compared with several prior hierarchical classification methods. In addition, the experimental results verify the FIL strategy indeed enhance the classification accuracy and make the convergence process faster.

Algorithm 1. Feedback Incremental Learning Strategy

---

for the classifier τ_c
while training loss has not converged **do**
    (1)Sampling
    let wd$(\tau_c) = \{c_1, c_2, ..., c_n\}$
    denote c_{n+1} as dustbin category
    for i = 1, ..., n **do**
        Draw k samples from the dataset$\{(x_{ij}, y_{ij})\}_{j=1}^{k}$ satisfy $y_{ij} = c_i$ according to probability p_{ij}
    for i = n+1, ..., 2n **do**
        Draw k samples from the $\{(x_{ij}, y_{ij})\}_{j=1}^{k}$ satisfy $y_{ij} \notin wd(\tau_c)$ according to probability p_{ij}
        let $y_{ij} = c_{n+1}$
    (2)Classification Network Optimization
    update θ using SGD

$$\nabla_\theta - \frac{1}{2kn} \sum_{i=1}^{2n} \sum_{j=1}^{k} \sum_{k=1}^{n+1} \mathbb{I}\{y_{ij} = c_k\} \, ln(G_\theta^{(k)}(x_{ij})) + \frac{\lambda}{4kn} \sum_\omega \omega^2$$

    (3)Feedback
    for i = 1, ..., 2n **do**
        for j = 1, ..., k **do**
            if the sample x_{ij} is detected as blocking misjudgment **then**
                $w_{ij} = w_{ij}/\alpha$
            else if the sample x_{ij} is detected as blocking correction **then**
                $w_{ij} = \alpha * w_{ij}$
            $p_{ij} = w_{ij}/\sum_{x=1}^{2n} \sum_{y=1}^{k} w_{xy}$

4.1 Experimental Dataset

The DeepFashion dataset contains over 800,000 diverse fashion images ranging from well-posed shop images to unconstrained consumer photos. Each image in this dataset is labeled with 50 categories. In actual experiments, we only use a subset of the DeepFashion dataset, including 289,222 images. DeepFashion dataset provides labels with a three-level category hierarchy: high-level (has 3 categories), middle-level (has 50 categories), and the low-level (has 5620 categories). In this work, we only consider high-level and middle-layer of DeepFashion dataset.

4.2 Evaluation Metrics

In this paper, we use a variety of metrics to evaluate the models, including accuracy, F1-measure and so on.

Accuracy. Different from the evaluation metric of the flat classification, we take into account hierarchical distance between the true label and predicted label for evaluating the classifier performance. In general, the samples that are closer to the actual class have a lower error rate than samples that are farther from the true class with respect to the hierarchy [23].

$$Accuracy = \frac{\sum_{i=1}^{N} |A(\hat{y}_i) \cap A(y_i)|}{\sum_{i=1}^{N} |A(y_i)|} \tag{5}$$

where $A(\hat{y}_i)$ and $A(y_i)$ are respectively the set of ancestors of the true label and predicted label which include the label itself.

F1-Measure. The Micro-F1 score takes into account the precision and recall of the classification model.

$$F1 = \frac{2PR}{P + R} \tag{6}$$

where P and R are respectively the precision rate and recall rate of the model. Moreover, we take the Macro-F1 score to evaluate the models. The Macro-F1 score calculates the F1 value of each category and then calculate the average.

Blocking Error and Base Classifier Error. Unlike flat classification, there are two types of classification errors in hierarchical classification, the blocking error and base classifier error. Blocking error refers to classification errors made by middle-layer classifiers. Moreover, if the sample has been correctly assigned to the corresponding base classifier but is eventually misclassified, we call it basic classifier error.

4.3 Comparison Methods.

We compare our proposed method with various methods on public fashion image classification benchmark DeepFashion [20] to verify the effectiveness of our proposed methods.

FC: We train the flat classification (FC) model by fine-tuning a well pre-trained CNN on DeepFashion dataset. The accuracy is 68.31% and the Micro-F1 score is 66.39%. It is worth noting that all the base classifiers used in the HC models mentioned in this paper, including our proposed DBHC model, are trained by fine-tuning the pre-trained CNN on DeepFashion dataset.

SHC: We use the original hierarchy structure in Fig. 1 to build the standard hierarchical classification (SHC) model. The accuracy is 66.86% and the Micro-F1 score is 66.18%. Among the error samples, 4,987 are blocking error samples, and 8,000 are base classifier error samples.

PKHC: Follow the model architecture in paper [10], we train our PKHC model on DeepFashion dataset as a baseline. The accuracy is 68.72% and the Micro-F1 score is 66.73%. Among the error samples, 4,469 are blocking error samples, and 7,895 are base classifier error samples.

4.4 Experimental Results

Table 1 shows the original blocking distribution of our DBHC model without introducing dustbin category. We can observe that the blocking phenomenon occurs frequently and the samples are easily misclassified. Tables 2 and 3 are respectively the blocking correction and blocking misjudgment distribution of the DBHC model after introducing dustbin category. We can see from Tables 2 and 3 that the blocking is reduced by introducing dustbin category.

Table 1. The original blocking distribution of the DBHC model

	Upper	Lower	Full
Upper		1732	2434
Lower	3600		898
Full	2390	458	

Table 2. The blocking correction distribution of the DBHC model

	Upper	Lower	Full
Upper		78	382
Lower	1161		168
Full	845	37	

Table 3. The blocking misjudgment distribution of the DBHC model

Upper	Lower	Full
2723	110	82

Table 4 shows the accuracy (%) and F1-Measure (%) of the comparison methods and our proposed DBHC model on the DeepFashion Dataset. From these results, we can observe that our DBHC model achieves an accuracy of 69.44%, which is 1.13% higher than FC. Moreover, in terms of F1-score, DBHC achieves a Micro-F1 score of 67.24%, which is 0.85% higher than FC. However, none of the HC models can exceed FC models on the Macro-F1 metric because the model will inevitably sacrifice the accuracy of certain categories when reducing blocking problem. Nonetheless, the Macro-F1 scores of the proposed methods in this paper are relatively high, which is 0.96% higher than SHC model. In addition, we can see from Table 4 that our FIL-DBHC model achieves an accuracy of 69.46% in 1000 iterations by introducing our feedback incremental learning strategy, which is 0.02% higher than DBHC model with 3000 iterations. Moreover, we can observe that our FIL-DBHC achieves the highest accuracy (69.49%) and Micro-F1 score (67.46%). Through the experimental verification, our FIL strategy indeed enhance the classification accuracy and accelerate the convergence process.

Table 4. Comparison of different methods on the DeepFashion dataset

Method	Top-1 accuracy	Micro-F1	Macro-F1
FC	68.31	66.39	**57.71**
SHC	66.86	66.18	55.36
PKHC	68.72	66.73	55.54
DBHC(iter3000)	69.44	67.24	56.32
FIL-DBHC(iter1000)	69.46	67.42	56.11
FIL-DBHC(iter2000)	**69.49**	**67.46**	56.62
FIL-DBHC(iter3000)	69.47	67.41	56.35

Figure 4 shows the error distributions comparison of different models. The proposed FIL-DBHC achieve the best performance in blocking reduction. Compared with PKHC, FIL-DBHC better balances the two types of errors. It not only achieves the best classification performance, but it also has the lowest impact on other categories. The comparison results indicate that our proposed FIL-DBHC is a comprehensive and excellent model.

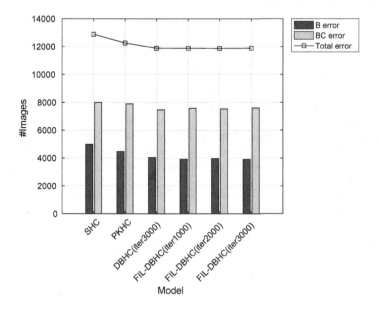

Fig. 4. Error distributions comparison of different models.

5 Conclusion

In this paper, we present a novel DBHC model for fashion image classification. By adding a virtual dustbin category for each middle-layer classifier, the proposed model can capture potential blockages and ultimately achieve better performance in fashion image classification task. Moreover, take into account the weights of samples, we intuitively propose a feedback incremental learning strategy to further improve the classification accuracy and make the convergence faster. Extensive experiments on DeepFashion demonstrate the superiority of our model compared with several prior hierarchical classification methods. Nevertheless, there is still room to improve the hierarchical classification accuracy. In the future, we intend to apply the model to more tasks to verify the robustness of our model.

Acknowledgment. The work is partially supported by the National Key Research and Development Project (No. 213), the National Nature Science Foundation of China (No. 61573259, No. 61673299, No. 61673301, No. 61573255), the Key Lab of Information Network Security, Ministry of Public Security (No. C18608) and Shanghai Health and Family Planning Commission Chinese Medicine and Technology Innovation Project (No. ZYKC201702005).

References

1. Krizhevsky, A., Sutskever, I., Hinton, G.E.: Imagenet classification with deep convolutional neural networks. In: Advances in Neural Information Processing Systems, pp. 1097–1105 (2012)
2. Yang, X., et al.: Co-trained convolutional neural networks for automated detection of prostate cancer in multi-parametric MRI. Med. Image Anal. **42**, 212–227 (2017)
3. He, K., Zhang, X., Ren, S., Sun, J.: Deep residual learning for image recognition. In: Proceedings of the IEEE Conference on Computer Vision and Pattern Recognition, pp. 770–778 (2016)
4. Simonyan, K., Zisserman, A.: Very deep convolutional networks for large-scale image recognition. arXiv preprint arXiv:1409.1556 (2014)
5. Moeslund, T.B., Granum, E.: A survey of computer vision-based human motion capture. Comput. Vis. Image Underst. **81**(3), 231–268 (2001)
6. Bhaskar, H., Hoyle, D.C., Singh, S.: Machine learning in bioinformatics: a brief survey and recommendations for practitioners. Comput. Biol. Med. **36**(10), 1104–1125 (2006)
7. Greiner, R., Grove, A., Schuurmans, D.: On learning hierarchical classifications. In: ResearchIndex; The NECI Scientifc Literature Digital Libraray, Citado em, vol. 32, pp. 34–40 (1997)
8. Dumais, S., Chen, H.: Hierarchical classification of web content. In: Proceedings of the 23rd Annual International ACM SIGIR Conference on Research and Development in Information Retrieval, pp. 256–263. ACM (2000)
9. Sun, A., Lim, E.P., Ng, W.K., Srivastava, J.: Blocking reduction strategies in hierarchical text classification. IEEE Trans. Knowl. Data Eng. **16**(10), 1305–1308 (2004)

10. Wen, L., Duo-Qian, M., Zhi-Hua, W., Wei-Li, W.: Hierarchical text classification model based on blocking priori knowledge. Pattern Recognit. Artif Intell. **23**(4), 456–463 (2010)

11. Koller, D., Sahami, M.: Hierarchically classifying documents using very few words. Technical report, Stanford InfoLab (1997)

12. Liu, T.Y., Yang, Y., Wan, H., Zeng, H.J., Chen, Z., Ma, W.Y.: Support vector machines classification with a very large-scale taxonomy. ACM SIGKDD Explora. Newsl. **7**(1), 36–43 (2005)

13. Xue, G.R., Xing, D., Yang, Q., Yu, Y.: Deep classification in large-scale text hierarchies. In: Proceedings of the 31st Annual International ACM SIGIR Conference on Research and Development in Information Retrieval, pp. 619–626. ACM (2008)

14. Zhu, S., Wei, X.Y., Ngo, C.W.: Collaborative error reduction for hierarchical classification. Comput. Vis. Image Underst. **124**, 79–90 (2014)

15. Naik, A., Rangwala, H.: Improving large-scale hierarchical classification by rewiring: a data-driven filter based approach. J. Intell. Inf. Syst. **52**(1), 141–164 (2019)

16. Naik, A., Rangwala, H.: Filter based taxonomy modification for improving hierarchical classification. arXiv preprint arXiv:1603.00772 (2016)

17. Nooka, S.P., Chennupati, S., Veerabhadra, K., Sah, S., Ptucha, R.: Adaptive hierarchical classification networks. In: 2016 23rd International Conference on Pattern Recognition (ICPR), pp. 3578–3583. IEEE (2016)

18. Wang, X., Zhang, T.: Clothes search in consumer photos via color matching and attribute learning. In: Proceedings of the 19th ACM international conference on Multimedia, pp. 1353–1356. ACM (2011)

19. Fu, J., Wang, J., Li, Z., Xu, M., Lu, H.: Efficient clothing retrieval with semantic-preserving visual phrases. In: Lee, K.M., Matsushita, Y., Rehg, J.M., Hu, Z. (eds.) ACCV 2012. LNCS, vol. 7725, pp. 420–431. Springer, Heidelberg (2013). https://doi.org/10.1007/978-3-642-37444-9_33

20. Liu, Z., Luo, P., Qiu, S., Wang, X., Tang, X.: DeepFashion: powering robust clothes recognition and retrieval with rich annotations. In: Proceedings of the IEEE Conference on Computer Vision and Pattern Recognition, pp. 1096–1104 (2016)

21. Di, W., Wah, C., Bhardwaj, A., Piramuthu, R., Sundaresan, N.: Style finder: fine-grained clothing style detection and retrieval. In: Proceedings of the IEEE Conference on Computer Vision and Pattern Recognition Workshops, pp. 8–13 (2013)

22. Ke, S.W., Lin, W.C., Tsai, C.F., Hu, Y.H.: Soft estimation by hierarchical classification and regression. Neurocomputing **234**, 27–37 (2017)

23. Naik, A., Rangwala, H.: Inconsistent node flattening for improving top-down hierarchical classification. In: 2016 IEEE International Conference on Data Science and Advanced Analytics (DSAA), pp. 379–388. IEEE (2016)

Spatial-temporal Fusion Network with Residual Learning and Attention Mechanism: A Benchmark for Video-Based Group Re-ID

Qiling Xu, Hua Yang[(✉)], and Lin Chen

Institution of Image Communication and Network Engineering,
Shanghai Jiao Tong University, Shanghai, China
{xuqiling0906,hyang,SJChenLin}@sjtu.edu.cn

Abstract. Video-based group re-identification (Re-ID) remains to be a meaningful task under rare study. Group Re-ID contains the information of the relationship between pedestrians, while the video sequences provide more frames to identify the person. In this paper, we propose a spatial-temporal fusion network for the group Re-ID. The network composes of the residual learning played between the CNN and the RNN in a unified network, and the attention mechanism which makes the system focus on the discriminative features. We also propose a new group Re-ID dataset DukeGroupVid to evaluate the performance of our spatial-temporal fusion network. Comprehensive experimental results on the proposed dataset and other video-based datasets, PRID-2011, i-LIDS-VID and MARS, demonstrate the effectiveness of our model.

Keywords: Residual learning · Spatial-temporal Attention · Group Re-ID · Video-based

1 Introduction

Group re-identification (Re-ID) is a significant but relatively less studied task in video surveillance systems [1,2]. Given a group sequence in one camera, the task of group Re-ID is to find matching sequences of the same group with the same people under different cameras. At present, the methods of group Re-ID are mainly image-based. The video-based group Re-ID task is rarely studied and remains to be promising and unsolved.

Group Re-ID has many connections with person Re-ID, making group Re-ID not a completely independent task. The group contains a plurality of pedestrian individuals whose movement direction and speed are basically the same, meaning that the group Re-ID solves the task of the Re-ID from a holistic perspective. Group Re-ID also includes challenges such as illumination, variations across

---

The first author is a student.

Z. Lin et al. (Eds.): PRCV 2019, LNCS 11857, pp. 492–504, 2019.
https://doi.org/10.1007/978-3-030-31654-9_42

different viewpoints, scale changes and occlusion that exist under person Re-ID. Recent works about person Re-ID widely utilize the convolutional neural networks (CNN) to extract the spatial information of the pedestrians [3–6] and adopt the recurrent neural networks (RNN or LSTM) to extract reliable temporal features for person Re-ID [7,8].

In addition to the commonality, there are many differences between the group Re-ID and the person Re-ID. Group Re-ID has more challenges than person Re-ID, including self-occlusion in groups, misalignment between group videos, changes in relative positions between pedestrians in groups, and interference caused by other pedestrians which make group Re-ID remain to be a challenging issue.

Since there are little researches for the video-based group Re-ID task, the traditional video-based person Re-ID methods are potentially helpful for video-based group Re-ID task. The works of [9,10] utilize the deep recurrent network (RNN) to extract the temporal information for the person sequences, achieving considerable improvements of performance. The work of [5] utilizes attention model to pay emphasis on the more important area and frames to make the learned features by the RNN more effective. These network architectures independently utilize the CNN or RNN layer, making the output features lack comprehensiveness. Since RNN cannot completely integrate all long-term information of all the sequence frames, the spatial and temporal features should be effectively fused for performance improvement. The work of [11] proposes a residual learning framework to make the deep layers indirectly better fit a desired optimal mapping by learning the residual, the residual learning can be helpful in the adaptive fusion of the spatial and temporal features for group Re-ID task.

In this paper, we propose a spatial-temporal fusion network with the residual learning mechanism which composes of the element-wise addition between the CNN and the recurrent layer in a unified network. The spatial features learned by the CNN are sent to the recurrent neural networks (RNN [12] or LSTM) for the temporal features learning. The element-wise addition is done between the extracted temporal and spatial features to obtain more discriminative fusion features which can improve the video-based group Re-ID.

Furthermore, we incorporate the spatial-temporal attention mechanism in the model to extract more discriminative group features. For spatial features, we use both position attention and channel attention for feature representation. For the temporal features, we utilize the temporal attention to integrate sequence information. In this paper, after the spatial-temporal attention is integrated into the model, the results have been greatly improved.

To demonstrate the effectiveness of our proposed method, we deploy our spatial-temporal fusion network on multiple datasets. We create a new dataset called DukeGroupVid based on DUKEMTMC [13] dataset. To the best of our knowledge, the proposed DukeGroupVid is the first video-based group Re-ID dataset that can be used for deep learning training, containing varied challenges such as misalignment and self-occlusion within the group. DukeGroupVid consists of 371 different groups and 890 tracklets with 8 cameras in the dataset.

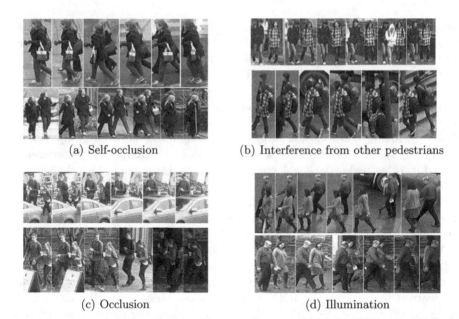

(a) Self-occlusion   (b) Interference from other pedestrians

(c) Occlusion   (d) Illumination

Fig. 1. Samples of DukeGroupVid datasets. The dataset contains different kinds of challenges, such as illumination, occlusion and interference from other pedestrians.

Tracklets contain 12 to 6444 frames, while most of IDs are captured by 2 to 4 cameras. This dataset remains challenging and necessary to evaluate the performance of the video-based group Re-ID methods. Samples of DukeGroupVid dataset with multiple challenges is shown in Fig. 1.

In conclusion, the main contribution of this paper is of three points:

– We propose a spatial-temporal fusion network for the video-based group Re-ID. Instead of only utilizing CNN or recurrent layer to extract features, We introduce the residual learning played between the RNN and CNN in a unified network for performance improvement.
– We propose multiple attention mechanism in the residual learning model to make the network emphasize more on important parts and frames, making our network learning characteristics more effective.
– A new dataset called DukeGroupVid based on DUKEMTMC [13] dataset is created. Comprehensive experimental results are conducted on the proposed dataset and other wildly utilized datasets, demonstrating the effectiveness of our model.

2   Proposed Method

The key point of our spatial-temporal fusion network is to learn and fuse both the spatial and temporal features of the certain group. We learn the spatial and temporal information respectively and incorporate the CNN and RNN/LSTM in a unified network. The residual learning is carried out by element-wise addition between the spatial and temporal features to obtain more discriminative fusion features that is able to improve the video-based group Re-ID. We have considered a variety of attention mechanisms and fuse spatial-temporal attention mechanism to the network which enables the network to extract more resolving sequence features under a multi-attention mechanism. In conclusion, we deploy our residual learning with spatial-temporal attention mechanism and propose improved spatial-temporal fusion network with performance improvements on the video-based group Re-ID task.

2.1   Model Structure

For video-based group Re-ID task, the spatial features extracted by the convolutional neural network (CNN) typically consider spatial characteristics and cannot integrate time domain information. At the same time, although the recurrent neural network (RNN) can accept a wide range of sequence inputs, it cannot fully integrate all the sequence information of the frame. [9,10] adopted the temporal pooling after recurrent layers to do an average within the output of the whole person sequences, which can not commendably solve this problem.

In this paper, we propose a spatial-temporal fusion network with the residual learning mechanism which composes of the element-wise addition between the CNN and the recurrent layer in a unified network. At the same time, we propose multiple attention mechanism in the residual learning model to make the network emphasize more on important parts and frames, making our network learning characteristics more effective. Our spatial-temporal fusion network is shown in Fig. 2.

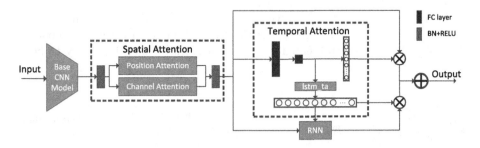

Fig. 2. The illustration of our proposed spatial-temporal fusion network based on residual learning and spatial-temporal attention. The spatial-temporal fusion network consists of four main parts: Base CNN Model, spatial attention mechanism, temporal attention mechanism and residual learning of spatial-temporal features.

The spatial-temporal fusion network consists of four main parts. As shown in Fig. 2, the first part is the Base CNN Model. The network architectures with residual learning mechanism and spatial-temporal attention is based on the original CNN model such as ResNet [11] and Densenet [14]. The second part is spatial attention mechanism. Considering the challenges like self-occlusion and interference from others outside the group, features extracted from the group sequence should concentrate more on the important parts and pedestrians of the frames. The model should be robust, reducing interference caused by backgrounds or other pedestrians. The third part is temporal attention mechanism. Video sequences containing multiple frames provides more information and also need to be better selected for effective information with resolution. There are often challenges with image misalignment, illumination changes inside the sequences. The time domain attention mechanism can help find more valuable frames and assign higher weights to these frames, thus enabling efficient use of these discriminative information. The last part is residual learning. Since the RNN model cannot fully integrate all the sequence information of the frame., and the spatial pooling can only bring very limit improvement, we propose a residual learning method and propose a new model that can extract the spatial-temporal fusion features which addresses the limitations of models such as RNN and time domain pooling. We deploy our adaptive spatial-temporal feature extraction mechanism to make the temporal features extracted by RNN in tune with the spatial features extracted by the original CNN, and apply attention mechanism to make the network more discriminative.

2.2 Residual Learning Mechanism

The performance of temporal features extracted by the recurrent layer is inferior, even lower than the image-based model [15]. To solve this problem, in this paper, we propose a spatial-temporal fusion network that combines residual learning mechanism with spatial-temporal features to enhance video-based Re-ID. The model structure is illustrated in Fig. 3.

Residual learning [11] is to solve the problem of degradation. Optimizing the residual map is easier than optimizing the original unreferenced map. Therefore, the residual learning represented by the recursive layer has the ability to help

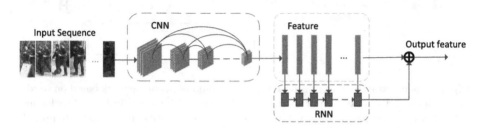

Fig. 3. An illustration of Residual Learning between RNN and CNN. Residual learning mechanism composes of the element-wise addition between the CNN and the recurrent layer in a unified network.

the two-dimensional CNN to be further optimized, and can make the learned features more discriminating.

Specifically, given an input sequence $s = (s^0, s^1, ..., s^{T-1})$, T is the sequence length, s^t denotes the person image at time t. The feature vectors obtained after the CNN are abbreviated as

$$f^{(t)} = C(s^{(t)}) \tag{1}$$

where the C function refers to the simplification of the feature extraction procedure by the CNN layers (such as ResNet [11] and DenseNet [14]). After synthesizing the features extracted from CNN, there is an RNN layers in the network to receive the output feature vectors from the CNN layers for accumulating features from anterior images within the video sequence. The input of the recurrent layer is the feature vectors $f^{(t)}$ obtained after the CNN. The recurrent layer learns long-term dependencies and remembers information for long periods of time within person sequence, which can be denoted in the following formula:

$$o^{(t)} = W_i f^{(t)} + W_s r^{(t-1)} \tag{2}$$

$$r^{(t)} = Tanh(o^{(t)}) \tag{3}$$

where $r^{(t)}$ remembers information at the previous time-step and $o^{(t)}$ produces an output based on both the current input and information from the previous time-steps. The $o^{(t)}$ and the $f^{(t)}$ both go through a linear combination to produce a feature vector with a dimension N. Then $o^{(t)}$ is connected to a temporal pooling layer, to produce a single feature vector which accumulates the appearance information of sequences to gain the periodic characteristics of certain person image sequence, which can be denoted as

$$x_R = \frac{1}{T} \sum_{t=1}^{T} o^{(t)} \tag{4}$$

where x_R is the temporal feature we need. In our case, to make the element-wise addition in the residual learning adaptive and concordant, the feature vectors $f^{(t)}$ from the CNN is also connected to a temporal pooling layer to produce a single feature vector representing the information averaged over the whole input sequence of the certain person, i.e. averaged spatial features, denoted by following formula:

$$x_C = \frac{1}{T} \sum_{t=1}^{T} f^{(t)} \tag{5}$$

where the x_C refers to the spatial features extracted by the CNN layer in the improved network. Furthermore, compared to the prior work by [12], which utilizes the one-stream network to process the image sequence from different camera views, where the spatial features from CNN is sent to the RNN for corresponding temporal feature extraction. We further improve the network by two-stream separated CNN and RNN layer to respectively extract the spatial and temporal features for more adaptive spatial-temporal fusion, bridging the gap between different camera view variations. The fusion operation is formulated as:

$$x_F = x_C + x_R \tag{6}$$

where the "+" denotes the element-wise addition in the cascade residual learning.

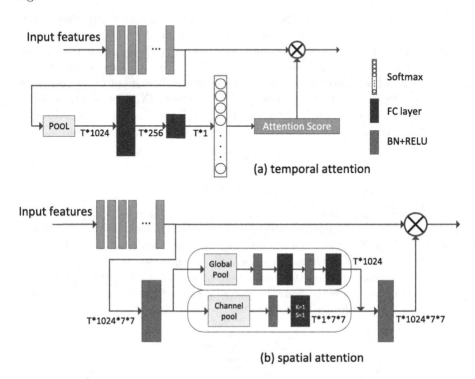

Fig. 4. The illustration of temporal attention and spatial attention mechanism used in our proposed spatial-temporal fusion network. Attention mechanism is used to make the feature extraction model focus more on resolving features.

2.3 Improved Spatial-temporal Attention Mechanism

In this section, we further optimize the network structure with the spatial-temporal attention mechanism which is adopted to replace the temporal pooling in the previous model. Since the pooling operation is to average the features of all frames in the sequence features, there is no higher focus on the more important frames. The operation of temporal pooling is relatively simple, but it is important to assign different weights to the characteristics of different frames.

Sequence features based on the temporal attention mechanism can be calculated as,

$$f_{ta}^{(t)} = \frac{1}{T} \sum_{t=1}^{T} attn_t^{(t)} f^{(t)} \tag{7}$$

where $attn_t^{(t)}$ is the attention weight of frame t of the sequence features. The temporal attention network takes the image-level sequence features [T,1024,w,h] (take DenseNet121 [14] for example) as inputs, and attention scores of length T. Temporal attention network is shown in Fig. 4. We apply a convolution layer with hidden dim of d_t and a Fully-Connected (FC) layer output dim of 1. The output of the convolution layer is the scalar vector score $s^{(t)}$. The attention score for the frame t of sequence can be calculated as,

$$attn_t^{(t)} = \frac{e^{s^{(t)}}}{\sum_{t=1}^{T} e^{s^{(t)}}} \tag{8}$$

Besides temporal attention, we apply the multi-spatial-attention mechanism to applied to extract more discriminative spatial features. For the channel attention part, we first perform a squeeze operation [16] with a global average pooling layer and get the shrinking feature f_c. This operation turn each 2D feature map into a real number f_c which is calculated by

$$f_c = \frac{1}{h \times w} \sum_{i=1}^{w} \sum_{j=1}^{h} \mathbf{X}_{1:h,1:w,c} \tag{9}$$

The dimensions of the squeeze operation output are the same as the number of input feature channels. The second operation is excitation and a bottleneck structure is used to get channel attention. Two FC layers are leveraged to form a bottleneck structure to model the correlation between channels. For the position attention, the first operation is cross-channel pooling before learning the position attention map. The position attention is modeled by a convolution layer of 1 × 1 filter with stride 1. Spatial attention network is shown in Fig. 4.

3   Experiment and Results

3.1   Proposed Dataset

A new dataset called DukeGroupVid based on DUKEMTMC [13] dataset is created. This dataset, which is the first known video-based group Re-ID dataset that can be used for deep learning training, contains different kinds of challenges such as misalignment and self-occlusion within the group. As an extension of the DUKEMTMC dataset [13], it consists of 371 different groups and 890 tracklets. There are totally 8 cameras in the dataset. Tracklets contain 12 to 6444 frames, while most IDs are captured by 2 to 4 cameras. This dataset remains challenging and necessary to evaluate the performance of the proposed video-based group Re-ID methods.

3.2   Evaluation Metrics

In order to test the performance of our method, following the common person Re-ID researches, we use the cumulative matching characteristic (CMC) to measure the performance of our spatial-temporal fusion network. We show the Rank1, Rank5 and Rank20 results in Table 1 and compare them with other methods. We also adopt mean averaged precision (mAP) as the other metric. Averaged precision (AP) is computed for each target person image based on the precision-recall curve. Therefore, mAP is the average of AP across all target tracklets.

3.3   Results

We make comparisons of our spatial-temporal fusion network with some baseline networks. To better illustrate the effectiveness of the spatial and temporal features in the networks after our residual learning mechanism, we deploy the model to separably extract different features by CNN and RNN and attention model for comparing the performance. RNN is known to have the problem of gradient vanishing, which makes it have better integration for adjacent frames but cannot completely integrate the periodic information from all sequence frames, especially the earlier image frames. In this section, we further compare the performance between different kinds of CNN to compare their respective effectiveness in different deep networks.

Table 1. Comparisons of our spatial-temporal fusion network with some baseline networks.

Method	Rank-1	Rank5	Rank-20	mAP
RRU [19]	54.2%	72.9%	79.9%	54.3%
RNN	60.4%	83.3%	92.4%	64.1%
CNN + Temporal Pooling (ResNet50)	72.9%	91.7%	95.8%	77.4%
CNN + Temporal Attention (ResNet50)	76.4%	89.6%	94.4%	76.7%
Residual Learning + Temporal Pooling (ResNet50)	76.4%	92.4%	97.9%	78.2%
Residual Learning + Spatial-temporal Attention (ResNet50)	81.9%	94.4%	98.6%	82.3%
Residual Learning + Spatial-temporal Attention (DenseNet121)	**82.6%**	**97.9%**	**98.6%**	**85.6%**

Group Re-ID has some similarities with person Re-ID with more challenges than person Re-ID, such as misalignment of frames and more background information. Therefore, applying the method of person Re-ID to the group's task directly does not yield satisfactory results [19].

The performance of combining CNN and RNN is better than that only from CNN or RNN. The residual learning framework is to address the degradation problem to make the deep layers indirectly better fit a desired optimal mapping. The results demonstrate the effectiveness of our spatial-temporal fusion network with residual learning and attention mechanism that adding the information

extracted by the CNN to the RNN can make up for the lost information from
the RNN layer.

4   Discussion

4.1   Analysis of Different Layers

Table 2 shows the performance of different attention model with our proposed
residual learning network. The spatial-temporal attention mechanism provides
additional benefits for further extraction of discriminant features. We conduct
a comparative experiment of spatial attention and temporal attention. It can
be seen from the experimental results that both spatial attention and temporal
attention can improve the experimental results. These results on the dataset
demonstrate the validity of our spatial-temporal attention mechanism for spatial-
temporal fusion network of video-based group Re-ID task.

Table 2. Component analysis of different kinds of attention mechanism on residual
learning network. The base CNN model is ResNet50 and our spatial-temporal fusion
network performs the best.

Method	Rank-1	Rank-5	Rank-20	mAP
Residual Learning + Temporal Pooling	76.4%	92.4%	97.9%	78.2%
Residual Learning + Spatial Attention	77.1%	94.4%	97.9%	79.8%
Residual Learning + Temporal Attention	79.2%	91.7%	97.9%	78.6%
Residual Learning + Spatial-temporal Attention	**81.9%**	**94.4%**	**98.6%**	**82.3%**

4.2   Experiments on Video-Based Person Re-ID Datasets

In addition to verification our spatial-temporal fusion network on the group Re-
ID dataset, we validate our method on the video-based person Re-ID datasets.
Our network can not only apply to group Re-ID task, and can also perform well
in person Re-ID task. The results comparison with the state-of-the art methods
can prove the effectiveness of our method on video-based person Re-ID task.

Video-Based Person Re-ID Dataset. In this paper, we adopt three typical
datasets widely used on the problem of video-based person Re-ID to evaluate
the performance of our method on person Re-ID task.

PRID-2011: The PRID 2011 [17] dataset contains two camera views, but only
200 people from the two camera views are adjacent. There is 400 image sequence
pair on the dataset. Each image sequence has a variable length from 5 to 675.

i-LIDS-VID: The iLIDS-VID dataset [18] is captured on two camera views.
Each camera view contains coincident 300 people and each image sequence has
a variable length from 23 to 192 Due to clothing similarities among people,

lighting and viewpoint variations across camera views, cluttered background and occlusions, this dataset is much more challenging than the PRID-2011 dataset.

MARS: The MARS dataset [6] consists of 1261 different identities and 20715 tracklets. A large number of tracklets contain 25 to 50 frames, while most IDs are captured by 2 to 4 cameras and have 5 to 20 tracklets.

Table 3. Comparisons of our Spatial-temporal Fusion Network and the state-of-the-art methods on Video-based Person Re-ID Datasets. The top 1 and 2 results are in bold and italic.

Dataset	PRID-2011 [17]		i-LIDS-VID [18]		MARS [6]		
Method	R1	R5	R1	R5	R1	R5	mAP
Baseline [10]	70%	90%	58%	84%	–	–	–
RCN [9]	69.0%	88.4%	46.1%	76.8%	–	–	–
DRSTA [21]	**93.2%**	–	80.2%	–	82.3%	–	65.8%
RRU [19]	*92.7%*	**98.8%**	*84.3%*	*96.8%*	**84.4%**	*93.2%*	*72.7%*
RQEN [20]	92.4%	**98.8%**	76.1%	92.9%	73.7%	84.9%	51.7%
Ours	92.1%	*97.8%*	**85.3%**	**98.0%**	*82.5%*	**93.7%**	**73.3%**

Experiment Results. We adopt DenseNet121 [14] as our CNN-based architecture to extract high-level features and compare the results between multiple structures as shown in Table 3.

Comprehensive experimental results conducted on the three representative datasets, PRID-2011, i-LIDS-VID and MARS, show that the improved network after our approach performs favorably than the existing state-of-the-art methods, demonstrating the effectiveness of the proposed network.

5   Conclusion

In this paper, we propose a spatial-temporal fusion network for adaptive spatial-temporal feature extraction, incorporating the convolution neural network (CNN) and the recurrent neural network (RNN/LSTM) to jointly exploit the spatial and temporal information for improving the video-based group Re-ID. We propose to make the feature extraction model of the recurrent layers in tune with the CNN layers for constructing an adaptive element-wise addition in the residual learning mechanism. We incorporate the spatial-temporal attention mechanism in the model to extract discriminative features better and explore the proposed network on different deep state-of-the-art networks to obtain improved spatial-temporal fusion networks for better performance improvements.

To demonstrate the effectiveness of our proposed method, we propose a new dataset DukeGroupVid to validate our network. Further comparisons are also made to show the respective significance of CNN and recurrent layer in different kinds of networks. Besides, comprehensive experimental results conducted on the three representative datasets, PRID-2011, i-LIDS-VID and MARS, show that the improved network after our approach performs favorably than the existing state-of-the-art methods. The results demonstrate the effectiveness of the proposed spatial-temporal fusion network.

Acknowledgement. This work was supported in part by National Natural Science Foundation of China (NSFC, Grant No. 61771303 and 61671289), Science and Technology Commission of Shanghai Municipality (STCSM, Grant Nos. 17DZ1205602, 18DZ1200-102, 18DZ2270700), and SJTUYitu/Thinkforce Joint laboratory for visual computing and application. Funded by National Engineering Laboratory for Public Safety Risk Perception and Control by Big Data (PSRPC).

References

1. Xiao, H., et al.: Group re-identification: leveraging and integrating multi-grain information. In: 2018 ACM Multimedia Conference on Multimedia Conference, ACM (2018

2. Lisanti, G., et al.: Group re-identification via unsupervised transfer of sparse features encoding. In: Proceedings of the IEEE International Conference on Computer Vision (2017)

3. Li, W., Zhu, X., Gong, S.: Harmonious attention network for person re-identification. In: Proceedings of the IEEE Conference on Computer Vision and Pattern Recognition (2018)

4. Sun, Y., Zheng, L., Yang, Y., Tian, Q., Wang, S.: Beyond part models: person retrieval with refined part pooling (and a strong convolutional baseline). In: Ferrari, V., Hebert, M., Sminchisescu, C., Weiss, Y. (eds.) ECCV 2018. LNCS, vol. 11208, pp. 501–518. Springer, Cham (2018). https://doi.org/10.1007/978-3-030-01225-0_30

5. Xu, S., et al.: Jointly attentive spatial-temporal pooling networks for video-based person re-identification. In: Proceedings of the IEEE International Conference on Computer Vision (2017)

6. Zheng, L., et al.: MARS: a video benchmark for large-scale person re-identification. In: Leibe, B., Matas, J., Sebe, N., Welling, M. (eds.) ECCV 2016. LNCS, vol. 9910, pp. 868–884. Springer, Cham (2016). https://doi.org/10.1007/978-3-319-46466-4_52

7. Yan, Y., Ni, B., Song, Z., Ma, C., Yan, Y., Yang, X.: Person re-identification via recurrent feature aggregation. In: Leibe, B., Matas, J., Sebe, N., Welling, M. (eds.) ECCV 2016. LNCS, vol. 9910, pp. 701–716. Springer, Cham (2016). https://doi.org/10.1007/978-3-319-46466-4_42

8. Su, C., Zhang, S., Xing, J., Gao, W., Tian, Q.: Deep attributes driven multi-camera person re-identification. In: Leibe, B., Matas, J., Sebe, N., Welling, M. (eds.) ECCV 2016. LNCS, vol. 9906, pp. 475–491. Springer, Cham (2016). https://doi.org/10.1007/978-3-319-46475-6_30

9. Wu, L., Shen, C., van den Hengel, A.: Deep recurrent convolutional networks for video-based person re-identification: an end-to-end approach. arXiv preprint arXiv:1606.01609 (2016)

10. McLaughlin, N., del Rincon, J.M., Miller, P.: Recurrent convolutional network for video-based person re-identification. In: Proceedings of the IEEE Conference on Computer Vision and Pattern Recognition (2016)

11. He, K., et al.: Deep residual learning for image recognition. In: Proceedings of the IEEE Conference on Computer Vision and Pattern Recognition (2016)

12. Chen, L., et al.: Deep spatial-temporal fusion network for video-based person re-identification. In: Proceedings of the IEEE Conference on Computer Vision and Pattern Recognition Workshops (2017)

13. Ristani, E., Solera, F., Zou, R., Cucchiara, R., Tomasi, C.: Performance measures and a data set for multi-target, multi-camera tracking. In: Hua, G., Jégou, H. (eds.) ECCV 2016. LNCS, vol. 9914, pp. 17–35. Springer, Cham (2016). https://doi.org/10.1007/978-3-319-48881-3_2

14. Huang, G., et al.: Densely connected convolutional networks. In: Proceedings of the IEEE Conference on Computer Vision and Pattern Recognition (2017)

15. Gao, J., Nevatia, R.: Revisiting temporal modeling for video-based person ReID. arXiv preprint arXiv:1805.02104 (2018)

16. Hu, J., Shen, L., Sun, G.: Squeeze-and-excitation networks. In: Proceedings of the IEEE Conference on Computer Vision and Pattern Recognition (2018)

17. Hirzer, M., Beleznai, C., Roth, P.M., Bischof, H.: Person re-identification by descriptive and discriminative classification. In: Heyden, A., Kahl, F. (eds.) SCIA 2011. LNCS, vol. 6688, pp. 91–102. Springer, Heidelberg (2011). https://doi.org/10.1007/978-3-642-21227-7_9

18. Wei-Shi, Z., Shaogang, G., Tao, X.: Associating groups of people. In: Proceedings of the British Machine Vision Conference (2009)

19. Liu, Y., et al.: Spatial and temporal mutual promotion for video-based person re-identification. arXiv preprint arXiv:1812.10305 (2018)

20. Song, G., et al.: Region-based quality estimation network for large-scale person re-identification. In: Thirty-Second AAAI Conference on Artificial Intelligence (2018)

21. Li, S., et al.: Diversity regularized spatiotemporal attention for video-based person re-identification. In: Proceedings of the IEEE Conference on Computer Vision and Pattern Recognition (2018)

Architectural Style Classification Based on DNN Model

Peipei Zhao[1,2], Qiguang Miao[1,2(✉)], Ruyi Liu[1], and Jianfeng Song[1,2]

[1] Xidian University, Xian, Shaanxi, China
qgmiao@126.com
[2] Xi'an Key Laboratory of Big Data and Intelligent Vision, Xi'an, China

Abstract. Deep neural networks (DNN) have been widely used for image classification. One major hurdle of deep learning approaches is that large sets of labeled data are necessary, which can be prohibitively costly to obtain, particularly in architectural style classification. Data augmentation can alleviate this labeling effort. In this paper, we use data augmentation to increase the number of architectural style datasets. To extract building elements, the inputs are preprocessed by Deformable Part Model (DPM) first, and then the preprocessed images are sent to the data augmentation to increase the number of images. Next, we design a deep neural network based on GoogLeNet. The proposed network aims to learn robust feature embeddings to improve architectural style classification performance. Finally, architectural style can be classified by the robust feature embeddings. Experimental results show that our approach achieves promising performance and is superior to previous methods.

Keywords: Deep neural networks · Architectural style classification · Deformable Part Model · Data augmentation · GoogLeNet

1 Introduction

Buildings can be classified according to architectural style which can reflect a set of unique and distinguishing features.[1] Architectural style is a form of regional cultural representation in which it is influenced by the era of political, social, economic, materials of building and techniques of construction. There are also complicated relationships between different architectural styles.

Although numerous architectural style classification methods have been proposed, there are still great challenges. Firstly, to cope with the lack of publicly available datasets, [1] releases a new large-scale architectural style dataset containing twenty-five classes. Table 1 shows the number of images in 25-classes architectural styles. However, the number of images in each style varies from 60 to 300, which is still small compared to datasets such as ImageNet [2] and COCO [3]. Secondly, as shows in Fig. 1, in addition to buildings, there are non-building elements such as sky, lawn, roads and trees. These elements may disturb the classification since they are

---

[1] The first author is a student.

© Springer Nature Switzerland AG 2019
Z. Lin et al. (Eds.): PRCV 2019, LNCS 11857, pp. 505–516, 2019.
https://doi.org/10.1007/978-3-030-31654-9_43

uncorrelated with architectural style. Furthermore, with the booming of deep learning, Convolutional Neural Networks (CNN) are used for many classification problems, and achieve pleasing results compared with those traditional methods. However, due to the limited number of samples, CNN has not been used for architectural style classification.

In this paper, we propose an architectural style classification method based on data augmentation, which can increase the number of images. First of all, we use Deformable Part Model (DPM) [4] to extract building elements and remove building-irrelevant elements. The building elements are generated to help with avoiding the adverse impact of backgrounds on architectural style images. After the de-background process, in order to over-fitting, the data augmentation is used for increasing the number of samples. Next the features of RGB is extracted by our deep neural networks (DNN) based on GoogLeNet [5–8], a convolutional network model that builds high-level features from the low-level ones and the details which are not related with the target can be ignored. The final result is obtained with a softmax classifier. The flowchart of our method is depicted in Fig. 2. This paper benefits mainly from three contributions as summarized below:

- The de-background process with DPM models. Since there are many building-irrelevant features, like the background in the RGB images, the DPM models are employed to help with eliminating them, which focuses on the building elements. The de-background process helps to filter the background in RGB images out and boost the classification accuracy.
- Method for preventing over-fitting with data augmentation. As illustrated in Table 1, the number of images in each style varies from 60 to 300, and altogether the dataset contains approximately 5, 000 images. However, training a DNN requires a large amount of dataset. Obviously, the dataset in Table 1 is not enough. In order to increase the number of architectural style dataset, we choose data augmentation.
- The deep neural network based on GoogLeNet. Given the "data-hungry" nature of DNN and the difficulty of collecting large-scale architectural style dataset, the applicability of DNN to tasks with limited amount of training data appears as an important problem. To address this problem, we propose to transfer image representations learned with DNN on large datasets to architectural style classification tasks with limited training data. We design a method that uses ImageNet-trained layers of GoogLeNet to extract efficient high-level image representation for images in architectural style. We analyze the transfer performance and show promising results for architectural style classification.

The rest of this paper is organized as follows. In Sect. 2, the research on architectural style classification is reviewed briefly. Following, the details of the implementation of our proposed architectural style classification method is described in Sect. 3. After that in Sect. 4, experiments on our technique and other available methods are illustrated and compared to demonstrate the effectiveness of our strategies. Finally, in the last section, our approach is concluded and the work for future is given.

Table 1. Details of architectural style dataset

Classes	Sample size	Classes	Sample size	Classes	Sample size
Achaemenid	69	Byzantine	111	Novelty	212
American Foursquare	59	Chicago school	153	Palladian	113
American craftsman	195	Colonial	177	Postmodern	163
Ancient Egypt	256	Deconstructivism	213	Queen Anne	425
Art Deco	366	Edwardian	79	Romanesque	107
Art Nouveau	450	Georgian	154	Russian Revival	160
Baroque	239	Gothic	109	Tudor Revival	162
Bauhaus	92	Greek Revial	327		
Beaux-Arts	191	International style	207		

Fig. 1. Some examples of the architectural style dataset. There are building elements and no-building elements.

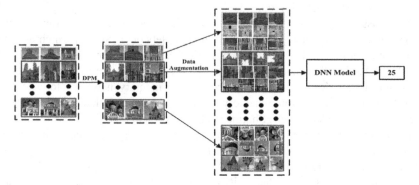

Fig. 2. Some examples of the architectural style dataset. There are building elements and no-building elements. The pipeline of our approach. First the input images are extracted locally remarkable building elements by DPM. Then data augmentation is used for increasing the number of images. Then the processed images are sent to our DNN model for feature extracting. Subsequently the features are classified via softmax classifier.

2 Related Work

Recent research in Architectural style classification has obtained some success. Providing efficient solutions to architectural style classification have a major focus on extracting elements or patterns [1, 4, 9–13]. Berg [9] addressed image parsing in the setting of architectural scenes by the generic recognition results boot-strap an image specific model. Chu [10] devised a representation to describe configurations of repetitive elements. By modeling spatial configurations, visual patterns were more discriminative than local features, and were able to tackle with object scaling, rotation, and deformation. Doersch [11] proposed to use a discriminative clustering approach able to take into account the weak geographic supervision. This method addressed a tremendously difficult task as the visual features distinguishing architectural elements of different places can be very subtle. Goel [12] explored, beyond the idea of buildings as instances, the possibility that buildings can be categorized based on the architectural style. Certain characteristic features distinguish an architectural style from others. Philbin [13] compared different scalable methods for building a vocabulary and introduced a novel quantization method based on randomized trees. This method addressed a major time and performance bottleneck. Xu [1] proposed a method that is based on Deformable Part-based Models (DPM) [4] and Multinomial Latent Logistic Regression (MLLR). DPM could capture morphological characteristics of basic architectural components. MLLR introduced the probabilistic analysis and tackled the multi-class problem in latent variable models.

With the development of deep learning and powerful hardwares like GPU, the Deep Neural Network (DNN) has made a great breakthrough on many computer vision tasks. DNN can build high-level features from the low-level ones and the details which are not related with the target can be ignored. Meanwhile, DNN shows to be invariant to surrounding clutter, rigid transformation and light. Song et al. [14] utilize long-range dependencies within the sentence being classified, using an LSTM, and short-span features, using a stacked CNN to tackle the problem that context is often ignored in the sentence classification task. Kitada et al. [15] fine-tune multiple pre-trained neural network models based on Squeeze-and-Excitation Networks (SENet) which achieved state-of-the-art results in the field of Skin Lesion Analysis towards Melanoma Detection. Many classification models work poorly on short texts due to data sparsity. To address this issue, Zeng et al. [16] propose topic memory networks for short text classification with a novel topic memory mechanism to encode latent topic representations indicative of class labels. Sharma et al. [17] present a unified CNN architecture that uses a range of enhancement filters that can enhance image-specific details via end-to-end dynamic filter learning. Wang et al. [18] propose a new architecture, termed as Appearance-and-Relation Network (ARTNet), to learn video representation in an end-to-end manner. It can be seen that DNN has been widely used in many classification tasks. Learning DNN amounts to estimating millions of parameters and requires a very large number of annotated image samples. However, architectural style dataset are only a few thousand data. Due to the lack of architectural style dataset, DNN has not been applied to this classification task. To address this issue, we use data augmentation to increase the number of architectural style images. Therefore, based on data augmentation, DNN can be applied to architectural style classification.

3 The Architectural Style Classification with De-background Data Based on Our DNN Model

Similar to precedent works, architectural style classification task, aiming at solving various architectural styles classification issues, experiences many difficulties in feature extraction. On the one hand, this task needs to filter the building-irrelevant factors, such as sky, trees, roads and so on. On the other hand, unlike the works like Song et al. [14] and Kitada et al. [15], this classification task doesn't have a sufficient dataset. In this paper, we propose a method which can address these issues based on GoogLeNet model. First of all, to eliminate the negative influence of background in images, we firstly use DPM models to extract representative building features. Then aiming at increasing the number of architectural style images, we generate data to train our DNN model. Following the features of these images are extracted respectively by our Deep Neural Network – the DNN model. After that, we obtain the finally classification results by a softmax classifier. The details of our DNN model implementation, the de-background process with DPM models and data augmentation strategy will be introduced in following subsections.

3.1 De-background Process with DPM Models

As mentioned in the first Section, the background is a building-irrelevant feature that disturbs the classification accuracy. To extract the features of buildings, more attention should be paid to filtering building-irrelevant part in the images. In order to reducing the influence of building-irrelevant factors and focus on the building elements, the DPM models are employed.

The Deformable Part-based Models (DPM) [4] consist of a coarse root filter that approximately covers an entire object, a set of part filters that cover smaller parts of the object and deformation costs. Consider building a model for an architectural style, the root filter can capture coarse resolution structure of buildings while the part filters can capture details such as towering spires and rose windows. Figure 3 shows a trained model for Gothic Style. The model for a building with m parts is formally defined by an $(m+2)$-tuple $(F_0, P_1, P_2, \ldots, P_m, b)$, where F_0 is a foot filter, P_i is a model for the i th part, b is a real-valued bias term. Each part model is defined by a 3-tuple (F_i, v_i, d_i), where F_i is a filter of the i th part, v_i is a two-dimensional vector that specifies the "reference" position of the i th part relative to the root position, and d_i is a 4-dimensional vector that specifies coefficients of a quadratic function that defines the deformation cost of each possible position of the part relative to the reference position.

In order to extract building-irrelevant elements, we choose a bounding box proportionally based on the size of the image. A bounding box slides over the image to form a number of sub-images $x = \{x_1, x_2, \ldots, x_n\}$, where n indicates the number of sub-images, x_i represents the i th sub-image. Each sub-image is matched to the model of the category it belongs to. Then we get scores $M = \{m_1, m_2, \ldots, m_n\}$, where $m_i = f(x_i)$ represents the matching degree between the i th sub-image x_i and the trained model of the style it belongs to. The matching degree is proportional to m_i. Then the highest matching sub-image is obtained by,

$$I = \text{argmax}_x f(x), x = \{x_1, x_2, \ldots, x_n\} \tag{1}$$

Following the image is replaced by sub-image I. As shown in Fig. 4, most of background is eliminated in the highest matching sub-images. And it is helpful to eliminate the building-irrelevant elements, so it can boost the performance.

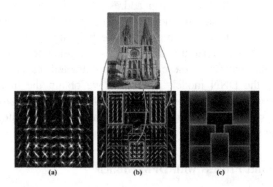

(a)   (b)   (c)

Fig. 3. The trained model for Gothic Style. (a) The model of a foot filter captures the overall structure of Gothic Style buildings. (b) A set of part filters can capture details of buildings such as towering spires and rose windows. Green boxes indicate correct detections with high scores given a part filter. (c) It is the deformation cost.

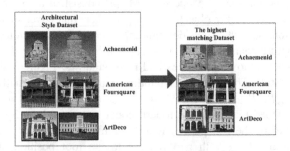

Fig. 4. These images are decomposed into many sub-images of the same size. The highest matching dataset are used to replace these images.

3.2   Data Augmentation Strategy

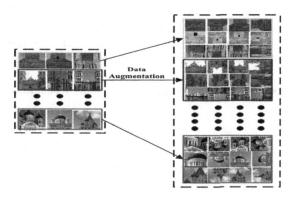

Fig. 5. Architecture style dataset increase the number of images by data augmentation.

As illustrated in Table 1, the problem with architecture style dataset is that our training model has insufficient data. In order to avoid the impact of insufficient data, we employ the data augmentation to increase the amount of architecture style training data. Data augmentation is a method to not only reduce over-fitting on models but also to augment data in a way such that to improve the performance of classifier. In this paper, we use traditional transformations, which consist of using a combination of affine transformations to manipulate the training data. The form of affine transformation is:

$$y_i = wx_i + b \tag{2}$$

Where x_i is the i th sub-image, w is the affine transformation, y_i is the image after the affine transformation. As can be seen in Fig. 5, we generate a larger dataset by data augmentation. For each input image, we generate a "duplicate" image that is rotated, shifted, flipped and zoomed in/out. Both image and duplicate are fed into our deep neural net. The data augmentation strategy improve classification accuracy, reduce over-fitting and help our deep neural networks converge faster. The results of data augmentation will be given in the next section.

3.3   Our Deep Neural Network Model

The architectural style image includes some building-irrelevant elements in addition to buildings. However, DNN can build high-level features from the low-level ones and the details which are not related with the target can be ignored. For the architectural style classification tasks, we employ the DNN model based on GoogLeNet to extract such high-level features.

The overall architecture of our DNN model is illustrated in Fig. 6. This model consists of 6 convolutional layers, 2 pooling layers, 3 Inception blocks and 2 fully-connected layers to learn features and a softmax layer to provide predicted label. All of convolution layers are with the same kernel size of 3×3 with strides 1 or 2, and the kernel size pooling 1 layer is 3×3, the kernel size pooling 2 layer is 8×8. These

Inception blocks are used to increase the depth and width of the network to improve the performance of deep neural network. Meanwhile, the factorization into small convolutions are introduced into these Inception blocks. As shown in Fig. 7, It breaks down a larger two-dimensional convolution into two smaller one-dimensional convolution, such as the kernel size of 7×7 is broken down into 1×7 and 7×1, or the kernel size of 3×3 is broken down into 1×3 and 3×1. Therefore, this method not only saves a lot of parameters but also increases the expression ability of a nonlinear extension model. These Inception blocks can extract more and richer spatial features and increase diversity of features.

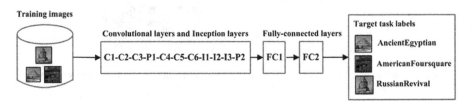

Fig. 6. The architecture of our DNN model. It consists of 6 convolutional layers, 2 pooling layers, 3 Inception blocks and 2 fully-connected layers.

However, training a deep neural network requires a large number of datasets since there are millions of parameters waiting to be adjusted. To address this problem, we design a method that uses ImageNet-trained layers of DNN to compute efficient mid-level image representation for images in architectural style dataset. The parameters of layers C1, C2, ..., C6, P1, P2, I1, I2 and I3 in Fig. 6 are first trained on the ImageNet task and kept fixed. Only the FC1 and FC2 layers are trained on the architectural style classification task training data as described next.

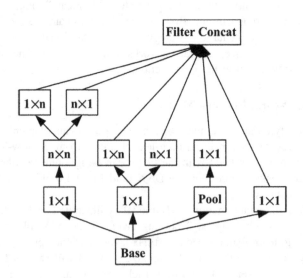

Fig. 7. The architecture of Inception block.

In order to achieve architectural style classification, we remove the output layers FCa and FCb of the pre-trained network and add an adaptation layer formed by two fully-connected layers FC1 and FC2 that use the output vector P2 of the layer FC1 as input. The FC1 and FC2 layers compute $Y_1 = \psi(W_1 P_2 + B_1)$ and $Y_2 = \psi(W_2 Y_1 + B_2)$, where W_1, B_1, W_2, B_2 are the trainable parameters. In our experiments, FC1 has size 2048, and FC2 has a size equal to the number of target categories. The effectiveness of this pre-training model has been verified by [19].

4   Experiments Results

In this section we demonstrate the effectiveness of each strategy of our method through experiments. First, we briefly introduce our experimental environment in Sect. 4.1, then the evaluation for the classification accuracy is given in Sect. 4.2, following the experiments that de-background process with DPM Models, data augmentation strategy and our deep neural network model are given in Sects. 4.3–4.5.

4.1   A Subsection Sample

Our experiments are processed on a PC with Intel Core i5-4590 CPU @ 3.30 GHZ 3.30 GHz, 8 GB RAM and Nvidia Tesla K40c GPU. The experiments of our deep neural network model are processed under Tensorflow framework on Linux Ubuntu 14.04 LTS, de-background process with DPM Models is implemented by matlab R2014a on 64-bit Windows 7.

4.2   The Evaluation for the Classification Accuracy

In order to get a fair comparison with the results in the architectural style classification task, the experimental strategy is the same as [1] and [20]. The classification accuracy is calculated by a ten-fold experiment.

4.3   De-background Process with DPM Models

In this subsection, we verify the effectiveness of de-background process. The classification results with de-background and original inputs are compared. As illustrated in Fig. 8, the employment of de-background data improves about 7% on the original data, because the building-irrelevant factors interfering the classification accuracy are filtered out by the participation of de-background data and the network can focus on capturing the building features.

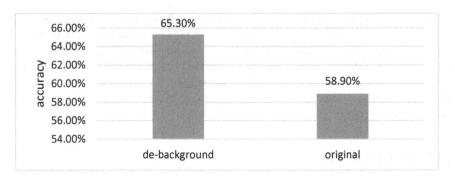

Fig. 8. Result comparison between the de-background data and original one. It can be find that the participation of DPM helps to improve the classification performance.

4.4 De-background Process with DPM Models

After the effectiveness of our de-background process has been proved, we verify the effectiveness of data augmentation strategy. Our data augmentation strategy consists of rotation, shift, flip and zoom in/out. Firstly, the architectural images are preprocessed with DPM. And then images are processed with data augmentation strategy. The experiments on data augmentation strategy are illustrated in Fig. 9.

As can be observed in Fig. 9, our data augmentation strategy helps to achieve higher accuracy. The improvement on data augmentation images is about 1.3%. That is because the data augmentation strategy can increase the number of images which can prevent over-fitting.

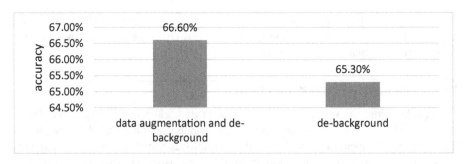

Fig. 9. Result comparison between the accuracy of data augmentation and without it. It can be find that the data augmentation strategy helps to improve the classification performance.

4.5 Our Deep Neural Network Model

In this subsection, we compare the proposed approach with the state-of-the-art approaches. The results of the comparison are shown in Fig. 10. It compares the classification results of our deep neural network model with other algorithms, including

MLLR+SP [1], IEP+LR [21], IEP+SVM [21] and our proposed method. The classification accuracy of our model has achieved the best results.

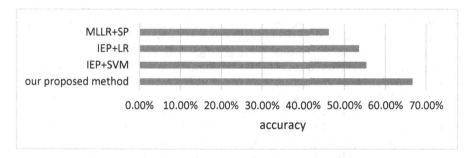

Fig. 10. The comparison of our proposed method and other methods.

4.6   Conclusions

In this paper, we propose a deep neural network with DPM model and data augmentation. We first use Deformable Part Model (DPM) to extract building elements and remove no-building elements. The de-background process helps to filter the background in RGB images out. After the de-background process, in order to over-fitting, the data augmentation is used for increasing the number of samples. Next the features of RGB is extracted by our deep neural networks (DNN) based on GoogLeNet. Experimental results show that our method achieves the best performance. The method is competitive comparing with other algorithms.

Acknowledgments. The work was jointly supported by the National Key R&D Program of China under Grant No. 2018YFC0807500, the National Key Research and Development Program of China No. 238, the National Natural Science Foundations of China under grant No. 61772396, 61472302, 61772392, the Fundamental Research Funds for the Central Universities under grant No. JBF180301, and Xi'an Key Laboratory of Big Data and Intelligent Vision under grant No. 201805053ZD4CG37.

References

1. Xu, Z., Tao, D., Zhang, Y., Wu, J., Tsoi, A.: Architectural style classification using multinomial latent logistic regression. In: Fleet, D., Pajdla, T., Schiele, B., Tuytelaars, T. (eds.) European Conference on Computer Vision, pp. 600–615. Springer, Cham (2014). https://doi.org/10.1007/978-3-319-10590-1_39
2. Krizhevsky, A., Sutskever, I., Hinton, G.E.: Imagenet classification with deep convolutional neural networks. In: Advances in Neural Information Processing Systems, pp. 1097–1105 (2012)
3. Peng, C., Xiao, T., Li, Z., et al.: MegDet: a large mini-batch object detector. arXiv preprint arXiv:1711.07240 (2017). 7

4. Felzenszwalb, P.F., Girshick, R.B., McAllester, D., Ramanan, D.: Object detection with discriminatively trained part-based models. IEEE Trans. Pattern Anal. Mach. Intell. **32**(9), 1627–1645 (2010)
5. Szegedy, C., Liu, W., Jia, Y., et al.: Going deeper with convolutions. In: Proceedings of the IEEE Conference on Computer Vision and Pattern Recognition, pp. 1–9 (2015)
6. Ioffe, S., Szegedy, C.: Batch normalization: accelerating deep network training by reducing internal covariate shift. arXiv preprint arXiv:1502.03167 (2015)
7. Szegedy, C., Vanhoucke, V., Ioffe, S., et al.: Rethinking the inception architecture for computer vision. In: Proceedings of the IEEE Conference on Computer Vision and Pattern Recognition, pp. 2818–2826 (2016)
8. Szegedy, C., Ioffe, S., Vanhoucke, V., et al.: Inception-v4, inception-resnet and the impact of residual connections on learning. In: AAAI, vol. 4, p. 12 (2017)
9. Berg, A.C., Grabler, F., Malik, J.: Parsing images of architectural scenes. In: 2007 IEEE 11th International Conference on Computer Vision, pp. 1–8. IEEE (2007)
10. Chu, W.T., Tsai, M.H.: Visual pattern discovery for architecture image classification and product image search. In: Proceedings of the 2nd ACM International Conference on Multimedia Retrieval, p. 27. ACM (2012)
11. Doersch, C., Singh, S., Gupta, A., Sivic, J., Efros, A.: What makes paris look like Paris? ACM Trans. Graph. **31**(4) (2015)
12. Goel, A., Juneja, M., Jawahar, C.V.: Are buildings only instances?: Exploration in architectural style categories. In: Proceedings of the Eighth Indian Conference on Computer Vision, Graphics and Image Processing, ACM (2012). Article number 1
13. Philbin, J., Chum, O., Isard, M., Sivic, J., Zisserman, A.: Object retrieval with large vocabularies and fast spatial matching. In: 2007 IEEE Conference on Computer Vision and Pattern Recognition, pp. 1–8. IEEE (2007)
14. Song, X., Petrak, J., Roberts, A.: A Deep Neural Network Sentence Level Classification Method with Context Information (2018)
15. Kitada, S., Iyatomi, H.: Skin lesion classification with ensemble of squeeze-and-excitation networks and semi-supervised learning. arXiv preprint arXiv:1809.02568 (2018)
16. Zeng, J., Li, J., Song, Y., Gao, C., Lyu, M.R., King, I.: Topic memory networks for short text classification. In EMNLP (2018)
17. Sharma, V., Diba, A., Neven, D., et al.: Classification-Driven Dynamic Image Enhancement. arXiv preprint arXiv:1710.07558 (2017)
18. Wang, L., Li, W., Li, W., et al.: Appearance-and-relation networks for video classification. arXiv preprint arXiv:1711.09125 (2017)
19. Tran, D., Bourdev, L., Fergus, R., Torresani, L., Paluri, M.: Learning spatiotemporal features with 3d convolutional networks. In: IEEE International Conference on Computer Vision, pp. 4489–4497. IEEE (2015)
20. Miao, Q., Liu, R., Zhao, P., et al.: A semi-supervised image classification model based on improved ensemble projection algorithm. IEEE Access **6**, 1372–1379 (2018)
21. Zhao, P.: 基于集成投影及卷积神经网络的建筑风格分类算法研究. Xidian University (2015)

DAEimp: Denoising Autoencoder-Based Imputation of Sleep Heart Health Study for Identification of Cardiovascular Diseases

Xiaoyun Dong[1,3], Jingjing Zhang[2], Gang Wang[2], and Yong Xia[1,3(✉)]

[1] Research and Development Institute of Northwestern Polytechnical University in ShenZhen, ShenZhen 518057, China
yxia@nwpu.edu.cn
[2] Department of Critical Care Medicine,
The Second Affiliated Hospital of Xi'an Jiaotong University, Xi'an 710004, China
[3] National Engineering Laboratory for Integrated Aero-Space-Ground-Ocean Big Data Application Technology, School of Computer Science and Engineering, Northwestern Polytechnical University, Xi'an 710072, China

Abstract. Since it has been recognized that the disordered breathing during sleep is related to cardiovascular diseases, it is possible to predict cardiovascular diseases from sleep breathing data, which however is usually inevitable to have missing data, resulted probability from the loss to follow-up, failure to attend medical appointments, lack of measurements, failure to send or retrieve questionnaires, and inaccurate data transfer. In this paper, we propose a denoising autoencoder-based imputation (DAEimp) algorithm to impute the missing values in the sleep heart health study (SHHS) dataset for the predication of cardiovascular diseases. This algorithm consists of three major steps: (1) based on the missing completely at random assumption, the random uniform noise is added to the positions of missing values to convert missing data imputation into a denoising problem, (2) feed the noisy data and a missing position indicator matrix into an autoencoder model and use the reconstruction error, divided into observation positions reconstruction error and missing positions error, for denoising, and (3) the logistic regression is applied to the generated complete dataset for the identification of cardiovascular diseases. Our results on the SHHS dataset indicate that the proposed DAEimp algorithm achieves state-of-the-art performance in missing data imputation and sleep breathing data-based identification of cardiovascular diseases.

Keywords: Missing data · Denoising autoencoder · Sleep heart health study · Cardiovascular disease identification

1 Introduction

The cardiovascular disease is one of the leading causes of death worldwide. Finding ways to predict the risk factors of this disease has become paramount [1]. The

© Springer Nature Switzerland AG 2019
Z. Lin et al. (Eds.): PRCV 2019, LNCS 11857, pp. 517–527, 2019.
https://doi.org/10.1007/978-3-030-31654-9_44

National Heart Lung & Blood Institute carried out a multi-center cohort study to determine the cardiovascular and other consequences of sleep-disordered breathing [3]. However, in medical longitudinal studies [8] like this one, it is inevitable to have missing data, which can occur for numerous grounds such as the loss to follow-up, failure to attend medical appointments, lack of measurements, failure to send or retrieve questionnaires, and inaccurate transfer data from paper registration to an electronic database [9]. Missing data is a complicated problem in data mining, since the lost information and highlighted uncertainty may confuse the model, result in unreliable output, and affect the generalizability in the data mining process.

Generally, there are two strategies to address the issue of missing data: complete-case analysis and missing value imputation. The complete-case analysis, also known as "list-wise deletion", removes the samples with missing values, which, however, reduces the size of datasets and may discard invaluable data. Various missing value imputation methods can be roughly categorized into two groups: statistical methods and learning-based methods. Typical statistical missing value imputation methods include (1) the mean imputation which replaces each missing value with the mean of the corresponding observed values, (2) regression imputation that fits the missing values based on observed ones, and (3) estimation imputation which samples the missing values from an estimated statistical model. These methods are easy to use, but their performance depends highly on the assumption of data distribution and observed data. Nevertheless, there are three types of missing data. The data is either missing at random (MAR) when the missing positions only depend on the observed variables, missing completely at random (MCAR) when the missing positions do not depend on any of the variables, or missing not at random (MNAR) when the missing positions depend on both observed variables and unobserved variables [11]. These statistical methods may fail in case of MCAR. The other group of missing value imputation methods are based on learning the latent distribution of incomplete data using deep neural networks, such as the generative adversarial imputation network (GAIN) [17] and multiple imputation using deep denoising autoencoder (MIDA) [15]. Despite their improved performance, GAIN is criticized for its less robustness and high complexity, and the initialized data used for training MIDA is obtained by replacing missing positions using mean imputation for continuous variables and frequent imputation for categorical variables, respectively, which may result in biased autoencoder.

In this paper, we propose a denoising autoencoder-based imputation (DAEimp) algorithm to impute the missing values in the sleep heart health study (SHHS) dataset for the predication of cardiovascular diseases. We assume that the missing data issue in the SHHS dataset is MCAR, and hence add random uniform noise to the positions of missing values to convert missing data imputation into a denoising problem. Then, we feed the generated noisy data and an indicator matrix, which tells the positions of missing values, into the DAEimp algorithm for denoising (i.e. generating the complete dataset). Finally, we apply the logistic regression to the generated complete dataset for prediction.

We have evaluated the proposed DAEimp algorithm against four existing missing value imputation methods, and our algorithm achieves the state-of-the-art performance.

2 Related Work

Statistical missing value imputation methods assume that the complete data follow a statistical distribution and impute missing values based on observed data. Buuren et al. [18] proposed the multivariate imputation by chained equations (MICE) algorithm to fit missing values. Song et al. [19] adopted KNN for missing data imputation, i.e. imputing each missing value using its k-nearest complete samples. John et al. [20] adopted the expectation maximization (EM) algorithm for missing data imputation, in which the conditional expectation of the underlying distribution of the complete data is evaluated in the E-step, and the expected evaluated in the E-step is maximized and new estimations for the parameters are obtained in the M-step.

Learning-based missing value imputation methods aim to learn the latent distribution of complete data. Yoon et al. [17] proposed the GAIN model, in which the generator imputes the missing positions conditioned on observed data, and the discriminator takes the imputed data and a hint vector as input and outputs a probability matrix (the probability of the observed data in every position). Gondara et al. [15] proposed the MIDA algorithm, which consists of three major steps: (a) initializing each missing value as the respective column average in case of continuous variables or most frequent label in case of categorical variables, (b) corrupting the initialized data by setting 50% of data to zero, and (c) using the corrupted data to train a denoising deep model, which can be used for missing value imputation. Despite its improved performance, this algorithm may suffer from the bias introduced in the data initialization process.

3 Method

3.1 Dataset

We validate the performance of our proposed algorithm DAEimp in the sleep heart health study (SHHS) dataset [4–7]. The original dataset has 5804 participants (samples) and 1281 variables (included 1 label variable), the label includes 2 categories, means the participant is dead or alive over a mean follow-up period of 14.6 ± 1.1 year. The 5804 participants, two had no outcomes, 4497 were alive and 1305 died. We select a complete sub dataset from sleep heart health study (SHHS) dataset to validate. The sub dataset includes 735 samples and 713 variables, which includes 573 alive participates and 162 dead. We simulate pseudo missing values by removing some values randomly in different proportions (5%, 10%, 15% and 20%). In the medical, imputing missing data whose missing rates more than 20% makes little sense. Thus, we compare the values we imputed and actually observed in the missing positions (the positions we randomly removed).

3.2   Problem Formulation

We consider the missing data imputation as a process that learns the distribution of incomplete data and generates complete data. Matrix X represents the incomplete data. Suppose that X has n independent samples and each sample consists of d variables. $X_i = (X_{i,1}, ..X_{i,j}, ..X_{i,d}), (i = 1, ..., n; j = 1, ..., d)$ represents a random draw from a multivariate distribution $P(X)$. M is an indicator matrix taking values in $\{0, 1\}^d$, and dependent on X, we define it in the following way:

$$M_{i,j} = \begin{cases} 1, & if \ X_{i,j} \ is \ observed \\ 0, & if \ X_{i,j} \ is \ missing \end{cases} \tag{1}$$

So that M indicates which components of X are observed.

Our goal is to impute the missing positions in X (the positions correspond to 0 in M). Formally, we want to generate complete data from X and let the learned distribution from X as similar as $P(X)$.

3.3   Our Method

Missing data is a special case of noisy data, which makes denoising autoencoder (DAE) as an ideal imputation model. In this section, we introduce our imputation algorithm DAEimp motivated by DAE.

Autoencoder and Denoising Autoencoder. An autoencoder takes $x \in [0, 1]^d$ as an input and encodes x to an intermediate representation $h \in [0, 1]^d$ using an encoder. Where d represents dimensional subspace of x. Then it decodes the intermediate representation h back to the original d dimensional space $\hat{x}$ using a decoder. During the training phase, the purpose of autoencoder is to minimize the reconstruction error between x and $\hat{x}$. Encoder and decoder are both artificial neural networks. The encoder and decoder stages are represented as in the following:

$$h = f(Wx + b) \tag{2}$$

$$\hat{x} = f(W'h + b') \tag{3}$$

Where $\hat{x}$ is the decode result, f is any nonlinear function, W and W' are the weight vector, b and b' are the bias.

Denoising autoencoder is a natural extension to autoencoder [14], it is designed to recover clean output from noisy input and discover robust representations. It forces the hidden layers h to learn robust features from corrupted input and lets the network reconstruct the clean output $\hat{x}$. Corruptions can be applied in different ways, such as randomly setting some input values to zero.

Our Method DAEimp in Imputation. In our proposed DAEimp algorithm, we add random uniform noise to the missing positions in incomplete data to convert the missing data imputation into a denoising problem. And then we takes the noisy data as the denoising autoencoder partial input in the training phase. The denoising autoencoder will output a complete data according to reconstruction error we defined (see Eq. (9)). The pipeline of our algorithm is shown in Fig. 1.

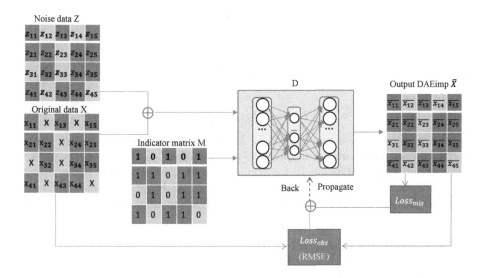

Fig. 1. The architecture of DAEimp algorithm

In our proposed DAEimp algorithm, we first generate a uniform distribution of intervals $[0, 0.1]$ noise matrix Z, and then we replace the missing positions in incomplete data X with correspond data in Z to generate a noisy data $\hat{X}$, and finally we take $\hat{X}$ and indicator M as inputs of DAEimp. Let DAEimp: $\hat{X} \times \{0, 1\}^d \rightarrow \bar{X}$ be a function, we define the random variable $\hat{X}$, $\bar{X}$ in the following way:

$$\hat{X} = X \odot M + Z \odot (1 - M) \tag{4}$$

$$\bar{X} = D(\hat{X}, M) \tag{5}$$

$$X_{out} = X \odot M + \bar{X} \odot (1 - M) \tag{6}$$

Where $\odot$ denotes element-wise (Hadamard) product of two vectors, D represents the network of denoising autoencoder. $\bar{X}$ is the output of DAE (DAE outputs a value for every position in X, even if the positions value is observed) and X_{out} is the results we want, the results replace each missing positions in X with the correspond positions value in $\bar{X}$.

Loss Function in DAEimp. As is known to all, DAE reconstructs clean output from corrupted data by minimizing the reconstruction error between output and complete data. However, obtaining a complete dataset is impossible in some cases. In order to tackle this problem, we divide the reconstruction error into observed positions reconstruction error L_{obs} and missing positions error L_{mis}, which is motivated by the generator loss function in GAIN [18]. Then we set the observed positions reconstruction error and missing positions error linear combination as the error L_{err}. We define the loss function L_{obs}, L_{mis},L_{err} in the following way:

$$L_{obs} = \sqrt{\frac{\sum m_i(x_i - \bar{x}_i)^2}{\sum m_i}} \tag{7}$$

$$L_{mis} = -\sum(1 - m_i)\log(|\bar{x}_i|) \tag{8}$$

$$L_{err} = \alpha L_{mis} + \beta L_{obs} \tag{9}$$

Where $m_i, x_i, \bar{x}_i$ are an observation in M, X and $\bar{X}$ respectively, α and β are positive hyper-parameters. Our goal is to minimize the L_{err} in the training phase. We use the AdadeltaOptimizer for gradient descent, it is dynamically adapted over time and has minimal computational overhead beyond vanilla stochastic gradient descent and appears robust to noisy gradient information.

4 Experiments and Results

4.1 Experiment Settings

In the first set of experiment, we did ablation experiment to qualitatively analyze the properties of DAEimp. In the second experiment we compare DAEimp against four existing missing value imputation methods under different missing rates to evaluate the root mean square error (RMSE) (see Eq. (10)). In the third experiment we compare DAEimp against four existing missing value imputation methods under different missing rates to predict the cardiovascular disease using logistic regression. In the last experiment we compare DAEimp against four existing missing value imputation methods to estimate the congeniality of DAEimp.

$$RMSE = \sqrt{\frac{\sum_{i=1}^{p}(x_i - \bar{x}_i)^2}{p}} \tag{10}$$

Where p is the numbers of missing values, x_i is the true value, and $\bar{x}_i$ is the imputed value.

All experiments are implemented in TensorFlow except the MIDA [15], which is implemented in PyTorch. In our proposed algorithm, the depth of network is set to three, the number of hidden nodes in each layer is d, $d/4$ and d, respectively. We use tanh as the activation functions of each layer, the number of batches K_{mb} is 64. We conducted each experiment 10 times, the ratio of training set and test set was 8:2.

4.2 Results

Ablation Experiment. The innovation of our method DAEimp has two parts, the input of DAEimp and the reconstruction error in the training phase. First, our proposed algorithm DAEimp takes the generated noisy data (random uniform noises replace the missing positions in original incomplete data) and the indicator matrix M as input. Next, we divide the reconstruction error into observed positions reconstruction error L_{obs} and missing positions error L_{mis}. We did an ablation experiment, which removes one or two components of our algorithm DAEimp to compare the performance. Table 1 shows that the performance of DAEimp is improved when all components are included.

Table 1. Ablation experiment of DAEimp algorithm (missing rates 20%)

Method	RMSE	ACC
DAEimp $wo/(L_{mis}\&M)$	$.1324 \pm .0017$	$.7392 \pm .1121$
DAEimp wo/M	$.1330 \pm .0036$	$.7091 \pm .1080$
DAEimp wo/L_{mis}	$.1361 \pm .0018$	$.7322 \pm .0901$
DAEimp	$\mathbf{.1287 \pm .0018}$	$\mathbf{.8001 \pm .0389}$

wo/: without

Root Mean Square Error (RMSE) in Imputation Method. RMSE measures how close the imputed data and the true data in the missing positions. It directly reflects the precision of imputation method, the lower the value, the closer the imputed is to the true. We compared our proposed DAEimp against four existing method under different missing rates to evaluate RMSE. Table 2 shows that DAEimp performs better than other four existing methods.

Table 2. RMSE comparison under different missing rates

Missing rates	RMSE ($Average \pm Std$)				
	DAEimp	GAIN [17]	MIDA [15]	MICE [18]	KNN [19]
5%	$\mathbf{.1209 \pm .0023}$	$.1295 \pm .0040$	$.1321 \pm .0039$	$.1640 \pm .0013$	$.1499 \pm .0016$
10%	$\mathbf{.1222 \pm .0021}$	$.1313 \pm .0027$	$.1341 \pm .0027$	$.1638 \pm .0010$	$.1512 \pm .0012$
15%	$\mathbf{.1266 \pm .0027}$	$.1329 \pm .0032$	$.1365 \pm .0025$	$.1640 \pm .0007$	$.1530 \pm .0006$
20%	$\mathbf{.1287 \pm .0018}$	$.1366 \pm .0027$	$.1389 \pm .0022$	$.1650 \pm .0004$	$.1543 \pm .0003$

Prediction Performance in Imputation Method. In this experiment, we compare DAEimp against four existing missing value imputation methods under different missing rates to predict the cardiovascular disease using logistic regression. Table 3 shows that DAEimp performs better than other four existing methods.

Table 3. Prediction performance comparison under different missing rates

Missing rates	ACC (Average ± Std)				
	DAEimp	GAIN [17]	MIDA [15]	MICE [18]	KNN [19]
5%	**.7728 ± .0472**	.7646 ± .0432	.7689 ± .0472	.7687 ± .0426	**.7728 ± .0407**
10%	**.7784 ± .0397**	.7715 ± .0391	.7700 ± .0406	.7648 ± .0456	.7701 ± .0420
15%	**.8028 ± .0422**	.7892 ± .0384	.7771 ± .0535	.7565 ± .0594	.7675 ± .0492
20%	**.8001 ± .0389**	.7891 ± .0452	.7689 ± .0438	.7836 ± .0361	.7727 ± .0422

Congeniality in Imputation Method. The congeniality of an imputation method measures the ability that imputed data keeps the variable-label relationship [17]. In this experiment, we compare the mean bias and mean square error between post-imputation parameters $\hat{w}$ and the complete parameters w in logistic regression. These quantities being lower, the congeniality being higher, with equal to keeps more the variable-label relationship and the better the imputation method. Table 4 shows that DAEimp performs better than other existing four methods.

Table 4. Congeniality comparison (missing rates 20%)

Method	Mean bias ($\|w - \hat{w}\|_1$)	Mean square error ($\|w - \hat{w}\|_2$)
DAEimp	**0.9163 ± 0.0629**	**5.0077 ± 0.0916**
GAIN [17]	0.9408 ± 0.1418	5.7430 ± 0.1005
MIDA [15]	0.9904 ± 0.1301	6.1308 ± 0.1221
MICE [18]	1.1060 ± 0.1175	6.8898 ± 0.1300
KNN [19]	1.2260 ± 0.1406	6.4309 ± 0.1252

5   Discussion

5.1   Ablation Experiment Analysis

From Table 1, we found that the performance without L_{mis}&M is better than without L_{mis} or without M. It is because that the latent relationship between M and L_{mis}, that is M hints the network that where observed positions and missing positions in the input, from this, the denoising autoencoder can get the position of missing data and calculate L_{mis} and L_{obs} to reconstruct complete data as close as possible to true data.

5.2   Parameters Design

In the training phase of our DAEimp, we divide the reconstruction error into observed positions reconstruction error and missing positions error (see Eq. (9)).

In our experiments, the parameters α (the coefficient of observed positions reconstruction error) and β (the coefficient of missing positions error) are designed in 0.18 and 9 respectively. From the components of reconstruction error, we should pay more attention to observed positions reconstruction error to impute the missing positions precisely. So we should set $\beta > \alpha$. After preliminary experiment verification, we set α range from 0.10 to 0.18, β range from 1 to 15 and then to find the optimal parameters. Figure 2 shows the RMSE under different settings.

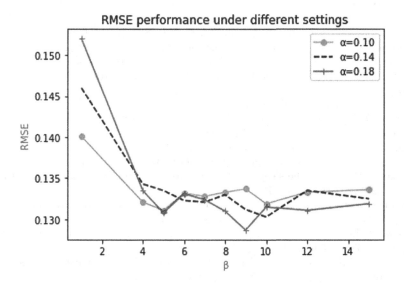

Fig. 2. RMSE performance under different settings (missing rates is 20%). The α and β represent the coefficient of observed positions reconstruction error and the coefficient of missing positions error in the reconstruction error (see Eq. (9)). The RMSE is calculated by the imputed data and true data in the missing positions in the test set.

6   Conclusion

In this paper, we propose denoising autoencoder-based imputation algorithm (DAEimp), which is designed to impute the missing positions more accurate in the data mining preprocess. Our method DAEimp takes the indicator matrix and generated noisy data as input and divides the reconstruction error into observed positions reconstruction error and missing positions error. Our results on the sleep heart health study dataset indicates that the proposed algorithm can impute the missing positions more precise than four existing methods.

Acknowledgement. This work was supported in part by the Science and Technology Innovation Committee of Shenzhen Municipality, China, under Grants JCYJ20180 306171334997, in part by the National Natural Science Foundation of China under Grants 61771397, in part by Synergy Innovation Foundation of the University and Enterprise for Graduate Students in Northwestern Polytechnical University (NPU) under Grants XQ201911, in part by the Seed Foundation of Innovation and Creation for Graduate Students in NPU under Grants ZZ2019029, and in part by the Project for Graduate Innovation team of NPU.

References

1. Koene, R.J., Prizment, A.E., Blaes, A., Konety, S.H.: Shared risk factors in cardiovascular disease and cancer. Circulation **133**(11), 1104–1114 (2016)
2. Shahar, E., et al.: Sleep-disordered breathing and cardiovascular disease: cross-sectional results of the sleep heart health study. Am. J. Respir. Crit. Care Med. **163**(1), 19–25 (2001)
3. Sleep Heart Health Study Homepage. https://sleepdata.org/datasets/shhs/
4. Dean, D.A., et al.: Scaling up scientific discovery in sleep medicine: the national sleep research resource. Sleep **39**(5), 1151–1164 (2016)
5. Zhang, G.Q., et al.: The national sleep research resource: towards a sleep data commons. J. Am. Med. Inform. Assoc. **25**(10), 1351–1358 (2018)
6. Quan, S.F., et al.: The sleep heart health study: design, rationale, and methods. Sleep **20**(12), 1077–1085 (1997)
7. Redline, S., et al.: Methods for obtaining and analyzing unattended polysomnography data for a multicenter study. Sleep **21**(7), 759–767 (1998)
8. Edward, J.C., Marius, R., Jules, H., Piergiorgio, S.: Longitudinal studies. J. Thorac. Dis. **7**(11), 537–540 (2015)
9. Pedersen, A.B.: Missing data and multiple imputation in clinical epidemiological research. Clin. Epidemil. **9**, 157–165 (2017)
10. Rubin, D.B.: Multiple imputation after 18+ years (with discussion). J. Am. Stat. Assoc. **91**, 473–489 (1996)
11. Barnard, J., Meng, X.-L.: Applications of multiple imputation in medical studies: from AIDS to NHANES. Stat. Methods Med. Res. **8**(1), 17–36 (1999)
12. Mackinnon, A.: The use and reporting of multiple imputation in medical research-a review. J. Intern. Med. **268**(6), 586–593 (2010)
13. Sterne, J.A., et al.: Multiple imputation for missing data in epidemiological and clinical research: potential and pitfalls. BMJ **338**, b2393 (2009)
14. Vincent, P., Larochelle, H., Bengio, Y., Manzagol, P.-A.: Extracting and composing robust features with denoising autoencoders. In: Proceedings of the 25th International Conference on Machine Learning, pp. 1096–1103. ACM, Finland (2008)
15. Gondara, L., Wang, K.: MIDA: multiple imputation using denoising autoencoders. In: Phung, D., Tseng, V.S., Webb, G.I., Ho, B., Ganji, M., Rashidi, L. (eds.) PAKDD 2018. LNCS (LNAI), vol. 10939, pp. 260–272. Springer, Cham (2018). https://doi.org/10.1007/978-3-319-93040-4_21
16. Bengio, Y., Yao, L., Alain, G., Vincent, P.: Generalized denoising auto-encoders as generative models. In: Advances in Neural Information Processing Systems, Spain, pp. 899–907 (2013)
17. Yoon, J., Jordon, J, van der Schaar, M.: GAIN: missing data imputation using generative adversarial nets. In: 35th International Conference on Machine Learning, ICML 2018, pp. 9042–9051. ACM, Sweden (2018)

18. Buuren, S., Groothuis-Oudshoorn, K.: MICE: multivariate imputation by chained equations in R. J. Stat. Softw. **45**(3), 1–67 (2011)
19. Song, Q., Shepperd, M., Chen, X., et al.: Can k-NN imputation improve the performance of C4.5 with small software project data sets? A comparative evaluation. J. Syst. Softw. **81**(12), 2361–2370 (2008)
20. John, R., Mandl, L.A., Ghomrawi Hassan, M.K., et al.: Is there a role for expectation maximization imputation in addressing missing data in research using WOMAC questionnaire? Comparison to the standard mean approach and a tutorial. BMC Musculoskelet. Disord. **12**(1), 109 (2011)

Fabric Defect Detection Based on Lightweight Neural Network

Zhoufeng Liu, Jian Cui$^{(\boxtimes)}$, Chunlei Li, Miaomiao Wei, and Yan Yang

School of Electrical and Information Engineering,
Zhongyuan University of Technology, Zhengzhou 450007, China
1342332327@qq.com

Abstract. Owing to the variety and complexity of defects in the fabric texture image, automatic fabric defect detection is a challenging task in the fields of machine vision. Deep convolutional neural network (CNN) has achieved remarkable progress in the field of target detection, and the application of deep CNN model to fabric defect detection has achieved better results. However, with the detection accuracy increasing of deep CNNs, comes the drawbacks of significant increase in computational costs and storage services, which seriously hinders the usages of CNN on resource-limited environments such as mobile or embedded devices. In this paper, a fabric defect detection method using lightweight CNN is proposed. We introduce an extremely computation-efficient CNN architecture named YOLO-LFD, which adopts continuous 3 × 3 and 1 × 1 convolution layers for dimensionality reduction and feature fusion. We use multi-scale feature extraction method to improve the detection ability of the model for different size targets, and adopt K-means clustering method on the fabric defect image dataset to find the optimal size of anchor boxes. Experimental results demonstrate that the proposed scheme improves the detection accuracy of fabric defects, greatly reduces the model parameters, and improves the detection speed, which can provide real-time fabric defects detection on embedded devices.

Keywords: Deep learning · YOLO-v3 · Fabric defect detection · Optimization model

1 Introduction

Fabric defect impairs the textile quality, thereby reduce the product price and profit. As a quality control method, fabric defect detection is very significant in the process of textile production. Traditional fabric defect detection is mainly carried out by inspectors, and it has low detection speed, high missed detection rate and cannot meet the requirement of rapid and high-quality product production [1]. With the development of machine vision technology, automatic fabric defect detection has been a research focus.

Existing automatic fabric defect detection methods can be divided into statistical analysis [2,3], spectral [4], structure method, model method [5] and so on.

© Springer Nature Switzerland AG 2019
Z. Lin et al. (Eds.): PRCV 2019, LNCS 11857, pp. 528–539, 2019.
https://doi.org/10.1007/978-3-030-31654-9_45

Statistical analysis methods detect the fabric defect by calculating the gray values contrasted with their surroundings. The detection results largely rely on the selected window size; moreover, it is difficult to detect the defects with smaller size. Spectral methods transform the test image into the frequency domain, then detect the defect by calculating the difference between the spectral coefficients, it includes Fourier transform method, wavelet transform method, Gabor transform method. The detection performance of these methods mainly depends on the selected filter banks, and has high computational complexity. Model-based methods first model the non-defective image texture features through parameter estimation techniques, then detect the defect by discriminating whether the test image conforms with the normal texture model. The model-based detection methods share a high computational complexity, and cannot efficiently detect the defects with smaller size.

Recently, deep learning algorithms, especially convolutional neural networks (CNNs), have shown their much stronger feature representation power in computer vision. Deep learning algorithms allow computational models that are composed of multiple processing layers to learn representations of data with multiple levels of abstraction [6] and have shown their much stronger feature representation power in computer vision. Therefore, it has been widely used in the field of object detection, and several effective detection models have been proposed. More recently, [7–9] have adopted the deep learning technology to detect the fabric defect, and achieve the good detection results. However, there are some issues need to be improved for the above-mentioned methods: (1) it is difficult to detect the defects with smaller size; (2) the computational costs and storage of the deep learning model need to be simplified.

In general, object detection based on deep learning algorithms can be mainly divided into two categories: one is Region Proposal-based algorithms, such as "Rich feature hierarchies for accurate object detection and semantic segmentation", Girshick, Ross, et al. [10], Fast R-CNN [11], Faster R-CNN, which uses the regional proposal network (RPN) to generate regional proposals, and then conducts classification and regression on region proposal. These methods possess accurate detection, but has a large amount of calculation and a slow detection speed. The other includes YOLO, SSD and other regression-based target detection algorithms, which deal with the detection problem as a regression problem, and uses only one convolutional neural network to directly predict the classification and location of different targets. These methods have high detection speed, but cannot effectively detect the small targets. YOLO-v3 is the newest version of YOLO series. It adopts the regression-based algorithm to predict the category and location of targets, which improves the detection speed, and adds Feature Pyramid Network (FPN) to improve detection accuracy [12].

However, with the increasing performance of CNN models, the model becomes more complex and requires high storage space for hardware, which restricts the application of CNNs in embedded system. Moreover, too many network model parameters cause a lot of redundant information, which affect the detection accuracy [13]. Therefore, the compression and acceleration of the deep learning model has become a hot research field. In this paper, an effective framework YOLO-LFN is proposed for real-time fabric defects detection, which is designed inspired by YOLO-v3 network. The model can greatly reduce computation cost while maintaining accuracy.

Our contributions are summarized as follows:

(1) A lightweight network structure is designed for fabric defect detection. The 3 × 3 and 1 × 1 convolution layers are added to the network structure, which enhances the ability of feature fusion and improves the detection accuracy.
(2) The multi-scale feature extraction method is adopted by considering the fabric texture characteristics, in order to extract different scale features and improve the detection ability of different size targets.
(3) K-means clustering algorithm is used to cluster the ground truth size of the fabric defect database, and get the size of priori anchor box to improves the target location accuracy.

2   YOLO-v3 Model

YOLO-v3 network conduct the object detection using a regression operation, and combining the inception structure of Googlenet with short cut structure of Resnet [14]. Comparing with the YOLO model, YOLO-v3 constructs the full convolution network structure and removes the full connection layer of YOLO network. In addition, the anchor mechanism is added to predict bounding box and its coordinate value. The network structure of fabric defect detection based on YOLO-v3 model is shown in Fig. 1.

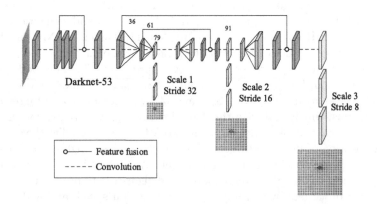

Fig. 1. The network structure diagram of YOLO-v3 model.

YOLO-v3 adopts Feature Pyramid Network (FPN) to extract information at different scale feature layers, and extracts features from feature maps obtained by 32×, 16× and 8× downsampled respectively.

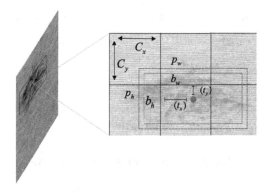

Fig. 2. Bounding box with dimension priors and location prediction.

The network predicts 3 bounding boxes at each cell in the output feature map. Instead of predicting offsets the model predict location coordinates relative to the location of the grid cell. The bounding box with dimension priors and location prediction is shown in Fig. 2.

It predicts the width and height of the box as offsets from cluster centroids, and predicts the center coordinates of the box which is relative to the location of filter application using a sigmoid function [15]. The position of the prediction box can be calculated as follows

$$b_x = \sigma(t_x) + c_x, b_y = \sigma(t_y) + c_y, b_w = p_w e^{t_w}, b_h = p_h e^{t_h} \tag{1}$$

where (b_w, b_h, b_x, b_y) are the length, width and central point coordinates of the forecasting frame; (t_x, t_y) are the offset of the target central point relative to the upper left corner of the grid where the point is located; (c_x, c_y) are the number of lattices with the difference between the upper left corner and the upper left corner of the grid where the point is located; (p_w, p_h) are the edge lengths of the anchor box, and (t_w, t_h) are the width and height of the forecasting frame.

YOLO obtains the coordinate value of bounding box by predicting offset and confidence for each box. Predicting offset instead of coordinates simplifies practical problems and is beneficial to the learning of neural networks. YOLO-v3 predicts an objectness score for each bounding box using logistic regression, and uses FPN to extract information at different scale feature layers. The model has high detection accuracy in target detection, but there are too many parameters in the model, which requires high storage space of hardware and time-consuming calculation. It is difficult to meet the requirements of real-time detection.

3   Acceleration and Compression

In order to compress the model parameters and improve the detection speed without reducing the detection accuracy, a novel network structure is proposed to accelerate and compress the original YOLO-v3 model. Its fewer storage enable the network can be directly applied in industrial field and embedded systems, and can real-time monitor the fabric defect.

3.1   Network Architecture

YOLO-v3 adopts Darknet-53 network framework which is a hybrid approach between residual network and the network Darknet-19 used in YOLO-v2. Its network framework is shown in the following Table 1.

Table 1. The framework of Darknet-53.

	Type	Filters	Size	Output
	Convolutional	32	3×3	256×256
	Convolutional	64	3×3/2	128×128
	Convolutional	32	1×1	
1	Convolutional	64	3×3	
	Residual			128×128
	Convolutional	128	3×3/2	64×64
	Convolutional	64	1×1	
2	Convolutional	128	3×3	
	Residual			64×64
	Convolutional	256	3×3/2	32×32
	Convolutional	128	1×1	
8	Convolutional	256	3×3	
	Residual			32×32
	Convolutional	512	3×3/2	16×16
	Convolutional	256	1×1	
8	Convolutional	512	3×3	
	Residual			16×16
	Convolutional	1024	3×3/2	8×8
	Convolutional	512	1×1	
4	Convolutional	1024	3×3	
	Residual			8×8
	Avgpool		Global	
	Connected		1000	
	Softmax			

Fabric defect image is mainly composed of direction, border and curvature information, so the network should mainly extract the low-level features of the image when detecting fabric defect. For this reason, we design a simpler framework YOLO-LFD based on Darknet-53.

In the YOLO-LFD network, we use continuous 3 × 3 and 1 × 1 convolution layers for dimensionality reduction and feature fusion. In the forward propagation process, the dimension transformation of tensor is realized by adjusting the step size of convolution core instead of max pooling layer, which ensures the high resolution of convolution output and improves the detection accuracy. The proposed YOLO-LFD framework can be shown in Table 2.

Table 2. The framework of YOLO-LFD.

L	Layer type	Filter size (w × h, n)	Stride	Output size w × h × d
0	Input	–	–	512 × 512 × 3
1	Convolution	3 × 3, 16	2	256 × 256×16
	Convolution	1 × 1, 8	–	256 × 256×8
2	Convolution	3 × 3, 32	2	128 × 128×32
	Convolution	1 × 1, 16	–	128 × 128×16
3	Convolution	3 × 3, 64	2	64 × 64×64
	Convolution	1 × 1, 32	–	64 × 64×32
4	Convolution	3 × 3, 128	2	32 × 32×128
	Convolution	1 × 1, 64	–	32 × 32×64
5	Convolution	3 × 3, 256	1	32 × 32 × 256
6	Convolution	1 × 1, 128	–	32 × 32 × 128
	Convolution	3 × 3, 256	2	16 × 16 × 256
7	Convolution	1 × 1, 128	–	16 × 16 × 128
	Convolution	3 × 3, 256	1	16 × 16 × 256
8	Convolution	1 × 1, 128	–	16 × 16 × 128
	Convolution	3 × 3, 256	1	16 × 16 × 256

Feature maps on different channels can be fused by 1×1 convolutional layers, which can highlight the features of the detection target, increase the depth of the network and improve the detection accuracy. Another key role is to reduce the computational complexity as a dimension reduction module [16]. The advantage of this method is that the convolution results of the previous layer can be fused by 1×1 convolutional layers, which improve the ability of feature fusion and reduce the computational complexity.

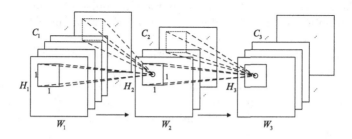

Fig. 3. Feature fusion of 1×1 convolutional layers.

1×1 convolutional layers can reduce or increase the dimension of feature map freely. It can be used to normalize the size of different features or to fuse the features on different channels. Characteristic fusion sketch of 1×1 convolution layers as shown in Fig. 3.

3.2   Multi-scale Feature Extraction

Fabric defect image is mainly composed of direction, boundary and curvature information. In addition, most fabric defect sizes are too small to be detected. Therefore, we adopt multi-scale feature extraction in the low-level features and medium-level features.   In order to tackle with the defect with small size, we

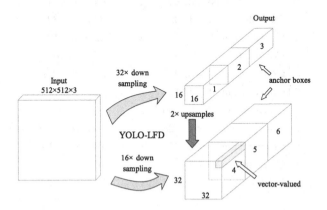

Fig. 4. The improved multi-scale detection module. When the size of the input image is $512 \times 512 \times 3$, the network will generate $16 \times 16 \times 3 + 32 \times 32 \times 3$ prediction boxes.

revise the multi-scale detection module of YOLO-v3 by using two different scale feature maps to extract features, which can make use of both high-resolution information of low-level features and high-semantic information of high-level features. We extract the features from the feature maps after $16\times$ and $32\times$ downsampled, and fuse the features between the two layers of feature maps. This method can improve the feature extraction ability of small targets and get more meaningful semantic information from the upsampled features. The structure diagram is shown in the following Fig. 4.

YOLO-LFD extract features from multiple scales. From the basic feature extractor, several convolution layers are utilized to predict bounding box, objectness, and class predictions. The model predicts three different scales boxes in each feature layer. Therefore, a total of 6 anchor boxes with different scales are needed for the 2 feature layers. The initial value of anchor box is obtained by K-means clustering algorithm.

3.3   K-means Clustering Algorithm

K-means clustering algorithm is a classical distance-based clustering algorithm, which uses distance as the evaluation index of similarity. The algorithm considers that clusters are composed of objects close to each other [17]. Therefore, the final goal of the algorithm is to get compact and independent clusters, and the data can be classified into different categories according to the distance relationship.

The traditional K-means clustering method uses the Euclidean Distance function, but this means that larger bounding boxes have produced greater errors than smaller bounding box, and the clustering result may deviate. To this end, the overlap ratio of the generated candidate box and the original marker box (IOU) is used to distance calculation [18,19], and appropriate priori box is generated by clustering, thus avoiding the error caused by the scale of the box. The distance function can be computed as the following formula:

$$D(box, centroid) = 1 - IOU(box, centroid) \tag{2}$$

According to the texture characteristics of fabric defects, we use K-means clustering algorithm to cluster the size of ground truth in fabric image database,and get anchor boxes which are closest to the size of the fabric defects bounding box. This priori knowledge is great helpful for the initialization of the bounding box.

4   Experimental Results and Analysis

The model was tested on the fabric image dataset, and compared the experimental results with SSD, YOLO-v3 and Tiny-Yolo-v3 tested by the same equipment. Experiments show that the detection accuracy of our model is close to YOLO-v3, and higher than SSD, Tiny-Yolo-v3. The detection speed is much higher than them, and the model parameters are far fewer than these networks.

4.1   Dataset

The dataset includes 3000 fabric defect images, which contains five classes (holes, surface debris, oil stains, longitude and weft breakage) of defects. Among them, 2000 pictures were randomly selected as the training set, and 1000 pictures as the test set. Part of the fabric defect images are shown in Fig. 5 below.

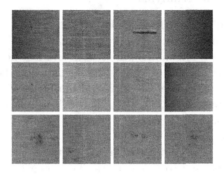

Fig. 5. Fabric defect image dataset.

4.2   Training Parameters

Keras framework is used to train the model. The operating system is Windows 10, the processors are two Intel Xeon (R) E5-2650-v4 CPUS and the system includes two NVIDIA Quadro M5000 graphics processing units GPUs. The initial training parameters of the YOLO-LFD are shown in Table 3.

Table 3. Initialization parameters of YOLO-LFD network.

Size of input images	Batch	Learning rate	Decay	Iteration steps
512×512	5	0.001	0.0005	500200

4.3   Fine-Tuning

The extraction of underlying features is very important for CNNs. Because there are fewer images of fabric defect datasets, the ability of neural network to extract the underlying features is insufficient, which has a great impact on the detection accuracy. The most fruitful and therefore most often applied approach is to pre-train a CNN on a large corpus of outside data and to fine-tune parameters on the target data.

COCO dataset contains photos of 91 objects types, with a total of 2.5 million labeled instances in 328k images [20]. Supervised pretraining on external data followed by domain specific fine-tuning yields a significant performance boost when external data and target domain show similar visual characteristics.

We present result for the model pre-trained on the entire COCO dataset, followed by domain-specific fine-tuning on fabric defect dataset. Firstly, the model parameters trained on COCO dataset are used as initial parameters. Freeze all the network layers except the last three layers, and train 50 epochs to train on the fabric defect dataset, thus retaining the underlying features. Then, thaw all layers and then train for another 50 epochs on fabric defect dataset.

4.4   Test Results and Analysis

The experimental results show that YOLO-LFD has a good effect on fabric image defect detection. Our neural network not only can accurately detect the location of defects, but also has a few model parameters and fast detection speed.

K-means clustering algorithm is used to calculate the bounding box of the fabric defect training set, and get the initial anchor boxes of size (12, 8), (35, 19), (57, 48), (117, 67), (139, 30), (203, 129). Through this method, the model can find the defect location more accurately. The test results of K-means clustering algorithm are shown in Fig. 6.

Experiments show that under the same network structure, when K-means clustering algorithm is used to calculate the bounding box of training set, the

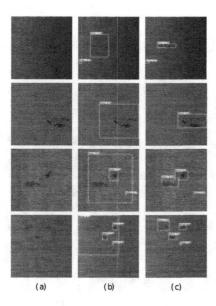

(a)   (b)   (c)

Fig. 6. Test results of k-mean algorithm. (a) the original test picture, (b) the test result without K-means clustering algorithm, (c) the test result with K-means clustering algorithm.

initialization anchor box can obviously improve the detection accuracy of defective targets, enhance the positioning ability of targets, and make the algorithm more applicable.

The experimental result of YOLO-LFD on fabric defect detection is shown in Fig. 7, which shows that the new neural network model has a good detection effect on fabric defects. It can detect various types of fabric defects. The detection effect is better than other neural networks, especially for small targets and less significant targets. The proposed algorithm YOLO-LFD is compared with YOLO-v3, Tiny-Yolo-v3 and SSD. We use the same training set and test set to experiment on the same hardware environment. The model performance comparison results are shown in Table 4.

Table 4. Comparison of the accuracy, speed and parameter size of each model in fabric defect detection task.

	ACC (%)	Speed (ms)	Model size (MB)
SSD	75.3	420.2	163
YOLO-v3	98.0	132.2	241
Tiny-Yolo-v3	86.1	56.5	34
YOLO-LFD	97.2	51.0	8

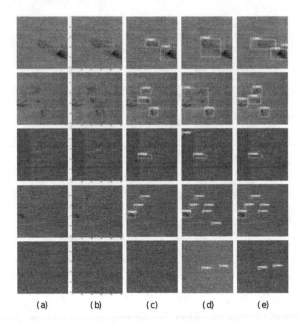

(a)   (b)   (c)   (d)   (e)

Fig. 7. Comparison of defect detection results. (a) The original test picture, (b) Detection results of SSD, (c) Detection results of Tiny-Yolo-v3, (d) Detection results of YOLO-v3, (e) Detection results of YOLO-LFD.

According to our experiments, the detection accuracy of the model reaches 97.2%, which is close to YOLO-v3. However, the model size is 30× smaller than that of YOLO-v3, and the detection speed is increased by 2.6×.

5   Conclusion

In this paper, a new lightweight deep convolution neural network, YOLO-LFD is proposed to detect fabric defects. The 1 × 1 convolution layer is used to fuse the feature map, which to improve the detection accuracy. We use K-means clustering algorithm to calculate the sizes of ground trues and get the initial anchor boxes. We compressed YOLO-v3 model from 241 MB to 8 MB, the detection speed is increased by 2.6×, and the accuracy is almost unchanged. The model is pre-trained on the entire COCO dataset, and then domain-specific fine-tuning on fabric defect dataset, which solves the problem of insufficient training set. Our work achieves the goal of lightening the deep convolution neural network, the model can greatly reduce computation cost while maintaining accuracy. In the future, we will explore how to embed the algorithm into the automatic defect detection system to achieve industrial applications.

References

1. Li, Y., Zhao, W., Pan, J.: Deformable patterned fabric defect detection with fisher criterion-based deep learning. IEEE Trans. Autom. Sci. Eng. **14**(2), 1256–1264 (2017)
2. Zhao, X., Deng, Z., Ran, Y.: Detection of fabric defect based on weighted local entropy. Cotton Text. Technol. **40**(10), 20–23 (2012)
3. Xiaobo, Y.: Fabric defect detection of statistic aberration feature based on GMRF model. J. Text. Res. **34**(4), 137–142 (2013)
4. Shuai, Z., Fengsheng, Z., Fucai, L.: Feature extraction of fabric defects based on wavelet transform. J. QingDao Univ. **28**(2), 53–59 (2013)
5. Yuan, L., Li, F., Yang, Y., et al.: Analysis of texture feature extracted by gray level co-occurrence matrix. Comput. Appl. **29**(4), 1019–1021 (2009)
6. Lecun, Y., Bengio, Y., Hinton, G.: Deep learning. Nature **521**(7553), 436 (2015)
7. Jing, J., Dong, A., Li, P., et al.: Yarn-dyed fabric defect classification based on convolutional neural network. Opt. Eng. **56**(9), 093104 (2017)
8. Shi, Y., Li, Y., Wei, X., et al.: A faster-RCNN based chemical fiber paper tube defect detection method. In: 2017 5th International Conference on Enterprise Systems (ES), pp. 173–177. IEEE (2017)
9. Tao, X., Zhang, D., Ma, W., et al.: Automatic metallic surface defect detection and recognition with convolutional neural networks. Appl. Sci. **8**(9), 1575 (2018)
10. Girshick, R., Donahue, J., Darrell, T., et al.: Rich feature hierarchies for accurate object detection and semantic segmentation. In: Proceedings of the IEEE Conference on Computer Vision and Pattern Recognition, pp. 580–587 (2014)
11. Girshick, R.: Fast R-CNN. Comput. Sci. (2015)
12. Lin, T.Y., Dollr, P., Girshick, R., et al.: Feature pyramid networks for object detection (2016)
13. Han, S., Liu, X., Mao, H., et al.: EIE: efficient inference engine on compressed deep neural network. In: ISCA. IEEE Computer Society (2016)
14. He, K., Zhang, X., Ren, S., et al.: Deep residual learning for image recognition (2015)
15. Redmon, J., Farhadi, A.: YOLO9000: better, faster, stronger. In: 2017 IEEE Conference on Computer Vision and Pattern Recognition (CVPR), pp. 6517–6525. IEEE (2017)
16. Szegedy, C., Liu, W., Jia, Y., et al.: Going deeper with convolutions. In: 2015 IEEE Conference on Computer Vision and Pattern Recognition (CVPR). IEEE (2015)
17. Dhanachandra, N., Manglem, K., Chanu, Y.J.: Image segmentation using K-means clustering algorithm and subtractive clustering algorithm. Proc. Comput. Sci. **54**, 764–771 (2015)
18. Nowozin, S.: Optimal decisions from probabilistic models: the intersection-over-union case. In: IEEE Conference on Computer Vision and Pattern Recognition. IEEE Computer Society (2014)
19. Ahmed, F., Tarlow, D., Batra, D.: Optimizing expected intersection-over-union with candidate-constrained CRFs. In: IEEE International Conference on Computer Vision (2016)
20. Lin, T.Y., et al.: Microsoft COCO: common objects in context. In: Fleet, D., Pajdla, T., Schiele, B., Tuytelaars, T. (eds.) ECCV 2014. LNCS, vol. 8693, pp. 740–755. Springer, Cham (2014). https://doi.org/10.1007/978-3-319-10602-1_48

Person Re-identification with Neural Architecture Search

Shizhou Zhang[1], Rui Cao[2], Xing Wei[3], Peng Wang[1(✉)], and Yanning Zhang[1]

[1] National Engineering Laboratory for Integrated Aero-Space-Ground-Ocean Big
Data Application Technology, School of Computer Science, Northwestern
Polytechnical University, Xi'an 710072, China
peng.wang@nwpu.edu.cn
[2] School of Information Science and Technology, Northwest University,
Xi'an 710127, China
[3] Institute of Artificial Intelligence and Robotics, College of Artificial Intelligence,
Xi'an Jiaotong University, Xi'an 710049, China

Abstract. Most of the existing person re-identification (ReID) methods
use a classification network pre-trained on external data as the backbone and then fine-tune it, which results in a network architecture that
is fixed and dependent on pre-training of external data. There are also
some methods that are specifically designed by human experts for ReID,
but manual network design becomes more difficult as network requirements increase and often fails to achieve optimal settings. In this paper,
we consider using emerging neural architecture search (NAS) technology
as a tool to solve above problems. However, most of NAS methods deal
with classification tasks, which causes NAS to not be directly extended
to ReID. In order to coordinate the inconsistency between the two optimization goals, we propose to establish an objective function with the
assistant of the triplet loss to guide the direction of architecture search.
Finally, it is no longer dependent on external data to automatically generate a ReID network with excellent performance using NAS directly on
the target dataset. The experimental results on three public datasets validate that our method can automatically and efficiently find the network
architecture suitable for ReID.

Keywords: Person re-identification · Neural architecture search

1 Introduction

Person re-identification (ReID) is a particularly challenging task, which aims at
retrieving images of the specific person across different cameras. With the rapid

S. Zhang and R. Cao—Denotes co-first authors. This work is partifically supported
by Natural Science Basic Research Plan in Shaanxi Province of China (Program No.
2019JQ158), China Postdoctoral Science Foundation funded project under Grant No.
2018M633577, the Fundamental Research Funds for Central Universities of China under
Grant No. G2018KY0303, and National Science Foundation of China under Grant No.
61801395, 61801393 and 61801391.

© Springer Nature Switzerland AG 2019
Z. Lin et al. (Eds.): PRCV 2019, LNCS 11857, pp. 540–551, 2019.
https://doi.org/10.1007/978-3-030-31654-9_46

development of deep learning [2,8,12,13,30,32,34,35], ReID methods based on deep neural network have made remarkable progresses [14,43]. However, developing state-of-the-art neural network architectures requires considerable effort of human experts through trial and error. Recently, some researchers have begun to study algorithms to automatically learn neural network architectures, which is so-called neural architecture search [6] (NAS). Moreover, the neural architectures searched by NAS algorithms automatically have achieved competitive performance compared with the state-of-the-arts invented by human experts in some tasks. For the ReID problem, most of the existing methods are first to pretrain a network in the classification task through external data, and then fine-tune it on the ReID datasets. This approach results in a network architecture that is relatively fixed and dependent on external datasets. If changing to a new baseline network architecture requires retraining on the external datasets, which is very time-consuming and cannot achieve optimal settings for the network architecture.

In order to overcome the above drawbacks, we need to search for an optimal network architecture directly from the ReID datasets without the help of external datasets. But if the existing NAS is directly extended to the ReID task, there is a problem that the ReID is evaluated differently than the classification task. The training pedestrian classes in the ReID do not intersect with the test pedestrian classes and the performance evaluation metric is similar to the ranking result rather than the classification accuracy, which is inconsistent with the optimization goal of NAS on the classification task. Performing performance evaluation on the searched candidate network architecture based only on the classification accuracy, and then guiding the direction of the network search according to the classification accuracy of the feedback does not ensure that the searched network can be effective for the ReID task. Therefore, we need to conduct an architectural search in a manner consistent with the real evaluation of the ReID, and the ultimate goal is that it is no longer necessary to pretrain external datasets to utilize neural architecture search algorithms directly on ReID datasets in the hope of automatically finding an optimal or sub-optimal network architecture suitable for this task.

2   Related Work

2.1   Person Re-identification

ReID has been studied intensively as a classic research topic. In the past few years, there are two main methods for the study of ReID: one is representation learning [1,7,19,29,31,38] and the other is metric learning [4,9,24,40,46]. The methods based on representation learning are to obtain robust and discriminative pedestrian features. Su et al. [31] proposed a pose-driven deep convolution model that uses human body cues to alleviate posture variations and adaptively learn more discriminative feature fusions from the global human body and different local body parts. Geng et al. [7] used a deep basic network to extract features and combined with the classification subnet and verification subnet to make full use of identity information. Lin et al. [19] combine the pedestrian attribute recognition, which performs well on local features, with the ReID method, which focuses on learning global features, to improve the performance of ReID. The methods based on metric learning learn the similarity between image pairs by designing a suitable distance metric function, aiming to make the distance of the same identity images as small as possible and the distance of different identities images as large as possible. Hermans et al. [9] proposed an improved triplet loss function with the batch hard sample mining. Cheng et al. [4] considered the absolute distance between positive sample pairs on the basis of [9] to propose an improved triplet loss function for training. Paisitkriangkrai et al. [24] proposed an effective structured learning based approach which learns the weights of different metric distance functions by optimizing the relative distance between the triple samples and maximizing the average rank-k precision. Many of the above methods are based on the classic classification neural architecture (such as the famous ResNet50 [8], Inception [32] and DenseNet [10]) as a baseline network, which need to rely on external data for pre-training before fine-tuning the improved network with target ReID data. In addition, there are some methods in which the human experts design the network specifically for the ReID [1,16,33,38], but it requires a lot of professional knowledge and experience, and it is relatively more difficult to design the network reasonably as the complex network requirements increase.

2.2 Neural Architecture Search

In 2017, Zoph and Le [47] proposed a pioneering work to train a recurrent neural network controller using the reinforcement learning mechanism to automatically search a neural network without human intervention, which has achieved competitive performance compared with the best architecture designed by human experts on the classification task of the cifar10 dataset. This work provides a new direction for the automatic generation of excellent neural network architecture. Since then, NAS has attracted extensive attention from academia and industry, and has become one of the mainstream research topics in the field of machine learning. In addition to methods based on reinforcement learning [3,47,48], there are evolutionary algorithms [26,27,39], gradient-based methods [21,22], SMBO [20], MCTS [23], Bayesian Optimization [11], etc, all of which have achieved good performance. Considering the low scalability due to the excessive computational resource requirements of the NAS algorithm. More recent research efforts have focused on how to achieve further competitive performance with fewer computing resources. For example, Zoph et al. [48] proposed NASNet that uses cells as the architectural building block to repeatedly stack into the final architecture, thus simplifying the search architecture to search for the best cell, which has made a breakthrough improvement on the basis of [47]. Elsken et al. [5] proposed NASH based on the hill climbing algorithm. Pham et al. [25] proposed ENAS that shares the weight of all subnetworks. Liu et al. [21] proposed DARTS to make discrete search spaces continuous for differentiable operations by a continuous relaxation scheme. Although NAS has gradually overcome its computational cost and time-consuming defects and achieved very competitive performance with human-invented networks, most of the existing NAS methods are aimed at solving image classification, which is characterized by sufficient training data, i.e., number of samples per class ranges from dozens to tens of thousands. Unlike most existing work on NAS, our approach aims to extend NAS technology to the ReID field.

3   The Proposed Method

3.1   Background

Recently, many NAS algorithms use cell as the basic building block of the neural architecture [20,21,37,48]. By repeatedly stacking these cells to form the final complex architecture, the search of the neural network is transformed into a search for the cell. Assuming that the network architecture is repeatedly stacked by K cells, and the cell is abstracted into a directed acyclic graph composed of N ordered nodes. Following [21,48], each $cell_k$ has two input nodes, N-3 intermediate nodes and one output node. The input nodes respectively receive the outputs of $cell_{k-1}$ and $cell_{k-2}$, and the transformation formula of the intermediate nodes is:

$$n_j = \sum_{i<j} o_{i,j}(n_i),\tag{1}$$

where n_i and n_j represent the i-th node and the j-th node, respectively, and $o_{i,j}$ represents a certain neural computational operation employed by n_i to n_j. The output node is obtained by concatenation operation on all intermediate nodes.

There are many different search strategies that are proposed to efficiently search for the optimal network architecture. From the perspective of the ReID, we decided to draw on the search strategy of DARTS [21] to complete the search for the network architecture of the ReID after carefully comparing various NAS algorithms. The DARTS algorithm implements efficient convolutional neural network architecture search for classification tasks on cifar10, and the entire search process requires only a single GPU to complete compared to the high computational resource requirements of most other algorithms. DARTS develops a continuous relaxation scheme for the discrete search space, i.e., continuous relaxation of the search space by placing a mixture of candidate operations on each edge:

$$\bar{o}_{i,j}(n) = \sum_{o\in O} \frac{\exp\left(\alpha_o^{(i,j)}\right)}{\sum_{o'\in O}\exp\left(\alpha_{o'}^{(i,j)}\right)} o(n),\tag{2}$$

where O represents a set of all candidate operations, which in our method include depth-wise separable convolution (3×3, 5×5, and 7×7), dilated convolution (3×3, and 5×5), average pooling (3×3), max pooling (3×3), skip connection and zero operation. And $\alpha_o^{(i,j)}$ represents the operation mixing weight between nodes i and j. After the continuous relaxation in Eq. (2), the task of model structure search is transformed into the learning of continuous variable set $\alpha = \{\alpha^{(i,j)}\}$, and α is called the architecture parameters. At the end of the search, the mixed operation $\bar{o}^{(i,j)}$ is replaced by the maximum possible operation $\max_{o \in \mathcal{O}, o \neq zero} \frac{\exp\left(\alpha_o^{(i,j)}\right)}{\sum_{o' \in \mathcal{O}} \exp\left(\alpha_{o'}^{(i,j)}\right)}$ to obtain a discrete network architecture. Through such a scheme, the network architecture is also treated as a continuous variable to perform gradient descent optimization, so that the joint optimization goal of the architecture α and the network weights w is differentiable to utilize the gradient-based optimization algorithms for efficient search.

3.2   Searching for Convolutional Cells on ReID Datasets

We search the convolutional cells as the building blocks for the final architecture. A cell is represented as a directed acyclic graph composed of seven nodes. In order to search the convolutional cells on the ReID datasets, we first treat the ReID as a classification problem of small data. The persons with the same identity are the same class. And then we randomly confuse the training set and split it into two parts of the training set and the validation set with a ratio of 1:1. We designed a class sampler to ensure that both the training set and the validation set contain all classes. The training set is to train the network weight w, and the validation set is for searching the network architecture α.

For the ReID task, the identity classes of the test set are other identities that do not overlap at all with the training set, which causes a difference with the optimization goal of the classification task. Therefore, we establish an objective function with the assistant of the triplet loss to guide the neural architecture search process. Our objective function is:

$$
\begin{aligned}
\mathcal{L} = &\sum_{i=1}^{M} -y_i \log\left(\mathcal{S}\left(x_i\right)\right) \\
&+ \sum_{i=1}^{M} \left(\left\|\mathcal{F}\left(x_i\right) - \mathcal{F}\left(x_i^{+}\right)\right\|_2 - \left\|\mathcal{F}\left(x_i\right) - \mathcal{F}\left(x_i^{-}\right)\right\|_2 + d\right)_{+},
\end{aligned}
\tag{3}
$$

where the first term is the cross entropy loss and the second one is the triplet loss. And M is the number of training samples, x_i represents the i-th sample, x_i^{+} is a positive sample with the same identity as x_i, x_i^{-} is a negative sample with a different identity from x_i, y_i is the ground-truth one-hot encoded label of the i-th sample, $\mathcal{S}(\cdot)$ indicates the output of the network classifier after softmax activation, $\mathcal{F}(\cdot)$ indicates the network feature extractor before the classification layer, $(z)_{+}$ indicates $max(z, 0)$, and d indicates a margin parameter. Our goal is to minimize this meta-objective function and search the strategy to follow DARTS. A small network of K = 8 cells is stacked to search on the divided training set, and finally the best convolution cell based on the ReID is obtained through training.

3.3   Retraining and Ranking

Retraining. We use the best convolution cell trained in the previous stage to repeatedly stack a large network of K = 20 cells, and retrain the network weight w of this large network with all the training sets including the previous validation set used to search the network architecture.

Ranking. In order to evaluate the ReID model we found through the network architecture search algorithm, the test datasets is usually divided into a query set and a gallery set, and we need to evaluate the similarity score of the query-gallery image pairs. We remove the last classification layer of the trained large network and use it as the feature extractor, then input the person images into the network to extract the corresponding deep convolutional feature maps. We use the simple L_2 Euclidean distance to calculate the similarity score between image feature vectors:

$$d_{q_i,g_j} = \|\mathcal{F}_{NAS}(q_i) - \mathcal{F}_{NAS}(g_j)\|_2 , \tag{4}$$

where $\mathcal{F}_{NAS}(\cdot)$ denotes the feature extraction operation using the final network architecture, q_i and g_j denote the i-th query images and the j-th gallery images.

4   Experiments and Results

4.1   Person ReID Datasets and Evaluation Metrics

In this paper, we report the performance evaluation of our model on the three authoritative datasets Market1501 [42], CUHK03 [16], and DukeMTMC-reID [44]. The Market-1501 dataset [42] has a total of 32,668 images of 1501 identities, of which 12,936 images of 751 identities are divided into the training set, and 19,732 images of the other 750 identities form the test set. The CUHK03 dataset [16] contained 14,097 images with 1467 different identities. It is divided into a detected set that draw pedestrian bounding boxes by a pedestrian detector and a labeled set manually cropped bounding boxes. We use the detected set to train and test in this paper. The DukeMTMC-reID dataset [44] is a subset of the DukeMTMC dataset [28], which consists of 16,522 images of 702 identities in the training set and 19,889 images of the other 702 identities in the test set.

We use the universal cumulative matching characteristics (CMC) and mean average precision (mAP) [42] to evaluate the performance of the automatically learned neural network model. We follow the original evaluation protocol for each dataset. The following Table 1 gives dataset split instructions in this paper. (Train Images, Train IDs) and (Val Images, Val IDs) indicate the split details in the first stage (i.e., search architecture), (Trainval Images, Trainval IDs) and the remaining ones are respectively listed is for the second stage of retraining and ranking.

Table 1. Dataset split instructions.

Dataset	Market1501	CUHK03	DukeMTMC-reID
Train IDs	751	1,367	702
Train images	6,468	6,557	8,261
Val IDs	751	1,367	702
Val images	6,468	6,556	8,261
Trainval IDs	751	1,367	702
Trainval images	12,936	13,113	16,522
Test IDs	750	100	702
Query images	3,368	984	2,228
Gallery images	19,732	984	17,661

4.2   Implementation Details

Stage 1: Searching. The input image is resized to 128×64, and we use random horizontal flip and random crop for data augmentation. In order to adapt to search the architecture on a single 1080Ti GPU condition, our experimental parameter settings are: we train the network of 8 cell with 100 epoch and the mini-batch size is set to 16, in which each identity has 4 samples. The optimizer uses Adam to optimize the architecture α with the initial learning rate of 0.0003 and momentum (0.9, 0.999). The optimizer uses momentum SGD to optimize the weight w with momentum 0.9 and adopts a cosine schedule to reduce the original learning rate from 0.025 to 0.001. We set d is 0.3 and weight decay is 0.0005. This search process takes about 2 day or so using a single GeForce GTX 1080Ti GPU. Finally, the two types of cells, normal cells and reduction cells, are optimized through training.

Stage 2: Retraining. We first use the best convolutional cell we get in Stage 1 to repeat stacking a large network of 20 cells. We use random horizontal flip and random crop for data augmentation. We retrain the large network with 600 epoch and the mini-batch size is set to 64. The setup of other hyperparameters follows the stage 1. We adopt L_2 Euclidean distance as the similarity score for ranking.

4.3   Comparison with State-of-the-Arts

In this section, we compare our method with the state-of-art ReID methods. For the baseline Resnet-50 is pre-trained on the ImageNet. And our method and the baseline Inception are trained from scratch. We use L_2 Euclidean distance for ranking throughout the paper.

Results on Market1501 Dataset. our method achieve 78.8% rank-1 accuracy and 59.2% mAP exceeding baseline ResNet-50 by 1.5% and 3.3% respectively.

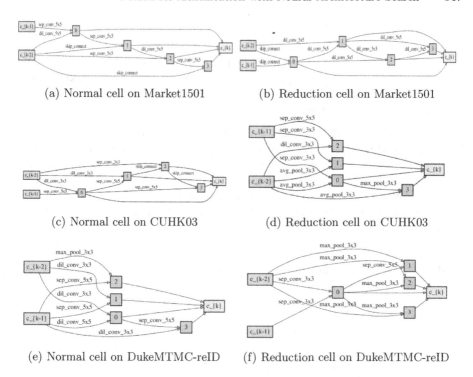

(a) Normal cell on Market1501

(b) Reduction cell on Market1501

(c) Normal cell on CUHK03

(d) Reduction cell on CUHK03

(e) Normal cell on DukeMTMC-reID

(f) Reduction cell on DukeMTMC-reID

Fig. 1. The normal and reduction cells searched on the Market1501, CUHK03 and DukeMTMC-reID datasets.

Fig. 2. The leftmost column is the query images, and the right side is the rank-k (k = 10) result on Market-1501 gallery set. The red frame circled the pedestrian images with the wrong identification, and the green frame circled to identify the correct images.

The results are listed in Table 2. Compared with methods using ImageNet pre-training, such as Basel. + LSRO [44], Our method improves the Rank-1 and mAP by 0.7% and 3.0% respectively. Our method also exceeds the specially designed network MSCAN [15] by 2.5% and 6.1% on rank-1 and mAP respectively, and outperforms the baseline Inception by 3.0% and 7.4% on rank-1 and mAP respectively (Figs. 1 and 2).

Results on CUHK03 Dataset. In Table 3, our method achieve 78.9% rank-1 accuracy and 68.3% mAP. Our method outperforms the baseline ResNet-50 by 8.1% and 5.6% on rank-1 and mAP respectively, and achieve competitive results for rank-5 and rank-10. Besides approaches such as baseline Inception and MSCAN [15], which have been introduced previously, our proposed method also outperforms LOMO+XQDA [17] by 32.6% and Gated Reid [33] by 10.8% on rank-1 accuracy.

Table 2. CMC rank-1, rank-5, rank-10 accuracies, and mAP by compared methods on the Market1501 dataset.

Method	Market1501			
	Rank-1	Rank-5	Rank-10	mAP
Inception [32]	75.8	–	–	51.8
ResNet-50 [8]	77.3	90.8	93.3	55.9
Basel. + LSRO [44]	78.1	–	–	56.2
MSCAN [15]	76.3	–	–	53.1
SpindleNet [41]	76.9	91.5	94.5	–
CADL [18]	73.8	–	–	47.1
Ours	78.8	92.7	95.3	59.2

Table 3. CMC rank-1, rank-5, rank-10 accuracies, and mAP by compared methods on the CUHK03 dataset.

Method	CUHK03			
	Rank-1	Rank-5	Rank-10	mAP
Inception [32]	73.2	–	–	65.8
ResNet-50 [8]	70.8	–	–	62.7
LOMO+XQDA [17]	46.3	78.9	88.6	–
Gated Reid [33]	68.1	88.1	94.6	58.8
k-reciprocal [45]	61.6	–	–	67.6
OL-MANS [46]	61.7	88.4	95.2	–
MSCAN [15]	74.2	94.3	97.5	–
Ours	78.9	95.2	98.0	68.3

Results on DukeMTMC-reID Dataset. The rank-1 accuracy and mAP of our method are 69.5% and 48.0%, respectively. The proposed method exceeds baseline ResNet-50 by 7.0% and baseline Inception by 15.1% on rank-1 accuracy. Our method exceeds all the compared methods in Table 4.

Table 4. CMC rank-1, rank-5, rank-10 accuracies, and mAP by compared methods on the DukeMTMC-reID dataset.

Method	DukeMTMC-reID			
	Rank-1	Rank-5	Rank-10	mAP
BoW+KISSME [42]	25.1	–	–	12.2
LOMO+XQDA [17]	37.8	–	–	17.0
Inception [32]	54.4	–	–	34.0
ResNet-50 [8]	62.5	–	–	40.7
Basel.+LSRO [44]	67.7	–	–	47.1
OMI loss [36]	68.1	–	–	47.4
Ours	69.5	81.3	85.1	48.0

5   Conclusion

In this paper, we treat ReID as a small data problem, and use the improved neural architecture search algorithm to automatically generate a neural network suitable for the person ReID task directly on the target dataset without relying on the pre-training of the external data set. Our experiments validate that using NAS automatically generates a ReID network with better performance, which not only surpasses some networks pre-trained with external data, but also better than some ReID networks specially designed by human experts.

References

1. Ahmed, E., Jones, M., Marks, T.K.: An improved deep learning architecture for person re-identification. In: CVPR (2015)
2. Arandjelovic, R., Gronat, P., Torii, A., Pajdla, T., Sivic, J.: NETVLAD: CNN architecture for weakly supervised place recognition. In: CVPR, pp. 5297–5307 (2016)
3. Baker, B., Gupta, O., Naik, N., Raskar, R.: Designing neural network architectures using reinforcement learning. In: ICLR (2017)
4. Cheng, D., Gong, Y., Zhou, S., Wang, J., Zheng, N.: Person re-identification by multi-channel parts-based CNN with improved triplet loss function. In: CVPR (2016)
5. Elsken, T., Metzen, J.H., Hutter, F.: Simple and efficient architecture search for convolutional neural networks. In: ICLR (2018)
6. Elsken, T., Metzen, J.H., Hutter, F.: Neural architecture search: a survey. J. Mach. Learn. Res. **20**, 55:1–55:21 (2019)

7. Geng, M., Wang, Y., Xiang, T., Tian, Y.: Deep transfer learning for person re-identification. CoRR (2016)
8. He, K., Zhang, X., Ren, S., Sun, J.: Deep residual learning for image recognition. In: CVPR, pp. 770–778 (2016)
9. Hermans, A., Beyer, L., Leibe, B.: In defense of the triplet loss for person re-identification. CoRR (2017)
10. Huang, G., Liu, Z., Weinberger, K.Q.: Densely connected convolutional networks. CoRR (2016)
11. Kandasamy, K., Neiswanger, W., Schneider, J., Póczos, B., Xing, E.P.: Neural architecture search with Bayesian optimisation and optimal transport. In: NeurIPS, pp. 2020–2029 (2018)
12. Kim, E., Hannan, D., Kenyon, G.: Deep sparse coding for invariant multimodal halle berry neurons. In: CVPR (2018)
13. Krizhevsky, A., Sutskever, I., Hinton, G.E.: ImageNet classification with deep convolutional neural networks. In: NIPS, pp. 1097–1105 (2012)
14. Lavi, B., Serj, M.F., Ullah, I.: Survey on deep learning techniques for person re-identification task. CoRR (2018)
15. Li, D., Chen, X., Zhang, Z., Huang, K.: Learning deep context-aware features over body and latent parts for person re-identification. In: CVPR, pp. 7398–7407 (2017)
16. Li, W., Zhao, R., Xiao, T., Wang, X.: DeepReID: deep filter pairing neural network for person re-identification. In: CVPR (2014)
17. Liao, S., Hu, Y., Zhu, X., Li, S.Z.: Person re-identification by local maximal occurrence representation and metric learning. In: CVPR, pp. 2197–2206 (2015)
18. Lin, J., Ren, L., Lu, J., Feng, J., Zhou, J.: Consistent-aware deep learning for person re-identification in a camera network. In: CVPR, pp. 3396–3405 (2017)
19. Lin, Y., Zheng, L., Zheng, Z., Wu, Y., Yang, Y.: Improving person re-identification by attribute and identity learning. CoRR (2017)
20. Liu, C., et al.: Progressive neural architecture search. In: Ferrari, V., Hebert, M., Sminchisescu, C., Weiss, Y. (eds.) ECCV 2018. LNCS, vol. 11205, pp. 19–35. Springer, Cham (2018). https://doi.org/10.1007/978-3-030-01246-5_2
21. Liu, H., Simonyan, K., Yang, Y.: DARTS: differentiable architecture search. CoRR (2018)
22. Luo, R., Tian, F., Qin, T., Liu, T.: Neural architecture optimization. CoRR (2018)
23. Negrinho, R., Gordon, G.J.: DeepArchitect: automatically designing and training deep architectures. CoRR (2017)
24. Paisitkriangkrai, S., Shen, C., van den Hengel, A.: Learning to rank in person re-identification with metric ensembles. In: CVPR (2015)
25. Pham, H., Guan, M.Y., Zoph, B., Le, Q.V., Dean, J.: Efficient neural architecture search via parameter sharing. In: The International Conference on Machine Learning (ICML), pp. 4092–4101 (2018)
26. Real, E., Aggarwal, A., Huang, Y., Le, Q.V.: Regularized evolution for image classifier architecture search. CoRR (2018)
27. Real, E., et al.: Large-scale evolution of image classifiers. In: Proceedings of the 34th International Conference on Machine Learning, ICML 2017, Sydney, NSW, Australia, 6–11 August 2017, pp. 2902–2911 (2017)
28. Ristani, E., Solera, F., Zou, R., Cucchiara, R., Tomasi, C.: Performance measures and a data set for multi-target, multi-camera tracking. In: Hua, G., Jégou, H. (eds.) ECCV 2016. LNCS, vol. 9914, pp. 17–35. Springer, Cham (2016). https://doi.org/10.1007/978-3-319-48881-3_2
29. Shen, Y., Xiao, T., Li, H., Yi, S., Wang, X.: End-to-end deep Kronecker-product matching for person re-identification. In: CVPR (2018)

30. Simonyan, K., Zisserman, A.: Very deep convolutional networks for large-scale image recognition. In: ICLR (2015)
31. Su, C., Li, J., Zhang, S., Xing, J., Gao, W., Tian, Q.: Pose-driven deep convolutional model for person re-identification. In: ICCV (2017)
32. Szegedy, C., et al.: Going deeper with convolutions. In: CVPR (2015)
33. Varior, R.R., Haloi, M., Wang, G.: Gated siamese convolutional neural network architecture for human re-identification. In: Leibe, B., Matas, J., Sebe, N., Welling, M. (eds.) ECCV 2016. LNCS, vol. 9912, pp. 791–808. Springer, Cham (2016). https://doi.org/10.1007/978-3-319-46484-8_48
34. Wei, X., Zhang, Y., Gong, Y., Zhang, J., Zheng, N.: Grassmann pooling as compact homogeneous bilinear pooling for fine-grained visual classification. In: Ferrari, V., Hebert, M., Sminchisescu, C., Weiss, Y. (eds.) ECCV 2018. LNCS, vol. 11207, pp. 365–380. Springer, Cham (2018). https://doi.org/10.1007/978-3-030-01219-9_22
35. Wei, X., Zhang, Y., Gong, Y., Zheng, N.: Kernelized subspace pooling for deep local descriptors. In: CVPR, pp. 1867–1875 (2018)
36. Xiao, T., Li, S., Wang, B., Lin, L., Wang, X.: Joint detection and identification feature learning for person search. In: CVPR, pp. 3376–3385 (2017)
37. Xie, S., Zheng, H., Liu, C., Lin, L.: SNAS: stochastic neural architecture search. CoRR (2018)
38. Yi, D., Lei, Z., Liao, S., Li, S.Z.: Deep metric learning for person re-identification. In: ICPR, pp. 34–39 (2014)
39. Zhang, H., Kiranyaz, S., Gabbouj, M.: Finding better topologies for deep convolutional neural networks by evolution. CoRR (2018)
40. Zhang, S., Zhang, Q., Wei, X., Zhang, Y., Xia, Y.: Person re-identification with triplet focal loss. IEEE Access 6, 78092–78099 (2018)
41. Zhao, H., eet al.: Spindle net: Person re-identification with human body region guided feature decomposition and fusion. In: CVPR, pp. 907–915 (2017)
42. Zheng, L., Shen, L., Tian, L., Wang, S., Wang, J., Tian, Q.: Scalable person re-identification: a benchmark. In: ICCV, pp. 1116–1124 (2015)
43. Zheng, L., Yang, Y., Hauptmann, A.G.: Person re-identification: past, present and future. CoRR (2016)
44. Zheng, Z., Zheng, L., Yang, Y.: Unlabeled samples generated by GAN improve the person re-identification baseline in vitro. In: ICCV, pp. 3774–3782 (2017)
45. Zhong, Z., Zheng, L., Cao, D., Li, S.: Re-ranking person re-identification with k-reciprocal encoding. In: CVPR, pp. 3652–3661 (2017)
46. Zhou, J., Yu, P., Tang, W., Wu, Y.: Efficient online local metric adaptation via negative samples for person re-identification. In: ICCV, pp. 2439–2447 (2017)
47. Zoph, B., Le, Q.V.: Neural architecture search with reinforcement learning. In: ICLR (2017)
48. Zoph, B., Vasudevan, V., Shlens, J., Le, Q.V.: Learning transferable architectures for scalable image recognition. In: CVPR, pp. 8697–8710 (2018)

Deep Convolutional Center-Based Clustering

Qinhong Yan[1,2], Meihan Tang[1,2], Weifu Chen[1,2(✉)], and Guocan Feng[1,2]

[1] School of Mathematics, Sun Yat-sen University, Guangzhou, China
yanqh095@gmail.com, tangtang_tmh@163.com,
{chenwf26,mcsfgc}@mail.sysu.edu.cn
[2] Guangdong Province Key Laboratory, Sun Yat-sen University, Guangzhou, China

Abstract. Deep clustering utilizes deep neural networks to learn feature representation which is suitable for clustering. One popular category of deep clustering algorithms combines stacked autoencoder and k-means clustering by defining objectives including both clustering loss and reconstruction loss so that the feature representation and the cluster assignment could be learned simultaneously by the networks. However, we observe that the optimization direction of two terms are not consistent. To address this issue, in this paper, we propose a model called Deep Convolutional Center-Based Clustering (DCCBC), which replaces the usual reconstruction loss by a novel reconstruction loss based on cluster centers. The model can produce compact feature representation and capture the salient features of instances in different clusters. The optimization problem can be efficiently solved by mini-batch stochastic gradient descent and back propagation. Experiments on several benchmark datasets showed that the proposed model could achieve competitive results and outperformed some popular state-of-the-art clustering algorithms.

Keywords: Deep Clustering · Convolutional Autoencoders · Unsupervised learning

1 Introduction

Clustering is one of the most fundamental tasks in data mining and machine learning, which groups instances into several groups so that instances in the same group (called a cluster) are more similar to each other than to those in other groups. When clustering with high-dimensional and complicated data, traditional methods first extract features according to domain-specific knowledge and then employ other clustering algorithms such as K-means on the extracted features. However, the extracted features are not necessarily suitable for clustering because of the separation of two phases. Thanks to deep learning approaches [5], some work combines feature learning and clustering into a unified framework

---

The first author is a student.

© Springer Nature Switzerland AG 2019
Z. Lin et al. (Eds.): PRCV 2019, LNCS 11857, pp. 552–561, 2019.
https://doi.org/10.1007/978-3-030-31654-9_47

which can simultaneously give out cluster assignment and the underlying feature representation [6,7,14,15,17,18]. Researchers refer it as *Deep Clustering* [7].

The most widely used neural network in deep clustering algorithms is Stacked AutoEncoders (SAE) [11]. A simple approach is to train a SAE on a dataset and use the features extracted from hidden layers for clustering. However, the features may not be suitable for clustering because SAE aims to minimize the reconstruction loss. Some works [6,7,17,18] define a clustering oriented loss function based on SAE to force the networks to learn representations that are suitable for clustering. We refer this category of clustering algorithms as *AutoEncoder-Based Clustering*.

The Deep Clustering Network (DCN) algorithm [18] builds up a SAE and performs k-means clustering on the embedded layer to drive the network to output k-means friendly representations. The loss function is weighted combination of reconstruction loss and center square loss on the hidden layer, which only considers features in the same clusters but neglects the features in different clusters. The Deep Embedded Clustering (DEC) algorithm [17] defines a centroid-based probability distribution and minimizes the KL divergence to an auxiliary target distribution. DEC is first initializes with a SAE to obtain semantically meaningful and well-seperated representations, removes the decoder part and tunes the network with clustering losses. To some extent, it aims to reduce the distance of instance features in the same cluster and enlarge the distance of instance features among different clusters. On the basis of DEC, the Improved Deep Embedded Clustering (IDEC) [6] and Deep Convolutional Embedded Clustering (DCEC) [7] propose to incorporate the reconstruction loss in the finetune phase. The reconstruction loss can preserve local structure of data generating distribution, which can avoid corruption of the embedded space. Specially, DCEC replaces the SAE with the Convolutional AutoEncoder network (CAE) to better capture spatial information of images. Though the reconstruction loss of CAE improves the clustering performance, the optimization directions of the clustering loss and the reconstruction loss are not consistent, which can be further improved.

In this paper, we present a cluster center-based reconstruction loss, which aims to minimize the mean squared error between instance reconstructions and their corresponding clustering center reconstructions. We improve the DCEC algorithm by replacing the CAE reconstruction loss with the new reconstruction loss. The new model can output more impact representation and capture the salient feature of instances in different clusters. We name our algorithm as Deep Convolutional Center-Based Clustering (DCCBC). The optimization of DCCBC can directly perform mini-batch stochastic gradient descent and back propagation. Experiments are conducted on several benchmark image datasets. The results validate the effectiveness of DCCBC. Our contributions include:

- We propose the Deep Convolutional Center-Based Clustering (DCCBC) algorithm to simultaneously learn the cluster assignment and the feature representation. The optimization problem can be efficiently solved by mini-batch stochastic gradient descent and back propagation algorithm.

- The new loss function forces the network to output compact representations that capture the salient features of instances in different clusters.
- Experiments conducted on benchmark image datasets validate the effectiveness of DCCBC.

2   Deep Convolutional Center-Based Clustering

In this section, we will introduce the Deep Convolutional Center-Based Clustering (DCCBC). First we will show the structure of the network and then introduce the elements of the model, that is Convolutional AntoEncoder (CAE), Clustering layer and loss function in sequence. At last, the optimization procedure is provided.

We first introduce the notations used below. Denote X as the image dataset, N is the number of instances in the X, K is the number of clusters. Let f and g be the encoder and the decoder respectively in CAE. They can be treated as two nonlinear mappings. Let d denote the number of units in the embedded layer and $Z \in R^{N \times d}$ be the hidden representation of X given by the embedded layer. For clustering, let Q, M denote the assignment probability and assignment matrix, the dimension of which are both $N \times K$. Denote $U \in R^{K \times d}$ as the cluster center matrix.

2.1   Structure of Model

We first introduce the architecture of DCCBC briefly. DCCBC consists of three parts, encoder, decoder and clustering layer, as depicted in Fig. 1. The encoder and decoder module are built with Convolutional AutoEncoder (see Fig. 2), the detail of which will be given in next part. Given the input X, we first obtain the hidden representation $Z = f(X)$ (see Eq. (2)). The clustering layer maps Z into probability distribution Q (see Eq. (5)), and generate the cluster assignment matrix M (see Eq. (8)). Then we get the corresponding cluster centers MU. Through the decoder g (see Eq. (3)), we get both instance reconstruction and cluster centers reconstruction $g(Z)$ and $g(MU)$.

The objective function is

$$L = L_c + \gamma L_{cr} \tag{1}$$

where L_{cr} (Eq. (9)) and L_c (Eq. (6)) are center-based reconstruction loss and clustering loss respectively, and $\gamma > 0$ is a balancing coefficient.

2.2   Convolutional AutoEncoder

Autoencoder networks aim to find a code for each input instance by minimizing the mean squared errors between inputs and outputs. A convolutional autoencoder is generally composed of two parts, encoder and decoder. They are defined as

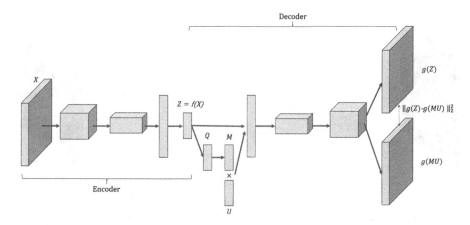

Fig. 1. The structure of Deep Convolutional Center-Based Clustering (DCCBC). It is composed of a convolutional autoencoders and a clustering layer connected to embedded layer of autoencoder.

$$z = f(x) = \sigma(x * W_E) \tag{2}$$
$$g(z) = \sigma(z * W_D) \tag{3}$$

where x and z are tensors, σ is an activation function like ReLU, sigmoid. $*$ is convolutional operator and W_E, W_D are convolutional filters.

The structure of Convolutional AutoEncoders used in DCCBC is as Fig. 2. Note that we haven't modify the structure of CAE and incorporate it in our model. First, some convolutional layers are stacked on the input images to extract hierarchical features. Then flatten all units in the last convolutional layer and form a vector, followed by a fully connected layer with 10 units, which is called the embedded layer. Then another fully connected layer and some convolutional transpose layers are built to transform embedded feature back to original image. The parameters of network are update by minimizing the reconstruction error:

$$L = \|g(f(X)) - X\|_2^2. \tag{4}$$

Clustering Layer and Clustering Loss. The clustering layer and loss are directly borrowed from DEC. We briefly review their definition for completeness of Model structure.

The clustering layer maintains cluster centers U and maps each embedded point z_i into soft label q_i by Student's t-distribution:

$$q_{ij} = \frac{(1 + \|z_i - \mu_j\|_2^2/\alpha)^{-\frac{\alpha+1}{2}}}{\sum_j (1 + \|z_i - \mu_j\|_2^2/\alpha)^{-\frac{\alpha+1}{2}}}, \tag{5}$$

where q_{ij} is the jth component of q_i, representing the probability of assigning sample i to cluster j. α is the degree of freedom of the Student's t-distribution and we let $\alpha = 1$ for all experiments.

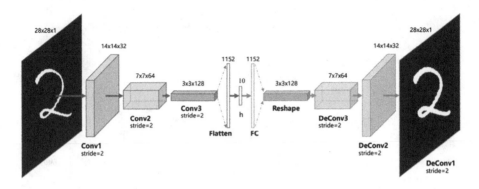

Fig. 2. The structure of Convolutional AutoEncoders for MNIST [7]. In the middle there is a fully connected autoencoder with 10 units embedded layer. The rest are convolutional layers and convolutional transpose layers (some work refers to as Deconvolutional layer).

The clustering loss is defined as

$$L_c = KL(P \parallel Q) = \sum_i \sum_j p_{ij} log \frac{p_{ij}}{q_{ij}}, \tag{6}$$

where P is the target distribution, defined as

$$p_{ij} = \frac{q_{ij}^2 / \sum_i q_{ij}}{\sum_k (q_{jk}^2 / \sum_i q_{ik})}. \tag{7}$$

From the definition of p_{ij}, we can see that minimizing the clustering loss L_c fores the samples to converge to the clusters with highest probability.

2.3   Cluster Center Reconstruction Loss

After pretraining, CAE-based algorithms try to use the CAE reconstruction loss in the finetune phase to preserve the local structure of data generating distribution. However, the optimization directions of the two loss terms are not consistent. In order to tackle this problem, we introduce a novel reconstruction loss based on cluster centers. Instead of reconstructing the instances as their origin inputs, we hope each instance can be represented by their cluster centers. Given input X, we can obtain the cluster assignment matrix M according to Eq. (8)

$$M_{ij} = \begin{cases} 1, & j = \arg\max_j q_{ij} \\ 0 & otherwise \end{cases}, \tag{8}$$

which assigns each instance to the cluster with highest probability. Then we get the corresponding cluster centers MU and its reconstruction $g(MU)$. we Define the cluster center reconstruction loss as Eq. (9).

$$L_{cr} = \|g(f(X)) - g(MU)\|_2^2. \tag{9}$$

The approximation of instance reconstruction and corresponding cluster center reconstruction reflects on the approximation of instance representation to their cluster centers, which makes the representation of instances in same cluster more compact. Meanwhile, it actually maps the instances in the same cluster into almost the same representations that capture the salient features of the cluster and remove the irrelevant details.

2.4 Optimization

First pretrain the parameter of CAE according to loss function Eq. 4 to get meaningful target distribution. After pretraining, the cluster centers are initialized by performing k-means on embedded features on the dataset. Then set $\gamma = 0.1$ and update parameters of CAE, cluster centers and target distribution as follows.

Update Autoencoder's Weights and Cluster Centers. As $\frac{\partial L_c}{\partial z_i}$ and $\frac{\partial L_c}{\partial \mu_j}$ are easily calculated, then the weights and centers can be updated by using backpropagation and mini-batch SGD.

Upadte Target Distribution. To avoid instability, update the target distribution P using all embedded points each iterations.

The training process terminates if the changes of label assignments between two consecutive updates for target distribution is less than a predefined threshold δ.

3 Experiment

To demonstrate the effectiveness of our DCCBC algorithm, we compared it with DEC, DCN, IDEC and DCEC. For reference, two classical clustering algorithms, k-means and Spectral Embedded Clustering [13] and some clustering algorithm raised recent year, i.e. LDGMI [20], JULE [19], DEPICT [4] were also included in comparison. Note that LDGMI is improved spectral clustering algorithm, JULE and DEPICT are some kind Deep Clustering algorithms.

3.1 DataSets

The proposed DCCBC model is evaluated on five image datasets:

- MNIST [10]: contains 70000 grey-scale handwritten digits of 28 × 28 pixels, 10 classes.
- USPS [8]: contains 9298 gray-scale handwritten digits of 16 × 16 pixels, 10 classes.
- Fashion-MNIST [16]: Zalando's article images, totally 70000 grey-scale of 28 × 28 pixels, 10 classes.
- Coil100 [12]: RGB images of 100 objects with different views, 128 × 128 × 3 pixels, 100 classes.
- YaleB [3]: contains 2414 grey-scale face images with size 192 × 168 pixels, 38 classes.

3.2   Parameter Settings

The structure of network is the same as DCEC. For MNIST and USPS, the encoder network structure is $conv_{32}^5 \rightarrow conv_{64}^5 \rightarrow conv_{128}^3 \rightarrow fc_{10}$, where $conv_n^k$ denotes a convolutional layer with n filters, kernel size of $k \times k$ and stride length 2. The decoder is a mirror of encoder. For YaleB, the structure is $conv_{32}^5 \rightarrow conv_{64}^5 \rightarrow conv_{64}^5 \rightarrow conv_{128}^3 \rightarrow fc_{10}$. The CAE is pretrained end-to-end for 200 epochs using Adam [9] with default parameters. The convergence threshold is set to $\delta = 0.1\%$.

All experiments were implemented on Keras [1] platform with a single NVIDIA Titan X GPU. For other algorithms over benchmark datasets, we report the best result from the papers.

3.3   Evaluation Metrics

We adopt standard metrics for evaluating clustering performance: normalized mutual information (NMI) and clustering accuracy (ACC). In a nutshell, both the two metrics are commonly used in clustering literature and both have pros and cons. But using them together suffices to demonstrate the effectiveness of the clustering algorithms. Note that both of them lies in the range from zero to one, with one being the perfect clustering result and zero the worst.

3.4   Comparing Results

The results are shown in Table 1. DCCBC outperformed classical clustering algorithms in both terms of ACC and NMI on all dataset. Comparing with AutoEncoder-Based clustering models, DCN, DEC, IDEC and DCEC, DCCBC obtained significant improvements. Comparing with advanced clustering algorithms LDGMI, JULE and DEPICT, though the metrics of DCCBC on USPS and Coil100 were not the best, the proposed approach also obtained competitive performance.

Table 1. Comparing of clustering performance in terms of NMI (%) and ACC (%).

Model	MNIST		USPS		Fashion-MNIST		Coil100		YaleB	
	NMI (%)	ACC (%)	NMI (%)	ACC (%)	NMI (%)	ACC (%)	NMI (%)	ACC (%)	NMI (%)	ACC (%)
Kmeans	49.97	57.23	45.00	46.00	51.16	47.33	80.30	62.1	61.5	51.4
SEC	66.26	69.58	68.10	65.90	–	–	84.90	64.80	84.90	72.1
LDGMI	76.10	72.30	56.30	58.00	–	–	88.80	76.30	94.50	90.10
JULE	91.30	96.40	91.30	95.00	–	–	**97.90**	**91.10**	**99.00**	97.00
DEPICT	91.90	96.80	**92.70**	**96.40**	–	–	66.70	42.00	98.90	96.50
DCN	57.00	56.00	68.30	68.80	55.80	50.10	81.10	62.00	59.00	43.00
DEC	77.16	84.30	70.18	69.28	54.60	51.80	81.50	61.10	–	–
IDEC	86.72	88.06	78.46	76.05	55.70	52.90	81.40	61.50	–	–
DCEC	88.49	88.97	82.57	79.00	58.48	55.34	83.30	62.70	–	–
DCCBC	**94.90**	**98.09**	85.21	81.13	**64.90**	**59.13**	85.51	62.83	98.52	**97.10**

3.5   Visualization

To demonstrate that DCCBC can give out compact representation and capture salient features of instances in different clusters. We made some visualization on MNIST.

Compact Representation. The center-based reconstruction loss could drive the network to produce compact representation in each cluster. We validated this property by visualizing the embedded features. We randomly sampled 7000 images, after pretraining, three and six epochs training, and took the embedded features of samples. Then we used t-SNE visualization [2] to reduce the dimension of the features to two and the result is shown in Fig. 3. Different colors refer to different labels. The feature representations of handwritten digits were well separated. The representation became compact after model training.

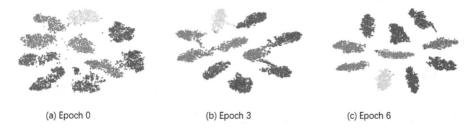

(a) Epoch 0   (b) Epoch 3   (c) Epoch 6

Fig. 3. Visualization of clustering results on subset of MNIST. Different colors mark different clusters. The structure of the representation tends to be more compact. (Color figure online)

Capture Salient Features. Using number three and six as examples, we randomly selected some images and computed the corresponding network output. The result is shown as Fig. 4. The first line is the origin images and the second line the network reconstructions. DCCBC can exclude the influence of font size, angle and other variations and capture the salient features of the handwritten digits, which is powerful for clustering.

Fig. 4. Compare with input images and DCCBC reconstruction images with number three and six as examples. The first line is the input images and the second line network output.

4   Conclusion

In this paper, we proposed a new deep clustering algorithm called Deep Convolutional Center-Based Clustering. DCCBC is a framework that jointly learns representation of images and perform clustering. It can output compact representation than some other deep clustering algorithms and capture the salient feature of instances in different clusters. Experimental results on benchmark datasets showed that the proposed model outperformed some state-of-the-art models, which indicated the advantages of the proposed model.

Directions for future work include modifying the structure or loss function to avoid pretraining.

Acknowledgement. This work is partially supported by the NSFC under grants Nos. 61673018, 61272338, 61703443 and Guangzhou Science and Technology Founding Committee under grant No. 201804010255 and Guangdong Province Key Laboratory of Computer Science.

References

1. Chollet, F., et al.: Keras (2015). https://github.com/fchollet/keras
2. Der Maaten, L.V., Hinton, G.E.: Visualizing data using t-SNE. J. Mach. Learn. Res. **9**, 2579–2605 (2008)
3. Georghiades, A., Belhumeur, P., Kriegman, D.: From few to many: illumination cone models for face recognition under variable lighting and pose. IEEE Trans. Pattern Anal. Mach. Intell. **23**(6), 643–660 (2001)
4. Ghasedi Dizaji, K., Herandi, A., Deng, C., Cai, W., Huang, H.: Deep clustering via joint convolutional autoencoder embedding and relative entropy minimization. In: The IEEE International Conference on Computer Vision (ICCV), October 2017
5. Goodfellow, I., Bengio, Y., Courville, A.: Deep Learning. MIT Press, Cambridge (2016). http://www.deeplearningbook.org
6. Guo, X., Gao, L., Liu, X., Yin, J.: Improved deep embedded clustering with local structure preservation. In: IJCAI, pp. 1753–1759 (2017)
7. Guo, X., Liu, X., Zhu, E., Yin, J.: Deep clustering with convolutional autoencoders. In: Liu, D., Xie, S., Li, Y., Zhao, D., El-Alfy, E.S. (eds.) ICONIP 2017. LNCS, vol. 10635, pp. 373–382. Springer, Cham (2017). https://doi.org/10.1007/978-3-319-70096-0_39
8. Hastie, Trevor, Tibshirani, Robert, Friedman, Jerome: The Elements of Statistical Learning: Data Mining, Inference, and Prediction. SSS. Springer, New York (2009). https://doi.org/10.1007/978-0-387-84858-7
9. Kingma, D.P., Ba, J.: Adam: a method for stochastic optimization. arXiv preprint arXiv:1412.6980 (2014)
10. LeCun, Y., Bottou, L., Bengio, Y., Haffner, P.: Gradient-based learning applied to document recognition. Proc. IEEE **86**(11), 2278–2324 (1998)
11. Masci, J., Meier, U., Cireşan, D., Schmidhuber, J.: Stacked convolutional auto-encoders for hierarchical feature extraction. In: Honkela, T., Duch, W., Girolami, M., Kaski, S. (eds.) ICANN 2011. LNCS, vol. 6791, pp. 52–59. Springer, Heidelberg (2011). https://doi.org/10.1007/978-3-642-21735-7_7

12. Nene, S.A., Nayar, S.K., Murase, H.: Columbia object image library (coil-100). Technical report, Technical Report CUCS-006-96, February 1996
13. Nie, F., Zeng, Z., Tsang, I.W., Xu, D., Zhang, C.: Spectral embedded clustering: a framework for in-sample and out-of-sample spectral clustering. IEEE Trans. Neural Netw. **22**(11), 1796–1808 (2011)
14. Peng, X., Feng, J., Lu, J., Yau, W.Y., Yi, Z.: Cascade subspace clustering. In: Thirty-First AAAI Conference on Artificial Intelligence (2017)
15. Peng, X., Xiao, S., Feng, J., Yau, W.Y., Yi, Z.: Deep subspace clustering with sparsity prior. In: IJCAI, pp. 1925–1931 (2016)
16. Xiao, H., Rasul, K., Vollgraf, R.: Fashion-MNIST: a novel image dataset for benchmarking machine learning algorithms (2017)
17. Xie, J., Girshick, R., Farhadi, A.: Unsupervised deep embedding for clustering analysis. In: International Conference on Machine Learning, pp. 478–487 (2016)
18. Yang, B., Fu, X., Sidiropoulos, N.D., Hong, M.: Towards k-means-friendly spaces: simultaneous deep learning and clustering. In: International Conference on Machine Learning, pp. 3861–3870 (2017)
19. Yang, J., Parikh, D., Batra, D.: Joint unsupervised learning of deep representations and image clusters. In: Computer Vision and Pattern Recognition, pp. 5147–5156 (2016)
20. Yang, Y., Xu, D., Nie, F., Yan, S., Zhuang, Y.: Image clustering using local discriminant models and global integration. IEEE Trans. Image Process. **19**(10), 2761–2773 (2010)

Exponential Moving Averaged Q-Network for DDPG

Xiangxiang Shen[1], Chuanhuan Yin[1(✉)], Yekun Chai[2], and Xinwen Hou[2]

[1] School of Computer and Information Technology, Beijing Jiaotong University,
Beijing, China
chyin@bjtu.edu.cn
[2] Center for Research on Intelligent System and Engineering,
Institute of Automation Chinese Academy of Sciences, Beijing, China

Abstract. The characteristics of instability and high-variance of Q-network result in the overestimation bias in the Deep Q-network (DQN). In contrast, Double DQN and averaged DQN have mitigated this problem from different approaches. By improving on the Averaged-DQN, we theoretically prove that the effective variance reduction of the Exponential Moving Average (EMA) in DQN, further illustrating its efficiency in the target network of Deep Deterministic Policy Gradient. We further propose the A3QDDPG algorithm by introducing the EMA Q-Network which is independent of the target Q-network when updating the policy. Experiments on ten continuous control environments of MuJoCo show that A3QDDPG achieves better performance than DDPG in terms of the average return, and the overestimation phenomenon of DDPG can also be observed under some environment in terms of average Q value.

Keywords: DQN · Exponential moving averaged Q-network · DDPG · Variance reduction · Overestimation bias

1 Introduction

In reinforcement learning (RL), the combination of model-free algorithms such as Q-learning [5] with non-linear function approximators could cause the Q function to diverge [15]. However, the Deep Q-network (DQN) [9,10] is the first to combine the Q-learning algorithm with the Convolutional Neural Network (CNN), matching the performance of human level in the Atari games. The crucial contribution of the DQN is bridging the gap between the RL and Supervised Learning by introducing the target Q-network and experience replay buffer.

With novel skills, DQN reduces the inability of theoretical convergence. Nevertheless, it is unavoidable that the Target Approximation Error (TAE) [1] exists in the function approximation settings, especially in the temporal difference (TD) learning [12]. This is because the error of Q-network estimates could propagate forward, leading to the accumulated TAE during the training process. Hence,

---

The first author is a student.

© Springer Nature Switzerland AG 2019
Z. Lin et al. (Eds.): PRCV 2019, LNCS 11857, pp. 562–572, 2019.
https://doi.org/10.1007/978-3-030-31654-9_48

Q-network is known to possess a high variance. Furthermore, the update of Q-network employs the maximum of the Q-function. This could produce the overestimation bias [14], resulting in that the action-state pair not taken by the Q-network might have a better contribution than the maximum Q-function value. To handle this, Double DQN [16] and Averaged-DQN [1] adopted different methods to mitigate the effects of the overestimated bias.

Although DQN is shown to be effective on multiple RL tasks, it can not be applied in the continuous action space. DDPG (Deep Deterministic policy gradient) [8] was shown to overcome this problem by combining the DQN and Deterministic Policy Gradient (DPG) [11]. Based on Averaged-DQN, we propose an EMA Q-network as the target Q-network combined with DQN, which we call EMA-DQN. There are three contributions in this paper: First EMA-DQN overcomes the drawback that Averaged-DQN requires multiple versions of Q-networks needed for average operation, and shows lower TAE variance. Second we introduce an additional EMA Q-network in the policy gradient update of the actor network and achieves better stability, where uses the original Q-network is not stable since the Q-network has larger variance. Third we propose A3QDDPG by introducing the EMA Q-network into DDPG to ensure its independency of the target Q-network and its stability because of low variance during training.

Due to the fact that the approach we utilize three Q-networks, it is thus called A3QDDPG. It is shown to take effects when experimenting on the MuJuCo simulation environment [4].

2   Background

2.1   Related Work

In conventional RL scenarios, the agent executes the action a_t following the policy π, a mapping from the state s_t to action a_t in terms of the interaction with environments. The policy π is gradually updated with the subsequent states and rewards from the follow-up environmental response. The return can be written as:

$$R(s_t) = \sum_{k=0}^{T} \gamma^k r(s_{t+k}, a_{t+k}) \tag{1}$$

where $\gamma \in (0,1)$ represents the discount factor, $a.$ follows the policy π, T denotes the total time steps, and r is the reward received from the environment. The action-value function $Q^\pi(s, a)$ represents the expected return when taking the action a at the state s:

$$Q^\pi(s, a) = E_\pi[R(s_t)|s_t = s, a] \tag{2}$$

where a follows the current policy π.

Efficient Q function is the hinge of the value approximation in Q-learning based RL algorithms. Nevertheless, a couple of RL methods wrongly predict the

Q-function with overoptimistic biases, e.g. DQN, thus impeding the guarantees of optimal polices.

There exist numerous kinds of improvements on the DQN, aiming to handle its high variances and overestimated biases. Double DQN [16] leveraged two almost independent networks, i.e. Q-network and target Q-network, to reduce the overestimation. [6] introduced an intrinsic penalty signal whilst Averaged-DQN [1] took the average of multiple Q-networks to mitigate the Q-value overestimation. LS-DQN [7] adopted a rich feature representation from a Deep RL algorithm with the linear least squares method.

EMA is often used to handle time series data in financial and technical community. In multi-agent RL, [2] and [3] learned the Q functions and policies with the EMA. By contrast, our A3QDDPG capitalizes on EMA for the parameter optimization of Q-networks in terms of single-agent RL.

2.2 Averaged-DQN

As a crucial improvement of the DQN, target Q-network takes the average Q value from previous k Q-networks at each training process of the Averaged-DQN, instead of directly copying the value from the target Q-network after a fixed-length time step. It could stabilize the whole training process by reducing the variance of the TAE.

Let $Q(s, a|\theta_n)$ be the value function at iteration n, and $y_{s,a}^n$ be the DQN target:

$$y_{s,a}^n = r(s, a) + E_{\mathcal{B}}[\gamma max_{a'} Q(s', a'|\theta_{n-1})] \tag{3}$$

where $\mathcal{B}$ represents the data distribution in experience replay buffer, $Z_{s,a}^n$ refers to the TAE:

$$Z_{s,a}^n = Q(s, a|\theta_n) - y_{s,a}^n \tag{4}$$

In the Averaged-DQN:

$$Q_{n-1}^A(s, a) = \frac{1}{K} \sum_{k=1}^{K} Q(s, a|\theta_{n-k}) \tag{5}$$

$$y_{s,a}^n = r(s, a) + E_{\mathcal{B}}[\gamma max_{a'} Q_{n-1}^A(s', a'|s, a)] \tag{6}$$

$Z_{s,a}^n$ is usually regarded as a random variable following uniform distribution, by reducing whose variance we could mitigate the effect of overestimation [1]. In order to explore the reduction of TAE in the Averaged-DQN, they made an assumption in the Markov Decision Process (MDP) that the agent applies fixed policy interacting with the environment, during which all the reward signals are zero. This assumption was based on the fact that the policy and reward function have no effect on the TAE. $Z_{s,a}^n$ has the following properties:

$$E[Z_{s,a}^n] = 0 \tag{7}$$

$$Var[Z_{s,a}^n] = \sigma_s^2 \tag{8}$$

$$Cov[Z_{s,a}^n, Z_{s',a'}^j] = 0, n \neq j \qquad (9)$$

Thus we could analyze the effect of accumulated TAE on the Q-network according to the variance of the Q function in DQN. According to [1], we can get:

$$Var[Q^{DQN}(s_0, a; \theta_n)] = \sum_{m=0}^{M-1} \gamma^{2m} \sigma_{s_m}^2 \qquad (10)$$

$$Var[Q_n^A(s_0, a)] \leq \frac{1}{K} Var[Q^{DQN}(s_0, a; \theta_n)] \qquad (11)$$

where s_0 denotes the initial state of the MDP, and s_{M-1} is the terminal state.

This proof further supports the evidence that the Averaged-DQN algorithm is of benefit in terms of the stability of the training process.

2.3 Deep Deterministic Policy Gradient (DDPG)

DDPG leveraged the general Actor-Critic architecure, by combing DPG with DQN. It deals with the problem that the DQN is of no effect in continuous action space. The formula of gradient when updating the policy is:

$$\nabla_{\theta^\mu} J = E_{\mathcal{B}}[\nabla_a Q(s, a|\theta^Q)|_{a=\mu(s)} \nabla_{\theta^\mu} \mu(s|\theta^\mu)] \qquad (12)$$

As shown in the formula of gradient, the estimate of Q-function is the uppermost during the RL training process. DDPG employs nearly the same method as the DQN when training the Q-network.

3   Exponential Moving Averaged Q-Network for DDPG

3.1   High Variance Reduction

It is obvious that the performance of Averaged-DQN goes up with the increase of the K value. In other words, more neural networks are required to store the parameters in order to achieve a better policy. However, amounts of memories are required for computation.

Exponential Moving Averaged DQN. Aiming at handling the need for overmany neural networks, we adopt the recursive forms as shown in Eq. (13) rather than reducing the variance of the TAE as in the Averaged-DQN.

$$\theta_n^{EMA} = \alpha \theta_n + (1 - \alpha) \theta_{n-1}^{EMA} \qquad (13)$$

Then we illustrate that by applying the averaging method, the effects of accumulated TAE on the variance of Q-network are effectively alleviated.

Assume that in the training process of Q-network in DQN, the corresponding parameter sequence $\theta_0, \theta_1, ..., \theta_i, \cdots, \theta_n$ of $Q(s, a|\theta_0), Q(s, a|\theta_1), \cdots,$

$Q(s, a|\theta_i), \cdots, Q(s, a|\theta_n)$ obeys the independent identical distribution (i.i.d), $E[\theta_i] = \theta^*, Var[\theta_i] = \sigma^2$. The EMA of θ is as Eq. (13).

Further, we assume:

$$\theta_0^{EMA} = \theta_0 = 0 \tag{14}$$

We can get:

$$\theta_n^{EMA} = w_1\theta_1 + w_2\theta_2 + ... + w_n\theta_n \tag{15}$$

where $w_1 = (1-\alpha)^{n-1}\alpha, w_2 = (1-\alpha)^{n-2}\alpha, ..., w_n = \alpha$. Assume that n is infinite:

$$w_1 + w_2 + ... + w_n = (1-\alpha)^{n-1}\alpha + (1-\alpha)^{n-2}\alpha + ... + \alpha \tag{16}$$
$$= 1 - (1-\alpha)^n \tag{17}$$
$$\approx 1 \tag{18}$$

Since the sum of the weight approximates 1, we have the following equations:

$$\theta_n^{EMA} - \theta^* \approx w_1(\theta_1 - \theta^*) + w_2(\theta_1 - \theta^*) + ... + w_n(\theta_1 - \theta^*) \tag{19}$$
$$E[\theta_n^{EMA}] \approx \theta^* \tag{20}$$
$$Var[\theta_n^{EMA}] \approx E\|\theta_n^{EMA} - \theta^*\|^2 \tag{21}$$
$$\approx w_1^2 E\|(\theta_1 - \theta^*)\|^2 + w_2^2 E\|(\theta_2 - \theta^*)\|^2 + ... \tag{22}$$
$$+ w_n^2 E\|(\theta_n - \theta^*)\|^2 \tag{23}$$
$$= (w_1^2 + w_2^2 + ... + w_n^2)Var[\theta_n] \tag{24}$$
$$= \alpha^2 \frac{1 - (1-\alpha)^{2n}}{1 - (1-\alpha)^2}\sigma^2 \tag{25}$$
$$= \frac{\alpha}{2-\alpha}\sigma^2 \tag{26}$$
$$\approx \frac{\alpha}{2}\sigma^2 \tag{27}$$

From the lipschitz continuity condition of the Q function:

$$|Q^{EMA}(s, a|\theta_n^{EMA}) - Q(s, a|\theta^*)|^2 \leq \|Q\|_{Lip}^2\|\theta_n^{EMA} - \theta^*\|^2 \tag{28}$$
$$Var[Q^{EMA}(s, a|\theta_n^{EMA})] = E|Q^{EMA}(s, a|\theta_n^{EMA}) - Q(s, a|\theta^*)|^2 \tag{29}$$
$$\leq \|Q\|_{Lip}^2 E\|\theta_n^{EMA} - \theta^*\|^2 \tag{30}$$
$$\approx \frac{\alpha}{2}\|Q\|_{Lip}^2\sigma^2 \tag{31}$$

Also, we can get:

$$Var[Q(s, a|\theta_n)] \leq \|Q\|_{Lip}^2\sigma^2 \tag{32}$$

Assuming that $\alpha = \frac{1}{K}$ in the EMA-DQN:

$$Var[Q_n^A(s, a)] \leq \frac{1}{K}\|Q\|_{Lip}^2\sigma^2 \tag{33}$$

$$Var[Q^{EMA}(s, a|\theta_n^{EMA})] \leq \frac{1}{2K}||Q||_{Lip}^2 \sigma^2 \tag{34}$$

Compared with the variance estimation Eq. (11) of Averaged-DQN, the EMA approach is more effective with only half the variance, which supports the fact that applying the EMA on the target Q-networks could greatly improve the stability during training.

In theory there is not a substantially gap between the variance reduction effects of such two algorithms, but in practice the EMA-DQN outperforms the Averaged-DQN approach by breaking through the limitation of memory hardware since the parameter K in Averaged DQN cannot be too large, whereas α can be set to arbitrarily small without cost.

Algorithm 1. EMA-DQN

Randomly initialize Q-network $Q(s, a|\theta^Q)$ with weights θ^Q
Initialize EMA Q-network Q^{EMA} with weights $\theta^{EMA} \leftarrow \theta^Q$
Initialize replay buffer $\mathcal{B}$
while *episode* **do**
> Receive initial observation state s_0
> **while** $t = 1, T$ **do**
>> With probability ϵ select a random action a_t
>> Otherwise select $a_t = argmax_a Q(s, a|\theta^Q)$
>> Execute action a_t and observe reward r_t and observe new state s_{t+1}
>> Store transition (s_t, a_t, r_t, s_{t+1}) in $\mathcal{B}$
>> Sample a random minibatch of N transitions (s_i, a_i, r_i, s_{i+1}) from $\mathcal{B}$
>> Set $y_i = r_i + \gamma max_{a'} Q^{EMA}(s_{i+1}, a'|\theta^{Q^{EMA}})$
>> Update Q-network by minimizing the loss: $L = \frac{1}{N} \sum_i (y_i - Q(s_i, a_i|\theta^Q))^2$
>> Update the EMA Q-network:
>> $\theta^{EMA} \leftarrow \alpha\theta^Q + (1 - \alpha)\theta^{EMA}$ (Eq. 13)
> **end**
end

3.2   A3QDDPG

Double Q-learning adopts two independent Q-networks to get the target values, avoiding the overestimation bias. By contrast, DDPG applies Q-network and target Q-network, where the application of Q-networks could definitely lead to the instability when updating the target. In this section, we introduce an additional EMA Q-network corporate with the target Q-network to get the target update values, and propose A3QDDPG based on this idea and DDPG. From the algorithm 2, it applies the additional EMA Q-network in the policy gradient update (see Eq. 35). While the update method of original DDPG provides a noisy gradient and slows the training speed due to the Q-network with the high variance [13].

$$\nabla_{\theta^\mu} J = E_\mathcal{B}[\nabla_a Q^{EMA}(s, a|\theta^{EMA})|_{a=\mu(s)} \nabla_{\theta^\mu} \mu(s|\theta^\mu)] \tag{35}$$

Algorithm 2. A3QDDPG

Randomly initialize critic network $Q(s, a|\theta^Q)$ and actor $\mu(s|\theta^\mu)$ with weights θ^Q and θ^μ

Initialize EMA network Q^{EMA} with weights $\theta^{EMA} \leftarrow \theta^Q$

Initialize target network Q' and μ' with weights $\theta^{Q'} \leftarrow \theta^Q$, $\theta^{\mu'} \leftarrow \theta^\mu$

Initialize replay buffer $\mathcal{B}$

while *episode* **do**

    Initialize a random process $\mathcal{N}$ for action exploration

    Receive initial observation state s_0

    while $t = 0, T$ **do**

        Select action $a_t = \mu(s_t|\theta^\mu) + \mathcal{N}_t$ according to the current policy and exploration noise

        Execute action a_t and observe reward r_t and observe new state s_{t+1}

        Store transition (s_t, a_t, r_t, s_{t+1}) in $\mathcal{B}$

        Sample a random minibatch of N transitions (s_i, a_i, r_i, s_{i+1}) from $\mathcal{B}$

        Set $y_i = r_i + \gamma Q'(s_{i+1}, \mu'(s_{i+1})|\theta^{Q'})$

        Update critic by minimizing the loss:$L = \frac{1}{N}\sum_i(y_i - Q(s_i, a_i|\theta^Q))^2$

        Update the actor policy using the sampled policy gradient:

        $\nabla_{\theta^\mu} J \approx \frac{1}{N}\sum_i \nabla_a Q^{EMA}(s, a|\theta^{EMA})|_{s=s_i, a=\mu(s_i)} \nabla_{\theta^\mu}\mu(s|\theta^\mu)|_{s_i}$(Eq.35)

        Update the target networks:
$$\theta^{EMA} \leftarrow \alpha\theta^Q + (1-\alpha)\theta^{EMA}$$
$$\theta^{Q'} \leftarrow \tau\theta^Q + (1-\tau)\theta^{Q'}$$
$$\theta^{\mu'} \leftarrow \beta\theta^\mu + (1-\beta)\theta^{\mu'}$$

    end

end

---

4   Experiments

4.1   Experiment Settings

In our experiments, the common hyperparameters of DDPG and A3QDDPG are the same, where the code is written in Pytorch. The agent is trained by Adam optimizer with a batch size of 100, where the learning rates of the Critic and Actor networks are set to 0.001 and 0.0001 respectively. The discounted factor of the action-value function is set to 0.99. We experimented on the 8 GB memory storage, GeForce GTX 1070 GPUs with the 8 GB memory storage, and 8 CPUs with 4.2 GHz. Almost agent is trained with totally 1,000,000 time steps, costing approximately 1–2 h. All the neural networks consist of two fully-connected feedforward layers, where the hidden units in the Q-network and policy network are both 64. The output dimension of the Q network is 1 whereas the counterpart of policy networks depends on the actual action space (as Table 1).

Table 1. The information of action space and observation space in simulation environments

Env-id	Action space	Observation space
Ant-v2	Box(8)	Box(111)
Humanoid-v2	Box(17)	Box(376)
HalfCheetah-v2	Box(6)	Box(17)
opper-v2	Box(3)	Box(11)
HumanoidStandup-v2	Box(17)	Box(376)
InvertedDoublePendulum-v2	Box(1)	Box(11)
InvertedPendulum-v2	Box(1)	Box(4)
Reacher-v2	Box(2)	Box(11)
Swimmer-v2	Box(2)	Box(8)
Walker2d-v2	Box(6)	Box(17)

Box is the unit of describing the action or state space in the *gym* environment interface [4]. Digits in brackets denotes the dimension of action or observation space, which implying the complexity degree of simulation environments.

4.2 Experiment Results Analysis

Though agents require completing different tasks in simulation environments, the adopted evaluation metric is the average return of each simulation environment after the training process of agents stabilize.

We leveraged DDPG and A3QDDPG on the aforementioned ten simulation environments, where the average return of each episode is shown as Fig. 1. It can be seen that except for HalfCheetah-v2, A3QDDPG achieved obvious higher performance than DDPG in terms of the average return, among almost all of ten environments, wherein Ant-v2, Humanoid-v2 and HumanoidStandup-v2 agents obtain top 3 performance. Due to the fact that these three environments have the relatively high dimension in terms of the action space and observation space, it can be illustrated that the high TAE resulting from the complexity of environments can be better handled by A3QDDPG compared with DDPG.

Figure 1 also illustrates the instability of DDPG, in which average returns go up at first, followed by a decreasing trend in Humanoid-v2, Reacher-v2, and InvertedDoublePendulum-v2. In contrast, the curves of A3QDDPG are more smooth and stable during the whole training process, indicating the stability of policy networks in A3QDDPG.

Further, we plot the line curve of average Q values in InvertedDouble-Pendulum-v2 and Reacher-v2 (see Fig. 2). In InvertedDoublePendulum-v2, the average Q value in DDPG are higher than those in A3QDDPG at most of the time, whereas in Fig. 1 the average return of A3QDDPG match those of DDPG in the first 400,000 time steps during training. Accordingly, it is concluded that DDPG does not effectively deal with the overestimation bias problem despite the usage of the double Q networks. However, A3QDDPG has effectively mitigated

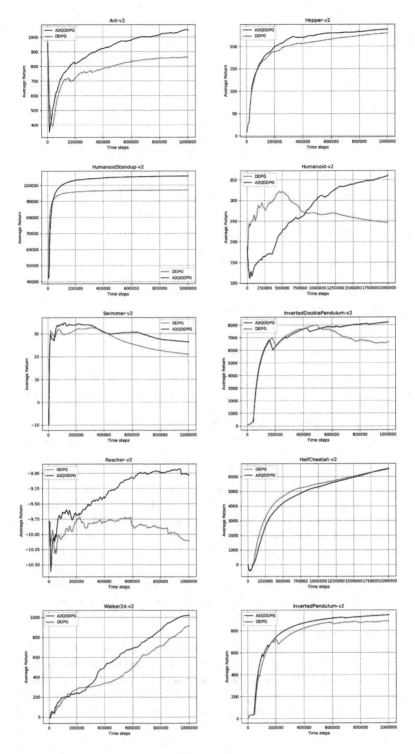

Fig. 1. The curve of average returns in ten simulation environments.

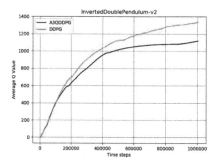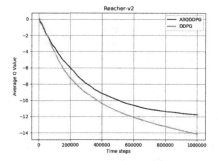

Fig. 2. The average Q value in InvertedDoublePendulum-v2 and Reacher-v2 environments.

the overestimation problem, and the average return has shown an increasing trend during the whole process. In fact, not all environments obtain similar results like in InvertedDoublePendulum-v2. For example, it can be observed that in Reacher-v2 the average Q value and the average return in A3QDDPG are both higher than those in DDPG (as in Figs. 2 and 1). We can conjecture that the observation of overestimation bias varies due to the real condition of simulation environments.

5   Conclusion

We proposed the method of EMA in order to handle the drawbacks of Averaged-DQN and has proved the effectiveness of EMA-DQN theoretically. Based on DDPG, we further employed EMA Q-network to improve the policy gradient in DDPG, called A3QDDPG. Our experiments applied the A3QDDPG in ten MuJoCo simulation environments, showing that the average return of the A3QDDPG outperforms that of DDPG.

Acknowledgement. This work is supported by the Fundamental Research Funds for the Central Universities (No. 2018JBZ006).

References

1. Anschel, O., Baram, N., Shimkin, N.: Averaged-DQN: variance reduction and stabilization for deep reinforcement learning. In: ICML (2017)
2. Awheda, M.D., Schwartz, H.M.: Exponential moving average Q-learning algorithm. In: 2013 IEEE Symposium on Adaptive Dynamic Programming and Reinforcement Learning (ADPRL), pp. 31–38. IEEE (2013)
3. Awheda, M.D., Schwartz, H.M.: Exponential moving average based multiagent reinforcement learning algorithms. Artif. Intell. Rev. **45**(3), 299–332 (2016)
4. Brockman, G., et al.: Openai gym (2016)
5. Krose, B.J.A.: Learning from delayed rewards. Robot. Auton. Syst. **15**(4), 233–235 (1995)

6. Leibfried, F., Graumoya, J., Bouammar, H.: An information-theoretic optimality principle for deep reinforcement learning. arXiv Artificial Intelligence (2017)

7. Levine, N., Zahavy, T., Mankowitz, D.J., Tamar, A., Mannor, S.: Shallow updates for deep reinforcement learning. In: Neural Information Processing Systems, pp. 3135–3145 (2017)

8. Lillicrap, T.P., et al.: Continuous control with deep reinforcement learning. In: International Conference on Learning Representations (2016)

9. Mnih, V., et al.: Playing atari with deep reinforcement learning. arXiv Learning (2013)

10. Mnih, V., et al.: Human-level control through deep reinforcement learning. Nature **518**(7540), 529–533 (2015)

11. Silver, D., Lever, G., Heess, N., Degris, T., Wierstra, D., Riedmiller, M.A.: Deterministic policy gradient algorithms. In: ICML (2014)

12. Sutton, R.S.: Learning to predict by the methods of temporal differences. Mach. Learn. **3**(1), 9–44 (1988)

13. Sutton, R.S., Barto, A.G.: Reinforcement learning: an introduction. IEEE Trans. Neural Netw. **16**, 285–286 (1988)

14. Thrun, S., Schwartz, A.: Issues in using function approximation for reinforcement learning. In: Proceedings of the 1993 Connectionist Models Summer School Hillsdale, NJ. Lawrence Erlbaum (1993)

15. Tsitsiklis, J.N., Van Roy, B.: An analysis of temporal-difference learning with function approximation. IEEE Trans. Autom. Control **42**(5), 674–690 (1997)

16. Van Hasselt, H., Guez, A., Silver, D.: Deep reinforcement learning with double Q-learning. In: International Conference on Artificial Intelligence, pp. 2094–2100 (2016)

Multi-scale Convolutional Neural Network Based on 3D Context Fusion for Lesion Detection

Zebiao Wu[1], Jinshan Chen[1], Zongyue Wang[1], Jinhe Su[1],
and Guorong Cai[1,2(✉)]

[1] Computer Engineering College, Jimei University, Xiamen 360121, China
`guorongcai.jmu@gmail.com`
[2] Fujian Collaborative Innovation Center for Big Data Applications in Governments,
Fuzhou 350003, China

Abstract. Lesion detection is an essential technique in medical diagnostic systems. Since there are great differences in intensity and appearance within a same lesion category, lesion detection from computed tomography (CT) scans is still a challenging task. Sufficiently using 3D context information become the research hotpot in lesion detection area, since algorithms can benefit from geometry and texture of lesions. Motivated by this trend, we propose a multi-scale CNN based on 3D context fusion, called M3DCF, for extracting lesion area from CT scans. In order to speed up the algorithm, the one-stage regression-based detector, rather than region proposal network, is adopted. Specifically, we employ 3D context fusion strategy that allows M3DCF fusing features from neighboring slices. Finally, we use a multi-scale scheme to combine low-level and high-level features. This strategy allows us to get more meaningful semantic information. The experimental results conducted on DeepLesion dataset indicates that the proposed method outperformed state-of-the-arts, including RetinaNet, Faster R-CNN, and 3DCE. The source code is available on https://github.com/JMUAIA/M3DCF.

Keywords: Lesion detection · One-stage neural network · 3D context

1 Introduction

Computed tomography (CT) scans are the most frequently used medical images for high-precision X-ray measurement. Hence, lesion can be identified by a specialist based on CT images' density. Different from common images, CT images have more details and self-similar texture. So far, machine learning based automatic diagnosis from CT scans cannot make a breakthrough due to the fact that there is lack of large-scale annotated lesion database. Recently, NIHCC

The first author is a student. This work is supported by the National Natural Science Foundation of China under Grant No. 61702251, the Key Technical Project of Fujian Province under Grant No. 2017H6015.

© Springer Nature Switzerland AG 2019
Z. Lin et al. (Eds.): PRCV 2019, LNCS 11857, pp. 573–585, 2019.
https://doi.org/10.1007/978-3-030-31654-9_49

released a large-scale medicine database called DeepLesion [1] on July 20, 2018. The DeepLesion dataset contains 32,735 lesions on 32,120 axial slices, which are annotated from 10,594 CT studies of 4,427 unique patients. Different from existing datasets that typically focus on one type of lesion, DeepLesion contains a variety of lesions including those in *Abdomen*, *Liver*, *Mediastinum*, etc. Basically, DeepLesion provides a good chance to handle the task of general lesion extraction, since mainstream object detection algorithms are mainly depended on large scale annotated data.

In the past five years, algorithms of object detection can be divided into two classes. The first one is based on two-stages scheme, which is based on proposal driven mechanism. The second scheme employs an end-to-end CNN [2] framework to regress the coordinates and the confidences of each target.

In the development of the two-stages network structures, R-CNN [3] (Region CNN) was the first use of deep learning for object detection. The author of RCNN has won awards in PASCAL VOC [4] at that time. R-CNN adopted selective search [5] to generate possible ROIs (Regions of Interest), then the proposals are classified by standard convolutional neural networks. Fast R-CNN [6] is an improved version of R-CNN that adopted ROI Pooling (Region of Interest Pooling) to share parameters. Faster R-CNN [7] integrates object proposal generation with classifier into a single convolution network, which is faster than Fast R-CNN since Region Proposal Network (RPN) shares full-image convolutional features. Mainstream two-stage algorithms including R-CNN, SPP-Net [8], Fast R-CNN, Faster R-CNN, R-FCN [9], etc.

OverFeat [10] is a first one-stage object detector based on CNNs. Recently, YOLO [13–15], SSD [11], DSSD [16] and RetinaNet [12] have innovative behavior in one-stage methods. SSD adopted multi-scale feature maps for object detection, 3 × 3 convolution kernels are used for fewer parameters. Besides this, anchor boxes are used for easier training, which are popular used in two-stages method. Since the featues SSD extracted are not as great as two-stages' features, DSSD adopted better backbone and deconvolution layers for feature extraction, therefore more expressive features are obtained. In addition, since imbalanced proportion of positive and negative samples have serious impacts on network training, a novel loss and well-designed network are used by RetinaNet and which achieves promising results.

Although deep learning achieves enduring greatness on the field of object detection. Most object detectors are designed for 2D images. Different from traditional 2D images, lesions in CT images have self-similar texture, which means non-lesions and true lesions areas may have similar appearances. Under such circumstances, using 3D context information to improve the performance of lesion detection becomes the research hotspot. To this end, Dou et al. [17] attempted to predict microbleeds in brain MRI by using a modified 3D CNN. Hwang and Kim [18] adopted weakly-supervised deep learning to detect nodules in chest radiographs and lesions in mammography. Besides, Teramoto et al. [19] proposed a novel CNNs for handling multi-model fusion task.

Recently, the DeepLesion team proposed a 3D Context Enhanced Region-based Convolutional Neural Network [20] (3DCE) for extracting lesion areas from CT scans. It is worth noting that this 3DCE adopts 3D context fusion strategy in the pipeline. The neighbor slices of target image are used to be the input to CNNs. Then the Region Proposal Network (RPN) of 3DCE generates a sparse set of candidate lesions. Finally, the feature maps of each candidate are used to lesion type classification. Although 3DCE CNN is a cost-efficient solution, the algorithm suffers from too much false positives. Since the proposed method is motivated by 3DCE, their results on Deeplesion are regarded as the baseline.

In this paper, we propose a novel method called Multi-scale Convolutional Neural Network based on 3D Context Fusion for lesion detection (M3DCF). First, we adopt one-stage framework rather than region proposal network. The purpose is to speed up the algorithm. Second, we designed multi-scale prediction scheme to fuse 3D context information. Third, our method performs bounding box regression directly from the last layer of our neural network. The experimental results show that the proposed method achieves state-of-the-art accuracy with faster speed than the mainstream algorithms such as RetinaNet, Faster R-CNN and 3DCE.

2   The Proposed Method

2.1   3D Context Features Fusion Network

Figure 1 describes the pipeline of the proposed method. First, we used three neighboring axial slices to compose a three-channel image. Second, 3*M

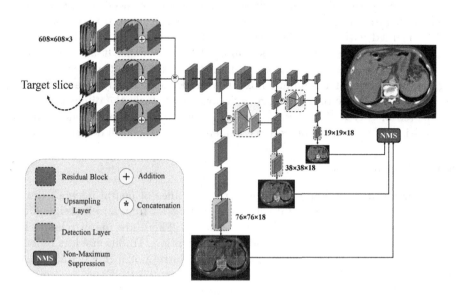

Fig. 1. Structure of the neural network we proposed

sequential slices have been divided into M images as the input of M3DCF. Note that the middlemost slice is the target slice with annotation. The main advantage of our fusion strategy is that it makes full use of shape information through 3D context, thus can enhance the discrimination ability of features.

Third, each image is fed into a respective convolutional neural network for performing feature extraction. M3DCF uses the Darknet-53 as its backbone network, since Darknet-53 is an efficient architecture that suitable for one stage object detection. In particular, Batch Normalization [21] (BN) is used in the backbone with each convolution layer. Moreover, we adopt the Rectified Linear Unit [22] (Relu) as our activation function after BN. The Convolution + Batch Norm + LeakyRelu (CBL) is a fundamental module in the pipeline of our framework. Additionally, residual modules [23] are proposed to improve the training of a deeper neural network. To ensure efficient training, we adopt residual modules of layer 1, 2 and 8. As shown in Fig. 1, we concatenate feature maps which are generated after several residual modules to construct a 3D context features. The concatenation of extracted features is a key component of M3DCF, which ensure more expressive features can be obtained. Different from simple addition, the concatenation in our method will expand the dimension of feature.

Most worthy of mention is that we adopt a multi-scale prediction strategy. The design of multi-scale anchors is an essential component for sharing features. Besides, the resolution of feature maps can be easily adjusted by changing the stride of convolution layer. In this way, we can transform the dimensions of tensor without any pooling layer and fully connected layer. As shown in Fig. 1, the input images are reduced to 1/32 of its original size in the first branch. For example, using stride as (2, 2) can halve the width and the height of the input size, then an input image with the size of 608 × 608 will be resized into 19×19.

Moreover, with the goal of multi-scale prediction, we need to combine low-level and high-level features. As shown in Fig. 1, feature map from former layers will be merged with upsampled features from latter layers. After that, convolutional layers are used to process combined feature maps. It is worth noting that our method predicts 3 boxes at different scales. The output tensor encoding the coordinates of a bounding box, the confidence of an object, and the class predictions. Since the only category is 'lesion' in our task, the dimension of the output tensor is $N \times N \times [3 \times (4 + 1 + 1)]$. Finally, we perform non-maximum suppression (NMS) on the detection confidence maps to obtain detection results.

2.2 Loss Function

Loss function has the important guiding significance of neural network during the training process. The neural network benefits a lot from a well-designed loss function and achieves competitive performance. There are many reliable loss functions and most of them have widespread adoption. Traditional loss function such as Mean Square Error [24] (MSE), Cross-Entropy [25] (CE), Root means squared error [26] (RMSE) and Sum Square Error [27] (SSE) are successfully used in different situations. Therefore, using a well-designed loss function for the practical problem may produce better results. As for object detection, there are

4 attributions need to be considered, such as location, size, class, and confidence. It's worth noting that there is only one category in the DeepLesion database and thus we haven't taken the category error into consideration.

2.2.1 Bounding Box Location Loss

First, we use binary cross-entropy loss for the location predictions. Thus, this formulation will be helpful when we move to more complex domains like the area of *Pelvis*. Since lesion detection has distinct difference of probability distribution, cross-entropy loss function is more suitable when there is large error between the predicted bounding boxes and the ground truths. Cross-entropy loss function makes the weights update faster, which accelerates the training process of CNNs. The location loss is defined as the following equation.

$$Loss_{location} = \sum_{l=1}^{L} \alpha_l \sum_{i=0}^{S_l^2} \sum_{j=0}^{B} \tau_{ij}^{obj} CrossEntropy[(x_i, y_i), (\hat{x}_i, \hat{y}_i)] \qquad (1)$$

where $l = 1, 2..., L$ denotes the number of different resolutions of the output layer. x and y represent the upper-left coordinates of predicted bounding boxes, respectively. $\hat{x}$ and $\hat{y}$ stand for the ground truths. S_l^2 denotes the number of cells in each resolution, B indicates the number of boxes predicted in each cell. α_l is a weighting factor of the lth resolution loss term. Additionally, τ_{ij}^{obj} stand for whether the Intersection over Union (IoU) of jth window predicted by the ith cell is higher than a specific threshold, which value is set to be 0 or 1. Generally, the IoU threshold is set to be 0.5.

2.2.2 Bounding Box Size Loss

As sum of squared error loss has been widely used in the object detection domain. We adopt sum of squared error loss as our bounding box size loss, and the formulation of bounding box size loss is shown as follow.

$$Loss_{size} = \sum_{l=1}^{L} \alpha_l \sum_{i=0}^{S_l^2} \sum_{j=0}^{B} \tau_{ij}^{obj} \cdot [(\sqrt{w_i} - \sqrt{\hat{w}_i})^2 + (\sqrt{h_i} - \sqrt{\hat{h}_i})^2] \qquad (2)$$

where w and h denote the size of predicted bounding boxes, respectively. $\hat{w}$ and $\hat{h}$ respectively stand for the ground truths. The other symbols are defined in Sect. 2.2.1.

2.2.3 Confidence Loss

The last component represents whether a predicted bounding box contains a lesion or not. Since confidence describes the terms of probability distribution, we adopt the cross entropy to construct the confidence loss. Since the values of confidence ranges from 0 to 1, there is not weighting factor in the confidence loss for different resolutions. Hence, if regressed bounding box contains a lesion, the confidence loss is given as the following equation.

$$Loss_{object} = \sum_{l=1}^{L} \sum_{i=0}^{S_l^2} \sum_{j=0}^{B} \tau_{ij}^{obj} \cdot CrossEntropy(C_i, \hat{C}_i) \tag{3}$$

The definitions of L, S_l^2, B, τ_{ij}^{obj} are given in Sect. 2.2.1. As shown in Eq. 3, the loss combines the confidence errors in all proposal bounding boxes from different scales. On the contrary, if a regressed bounding box does not contain a lesion, the confidence loss is defined as Eq. 4.

$$Loss_{noobj} = \sum_{l=1}^{L} \sum_{i=0}^{S_l^2} \sum_{j=0}^{B} \tau_{ij}^{noobj} \cdot CrossEntropy(C_i, \hat{C}_i) \tag{4}$$

where τ_{ij}^{noobj} denotes whether the jth bounding box that predicted by i^{th} cell contains a lesion or not. If the intersection over union (IoU) of prediction and the ground truth is below a well-setting threshold, τ_{ij}^{noobj} is set to be 0. As is mentioned in Sect. 2.2.1, we set $IoU = 0.5$ in the confidence loss function.

2.2.4   Overall Loss Function

In summary, the loss function of M3DCF is a combination of the mentioned components, and which is defined as the following equation.

$$Loss = \lambda_{coord} L_{location} + \lambda_{coord} L_{size} + L_{object} + \lambda_{noobj} L_{noobj} \tag{5}$$

where λ_{coord} and λ_{noobj} are respectively the weighting factors, which are designed for addressing imbalance of coordinate and confidence loss. For the reason that the ranges of location, size and confidence are different, the values of λ_{coord} and λ_{noobj} should depend on the ratio of their range. Generally, YOLO v3 recommends that the weights of location and the size can be the same, where the values should relate to the size of input object. Based on this scheme, we analysis the resolution of lesions in DeepLesion database. It's worth noting that the loss ranges of location, size and confidence will achieve stabilization during the training process when $\lambda_{coord} = 0.5$ and $\lambda_{noobj} = 0.5$.

3   Experiments

3.1   Experiment Setup

The experiments are conducted on DeepLesion dataset to evaluate the performance of the proposed algorithm. Specially, the training and the testing processes of all methods are performed on NVIDIA 1080Ti GPU. The DeepLesion is divided into training (70%, 22,901 lesions), validation (15%, 4887 lesions), and testing (15%, 4912 lesions) sets. There are several categories of DeepLesion, including *Bone*, *Mediastinum*, *Abdomen*, *Liver*, *Softtissue*, *Lung*, *Kidney*, and *Pelvis*. With the goal of encoding 3D information, we used three axial slices to compose three-channel images, and then each image is used to be the input to CNN. Note that only the target CT slice that contains the ground truth bounding box. As for state-of-the-arts, we chose 3DCE, Faster R-CNN and RetinaNet as the baselines. As for Faster R-CNN, we use VGG-16 [28] pretrained on ImageNet as the backbone. The learning rate is set to be 0.001, and the batch is set to be 1 with the momentum is 0.9. RetinaNet is trained with Resnet-50 [23] where the input image size is $600 \times 1000 \times 3$. The initial learning rate of RetinaNet is set to be 0.00001, where the batch and the momentum is respectively as 1 and 0.9. As for 3DCE, we used VGG-16 as its pretrained backbone. The input image is with sized of $512 \times 512 \times 3$ (or $512 \times 512 \times 9$), the batch and the gradient descent momentum is set to be 1 and 0.9, respectively.

3.2   Results and Discussions

3.2.1   Overall Evaluation

Most existing works use sensitivity as their evaluative criteria, since the sensitivity measures the proportion of actual positives that are correctly identified as such (e.g., the percentage of lesions which are correctly identified as having the condition). The 3DCE adopts "sensitivity at 4 false positives per image" as their assessment criteria. In 3DCE, they drew the sensitivity curve with average false positives per image, then the sensitivity rise as more false predictions allowed. In order to obtain more general evaluation, we considered this general object detection evaluation metric, namely mean average precision, to measure the performance of each algorithm. Specifically, we draw precision-recall curve to visualize the results of all methods.

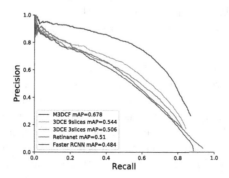

Fig. 2. Precision-recall curve and mAPs of different algorithms.

Figure 2 shows the precision-recall curve and the Mean Average Precision of all methods, respectively. It is obvious that the proposed algorithm significantly outperforms the other methods. Noteworthy that our method increases at least 0.13 mAP than state-of-the-art methods, such as 3DCE 9 slices. The results of 3DCE 9 slices indicates 3D context feature fusion drastically improve the discriminant ability of lesion features that extracted from different scales. Moreover, one can see that the accuracy of all algorithms dropped significantly when recall reaches a high level such as recall > 0.8. This phenomenon means that there will be a large proportion of false positives with high confidence. It is worth noting that our method has significant produces a better result while M3DCF maintains the precision with 0.4. M3DCF obviously achieves state-of-the-art accuracy with faster than the other existing lesion detectors.

Table 1. The mAP and AP of the experimented algorithms.

Method	mAP	AP							
		Bone	Abdomen	Mediastinum	Liver	Lung	Kidney	Softtissue	Pelvis
RetinaNet	0.510	0.510	0.418	0.543	0.515	0.603	0.415	0.440	0.407
Faster R-CNN	0.484	0.530	0.369	0.495	0.541	0.574	0.411	0.422	0.362
3DCE 9slices	0.544	0.475	0.451	0.560	0.553	0.648	0.468	0.426	0.451
3DCE 3slices	0.506	0.423	0.408	0.507	0.537	0.617	0.415	0.413	404
3DCFF	**0.678**	**0.671**	**0.629**	**0.761**	**0.722**	**0.689**	**0.591**	**0.524**	**0.681**

As shown in Table 1, M3DCF has higher mAP and APs in all categories, which indicates that the feature fusion scheme M3DCF has significant benefits over the other lesion detection algorithms. Actually, M3DCF achieves an approximately 0.13 higher mAP than the other methods. Noteworthy that we achieve at least 0.2 mAP higher than the other lesion detectors in the categories of *Pelvis* and *Mediastinum*. Furthermore, our method also produces better qualitative results in *Bone*, *Abdomen*, *Liver*, *Kidney*, etc. General speaking, 3D feature fusion schemes are always better than detectors that only depend on one target image as the input. The exceptional thing is that RetinaNet and Faster R-CNN obtain better AP in category of *Bone* than 3DCE 9 slices.

3.2.2   Evaluation of Each Part

We plot the precision-recall curves of all algorithms shown in Fig. 3a, which was experimented in the area of *Mediastinum*. We can empirically observe that the average precision of most algorithms is above 0.5 while our method achieves an excellent result for $AP = 0.761$. Specially, the result of our method is close to the standard of practical application and which is 0.20 higher than 3DCE 9 slices. In addition, when the recall reaches 0.8, our method maintains the precision above 0.6 while the other methods drop rapidly. Figure 4 shows the detection results of experiments. It's shown that the texture of lesion is similar with surrounding areas and the lesion entirely blend with adjacent tissues. The 3DCE and Faster R-CNN which is based on Region Proposal Network generate a lot of candidate boxes, however, it's an extremely challenging task to recognize lesions under such conditions. Therefore, 3DCE and Faster R-CNN generate many useless false positives. Also, RetinaNet cannot handle this problem. On the contrary, the method we proposed successfully extract the lesion without any false positives. Meanwhile, we can infer that the fusion and multi-scale prediction strategy we designed can regress lesions precisely.

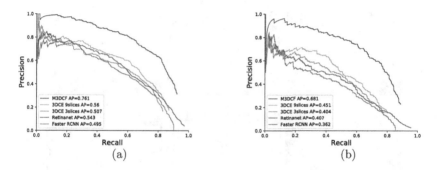

Fig. 3. Precision-recall curve of *Mediastinum* (a) and *Pelvis* (b)

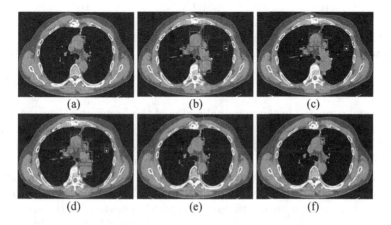

Fig. 4. The detection results on the position of *Mediastinum* (No. 000238 10 01 130), with (a) Ground truth; (b) 3DCE 3slices; (c) 3DCE 9slices; (d) Faster R-CNN; (e) RetinaNet; (f) M3DCF.

Figure 5 shows a typical slice of the area of *Pelvis*, the lesion located on the top left corner. It's an extremely challenging task to extract lesion since surrounding areas environmentally similar to the target area. Under such circumstances, current algorithms have poor performance on detection. It's worth noting that the average precision of 3DCE 9 slices is below 0.46 while Faster RCNN at 0.362 AP. However, our method achieves $AP = 0.681$ and which exceeds 0.2 accuracy. Besides, M3DCF has a competitive balance in the precision-recall trade off since the other algorithms generate a large proportion of false positives in a high recall. Obviously the strategy adopted is surprisingly effective.

3.2.3 Typical Fail Condition

We show representative failure cases in Fig. 6. CT slices' low-resolution, similar texture with surrounding, making the association of tissues complex. The results in Fig. 6 are difficult to regress precisely for M3DCF. As we can observe, the lesion

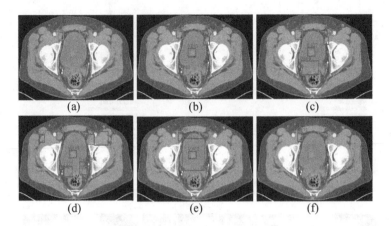

Fig. 5. The detection results on the position of *Pelvis* (No. 000268 03 01 127), with (a) Ground truth; (b) 3DCE 3slices; (c) 3DCE 9slices; (d) Faster R-CNN; (e) RetinaNet; (f) M3DCF.

of Fig. 6a and c located in the marginal region of the *Lung*, and there is plenty of similar tissues which make the performance worse. Since the lesion in Fig. 6b surrounded by the tissues and affected by light intensity, the method we proposed cannot extract the lesion well and makes a poor performance. In such cases, the algorithm is required to have strong edge sensitivity. Figure 6d and e are the slices of *Pelvis*, compared with other regions, more complex information like composition and texture bring more interference. Figure 6f shows the *Softtissue* area, it's difficult to recognize the lesion since the target is wrapped by tissues. In general, it is intractable for our method to detect the lesion especially for complicated shape, low-resolution, wrapped by surrounding tissues, etc.

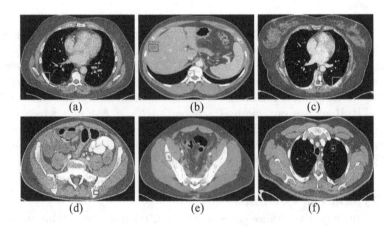

Fig. 6. The detection results on the position of *Pelvis* (No. 000268 03 01 127), with (a) Ground truth; (b) 3DCE 3slices; (c) 3DCE 9slices; (d) Faster R-CNN; (e) RetinaNet; (f) M3DCF.

Table 2. The average runtime of experimented algorithms.

Method	Average runtime (ms)
Faster R-CNN	159
RetinaNet	154
3DCE - 3 slices	79
3DCE - 9 slices	148
M3DCF	49

4 Runtime Evaluation

Runtime results for lesion detection are shown in Table 2. And runtimes are measured on a NVIDIA 1080 Ti. As shown in the experiment, since mainstream algorithms such as Faster RCNN and 3DCE adopt Region Proposal Network (RPN) for proposal generation proceeding. In addition, the backbone of Faster R-CNN for feature extraction is a relatively complicated network and which cost a lot of time. As shown in Table 2, the average processing time of Faster R-CNN is 159 ms. It is worth noting that the processing time of RetinaNet is 154 ms closed to Faster R-CNN. 3DCE 3 slices takes the half time of 3DCE 9 slices, which obviously proved that method based on 3DCE has not made a tradeoff of speed and accuracy. Most worthy of mention is that the extra time cost can be reduced by using Darknet-53 for its significant time efficiency. At 608×608 our method runs 49 ms at 67.8 mAP with three times faster than 3DCE 9 slices.

5 Conclusion

In this paper, we propose a new method called M3DCF that acts as a more effective alternative to previous approaches for lesion detection. First, we adopt a one-stage detector to enable the network is faster and simpler. And which gives rise to effective results. Second, for characteristics of computed tomography (CT) scans, we propose a novel feature fusion strategy based on 3D context to sufficiently fuse the extracted feature of multiple neighboring slices. Third, based on our 3D context fusion strategy, the multi-scale strategy allows us to get more meaningful semantic information, and it obviously improves the performance on the test set of DeepLesion database. The experimental results conducted on DeepLesion dataset indicates that the proposed method surpass the accuracy of the mainstream algorithms such as Faster R-CNN, RetinaNet, and 3DCE, while still being faster.

References

1. Yan, K., et al.: DeepLesion: automated mining of large-scale lesion annotations and universal lesion detection with deep learning. J. Med. Imaging **5**(3), 036501 (2018)
2. Krizhevsky, A., Sutskever, I. , Hinton, G.E.: ImageNet classification with deep convolutional neural networks. In: Advances in Neural Information Processing Systems (2012)
3. Girshick, R., et al.: Rich feature hierarchies for accurate object detection and semantic segmentation. In: Proceedings of the IEEE Conference on Computer Vision and Pattern Recognition (2014)
4. Everingham, M., et al.: The pascal visual object classes (VOC) challenge. Int. J. Comput. Vis. **88**(2), 303–338 (2010)
5. Uijlings, J.R.R., et al.: Selective search for object recognition. Int. J. Comput. Vis. **104**(2), 154–171 (2013)
6. Girshick, R.: Fast R-CNN. In: Proceedings of the IEEE International Conference on Computer Vision (2015)
7. Ren, S., et al.: Faster R-CNN: towards real-time object detection with region proposal networks. In: Advances in Neural Information Processing Systems (2015)
8. He, K., et al.: Spatial pyramid pooling in deep convolutional networks for visual recognition. IEEE Trans. Pattern Anal. Mach. Intell. **37**(9), 1904–1916 (2015)
9. Dai, J., et al.: R-FCN: object detection via region-based fully convolutional networks. In: Advances in Neural Information Processing Systems (2016)
10. Sermanet, P., et al.: OverFeat: integrated recognition, localization and detection using convolutional networks. arXiv preprint arXiv:1312.6229 (2013)
11. Liu, W., et al.: SSD: single shot multibox detector. In: Leibe, B., Matas, J., Sebe, N., Welling, M. (eds.) ECCV 2016. LNCS, vol. 9905, pp. 21–37. Springer, Cham (2016). https://doi.org/10.1007/978-3-319-46448-0_2
12. Lin, T.-Y., et al.: Focal loss for dense object detection. In: Proceedings of the IEEE International Conference on Computer Vision (2017)
13. Redmon, J., et al.: You only look once: unified, real-time object detection. In: Proceedings of the IEEE Conference on Computer Vision and Pattern Recognition (2016)
14. Redmon, J., Farhadi, A.: YOLO9000: better, faster, stronger. In: Proceedings of the IEEE Conference on Computer Vision and Pattern Recognition (2017)
15. Redmon, J., Farhadi, A.: YOLOv3: an incremental improvement. arXiv preprint arXiv:1804.02767 (2018)
16. Fu, C.-Y., et al.: DSSD: deconvolutional single shot detector. arXiv preprint arXiv:1701.06659 (2017)
17. Dou, Q., Chen, H., Yu, L., et al.: Automatic detection of cerebral microbleeds from MR images via 3D convolutional neural networks. IEEE Trans. Med. Imaging **35**(5), 1182–1195 (2016)
18. Hwang, S., Kim, H.E.: Self-transfer learning for fully weakly supervised object localization. arXiv preprint arXiv:1602.01625 (2016)
19. Teramoto, A., Fujita, H., Yamamuro, O., et al.: Automated detection of pulmonary nodules in PET/CT images: ensemble false-positive reduction using a convolutional neural network technique. Med. phys. **43**(6Part1), 2821–2827 (2016)

20. Yan, K., Bagheri, M., Summers, R.M.: 3D context enhanced region-based convolutional neural network for end-to-end lesion detection. In: Frangi, A.F., Schnabel, J.A., Davatzikos, C., Alberola-López, C., Fichtinger, G. (eds.) MICCAI 2018. LNCS, vol. 11070, pp. 511–519. Springer, Cham (2018). https://doi.org/10.1007/978-3-030-00928-1_58

21. Courbariaux, M., et al.: Binarized neural networks: training deep neural networks with weights and activations constrained to +1 or −1. arXiv preprint arXiv:1602.02830 (2016)

22. Nair, V., Hinton, G.E.: Rectified linear units improve restricted Boltzmann machines. In: Proceedings of the 27th International Conference on Machine Learning (ICML-10) (2010)

23. He, K., et al.: Deep residual learning for image recognition. In: Proceedings of the IEEE Conference on Computer Vision and Pattern Recognition (2016)

24. Ephraim, Y., Malah, D.: Speech enhancement using a minimum-mean square error short-time spectral amplitude estimator. IEEE Trans. Acoust. Speech Signal Process. **32**(6), 1109–1121 (1984)

25. De Boer, P.-T., et al.: A tutorial on the cross-entropy method. Ann. Oper. Res. **134**(1), 19–67 (2005)

26. Levinson, N.: The Wiener (root mean square) error criterion in filter design and prediction. J. Math. Phys. **25**(1–4), 261–278 (1946)

27. Willmott, C.J., Matsuura, K.: Advantages of the mean absolute error (MAE) over the root mean square error (RMSE) in assessing average model performance. Clim. Res **30**(1), 79–82 (2005)

28. Simonyan, K., Zisserman, A.: Very deep convolutional networks for large-scale image recognition. arXiv preprint arXiv:1409.1556 (2014)

Orientation Adaptive YOLOv3 for Object Detection in Remote Sensing Images

Jiahui Lei$^{(\boxtimes)}$, Chongjun Gao, Jing Hu, Changxin Gao, and Nong Sang

National Key Laboratory of Science and Technology on Multispectral Information Processing, School of Artificial Intelligence and Automation, Huazhong University of Science and Technology, Wuhan, China
{makuragami,gaochongjun,1999010174,cgao,nsang}@hust.edu.cn

Abstract. Object detection in remote sensing images is full of challenges. The large scale of detection region, and the difficulty of dense object detection are the main problems needed to solve. Although YOLOv3 perform better and faster, it is not suitable to the orientation which means it is not friendly to NMS operation on dense objects area. This drawback would lead to an increase in miss rate in dense object detection. In this paper, we modified YOLOv3 based on the oriented bounding box (OBB) for object detection in remote images to solve the problems above. This model is based on YOLOv3 which performs better on small target compared with YOLOv2. We modified the architecture of YOLOv3 to predict oriented bounding box. In this way, we can obtain bounding boxes more suitable for large aspect ratio objects. Moreover, in a dense area such as parking lot, it can also achieve a good performance.

Keywords: Remote sensing · Object detection · Convolutional neural network

1 Introduction

Object detection in remote sensing images (RSIs) is to determine if a given high-resolution aerial image includes one or more objects which belong to the categories needed and locate the position of each predicted object in the image [1]. Usually, the category of object refers to some representative human-made objects (e.g. vehicles, ships, planes, etc.). As a fundamental problem in the field of intelligent interpretation of remote sensing images, object detection in RSIs plays a vital role in a wide range of scenarios. Different from conventional perspective images, object detection in RSIs suffers from more challenges including background clutter, small target. Objects with large aspect ratio (such as vehicles, ships,etc.) may also make object detection become more difficult than other object detections, shown as Fig. 1.

In recent years, the development of deep learning provides effective frameworks for object detection. The mostly adopted frameworks are R-CNN [2], SSP-Net [3], Fast R-CNN [4], Faster R-CNN [5] which are two-stage, and YOLO

© Springer Nature Switzerland AG 2019
Z. Lin et al. (Eds.): PRCV 2019, LNCS 11857, pp. 586–597, 2019.
https://doi.org/10.1007/978-3-030-31654-9_50

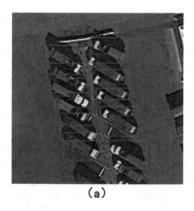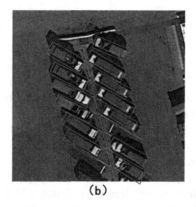

Fig. 1. Horizontal bounding box (a) and Oriented bounding box (b). It is obvious that oriented bounding boxes are more suitable for objects and would be less influenced by NMS operation.

[6–8], SSD [9] which are one-stage. Besides, special kind of CNN, FCN [10], is popularly used in segmentation, and R-FCN [11], builds a fully convolutional network which greatly improves the speed of detection with a good effect. The method above are all known as horizontal region detection, which are not suitable for object with large aspect ratio in remote sensing. In remote sensing images, the vehicles, ships are often densely arranged in complex scenes, the redundant regions of horizontal bounding box will lead a bad influence on feature extraction. And the regions overlap between two objects will be disadvantage of recall rate.

In this paper, we proposed an adaptive orientation method based on YOLOv3 to get oriented bounding boxes instead of horizontal bounding boxes to reduce the miss detection rate in intensive object area. We can get a suitable bounding box helping to extract better features simultaneously. By using a structure similar to FPN [12], the performance of small target detection has been significantly improved. Moreover, in order not to lose information during resizing RSIs, we crop the images into 1024 × 1024 with 100 × 1024 pixel overlap area. NMS of this area is necessary to refine the detection at the edge of each piece of RSIs.

2   Related Work

CNN is widely used in image related tasks and performs much better than typical methods. Current CNN-based object detection methods are commonly used in the vision community. Faster R-CNN [5] introduces a region proposal network (RPN) to get proposal regions. The features for each region are extracted from feature maps using ROI-pooling. YOLO [6] frames object detection as a regression problem to spatially separated bounding boxes and associated class probabilities. Features are extracted based on the boxes from feature maps. SSD [9] discretizes the output space of bounding boxes into a set of default boxes over different aspect ratios and scales per feature map location. It extracts different features for different default boxes at the same location from different feature layers. Due to the extremely effective performance of CNN-based features, hand-crafted features gradually fade out from recent detection systems.

Considering the different size of the object which we are interested and the large scale of remote sensing images, researchers proposed many specific methods to improve the performance of CNN-based detection models. Lin [13] utilize an FCN to tackle the problem of inshore ship detection and design a ship detection framework that possesses a more simplified procedure and a more robust performance. Kang [14] take the objects proposals generated by Faster R-CNN for the guard windows of CFAR algorithm, then pick up the small objects, thus reevaluating the bounding boxes which have relatively low classification scores in detection network. Zhang [15] propose a new ship detection model based on CNN which is called SCNN, fed with specially designed proposals extracted from the ship model combined with an improved saliency detection method. Kang [16] build a contextual region-based CNN with multi-layer fusion for ship detection in RSIs, which is an elaborately designed deep hierarchical network, and composed of an RPN with high network resolution and an object detection network with contextual features. Etten [17] proposed a new architecture which is exploited for high-level feature representation and classification at high speed. Redmon proposed YOLOv3 [8] which is sensitive to a small target, and performed better than SSD and YOLOv2 [7] at little expense of speed.

Although these machine-learning-based remote sensing object detection algorithm above have shown promising performance, they have poor practicability in areas with dense objects because of the horizontal bounding boxes and NMS operation. To solve this problem, using oriented bounding boxes instead of horizontal bounding boxes is a good idea. It is also necessary to get the orientation information in the OCR field. Ma [18] first proposed Rotation Region Proposal Network (RRPN) and Rotation ROI Pooling (RROI), which can obtain oriented bounding boxes to detect text in natural scenarios accurately by using R-anchors. Jiang [19] proposed Rotation Region CNN for detecting arbitrary-oriented texts in natural scene images. But Ma's and Jiang's models are all based on Faster R-CNN, which means a high cost of calculation. The speed of this model is too slow. Shi [20] introduced oriented information by modifying SSD and performed well on oriented text, achieved a high performance with a high speed. However, SSD has poor performance on small target detection, which is the primary target in RSIs. This year in the field of object detection in remote sensing images, Xia [21] proposed new datasets with over 188,000 oriented bounding boxes in 2,806 images, and furthermore, they also modify Faster R-CNN with oriented bounding boxes, and obtain a higher mAP than other horizontal methods. Additionally, Yang [22] proposed Multitask Rotation Region CNN and performances great on DOTAdataset. But as same as RRPN, these algorithms are not efficient enough, could not meet the requirements of real-time.

To demonstrate the challenges of object detection remote sensing images, we proposed an adaptive orientation algorithm based on YOLOv3. The architecture

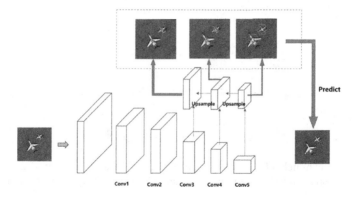

Fig. 2. Network architecture. The network consists of convolutional feature layers (shown as blocks) and convolutional predictors (shown as arrows).

of YOLOv3 is modified to obtain oriented bounding boxes. And we train the model with 1024 × 1024 pixel cutouts of DOTAdataset. Due to the increase in input size, the ability of small target detection of our model has also increased.

3   Method

3.1   Overview

To solve the problems discussed in Sect. 2, we implement an object detection framework based on YOLOv3, which has achieved a good balance of performance and efficiency.

The architecture of our framework is illustrated in Fig. 2. Our network uses a pre-trained Darknet-53 network as its essential feature extracted network.

3.2   Predict Oriented Bounding Box

In our model, the predicted bounding box is a rotated rectangle denoted by $b = (x_b, y_b, w_b, h_b, \theta_b)$, where b_x, b_y are the coordinates of the grid cell, b_w, b_h are the width and height of bounding box, b_θ is the angle. The height b_h is set as the short side of the bounding box, and the width b_w is set as the long side of the rectangle. The orientation θ is the angle from the positive direction of the x-axis to the direction parallel to the long side of the rotated bounding box. Here we just let orientation parameter b_θ covers 180° space. Defining the orientation of a rotated box is θ, there exists one and only one integer k ensuring that $\theta + k\pi$ is within the interval $\left[-\frac{\pi}{4}, \frac{3\pi}{4}\right)$, and we regard $b_\theta + k\pi$ as b_θ. We detect objects by estimating the confidence scores and offsets to a series of default boxes on feature map (shown as Fig. 3). Each default box is associated with a location, and the feature at that location predicts the score and offsets. One feature map location associates three default box.

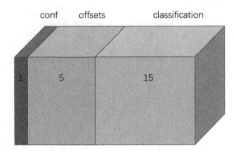

Fig. 3. Output channels of a convolutional predictor. The dimension of output is 21, confidence has one channel, offsets have 5 channels refer to (x, y, w, h, θ), and 15 channels apply to 15 categories.

The convolutional predictor produces 5 channels for object detection, predicts an object score for each bounding box using logistic regression. This should be 1 if the bounding box prior overlaps a ground truth object by more than any other bounding box prior. If the bounding box prior is not the best but does overlap a ground truth object by more than some threshold, we ignore the prediction. The rest 5 are the geometric offsets. Considering a location (x, y) on the map, we denote the vector at this location along the depth by $(\Delta b_s, \Delta b_y, \Delta b_w, \Delta b_h, \Delta b_\theta)$. Then, the predict bounding box at this location is calculated by:

$$b_x = \sigma\left(t_x\right) + c_x,$$
$$b_y = \sigma\left(t_y\right) + c_y,$$
$$b_w = p_w e^{t_w},$$
$$b_h = p_h e^{t_h},$$
$$b_\theta = \Delta\theta_s.$$

During training, we use a sum of squared error loss. If the ground truth for some coordinate prediction is $\hat{t}_*$ our gradient is the ground truth value (computed from the ground truth box) minus our prediction: $\hat{t}_* - t_*$. This ground truth value can be easily calculated by inverting the equations above.

3.3   Rotation IoU Algorithm

The predict bounding box can be generated in any orientations. So the IoU computation for horizontal bounding box may lead to an inaccurate IoU of skew interactive proposals and further get negative influence on the predictor learning. As shown in Fig. 4, we show the geometric principles to calculate offsets on positive default boxes. Given a set of skew rectangles, we need to compute the IoU for each pair rectangle. Because of the irregularity of the intersection regions, normal IoU algorithms could not get an accurate result. So we need to divide this intersection area into several triangular regions. Then we can efficiently compute the region of each of these triangular areas. For example, we assume that there

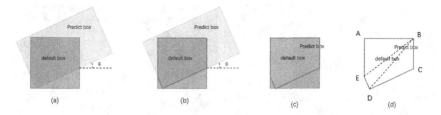

Fig. 4. IoU algorithms. Offsets calculation steps: (a) shows the scenarios that default box, predict bounding box has different angle; (b)–(c) get the bounding of intersection area; (d) divides the intersection area into several triangular areas, and calculates this area $Area(\text{ABCDE}) = Area(\triangle\text{ABE}) + Area(\triangle\text{BDE}) + Area(\triangle\text{BCD})$.

is only one ground truth object on the input image. A default box is labeled as a positive bounding box. Offsets are calculated on positive default boxes.

3.4 Rotation Non-maximun Suppression

Traditional NMS operation takes only the IoU result into consideration, but it is not enough for oriented bounding boxes because of the angle information. For instance, an anchor with a ratio of 1:8 and an angle difference of $\frac{\pi}{12}$ has an IoU of 0.31, which is less than 0.7; however, it may be regarded as a positive sample. Therefore, the Rotation NMS similar to Soft-NMS [23] consists of 4 phases:

(i) keep the max IoU for proposals with an IoU larger than 0.7;
(ii) if all proposals have an IoU in the range [0.3, 0.7], keep the proposal with the minimum angle difference concerning the ground truth (the angle difference should be less than $\frac{\pi}{12}$).
(iii) if the aspect ratio of bounding boxes exceed 1:20, it means this bounding box is false except it was predicted to be a harbor.
(iv) if the IoU is in the range of [0.3, 0.7], discard the prediction results that the angle difference is greater than 15°.

3.5 Loss Function

During training of our model, each anchor is associated with a class label and five parantric coordinates. Our network model is trained by simultaneously minimizing the losses on object classification and offsets regression. Overall, the loss function is a weighted sum of the two losses (Fig. 5):

$$L(x, c, l, g) = \frac{1}{N}(L_{conf}(x, c) + \lambda L_{loc}(x, l, g)) \tag{1}$$

where x is indicator for matching the i-th default box to the j-th ground truth box of category s. $c = 1$ if the i-th default box is labeled as positive, and 0 otherwise. L_{conf} is the softmax loss over the predicted object, respectively c and l. L_{loc} is the $SmoothL1$ regression loss over the predicted bounding box x and the ground truth g. The losses on objects classification and regression are normalized by N_s,

Fig. 5. Samples of annotated images in DOTAdataset. Compared with horizontal bounding boxes, oriented bounding boxes are more suitable to object with large aspect ratio (e.g. vehicles, ships).

4   Experiment

4.1   Dataset

In this section, we evaluate the proposed method on a public dataset, namely DOTA [21]. DOTAdataset contains fifteen categories include plane, ship, storage tank, baseball diamond, tennis court, basketball court, ground track field, harbor, bridge, large vehicle, small vehicle, helicopter, roundabout, soccer ball field and basketball court. There are 2806 images about 4000 × 4000 pixels and 188,282 oriented bounding boxes instance, each of which is labeled in $(x_1, y_1, x_2, y_2, x_3, y_3, x_4, y_4)$ form. Because the input of YOLOv3 is different from DOTAdataset, first we transformed the labels into (x, y, w, h, θ) shape. Furthermore, θ is calculated by

$$\theta = \frac{\left(\frac{y_2 - y_1}{x_2 - x_1} + \frac{y_3 - y_4}{x_3 - x_4} \right)}{2} \tag{2}$$

Table 1. Numerical results (AP) of baseline models from DOTA compared with our method evaluated with OBB ground truth. The short names for categories are defined as *BD-Baseball diamond, GTF-Ground field track, SV-Small vehicle, LV-Large vehicle, TC-Tennis court, BC-Basketball court, ST-Storage tank, SBF-Soccer-ball Field, RA-Roundabout, SP-Swimming pool, and HC-Helicopter.* FR-O means Faster R-CNN with Oriented bounding box. Ours means YOLOv3 trained on Oriented bounding box.

	YOLOv2	SSD	R-FCN	FR	FR-O	Ours
Plane	39.57	39.83	37.8	47.16	**79.09**	65.3
BD	20.29	9.09	38.21	61	**69.12**	22.12
Bridge	26.58	0.64	3.64	9.8	17.17	**33.28**
GTF	23.42	13.18	37.26	51.74	**63.49**	54.27
SV	8.85	0.26	6.74	14.87	**34.2**	29.96
LV	2.09	0.39	2.60	12.8	37.16	**43.58**
Ship	4.82	1.11	5.59	6.88	36.2	**38.46**
TC	44.34	16.24	22.85	56.26	**89.19**	65.39
BC	38.25	27.57	46.93	59.97	**69.6**	60.51
ST	34.65	9.23	66.04	57.32	**58.96**	49.25
SBF	16.02	27.16	33.37	47.83	**49.4**	28.16
RA	37.62	9.09	47.15	48.7	**52.52**	45.18
Harbor	47.23	3.03	10.6	8.23	46.69	**57.53**
SP	25.5	1.05	25.19	37.25	**44.8**	32.41
HC	7.45	1.01	17.96	23.05	**46.3**	29.74
Avg.	21.39	10.59	26.79	36.29	**52.93**	43.66
FPS	–	–	–	–	4.2	**11.4**

4.2 Setting

Our network is based on YOLOv3, fine-tuned on DOTA dataset. It is optimized by the standard SGD algorithms with a momentum of 0.9. Before training, all Images are cropped to 1024×1024 with a 200-pixel redundant area. Since our model is fully-convolutional, we can train it on a certain size and apply it to other sizes during testing. Batch size is set to 8. In pre-training, the learning is set to 10^{-3} for the first 30k iterations, then decayed to 10^{-4} for the rest 20k iterations. During fine-tune, the learning rate is fixed to 10^{-4} for 10k iterations. The number of fine-tune iterations depends on the size of the dataset.

While testing our method, because of the oriented bounding boxes, we could not use rectangle function to draw annotations. So we need to transform the label form back to $(x_1, y_1, x_2, y_2, x_3, y_3, x_4, y_4)$ form.

Our method is implemented using MXNET [24]. All the experiments are carried out on a workstation with 4 TitanX Graphics Cards.

Fig. 6. As shown in this figure, almost all objects are accurately detected, especially vehicles in the parking.

4.3   Results

Table 1 compares our method with other mainstream methods such as YOLOv2, SSD, R-FCN, Faster R-CNN and Faster R-CNN with OBB (FR-O). In the comparison of traditional detection methods, the method with OBB (FR-O and our methods) has a better performance. Because there are fewer redundant areas in OBB, the model can extract higher quality features. And there are fewer miss detection due to NMS. Benefit from FPN structure, our method is superior to FR-O in large vehicle (43.58), ship (38.46) (Fig. 6).

The FPS shows the speed of Faster RCNN with OBB and YOLOv3 with OBB, we can find that although FR-O obtains the highest mAP, our method is only second, but our method is faster than FR-O. Our method is more than 2× faster, and only sacrificed a little performance. For example, we assume the raw remote sensing images of the 4000 *times* 4000 size cropped into 100 parts. It means orientation adaptive YOLOv3 only need about 9 s while Faster RCNN would run more 20 s. In short, our method gets a right balance between speed and performance.

However, in some complex scene, such as a port or a parking lot with containers, or the shadow between two objects, which have similar aspect ratios, would cause false alarms on the detector. As shown in Fig. 7, the aircraft carrier was not detected. And the model incorrectly detected the text as planes.

Figure 8 shows example results on validation dataset. We can find that in dense area, our model can predict suitable oriented bounding box to avoid unexpected NMS operation, which would raise the miss rate. Moreover, the second images, planes with different scale did not reduce the performance of our mode.

Fig. 7. False detection results.

Fig. 8. Multi categorize results.

5   Conclusion

In this paper, we proposed an end to end remote sensing object detection framework with oriented bounding box which can handle different complex scenarios, detect dense objects. This framework absorbs many advantages of mainstream algorithms, combined oriented information with one-stage network YOLOv3, achieves a good balance of performance and efficiency. By using oriented bounding box, the model can extract features with high quality, and reduce the loss of NMS operation. On the other hand, this model can process data at high speed, means this model can be applied in many scenarios. Experiments show that adaptive orientation YOLOv3 has a good performance in DOTAdataset, better than other horizontal bounding box method. Although our method can not achieve the same performance with Faster R-CNN with the oriented bounding box, our method is nearly 3x faster than Faster R-CNN.

Despite the performance and speed, there are still many problem need to solve. We need to find why there are many false alarms and misjudgment. Moreover, we need further improve the architecture to have a similar performance as Faster R-CNN, or even better.

References

1. Cheng, G., Han, J.: A survey on object detection in optical remote sensing images. Isprs J. Photogr. Remote Sens. **117**, 11–28 (2016)
2. Girshick, R., Donahue, J., Darrell, T., Malik, J.: Region-based convolutional networks for accurate object detection and segmentation. IEEE Trans. Pattern Anal. Mach. Intell. **38**(1), 142–158 (2016)
3. He, K., Zhang, X., Ren, S., Sun, J.: Spatial pyramid pooling in deep convolutional networks for visual recognition. IEEE Trans. Pattern Anal. Mach. Intell. **37**(9), 1904–16 (2014)
4. Girshick, R.: FAST R-CNN. In: IEEE International Conference on Computer Vision (2015)
5. Ren, S., He, K., Girshick, R., Sun, J.: Faster R-CNN: towards real-time object detection with region proposal networks. In: International Conference on Neural Information Processing Systems (2015)
6. Redmon, J., Divvala, S., Girshick, R., Farhadi, A.: You only look once: unified, real-time object detection. In: IEEE Conference on Computer Vision and Pattern Recognition, pp. 779–788 (2016)
7. Redmon, J., Farhadi, A.: YOLO9000: better, faster, stronger. In: IEEE Conference on Computer Vision and Pattern Recognition (2017)
8. Redmon, J., Farhadi, A.: YOLOv3: an incremental improvement. arXiv (2018)
9. Liu, W., et al.: SSD: single shot multibox detector. In: Leibe, B., Matas, J., Sebe, N., Welling, M. (eds.) ECCV 2016. LNCS, vol. 9905, pp. 21–37. Springer, Cham (2016). https://doi.org/10.1007/978-3-319-46448-0_2
10. Shelhamer, E., Long, J., Darrell, T.: Fully convolutional networks for semantic segmentation. IEEE Trans. Pattern Anal. Mach. Intell. **PP**(99), 1–1 (2014)
11. Dai, J., Li, Y., He, K., Sun, J.: R-FCN: Object detection via region-based fully convolutional networks. In: Neural Information Processing Systems (2016)
12. Lin, T.Y., Dollár, P., Girshick, R., He, K., Hariharan,B., Belongie, S.: Feature pyramid networks for object detection. In IEEE Conference on Computer Vision and Pattern Recognition (2017)
13. Lin, H., Shi, Z., Zou, Z.: Fully convolutional network with task partitioning for inshore ship detection in optical remote sensing images. IEEE Geosci. Remote Sens. Lett. **PP**(99), 1–5 (2017)

14. Kang, M., Leng, X., Lin, Z., Ji, K.: A modified faster R-CNN based on CFAR algorithm for SAR ship detection. In: International Workshop on Remote Sensing with Intelligent Processing (2017)
15. Zhang, R., Yao, J., Zhang, K., Feng, C., Zhang, J.: S-CNN-based ship detection from high-resolution remote sensing images. Int. Arch. Photogr. Sens. Spat. Inform. Sci. **XLI–B7**, 423–430 (2016)
16. Kang, M., Ji, K., Leng, X., Lin, Z.: Contextual region-based convolutional neural network with multilayer fusion for SAR ship detection. Remote Sens. **9**(8), 860 (2017)
17. Van Etten, A.: You only look twice: rapid multi-scale object detection in satellite imagery. arXiv (2018)
18. Ma, J.: Arbitrary-oriented scene text detection via rotation proposals. IEEE Trans. Multimed. **PP**(99), 1 (2017)
19. Jiang, Y.: R2CNN: rotational region CNN for orientation robust scene text detection. arXiv (2017)
20. Shi, B., Bai, X., Belongie, S.: Detecting oriented text in natural images by linking segments. In: IEEE Conference on Computer Vision and Pattern Recognition (2017)
21. Xia, G.-S.: DOTA: a large-scale dataset for object detection in aerial images. In: The IEEE Conference on Computer Vision and Pattern Recognition (2018)
22. Yang, X., Sun, H., Sun, X., Yan, M., Guo, Z., Kun, F.: Position detection and direction prediction for arbitrary-oriented ships via multitask rotation region convolutional neural network. IEEE Access **6**, 50839–50849 (2018)
23. Bodla, N., Singh, B., Chellappa, R., Davis, L.S.: Soft-NMS–improving object detection with one line of code. In: IEEE International Conference on Computer Vision, pp. 5562–5570. IEEE (2017)
24. Chen, T.: MXNet: a flexible and efficient machine learning library for heterogeneous distributed systems. arXiv (2015)

Neural Ordinary Differential Equations with Evolutionary Weights

Lingshen He, Xingyu Xie, and Zhouchen Lin$^{(\boxtimes)}$

Key Laboratory of Machine Perception, School of EECS,
Peking University, Beijing, China
zlin@pku.edu.cn

Abstract. Neural networks have been very successful in many learning tasks, for their powerful ability to fit the data. Recently, to understand the success of neural networks, much attention has been paid to the relationship between differential equations and neural networks. Some research suggests that the depth of neural networks is important for their success. However, the understanding of neural networks from the differential equation perspective is still very preliminary. In this work, also connecting with the differential equation, we extend the depth of neural networks to infinity, and remove the existing constraint that parameters of every layer have to be the same by using another ordinary differential equation(ODE) to model the evolution of the weights. We prove that the ODE can model any continuous evolutionary weights and validate it by an experiment. Meanwhile, we propose a new training strategy to overcome the inefficiency of pure adjoint method. This strategy allows us to further understand the relationship between ResNet with finite layers and that with infinite layers. Our experiment indicates that the former can be a good initialization of the latter. Finally, we give a heuristic explanation on why the new training method works better than pure adjoint method. Further experiments show that our neural ODE with evolutionary weights converges faster than that with fixed weights.

Keywords: Neural network · ODE · Adjoint method

1 Introduction

Deep neural networks have become a very powerful tool in machine learning [1]. The great success of deep neural networks mainly attributes to its ability to extract useful features from data by end-to-end learning.

The performance of neural networks with different structures vary greatly even on the same dataset. For example, convolutional neural networks (CNNs)

The first author is a student.

Electronic supplementary material The online version of this chapter (https:// doi.org/10.1007/978-3-030-31654-9_51) contains supplementary material, which is available to authorized users.

achieves the state-of-the-art results on object recognition and detection [14,24] while the fully connected networks fail. Unfortunately, the universal structure design rules remain unknown. Many researchers make efforts in order to better understand deep learning structures. The works in [26] visualized the learning procedure during training, which tried to figure out the connection between network structures and extracted features visually. However, neural networks visualization may not provide a theoretically sound designing guidance for good neural networks. Another line of works focus on the landscape of deep models. A lot of interesting theoretical results have been established to analyze the loss surface of neural networks [15,29]. However, the current theoretical analysis is still very preliminary as it normally imposes strong assumptions on data and shallow neural networks. So the theoretical analysis cannot provide designing guidance either.

One common problem of all the above investigations is that they cannot describe the behavior of networks when the depth approaches infinity. In general, it is hard to analyze ultra deep networks, since the instabilities will cause the over-expansion or decline of the network output [6]. Another problem is that the previous theoretical works cannot perfectly match the empirical success of ResNet [10] which is one of the most successful CNN structures. To understand the success of ResNet and its variants [25,27], the works [4,7] try to interpret ResNet from the perspective of dynamic systems. However, their analysis is still very preliminary, and the theoretical exploration on ResNet is still ongoing [8,11].

Recently, an interesting and theoretically sound combination of ordinary differential equation (ODE) and neural network architecture provides a new perspective on understanding ultra deep ResNet [3,4,22]. It is natural to adopt a differential equation to parameterize the continuous dynamics of hidden units in ResNet because the residual block of ResNet can be written as:

$$\mathbf{u}_{n+1} = \mathbf{u}_n + f_n(\mathbf{u}_n), \tag{1}$$

where $\mathbf{u} \in \mathbb{R}^n$ and f_n is a continuous function. Equation (1) is exactly one step of forward Euler discretization in ODE. Actually, many neural networks can be viewed as numerical ODEs [25,28,30]. Conversely, different types of numerical schemes of ODE can also be translated as neural networks [22].

In practice, we observe that a deeper ResNet obtains better performance and the ℓ_2-norm of $f_n(\mathbf{u}_n)$ becomes smaller as the network goes deeper [2]. In other words, a deeper ResNet resembles an ODE numerical scheme with a smaller time step. Based on these observations, in this paper we propose an ODE system— *Neural Ordinary Differential Equations with Evolutionary Weights* (NODE-EW), which is a continuous version of a deep ResNet. Our NODE-EW makes analyzing ultra deep ResNet possible. In our system, ODE is used in two places. Besides the discrete version ODE shown in Eq. (1), we also model the $\boldsymbol{\theta}_n$ as a trajectory of ODE, where $\boldsymbol{\theta}_n$ is the parameters of the function f_n. The double using of ODE brings two advantages. Besides larger model capacity and more representation power, the practical ResNet and its variants can be more accurately modeled by our NODE-EW than by the previous ODE works [3], in which

$f_n = f$ for all n, where f is a shared function. Moreover, we rigorously prove that the ODE system proposed in [3] can approximate any continuous trajectory, which implies that NODE-EW is very general and has more expressive power than the ODE system in [3] since the latter uses fixed weights. In general, numerical methods for solving ODE consume too many iteration steps. To make a trade off between memory and efficiency, we propose a backpropagation initialized training strategy to train our NODE-EW. To be specific, we discretize the ODE system w.r.t. θ_n and first train the weights in the corresponding neural networks by the gradient-based method. With such an initialization, we adopt the adjoint method to fine-tuning the weights. Notably, the speed of the proposed training strategy is much faster than the pure adjoint method. Our training method bridges the popular continuous and discrete training strategies and provides a new insight into solving ODEs numerically. Another notable addition of the proposed ODE system is its memory efficiency. The consumed memory of NODE-EW is independent of the depth, hence it allows the network depth to go to infinity. At last, our network is reversible, which is important for mobile devices. We summarize our contributions as follows:

1. We propose an ODE system—NODE-EW, which is a continuous version of ResNet. Specifically, we model the learnable weights of residual blocks as a trajectory of ODE, by which NODE-EW obtains larger model capacity and describes the behavior of deep ResNet more accurately than the neural ODE with fixed weights [3].
2. To address the time-consuming issue of adjoint method, we propose a new training strategy which combines the backpropagation and the adjoint method. Our strategy bridges the continuous and discrete training methods.
3. We prove that our ODE system is able to approximate any continuous trajectory. We also validate the expressive power of our ODE system empirically.

2　Preliminaries and Related Work

2.1　ResNet and Its Variants

Resnet [10] is a deep neural network consisting of multiple residual blocks. It contains skip-connections bypassing residual layers. It solves the gradient explosion/vanishing and accuracy degradation issues [9] existing in the deep neural networks. After the success of ResNet, lots of variants of ResNet appear. Some adjust the structure of residual block [25], then the single convolution becomes a multi-branch convolution. Others create novel topological structures to replace the skip-connections [28,30].

2.2　Learning Partial Differential Equations

In the past few decades, partial differential equations (PDEs) have been very popular in low-level image processing. However, designing the PDE systems by hand requires a lot of tricks and prior knowledge. To deal with this problem,

[19,20] proposed frameworks to learn PDEs from data. They use the differential invariants that are invariant under rotation and translation as bases of PDE and learn the coefficient from data using the adjoint method. [5] also indicated that PDE systems can learn good features in face recognition. [18,21] first used learnt PDEs with learnable boundary conditions for saliency detection and object tracking. So far, the learning-based PDEs have been used in many image processing tasks, such as image denoising, color to gray and demosaicing [16,17,19].

2.3 Neural ODE

Yet, the previous systems [19,20] discretize the differential equations first and then learn the weights at each time step by the adjoint method. [3] proposed another learning system called *Neural ODE*, which does not discretize the differential equation and updates the weights by the adjoint method directly. It reduces the memory consumption to $O(1)$. Neural ODE can be viewed as ResNet with infinite layers. From this perspective, the weights of ResNet at every layer should be different, however, those of Neural ODE are the same. So Neural ODE is not a continuous version of ResNet in a more rigorous sense.

2.3.1 Overview of Neural ODE

We introduce Neural ODE [3] in this section. Given $\mathbf{x}_0$ and $\mathbf{y} \in \mathbb{R}^n$ as the input and the output, respectively, Neural ODE reads as:

$$\frac{d\mathbf{x}(t)}{dt} = f(\mathbf{x}(t), t, \boldsymbol{\theta}), \quad \forall t \in [0, T],$$

where $f : \mathbb{R}^n \to \mathbb{R}^n$ is a continuous function and $\boldsymbol{\theta}$ is the parameters of f. Starting from the input layer $\mathbf{x}(0) = \mathbf{x}_0$, we can let the output layer $\mathbf{x}(T) = \mathbf{y}$ be the output of our system. The above equation is solved by a black-box ODE solver with desired accuracy.

2.3.2 Connection with ResNet

In Neural ODE, f is chosen as a neural network. The discretized version of Neural ODE is:

$$\mathbf{x}_{k+1} = \mathbf{x}_k + \Delta t \cdot f(\mathbf{x}_k, k\Delta t, \boldsymbol{\theta}), \tag{2}$$

where Δt is the time step of the numerical scheme and $\mathbf{x}_k$ means the numerical solution at time $k\Delta t$. Equation (2) is equivalent to a special type of ResNet whose weights $\boldsymbol{\theta}$ are identical at every layer.

3 Nerual ODE with Evolutionary Weights

In this section, we provide our ODE system which is a continuous version of the general deep ResNet. As mentioned above, although the weights of residual function f in Neural ODE are learnable, the identical f at different layers limits the expressive power of this ODE system and thus Neural ODE is actually not a continuous version of ResNet in a rigorous sense.

3.1 Formulation

To address the issue, we propose a new ODE system named *Neural Ordinary Differential Equaitons with Evolutionary Weights* (NODE-EW). In NODE-EW, the function f can vary at different time, i.e., $\boldsymbol{\theta}$ is a function of time t:

$$\frac{d\mathbf{x}(t)}{dt} = f(\mathbf{x}(t), t, \boldsymbol{\theta}(t)), \quad \forall t \in [0, T],$$

where $\mathbf{x}(0) = \mathbf{x}_0$. In order to find the optimal function $\boldsymbol{\theta}(t)$, we aim to solve a standard optimal control problem with a loss function L. L can be an arbitrary continuous loss such as mean squared error or cross entropy. The optimization problem is:

$$\min_{\theta(t)} L(\mathbf{x}(T), \mathbf{y}). \tag{3}$$

In order to make the function space computable, here we use another Neural ODE to model the evolution of $\boldsymbol{\theta}(t)$. Given $\boldsymbol{\theta}(0) = \boldsymbol{\theta}_0$, we assume

$$\frac{d\boldsymbol{\theta}(t)}{dt} = g(\boldsymbol{\theta}(t), t, \boldsymbol{\theta}_1), \tag{4}$$

where g is another neural network and $\boldsymbol{\theta}_0$ and $\boldsymbol{\theta}_1$ are the parameters to characterize $\boldsymbol{\theta}(t)$.

3.2 Training NODE-EW

3.2.1 Adjoint Method

As mentioned in [3], the relative error of the ODE solver depends on the magnitude of time step Δt. When there is a strict requirement on the error of the system, there will be a lot of intermediate steps which will consume a lot of memory if the system is trained with backpropagation. So [3] proposed the adjoint method. This method makes the systems require only memory of $O(1)$, despite its infinite layers. In contrast, an ordinary residual networks requires the memory proportional to its number of layers.

The adjoint of the system is defined as: $\mathbf{a}(t) = \frac{\partial L}{\partial \mathbf{x}(t)}$ and $\mathbf{b}(t) = \frac{\partial L}{\partial \boldsymbol{\theta}(t)}$. The following ODEs are satisfied:

$$\frac{d\mathbf{a}(t)}{dt} = -\left(\frac{\partial f(\mathbf{x}(t), \boldsymbol{\theta}(t))}{\partial \mathbf{x}(t)}\right)^{\top} \mathbf{a}(t),$$

$$\frac{d\mathbf{b}(t)}{dt} = -\left(\frac{\partial g(\boldsymbol{\theta}(t), \boldsymbol{\theta}_1)}{\partial \boldsymbol{\theta}(t)}\right)^{\top} \mathbf{b}(t). \tag{5}$$

According to the definition, $\frac{\partial L}{\partial \mathbf{x}(0)} = a(0)$ and $\frac{\partial L}{\partial \boldsymbol{\theta}_0} = b(0)$. Computing the derivative of L with respect to $\boldsymbol{\theta}_1$ requires evaluation of an integral

$$\frac{\partial L}{\partial \boldsymbol{\theta}_1} = \left(\int_0^T \frac{\partial g(\boldsymbol{\theta}(t), \boldsymbol{\theta}_1)}{\partial \boldsymbol{\theta}_1}\right)^{\top} \mathbf{b}(t).$$

If we define $\mathbf{c}(t)$ to satisfy the following equation:

$$\frac{d\mathbf{c}(t)}{dt} = -\left(\frac{\partial g(\boldsymbol{\theta}(t), \boldsymbol{\theta}_1)}{\partial \boldsymbol{\theta}_1}\right)^\top \mathbf{b}(t), \quad \mathbf{c}(T) = 0.$$

Then $\mathbf{c}(0) = \frac{\partial L}{\partial \boldsymbol{\theta}_1}$. We can summarize the above equations in a more concise way. Define the function $aug\_dynamics$ to be:

$$aug\_dynamics([\mathbf{x}(t), \mathbf{a}(t), \mathbf{b}(t), \mathbf{c}(t), t, \boldsymbol{\theta}_1])$$

$$= \left[f(\mathbf{x}(t), t, \boldsymbol{\theta}), -\left(\frac{\partial f}{\partial \mathbf{x}}\right)^\top \mathbf{a}(t), -\left(\frac{\partial g}{\partial \boldsymbol{\theta}(t)}\right)^\top \mathbf{b}(t), -\left(\frac{\partial g}{\partial \boldsymbol{\theta}_1}\right)^\top \mathbf{b}(t)\right]. \quad (6)$$

To compute the derivative of L respect to various quantities of the system, we need to solve the following ODE terminal value problem:

$$\frac{d}{dt}[\mathbf{x}(t), \mathbf{a}(t), \mathbf{b}(t), \mathbf{c}(t)] = aug\_dynamics([\mathbf{x}(t), \mathbf{a}(t), \mathbf{b}(t), \mathbf{c}(t), t, \boldsymbol{\theta}_1])$$

$$\mathbf{x}(T) = \mathbf{x}(T), \quad \mathbf{a}(T) = \frac{\partial L}{\partial \mathbf{x}(T)}, \quad \mathbf{b}(T) = 0, \quad \mathbf{c}(T) = 0.$$

Then we get $\frac{\partial L}{\partial \mathbf{x}(0)} = \mathbf{a}(0)$, $\frac{\partial L}{\partial \boldsymbol{\theta}_0} = \mathbf{b}(0)$, and $\frac{\partial L}{\partial \boldsymbol{\theta}_1} = \mathbf{c}(0)$.

The whole process of computing the derivative is summarized in Algorithm 1, Where ODESOLVE is an ODE solver.

Algorithm 1. Computing derivative of NODE-EW

Input: parameters $\boldsymbol{\theta}_1$, $\boldsymbol{\theta}(T)$, the final state $\mathbf{x}(T)$, and loss gradient $\frac{\partial L}{\partial \mathbf{x}(T)}$

$\mathbf{s}_0 = [\mathbf{x}(T), \boldsymbol{\theta}(T), \frac{\partial L}{\partial \mathbf{x}(T)}, \mathbf{0}, \mathbf{0}]$

   def aug_dynamic($[\mathbf{x}(t), \mathbf{a}(t), \mathbf{b}(t), \mathbf{c}(t)], t, \boldsymbol{\theta}_1$)

      Return $[f(\mathbf{x}(t), t, \boldsymbol{\theta}), -\left(\frac{\partial f}{\partial \mathbf{x}}\right)^\top \mathbf{a}(t), -\left(\frac{\partial g}{\partial \boldsymbol{\theta}(t)}\right)^\top \mathbf{b}(t), -\left(\frac{\partial g}{\partial \boldsymbol{\theta}_1}\right)^\top \mathbf{b}(t)]$

$[\mathbf{x}(0), \frac{\partial L}{\partial \mathbf{x}(0)}, \frac{\partial L}{\partial \boldsymbol{\theta}_0}, \frac{\partial L}{\partial \boldsymbol{\theta}_1}] = $ ODESOLVE$(\mathbf{s}_0, aug\_dynamic, T, 0, \boldsymbol{\theta}_1)$

Return $[\frac{\partial L}{\partial \mathbf{x}(0)}, \frac{\partial L}{\partial \boldsymbol{\theta}_0}, \frac{\partial L}{\partial \boldsymbol{\theta}_1}]$

When $g(\cdot) = 0$, NODE-EW degenerates to the original Neural ODE. So NODE-EW is a generalization of Neural ODE. Because the computing of an ODE system is reversible, there is no need to save the intermediate variables for backpropagation. In other words, Algorithm 1 consumes $O(1)$ memory for training. Comparing to Neural ODE, computation of $\boldsymbol{\theta}(t)$ indeed brings some extra computation. Fortunately, neural networks are usually trained in a batch way. As the batch-size increases, the extra computation is negligible.

3.2.2   Acceleration of Training

The problem of the adjoint method is that we have to solve an ODE in the feed forward propagation and solve another to compute the derivative. To achieve the required errors, we need to discreticize the interval into many time steps which is very time consuming. On the other hand, it is not easy to tune the error tolerance of ODE solver during training. Hence we propose a new training strategy, which can significantly accelerate the training process when the memory requirement can be kept low.

1. At the beginning of the training, we discretize the ODE system using the Euler forward scheme with constant step size. Then we train the weights of ODE system with backpropagation until the discrete system reaches a desirable loss.
2. Fine-tune the ODE system by the adjoint method at the rest of the training epochs.

Our strategy only requires to compute fixed steps of the Euler forward scheme (we choose the time steps to be small), which can significantly reduce the training time and not introduce too much memory burden. Of course, our method make a trade off between the training speed and the memory cost depending on the steps size we choose. As is shown in Sect. 4, our method not only reduces the training time, but also boosts the performance on the image classification tasks.

3.3   Expressive Power of NODE-EW

In this section, we prove that our ODE system has a strong expressive power as described in Theorem 1. The proof can be found in the supplementary material.

Theorem 1. *Define a continuous function* $s : [0, T] \to \mathbb{R}^n$ *such that* $s(a) = s(b)$ *if and only if* $a = b$. *Given any* $\sigma > 0$, *there always exists a Neural ODE defined on the interval* $[0, T]$ *and its solution* $\mathbf{y}(t)$ *satisfies:* $|\mathbf{y}(t) - s(t)| \leq \sigma, \quad \forall t \in [0, T]$.

Theorem 1 states that any continuous trajectory can be approximated by a Neural ODE with an arbitrary accuracy. So it is sufficient to use a Neural ODE [3] to model the evolution of weights $\boldsymbol{\theta}(t)$.

4   Experiment Results

4.1   Verification of Theorem 1

In this section, we conduct an experiment to verify Theorem 1. In the theorem, we have proved that any continuous trajectory can be approximated by a solution of some Nerual ODE. We take a continuous curve in the 3-dimensional space, such that: $\mathbf{x}(t) = [\sin(t)\cos(t), \sin^2(t) + \cosh^2(t), \exp(t)], t \in [0, 1]$. f in the experiment is a two-layer neural network with 1,000 hidden units in each layer.

We take ReLu to be the activation function. We discretize the interval $[0,1]$ into 100 pieces uniformly and try to fit the curve at the 100 points. Hence we adopt the following loss function:

$$loss = \sum_{i=1}^{100} \|\mathbf{x}(i\Delta t) - \boldsymbol{\theta}(i\Delta t)\|^2,$$

where $\Delta t = \frac{1}{100}$, and $\boldsymbol{\theta}(t)$ is the solution generated by Neural ODE. In our experiment, if we use the black-box solver to solve the Neural ODE and train the weights in f using the adjoint method, the whole process will be very time consuming. So we adopt the training strategy introduced in Sect. 3.2.2. We first train the weights in f using the backpropagation as initialization at first 5k iterations, then use the adjoint method to fine tune at the rest 100 iterations. The training time is reduced to 30 times shorter compared to the original pure adjoint method. The experiment results are shown in the Fig. 1.

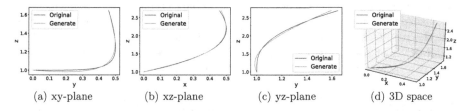

(a) xy-plane   (b) xz-plane   (c) yz-plane   (d) 3D space

Fig. 1. The three Figs. 1(a), (c) and (b) display the projection of the curve in the 3 orthogonal planes. In the 3D space 1(d), we can see the curve generated by our ODE system approximates well to the original curve.

4.2   Supervised Learning on MNIST

To compare the accuracy of Neural ODE and NODE-EW on MNIST, we utilize the structure mentioned in [3]. It first downsamples the input twice and then applies the kernel model. The figure of NODE-EW is presented in the supplementary material.

We train the two models under the same setting. We train both of them 300 epochs. The learning rate is set as 0.1 and it reduces by 0.1 after each 100 epochs. No data augmentation is used . The error rate on the test set for our NODE-EW is 0.35% which is lower than that of Neural ODE, 0.38%.

Adjoint method costs too much time for solving the ODE equations during training NODE-EW. Hence, we apply our speed-up training method proposed in Sect. 3.2.2 to train NODE-EW in this experiment. We discretize NODE-EW to 10 discrete steps, and we train the model by gradient-based backpropagation method for 80 epochs with learning rate 0.01. Then, we fine-tune the backprop-agation initialized weights with learning rate 0.001 by adjoint method for 80 epochs. For comparison, we train another model by pure adjoint method for 160 epochs.

The result is summarized in Table 1 and the training process is displayed in Fig. 2. We can see that our NODE-EW finishes the training in less time and obtains better accuracy on both training and testing data sets. The speed-up training method consumes 23.18s each epoch for the first 80 epochs, while that of the adjoint method is 88.19s. The peak of the accuracy appears after 80 epochs, so we compare the mean accuracy for the last 80 epochs. The speed-up method achieves 99.57% mean accuracy on the training set while pure adjoint method only achieves 99.65%.

As is shown Fig. 2, our speed-up method boosts the accuracy during the training. The training accuracy oscillates at the first 80 epochs for our training method. We attribute this phenomenon to that direct discretization will introduce more error compared to the original ODE solver. Meanwhile, it can also have more chance to escape the saddle points, which heuristically explain why the speed-up method can boost accuracy. Note that at the 80th epoch, the speed-up training method does not have accuracy degradation, which demonstrates that discretization + backpropagation can indeed train the parameters in a continuous ODE system. So, for efficiency, it is reasonable to replace the adjoint method with backpropagation at the beginning of the training. Our observation agrees with the results in [2] which demonstrate that shallow ResNet can be a good initialization of deep ResNet. In our case, we can see that ResNet with finite layers can be a good initialization of ResNet with infinite layers.

Table 1. Training results for the pure adjoint method and the out new training strategy.

	Adjoint method	BP+Adjoint method
Mean Test Acc	99.57%	99.65%
Mean Train Acc	99.97%	99.98%
Time/epoch	89.76s	62.54s

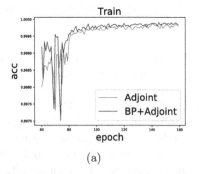
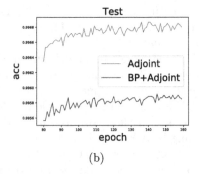

(a)   (b)

Fig. 2. Accuracies of supervised learning on the training set (left) and the testing set (right) of MNIST.

4.3   Normalizing Flow

The application of Neural ODE in the normalizing flow is very attractive, for it can bring down the computational cost from computing the determinant of Jacobian whose complexity is $O(n^3)$ to only solving a differential equation whose computational cost is $O(n)$.

Normalizing flow stacks many layers of invertible transformation to attain a complex distribution from very simple distribution such as the Gaussian distribution. The method has been used in variational inference [23] and generative model [13] recently.

For a discrete model, it relys on the *Change of Variable Theorem*: Let h be an invertible smooth mapping from $\mathbb{R}^n$ to $\mathbb{R}^n$, $\mathbf{x}$ be a random variable with distribution $p(\mathbf{x})$ and $\mathbf{x}_1 = h(\mathbf{x})$, then

$$\log(p(\mathbf{x}_1)) = \log(p(\mathbf{x})) + \log\left(\det\left(\frac{\partial h}{\partial \mathbf{x}}\right)\right).$$

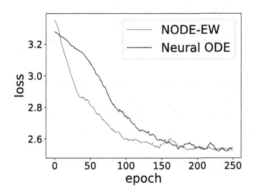

Fig. 3. The training curve of the Neural ODE and the NODE-EW (where the vertical axis represents loss and the horizontal one represents number of iterations): We can see that the new model descent the loss faster than the original one.

If the transformation is placed by an ODE, the following theorem is proposed by [3].

Instantaneous Change of Variables Theorem: Let $\mathbf{x}(t)$ is a continuous random variable depending on time which is described by a differential equation: $\frac{d\mathbf{x}}{dt} = f(\mathbf{x}(t), t)$, then the log of its density function follows:

$$\frac{\partial \log(p(\mathbf{x}(t)))}{\partial t} = -\text{tr}\left(\frac{\partial f}{\partial \mathbf{x}(t)}\right).$$

The proof can be found in [3].

By an easy derivation, the above rule is also true for our NODE-EW. We conduct an experiment to generate a target 2D distribution to compare the performance of the two models. Here, we consider the maximum likelihood training, that is to maximize $E(p(x))$, where the p is the density of the model, x is the sample and E is the expectation operator. We adopt the Adam [12] optimizer and train the model $1,000$ epochs, taking 100 data points in every epoch.

We found that the training of two models can achieve the almost the same loss ultimately. However, NODE-EW can achieve the minimum value in less epochs, which is shown in Fig. 3.

5   Conclusions

In this work, we demonstrate that the weights a of continuous ResNet can be modeled by an ODE system. It provides us with a new tool for the further research about the neural networks with infinite layers. ResNet of finite layers is a good initialization of ResNet of infinite layers, which indicates a close relationship between them. This helps us to accelerate the pure adjoint training method. As the experiment indicates, equipped with evolutionary weights, our NODE-EW acquires more capacity and expressive power and it can arrive at the minimum loss in less epochs. So our NODE-EW is a more accurate and better continuous ODE model of the discrete ResNet.

Acknowledgments. The work of Zhouchen Lin is supported in part by 973 Program of China under Grant 2015CB352502, in part by NSF of China under Grants 61625301 and 61731018, and in part by Beijing Academy of Artificial Intelligence (BAAI) and Microsoft Research Asia.

References

1. Bengio, Y., et al.: Learning deep architectures for AI. Found. Trends Mach. Learn. **2**(1), 1–127 (2009)
2. Chang, B., Meng, L., Haber, E., Tung, F., Begert, D.: Multi-level residual networks from dynamical systems view. arXiv preprint arXiv:1710.10348 (2017)
3. Chen, T.Q., Rubanova, Y., Bettencourt, J., Duvenaud, D.K.: Neural ordinary differential equations. In: Advances in Neural Information Processing Systems, pp. 6571–6583 (2018)
4. Weinan, E.: A proposal on machine learning via dynamical systems. Commun. Math. Stat. **5**(5), 1–11 (2017)
5. Fang, C., Zhao, Z., Zhou, P., Lin, Z.: Feature learning via partial differential equation with applications to face recognition. Pattern Recogn. **69**, 14–25 (2017)
6. Haber, E., Ruthotto, L.: Stable architectures for deep neural networks. Inverse Prob. **34**(1), 014004 (2017)
7. Haber, E., Ruthotto, L., Holtham, E., Jun, S-H.: Learning across scales–Multiscale methods for convolution neural networks. In: AAAI Conference on Artificial Intelligence (2018)
8. Hardt, M., Ma, T.: Identity matters in deep learning. arXiv preprint arXiv:1611.04231 (2016)

9. He, K., Sun, J.: Convolutional neural networks at constrained time cost. In: Computer Vision and Pattern Recognition, pp. 5353–5360 (2015)

10. He, K., Zhang, X., Ren, S., Sun, J.: Deep residual learning for image recognition. In: Computer Vision and Pattern Recognition, pp. 770–778 (2016)

11. Jastrzebski, S., Arpit, D., Ballas, N., Verma, V., Che, T., Bengio, Y.: Residual connections encourage iterative inference. arXiv preprint arXiv:1710.04773 (2017)

12. Kingma, D.P., Ba, J.: Adam: a method for stochastic optimization. arXiv preprint arXiv:1412.6980 (2014)

13. Kingma, D.P., Dhariwal, P.: Glow: Generative flow with invertible 1x1 convolutions. In: Advances in Neural Information Processing Systems, pp. 10215–10224 (2018)

14. Krizhevsky, A., Sutskever, I., Hinton, G.E.: ImageNet classification with deep convolutional neural networks. In: Advances in Neural Information Processing Systems, pp. 1097–1105 (2012)

15. Li, H., Xu, Z., Taylor, G., Studer, C., Goldstein, T.: Visualizing the loss landscape of neural nets. In Advances in Neural Information Processing Systems, pp. 6389–6399 (2018)

16. Lin, Z., Zhang, W., Tang, X.: Learning partial differential equations for computer vision. MSR-TR-2008-189 (2008)

17. Lin, Z., Zhang, W., Tang, X.: Designing partial differential equations for image processing by combining differential invariants. MSR-TR-2009-192 (2009)

18. Liu, R., Cao, J., Lin, Z., Shan, S.: Adaptive partial differential equation learning for visual saliency detection. In: Computer Vision and Pattern Recognition, pp. 3866–3873 (2014)

19. Liu, R., Lin, Z., Zhang, W., Su, Z.: Learning PDEs for image restoration via optimal control. In: Daniilidis, K., Maragos, P., Paragios, N. (eds.) ECCV 2010. LNCS, vol. 6311, pp. 115–128. Springer, Heidelberg (2010). https://doi.org/10.1007/978-3-642-15549-9_9

20. Liu, R., Lin, Z., Zhang, W., Tang, K., Zhixun, S.: Toward designing intelligent PDEs for computer vision: an optimal control approach. Image Vis. Comput. 31(1), 43–56 (2013)

21. Liu, R., Zhong, G., Cao, J., Lin, Z., Shan, S., Luo, Z.: Learning to diffuse: a new perspective to design pdes for visual analysis. IEEE Trans. Pattern Anal. Mach. Intell. 38(12), 2457–2471 (2016)

22. Lu, Y., Zhong, A., Li, Q., Dong, B.: Beyond finite layer neural networks: Bridging deep architectures and numerical differential equations. In International Conference on Machine Learning (2017)

23. Rezende, D.J., Mohamed, S.: Variational inference with normalizing flows. In: International Conference on Machine Learning, pp. 1530–1538. JMLR (2015)

24. Szegedy, C., et al.: Going deeper with convolutions. In: Computer Vision and Pattern Recognition, pp. 1–9 (2015)

25. Xie, S., Girshick, R., Dollár, P., Tu, Z., He, K.: Aggregated residual transformations for deep neural networks. In: Computer Vision and Pattern Recognition, pp. 1492–1500 (2017)

26. Yosinski, J., Clune, J., Nguyen, A., Fuchs, T., Lipson, H.: Understanding neural networks through deep visualization. arXiv preprint arXiv:1506.06579 (2015)

27. Zagoruyko, S., Komodakis, N.: Wide residual networks. arXiv preprint arXiv:1605.07146 (2016)

28. Zagoruyko, S., Komodakis, N.: DiracNets: Training very deep neural networks without skip-connections. arXiv preprint arXiv:1706.00388 (2017)

29. Zhang, H., Shao, J., Salakhutdinov, R.: Deep neural networks with multi-branch architectures are less non-convex. arXiv preprint arXiv:1806.01845 (2018)
30. Zhang, X., Li, Z., Loy, C.C., Lin, D.: PolyNet: a pursuit of structural diversity in very deep networks. In: Computer Vision and Pattern Recognition, pp. 718–726 (2017)

Infrared Image Segmentation for Photovoltaic Panels Based on Res-UNet

Hao Zhang⑩, Xianggong Hong$^{(\boxtimes)}$, Shifen Zhou, and Qingcai Wang

School of Information Engineering, Nanchang University, Nanchang, China
hongxianggong@ncu.edu.cn

Abstract. Infrared image segmentation is the basis of error detection for photovoltaic panels. In this work, the infrared image data are collected by infrared thermal imager from the view of unmanned aerial vehicle (UAV). A semantic segmentation neural network named Deep Res-UNet, which combines the strengths of residual learning, transfer learning, and U-Net, is proposed for infrared image segmentation. Residual units are applied in both the encoding and decoding path, which makes the whole deep network ease to train. A modified ResNet-34 with pre-trained weights is utilized to get better feature representation. In the modified ResNet-34, maxpooling layer is removed for reducing the loss in resolution, an additional conv1 stage is added to copy features for the corresponding decoding path and the skip block with dilated residual block is added to generate features with larger resolution and larger receptive field. A new loss function combining Binary Cross-Entropy (BCE) and Dice is proposed to get better results. Additionally, Conditional Random Field (CRF) is integrated into the model as a post-process. The experimental results show that the prediction results of the proposed model are **97.11%** and **94.47%** respectively on the two evaluation indexes of F_1 and Jaccard index, which is better than FCN-8s, SegNet, U-Net and two descendants of U-Net and ResNet: ResUnet and ResNet34-Unet.

Keywords: Infrared image · Semantic segmentation · Photovoltaic panels · U-Net

1 Introduction

Infrared Thermography (IRT) plays a vital role in monitoring and inspecting thermal defects of photovoltaic panels. It has many advantages such as non-contact detection, safety, reliability and providing broad inspection coverage. The unmanned aerial vehicle (UAV) equipped with infrared thermal imager inspects the solar panel group overhead, getting infrared images of the photovoltaic plate area. The limitation of the infrared thermal imager, the flight height of UAV and other factors will result in the low-resolution photos which are hard for the human view. How to analyze these infrared images automatically is the key to detect the fault area of solar panels efficiently and accurately.

H. Zhang—Student.

© Springer Nature Switzerland AG 2019
Z. Lin et al. (Eds.): PRCV 2019, LNCS 11857, pp. 611–622, 2019.
https://doi.org/10.1007/978-3-030-31654-9_52

Infrared image segmentation is a fundamental and challenging problem in IRT for its over-centralized distributions and low-intensity contrasts.

A variety of methods have been proposed to segment infrared images in recent years. These algorithms can be categorised into threshold based [5,13], textural analysis [8,14], fuzzy based [23], region based [12,21]. The key of the threshold based methods is to choose a appropriate threshold. Kapur [13] adopted the entropy of the histogram to get grey-level picture thresholding. Chen [5] used the gray level and local entropy information to construct a new tow-dimension histogram to achieve the segmentation. Edge, color, texture, and motion are integrated to segment objects within an image [8,14]. Wu [23] utilized fast fuzzy c-means with spatial information to segment infrared images. Region-based segmentation algorithms can be classified into region growing and region division and merge. According to [12], region-based methods are better than other algorithms for image segmentation. For infrared image segmentation, a region of interest (RoI) extraction method based on gray level co-occurrence matrix (GLCM) characteristic imitate gradient proposed in [21], and it achieves better performance than grab cut. In [27], a FAsT-Match algorithm is proposed for infrared images segmentation of electrical equipment, getting comparable result with other traditional methods. However, these methods can only segment images based on low-level semantic information, which perform worse and often cause over-segmented.

Recent years have witnessed the broad application of deep learning in the field of computer vision and image processing, such as image classification [9], object detection [25], and image denoising [2]. The powerful feature extraction ability of convolutional neural network has also been applied in semantic segmentation [1,17,20]. Semantic segmentation can be treated as a pixel-level classification problem, labeling each pixel in the image with a specific category. The common pipeline of semantic segmentation can be divided into an encoder and a decoder, where the encoder is responsible for feature extraction for the classification of pixels while the decoder is utilized to restore information lost in the encoder process. The encoder could be a reduced classification model, like VGG-16 [22] or ResNet [11], which has excellent feature representation ability. The decoder often consists of several up-sampling layers or deconvolution layers, recovering the resolution of downsampled features. Long et al. utilizes FCN [17] (fully convolutional network) which replaced the fully connected layer with convolutional layer, achieving pixel-level segmentation. Chen et al. combined the FCN with a conditional random field (CRF) [15] to extract a DeepLab [7] model, using FCN to segment the image and optimizing the result through CRF. Yu et al. [24] introduced dilated convolutions into the segmentation pipeline instead of pooling layer to realize multi-scale contextual information for better accuracy.

Lots of works have suggested that deeper networks would bring better performance [22]. However, it is very difficult to train a very deep network for the emergence of problems such as vanishing gradients with the increasing of layers. He et al. [11] introduced the deep residual learning framework that employs an identity mapping. Instead of using skip connection in fully convolutional net-

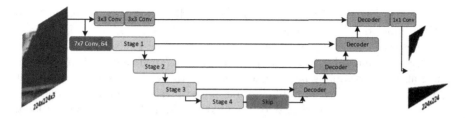

Fig. 1. The pipeline of our proposed deep Res-UNet.

works [17], Ronneberger *et al.* proposed that which combines different level of semantic information to get a finer result for medical image segmentation. To achieve this, U-Net copies low-level features to the corresponding high levels through concatenation operation.

In this work, we inherit the benefit of the U-Net [20] architecture with improvement by substituting the plain unit with multiple residual units [11]. We propose a deep residual U-Net, named Deep Res-UNet, an architecture that takes advantage of strengths from both deep residual learning and U-Net architecture. A modified ResNet-34 is utilized to extract features in the encoding path, and residual block is adopted in decoding path to ease the training of deep networks. We remove the maxpooling layer in the original ResNet-34 to keep a larger resolution, and a skip block with dialted residual unit is used to enlarge the receptive field while keep the resolution simultaneously. A new loss function which combines the Binary Cross-Entropy and Dice coefficient is proposed in this work. Additionally, Conditional Random Field (CRF) is integrated into the model as a post-processing to achieve a better boundary recovery. The experimental results show that the results of the proposed model are 97.11% and 94.47% respectively on the two evaluation indexes of F_1 and Jaccard index, which is better than FCN-8s [17], SegNet [1], U-Net [20], and two variants of U-Net: ResUnet [26] and ResNet34-Unet [3].

2   Method

2.1   The Structure of Proposed Deep Res-UNet

The proposed Deep Res-UNet (Fig. 1 and Table 1) in this paper was designed based on ResNet [11], which has shown excellent performance in image classification task, and has been applied in many tasks. ResNet with a series of stacked residual blocks is powerful enough to extract features and strength the feature propagation during training and testing. Meanwhile, encouraged by the excellent performance the symmetrical structure of U-Net [20] for biomedical image segmentation, we utilize a multi-stage architecture of Deep Res-UNet for infrared image segmentation with two parts (Fig. 1). The first part (encoding part) is designed to extract the features using the modified ResNet-34, also known as the "contracting" path in U-Net. The second part (decoding part, or "expansive" path in U-Net) is utilized to generate the classification map using the extracted features at different stages of the encoding part. The proposed Deep Res-UNet inherits both the benefits of ResNet and U-Net, and to get better feature representations from the encoding part, a modified ResNet-34 is utilized.

The conventional ResNet [11] starts with 7×7 convolutional layers with stride 2 and a max-pooling layer to down-sample the size of feature map for fast computation. Four stages with different numbers of residual blocks with two convolutional layers (shown in Fig. 2(b)) are followed by, and the first convolutional layer of the first residual block in stage 2–4 is with stride 2 while the other is 1. Specificly, ResNet-34 has $[3, 4, 6, 3]$ residual blocks and total 33 convolutional layers and 1 fully connected layer, so called ResNet-34. There are 5 downsampling operations in ResNet, and the size of the final feature maps is $32\times$ smaller than the original input size, *e.g.*, a 7×7 feature map is generated with the input of 224×224. We modified ResNet-34 as the Encoder part (as illustrated in Fig. 1 and Table 1) from three aspects: (1) an additional `conv1` stage with two 3×3 convolution layers to keep the resolution of the input size instead of downsampling it directly with convolutional layers with a kernel of size 7×7 and stride 2; (2) removal of the maxpooling operation after the first convolution layer which will bring loss in information; (3) an additional skip block is attached after Stage 4 to expand the receptive field while keep the resolution.

Actually, the combination of ResNet [11] and U-Net [20] has two options: (1) replace the plain block of U-Net with residual block in ResNet; (2) replace the Encoder part of U-Net with a reduced ResNet. Zhang *et al.* [26] proposed the combination of residual learning and U-Net with replacing the plain block of U-Net with residual units for road extraction. Buslaev *et al.* [3] adopted ResNet-34 pre-trained on ImageNet [9] and decoder adapted from vanilla U-Net. Besides these two options, we inherit both the benefits of the two choices: the residual blocks ease training of deep networks in both the Encoder and Decoder parts; the pre-trained ResNet-34 has more powerful feature extraction ability.

As illustrated in Fig. 1, the Encoder consists of both plain block, residual block and dilated residual block, which are shown in Fig. 2(a)–(c). These three types of blocks allow us to effectively capture the multi-scale context, where the plain block in the first layer can extract the shallow information of the input image, the residual blocks capture the semantic information through deep stacked network, and the last skip layer with dilated convolution can effectively enlarge the field of view of filters to incorporate deep semantic information without downsampling the size of feature maps. The Encoder part encodes the input image into compact representations.

The right part of Fig. 1 and Fig. 2(d) have shown the Decoder of the proposed Deep Res-UNet. Low-level features are upsampled first and then concated with feature maps from the corresponding encoding path. The plain block of the vanilla decoder of U-Net is replaced by the residual block. The last stage of the decoding path, a 1×1 convolution layer and a sigmoid activation layer is utilized to project the multi-channel feature maps into the desired segmentation result. The Decoder part recovers the representations to a pixel-wise classification, i.e., semantic segmentation.

Table 1. Network structure

Layer name	Output size	Encoder		Decoder	
conv1	224×224	$\begin{bmatrix} 3 \times 3, 64 \\ 3 \times 3, 64 \end{bmatrix}$	$\times 1$	$1 \times 1, 64$	
Stage1	112×112	$7 \times 7, 64$ stride 2		$\begin{bmatrix} 3 \times 3, 64 \\ 3 \times 3, 64 \end{bmatrix}$	$\times 2$
		$\begin{bmatrix} 3 \times 3, 64 \\ 3 \times 3, 64 \end{bmatrix}$	$\times 3$		
Stage2	56×56	$\begin{bmatrix} 3 \times 3, 128 \\ 3 \times 3, 128 \end{bmatrix}$	$\times 4$	$\begin{bmatrix} 3 \times 3, 64 \\ 3 \times 3, 64 \end{bmatrix}$	$\times 2$
Stage3	28×28	$\begin{bmatrix} 3 \times 3, 256 \\ 3 \times 3, 256 \end{bmatrix}$	$\times 6$	$\begin{bmatrix} 3 \times 3, 128 \\ 3 \times 3, 128 \end{bmatrix}$	$\times 2$
Stage4	14×14	$\begin{bmatrix} 3 \times 3, 512 \\ 3 \times 3, 512 \end{bmatrix}$	$\times 3$	$\begin{bmatrix} 3 \times 3, 256 \\ 3 \times 3, 256 \end{bmatrix}$	$\times 2$
Skip	14×14	$[3 \times 3, 512]$, dilation 2			

2.2 Residual Block

As illustrated in Fig. 2(a) and (b), U-Net [20] adopted the plain blocks with two 3×3 convolutional layers with batch normalization (BN) and ReLU layers, and the residual blockd with skip connection can be stacked to a very deep network. We replace the original plain block in U-Net with residual block in both the Encoder and the Decoder parts. In the encoding path, the modified ResNet-34 pre-trained on ImageNet [9] has powerful feature extraction ability than randomly initialized.

More importantly, a dilated residual block is proposed to fix the removal the maxpooling in the conventional ResNet-34 [11]. Dilated convolution, also known as atrous convolution, has been demonstrated effective in semantic segmentation [6,7,24]. Dilated convolution allows us to repurpose ImageNet [9] pre-trained models to extract denser feature maps by removing the downsampling operation, which can control the resolution without requiring learning extra parameters. Actually, Li *et al.* [16] pointed out that there is gap between the image classification and object detection, so large downsampling factor in image classification networks brings large valid receptive field which is good for image classification but compromises the object location ability. As for semantic segmentation, pre-trained ResNet [11] with $32\times$ downsampling factor performs well for extracting semantic features for classification, but it harms pixel-level classification or segmentation for the downsampled information can not be recovered accurately through up-sampling operation. So we modified the original ResNet-34 with the removing of maxpooling layer and adding a dilated residual block, named Skip Block.

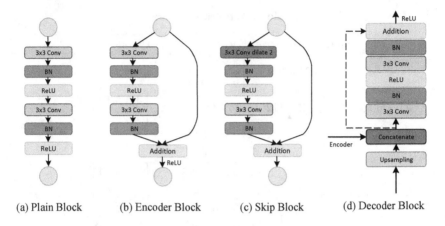

(a) Plain Block   (b) Encoder Block   (c) Skip Block   (d) Decoder Block

Fig. 2. Basic blocks of the Encoder & Decoder.

As illustrated in Fig. 2(c), the Skip Block is based on the residual block in ResNet-34 with simply replacing the first convolutional layer with dialted convolution with dilated rate 2. The dilated convolution will enlarge the receptive field of the filters without downsampling the resolution.

2.3 Loss Function

Semantic segmentation can be treated as pixel-level classification task, so it often adopts cross entropy loss or mean square error (MSE) as loss function. In this paper, we use pixel-wise cross entropy as loss function following U-Net [20], which can be formulated as:

$$L(g,p) = -\sum_i g_i \log p_i \tag{1}$$

where i is the categor y, specifically $(0,1)$ in our task, p_i is the predicted label, and g_i is the true label. The loss caculate the result of every pixel averagely without considering the imbalance problem between classes.

Dice coefficient is often used to evaluate the performance of sementation, representing for the overlapping between two samples.

$$D(G,P) = \frac{2|G \cap P|}{|G| + |P|} \tag{2}$$

where G is the true object region, and P is the predicted object region. The Dice coefficient can be generalized in 2D segmentation [4,10], where predict label $p_i \in 0,1$, soft Dice can be formulated as:

$$D_{soft}(g,p) = \frac{2\sum_i p_i \times g_i}{\sum_i p_i + \sum_i g_i} \tag{3}$$

where $p_i \in [0,1]$ is the value after sigmoid function, $g_i \in [0,1]$ is the true label. We combine the Dice coefficient and Binary Cross-Entropy (BCE) Loss as blew:

$$L(g,p) = (1 - \beta)(\sum_i g_i \log(p_i)) - \beta \log(\frac{2\sum_i p_i \times g_i + smooth}{\sum_i p_i + \sum_i g_i + smooth}) \qquad (4)$$

where $smooth$ is often an extreme small number, e.g. $1e-15$ to prevent from dividing by zero. β is set as 0.75 empirically.

2.4 Post Processing

For accurate boundary recovery, fully connected Conditional Random Field (CRF) is integrated into our system as a post-process from [15]. The model employs the energy function

$$E(x) = \sum_i \theta_i (x_i) + \sum_{ij} \theta_{ij} (x_i, x_j) \qquad (5)$$

where x is the label assignment for pixels. We use as unary potential $\theta_i (x_i) = -\log P(x_i)$, where $P(x_i)$ is the label assignment probability at pixel i as computed by a DCNN. The pairwise potential has a form that allows for efficient inference while using a fully-connected graph, i.e., when connecting all pairs of image pixels, i; j. In particular, as in [15], we use the following expression

$$\theta_{ij} (x_i, x_j) = \mu(x_i, x_j) \left[w_1 \exp\left(-\frac{\|p_i - p_j\|^2}{2\sigma_\alpha^2} - \frac{\|I_i - I_j\|^2}{2\sigma_\beta^2}\right) + w_2 \exp\left(-\frac{\|p_i - p_j\|^2}{2\sigma_\gamma^2}\right)\right] \qquad (6)$$

where $\mu(x_i, x_j) = 1$ if $x_i \neq x_j$, and zero otherwise, which, as in the Potts model, means that only nodes with distinct labels are penalized. The remaining expression uses two Gaussian kernels in different feature spaces; the first, *appearance kernel* depends on both pixel positions (denoted as p) and RGB color (denoted as I), and the second kernel, *smoothness kernel* only depends on pixel positions. The degrees of nearness and similarity are controlled by parameters θ_α and θ_β.

3 Results

3.1 Dataset and Augmentation

The image data are collected from Jiangsu LINYANG Power Station, located at the No. 666, LINYANG Road, Qidong Economic Development Area, Jiangsu Province 226220, China, with the coordinate position on the map of (121.639278, 31.817825). The imaginary thermal instrument adopted here is DM63 series, manufactured by Zhejiang Dali Technology Co., Ltd... The images were shot in the morning, high noon and evening respectively from Jul. to Aug. 2016, when sunny and cloudy weather. The pixel of the adopted thermal imager instrument

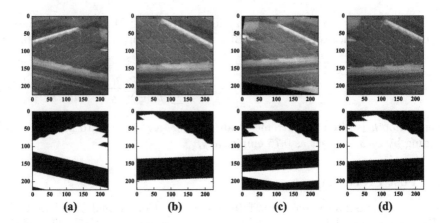

Fig. 3. Data augmentation with random crop (**a**), horizontal flip (**b**), shift scale rotate (**c**), random brightness contrast (**d**).

is 320×240. The training set involves 216 images and the testing set is 19. All images are annotated manually with two kinds of pixels: including "panels" and "others".

To prevent overfitting and make the model more robust, we use some data augmentation methods when training. These methods include random crop, horizontal flip, shift scale rotate, random brightness contrast, as shown in Fig. 3. All these methods are combined only when training for all experiments in this paper.

3.2   Experimental Setup and Results

The proposed model was implemented using PyTorch [19]. The encoding part (Stage 1–4) of our deep Res-UNet is initialized from the pre-trained model on ImageNet [9], and the other part is initialized randomly. The initial learning rate is 0.0001, and SGD is used to optimize the model. We start training the model with a minibatch size of 16 on an NVIDIA GTX 1080 GPU with 8 GB onboard memory, Intel(R) Xeon(R) CPU E5-2683 v3 @2.00 GHz.

Evaluation Metrics. To assess the quantitative performance of the proposed Deep Res-UNet for infrared image segmentation, the precision (P) and recall (R) are introduced, as well as the F_1 score [18] and Jaccard index. The F_1 score is calculated by P and R, which is an evaluation metric for the harmonic mean of P and R, and it can be calculated as follows:

$$F_1 = 2 \times \frac{P \times R}{P + R} \tag{7}$$

where

$$P = \frac{TP}{TP + FP}, R = \frac{TP}{TP + FN} \tag{8}$$

Here, TP, FP and FN represent for the number of true positives, false positives and false positives, respectively. P measures the proportion of matched pixels in the predicted results and R is the percentage of matched pixels in the ground truth. Jaccard index (Intersection Over Union) measures the similarity of the predicted result and the ground truth, and it can be calculated as:

$$J(Gr, Pr) = \frac{|Pr \cap Gr|}{|Pr| + |Gr| - |Pr \cap Gr|} \tag{9}$$

where Gr is the true object region, and Pr is the predicted object region.

Results. As shown is Table 2, our proposed Deep Res-UNet achieves a performance of 96.30%, 98.03%, 97.11%, and 94.47% with the highest in R, F_1, and Jaccard metrics under $\beta = 0.75$. Compared to the original U-Net [20], the Deep Res-UNet gets 1.06 and 1.82 points in F_1 and Jaccard respectively. ResUnet [26] got the highest P of 97.25% also the lowest R of 94.29%, F_1 of 95.54% and Jaccard of 91.83% mainly for it only has 15 convolutional layers which has weak ability to extract features. As for ResNet34-Unet [3], it performs quite better compared to U-Net and ResUnet mainly due to the pre-trained ResNet34 [11]. To demonstrate the pre-trained model helps extract features, we trained our model without per-trained on ImageNet [9], we received a performance of 96.04%, 95.76%, 95.90%, and 91.84% in P, R, F_1, and Jaccard, even worse than U-Net.

We visualised some of the results of FCN-8s [17], SegNet [1], UNet [20], ResUnet [26], ResNet34-Unet [3], and our Deep Res-UNet in Fig. 4. All the output of these models are post-processed with conditional random field (CRF) to get a better boundary. As shown in the second row, our proposed Deep Res-UNet performs better in the area with complex shapes, which is mainly because of the pre-trained model of the deep network. Similarly, ResNet34-UNet has shown the same signature mainly for the same reason. After the post-process of CRF, all models can detect the main area of photovoltaic panels correctly.

Table 2. Experimental comparison

Method	β	Precision	Recall	F1	Jaccard
FCN8s [17]	0	95.64	95.85	95.43	92.01
SegNet [1]	0	95.84	97.07	96.35	93.17
UNet [20]	0	96.11	96.30	96.05	92.65
ResUnet [26]	0	**97.25**	94.29	95.54	91.83
ResNet34-UNet [3]	0	95.52	97.21	96.24	92.94
Ours w/o	0	96.04	95.76	95.90	91.84
Ours	0	96.34	96.59	96.25	93.10
Ours	0.75	96.30	**98.03**	**97.11**	**94.47**

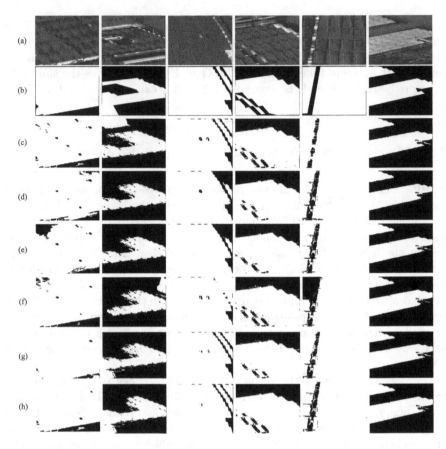

Fig. 4. Some visulized results of different models. (a) Image; (b) Groun-truth; (c) FCN-8s [17]; (d) SegNet [1]; (e) U-Net [20]; (f) ResUnet [26]; (g) ResNet34-UNet [3]; (h) Our Deep Res-UNet.

4   Conclusions

In this work, we propose Deep Res-UNet for segmentation of UAV-based infrared images for photovoltaic panels. Infrared images are collected by the UAV equipped with infrared thermal imager, inspecting the solar panel group over-head. The proposed network combines the strengths of residual learning and U-Net. Both the Encoder and Decoder are constructed by residual units, which make the whole deep network easy to train. ResNet-34 with modifications is uti-lized to learn the feature representations. The modifications including: the addi-tion of conv1 stage for copying features for the original input size, the removal of maxpooling layer for remaining a larger resolution, and the adding of Skip block with dilated residual unit to enlarge the received field. To get a finer result of the network, a modified loss function, which inherits both Binary Cross-Entropy (BCE) and Dice is utilized, and we reached the best result of our model at

$\beta = 0.75$. Besides, Conditional Random Field (CRF) is integrated into the segmentation pipeline as a post-process. Experiments in this work demonstrate the superiority of our proposed Deep Res-UNet, which exceeds FCN-8s [17], SegNet [1], U-Net [20] and its variants ResUnet [26] and ResNet34-Unet [3].

References

1. Badrinarayanan, V., Kendall, A., Cipolla, R.: SegNet: a deep convolutional encoder-decoder architecture for image segmentation. IEEE Trans. Pattern Anal. Mach. Intell. **39**(12), 2481–2495 (2017)
2. Burger, H.C., Schuler, C.J., Harmeling, S.: Image denoising: can plain neural networks compete with BM3D? (2012)
3. Buslaev, A., Seferbekov, S.S., Iglovikov, V., Shvets, A.: Fully convolutional network for automatic road extraction from satellite imagery. In: CVPR Workshops, pp. 207–210 (2018)
4. Chang, H.H., Zhuang, A.H., Valentino, D.J., Chu, W.C.: Performance measure characterization for evaluating neuroimage segmentation algorithms. Neuroimage **47**(1), 122–135 (2009)
5. Chen, J., Guan, B., Wang, H., Zhang, X., Tang, Y., Hu, W.: Image thresholding segmentation based on two dimensional histogram using gray level and local entropy information. IEEE Access **6**, 5269–5275 (2018)
6. Chen, L.C., Papandreou, G., Kokkinos, I., Murphy, K., Yuille, A.L.: Semantic image segmentation with deep convolutional nets and fully connected CRFs. arXiv preprint arXiv:1412.7062 (2014)
7. Chen, L.C., Papandreou, G., Kokkinos, I., Murphy, K., Yuille, A.L.: DeepLab: semantic image segmentation with deep convolutional nets, atrous convolution, and fully connected CRFs. IEEE Trans. Pattern Anal. Mach. Intell. **40**(4), 834–848 (2018)
8. Cremers, D., Rousson, M., Deriche, R.: A review of statistical approaches to level set segmentation: integrating color, texture, motion and shape. Int. J. Comput. Vis. **72**(2), 195–215 (2007)
9. Deng, J., Dong, W., Socher, R., Li, L.J., Li, K., Fei-Fei, L.: Imagenet: a large-scale hierarchical image database. In: 2009 IEEE Conference on Computer Vision and Pattern Recognition, pp. 248–255. IEEE (2009)
10. Fidon, L., Li, W., Garcia-Peraza-Herrera, L.C., Ekanayake, J., Kitchen, N., Ourselin, S., Vercauteren, T.: Generalised Wasserstein dice score for imbalanced multi-class segmentation using holistic convolutional networks. In: Crimi, A., Bakas, S., Kuijf, H., Menze, B., Reyes, M. (eds.) BrainLes 2017. LNCS, vol. 10670, pp. 64–76. Springer, Cham (2018). https://doi.org/10.1007/978-3-319-75238-9_6
11. He, K., Zhang, X., Ren, S., Sun, J.: Deep residual learning for image recognition. In: Proceedings of the IEEE Conference on Computer Vision and Pattern Recognition, pp. 770–778 (2016)
12. Jaffery, Z., I.: Performance comparison of image segmentation techniques for infrared images, December 2015. https://doi.org/10.1109/INDICON.2015.7443391
13. Kapur, J.N., Sahoo, P.K., Wong, A.K.: A new method for gray-level picture thresholding using the entropy of the histogram. Comput. Vis. Graph. Image Process. **29**(3), 273–285 (1985)
14. Kaur, S., Kaur, P.: An edge detection technique with image segmentation using ant colony optimization: a review. In: 2016 Online International Conference on Green Engineering and Technologies (IC-GET), pp. 1–5. IEEE (2016)

15. Krähenbühl, P., Koltun, V.: Efficient inference in fully connected CRFs with gaussian edge potentials. In: Advances in Neural Information Processing Systems, pp. 109–117 (2011)
16. Li, Z., Peng, C., Yu, G., Zhang, X., Deng, Y., Sun, J.: DetNet: design backbone for object detection. In: Proceedings of the European Conference on Computer Vision (ECCV), pp. 334–350 (2018)
17. Long, J., Shelhamer, E., Darrell, T.: Fully convolutional networks for semantic segmentation. In: Proceedings of the IEEE Conference on Computer Vision and Pattern Recognition, pp. 3431–3440 (2015)
18. Martin, D.R., Fowlkes, C.C., Malik, J.: Learning to detect natural image boundaries using local brightness, color, and texture cues. IEEE Trans. Pattern Anal. Mach. Intell. **5**, 530–549 (2004)
19. Paszke, A., Gross, S., Chintala, S., Chanan, G.: PyTorch: Tensors and dynamic neural networks in python with strong GPU acceleration. **6** (2017). https://pytorch.org/
20. Ronneberger, O., Fischer, P., Brox, T.: U-Net: convolutional networks for biomedical image segmentation. In: Navab, N., Hornegger, J., Wells, W.M., Frangi, A.F. (eds.) MICCAI 2015. LNCS, vol. 9351, pp. 234–241. Springer, Cham (2015). https://doi.org/10.1007/978-3-319-24574-4_28
21. Shen, H., Zhu, L., Hong, X., Chang, W.: ROI extraction method of infrared thermal image based on GLCM characteristic imitate gradient. In: Yang, J., Hu, Q., Cheng, M.-M., Wang, L., Liu, Q., Bai, X., Meng, D. (eds.) CCCV 2017. CCIS, vol. 771, pp. 192–205. Springer, Singapore (2017). https://doi.org/10.1007/978-981-10-7299-4_16
22. Simonyan, K., Zisserman, A.: Very deep convolutional networks for large-scale image recognition. arXiv preprint arXiv:1409.1556 (2014)
23. Wu, J., Li, J., Liu, J., Tian, J.: Infrared image segmentation via fast fuzzy C-means with spatial information. In: 2004 IEEE International Conference on Robotics and Biomimetics, pp. 742–745. IEEE (2004)
24. Yu, F., Koltun, V.: Multi-scale context aggregation by dilated convolutions. arXiv preprint arXiv:1511.07122 (2015)
25. Zhang, H., Hong, X.: Recent progresses on object detection: a brief review. Multimed. Tools Appl. (2019). https://doi.org/10.1007/s11042-019-07898-2
26. Zhang, Z., Liu, Q., Wang, Y.: Road extraction by deep residual U-Net. IEEE Geosci. Remote Sens. Lett. **15**(5), 749–753 (2018)
27. Zou, H., Huang, F.: Infrared image segmentation for electrical equipment based on fast-match algorithm. Infrared Technol. **38**(1), 21–27 (2016)

Author Index

An, Jianjing I-421

Bai, Zhengyao I-63
Bai, Zhimin I-14
Bao, Hujun III-283
Bao, Jiaqi II-102
Bian, Mingyun III-409
Bo, Qirong II-498
Bu, Qirong I-272
Bu, XiaoQing II-416

Cai, Guorong I-308, I-573
Cai, Songxin I-308
Cao, Rui I-540
Cao, Shan I-261
Cao, Zhongping II-644
Chai, Yekun I-562
Chai, Zhenhua II-725
Chan, Sixian I-147
Chen, Bingzhi II-682
Chen, Dihu I-386
Chen, Feiyu II-328
Chen, Huihui II-29
Chen, Jiaming I-456, III-528
Chen, Jianyu I-98
Chen, Jiaxin III-38
Chen, Jiaxing III-296
Chen, Jinshan I-308, I-573
Chen, Lin I-492
Chen, Liqing II-657
Chen, Peng II-714
Chen, Shengyong I-147
Chen, Shuya III-418
Chen, Wei III-199
Chen, Weifu I-552
Chen, Wenbai II-725
Chen, Xiaozhen II-694, III-272
Chen, Xiuxin I-251
Chen, Xuliang III-397
Chen, Yaxiong III-454
Chen, Yelin I-110
Chen, Yiman III-418
Chen, Ying I-480, II-126
Chen, Zhang III-353

Chen, Zhiyuan II-209
Cheng, Long III-366
Cheng, Yuehua II-241
Cheng, Zhanzhan I-193
Cui, Jian I-528, III-341
Cui, Zhi Gao II-761
Cui, Zhiying II-572

Dai, Guojun II-783
Dai, Lingzheng II-354
Dang, Fan I-295
Deng, Donghu II-475, III-62
Deng, Hongxia II-3
Deng, Rui II-303
Deng, Wei I-468
Ding, Kaiming I-308
Ding, Mengna II-620
Ding, Xinnan II-197
Ding, Yu II-354
Ding, Yuxuan III-62
Dong, Jing III-409
Dong, Minghao II-551
Dong, Ning II-487
Dong, Xiaoyun I-517
Dong, Xiwei III-3
Dong, Yan III-479
Du, Jiahao II-453
Du, Jiang I-3
Du, Wentao III-418
Duan, Lijuan II-267
Duan, Pengfei I-398
Duan, Yinong II-453

Fan, Haoxin I-421
Fan, Honghui II-91
Fan, Rongrong III-320
Fan, Xing-Rong III-211
Fan, Yingchun III-247
Fang, Yuming II-620
Feng, Guocan I-552
Feng, Hongwei II-498
Feng, Jun I-272
Feng, Wei II-542
Feng, Yachuang II-670, III-454

Ferede, Shambel I-3
Fraundorfer, Friedrich III-172
Fu, Jiahui I-349
Fu, Peng II-772
Fu, Ying II-221

Gan, Zongliang II-367, III-308
Gao, Changxin I-586, II-279
Gao, Chenyu II-582
Gao, Chongjun I-586
Gao, Cunyuan II-441
Gao, Wanshun II-66
Gao, Xinbo III-97
Gao, Ye II-582
Gao, Yukang II-429
Gao, Yun I-284
Gao, Zeng I-217
Gong, Ping III-366
Gu, Guanghua III-122
Guan, Banglei III-172
Guan, Shaoya II-380
Guo, Hantao I-431
Guo, Jinxiu II-3
Guo, Wenbo I-86
Guo, Xiaobao II-253
Guo, Xinqing III-353
Guo, Xuemei II-644

Han, Bin III-97
Han, Hong III-247
Han, Jungong II-114
Han, Mingfei I-123
Han, Qianqian III-38
Han, Shishuai II-607
Han, Xiaodong II-241
Han, Yu II-161
Hao, Huiling I-172
He, Guiqing II-703
He, Jishuai II-341
He, Lingshen I-598
He, Qi II-714
Hong, Xianggong I-611
Hou, Guofei II-316
Hou, Jinxiu II-3
Hou, Rong II-714
Hou, Shudong II-114, III-75
Hou, Xinwen I-562
Hu, Haifeng I-386
Hu, Jing I-586

Hu, Wenchao II-403
Hu, Xiaoming I-135
Hua, Songjian I-239
Huang, Hongfei II-783
Huang, Hua II-221
Huang, Kai III-283
Huang, Kaiqi II-291
Huang, Maochun I-160
Huang, Sheng II-138, II-328
Huang, Yan II-18
Huang, Yibin II-341
Huang, Ying III-110
Huang, Yun III-479
Huang, Zijun I-160
Huo, Xing III-52

Ji, Fanfan I-337
Ji, Jian II-316
Ji, Jiaqi II-703
Jia, Xibin III-390
Jia, Yunde I-181, II-391
Jian, Meng I-409
Jiang, Dong I-63
Jiang, Ke II-761
Jiang, Mengmeng III-62
Jiang, Shiling I-468
Jiang, Xinghao II-632
Jin, Dou II-542
Jin, Guanghao I-468, II-416, III-430
Jin, Xin II-41
Jin, Xing I-3
Jing, Xiao-Yuan III-3, III-259, III-491
Jing, Xin III-247

Kan, Haipeng III-110

Lai, Jian-Huang III-296
Lai, Zhihui II-102
Lee, Yilong II-197
Lei, Jiahui I-586
Lei, Qing I-284
Li, Ai Hua II-761
Li, Annan II-209
Li, Changsheng I-205
Li, Chunlei I-528, III-479
Li, Dong I-160, III-84
Li, Guangyao III-516
Li, Haifang II-3
Li, Haohao II-725

Li, Haoran   III-97
Li, Hongru   II-463
Li, Hui   III-503
Li, Jiafeng   II-487
Li, Jinyu   III-283
Li, Juanjuan   III-491
Li, Junwei   I-147
Li, Junxia   II-354
Li, Lemin   II-303
Li, Min   II-185
Li, Na   II-561
Li, Qianwen   I-480
Li, Qin   III-161
Li, Shengyang   I-123
Li, Shimin   I-308
Li, Sitong   II-316
Li, Siyuan   III-353
Li, Tianyu   III-466
Li, Wei   II-173
Li, Weijun   I-398
Li, Weiqi   II-694, III-272
Li, Wenge   II-173
Li, Xiaoguang   II-487
Li, Xiaoqi   I-228
Li, Yaodong   III-516
Li, Zhang   III-172
Li, Zhenbo   III-516
Li, Zhuoyi   III-122
Li, Zihao   II-291
Lian, Yuanfeng   II-508, III-378
Liang, Jiayu   I-468, II-416, III-430
Liang, Jimin   II-551
Liang, Lina   II-441
Liang, Shan   III-184
Liang, Zijun   I-110
Liao, Shirong   I-38
Lin, Jie   III-341
Lin, Junyu   II-197
Lin, Zhouchen   I-431, I-598
Liu, Aoli   II-794
Liu, Bing   I-409
Liu, Caihua   II-453
Liu, Chen   II-138
Liu, Danhua   III-341
Liu, Feng   II-367, III-308
Liu, Hao   III-27
Liu, Haoqi   II-3
Liu, Heng   II-114, III-62, III-75

Liu, Honghai   I-147
Liu, Jiahui   II-279
Liu, Jiangtao   III-122
Liu, Kunliang   I-468, II-416, III-430
Liu, Liangliang   II-197
Liu, Licheng   II-561
Liu, Min   I-50
Liu, Mingyang   I-284
Liu, Ning   II-102, II-714
Liu, Qingshan   II-354, III-320
Liu, Qiong   II-725
Liu, Ruyi   I-505
Liu, Shaofeng   III-247
Liu, Wenju   III-184
Liu, Xuning   I-409
Liu, Yujun   I-308
Liu, Yunfeng   III-390
Liu, Zhen   II-91
Liu, Zhoufeng   I-528, III-479
Liu, Ziyuan   III-366
Long, Zihan   I-361
Lou, Shuqin   II-79
Lu, Guangming   II-253, II-682
Lu, Haiwei   I-373
Lu, Hu   I-444
Lu, Jianglin   II-102
Lu, Wen   II-607
Lu, Xiaoqiang   III-454
Lu, Xin   II-185
Lu, Yao   II-682, II-694, III-272
Lu, Yuwu   II-102
Luo, Bin   II-596, II-749
Luo, Chao   III-52
Luo, Jie   II-498
Luo, Ling   II-161
Luo, Wei   I-50, I-110
Luo, Xiaokai   III-3
Lv, Xinbi   III-199

Ma, Kang   I-272
Ma, Kuan   II-498
Ma, Ming   I-468
Mao, Zihao   III-528
Meng, Cai   II-380
Meng, Jingke   III-296
Miao, Qiguang   I-505, II-316
Ming, Rui   III-211
Mo, Xianjie   I-50, I-110

Nie, Shuai   III-184
Ning, Xin   I-398
Niu, Chuang   II-551
Niu, Yi   I-193

Pan, Chunhong   III-442
Pei, Mingtao   I-172
Peng, Bo   III-409
Peng, Qinmu   III-15
Pi, Lihong   II-18

Qian, Jianjun   II-53
Qian, Likuan   III-378
Qiao, Chengyu   III-418
Qiao, Tianhao   I-261
Qiao, Yuanhua   II-267
Qin, Zengchang   III-110
Qiu, Guanghui   III-366
Qiu, Zhuling   I-74

Reda, Mohamed   II-736
Ren, Fen   II-316
Ren, Shenghan   II-551
Ren, Siyu   I-468
Rong, Yaru   II-794

Sang, Nong   I-586, II-279
Shao, Kun   III-52
Shen, Chunxu   II-341
Shen, Linghao   II-736
Shen, Weichao   II-391
Shen, Wen   I-480
Shen, Xiangxiang   I-562
Shen, Yan   II-79
Shi, Guangming   I-3, I-98, III-341
Shi, Haichao   I-205
Shi, Yuan   I-398
Shi, Yufeng   III-15
Shi, Zhenjun   I-228
Shi, Zhongchao   III-223
Shu, Zhenqiu   II-91
Shuai, Hui   I-337, I-373, III-320
Song, Hao   I-181
Song, Jianfeng   I-505
Su, Ang   III-172
Su, Jinhe   I-308, I-573
Su, Ming   I-251
Su, Songzhi   I-38
Su, Yan Zhao   II-761

Sui, Wei   III-442
Sun, Bin   III-110
Sun, Che   I-181
Sun, Kai   II-380
Sun, Ke   I-431
Sun, Ningning   I-135
Sun, Peng   I-86
Sun, Quansen   II-772
Sun, Tanfeng   II-632
Sun, Ying   III-259, III-491
Sun, Yukuan   I-468, II-416, III-430
Sun, Yunda   III-84

Tan, Jieqing   III-52
Tan, Zuowen   II-620
Tang, Jin   I-239, II-596, II-749
Tang, Meihan   I-552
Tang, Yiping   II-551
Tang, Yuliang   III-247
Tang, Yunqi   III-149
Tao, Wenbing   III-137
Tian, Chunna   II-475, III-62
Tian, Ming   II-475
Tu, Juanjuan   II-367
Tu, Tianqi   II-173
Tu, Zhengzheng   I-239

Wang, Cailing   III-3
Wang, Dianzhong   II-508
Wang, Ding   II-126
Wang, Dong   I-421
Wang, Dongyue   II-596, II-749
Wang, Fangzhao   I-361
Wang, Futian   I-239
Wang, Gang   I-517
Wang, Guoli   II-644
Wang, Haijian   III-503
Wang, Jianming   I-468, II-416, III-430
Wang, Jing   III-366
Wang, Junpu   III-479
Wang, Junqiu   III-235
Wang, Kaixuan   III-149
Wang, Kejun   II-197
Wang, Kun   II-328
Wang, Lei   II-475
Wang, Liang   II-18
Wang, Lianglin   I-38
Wang, Lingfeng   I-14, I-26
Wang, Ning   III-308

Wang, Peng   I-295, I-540, II-582, III-223
Wang, Qigang   III-223
Wang, Qingcai   I-611
Wang, Qiuli   II-138
Wang, Qiuyuan   III-235
Wang, Rui   I-272
Wang, Ruixuan   II-572
Wang, Shaocong   II-670
Wang, Shengwei   II-150
Wang, Shuo   III-15
Wang, Tao   II-761, II-772
Wang, Tianmiao   II-380
Wang, Wei   I-386, III-62, III-409
Wang, Weining   II-303
Wang, Wenjie   III-15
Wang, Xiao   I-239
Wang, Xin   III-235
Wang, Xiujun   III-75
Wang, Xuebo   II-694, III-272
Wang, Yaxin   II-508
Wang, Yifeng   II-794
Wang, Yilei   II-657
Wang, Ying   II-463, III-442
Wang, Yixuan   II-150
Wang, Yu   I-251, II-41
Wang, Yunhong   II-209
Wang, Zhengsheng   II-241
Wang, Zhiguang   II-403
Wang, Zhongli   II-79
Wang, Zhuo   II-291
Wang, Zijian   II-694, III-272
Wang, Zongyue   I-308, I-573
Wei, Lai   III-27
Wei, Miaomiao   I-528
Wei, Qian   III-378
Wei, Shaonan   III-430
Wei, Tingting   I-50, I-110
Wei, Wei   II-475, III-62
Wei, Xiaoming   II-725
Wei, Xing   I-540
Wei, Xueling   II-173
Wei, Zhihua   I-480
Wu, Chunli   II-267
Wu, Fei   III-3, III-259, III-491
Wu, Jian   II-341
Wu, Jinhua   III-84
Wu, Jinjian   I-98

Wu, Longshi   II-572
Wu, Ming   III-332
Wu, Shuangyuan   III-378
Wu, Songsong   III-259
Wu, Xiaofu   I-349, II-41
Wu, Xiaojun   II-91
Wu, Xinxiao   I-181, III-466
Wu, Yingjie   II-657
Wu, Yuwei   II-391
Wu, Zebiao   I-573
Wu, Zhaohui   II-530
Wu, Zhiyong   III-3

Xi, Runping   III-38
Xia, Yong   I-517
Xia, Zhaoqiang   II-703
Xiang, Shiming   III-442
Xiang, Yixi   II-221
Xiang, Zhiyu   III-418
Xiao, Yong   II-596, II-749
Xie, Bin   III-161
Xie, Jin   II-53
Xie, Xingyu   I-598
Xie, Xuemei   I-3, I-98
Xiong, Jian   II-41
Xu, Fan   II-267
Xu, Feiyu   III-223
Xu, Guili   II-241
Xu, Guoliang   III-211
Xu, Haiyan   II-185
Xu, Jiamiao   I-361
Xu, Ke   II-632
Xu, Qianqian   II-772
Xu, Qiling   I-492
Xu, Qin   II-596, II-749
Xu, Shugong   I-261
Xu, Tao   II-453
Xu, Tongtong   II-267
Xu, Wen   III-332
Xu, Xiangmin   II-303
Xu, Xun   I-98
Xu, Zhixin   II-253
Xuan, Shiyu   I-123
Xue, Fei   III-235
Xue, Shaohui   III-38
Xue, Yuting   II-475

Yan, Hongping   I-14, I-26
Yan, Qinhong   I-552
Yang, Bangbang   III-283
Yang, Beibei   II-279
Yang, Chuanwu   I-361
Yang, Dan   II-138
Yang, Dawei   III-390
Yang, Fengjia   II-632
Yang, Guanglu   I-217
Yang, Hua   I-492, II-429
Yang, Jiachen   II-607
Yang, Jian   II-53
Yang, Jisheng   I-160
Yang, Meng   I-456, III-503, III-528
Yang, Min   III-259
Yang, Qize   III-296
Yang, Xiaofeng   II-3
Yang, Xin   I-373
Yang, Yan   I-528
Yang, Yang   III-353
Yang, Yingchun   II-530
Yang, Yongguang   III-491
Yang, Yue   II-173
Yang, Zhenghan   III-390
Yao, Jintao   III-247
Yao, Qi   I-444
Yao, Rui   I-409, II-441
Ye, Linbin   III-503
Yin, Chuanhuan   I-562
Yin, Xiangyu   II-234
You, Congzhe   II-91
You, Xinge   I-361, III-15
Yu, Changqian   II-279
Yu, Hongyuan   II-18
Yu, Jingyi   III-353
Yu, Li   I-284, II-150
Yu, Qiang   III-442
Yu, Shifang   II-783
Yuan, Hejin   I-251
Yuan, Xiao-Tong   I-337, I-373
Yuan, Yuan   II-670
Yue, Jun   III-516

Zeng, Xianxian   I-160
Zha, Hongbin   III-235
Zha, Yufei   I-74
Zhang, Bin   I-228
Zhang, Cheng   I-239
Zhang, Chuang   III-332
Zhang, Chuyue   III-516

Zhang, Fei   I-74, III-52
Zhang, Guofeng   III-283
Zhang, Hao   I-611
Zhang, Houlu   III-149
Zhang, Houwang   II-519
Zhang, Hua   II-783
Zhang, Huanlong   I-217
Zhang, Jiajia   II-138
Zhang, Jianbin   II-508, III-378
Zhang, Jie   I-217
Zhang, Jingjing   I-517
Zhang, Junge   II-291
Zhang, Lei   II-221
Zhang, Li   III-84
Zhang, Liao   II-79
Zhang, Linjiang   I-295
Zhang, Nianrong   II-173
Zhang, Peng   I-193
Zhang, Qing   I-26
Zhang, Qiqi   II-703
Zhang, Shaojie   I-295
Zhang, Shaolin   I-398
Zhang, Shizhou   I-540
Zhang, Shu   I-98, II-291
Zhang, Shunqing   I-261
Zhang, Suofei   I-349
Zhang, Tuo   I-272
Zhang, Xiaohong   II-138, II-328
Zhang, Xiaoyu   I-205
Zhang, Xuejie   I-284
Zhang, Xuewu   II-185
Zhang, Yanning   I-540
Zhang, Yaping   III-184
Zhang, Yikun   II-441
Zhang, Yujun   III-97
Zhang, Yun   I-160
Zhang, Zhenchuan   II-530
Zhang, Zhichao   I-261
Zhang, Zhihe   II-714
Zhang, Zhulin   III-84
Zhang, Zhuo   II-185
Zhao, Cairong   III-199
Zhao, Di   II-267
Zhao, Jiaqi   I-409, II-441
Zhao, Meng   I-172
Zhao, Peipei   I-505
Zhao, Qijun   II-714
Zhao, Xi   II-66
Zhao, Xiaoxuan   I-50
Zhao, Yili   I-325

Zhao, Yongqiang   II-736
Zhao, Zifei   I-123
Zheng, Feng   III-15
Zheng, Haihong   II-794
Zheng, Longyu   III-137
Zheng, Ruishen   II-53
Zheng, Wei-Shi   II-572, III-296
Zheng, Xianghan   II-657
Zheng, Xiaoyu   II-114
Zheng, Xinyue   III-223
Zheng, Yi   I-409
Zhou, Hua   I-325
Zhou, Jun   III-259
Zhou, Pan   I-38
Zhou, Quan   I-349, II-41
Zhou, Shifen   I-611
Zhou, Shuigeng   I-193
Zhou, Xiaolong   I-147

Zhou, Yong   I-409, II-441
Zhou, Yuan   II-463, II-542
Zhou, Yue   III-397
Zhou, Ziheng   II-607
Zhu, Bing   III-466
Zhu, Jiajie   I-50
Zhu, Peng   I-74
Zhu, Shipeng   II-241
Zhu, Songhao   I-86
Zhu, Xinyu   I-193
Zhu, Yuan   II-519
Zhu, Yuanping   I-135
Zhu, Zhanxing   I-431
Zhuang, Jiankai   III-110
Zhuo, Li   II-487
Zhuo, Yifan   II-657
Zou, Nan   III-418
Zuo, Yifan   II-620

Printed in the United States
By Bookmasters